The Quotation Dictionary

Edited by ROBIN HYMAN

The Macmillan Company
NEW YORK

TO MY MOTHER AND FATHER
WHO TAUGHT ME TO ENJOY READING

Printed in the United States of America

Foreword

THIS DICTIONARY has been planned as a useful and comprehensive reference book of familiar quotations and proverbs and also as a book which it is hoped will give pleasure to the reader who uses it as an anthology. The selection of entries, as well as the arrangement in single rather than double column, is intended to encourage the browser in addition to anyone looking up specific quotations. The emphasis in selection is on what is likely to be familiar to the general reader of today. A few quotations are included from French, German, Greek, Italian, Latin and Spanish sources which seem likely to be known to many American readers. In all such cases a translation is given.

It is often extremely difficult to assess the degree of familiarity of quotations, and this is particularly true when considering what to include from contemporary writing and speech. An attempt has been made to decide what is likely to remain well known for several years, and this test means the exclusion of most current radio and television sayings, advertising slogans and political phrases, although many quotations from twentieth-century writers are included. The criterion in selection throughout has been what is familiar to readers rather than what ought to be familiar. Complete objectivity is impossible, but it is hoped that not too many entries have been included which reflect merely the compiler's own tastes. The number of quotations selected from an author is, of course, no indication of the compiler's assessment of the author's literary merit. Some authors, such as Pope and Wilde, wrote in an epigrammatic form which lends itself well to quotation; by comparison, few novelists, apart from Dickens, have this particular quality. As well as quotations, over 1,000 proverbs are included in this dictionary. Often one does not know whether a familiar phrase is proverbial or whether it has a specific literary origin. Because of this, it seemed helpful to include the best-known proverbs.

A comprehensive index with over 25,000 entries has been provided at the end of the dictionary, and this contains the key words in each quotation. The index gives not only the page reference but also the number of the quotation on the page. From this index it is easy to trace quickly a half-remembered quotation by looking up one of the key words, and also, should one refer to individual words in the index, such as *man, beauty*, etc., find quotations on these subjects.

The arrangement of entries is alphabetical by author, and, wherever possible, line references have been given in poems, and act and scene references in plays. References in most cases are to the Oxford Editions of Standard Authors, but line references obviously vary from edition to edition with authors, such as Shakespeare, who wrote partly in prose and partly in poetry. The name of the speaker has been given in all quotations from plays, and this enables one to find out without reference to the original text that, for example, it was Marcellus—not Hamlet or Horatio, as some might have supposed—who said, "Something is rotten in the state of Denmark."

Many friends have given encouragement and helpful advice during the five years of preparation of this book. Thanks are due in particular to the Reverend S. R. Cutt for his assistance in the selection of quotations from the Bible; Mrs. E. M. Hatt, who undertook the immense task of compiling the index; and Miss Barbara Hall and Miss Pamela Jones for their careful checking of the proofs. Librarians in the United States and England have answered numerous inquiries with great courtesy, and the staff of the British Museum in London have been especially helpful. The checking of contemporary references has in many cases been made easier by the ready cooperation of the writers and speakers themselves.

ROBIN HYMAN

The Quotation Dictionary

ACTON, John Emerich Edward Dalberg, 1st Baron, 1834–1902

1 Power tends to corrupt, and absolute power corrupts absolutely. Great men are almost always bad men . . . There is no worse heresy than that the office sanctifies the holder of it. *Historical Essays and Studies, Appendix, Letter to Bishop Mandell Creighton*

ADAMS, John Quincy, 1767–1848

2 Think of your forefathers! Think of your posterity! *Speech, Plymouth, Massachusetts, 22 Dec. 1802*

ADAMS, Sarah Flower, 1805–1848

3 Nearer, my God, to thee,
   Nearer to thee!
E'en though it be a cross
   That raiseth me. *Nearer, my God, to Thee*

ADDISON, Joseph, 1672–1719

4 'Tis not in mortals to command success,
But we'll do more, Sempronius; we'll deserve it. PORTIUS *Cato, Act 1, Scene 2*

5 The woman that deliberates is lost. MARCIA *Ib, Act 4, Scene 1*

6 Thus I live in the world rather as a Spectator of mankind, than as one of the species, by which means I have made myself a speculative statesman, soldier, merchant, and artisan, without ever meddling with any practical part of life. *The Spectator, No. 1, 1 March 1711*

7 Sunday clears away the rust of the whole week. *Ib, No. 112, 9 July 1711*

8 [*Sir Roger*] told them, with the air of a man who would not give his judgment rashly, that 'much might be said on both sides.' *Ib, No. 122, 20 July 1711*

9 The spacious firmament on high,
With all the blue ethereal sky,
And spangled heavens, a shining frame,
Their great Original proclaim. *Ib, No. 465, 23 Aug. 1712, Ode*

10 A woman seldom asks advice until she has bought her wedding clothes. *Ib, No. 475, 4 Sept. 1712*

11 We are always doing something for posterity, but I would fain see posterity do something for us. *Ib, No. 583, 20 Aug. 1714*

12 See in what peace a Christian can die. *Last words*

ADY, Thomas, c. 1655

13 Matthew, Mark, Luke, and John,
The bed be blest that I lie on.
Four angels to my bed,
Four angels round my head,
One to watch, and one to pray,
And two to bear my soul away. *A Candle in the Dark*

9

AKINS, Zoë, 1886—

1 The Greeks Had a Word For It. *Title of play, 1930*

ALCUIN, 735–804

2 *Vox populi, vox dei.* The voice of the people is the voice of God.
Letter to Charlemagne

ALDRICH, Henry, 1647–1710

3 If all be true that I do think,
There are five reasons we should drink:
Good wine—a friend—or being dry—
Or lest we should be by and by—
Or any other reason why. *Reasons for Drinking*

ALEXANDER, Cecil Frances, 1818–1895

4 All things bright and beautiful,
All creatures great and small,
All things wise and wonderful,
The Lord God made them all. *All Things Bright and Beautiful*

5 The rich man in his castle,
The poor man at his gate,
God made them, high or lowly,
And order'd their estate. *Ib*

6 Once in royal David's city
Stood a lowly cattle shed,
Where a Mother laid her Baby
In a manger for His bed:
Mary was that Mother mild,
Jesus Christ her little child. *Once in Royal David's City*

7 There is a green hill far away,
Without a city wall,
Where the dear Lord was crucified,
Who died to save us all. *There is a Green Hill*

ALLAINVAL, Abbé Léonor d', 1700–1753

8 *L'embarras des richesses.* A superfluity of good things. *Title of play, 1726*

ALLINGHAM, William, 1824–1889

9 Up the airy mountain
Down the rushy glen,
We daren't go a-hunting,
For fear of little men. *The Fairies*

AMBROSE, St., 340?–397?

10 *Si fueris Romae, Romano vivito more;*
Si fueris alibi, vivito sicut ibi.
When in Rome, live as the Romans do; when elsewhere, live as they live
elsewhere *Advice to St. Augustine, quoted by Jeremy Taylor*

ANDERSEN, Hans Christian, 1805–1875

11 The Ugly Duckling. *Title of story*

ANONYMOUS
Advertisements

1 Daddy, what did YOU do in the Great War?
Recruiting Poster, 1914–18 War

2 Drinka pinta milka day.   *Milk Marketing Board*

3 Friday night is Amami night.

4 Guinness is good for you.

5 Is your journey really necessary?   *Railway Poster, 1939–45 War*

6 That schoolgirl complexion.   *Palmolive Soap*

7 Stop me and buy one.   *Wall's Ice Cream*

8 They come as a boon and a blessing to men,
The Pickwick, The Owl, and the Waverley pen.

9 Top People take *The Times.*

10 Worth a guinea a box.   *Beecham's Pills*

11 You want the best seats; we have them.   *Keith Prowse & Co. Ltd.*

Ballads

12 In Scarlet town, where I was born,
    There was a fair maid dwellin',
    Made every youth cry *Well-a-way!*
       Her name was Barbara Allen.   *Barbara Allen's Cruelty, Stanza 1*

13 The King sits in Dunfermline town
       Drinking the blude red wine.   *Sir Patrick Spens, 1*

14 To Noroway, to Noroway,
    To Noroway o'er the faem;
    The King's daughter o' Noroway,
       'Tis thou must bring her hame.   *Ib, 13*

15 There were three ravens sat on a tree,
    They were as black as they might be.
    The one of them said to his make,
    'Where shall we our breakfast take?'   *The Three Ravens, 1*

16 As I was walking all alane
    I heard twa corbies making a mane:
    The tane unto the tither did say,
    'Whar shall we gang and dine the day?'   *The Twa Corbies*

Epitaphs

17 Here lie I and my four daughters,
    Killed by drinking Cheltenham waters.
    Had we but stuck to Epsom salts,
    We wouldn't have been in these here vaults.   *Cheltenham Waters*

18 Here lies a man who was killed by lightning;
    He died when his prospects seemed to be brightening.
    He might have cut a flash in this world of trouble,
    But the flash cut him, and he lies in the stubble.   *At Great Torrington,*
                                                              Devon

1 Here lies a poor woman who was always tired,
She lived in a house where help wasn't hired:
Her last words on earth were: 'Dear friends, I am going
To where there's no cooking, or washing, or sewing,
For everything there is exact to my wishes,
For where they don't eat there's no washing of dishes.
I'll be where loud anthems will always be ringing,
But having no voice I'll be quit of the singing.
Don't mourn for me now, don't mourn for me never,
I am going to do nothing for ever and ever.'   *On a Tired Housewife*

2 Here lies my wife,
Here lies she;
Hallelujah!
Hallelujee!   *At Leeds*

3 Here lies the body of Richard Hind,
Who was neither ingenious, sober, nor kind.   *On Richard Hind*

4 Here lies the body of Mary Ann Lowder,
She burst while drinking a seidlitz powder.
Called from the world to her heavenly rest,
She should have waited till it effervesced.   *On Mary Ann Lowder*

5 Here lies Will Smith—and, what's something rarish,
He was born, bred, and hanged, all in the same parish.   *On Will Smith*

6 Mary Ann has gone to rest,
Safe at last on Abraham's breast,
Which may be nuts for Mary Ann,
But is certainly rough on Abraham.   *Mary Ann*

7 Stranger! Approach this spot with gravity!
John Brown is filling his last cavity.   *A Dentist*

8 This is the grave of Mike O'Day
Who died maintaining his right of way.
His right was clear, his will was strong,
But he's just as dead as if he'd been wrong.   *20th century*

Limericks

9 There was a faith-healer of Deal,
Who said, 'Although pain isn't real,
    If I sit on a pin
    And it punctures my skin,
I dislike what I fancy I feel.'

10 There was a young lady of Riga,
Who went for a ride on a tiger;
    They returned from the ride
    With the lady inside,
And a smile on the face of the tiger.

11 There was a young man of Boulogne
Who sang a most topical song.
    It wasn't the words
    That frightened the birds,
But the horrible *double entendre*.

1 There was a young man of Japan
Whose limericks never would scan;
    When they said it was so,
    He replied, 'Yes, I know,
But I always try to get as many words into the last line as ever I possibly can.'

2 There was a young woman called Starkie,
Who had an affair with a darky.
    The result of her sins
    Was quadruplets, not twins—
One black, and one white, and two khaki.

3 There was an old man from Darjeeling,
Who boarded a bus bound for Ealing,
        He saw on the door:
        'Please don't spit on the floor',
So he stood up and spat on the ceiling.

4 There's a wonderful family called Stein,
There's Gert and there's Epp and there's Ein;
    Gert's poems are bunk,
    Epp's statues are junk,
And no one can understand Ein.

For other limericks, see Arnold Bennett (28:9), A. H. R. Buller (63:1), A. H. Euwer (109:1), M. E. Hare (128:11), R. A. Knox (155:14), Edward Lear (158:12 and 13), D. L. Merritt (170:6), and W. C. Monkhouse (183:1).

Play

5 Everyman, I will go with thee and be thy guide,
In thy most need to go by thy side.   KNOWLEDGE   *Everyman (15th century morality play)*

Poems and Sayings

6 A beast, but a just beast.   *Of Dr. Temple, Headmaster of Rugby*

7 From ghoulies and ghosties and long-leggety beasties
And things that go bump in the night,
Good Lord, deliver us!   *Scottish prayer*

8 He that fights and runs away
May live to fight another day.   *Musarum Deliciae (17th century)*

9 'How different, how very different, from the home life of our own dear Queen!'   *Irvin S. Cobb, A Laugh a Day.   Remark of Victorian lady after a performance of Antony and Cleopatra*

10 I always eat peas with honey
I've done it all my life,
They do taste kind of funny,
But it keeps them on the knife.   *Peas*

11 I know two things about the horse,
And one of them is rather coarse.   *The Horse (20th century)*

1 If all the world were paper,
And all the sea were ink,
And all the trees were bread and cheese,
What should we do for drink? *If All the World were Paper (17th century)*

2 King Charles the First walked and talked
Half an hour after his head was cut off. *Peter Puzzlewell, A Choice
Collection of Riddles, Charades, and Rebuses (18th century)*

3 Lizzie Borden took an axe
And gave her mother forty whacks;
When she saw what she had done,
She gave her father forty-one. *On an American Trial of the 1890's*

4 Miss Buss and Miss Beale
Cupid's darts do not feel.
How different from us,
Miss Beale and Miss Buss. *On Two Victorian Headmistresses*

5 Please to remember
The Fifth of November,
Gunpowder treason and plot. *Guy Fawkes Day*

6 The rabbit has a charming face;
Its private life is a disgrace. *The Rabbit (20th century)*

7 Sumer is icumen in
Lhude sing cucu!
Groweth sed and bloweth med
And springth the wude nu. *Sumer is Icumen In (13th century)*

Songs

8 Absence makes the heart grow fonder. *Davison, Poetical Rhapsody, 1602*

9 The animals went in one by one,
There's one more river to cross. *One More River*

10 As I sat on a sunny bank,
On Christmas Day in the morning,
I spied three ships come sailing by. *Carol, As I sat on a Sunny Bank*

11 Begone, dull care! I prithee begone from me!
Begone, dull care, you and I shall never agree. *Begone Dull Care*

12 The bells of hell go ting-a-ling-a-ling
For you but not for me. *Song of 1914–18 War*

13 The Campbells are comin', oho, oho. *The Campbells are Comin'*

14 Come, landlord, fill the flowing bowl,
Until it doth run over ...
    For to-night we'll merry, merry be,
    To-morrow we'll be sober. *Come, Landlord, Fill the Flowing Bowl*

15 Come lasses and lads, get leave of your dads,
And away to the Maypole hie,
For every he has got him a she,
And the fiddler's standing by. *Come Lasses and Lads*

1 Early one morning, just as the sun was rising,
  I heard a maid singing in the valley below:
  'Oh, don't deceive me; Oh, never leave me!
  How could you use a poor maiden so?'   *Early One Morning*

2 Frankie and Johnny were lovers, lordee, and how they could love,
  Swore to be true to each other, true as the stars above;
  He was her man, but he done her wrong.   *Frankie and Johnny*

3 God rest you merry, gentlemen,
  Let nothing you dismay.   *God Rest You Merry*

4 Greensleeves was all my joy,
    Greensleeves was my delight,
  Greensleeves was my heart of gold,
    And who but Lady Greensleeves.   *Greensleeves*

5 Ha, ha, ha, you and me,
  Little brown jug, don't I love thee!   *The Little Brown Jug*

6 Here's a health unto his Majesty, ...
  Confusion to his enemies, ...
  And he that will not drink his health,
  I wish him neither wit nor wealth,
  Nor yet a rope to hang himself.   *Here's a Health unto his Majesty*

7 Here we come gathering nuts in May
      Nuts in May,
  On a cold and frosty morning.   *Children's Song*

8 The holly and the ivy,
  When they are both full grown,
  Of all the trees that are in the wood,
  The holly bears the crown.
  The rising of the sun
  And the running of the deer,
  The playing of the merry organ,
  Sweet singing in the choir.   *Carol, The Holly and the Ivy*

9 I feel no pain, dear mother, now
  But oh, I am so dry!
  O take me to a brewery
  And leave me there to die.   *Shanty*

10 In Dublin's fair city, where the girls are so pretty,
  I first set my eyes on sweet Molly Malone,
  As she wheeled her wheelbarrow, through streets broad and narrow,
  Crying, Cockles and mussels! alive, alive, O!   *Cockles and Mussels*

11 She was a fishmonger, but sure 'twas no wonder,
  For so were her father and mother before.   *Ib*

12 In good King Charles's golden days,
  When loyalty no harm meant,
  A zealous High Churchman was I,
  And so I got preferment.   *The Vicar of Bray*

13 And this is law, that I'll maintain,
  Unto my dying day, Sir,
  That whatsoever King shall reign,
  I'll be the Vicar of Bray, Sir.   *Ib*

1 It is good to be merry and wise,
It is good to be honest and true,
It is best to be off with the old love,
Before you are on with the new.   *Songs of England and Scotland, 1835*

2 My Bonnie is over the ocean,
My Bonnie is over the sea,
My Bonnie is over the ocean,
Oh, bring back my Bonnie to me.   *My Bonnie*

3 Now I am a bachelor, I live by myself and I work at the weaving trade,
And the only only thing that I ever did wrong
Was to woo a fair young maid.   *Weaver's Song*

4 She sighed, she cried, she damned near died: she said 'What shall I do?'
So I took her into bed and covered up her head
Just to save her from the foggy, foggy dew.   *Ib*

5 Oh, I went down South for to see my Sal,
Sing 'Polly-wolly-doodle' all the day!   *Polly-Wolly-Doodle*

6 Oh, 'tis my delight on a shining night, in the season of the year.
                    The Lincolnshire Poacher

7 Old soldiers never die;
They only fade away.
                    War Song, 1914–18

8 O, No, John! No, John! No, John! No!   *O, No, John*

9 O, Shenandoah, I long to hear you
Away, you rolling river.   *Shenandoah*

10 O ye'll tak' the high road, and I'll tak' the low road,
And I'll be in Scotland afore ye,
But me and my true love will never meet again,
On the bonnie, bonnie banks o' Loch Lomon'.
                    The Bonnie Banks o' Loch Lomon'

11 She was poor but she was honest
Victim of a rich man's game.
First he loved her, then he left her,
And she lost her maiden name.   *She was Poor but she was Honest*

12 See her on the bridge at midnight,
Saying 'Farewell, blighted love.'
Then a scream, a splash and goodness,
What is she a-doin' of?   *Ib*

13 It's the same the whole world over,
It's the poor wot gets the blame,
It's the rich wot gets the gravy.
Ain't it all a bleedin' shame?   *Ib*

14 Some talk of Alexander, and some of Hercules,
Of Hector and Lysander, and such great names as these;
But of all the world's brave heroes there's none that can compare
With a tow, row, row, row, row, row for the British Grenadier.
                    The British Grenadiers

15 The sons of the prophet were brave men and bold,
And quite unaccustomed to fear,
But the bravest by far in the ranks of the Shah
Was Abdul the Bulbul Amir.   *Abdul the Bulbul Amir*

1 Swing low sweet chariot,
  Comin' for to carry me home,
  I looked over Jordan an' what did I see?
  A band of Angels coming after me,
  Comin' for to carry me home.   *Swing Low, Sweet Chariot*

2 There is a lady sweet and kind,
  Was never face so pleased my mind;
  I did but see her passing by,
  And yet I love her till I die.   *Passing By*

3 There is a tavern in the town,
  And there my dear love sits him down,
  And drinks his wine 'mid laughter free,
  And never, never thinks of me.   *There is a Tavern in the Town*

4 Fare thee well, for I must leave thee,
  Do not let this parting grieve thee,
  And remember that the best of friends must part.   *Ib*

5 Tom Pearse, Tom Pearse, lend me your grey mare,
  All along, down along, out along Lee.
  For I want for to go to Widdicombe Fair,
  Wi' Bill Brewer, Jan Stewer, Peter Gurney, Peter Davey, Dan'l Whiddon,
      Harry Hawk, Old Uncle Tom Cobbleigh and all.   *Widdicombe Fair*

6 We're here because we're here because we're here because we're here.
                                                    Army Song, 1914–18

7 What shall we do with the drunken sailor
  Early in the morning?
  Hoo-ray and up she rises
  Early in the morning.   *What shall we do with the Drunken Sailor?*

French

8 *Liberté! Égalité! Fraternité!* Liberty! Equality! Fraternity!   *French*
                                                                 Revolution

9 *Revenons à nos moutons.* Let us return to our sheep (i.e. to the subject).
                                                    Maistre Pierre Pathelin

Greek

10 Nothing in excess.   *In the temple at Delphi*

Latin

11 *Ad majorem Dei gloriam.* To the greater glory of God.   *Motto of the*
                                                         Society of Jesus

12 *Et in Arcadia ego.* I too am in Arcadia.   *Inscription on tomb*

13 *Gaudeamus igitur,*
   Iuvenes dum sumus.
   Let us be happy while we are young.   *Students' song (13th century)*

14 *Tempora mutantur, et nos mutamur in illis.* Times change, and we change
   with them.   *Quoted in Harrison, Description of Britain, 1577*

ARABIAN NIGHTS

1 Who will change old lamps for new ones? . . . new lamps for old ones?
The History of Aladdin

2 Open Sesame! *The History of Ali Baba*

ARCHIMEDES, 287–212 B.C.

3 Give me a firm place to stand, and I will move the earth. *On the Lever*

4 I have found it! [Eureka!] *On making a discovery*

ARISTOTLE, 384–322 B.C.

5 Man is by nature a political animal. *Politics, Book 1*

6 Inferiors revolt in order that they may be equal, and equals that they may be superior. Such is the state of mind which creates revolutions. *Ib, Book 5*

7 Plato is dear to me, but dearer still is truth. *Attributed*

ARNOLD, George, 1834–1865

8 The living need charity more than the dead. *The Jolly Old Pedagogue*

ARNOLD, Matthew, 1822–1888

9 The sea is calm to-night,
The tide is full, the moon lies fair
Upon the Straits. *Dover Beach*

10 Is it so small a thing
To have enjoy'd the sun,
To have lived light in the spring,
To have loved, to have thought, to have done? *Empedocles on Etna*

11 Come, dear children, let us away;
Down and away below. *The Forsaken Merman*

12 Children dear, was it yesterday
(Call yet once) that she went away? *Ib*

13 She left lonely for ever
The kings of the sea. *Ib*

14 Who saw life steadily, and saw it whole:
The mellow glory of the Attic stage. *Sonnets, To a Friend*

15 Wandering between two worlds, one dead,
The other powerless to be born. *The Grande Chartreuse*

16 Strew on her roses, roses,
And never a spray of yew.
In quiet she reposes:
Ah! would that I did too. *Requiescat*

17 To-night it doth inherit
The vasty Hall of Death. *Ib*

18 Go, for they call you, Shepherd, from the hill. *The Scholar Gipsy, 1*

19 All the live murmur of a summer's day. *Ib, 20*

20 Tired of knocking at Preferment's door. *Ib, 35*

21 Before this strange disease of modern life,
With its sick hurry, its divided aims. *Ib, 203*

1 Still nursing the unconquerable hope,
   Still clutching the inviolable shade.   *The Scholar Gipsy, 211*

2 Others abide our question. Thou art free.
   We ask and ask: Thou smilest and art still,
   Out-topping knowledge.   *Shakespeare*

3 Truth sits upon the lips of dying men.   *Sohrab and Rustum*

4 And that sweet City with her dreaming spires
   She needs not June for beauty's heightening.   *[Of Oxford] Thyrsis, 19*

5 The pursuit of perfection, then, is the pursuit of sweetness and light.
                                                         Culture and Anarchy

6 Thus we have got three distinct terms, Barbarians, Philistines, Populace,
   to denote roughly the three great classes into which our society is divided.
                                                                        Ib

7 Home of lost causes, and forsaken beliefs, and unpopular names, and
   impossible loyalties!   *[Of Oxford] Essays in Criticism, First Series, Preface*

8 I am bound by my own definition of criticism: a disinterested endeavour
   to learn and propagate the best that is known and thought in the world.
                                   Ib, Functions of Criticism at the Present Time

9 In poetry, no less than in life, he is 'a beautiful and ineffectual angel,
   beating in the void his luminous wings in vain.'
                                                   [Of Shelley] Ib, Second Series

10 Culture is the passion for sweetness and light, and (what is more) the passion
   for making them prevail.   *Literature and Dogma, Preface*

11 Culture, the acquainting ourselves with the best that has been known and
   said in the world, and thus with the history of the human spirit.   *Ib*

ARNOLD, Thomas, 1795-1842

12 What we must look for here is, first, religious and moral principles; secondly,
   gentlemanly conduct; thirdly, intellectual ability.   *Address to his Scholars
                                                                     at Rugby*

13 My object will be, if possible, to form Christian men, for Christian boys I
   can scarcely hope to make.   *Letter on appointment as Headmaster of
                                                                Rugby, 1828*

ASAF, George (George H. Powell), 1880-1951

14 What's the use of worrying?
      It never was worth while,
   So, pack up your troubles in your old kit-bag,
      And smile, smile, smile.
                          Pack up your Troubles in your old Kit-Bag (1915)

ASQUITH, Herbert Henry, 1st Earl of Oxford and Asquith, 1852-1928

15 Wait and see.   *Various Speeches, 1910*

AUDEN, Wystan Hugh, 1907—

16 To save your world you asked this man to die:
   Would this man, could he see you now, ask why?   *Epitaph for an
                                                               Unknown Soldier*

1 When statesmen gravely say—'We must be realistic—'
The chances are they're weak and therefore pacifistic:
But when they speak of Principles—look out—perhaps
Their generals are already poring over maps.   *Footnotes*

2 Lay your sleeping head, my love,
Human on my faithless arm.   *Lay your Sleeping Head*

3 To the man-in-the-street, who, I'm sorry to say
Is a keen observer of life,
The word Intellectual suggests straight away
A man who's untrue to his wife.   *Note on Intellectuals*

4 Our researchers into Public Opinion are content
That he held the proper opinions for the time of year;
When there was peace, he was for peace; when there was war, he went.
    The Unknown Citizen

AUGUSTINE, St., 354-430

5 Give me chastity and continence, but not yet.   *Confessions, 8*

AUSTEN, Jane, 1775-1817

6 The yeomanry are precisely the order of people with whom I feel I can have nothing to do. A degree or two lower, and . . . I might hope to be useful to their families in some way or other.   EMMA   *Emma, Ch. 4*

7 One half of the world cannot understand the pleasures of the other.
    EMMA   *Ib, Ch. 9*

8 Nobody is healthy in London, nobody can be.   MR WOODHOUSE
    Ib, Ch. 12

9 Human nature is so well disposed towards those who are in interesting situations, that a young person, who either marries or dies, is sure of being kindly spoken of.   *Ib, Ch. 22*

10 Business, you know, may bring money, but friendship hardly ever does.
    JOHN KNIGHTLEY   *Ib, Ch. 34*

11 It will, I believe, be everywhere found, that as the clergy are, or are not what they ought to be, so are the rest of the nation.   EDMUND
    Mansfield Park, Ch. 9

12 To sit in the shade on a fine day, and look upon verdure is the most perfect refreshment.   FANNY   *Ib, Ch. 9*

13 Let other pens dwell on guilt and misery.   *Ib, Ch. 48*

14 But are they all horrid, are you sure they are all horrid?
    CATHERINE MORLAND   *Northanger Abbey, Ch. 6*

15 A woman, especially if she have the misfortune of knowing anything, should conceal it as well as she can.   *Ib, Ch. 14*

16 One does not love a place the less for having suffered in it, unless it has all been suffering, nothing but suffering.   *Persuasion, Ch. 20*

17 It is a truth universally acknowledged, that a single man in possession of a good fortune must be in want of a wife.   *Pride and Prejudice, Ch. 1*

18 Happiness in marriage is entirely a matter of chance.   *Ib, Ch. 6*

19 How can you contrive to write so even?   MISS BINGLEY   *Ib, Ch. 10*

1 It is happy for you that you possess the talent of flattering with delicacy. May I ask whether these pleasing attentions proceed from the impulse of the moment, or are the result of previous study?   MR BENNET
Pride and Prejudice, Ch. 14

2 Nobody is on my side, nobody takes part with me: I am cruelly used, nobody feels for my poor nerves.   MRS BENNET   *Ib, Ch. 48*

3 'I am afraid' replied Elinor, 'that the pleasantness of an employment does not always evince its propriety.'   *Sense and Sensibility, Ch. 13*

4 What dreadful hot weather we have! It keeps me in a continual state of inelegance.   *Letter, 18 Sept. 1796*

AUSTIN, Alfred, 1835–1913

5 An earl by right, by courtesy a man.   *The Season*

6 Across the wires the electric message came:
'He is no better, he is much the same.'   *On the Illness of the Prince of Wales, Attributed*

BACON, Francis, 1st Baron Verulam, 1561–1626

7 My Essayes . . . come home, to Mens Businesse, and Bosomes.
Essays. Dedication

8 What is truth? said jesting Pilate, and would not stay for an answer.
Essay 1. Of Truth

9 Men fear death, as children fear to go in the dark; and as that natural fear in children is increased with tales, so is the other.   *2. Of Death*

10 It is as natural to die as to be born; and to a little infant, perhaps, the one is as painful as the other.   *Ib*

11 All colours will agree in the dark.   *3. Of Unity in Religion*

12 Revenge is a kind of wild justice; which the more man's nature runs to, the more ought law to weed it out.   *4. Of Revenge*

13 Prosperity is the blessing of the Old Testament; adversity is the blessing of the New.   *5. Of Adversity*

14 Prosperity is not without many fears and distastes; and adversity is not without comforts and hopes.   *Ib*

15 Prosperity doth best discover vice; but adversity doth best discover virtue.
Ib

16 He that talketh what he knoweth, will also talk what he knoweth not.
6. Of Simulation and Dissimulation

17 The joys of parents are secret, and so are their griefs and fears.
7. Of Parents and Children

18 Children sweeten labours, but they make misfortunes more bitter.   *Ib*

19 He that hath wife and children hath given hostages to fortune; for they are impediments to great enterprises, either of virtue or mischief.
8. Of Marriage and Single Life

20 Wives are young men's mistresses; companions for middle age; and old men's nurses.   *Ib*

21 He was reputed one of the wise men, that made answer to the question, when a man should marry? A young man not yet, an elder man not at all.
Ib

1 Nuptial love maketh mankind; friendly love perfecteth it; but wanton love corrupteth and embaseth it. *Essay 10. Of Love*

2 Men in great places are thrice servants: servants of the sovereign or state; servants of fame; and servants of business. *11. Of Great Place*

3 There is in human nature generally more of the fool than of the wise. *12. Of Boldness*

4 If the hill will not come to Mahomet, Mahomet will go to the hill. *Ib*

5 In charity there is no excess. *13. Of Goodness, and Goodness of Nature*

6 If a man be gracious and courteous to strangers, it shews he is a citizen of the world. *Ib*

7 New nobility is but the act of power; but ancient nobility is the act of time. *14. Of Nobility*

8 So when any of the four pillars of government are mainly shaken or weakened (which are religion, justice, counsel, and treasure), men had need to pray for fair weather. *15. Of Seditions and Troubles*

9 Money is like muck, not good except it be spread. *Ib*

10 The remedy is worse than the disease. *Ib*

11 A little philosophy inclineth man's mind to atheism; but depth in philosophy bringeth men's minds about to religion. *16. Of Atheism*

12 It were better to have no opinion of God at all, than such an opinion as is unworthy of him. *17. Of Superstition*

13 Travel, in the younger sort, is a part of education; in the elder, a part of experience. *18. Of Travel*

14 It is a miserable state of mind to have few things to desire and many things to fear. *19. Of Empire*

15 Nothing destroyeth authority so much as the unequal and untimely interchange of power pressed too far, and relaxed too much. *Ib*

16 There be that can pack the cards, and yet cannot play well. *22. Of Cunning*

17 Be so true to thyself, as thou be not false to others. *23. Of Wisdom for a Man's Self*

18 He that will not apply new remedies must expect new evils: for time is the greatest innovator. *24. Of Innovations*

19 To choose time is to save time. *25. Of Dispatch*

20 The French are wiser than they seem, and the Spaniards seem wiser than they are. *26. Of Seeming Wise*

21 Whosoever is delighted in solitude is either a wild beast or a god. *27. Of Friendship*

22 Riches are for spending. *28. Of Expense*

23 Age will not be defied. *30. Of Regiment of Health*

24 Suspicions amongst thoughts are like bats amongst birds, they ever fly by twilight. *31. Of Suspicion*

25 Of great riches there is no real use, except it be in the distribution. *34. Of Riches*

26 Nature is often hidden, sometimes overcome, seldom extinguished. *38. Of Nature in Men*

1 A man that is young in years may be old in hours, if he have lost no time
Essay 42. Of Youth and Age

2 Virtue is like a rich stone, best plain set.   *43. Of Beauty*

3 Houses are built to live in, and not to look on.   *45. Of Building*

4 God Almighty first planted a garden. And indeed it is the purest of human
pleasures.   *46. Of Gardens*

5 Studies serve for delight, for ornament, and for ability.   *50. Of Studies*

6 To spend too much time in studies is sloth.   *Ib*

7 Some books are to be tasted, others to be swallowed, and some few to be
chewed and digested.   *Ib*

8 Reading maketh a full man; conference a ready man; and writing an exact
man.   *Ib*

9 Histories make men wise; poets witty; the mathematics subtile; natural
philosophy deep; moral grave; logic and rhetoric able to contend.   *Ib*

10 Fame is like a river, that beareth up things light and swoln, and drowns
things weighty and solid.   *53. Of Praise*

11 The place of justice is an hallowed place.   *56. Of Judicature*

12 If a man will begin with certainties, he shall end in doubts, but if he will be
content to begin with doubts, he shall end in certainties.
The Advancement of Learning, 1, 5, 8

13 Hope is a good breakfast, but it is a bad supper.   *Apophthegms, 36*

14 I have taken all knowledge to be my province.   *Letter to Lord Burleigh,*
1592

15 God's first creature, which was light.   *The New Atlantis*

16 There are four classes of Idols which beset men's minds. To these for
distinction's sake I have assigned names—calling the first class, Idols of the
Tribe; the second, Idols of the Cave; the third, Idols of the Market-place;
the fourth, Idols of the Theatre.   *Novum Organum*

17 Nature, to be commanded, must be obeyed.   *Ib*

BAGEHOT, Walter, 1826–1877

18 *The Times* has made many ministries.   *The English Constitution, Ch. 1*

19 Women—one half the human race at least—care fifty times more for a
marriage than a ministry.   *Ib, Ch. 2*

20 Of all nations in the World, the English are perhaps the least a nation of pure
philosophers.   *Ib*

21 Poverty is an anomaly to rich people. It is very difficult to make out why
people who want dinner do not ring the bell.   *Literary Studies, 2*

BAIRNSFATHER, Charles Bruce, 1888–1959

22 Well, if you knows of a better 'ole, go to it.   *Fragments from France, 1*

BALFOUR, Arthur James, 1848–1930

23 The energies of our system will decay, the glory of the sun will be dimmed,
and the earth, tideless and inert, will no longer tolerate the race which has

for a moment disturbed its solitude. Man will go down into the pit, and all
his thoughts will perish. *The Foundations of Belief, Part 1, Ch. 1*

1 It is unfortunate, considering that enthusiasm moves the world, that so few
enthusiasts can be trusted to speak the truth. *Letter to Mrs Drew, 1918*

BALL, John, ?–1381

2 When Adam delved and Eve span,
Who was then the gentleman? *Text for sermon on Peasants' Revolt*

BARHAM, Richard Harris, 1788–1845

3 A servant's too often an impudent elf;
—If it's business of consequence, *do it yourself*! *The Ingoldsby Legends,*
The Ingoldsby Penance, Moral

4 The Jackdaw sat on the Cardinal's chair!
Bishop and abbot, and prior were there. *Ib, The Jackdaw of Rheims*

5 Never, I ween,
Was a prouder seen,
Read of in books, or dreamt of in dreams,
Than the Cardinal Lord Archbishop of Rheims! *Ib*

6 He long lived the pride of that country side,
And at last in the odour of sanctity died. *Ib*

7 He smiled and said, 'Sir, does your mother know that you are out?'
Ib, Misadventures at Margate

BARING-GOULD, Sabine, 1834–1924

8 Now the day is over,
Night is drawing nigh,
Shadows of the evening
Steal across the sky. *Now the Day is over*

9 Onward, Christian soldiers
Marching as to war,
With the Cross of Jesus
Going on before. *Onward, Christian Soldiers*

BARNUM, Phineas Taylor, 1810–1891

10 There's a sucker born every minute. *Attributed*

BARRIE, Sir James Matthew, 1860–1937

11 When the first baby laughed for the first time, the laugh broke into a thousand pieces and they all went skipping about, and that was the beginning of
fairies. PETER PAN *Peter Pan, Act 1*

12 Every time a child says 'I don't believe in fairies' there is a little fairy somewhere that falls down dead. PETER PAN *Ib*

13 To die will be an awfully big adventure. PETER PAN *Ib, Act 3*

14 Do you believe in fairies? Say quick that you believe. If you believe, clap
your hands! PETER PAN *Ib, Act 4*

15 One's religion is whatever he is most interested in, and yours is Success.
KATE *The Twelve-Pound Look*

1 You've forgotten the grandest moral attribute of a Scotsman, Maggie, that
he'll do nothing which might damage his career.   JOHN SHAND
What Every Woman Knows, Act 2

BARRINGTON, George, 1755–1810?

2 True patriots we; for be it understood,
We left our country for our country's good.   *Prologue for opening of*
Playhouse, Sydney, 16 Jan. 1796 by company of convicts

BATEMAN, Edgar, 19th century

3 Wiv a ladder and some glasses,
You could see to 'Ackney Marshes,
If it wasn't for the 'ouses in between.   *If it wasn't for the 'Ouses in between*

BATES, Katherine Lee, 1859–1929

4 America! America!
God shed His grace on thee
And crown thy good with brotherhood
From sea to shining sea!   *America the Beautiful*

BAYLY, Thomas Haynes, 1797–1839

5 Absence makes the heart grow fonder,
Isle of Beauty, Fare thee well!   *Isle of Beauty*

BEATTY, David, 1st Earl Beatty, 1871–1936

6 There's something wrong with our bloody ships to-day.
Remark during Battle of Jutland, 1916

BEAUMONT, Francis, 1584–1616

7   What things we have seen,
Done at the Mermaid! heard words that have been
So nimble, and so full of subtle flame,
As if that everyone from whence they came
Had meant to put his whole wit in a jest,
And had resolved to live a fool the rest
Of his dull life.   *Letter to Ben Jonson*

8 Mortality, behold and fear!
What a change of flesh is here.   *On the Tombs in Westminster Abbey*

BEAUMONT, Francis, 1584–1616, and FLETCHER, John, 1579–1625

9 But what is past my help is past my care.   *The Double Marriage, Act 1,*
Scene 1

10 There is no other purgatory but a woman.   ELDER LOVELESS
The Scornful Lady, Act 3, Scene 1

BECKETT, Samuel, 1906—

11 Nothing happens, nobody comes, nobody goes, it's awful!   ESTRAGON
Waiting for Godot, Act 1

1 VLADIMIR: That passed the time.
ESTRAGON: It would have passed in any case.
VLADIMIR: Yes, but not so rapidly.   *Waiting for Godot, Act 1*

2 Habit is a great deadener.   VLADIMIR   *Ib, Act 3*

BECKFORD, William, 1759–1844

3 I am not over-fond of resisting temptation.   *Vathek*

BECON, Thomas, 1512–1567

4 For when the wine is in, the wit is out.   *Catechism, 375*

BEE, Bernard Elliott, 1823–1861

5 There is Jackson standing like a stone wall.   *First Battle of Bull Run, 1861*

BEECHING, Henry Charles, 1859–1919

6 First come I; my name is Jowett.
There's no knowledge but I know it.
I am Master of this College:
What I don't know isn't knowledge.   *The Masque of Balliol*

BEERBOHM, Sir Max, 1872–1956

7 Most women are not so young as they are painted.   *A Defence of*
                                                              Cosmetics

8 Zuleika, on a desert island, would have spent most of her time in looking
for a man's footprint.   *Zuleika Dobson, Ch. 2*

9 She was one of the people who say, 'I don't know anything about music
really, but I know what I like.'   *Ib, Ch. 9*

BEERS, Ethel Lynn, 1827–1879

10 All quiet along the Potomac to-night,
   No sound save the rush of the river,
While soft falls the dew on the face of the dead—
   The picket's off duty forever.   *All Quiet Along the Potomac*

BEHN, Aphra, 1640–1689

11 Love ceases to be a pleasure, when it ceases to be a secret.
                        La Montre, or The Lover's Watch, Four o'clock

12 Variety is the soul of pleasure.   WILLMORE   *The Rover, Part 2, Act 1*

13 Fine clothes, rich furniture, jewels and plate are more inviting than beauty
unadorn'd.   PETRONELLA   *Ib, 4, 2*

BELLOC, Hilaire, 1870–1953

14 Child! do not throw this book about;
   Refrain from the unholy pleasure
Of cutting all the pictures out!
   Preserve it as your chiefest treasure.
            The Bad Child's Book of Beasts, Dedication

1 When people call this beast to mind,
  They marvel more and more
  At such a little tail behind,
  So large a trunk before.   *The Bad Child's Book of Beasts, The Elephant*

2 The Chief Defect of Henry King
  Was chewing little bits of String.   *Cautionary Tales, Henry King*

3 Physicians of the Utmost Fame
  Were called at once; but when they came
  They answered, as they took their Fees,
  'There is no Cure for this Disease.'   *Ib*

4 'Oh, my Friends, be warned by me,
  That Breakfast, Dinner, Lunch and Tea
  Are all the Human Frame requires. . . .'
  With that the Wretched Child expires.   *Ib*

5 When I am dead, I hope it may be said:
  'His sins were scarlet, but his books were read.'   *Epigrams, On His Books*

6 Lord Finchley tried to mend the Electric Light
  Himself. It struck him dead: And serve him right!
  It is the business of the wealthy man
  To give employment to the artisan.   *Ib, Lord Finchley*

7 The accursèd power which stands on Privilege
  (And goes with Women, and Champagne and Bridge)
  Broke—and Democracy resumed her reign:
  (Which goes with Bridge, and Women and Champagne).
                                     Ib, On a General Election

8 The Devil, having nothing else to do,
  Went off to tempt My Lady Poltagrue.
  My Lady, tempted by a private whim,
  To his extreme annoyance, tempted him.
                          Ib, On Lady Poltagrue, A Public Peril

9 I said to Heart, 'How goes it?' Heart replied:
  'Right as a Ribstone Pippin!' But it lied.   *The False Heart*

10 I'm tired of Love: I'm still more tired of Rhyme.
   But Money gives me pleasure all the time.   *Fatigue*

11 Birds in their little nests agree
   With Chinamen, but not with me.   *On Food*

12 Remote and ineffectual Don
   That dared attack my Chesterton.   *Lines to a Don*

13 The Microbe is so very small
   You cannot make him out at all.
                     More Beasts for Worse Children, The Microbe

14 Lord Hippo suffered fearful loss
   By putting money on a horse
   Which he believed, if it were pressed,
   Would run far faster than the rest.   *More Peers, Lord Hippo*

1 Lord Lucky, by a curious fluke,
   Became a most important duke.
   From living in a vile Hotel
   A long way east of Camberwell
   He rose in less than half an hour
   To riches, dignity and power.
              More Peers, Lord Lucky

2 When I am living in the Midlands
    That are sodden and unkind,
  I light my lamp in the evening:
    My work is left behind;
  And the great hills of the South Country
    Come back into my mind.
              The South Country

3 If I ever become a rich man,
    Or if ever I grow to be old,
  I will build a house with deep thatch
    To shelter me from the cold,
  And there shall the Sussex songs be sung
    And the story of Sussex told.
              Ib

4 I will hold my house in the high wood
    Within a walk of the sea,
  And the men that were boys when I was a boy
    Shall sit and drink with me.
              Ib

5 Do you remember an Inn,
  Miranda?
              Tarantella

BENNETT, Enoch Arnold, 1867–1931

6 'Ye can call it influenza if ye like,' said Mrs. Machin. 'There was no influenza in my young days. We called a cold a cold.'   *The Card, Ch. 8*

7 'And yet,' demanded Councillor Barlow . . . 'what great cause is he identified with?'
'He is identified,' said the speaker, 'with the great cause of cheering us all up.'   *Ib, Ch. 12*

8 Being a husband is a whole-time job. That is why so many husbands fail. They cannot give their entire attention to it.   CULVER *The Title, Act 1*

9 There was a young man of Montrose,
  Who had pockets in none of his clothes,
    When asked by his lass
    Where he carried his brass,
  He said, 'Darling, I pay through the nose.'
              Limerick

BENSON, Arthur Christopher, 1862–1925

10 Land of Hope and Glory, Mother of the Free,
  How shall we extol thee, who are born of thee?
  Wider still and wider shall thy bounds be set;
  God who made thee mighty, make thee mightier yet.
    Land of Hope and Glory (Music by Sir Edward Elgar)

BENTHAM, Jeremy, 1748–1832

1 The greatest happiness of the greatest number is the foundation of morals
and legislation.   *The Commonplace Book*

BENTLEY, Edmund Clerihew, 1875–1956

2 The Art of Biography
Is different from Geography.
Geography is about Maps,
But Biography is about Chaps.
                Biography for Beginners, Introductory Remarks

3 Sir Christopher Wren
Said, 'I am going to dine with some men.
If anybody calls
Say I am designing St. Paul's.'   *Ib, Sir Christopher Wren*

4 What I like about Clive
Is that he is no longer alive.
There is a great deal to be said
For being dead.   *Ib, Clive*

5 Sir Humphry Davy
Detested gravy.
He lived in the odium
Of having discovered Sodium.   *Ib, Sir Humphry Davy*

6 George the Third
Ought never to have occurred.
One can only wonder
At so grotesque a blunder.   *More Biography, George the Third*

7 When their lordships asked Bacon
How many bribes he had taken
He had at least the grace
To get very red in the face.   *Baseless Biography, Bacon*

BENTLEY, Nicolas Clerihew, 1907—

8 Cecil B. de Mille,
Rather against his will,
Was persuaded to leave Moses
Out of 'The Wars of the Roses'.   *Clerihew*

BERLIN, Irving, 1888—

9 Come on and hear, come on and hear, Alexander's Ragtime Band.
                                        Alexander's Ragtime Band

BERNARD, William Bayle, 1807–1875

10 A Storm in a Teacup.   *Title of Farce*

BETJEMAN, John, 1906—

11 The Church's Restoration
In eighteen-eighty-three
Has left for contemplation
Not what there used to be.   *Hymn*

12 Miss J. Hunter Dunn, Miss J. Hunter Dunn,
Furnish'd and burnish'd by Aldershot sun.   *A Subaltern's Love Song*

THE BIBLE

(Quotations are from the Authorised Version, 1611, unless otherwise stated)

Old Testament

Genesis

1 In the beginning God created the heaven and the earth.
And the earth was without form, and void. *1, 1–2*

2 And God said, Let there be light: and there was light. *1, 3*

3 So God created man in his own image, in the image of God created he him; male and female created he them. *1, 27*

4 Be fruitful, and multiply, and replenish the earth. *1, 28*

5 And God saw everything that he had made, and, behold, it was very good. *1, 31*

6 And the Lord God took the man, and put him into the garden of Eden to dress it and to keep it. *2, 15*

7 And the Lord God said, It is not good that the man should be alone; I will make him an help meet for him. *2, 18*

8 And the rib, which the Lord God had taken from man, made he a woman. *2, 22*

9 This is now bone of my bones, and flesh of my flesh. *2, 23*

10 And they were both naked, the man and his wife, and were not ashamed. *2, 25*

11 Ye shall be as gods, knowing good and evil. *3, 5*

12 And they sewed fig leaves together, and made themselves aprons. *3, 7*

13 In the sweat of thy face shalt thou eat bread. *3, 19*

14 For dust thou art, and unto dust shalt thou return. *3, 19*

15 The mother of all living. *3, 20*

16 Am I my brother's keeper? *4, 9*

17 And the Lord set a mark upon Cain. *4, 15*

18 And all the days of Methuselah were nine hundred sixty and nine years. *5, 27*

19 There were giants in the earth in those days. *6, 4*

20 There went in two and two unto Noah into the ark, the male and the female. *7, 9*

21 And the ark rested in the seventh month, on the seventeenth day of the month, upon the mountains of Ararat. *8, 4*

22 And the dove came in to him in the evening; and, lo, in her mouth was an olive leaf pluckt off. *8, 11*

23 While the earth remaineth, seedtime and harvest, and cold and heat, and summer and winter, and day and night shall not cease. *8, 22*

24 Whoso sheddeth man's blood, by man shall his blood be shed. *9, 6*

25 I do set my bow in the cloud. *9, 13*

26 Even as Nimrod the mighty hunter before the Lord. *10, 9*

27 Therefore is the name of it called Babel; because the Lord did there confound the language of all the earth. *11, 9*

1 His hand will be against every man, and every man's hand against him.
Genesis, 16, 12

2 Shall not the Judge of all the earth do right?   *18, 25*

3 If I find in Sodom fifty righteous within the city, then I will spare all the place for their sakes.   *18, 26*

4 But his wife looked back from behind him, and she became a pillar of salt.
19, 26

5 In thy seed shall all the nations of the earth be blessed.   *22, 18*

6 He sold his birthright unto Jacob.   *25, 33*

7 Esau my brother is a hairy man, and I am a smooth man.   *27, 11*

8 The voice is Jacob's voice, but the hands are the hands of Esau.   *27, 22*

9 A ladder set up on the earth, and the top of it reached to heaven.   *28, 12*

10 He made him a coat of many colours.   *37, 3*

11 Behold, this dreamer cometh.   *37, 19*

12 Jacob saw that there was corn in Egypt.   *42, 1*

13 Ye shall eat the fat of the land.   *45, 18*

14 Unstable as water, thou shalt not excel.   *49, 4*

Exodus

15 Now there arose up a new king over Egypt, which knew not Joseph.   *1, 8*

16 I have been a stranger in a strange land.   *2, 22*

17 Behold, the bush burned with fire, and the bush was not consumed.   *3, 2*

18 A land flowing with milk and honey.   *3, 8*

19 I AM THAT I AM.   *3, 14*

20 Ye shall no more give the people straw to make brick.   *5, 7*

21 Let my people go, that they may serve me.   *8, 1*

22 This is the finger of God.   *8, 19*

23 Darkness which may be felt.   *10, 21*

24 But the Lord hardened Pharaoh's heart, and he would not let them go.
10, 27

25 The Lord smote all the firstborn in the land of Egypt.   *12, 29*

26 And the children of Israel went into the midst of the sea upon the dry ground.   *14, 22*

27 Would to God we had died by the hand of the Lord in the land of Egypt, when we sat by the flesh pots, and when we did eat bread to the full.   *16, 3*

28 And when the children of Israel saw it, they said one to another, It is manna: for they wist not what it was. And Moses said unto them, This is the bread which the Lord hath given you to eat.   *16, 15*

29 I am the Lord thy God, which have brought thee out of the land of Egypt, out of the house of bondage.   *20, 2*

30 Thou shalt have no other gods before me.   *20, 3*

31 Thou shalt not make unto thee any graven image.   *20, 4*

1 For I the Lord thy God am a jealous God, visiting the iniquity of the fathers upon the children unto the third and fourth generation of them that hate me. *Exodus, 20, 5*

2 Thou shalt not take the name of the Lord thy God in vain. *20, 7*

3 Remember the sabbath day, to keep it holy.
Six days shalt thou labour, and do all thy work:
But the seventh day is the sabbath of the Lord thy God. *20, 8–10*

4 Honour thy father and thy mother: that thy days may be long upon the land which the Lord thy God giveth thee. *20, 12*

5 Thou shalt not kill. *20, 13*

6 Thou shalt not commit adultery. *20, 14*

7 Thou shalt not steal. *20, 15*

8 Thou shalt not bear false witness against thy neighbour. *20, 16*

9 Thou shalt not covet thy neighbour's house, thou shalt not covet thy neighbour's wife, nor his manservant, nor his maidservant, nor his ox, nor his ass, nor any thing that is thy neighbour's. *20, 17*

10 Thou shalt give life for life,
Eye for eye, tooth for tooth, hand for hand, foot for foot. *21, 23–24*

11 Thou shalt not suffer a witch to live. *22, 18*

12 Thou art a stiffnecked people. *33, 3*

Leviticus

13 Let him go for a scapegoat into the wilderness. *16, 10*

14 Ye shall be holy; for I the Lord your God am holy. *19, 2*

15 And thou shalt not glean thy vineyard, neither shalt thou gather every grape of thy vineyard; thou shalt leave them for the poor and stranger. *19, 10*

16 Thou shalt love thy neighbour as thyself. *19, 18*

17 Thou shalt rise up before the hoary head, and honour the face of the old man. *19, 32*

Numbers

18 The Lord bless thee, and keep thee: The Lord make his face shine upon thee, and be gracious unto thee: The Lord lift up his countenance upon thee, and give thee peace. *6, 24–26*

19 We will go by the king's high way. *20, 17*

20 Let me die the death of the righteous, and let my last end be like his! *23, 10*

Deuteronomy

21 Hear, O Israel: The Lord our God is one Lord. *6, 4*

22 And thou shalt love the Lord thy God with all thine heart, and with all thy soul, and with all thy might. *6, 5*

23 Man doth not live by bread only, but by every word that proceedeth out of the mouth of the Lord doth man live. *8, 3*

24 As a man chasteneth his son, so the Lord thy God chasteneth thee. *8, 5*

1 And now, Israel, what doth the Lord thy God require of thee, but to fear the Lord thy God, to walk in all his ways, and to love him and to serve the Lord thy God with all thy heart and with all thy soul.   *Deuteronomy, 10, 12*

2 Love ye therefore the stranger: for ye were strangers in the land of Egypt.
10, 19

3 For the poor shall never cease out of the land.   *15, 11*

4 Thou shalt not muzzle the ox when he treadeth out the corn.   *25, 4*

5 I have set before you life and death, blessing and cursing: therefore choose life, that both thou and thy seed may live.   *30, 19*

6 He kept him as the apple of his eye.   *32, 10*

7 Jeshurun waxed fat, and kicked.   *32, 15*

8 As thy days, so shall thy strength be.   *33, 25*

9 The eternal God is thy refuge, and underneath are the everlasting arms.
33, 27

Joshua

10 Be strong and of a good courage.   *1, 6*

11 Hewers of wood and drawers of water.   *9, 21*

12 Sun, stand thou still upon Gibeon; and thou, Moon, in the valley of Ajalon.
10, 12

Judges

13 I arose a mother in Israel.   *5, 7*

14 The stars in their courses fought against Sisera.   *5, 20*

15 She brought forth butter in a lordly dish.   *5, 25*

16 Have they not divided the prey; to every man a damsel or two?   *5, 30*

17 Faint, yet pursuing.   *8, 4*

18 Say now Shibboleth.   *12, 6*

19 Out of the eater came forth meat, and out of the strong came forth sweetness.
14, 14

20 He smote them hip and thigh.   *15, 8*

21 If I be shaven, then my strength will go from me.   *16, 17*

22 He bowed himself with all his might; and the house fell upon the lords, and upon all the people that were therein.   *16, 30*

23 From Dan even to Beer-sheba.   *20, 1*

24 Every man did that which was right in his own eyes.   *21, 25*

Ruth

25 Whither thou goest, I will go; and where thou lodgest, I will lodge: thy people shall be my people, and thy God my God.   *1, 16*

26 The Lord do so to me, and more also, if ought but death part thee and me.
1, 17

27 And she went, and came, and gleaned in the field after the reapers.   *2, 3*

1 Samuel

28 Speak, Lord; for thy servant heareth.   *3, 9*

29 It is the Lord: let him do what seemeth him good.   *3, 18*

1 Quit yourselves like men.   *I Samuel, 4, 9*

2 Is Saul also among the prophets?   *10, 11*

3 The Lord hath sought him a man after his own heart.   *13, 14*

4 Agag came unto him delicately.   *15, 32*

5 Man looketh on the outward appearance, but the Lord looketh on the heart.
    16, 7

6 David took an harp, and played with his hand.   *16, 23*

7 Saul hath slain his thousands, and David his ten thousands.   *18, 7*

8 David therefore departed thence, and escaped to the cave Adullam.   *22, 1*

2 Samuel

9 How are the mighty fallen!   *1, 19*

10 Tell it not in Gath, publish it not in the streets of Askelon; lest the daughters
of the Philistines rejoice, lest the daughters of the uncircumcised triumph.
    1, 20

11 Saul and Jonathan were lovely and pleasant in their lives, and in their death
they were not divided: they were swifter than eagles, they were stronger
than lions.   *1, 23*

12 Thy love to me was wonderful, passing the love of women.   *1, 26*

13 Abner with the hinder end of the spear smote him under the fifth rib.   *2, 23*

14 Would God I had died for thee, O Absalom, my son, my son!   *18, 33*

15 The sweet psalmist of Israel.   *23, 1*

1 Kings

16 Divide the living child in two.   *3, 25*

17 There came of all people to hear the wisdom of Solomon.   *4, 34*

18 The barrel of meal shall not waste, neither shall the cruse of oil fail.   *17, 14*

19 How long halt ye between two opinions?   *18, 21*

20 There ariseth a little cloud out of the sea, like a man's hand.   *18, 44*

21 A still small voice.   *19, 12*

22 Elijah passed by him, and cast his mantle upon him.   *19, 19*

2 Kings

23 Go up, thou bald head.   *2, 23*

24 There is death in the pot.   *4, 40*

25 The driving is like the driving of Jehu the son of Nimshi; for he driveth
furiously.   *9, 20*

Esther

26 Let it be written among the laws of the Persians and the Medes, that it be
not altered.   *1, 19*

27 The king loved Esther above all the women.   *2, 17*

Job

1 Naked came I out of my mother's womb, and naked shall I return thither: the Lord gave, and the Lord hath taken away; blessed be the name of the Lord.   *1, 21*

2 Shall mortal man be more just than God? shall a man be more pure than his maker?   *4, 17*

3 Man is born unto trouble, as the sparks fly upward.   *5, 7*

4 Though he slay me, yet will I trust in him.   *13, 15*

5 Man that is born of a woman is of few days, and full of trouble.   *14, 1*

6 Miserable comforters are ye all.   *16, 2*

7 I am escaped with the skin of my teeth.   *19, 20*

8 I know that my redeemer liveth.   *19, 25*

9 The price of wisdom is above rubies.   *28, 18*

10 I was eyes to the blind, and feet was I to the lame.   *29, 15*

11 Great men are not always wise.   *32, 9*

12 Who is this that darkeneth counsel by words without knowledge?   *38, 2*

13 Hath the rain a father?   *38, 28*

14 Canst thou draw out leviathan with an hook?   *41, 1*

15 I have heard of thee by the hearing of the ear: but now mine eye seeth thee.
42, 5

Psalms

16 Why do the heathen rage, and the people imagine a vain thing?   *2, 1*

17 Out of the mouth of babes and sucklings hast thou ordained strength.   *8, 2*

18 What is man, that thou art mindful of him?   *8, 4*

19 Thou hast made him a little lower than the angels.   *8, 5*

20 The fool hath said in his heart, There is no God.   *14, 1*

21 Keep me as the apple of the eye, hide me under the shadow of thy wings.
17, 8

22 The heavens declare the glory of God; and the firmament sheweth his handywork.   *19, 1*

23 Day unto day uttereth speech, and night unto night sheweth knowledge.
19, 2

24 More to be desired are they than gold, yea, than much fine gold: sweeter also than honey and the honeycomb.   *19, 10*

25 Let the words of my mouth, and the meditation of my heart, be acceptable in thy sight, O Lord, my strength, and my redeemer.   *19, 14*

26 Some trust in chariots, and some in horses: but we will remember the name of the Lord our God.   *20, 7*

27 The Lord is my shepherd; I shall not want.   *23, 1*

28 He maketh me to lie down in green pastures: he leadeth me beside the still waters.   *23, 2*

29 Yea, though I walk through the valley of the shadow of death, I will fear no evil: for thou art with me; thy rod and thy staff they comfort me.   *23, 4*

1 The earth is the Lord's, and the fulness thereof; the world, and they that dwell therein.
Psalms, 24, 1

2 Weeping may endure for a night, but joy cometh in the morning.   *30, 5*

3 Into thy hands I commend my spirit. *31, 6, Book of Common Prayer version*

4 Praise the Lord with harp: sing unto him with the psaltery and an instrument of ten strings.
33, 2

5 Sing unto him a new song; play skilfully with a loud noise.   *33, 3*

6 O taste and see that the Lord is good.   *34, 8*

7 The Lord is nigh unto them that are of a broken heart.   *34, 18*

8 But the meek shall inherit the earth.   *37, 11*

9 I have been young, and now am old; yet have I not seen the righteous forsaken, nor his seed begging bread.
37, 25

10 I myself have seen the ungodly in great power: and flourishing like a green bay-tree.
37, 36, Book of Common Prayer version

11 Lord, make me to know mine end, and the measure of my days.   *39, 4*

12 Blessed is he that considereth the poor.   *41, 1*

13 God is our refuge and strength, a very present help in trouble.   *46, 1*

14 Purge me with hyssop, and I shall be clean: wash me, and I shall be whiter than snow.
51, 7

15 The sacrifices of God are a broken spirit: a broken and a contrite heart, O God, thou wilt not despise.
51, 17

16 Oh that I had wings like a dove!   *55, 6*

17 They are like the deaf adder that stoppeth her ear.   *58, 4*

18 They grin like a dog, and run about through the city.
59, 6, Book of Common Prayer version

19 Make a joyful noise unto God.   *66, 1*

20 They go from strength to strength.   *84, 7*

21 I had rather be a doorkeeper in the house of my God, than to dwell in the tents of wickedness.
84, 10

22 For a thousand years in thy sight are but as yesterday when it is past, and as a watch in the night.
90, 4

23 The days of our years are threescore years and ten; and if by reason of strength they be fourscore years, yet is their strength labour and sorrow; for it is soon cut off, and we fly away.
90, 10

24 So teach us to number our days, that we may apply our hearts unto wisdom.
90, 12

25 He shall cover thee with his feathers, and under his wings shalt thou trust.
91, 4

26 Thou shalt not be afraid for the terror by night; nor for the arrow that flieth by day.
91, 5

27 Nor for the pestilence that walketh in darkness; nor for the destruction that wasteth at noonday.
91, 6

28 Like as a father pitieth his children, so the Lord pitieth them that fear him.
103, 13

1 As for man, his days are as grass: as a flower of the field, so he flourisheth.
Psalms, 103, 15

2 Wine that maketh glad the heart of man.   *104, 15*

3 The iron entered into his soul.   *105, 18, Book of Common Prayer version*

4 They that go down to the sea in ships, that do business in great waters.
107, 23

5 They reel to and fro, and stagger like a drunken man, and are at their wits'
end.   *107, 27*

6 The fear of the Lord is the beginning of wisdom.   *111, 10*

7 The mountains skipped like rams, and the little hills like lambs.   *114, 4*

8 They have mouths, but they speak not: eyes have they, but they see not.
115, 5

9 They have ears, but they hear not: noses have they, but they smell not.
115, 6

10 I said in my haste, All men are liars.   *116, 11*

11 Precious in the sight of the Lord is the death of his saints.   *116, 15*

12 It is better to trust in the Lord than to put confidence in man.   *118, 8*

13 The stone which the builders refused is become the head stone of the
corner.   *118, 22*

14 I am for peace: but when I speak, they are for war.   *120, 7*

15 I will lift up mine eyes unto the hills, from whence cometh my help. *121, 1*

16 The sun shall not smite thee by day, nor the moon by night.   *121, 6*

17 The Lord shall preserve thy going out and thy coming in from this time
forth, and even for evermore.   *121, 8*

18 They that sow in tears shall reap in joy.   *126, 5*

19 Except the Lord build the house, they labour in vain that build it. *127, 1*

20 It is vain for you to rise up early, to sit up late, to eat the bread of sorrows:
for so he giveth his beloved sleep.   *127, 2*

21 Behold, how good and how pleasant it is for brethren to dwell together in
unity!   *133, 1*

22 By the rivers of Babylon, there we sat down, yea, we wept, when we remembered Zion.   *137, 1*

23 We hanged our harps upon the willows in the midst thereof.   *137, 2*

24 Sing us one of the songs of Zion.   *137, 3*

25 How shall we sing the Lord's song in a strange land?   *137, 4*

26 If I forget thee, O Jerusalem, let my right hand forget her cunning. *137, 5*

27 If I do not remember thee, let my tongue cleave to the roof of my mouth.
137, 6

28 I am fearfully and wonderfully made.   *139, 14*

29 Set a watch, O Lord, before my mouth; keep the door of my lips.   *141, 3*

30 The eyes of all wait upon thee; and thou givest them their meat in due
season.   *145, 15*

31 Put not your trust in princes.   *146, 3*

Proverbs

1 The fear of the Lord is the beginning of knowledge.   *1, 7*

2 Whom the Lord loveth he correcteth.   *3, 12*

3 Her ways are ways of pleasantness, and all her paths are peace.   *3, 17*

4 Go to the ant, thou sluggard; consider her ways, and be wise.   *6, 6*

5 For wisdom is better than rubies.   *8, 11*

6 Wisdom hath builded her house, she hath hewn out her seven pillars. *9, 1*

7 Stolen waters are sweet, and bread eaten in secret is pleasant.   *9, 17*

8 A wise son maketh a glad father: but a foolish son is the heaviness of his
mother.   *10, 1*

9 The memory of the just is blessed.   *10, 7*

10 In the multitude of counsellers there is safety.   *11, 14*

11 As a jewel of gold in a swine's snout, so is a fair woman which is without
discretion.   *11, 22*

12 A virtuous woman is a crown to her husband: but she that maketh ashamed
is as rottenness in his bones.   *12, 4*

13 Hope deferred maketh the heart sick.   *13, 12*

14 He that spareth his rod hateth his son: but he that loveth him chasteneth
him betimes.   *13, 24*

15 Righteousness exalteth a nation.   *14, 34*

16 A soft answer turneth away wrath.   *15, 1*

17 A merry heart maketh a cheerful countenance.   *15, 13*

18 Better is a dinner of herbs where love is, than a stalled ox and hatred therewith.   *15, 17*

19 Pride goeth before destruction, and an haughty spirit before a fall. *16, 18*

20 Even a fool, when he holdeth his peace, is counted wise.   *17, 28*

21 Wealth maketh many friends.   *19, 4*

22 Wine is a mocker, strong drink is raging: and whosoever is deceived thereby
is not wise.   *20, 1*

23 Even a child is known by his doings.   *20, 11*

24 It is naught, it is naught, saith the buyer; but when he is gone his way, then
he boasteth.   *20, 14*

25 The glory of young men is their strength.   *20, 29*

26 A good name is rather to be chosen than great riches.   *22, 1*

27 Train up a child in the way he should go: and when he is old, he will not
depart from it.   *22, 6*

28 If thine enemy be hungry, give him bread to eat; and if he be thirsty, give
him water to drink:
For thou shalt heap coals of fire upon his head, and the Lord shall reward
thee.   *25, 21–22*

29 As cold waters to a thirsty soul, so is good news from a far country. *25, 25*

30 A whip for the horse, a bridle for the ass, and a rod for the fool's back. *26, 3*

31 As a dog returneth to his vomit, so a fool returneth to his folly.   *26, 11*

1 Whoso diggeth a pit shall fall therein.   *Proverbs, 26, 27*

2 Open rebuke is better than secret love.   *27, 5*

3 Faithful are the wounds of a friend.   *27, 6*

4 He that maketh haste to be rich shall not be innocent.   *28, 20*

5 Where there is no vision, the people perish.   *29, 18*

6 Give me neither poverty nor riches; feed me with food convenient for me.
                    30, 8

7 There be three things which are too wonderful for me, yea, four which I know not: The way of an eagle in the air; the way of a serpent upon a rock; the way of a ship in the midst of the sea; and the way of a man with a maid.
                    30, 18–19

8 Who can find a virtuous woman? for her price is far above rubies. *31, 10*

Ecclesiastes

9 Vanity of vanities, saith the Preacher, vanity of vanities; all is vanity. *1, 2*

10 What profit hath a man of all his labour which he taketh under the sun? *1, 3*

11 One generation passeth away, and another generation cometh: but the earth abideth for ever.   *1, 4*

12 There is no new thing under the sun.   *1, 9*

13 For in much wisdom is much grief: and he that increaseth knowledge increaseth sorrow.   *1, 18*

14 To every thing there is a season, and a time to every purpose under the heaven.   *3, 1*

15 A threefold cord is not quickly broken.   *4, 12*

16 God is in heaven, and thou upon earth: therefore let thy words be few. *5, 2*

17 The sleep of a labouring man is sweet.   *5, 12*

18 A good name is better than precious ointment; and the day of death than the day of one's birth.   *7, 1*

19 For as the crackling of thorns under a pot, so is the laughter of the fool. *7, 6*

20 Say not thou, What is the cause that the former days were better than these? for thou dost not inquire wisely concerning this.   *7, 10*

21 Be not righteous over much.   *7, 16*

22 Whatsoever thy hand findeth to do, do it with thy might.   *9, 10*

23 The race is not to the swift, nor the battle to the strong, neither yet bread to the wise, nor yet riches to men of understanding, nor yet favour to men of skill; but time and chance happeneth to them all.   *9, 11*

24 Cast thy bread upon the waters: for thou shalt find it after many days. *11, 1*

25 Rejoice, O young man, in thy youth.   *11, 9*

26 Remember now thy Creator in the days of thy youth, while the evil days come not, nor the years draw nigh, when thou shalt say, I have no pleasure in them.   *12, 1*

27 Man goeth to his long home.   *12, 5*

28 Of making many books there is no end; and much study is a weariness of the flesh.   *12, 12*

1 Let us hear the conclusion of the whole matter: Fear God, and keep his commandments: for this is the whole duty of man.   *Ecclesiastes, 12, 13*

The Song of Solomon

2 Let him kiss me with the kisses of his mouth: for thy love is better than wine.   *1, 2*

3 I am black, but comely, O ye daughters of Jerusalem.   *1, 5*

4 I am the rose of Sharon, and the lily of the valleys.   *2, 1*

5 His banner over me was love.   *2, 4*

6 Stay me with flagons, comfort me with apples: for I am sick of love.   *2, 5*

7 Rise up, my love, my fair one, and come away.   *2, 10*

8 For, lo, the winter is past, the rain is over and gone.   *2, 11*

9 The flowers appear on the earth; the time of the singing of birds is come, and the voice of the turtle is heard in our land.   *2, 12*

10 Our vines have tender grapes.   *2, 15*

11 Until the day break, and the shadows flee away.   *2, 17*

12 I sleep, but my heart waketh.   *5, 2*

13 Terrible as an army with banners.   *6, 4*

14 Love is strong as death; jealousy is cruel as the grave.   *8, 6*

15 Many waters cannot quench love.   *8, 7*

Isaiah

16 The ox knoweth his owner, and the ass his master's crib.   *1, 3*

17 Though your sins be as scarlet, they shall be as white as snow.   *1, 18*

18 They shall beat their swords into plowshares, and their spears into pruning-hooks: nation shall not lift up sword against nation, neither shall they learn war any more.   *2, 4*

19 What mean ye that ye beat my people to pieces, and grind the faces of the poor?   *3, 15*

20 Woe unto them that call evil good, and good evil.   *5, 20*

21 A virgin shall conceive, and bear a son, and shall call his name Immanuel.   *7, 14*

22 The people that walked in darkness have seen a great light.   *9, 2*

23 For unto us a child is born, unto us a son is given: and the government shall be upon his shoulder: and his name shall be called Wonderful, Counseller, The mighty God, The everlasting Father, The Prince of Peace.   *9, 6*

24 The wolf also shall dwell with the lamb, and the leopard shall lie down with the kid; and the calf and the young lion and the fatling together; and a little child shall lead them.   *11, 6*

25 How art thou fallen from heaven, O Lucifer, son of the morning!   *14, 12*

26 Watchman, what of the night?   *21, 11*

27 Let us eat and drink; for to-morrow we shall die.   *22, 13*

28 Set thine house in order: for thou shalt die.   *38, 1*

29 All flesh is grass.   *40, 6*

1 Behold, the nations are as a drop of a bucket.   *Isaiah, 40, 15*

2 A bruised reed shall he not break, and the smoking flax shall he not quench.
                                                                    42, 3

3 There is no peace, saith the Lord, unto the wicked.   *48, 22*

4 How beautiful upon the mountains are the feet of him that bringeth good
  tidings.   *52, 7*

5 He is despised and rejected of men; a man of sorrows, and acquainted with
  grief.   *53, 3*

6 All we like sheep have gone astray.   *53, 6*

7 He is brought as a lamb to the slaughter.   *53, 7*

8 Seek ye the Lord while he may be found, call ye upon him while he is near.
                                                                    55, 6

9 For my thoughts are not your thoughts, neither are your ways my ways,
  saith the Lord.   *55, 8*

10 Is it such a fast that I have chosen? a day for a man to afflict his soul? *58, 5*

11 To give unto them beauty for ashes, the oil of joy for mourning, the garment
   of praise for the spirit of heaviness.   *61, 3*

Jeremiah

12 They have healed also the hurt of the daughter of my people slightly,
   saying, Peace, peace; when there is no peace.   *6, 14*

13 Is there no balm in Gilead; is there no physician there?   *8, 22*

14 Can the Ethiopian change his skin, or the leopard his spots?   *13, 23*

15 As the clay is in the potter's hand, so are ye in mine hand, O house of Israel.
                                                                    18, 6

16 The fathers have eaten a sour grape, and the children's teeth are set on edge.
                                                                    31, 29

Lamentations

17 Is it nothing to you, all ye that pass by? behold, and see if there be any
   sorrow like unto my sorrow.   *1, 12*

18 Remembering mine affliction and my misery, the wormwood and the gall.
                                                                    3, 19

19 His compassions fail not. They are new every morning.   *3, 22-23*

20 It is good for a man that he bear the yoke in his youth.   *3, 27*

Ezekiel

21 They four had one likeness, as if a wheel had been in the midst of a wheel.
                                                                    10, 10

22 The king of Babylon stood at the parting of the way.   *21, 21*

23 O ye dry bones, hear the word of the Lord.   *37, 4*

24 Son of man, set thy face against Gog, the land of Magog.   *38, 2*

Daniel

25 And he commanded the most mighty men that were in his army to bind
   Shadrach, Meshach, and Abed-nego, and to cast them into the burning
   fiery furnace.   *3, 20*

1 MENE, MENE, TEKEL, UPHARSIN.	*Daniel, 5, 25*
2 Thou art weighed in the balances, and art found wanting.	*5, 27*
3 Thy kingdom is divided, and given to the Medes and Persians.	*5, 28*
4 The law of the Medes and Persians, which altereth not.	*6, 12*
5 They brought Daniel, and cast him into the den of lions.	*6, 16*
6 The Ancient of days.	*7, 13*
7 O Daniel, a man greatly beloved.	*10, 11*

Hosea

8 I desired mercy, and not sacrifice; and the knowledge of God more than burnt offerings. *6, 6*

9 They have sown the wind, and they shall reap the whirlwind. *8, 7*

10 I drew them with cords of a man, with bands of love. *11, 4*

Joel

11 Rend your heart, and not your garments. *2, 13*

12 The years that the locust hath eaten. *2, 25*

13 Your old men shall dream dreams, your young men shall see visions. *2, 28*

14 Multitudes in the valley of decision. *3, 14*

Amos

15 Can two walk together, except they be agreed? *3, 3*

16 Prepare to meet thy God. *4, 12*

17 Woe to them that are at ease in Zion. *6, 1*

Jonah

18 So they cast lots, and the lot fell upon Jonah. *1, 7*

19 Jonah was in the belly of the fish three days and three nights. *1, 17*

20 And God said to Jonah, Doest thou well to be angry for the gourd? *4, 9*

21 And should not I spare Nineveh, that great city, wherein are more than sixscore thousand persons that cannot discern between their right hand and their left hand; and also much cattle? *4, 11*

Micah

22 They shall sit every man under his vine and under his fig tree. *4, 4*

23 O my people, what have I done unto thee? and wherein have I wearied thee? *6, 3*

24 What doth the Lord require of thee, but to do justly, and to love mercy, and to walk humbly with thy God? *6, 8*

Habakkuk

25 Thou art of purer eyes than to behold evil. *1, 13*

26 Write the vision, and make it plain upon tables, that he may run that readeth it. *2, 2*

Haggai

1 The glory of this latter house shall be greater than of the former.   *2, 9*

Zechariah

2 Is not this a brand plucked out of the fire ?   *3, 2*

3 Who hath despised the day of small things ?   *4, 10*

4 What are these wounds in thine hands ? Then he shall answer, Those with which I was wounded in the house of my friends.   *13, 6*

Malachi

5 Have we not all one father ? hath not one God created us ?   *2, 10*

6 The Lord, whom ye seek, shall suddenly come to his temple.   *3, 1*

7 Unto you that fear my name shall the Sun of righteousness arise with healing in his wings.   *4, 2*

The New Testament

St. Matthew

8 Where is he that is born King of the Jews ? for we have seen his star in the east, and are come to worship him.   *2, 2*

9 Rachel weeping for her children, and would not be comforted, because they are not.   *2, 18*

10 Repent ye: for the kingdom of heaven is at hand.   *3, 2*

11 The voice of one crying in the wilderness.   *3, 3*

12 O generation of vipers, who hath warned you to flee from the wrath to come ?   *3, 7*

13 Man shall not live by bread alone, but by every word that proceedeth out of the mouth of God.   *4, 4*

14 Follow me, and I will make you fishers of men.   *4, 19*

15 Blessed are the meek: for they shall inherit the earth.   *5, 5*

16 Blessed are the pure in heart: for they shall see God.   *5, 8*

17 Ye are the salt of the earth: but if the salt have lost his savour, wherewith shall it be salted ?   *5, 13*

18 An eye for an eye, and a tooth for a tooth.   *5, 38*

19 Resist not evil: but whosoever shall smite thee on thy right cheek, turn to him the other also.   *5, 39*

20 Love your enemies.   *5, 44*

21 He maketh his sun to rise on the evil and on the good, and sendeth rain on the just and on the unjust.   *5, 45*

22 Let not thy left hand know what thy right hand doeth.   *6, 3*

23 Use not vain repetitions.   *6, 7*

24 After this manner therefore pray ye: Our Father which art in heaven, Hallowed be thy name. Thy kingdom come. Thy will be done in earth, as it is in heaven. Give us this day our daily bread. And forgive us our debts, as we forgive our debtors. And lead us not into temptation, but deliver us from evil: For thine is the kingdom, and the power, and the glory, for ever. Amen.   *6, 9–13*

1 No man can serve two masters. *St. Matthew, 6, 24*

2 Ye cannot serve God and mammon. *Ib*

3 Consider the lilies of the field, how they grow; they toil not, neither do they spin. *6, 28*

4 Sufficient unto the day is the evil thereof. *6, 34*

5 Judge not, that ye be not judged. *7, 1*

6 Neither cast ye your pearls before swine. *7, 6*

7 Therefore all things whatsoever ye would that men should do to you, do ye even so to them: for this is the law and the prophets. *7, 12*

8 Enter ye in at the strait gate. *7, 13*

9 Beware of false prophets, which come to you in sheep's clothing, but inwardly they are ravening wolves. *7, 15*

10 A man under authority. *8, 9*

11 What went ye out into the wilderness to see? A reed shaken with the wind? *11, 7*

12 He that is not with me is against me. *12, 30*

13 One pearl of great price. *13, 46*

14 A prophet is not without honour, save in his own country. *13, 57*

15 If the blind lead the blind, both shall fall into the ditch. *15, 14*

16 Thou art Peter, and upon this rock I will build my church; and the gates of hell shall not prevail against it. *16, 18*

17 The keys of the kingdom of heaven. *16, 19*

18 Get thee behind me, Satan. *16, 23*

19 Except ye be converted, and become as little children, ye shall not enter into the kingdom of heaven. *18, 3*

20 But whoso shall offend one of these little ones which believe in me, it were better for him that a millstone were hanged about his neck, and that he were drowned in the depth of the sea. *18, 6*

21 If thine eye offend thee, pluck it out. *18, 9*

22 Until seventy times seven. *18, 22*

23 It is easier for a camel to go through the eye of a needle, than for a rich man to enter into the kingdom of God. *19, 24*

24 For many are called, but few are chosen. *22, 14*

25 Render therefore unto Caesar the things which are Caesar's; and unto God the things that are God's. *22, 21*

26 Ye blind guides, which strain at a gnat, and swallow a camel. *23, 24*

27 Wars and rumours of wars. *24, 6*

28 For unto every one that hath shall be given, and he shall have abundance: but from him that hath not shall be taken away even that which he hath. *25, 29*

29 As a shepherd divideth his sheep from the goats. *25, 32*

30 Inasmuch as ye have done it unto one of the least of these my brethren, ye have done it unto me. *25, 40*

1 Ye have the poor always with you.   *St. Matthew, 26, 11*

2 Watch and pray, that ye enter not into temptation: the spirit indeed is willing, but the flesh is weak.   *26, 41*

3 He took water, and washed his hands before the multitude, saying, I am innocent of the blood of this just person.   *27, 24*

4 I am with you alway, even unto the end of the world.   *28, 20*

St. Mark

5 They that are whole have no need of the physician, but they that are sick.
2, 17

6 The sabbath was made for man, and not man for the sabbath.   *2, 27*

7 If a house be divided against itself, that house cannot stand.   *3, 25*

8 He that hath ears to hear, let him hear.   *4, 9*

9 My name is Legion: for we are many.   *5, 9*

10 For what shall it profit a man, if he shall gain the whole world, and lose his own soul?   *8, 36*

11 I believe: help thou mine unbelief.   *9, 24*

12 What therefore God hath joined together, let not man put asunder. *10, 9*

13 Suffer the little children to come unto me, and forbid them not: for of such is the kingdom of God.   *10, 14*

14 Is it not written, My house shall be called of all nations the house of prayer? but ye have made it a den of thieves.   *11, 17*

15 And there came a certain poor widow, and she threw in two mites, which make a farthing.   *12, 42*

16 Take ye heed, watch and pray.   *13, 33*

17 Before the cock crow twice, thou shalt deny me thrice.   *14, 30*

18 Crucify him.   *15, 13*

St. Luke

19 There was no room for them in the inn.   *2, 7*

20 And there were in the same country shepherds abiding in the field, keeping watch over their flock by night.   *2, 8*

21 Ye shall find the babe wrapped in swaddling clothes, lying in a manger. *2, 12*

22 Glory to God in the highest, and on earth peace, good will toward men.
2, 14

23 Be content with your wages.   *3, 14*

24 Physician, heal thyself.   *4, 23*

25 No man putteth new wine into old bottles.   *5, 37*

26 No man, having put his hand to the plough, and looking back, is fit for the kingdom of God.   *9, 62*

27 The labourer is worthy of his hire.   *10, 7*

28 Fell among thieves.   *10, 30*

29 He passed by on the other side.   *10, 31*

30 Friend, go up higher.   *14, 10*

1 The poor, and the maimed, and the halt, and the blind.   *St. Luke, 14, 21*

2 Joy shall be in heaven over one sinner that repenteth, more than over ninety and nine just persons, which need no repentance.   *15, 7*

3 And he would fain have filled his belly with the husks that the swine did eat.   *15, 16*

4 Bring hither the fatted calf, and kill it.   *15, 23*

5 I cannot dig; to beg I am ashamed.   *16, 3*

6 The children of this world are in their generation wiser than the children of light.   *16, 8*

7 Make to yourselves friends of the mammon of unrighteousness.   *16, 9*

8 The crumbs which fell from the rich man's table.   *16, 21*

9 Between us and you there is a great gulf fixed.   *16, 26*

10 Remember Lot's wife.   *17, 32*

11 I thank thee, that I am not as other men are.   *18, 11*

12 Out of thine own mouth will I judge thee.   *19, 22*

13 Father, forgive them; for they know not what they do.   *23, 34*

St. John

14 In the beginning was the Word, and the Word was with God, and the Word was God.   *1, 1*

15 The true Light, which lighteth every man that cometh into the world. *1, 9*

16 He came unto his own, and his own received him not.   *1, 11*

17 The Word was made flesh, and dwelt among us.   *1, 14*

18 Can there any good thing come out of Nazareth?   *1, 46*

19 Ye must be born again.   *3, 7*

20 The wind bloweth where it listeth.   *3, 8*

21 For God so loved the world, that he gave his only begotten Son, that whosoever believeth in him should not perish, but have everlasting life.   *3, 16*

22 Men loved darkness rather than light, because their deeds were evil. *3, 19*

23 Judge not according to the appearance, but judge righteous judgment. *7, 24*

24 He that is without sin among you, let him first cast a stone at her.   *8, 7*

25 I am the light of the world.   *8, 12*

26 The night cometh, when no man can work.   *9, 4*

27 The good shepherd giveth his life for the sheep.   *10, 11*

28 Jesus wept.   *11, 35*

29 A new commandment I give unto you, That ye love one another.   *13, 34*

30 In my Father's house are many mansions.   *14, 2*

31 Greater love hath no man than this, that a man lay down his life for his friends.   *15, 13*

32 Whither goest thou?   *16, 5*

33 Pilate saith unto him, What is truth?   *18, 38*

34 What I have written I have written.   *19, 22*

35 Blessed are they that have not seen, and yet have believed.   *20, 29*

Acts of the Apostles

1 Silver and gold have I none; but such as I have give I thee.   *3, 6*

2 Thy money perish with thee, because thou hast thought that the gift of God may be purchased with money.   *8, 20*

3 He went on his way rejoicing.   *8, 39*

4 It is hard for thee to kick against the pricks.   *9, 5*

5 God is no respecter of persons.   *10, 34*

6 In him we live, and move, and have our being.   *17, 28*

7 Great is Diana of the Ephesians.   *19, 34*

8 It is more blessed to give than to receive.   *20, 35*

9 A citizen of no mean city.   *21, 39*

10 Brought up in this city at the feet of Gamaliel.   *22, 3*

11 I appeal unto Caesar.   *25, 11*

12 Hast thou appealed unto Caesar? unto Caesar shalt thou go.   *25, 12*

13 I was not disobedient unto the heavenly vision.   *26, 19*

14 Almost thou persuadest me to be a Christian.   *26, 28*

Romans

15 The just shall live by faith.   *1, 17*

16 These, having not the law, are a law unto themselves.   *2, 14*

17 Death hath no more dominion over him.   *6, 9*

18 The wages of sin is death.   *6, 23*

19 For the good that I would I do not: but the evil which I would not, that I do.   *7, 19*

20 And we know that all things work together for good to them that love God.   *8, 28*

21 If God be for us, who can be against us?   *8, 31*

22 So we, being many, are one body in Christ, and every one members one of another.   *12, 5*

23 Let love be without dissimulation. Abhor that which is evil; cleave to that which is good.   *12, 9*

24 Rejoice with them that do rejoice, and weep with them that weep.   *12, 15*

25 Be not wise in your own conceits.   *12, 16*

26 Vengeance is mine; I will repay, saith the Lord.   *12, 19*

27 Be not overcome of evil, but overcome evil with good.   *12, 21*

28 The powers that be are ordained of God.   *13, 1*

29 Love worketh no ill to his neighbour: therefore love is the fulfilling of the law.   *13, 10*

30 None of us liveth to himself, and no man dieth to himself.   *14, 7*

31 We then that are strong ought to bear the infirmities of the weak.   *15, 1*

1 Corinthians

32 I have planted, Apollos watered; but God gave the increase.   *3, 6*

33 Absent in body, but present in spirit.   *5, 3*

1 Know ye not that a little leaven leaveneth the whole lump? *I Corinthians,*
5, 6

2 All things are lawful unto me, but all things are not expedient. *6, 12*

3 It is better to marry than to burn. *7, 9*

4 All things to all men. *9, 22*

5 If a woman have long hair, it is a glory to her. *11, 15*

6 When I became a man, I put away childish things. *13, 11*

7 Now we see through a glass, darkly; but then face to face. *13, 12*

8 And now abideth faith, hope, charity, these three; but the greatest of these
is charity. *13, 13*

9 Let your women keep silence in the churches. *14, 34*

10 Let all things be done decently and in order. *14, 40*

11 One born out of due time. *15, 8*

12 By the grace of God I am what I am. *15, 10*

13 O death, where is thy sting? O grave, where is thy victory? *15, 55*

2 Corinthians

14 The letter killeth, but the spirit giveth life. *3, 6*

15 We walk by faith, not by sight. *5, 7*

16 God loveth a cheerful giver. *9, 7*

17 For ye suffer fools gladly, seeing ye yourselves are wise. *11, 19*

18 A thorn in the flesh. *12, 7*

19 My grace is sufficient for thee: for my strength is made perfect in weakness.
12, 9

Galatians

20 The right hands of fellowship. *2, 9*

21 Ye are fallen from grace. *5, 4*

22 Bear ye one another's burdens. *6, 2*

23 Be not deceived; God is not mocked: for whatsoever a man soweth, that
shall he also reap. *6, 7*

Ephesians

24 Be ye angry, and sin not: let not the sun go down upon your wrath. *4, 26*

25 For this cause shall a man leave his father and mother, and shall be joined
unto his wife, and they two shall be one flesh. *5, 31*

26 Put on the whole armour of God. *6, 11*

27 For we wrestle not against flesh and blood, but against principalities, against
powers, against the rulers of the darkness of this world, against spiritual
wickedness in high places. *6, 12*

Philippians

28 Work out your own salvation with fear and trembling. *2, 12*

29 Whose God is their belly, and whose glory is in their shame. *2, 19*

30 Our conversation is in heaven. *3, 20*

31 The peace of God, which passeth all understanding. *4, 7*

1 Whatsoever things are true, whatsoever things are honest, whatsoever things are just, whatsoever things are pure, whatsoever things are lovely, whatsoever things are of good report; if there be any virtue, and if there be any praise, think on these things. *Philippians, 4, 8*

2 I have learned, in whatsoever state I am, therewith to be content. *4, 11*

Colossians

3 Touch not; taste not; handle not. *2, 21*

4 Set your affection on things above, not on things on the earth. *3, 2*

1 Thessalonians

5 Remembering without ceasing your work of faith, and labour of love. *1, 3*

6 Pray without ceasing. *5, 17*

7 Prove all things: hold fast that which is good. *5, 21*

2 Thessalonians

8 If any would not work, neither should he eat. *3, 10*

1 Timothy

9 Not greedy of filthy lucre. *3, 3*

10 Refuse profane and old wives' fables. *4, 7*

11 Let no man despise thy youth. *4, 12*

12 Drink no longer water, but use a little wine for thy stomach's sake and thine often infirmities. *5, 23*

13 For we brought nothing into this world, and it is certain we can carry nothing out. *6, 7*

14 The love of money is the root of all evil. *6, 10*

15 Fight the good fight of faith. *6, 12*

2 Timothy

16 All scripture is given by inspiration of God. *3, 16*

17 I have fought a good fight, I have finished my course, I have kept the faith. *4, 7*

Titus

18 Unto the pure all things are pure. *1, 15*

Hebrews

19 It is appointed unto men once to die, but after this the judgment. *9, 27*

20 It is a fearful thing to fall into the hands of the living God. *10, 31*

21 Faith is the substance of things hoped for, the evidence of things not seen. *11, 1*

22 Whom the Lord loveth he chasteneth. *12, 6*

23 Let brotherly love continue. *13, 1*

24 Jesus Christ the same yesterday, and today, and for ever. *13, 8*

James

25 Faith without works is dead. *2, 20*

1 The tongue can no man tame; it is an unruly evil.   *James, 3, 8*

2 Resist the devil, and he will flee from you.   *4, 7*

3 Ye have heard of the patience of Job.   *5, 11*

1 Peter

4 All flesh is as grass.   *1, 24*

5 Honour all men. Love the brotherhood. Fear God. Honour the king. *2, 17*

6 Giving honour unto the wife, as unto the weaker vessel.   *3, 7*

7 Charity shall cover the multitude of sins.   *4, 8*

8 Be sober, be vigilant; because your adversary the devil, as a roaring lion, walketh about, seeking whom he may devour.   *5, 8*

2 Peter

9 The dog is turned to his own vomit again; and the sow that was washed to her wallowing in the mire.   *2, 22*

10 One day is with the Lord as a thousand years, and a thousand years as one day.   *3, 8*

1 John

11 Shutteth up his bowels of compassion.   *3, 17*

12 God is love.   *4, 8*

13 There is no fear in love; but perfect love casteth out fear.   *4, 18*

2 John

14 The elder unto the elect lady.   *1, 1*

Revelation

15 I am Alpha and Omega, the beginning and the ending.   *1, 8*

16 Be thou faithful unto death, and I will give thee a crown of life.   *2, 10*

17 He shall rule them with a rod of iron.   *2, 27*

18 I will not blot out his name out of the book of life.   *3, 5*

19 Because thou art lukewarm, and neither cold nor hot, I will spue thee out of my mouth.   *3, 16*

20 Behold, I stand at the door, and knock.   *3, 20*

21 He went forth conquering, and to conquer.   *6, 2*

22 Behold a pale horse: and his name that sat on him was Death, and Hell followed with him.   *6, 8*

23 And when he had opened the seventh seal, there was silence in heaven about the space of half an hour.   *8, 1*

24 The bottomless pit.   *9, 1*

25 They had tails like unto scorpions, and there were stings in their tails. *9, 10*

26 Let him that hath understanding count the number of the beast: for it is the number of a man; and his number is Six hundred threescore and six.   *13, 18*

27 A place called in the Hebrew tongue Armageddon.   *16, 16*

1 And I saw a new heaven and a new earth: for the first heaven and the first earth were passed away; and there was no more sea.   *Revelation, 21, 1*

2 The holy city, new Jerusalem, coming down from God out of heaven, prepared as a bride adorned for her husband.   *21, 2*

3 And God shall wipe away all tears from their eyes; and there shall be no more death, neither sorrow, nor crying, neither shall there be any more pain: for the former things are passed away.   *21, 4*

4 If any man shall add unto these things, God shall add unto him the plagues that are written in this book.   *22, 18*

Apocrypha

1 Esdras

5 The first wrote, Wine is the strongest.
The second wrote, The king is strongest.
The third wrote, Women are strongest: but above all things Truth beareth away the victory.   *3, 10*

6 Great is Truth, and mighty above all things.   *4, 41*

2 Esdras

7 I shall light a candle of understanding in thine heart, which shall not be put out.   *14, 25*

Tobit

8 If thou hast abundance, give alms accordingly: if thou have but a little, be not afraid to give according to that little.   *4, 8*

9 So they went forth both, and the young man's dog with them.   *5, 16*

Wisdom of Solomon

10 Let us crown ourselves with rosebuds, before they be withered.   *2, 8*

11 Through envy of the devil came death into the world.   *2, 24*

12 The souls of the righteous are in the hand of God, and there shall no torment touch them.   *3, 1*

13 The corruptible body presseth down the soul.   *9, 15*

14 O Lord, thou lover of souls.   *11, 26*

Ecclesiasticus

15 My son, if thou come to serve the Lord, prepare thy soul for temptation.   *2, 1*

16 A faithful friend is the medicine of life.   *6, 16*

17 Miss not the discourse of the elders.   *8, 9*

18 Open not thine heart to every man.   *8, 19*

19 Give not thy soul unto a woman.   *9, 2*

20 Forsake not an old friend.   *9, 10*

21 Judge none blessed before his death.   *11, 28*

22 He that toucheth pitch shall be defiled therewith.   *13, 1*

23 Be not made a beggar by banqueting upon borrowing.   *18, 33*

1 All wickedness is but little to the wickedness of a woman. *Ecclesiasticus, 25, 19*

2 Let thy speech be short, comprehending much in few words. *32, 8*

3 Honour a physician with the honour due unto him. *38, 1*

4 How can he get wisdom . . . whose talk is of bullocks? *38, 25*

5 Let us now praise famous men, and our fathers that begat us. *44, 1*

6 Rich men furnished with ability, living peaceably in their habitations. *44, 6*

7 And some there be, which have no memorial. *44, 9*

8 Their bodies are buried in peace; but their name liveth for evermore. *44, 14*

1 Maccabees

9 Consider ye throughout all ages, that none that put their trust in him shall be overcome. *2, 61*

2 Maccabees

10 When he was at the last gasp. *7, 9*

11 It was an holy and good thought. *12, 45*

The Book of Common Prayer

12 We have erred, and strayed from thy ways like lost sheep.
Morning Prayer, General Confession

13 We have left undone those things which we ought to have done; And we have done those things which we ought not to have done. *Ib, Ib*

14 As it was in the beginning, is now, and ever shall be: world without end.
Ib, Gloria

15 The noble army of Martyrs. *Ib, Te Deum*

16 Give peace in our time, O Lord. *Ib, Versicles*

17 Whose service is perfect freedom. *Ib, Second Collect, for Peace*

18 In Quires and Places where they sing. *Ib, Rubric after Third Collect*

19 When two or three are gathered together in thy Name thou wilt grant their requests. *Ib, Prayer of St. Chrysostom*

20 Lighten our darkness. *Evening Prayer, Third Collect, for Aid against all Perils*

21 Defend us from all perils and dangers of this night. *Ib, Ib*

22 Have mercy upon us miserable sinners. *Litany*

23 Envy, hatred, and malice, and all uncharitableness. *Ib*

24 All the deceits of the world, the flesh, and the devil. *Ib*

25 In the hour of death, and in the day of judgement. *Ib*

26 Preserve to our use the kindly fruits of the earth. *Ib*

27 All sorts and conditions of men. *Prayer for all Conditions of men*

28 All who profess and call themselves Christians. *Ib*

29 Those who are any ways afflicted, or distressed, in mind, body, or estate. *Ib*

30 Patience under their sufferings, and a happy issue out of all their afflictions.
Ib

1 Our creation, preservation, and all the blessings of this life.   *A General Thanksgiving*

2 Read, mark, learn, and inwardly digest.   *Collect, 2nd Sunday in Advent*

3 All our doings without charity are nothing worth.   *Ib, Quinquagesima Sunday*

4 Jews, Turks, Infidels, and Hereticks.   *Ib, Third Collect for Good Friday*

5 A right judgement in all things.   *Ib, Whit-Sunday*

6 The author and giver of all good things.   *Ib, 7th Sunday after Trinity*

7 Whom truly to know is everlasting life.   *Ib, St. Philip and St. James's Day*

8 Constantly speak the truth, boldly rebuke vice, and patiently suffer for the truth's sake.   *Ib, St. John Baptist's Day*

9 An open and notorious evil liver.   *Holy Communion, Introductory Rubric*

10 Grant that the old Adam in this Child may be so buried, that the new man may be raised up in him.   *Publick Baptism of Infants, Blessing*

11 Renounce the devil and all his works.   *Ib*

12 The pomps and vanity of this wicked world.   *Catechism*

13 To order myself lowly and reverently to all my betters.   *Ib*

14 To keep my hands from picking and stealing.   *Ib*

15 To do my duty in that state of life, unto which it shall please God to call me.   *Ib*

16 An outward and visible sign of an inward and spiritual grace.   *Ib*

17 Being now come to the years of discretion.   *Order of Confirmation*

18 If any of you know cause, or just impediment.   *Solemnization of Matrimony*

19 Brute beasts that have no understanding.   *Ib*

20 Let him now speak, or else hereafter for ever hold his peace.   *Ib*

21 Wilt thou have this Woman to thy wedded wife?   *Ib*

22 To have and to hold from this day forward, for better for worse, for richer for poorer, in sickness and in health, to love and to cherish, till death us do part.   *Ib*

23 To love, cherish, and to obey.   *Ib*

24 With this Ring I thee wed, with my body I thee worship, and with all my worldly goods I thee endow.   *Ib*

25 Those whom God hath joined together let no man put asunder.   *Ib*

26 I pronounce that they be Man and Wife together.   *Ib*

27 The Office ensuing is not to be used for any that die unbaptized, or excommunicate, or have laid violent hands upon themselves.   *Burial of the Dead, Introductory Rubric*

28 Man that is born of a woman hath but a short time to live, and is full of misery.   *Ib*

29 In the midst of life we are in death.   *Ib*

30 We therefore commit his body to the ground; earth to earth, ashes to ashes, dust to dust.   *Ib*

BICKERSTAFFE, Isaac, 1735?–1812?

1 There was a jolly miller once
    Lived on the river Dee;
  He worked and sang from morn till night;
    No lark more blithe than he.   *Love in a Village, Act 1, Scene 5*

2 I care for nobody, not I,
    If no one cares for me.   *Ib*

3 But if I'm content with a little
    Enough is as good as a feast.   *Ib, Act 3, Scene 1*

BICKERSTETH, Edward Henry, 1825–1906

4 Peace, perfect peace, in this dark world of sin?
    The blood of Jesus whispers peace within.   *Songs in the House of
                                                        Pilgrimage*

BINYON, Laurence Robert, 1869–1943

5 They shall grow not old, as we that are left grow old:
    Age shall not weary them, nor the years condemn.
  At the going down of the sun and in the morning
    We will remember them.   *For the Fallen (1914–18)*

BIRRELL, Augustine, 1850–1933

6 That great dust-heap called 'history'.   *Obiter Dicta, 1st series, Carlyle*

BISMARCK, Otto von, 1815–1898

7 *Nach Canossa gehen wir nicht.* We will not go to Canossa.   *Speech,
                                                  Reichstag, 14 May 1872*

8 *Blut und Eisen.* Blood and Iron.   *Speech, Prussian Chamber, 28 Jan. 1886*

BLACKSTONE, Sir William, 1723–1780

9 The king never dies.   *Commentaries on the Laws of England, Book 1, 7*

10 That the king can do no wrong, is a necessary and fundamental principle of
   the English constitution.   *Ib, Book 3, 17*

11 It is better that ten guilty persons escape than one innocent suffer.
                                                    Ib, Book 4, 27

BLAIR, Eric, see ORWELL, George

BLAKE, William, 1757–1827

12 To see a World in a grain of sand,
   And a Heaven in a wild flower,
   Hold Infinity in the palm of your hand,
   And Eternity in an hour.   *Auguries of Innocence, 1*

13 A robin redbreast in a cage
   Puts all Heaven in a rage.   *Ib, 5*

14 A truth that's told with bad intent
   Beats all the lies you can invent.   *Ib, 53*

15 Man was made for joy and woe;
   And when this we rightly know,
   Thro' the world we safely go.   *Ib, 56*

1 God appears, and God is Light,
  To those poor souls who dwell in Night;
  But does a Human Form display
  To those who dwell in realms of Day.   *Auguries of Innocence, 129*

2 Does the Eagle know what is in the pit
  Or wilt thou go ask the Mole?
  Can Wisdom be put in a silver rod,
  Or Love in a golden bowl?   *The Book of Thel, Thel's Motto*

3 Mutual Forgiveness of each vice,
  Such are the Gates of Paradise.   *The Gates of Paradise, Prologue*

4 He who bends himself a Joy
  Doth the wingèd life destroy;
  But he who kisses the Joy as it flies
  Lives in Eternity's sunrise.

        Gnomic Verses, XVII, Several Questions Answered

5 For a Tear is an Intellectual thing;
  And a Sigh is the sword of an angel king;
  And the bitter groan of a Martyr's woe
  Is an arrow from the Almighty's bow.   *Jerusalem, f. 52*

6 He who would do good to another must do it in Minute Particulars.
  General Good is the plea of the scoundrel, hypocrite, and flatterer.
                                                                Ib, f. 55

7 I care not whether a man is Good or Evil; all that I care
  Is whether he is a Wise Man or a Fool. Go! put off Holiness,
  And put on Intellect.   *Ib, f. 91*

8 And did those feet in ancient time
      Walk upon England's mountains green?
  And was the holy Lamb of God
      On England's pleasant pastures seen?

  Bring me my bow of burning gold!
      Bring me my arrows of desire!
  Bring me my spear! O clouds, unfold!
      Bring me my chariot of fire!

  I will not cease from mental fight,
      Nor shall my sword sleep in my hand,
  Till we have built Jerusalem
      In England's green and pleasant land.   *Milton, Preface*

9 Mock on, mock on, Voltaire, Rousseau;
  Mock on, mock on; 'tis all in vain!
  You throw the sand against the wind,
  And the wind blows it back again.   *Mock on, mock on, Voltaire, Rousseau*

10 Never seek to tell thy love,
   Love that never told can be;
   For the gentle wind does move
   Silently, invisibly.   *Never seek to tell thy Love*

11 Soon as she was gone from me,
   A traveller came by,
   Silently, invisibly:
   He took her with a sigh.   *Ib*

1 A petty sneaking knave I knew—
  O! Mr. Cromek, how do ye do?   *On Cromek*

2 Love seeketh not itself to please,
  Nor for itself hath any care,
  But for another gives its ease,
  And builds a Heaven in Hell's despair.
                      Songs of Experience, The Clod and the Pebble

3 My mother groan'd, my father wept,
  Into the dangerous world I leapt;
  Helpless, naked, piping loud,
  Like a fiend hid in a cloud.   *Ib, Infant Sorrow*

4 But if at the Church they would give us some ale,
  And a pleasant fire our souls to regale,
  We'd sing and we'd pray all the livelong day,
  Nor ever once wish from the Church to stray.   *Ib, The Little Vagabond*

5 Tiger! Tiger! burning bright
  In the forests of the night,
  What immortal hand or eye
  Could frame thy fearful symmetry?   *Ib, The Tiger*

6 When the stars threw down their spears,
  And water'd heaven with their tears,
  Did he smile his work to see?
  Did he who made the Lamb make thee?   *Ib*

7 Piping down the valleys wild,
  Piping songs of pleasant glee,
  On a cloud I saw a child.   *Songs of Innocence, Introduction*

8 'Pipe a song about a Lamb!'
  So I piped with merry cheer.   *Ib*

9 Little Lamb, who made thee?
  Dost thou know who made thee?   *Ib, The Lamb*

10 My mother bore me in the southern wild,
   And I am black, but O! my soul is white.   *Ib, The Little Black Boy*

11 When the voices of children are heard on the green,
   And laughing is heard on the hill.   *Ib, Nurse's Song*

12 Can I see another's woe,
   And not be in sorrow too?   *Ib, On Another's Sorrow*

13 Whether on Ida's shady brow,
   Or in the chambers of the East,
   The chambers of the sun, that now
   From ancient melody have ceas'd.   *To the Muses*

14 How have you left the ancient love
   That bards of old enjoy'd in you!
   The languid strings do scarcely move!
   The sound is forc'd, the notes are few!   *Ib*

15 Without Contraries is no progression. Attraction and Repulsion, Reason
   and Energy, Love and Hate, are necessary to Human existence.
                      The Marriage of Heaven and Hell, The Argument

16 Energy is Eternal Delight.   *Ib, The Voice of the Devil*

1 The road of excess leads to the palace of wisdom.   *The Marriage of Heaven and Hell, Proverbs of Hell*

2 He who desires but acts not, breeds pestilence.   *Ib*

3 A fool sees not the same tree that a wise man sees.   *Ib*

4 Damn braces. Bless relaxes.   *Ib*

5 Exuberance is Beauty.   *Ib*

6 Where man is not, nature is barren.   *Ib*

7 If the doors of perception were cleansed everything would appear to man as it is, infinite.   *Ib, A Memorable Fancy*

BORROW, George Henry, 1803–1881

8 There's night and day, brother, both sweet things; sun, moon, and stars, brother, all sweet things; there's likewise a wind on the heath. Life is very sweet, brother; who would wish to die?   *Lavengro, Ch. 25*

BOSQUET, Marshal Pierre, 1810–1861

9 *C'est magnifique, mais ce n'est pas la guerre.* It is magnificent, but it is not war.
    Watching the Charge of the Light Brigade, Balaclava, 1854

BOSSIDY, John Collins, 1860–1928

10 And this is good old Boston,
    The Home of the bean and the cod,
    Where the Lowells talk to the Cabots,
    And the Cabots talk only to God.   *On the Aristocracy of Harvard*

BOULTON, Sir Harold Edwin, 1859–1935

11 When Adam and Eve were dispossessed
    Of the garden hard by Heaven,
    They planted another one down in the West,
    'Twas Devon, glorious Devon!   *Glorious Devon*

12 Speed, bonny boat, like a bird on the wing;
    'Onward!' the sailors cry;
    Carry the lad that's born to be king
    Over the sea to Skye.   *Skye Boat Song*

BOURDILLON, Francis William, 1852–1921

13 The night has a thousand eyes,
    And the day but one;
    Yet the light of the bright world dies
    With the dying sun.   *Light*

BOWEN, Charles, 1st Baron, 1835–1894

14 The rain it raineth on the just
    And also on the unjust fella:
    But chiefly on the just, because
    The unjust steals the just's umbrella.   *Sichel, Sands of Time*

BOWEN, Edward Ernest, 1836–1901

15 Forty years on, growing older and older,
    Shorter in wind, as in memory long.
    Feeble of foot, and rheumatic of shoulder,
    What will it help you that once you were strong?   *Forty Years On, Harrow School Song*

BRADFORD, John, 1510?–1555

1 There, but for the grace of God, goes John Bradford.   *Remark on seeing
some criminals led to execution*

BRATHWAITE, Richard, 1588?–1673

2 To Banbury came I, O profane one!
Where I saw a Puritane-one
Hanging of his cat on Monday,
For killing of a mouse on Sunday.   *Barnabee's Journal, 1*

BRIDGES, Robert, 1844–1930

3 Awake, my heart, to be loved, awake, awake!
The darkness silvers away, the morn doth break,
It leaps in the sky: unrisen lustres slake
The o'ertaken moon. Awake, O heart, awake!   *Awake, My Heart, to be
Loved*

4 I heard a linnet courting
    His lady in the spring.   *I heard a Linnet courting*

5 I never shall love the snow again
    Since Maurice died.   *I never shall love the Snow again*

6 Perfect little body, without fault or stain on thee,
With promise of strength and manhood full and fair!   *On a Dead Child*

7 When Death to either shall come,—
    I pray it be first to me.   *When Death to either shall come*

BRIGHT, John, 1811–1889

8 The Angel of Death has been abroad throughout the land; you may almost
hear the beating of his wings.   *Speech, House of Commons, 23 Feb. 1855*

9 England is the mother of parliaments.   *Speech, Birmingham, 18 Jan. 1865*

10 The right honourable gentleman . . . has retired into what may be called his
political Cave of Adullam.   *Speech, House of Commons, 13 March 1866*

11 Force is not a remedy.   *Speech, Birmingham, 16 Nov. 1880*

BRONTË, Emily, 1818–1848

12   No coward soul is mine,
No trembler in the world's storm-troubled sphere:
    I see Heaven's glories shine,
And faith shines equal, arming me from fear.   *Last Lines*

13   Vain are the thousand creeds
That move men's hearts: unutterably vain;
    Worthless as wither'd weeds.   *Ib*

14 Riches I hold in light esteem,
    And Love I laugh to scorn;
And lust of fame was but a dream
    That vanish'd with the morn.   *The Old Stoic*

15 O! dreadful is the check—intense the agony—
When the ear begins to hear, and the eye begins to see;
When the pulse begins to throb—the brain to think again—
The soul to feel the flesh, and the flesh to feel the chain.   *The Prisoner*

BROOKE, Rupert, 1887–1915

1 Blow out, you bugles, over the rich Dead.   *The Dead*

2 Just now the lilac is in bloom
  All before my little room.   *The Old Vicarage, Grantchester*

3 For England's the one land, I know,
  Where men with Splendid Hearts may go.   *Ib*

4 Stands the Church clock at ten to three?
  And is there honey still for tea?   *Ib*

5 If I should die, think only this of me:
  That there's some corner of a foreign field
  That is forever England.   *The Soldier*

6 A dust whom England bore, shaped, made aware,
  Gave, once, her flowers to love, her ways to roam,
  A body of England's, breathing English air,
  Washed by the rivers, blest by suns of home.   *Ib*

7 And laughter, learnt of friends; and gentleness,
  In hearts at peace, under an English heaven.   *Ib*

BROOKS, Phillips, 1835–1893

8 O little town of Bethlehem,
    How still we see thee lie;
  Above thy deep and dreamless sleep
    The silent stars go by.   *O Little Town of Bethlehem*

BROWN, Thomas, 1663–1704

9 I do not love thee, Doctor Fell,
  The reason why I cannot tell;
  But this alone I know full well,
  I do not love thee, Doctor Fell.   *Translation of Martial, Epigrams, 1, 32*

BROWN, Thomas Edward, 1830–1897

10 A garden is a lovesome thing, God wot!   *My Garden*

BROWNE, Charles Farrar, see WARD, Artemus

BROWNE, Sir Thomas, 1605–1682

11 He who discommendeth others obliquely commendeth himself.
                                                        Christian Morals

12 I dare, without usurpation, assume the honourable style of Christian.
                                                    Religio Medici, Part 1, 1

13 All things are artificial, for nature is the art of God.   *Ib, 16*

14 I am of a constitution so general that it consorts and sympathiseth with all
   things. I have no antipathy, or rather idiosyncrasy, in diet, humour, air,
   any-thing.   *Ib, Part 2, 1*

15 It is the common wonder of all men, how among so many million of faces,
   there should be none alike.   *Ib, 2*

16 No man can justly censure or condemn another, because indeed no man
   truly knows another.   *Ib, 4*

1 I could be content that we might procreate like trees, without conjunction, or that there were any way to perpetuate the world without this trivial and vulgar way of coition. *Religio Medici, Part 2, 9*

2 Lord, deliver me from myself. *Ib, 10*

3 Man is a noble animal, splendid in ashes, and pompous in the grave.
Urn Burial, Ch. 5

BROWNE, Sir William, 1692–1774

4 The King to Oxford sent a troop of horse,
For Tories own no argument but force:
With equal skill to Cambridge books he sent,
For Whigs admit no force but argument. *Reply to Trapp's Epigram*
(see 318:1)

BROWNING, Elizabeth Barrett, 1806–1861

5   Let no one till his death
Be called unhappy. Measure not the work
Until the day's out and the labour done. *Aurora Leigh, Book 5*

6 Since when was genius found respectable? *Ib, Book 6*

7 Do you hear the children weeping, O my brothers,
Ere the sorrow comes with years? *The Cry of the Children*

8 I tell you hopeless grief is passionless. *Grief*

9 What was he doing, the great god Pan,
Down in the reeds by the river? *A Musical Instrument*

BROWNING, Robert, 1812–1889

10   Love, we are in God's hand.
How strange now, looks the life he makes us lead!
So free we seem, so fettered fast we are! *Andrea del Sarto*

11 Ah, but a man's reach should exceed his grasp,
Or what's a heaven for? *Ib*

12 One who never turned his back but marched breast forward,
      Never doubted clouds would break,
Never dreamed, though right were worsted, wrong would triumph,
Held we fall to rise, are baffled to fight better,
      Sleep to wake. *Asolando, Epilogue*

13 Just when we are safest, there's a sunset-touch,
A fancy from a flower-bell, some one's death,
A chorus-ending from Euripides,—
And that's enough for fifty hopes and fears
As old and new at once as Nature's self,
To rap and knock and enter in our soul. *Bishop Blougram's Apology*

14 No, when the fight begins within himself,
A man's worth something. *Ib*

15 Oh, the little more, and how much it is!
      And the little less, and what worlds away! *By The Fire-side, 39*

16   We loved, sir—used to meet:
How sad and bad and mad it was—
      But then, how it was sweet! *Confessions*

1 Oh, to be in England
  Now that April's there,
  And whoever wakes in England
  Sees, some morning, unaware,
  That the lowest boughs and the brushwood sheaf
  Round the elm-tree bole are in tiny leaf,
  While the chaffinch sings on the orchard bough
  In England—now!   *Home-Thoughts, from Abroad*

2 And after April, when May follows,
  And the whitethroat builds, and all the swallows!   *Ib*

3 That's the wise thrush; he sings each song twice over,
  Lest you should think he never could recapture
  The first fine careless rapture!   *Ib*

4 Nobly, nobly Cape Saint Vincent to the North-west died away;
  Sunset ran, one glorious blood-red, reeking into Cadiz Bay.
                                      Home-Thoughts, from the Sea

5 Whoso turns as I, this evening, turn to God to praise and pray,
  While Jove's planet rises yonder, silent over Africa.   *Ib*

6 I sprang to the stirrup, and Joris, and he;
  I galloped, Dirck galloped, we galloped all three.
                          How they brought the Good News from Ghent to Aix

7   Escape me?
       Never—
       Beloved!
  While I am I, and you are you.   *Life in a Love*

8 Just for a handful of silver he left us,
       Just for a riband to stick in his coat.   *The Lost Leader*

9 Never glad confident morning again!   *Ib*

10 Ah, did you once see Shelley plain,
       And did he stop and speak to you?
   And did you speak to him again,
       How strange it seems, and new!   *Memorabilia*

11 Never the time and the place
       And the loved one all together!   *Never the Time and the Place*

12 Dante, who loved well because he hated,
   Hated wickedness that hinders loving.   *One Word More, 5*

13 Where my heart lies, let my brain lie also!   *Ib, 14*

14 God be thanked, the meanest of his creatures
   Boasts two soul-sides, one to face the world with,
   One to show a woman when he loves her.   *Ib, 17*

15 It was roses, roses all the way.   *The Patriot*

16   Hamelin Town's in Brunswick,
   By famous Hanover city;
       The river Weser, deep and wide,
       Washes its wall on the southern side.
                                      The Pied Piper of Hamelin, 1

17   Rats!
   They fought the dogs and killed the cats,
       And bit the babies in the cradles.   *Ib. 2*

1   With shrieking and squeaking
In fifty different sharps and flats.   *The Pied Piper of Hamelin, 2*

2 If I can rid your town of rats
Will you give me a thousand guilders?'
'One? fifty thousand!'—was the exclamation
Of the astonished Mayor and Corporation.   *Ib, 6*

3 And the muttering grew to a grumbling;
And the grumbling grew to a mighty rumbling;
And out of the houses the rats came tumbling.   *Ib, 7*

4 So, munch on, crunch on, take your nuncheon,
Breakfast, supper, dinner, luncheon!   *Ib*

5 'You threaten us, fellow? Do your worst,
Blow your pipe there till you burst!'   *Ib, 9*

6 All the little boys and girls,
With rosy cheeks and flaxen curls,
And sparkling eyes, and teeth like pearls,
Tripping and skipping, ran merrily after
The wonderful music with shouting and laughter.   *Ib, 12*

7 The year's at the spring,
And day's at the morn;
Morning's at seven;
The hill-side's dew-pearled;
The lark's on the wing;
The snail's on the thorn;
God's in His heaven—
All's right with the world.   *Pippa Passes, 1, Morning*

8 All service ranks the same with God—
With God, whose puppets, best and worst,
Are we: there is no last nor first.   *Ib, 4, Night*

9 Grow old along with me.
The best is yet to be,
The last of life, for which the first was made:
Our times are in His hand
Who saith 'A whole I planned,
Youth shows but half; trust God: see all nor be afraid!'   *Rabbi Ben Ezra*

10 Let age approve of youth, and death complete the same!   *Ib*

11 What of soul was left, I wonder, when the kissing had to stop?
    A Toccata of Galuppi's, 14

BUCHANAN, Robert Williams, 1841-1901

12 The Fleshly School of Poetry.   *Title of article in the Contemporary
Review, Oct. 1871*

13   She just wore
Enough for modesty—no more.   *White Rose and Red, Part 1, 5*

BUFFON, Georges Louis Leclerc, Comte de, 1707-1788

14 *Le style est l'homme même.* Style is the man himself.   *Discours sur le style*

BULLER, Arthur Henry Reginald, 1874–1944

1 There was a young lady named Bright,
  Whose speed was far faster than light;
      She set out one day
      In a relative way,
  And returned home the previous night.   *Limerick*

BULWER-LYTTON, Edward, 1803–1873

2 Here Stanley meets,—how Stanley scorns, the glance!
  The brilliant chief, irregularly great,
  Frank, haughty, rash,—the Rupert of Debate.   *The New Timon, 1, 6*

3 Beneath the rule of men entirely great,
  The pen is mightier than the sword.   *Richelieu, 2, 2*

BUNN, Alfred, 1796?–1860

4 I dreamt that I dwelt in marble halls,
  With vassals and serfs at my side.   ARLINE   *The Bohemian Girl, Act 2*

BUNYAN, John, 1628–1688

5 Some said, John, print it; others said, Not so;
  Some said, It might do good; others said, No.
                              Pilgrim's Progress, Author's Apology

6 As I walked through the wilderness of this world.   *Ib, Part 1*

7 The name of the slough was Despond.   *Ib*

8 The gentleman's name that met him was Mr. Worldly Wiseman.   *Ib*

9 It beareth the name of Vanity Fair, because the town where 'tis kept is
  lighter than vanity.   *Ib*

10 Mr. Facing-both-ways.   *Ib*

11 A castle called Doubting Castle, the owner whereof was Giant Despair. *Ib*

12 So I awoke, and behold it was a dream.   *Ib*

13 He who would valiant be
   'Gainst all disaster,
   Let him in constancy
         Follow the Master.
   There's no discouragement
   Shall make him once relent
   His first avowed intent
         To be a pilgrim.   *Ib, Part 2, English Hymnal Version*

14 I'll fear not what men say,
   I'll labour night and day
         To be a pilgrim.   *Ib*

15 He that is down needs fear no fall;
   He that is low, no pride.   *Ib, Shepherd Boy's Song*

16 So he passed over, and all the trumpets sounded for him on the other side.
                                                                 Ib

BURGESS, Gelett, 1866–1951

1 I never saw a Purple Cow,
 I never hope to see one;
 But I can tell you, anyhow,
 I'd rather see than be one.   *The Purple Cow*

2 Ah, yes, I wrote the 'Purple Cow'—
 I'm sorry, now, I wrote it!
 But I can tell you anyhow,
 I'll kill you if you quote it.   *Reply*

BURGON, John William, 1813–1888

3 Match me such marvel save in Eastern clime,
 A rose-red city half as old as time.   *Petra, 132*

BURKE, Edmund, 1729–1797

4 The concessions of the weak are the concessions of fear.
 Speech on Conciliation with America, 22 March 1775

5 The use of force alone is but *temporary*. It may subdue for a moment; but it does not remove the necessity of subduing again: and a nation is not governed, which is perpetually to be conquered.   *Ib*

6 I do not know the method of drawing up an indictment against an whole people.   *Ib*

7 All government, indeed every human benefit and enjoyment, every virtue, and every prudent act, is founded on compromise and barter.   *Ib*

8 The people are the masters.   *Speech on the Economical Reform, 11 Feb. 1780*

9 He was not merely a chip of the old block, but the old block itself.
 Of Pitt's first speech, 26 Feb. 1781

10 There is, however, a limit at which forbearance ceases to be a virtue.
 Observations on 'The Present State of the Nation', 1769

11 But the age of chivalry is gone. That of sophisters, economists, and calculators, has succeeded; and the glory of Europe is extinguished for ever.
 Reflections on the Revolution in France

12 Man is by his constitution a religious animal.   *Ib*

13 Superstition is the religion of feeble minds.   *Ib*

14 Good order is the foundation of all good things.   *Ib*

15 Example is the school of mankind, and they will learn at no other.
 Letters on a Regicide Peace, 1, 1796

16 And having looked to government for bread, on the very first scarcity they will turn and bite the hand that fed them.
 Thoughts and Details on Scarcity

17 If any ask me what a free government is, I answer, that, for any practical purpose, it is what the people think so.
 Letter to the Sheriffs of Bristol, 1777

18 Liberty, too, must be limited in order to be possessed.   *Ib*

19 Among a people generally corrupt, liberty cannot long exist.   *Ib*

20 The greater the power, the more dangerous the abuse.
 Speech, House of Commons, 7 Feb. 1771

1 I am convinced that we have a degree of delight, and that no small one, in the real misfortunes and pains of others.

On the Sublime and Beautiful, 1, 14

2 Power gradually extirpates from the mind every humane and gentle virtue.

A Vindication of Natural Society

BURNET, Bishop Gilbert, 1643–1715

3 There was a sure way to see it lost, and that was to die in the last ditch.

History of his own Times, 1

BURNEY, Fanny (Mme D'Arblay), 1752–1840

4 Dancing? Oh, dreadful! How it was ever adopted in a civilised country I cannot find out; 'tis certainly a Barbarian exercise, and of savage origin.

MR MEADOWS   *Cecilia, Bk. 3*

5 'True, very true ma'am,' said he, yawning, 'one really lives nowhere; one does but vegetate and wish it all at an end.'   MR MEADOWS   *Ib, Bk. 4*

6 Indeed, the freedom with which Dr. Johnson condemns whatever he disapproves is astonishing.   *Diary, 23 Aug. 1778*

BURNS, John, 1858–1943

7 Every drop of the Thames is liquid history.

Attributed by Sir Frederick Whyte

BURNS, Robert, 1759–1796

8 Ae fond kiss, and then we sever!   *Ae Fond Kiss, 1*

9 But to see her was to love her,
Love but her, and love for ever.   *Ib, 11*

10 Had we never lov'd sae kindly,
Had we never lov'd sae blindly,
Never met—or never parted,
We had ne'er been broken-hearted.   *Ib, 13*

11 Flow gently, sweet Afton, among thy green braes,
Flow gently, I'll sing thee a song in thy praise.   *Afton Water, 1*

12 Should auld acquaintance be forgot,
And never brought to min'?   *Auld Lang Syne, 1*

13 We'll tak a cup o' kindness yet,
For auld lang syne.   *Ib, 7*

14 Freedom and Whisky gang thegither!   *The Author's Earnest Cry and Prayer, 185*

15 Gin a body meet a body
Coming through the rye;
Gin a body kiss a body,
Need a body cry?   *Coming through the Rye, 5*

16 I wasna fou, but just had plenty.   *Death and Doctor Hornbrook, 14*

17 On ev'ry hand it will allow'd be,
He's just—nae better than he should be.

A Dedication to Gavin Hamilton, 25

18 A man's a man for a' that.   *For a' that and a' that, 12*

1 Green grow the rashes O,
    Green grow the rashes O;
The sweetest hours that e'er I spend,
    Are spent amang the lasses O!   *Green Grow the Rashes, 1*

2 The wisest man the warl' saw,
    He dearly lov'd the lasses O.   *Ib, 19*

3 The golden hours on angel wings
    Flew o'er me and my dearie;
For dear to me as light and life
    Was my sweet Highland Mary.   *Highland Mary, 13*

4 There's some are fou o' love divine,
    There's some are fou o' brandy.   *The Holy Fair, 239*

5 John Anderson my jo, John,
    When we were first acquent,
Your locks were like the raven,
    Your bonnie brow was brent.   *John Anderson My Jo, 1*

6 True it is, she had one failing,
    Had a woman ever less?   *Lines, written under picture of Miss Burns*

7   Nature's law,
That man was made to mourn.   *Man was Made to Mourn, 31*

8 Man's inhumanity to man
    Makes countless thousands mourn!   *Ib, 55*

9 O Mary, at thy window be,
    It is the wish'd, the trysted hour!   *Mary Morison, 1*

10 Wee, sleekit, cow'rin', tim'rous beastie,
    O what a panic's in thy breastie!   *To a Mouse, 1*

11 I'm truly sorry man's dominion
    Has broken Nature's social union.   *Ib, 7*

12 The best laid schemes o' mice an' men
                Gang aft a-gley,
An' lea'e us nought but grief an' pain
                For promis'd joy.   *Ib, 39*

13 Still thou art blest compar'd wi' me!
The present only toucheth thee:
But oh! I backward cast my e'e
                On prospects drear!
An' forward tho' I canna see,
                I guess an' fear!   *Ib, 43*

14 My heart's in the Highlands, my heart is not here;
My heart's in the Highlands a-chasing the deer;
Chasing the wild deer, and following the roe,
My heart's in the Highlands, wherever I go.
          My Heart's in the Highlands, 1

15 My love is like a red red rose
    That's newly sprung in June:
My love is like the melodie
    That's sweetly play'd in tune.   *A Red, Red Rose*

1 Scots, wha hae wi' Wallace bled,
  Scots, wham Bruce has aften led,
  Welcome to your gory bed,
    Or to victorie. *Scots, Wha Hae, 1*

2 Liberty's in every blow!
  Let us do or die! *Ib, 23*

3 Some hae meat, and canna eat,
    And some wad eat that want it;
  But we hae meat and we can eat,
    And sae the Lord be thankit. *The Selkirk Grace*

4 But pleasures are like poppies spread—
  You seize the flow'r, its bloom is shed;
  Or like the snow falls in the river—
  A moment white, then melts for ever. *Tam o' Shanter, 59*

5 Ye banks and braes o' bonnie Doon,
    How can ye bloom sae fresh and fair?
  How can ye chant, ye little birds,
    And I sae weary fu' o' care? *Ye Banks and Braes, 1*

6 Thou minds me o' departed joys,
    Departed never to return. *Ib, 7*

7 And my fause lover stole my rose,
    But ah! he left the thorn wi' me. *Ib, 15*

BURTON, Robert, 1577–1640

8 All my joys to this are folly,
  Naught so sweet as Melancholy. *Anatomy of Melancholy, Author's*
  Abstract of Melancholy

9 *Hinc quam sit calamus saevior ense patet.* From this it is clear how much more
  cruel the pen is than the sword. *Ib, Part 1*

10 England is a paradise for women, and hell for horses: Italy a paradise for
  horses, hell for women. *Ib, Part 3*

11 One religion is as true as another. *Ib*

12 Be not solitary, be not idle. *Ib, Last words*

BUSSY-RABUTIN, Comte de, 1618–1693

13 *L'absence est à l'amour ce qu'est au feu le vent; il éteint le petit, il allume le*
  grand. Absence is to love what wind is to fire; it extinguishes the small, it
  inflames the great. *Histoire Amoureuse des Gaules*

BUTLER, Samuel, 1612–1680

14 When civil fury first grew high,
  And men fell out they knew not why. *Hudibras, 1, 1, 1*

15 For every why he had a wherefore. *Ib, 1, 1, 132*

16 Oaths are but words, and words but wind. *Ib, 2, 2, 107*

17 What makes all doctrines plain and clear?
  About two hundred pounds a year.
  And that which was prov'd true before
  Prove false again? Two hundred more. *Ib, 3, 1, 1277*

1 He that complies against his will,
  Is of his own opinion still.   *Hudibras, 3, 3, 547*

2 The souls of women are so small,
  That some believe they've none at all.   *Miscellaneous Thoughts*

BUTLER, Samuel, 1835–1902

3 It has been said that the love of money is the root of all evil. The want of
  money is so quite as truly.   *Erewhon, Ch. 20*

4 I keep my books at the British Museum and at Mudie's.
                     The Humour of Homer, Ramblings in Cheapside

5 Life is one long process of getting tired.   *Note-books, Life, 7*

6 Life is the art of drawing sufficient conclusions from insufficient premises.
                                                   Ib, 9

7 All progress is based upon a universal innate desire on the part of every
  organism to live beyond its income.   *Ib, 16*

8 To live is like love, all reason is against it, and all healthy instinct for it.
                     Ib, Higgledy-Piggledy, Life and Love

9 Stowed away in a Montreal lumber room
  The Discobolus standeth and turneth his face to the wall;
  Dusty, cobweb-covered, maimed and set at naught,
  Beauty crieth in an attic and no man regardeth.
      O God! O Montreal!   *A Psalm of Montreal*

10 The advantage of doing one's praising for oneself is that one can lay it on
   so thick and exactly in the right places.   *The Way of All Flesh, Ch. 34*

11 A man's friendships are, like his will, invalidated by marriage—but they
   are also no less invalidated by the marriage of his friends.   *Ib, Ch. 75*

12 'Tis better to have loved and lost than never to have lost at all.   *Ib, Ch. 77*
                     (see also *84:18 and 312:13*)

13 Brigands demand your money or your life; women require both.
                                                   Attributed

BYROM, John, 1692–1763

14 Christians awake, salute the happy morn,
   Whereon the Saviour of the world was born.   *Hymn for Christmas Day*

15 God bless the King, I mean the Faith's Defender;
   God bless—no harm in blessing—the Pretender;
   But who Pretender is, or who is King,
   God bless us all—that's quite another thing.   *To an Officer in the Army*

BYRON, George Gordon, 6th Baron, 1788–1824

16 In short, he was a perfect cavaliero,
   And to his very valet seem'd a hero.   *Beppo, 33*

17 I like the weather, when it is not rainy,
   That is, I like two months of every year.   *Ib, 48*

18 Maidens, like moths, are ever caught by glare,
   And Mammon wins his way where Seraphs might despair.
                     Childe Harold's Pilgrimage, Canto 1, 9

1 Adieu, adieu! my native shore
  Fades o'er the waters blue.   *Childe Harold's Pilgrimage, Canto 1, 13*

2 My native Land—Good Night!   *Ib*

3 There was a sound of revelry by night,
  And Belgium's capital had gather'd then
  Her Beauty and her Chivalry, and bright
  The lamps shone o'er fair women and brave men.   *Ib, Canto 3, 21*

4 On with the dance! let joy be unconfined;
  No sleep till morn, when Youth and Pleasure meet
  To chase the glowing Hours with flying feet.   *Ib, 3, 22*

5 I have not loved the world, nor the world me;
  I have not flatter'd its rank breath, nor bow'd
  To its idolatries a patient knee.   *Ib, 3, 113*

6 I stood in Venice, on the Bridge of Sighs;
  A palace and a prison on each hand.   *Ib, Canto 4, 1*

7 Yet, Freedom! yet thy banner, torn, but flying,
  Streams like the thunder-storm *against* the wind.   *Ib, 4, 98*

8 While stands the Coliseum, Rome shall stand;
  When falls the Coliseum, Rome shall fall;
  And when Rome falls—the World.   *Ib, 4, 145*

9 There is a pleasure in the pathless woods,
  There is a rapture on the lonely shore,
  There is society, where none intrudes,
  By the deep Sea, and music in its roar:
  I love not Man the less, but Nature more.   *Ib, 4, 178*

10 What men call gallantry, and gods adultery,
  Is much more common where the climate's sultry.   *Don Juan, Canto 1, 63*

11 A little still she strove, and much repented,
  And whispering 'I will ne'er consent'—consented.   *Ib, 1, 117*

12 Sweet is revenge—especially to women.   *Ib, 1, 124*

13 Pleasure's a sin, and sometimes sin's a pleasure.   *Ib, 1, 133*

14 Man's love is of man's life a thing apart,
  'Tis woman's whole existence.   *Ib, 1, 194*

15 Man, being reasonable, must get drunk;
  The best of life is but intoxication.   *Ib, Canto 2, 179*

16 Alas! the love of women! it is known
  To be a lovely and a fearful thing.   *Ib, 2, 199*

17 In her first passion woman loves her lover,
  In all the others all she loves is love.   *Ib, Canto 3, 3*

18 'Tis melancholy, and a fearful sign
  Of human frailty, folly, also crime,
  That love and marriage rarely can combine.   *Ib, 3, 5*

19 All tragedies are finish'd by a death,
  All comedies are ended by a marriage.   *Ib, 3, 9*

20 Dreading that climax of all human ills
  The inflammation of his weekly bills.   *Ib, 3, 35*

21 The isles of Greece, the isles of Greece!
  Where burning Sappho loved and sung,

Where grew the arts of war and peace,
    Where Delos rose, and Phoebus sprung!
Eternal summer gilds them yet,
    But all, except their sun, is set.   *Don Juan, Canto 3, 86, 1*

1 The mountains look on Marathon—
    And Marathon looks on the sea;
And musing there an hour alone,
    I dream'd that Greece might still be free.   *Ib, 3, 86, 3*

2 And if I laugh at any mortal thing,
    'Tis that I may not weep.   *Ib, Canto 4, 4*

3 There is a tide in the affairs of women,
    Which, taken at the flood, leads—God knows where.   *Ib, Canto 6, 2*

4   A lady of a 'certain age,' which means
Certainly aged.   *Ib, 6, 69*

5 And, after all, what is a lie? 'Tis but
    The truth in masquerade.   *Ib, Canto 11, 37*

6 'Tis strange the mind, that very fiery particle,
    Should let itself be snuff'd out by an article.   [*John Keats*]   *Ib, 11, 60*

7 Now hatred is by far the longest pleasure;
    Men love in haste, but they detest at leisure.   *Ib, Canto 13, 6*

8 The English winter—ending in July,
    To recommence in August.   *Ib, 13, 42*

9 Society is now one polish'd horde,
    Form'd of two mighty tribes, the *Bores* and *Bored*.   *Ib, 13, 95*

10 'Tis strange,—but true; for truth is always strange;
    Stranger than fiction: if it could be told,
How much would novels gain by the exchange!   *Ib, Canto 14, 101*

11   I'll publish, right or wrong:
Fools are my theme, let satire be my song.
        English Bards and Scotch Reviewers, 5

12 'Tis pleasant, sure, to see one's name in print;
    A book's a book, although there's nothing in't.   *Ib, 51*

13 A man must serve his time to every trade
    Save censure—critics all are ready made.   *Ib, 63*

14   As soon
Seek roses in December—ice in June;
Hope constancy in wind, or corn in chaff;
Believe a woman or an epitaph,
Or any other thing that's false, before
You trust in critics, who themselves are sore.   *Ib, 75*

15 Better to err with Pope, than shine with Pye.   *Ib, 102*

16 Fare thee well! and if for ever,
    Still for ever, fare thee well.   *Fare Thee Well, 1*

17 Who kill'd John Keats?
    'I,' says the Quarterly,
    So savage and Tartarly;
    ''Twas one of my feats.'   *John Keats*

1 Maid of Athens, ere we part,
Give, oh give me back my heart!   *Maid of Athens, ere we Part*

2 She walks in beauty, like the night
 Of cloudless climes and starry skies;
And all that's best of dark and bright
 Meet in her aspect and her eyes.   *She Walks in Beauty*

3 So, we'll go no more a roving
 So late into the night,
Though the heart be still as loving,
 And the moon be still as bright.   *So, we'll go no more a roving*

4 Though the night was made for loving,
 And the day returns too soon,
Yet we'll go no more a roving
 By the light of the moon.   *Ib*

5 When we two parted
 In silence and tears,
Half broken-hearted
 To sever for years,
Pale grew thy cheek and cold,
 Colder thy kiss;
Truly that hour foretold
 Sorrow to this.   *When we two parted*

6 If I should meet thee
 After long years,
How should I greet thee?—
 With silence and tears.   *Ib*

7 I awoke one morning and found myself famous.   *Entry in Memoranda*
after publication of Childe Harold

BYRON, Henry James, 1834–1884
8 Life's too short for chess.   *Our Boys, Act I*

CAESAR, Augustus, 63 B.C.–A.D. 14
9 *Quintili Vare, legiones redde.* Quintilius Varus, give me back my legions.
Suetonius, Divus Augustus, 23
10 *Ad Kalendas Graecas soluturos.* To be paid at the Greek Kalends.   *Ib, 87*

CAESAR, Julius, 102?–44 B.C
11 *Gallia est omnis divisa in partes tres.* All Gaul is divided into three parts.
De Bello Gallico, I, I
12 *Iacta alea est.* The die is cast.   *On Crossing the Rubicon, 49 B.C.*
13 *Veni, vidi, vici.* I came, I saw, I conquered.   *After Victory at Zela, 47 B.C.*
14 *Et tu, Brute.* You too, Brutus?   *Last Words, attributed*
15 Caesar's wife must be above suspicion.   *Plutarch, Life of Caesar*

CALVERLEY, Charles Stuart, 1831–1884
16 The auld wife sat at her ivied door
 (Butter and eggs and a pound of cheese)
A thing she had frequently done before;
 And her spectacles lay on her aproned knees.   *Ballad*

1 The heart which grief hath cankered
Hath one unfailing remedy—the Tankard. *Beer*

2 For I've read in many a novel that, unless they've souls that grovel,
Folks *prefer* in fact a hovel to your dreary marble halls. *In the Gloaming*

3 How Eugene Aram, though a thief, a liar, and a murderer
Yet, being intellectual, was amongst the noblest of mankind. *Of Reading*

4 I have a liking old
For thee, though manifold
Stories, I know, are told,
Not to thy credit. *Ode to Tobacco*

CAMDEN, William, 1551–1623

5 Betwixt the stirrup and the ground
Mercy I asked, mercy I found. *Epitaph for a Man killed by falling from his Horse*

CAMPBELL, Roy, 1902–1957

6 You praise the firm restraint with which they write,
I'm with you there, of course:
They use the snaffle and the curb all right,
But where's the bloody horse? *On Some South African Novelists*

CAMPBELL, Thomas, 1777–1844

7 O leave this barren spot to me!
Spare, woodman, spare the beechen tree. *The Beech-Tree's Petition*

8 A chieftain to the Highlands bound
Cries 'Boatman, do not tarry!
And I'll give thee a silver pound
To row us o'er the ferry.' *Lord Ullin's Daughter*

9 'Tis distance lends enchantment to the view,
And robes the mountain in its azure hue. *Pleasures of Hope, 1, 7*

10 Ye mariners of England
That guard our native seas,
Whose flag has braved, a thousand years,
The battle and the breeze. *Ye Mariners of England*

11 Now Barabbas was a publisher. *Attributed*

CAMPION, Thomas, 1567–1620

12 Follow thy fair sun, unhappy shadow. *Follow thy Fair Sun*

13 There is a garden in her face,
Where roses and white lilies grow. *There is a Garden in her Face*

14 There cherries grow, which none may buy
Till 'Cherry Ripe' themselves do cry. *Ib*

CANNING, George, 1770–1827

15 I called the New World into existence to redress the balance of the Old.
Speech, 12 Dec. 1826

16 But of all plagues, good Heaven, thy wrath can send,
Save me, oh, save me, from the candid friend. *New Morality, 209*

17 Pitt is to Addington
As London is to Paddington. *The Oracle*

CAREY, Henry, 1693?–1743

1 God save our Gracious King,
   Long live our noble King,
   God save the King.
   Send him victorious,
   Happy and glorious.   *God Save the King. Origin is disputed.*
                        See Dr. Percy A. Scholes, God Save the Queen, 1954

2 Confound their politics
   Frustrate their knavish tricks.   *Ib*

3 Of all the girls that are so smart
      There's none like pretty Sally;
   She is the darling of my heart
      And she lives in our alley.   *Sally in our Alley*

CARLYLE, Thomas, 1795–1881

4 A witty statesman said, you might prove anything by figures.
                                            Essay on Chartism

5 Genius (which means transcendent capacity of taking trouble, first of all).
                                     Frederick the Great, Bk. 4, Ch. 3

6 A whiff of grapeshot.   *History of the French Revolution, 1, 5, 3*

7 The seagreen Incorruptible. [*Robespierre*]   *Ib, 2, 4, 4*

8 No great man lives in vain. The history of the world is but the biography
   of great men.   *Heroes and Hero-Worship, 1, The Hero as Divinity*

9 The true University of these days is a collection of books.
                          Ib, 5, The Hero as Man of Letters

10 History is the essence of innumerable biographies.   *Essay on History*

11 No man who has once heartily and wholly laughed can be altogether
    irreclaimably bad.   *Sartor Resartus, Bk. 1, Ch. 4*

CARNEGIE, Dale, 1888—

12 How to Win Friends and Influence People.   *Title of Book*

CARNEY, Julia A. Fletcher, 1823–1908

13 Little drops of water, little grains of sand,
    Make the mighty ocean and the pleasant land.
    So the little minutes, humble though they be,
    Make the mighty ages of eternity.   *Little Things*

CARROLL, Lewis (Charles Lutwidge Dodgson), 1832–1898

14 'What is the use of a book,' thought Alice, 'without pictures or conversa-
    tion?'   *Alice's Adventures in Wonderland, Ch. 1*

15 She found a little bottle on it, ('which certainly was not here before,' said
    Alice,) and round its neck a paper label, with the words 'DRINK ME'
    beautifully printed on it in large letters.   *Ib, Ch. 1*

16 'Curiouser and curiouser!' cried Alice.   *Ib, Ch. 2*

17 How doth the little crocodile
       Improve his shining tail,
    And pour the waters of the Nile
       On every golden scale!

How cheerfully he seems to grin,
   How neatly spread his claws,
And welcomes little fishes in
   With gently smiling jaws!   ALICE   *Alice's Adventures in Wonderland,*
   Ch. 2

1 'I'll be judge, I'll be jury,' said cunning old Fury: 'I'll try the whole cause,
and condemn you to death.'   *Ib, Ch. 3*

2 The Duchess! The Duchess! Oh my dear paws! Oh my fur and whiskers!
   THE WHITE RABBIT   *Ib, Ch. 4*

3 'You are old, Father William,' the young man said,
   'And your hair has become very white;
And yet you incessantly stand on your head—
   Do you think at your age, it is right?'
'In my youth,' Father William replied to his son,
   'I feared it might injure the brain;
But, now that I'm perfectly sure I have none,
   Why, I do it again and again.'   ALICE   *Ib, Ch. 5*

4 'I have answered three questions, and that is enough,'
   Said his father; 'don't give yourself airs!
Do you think I can listen all day to such stuff?
   Be off or I'll kick you downstairs!'   ALICE   *Ib, Ch. 5*

5 'If everybody minded their own business,' the Duchess said in a hoarse
growl, 'the world would go round a deal faster than it does.'   *Ib, Ch. 6*

6 Speak roughly to your little boy,
   And beat him when he sneezes:
He only does it to annoy,
   Because he knows it teases.   THE DUCHESS   *Ib, Ch. 6*

7 I speak severely to my boy,
   I beat him when he sneezes;
For he can thoroughly enjoy
   The pepper when he pleases!   THE DUCHESS   *Ib, Ch. 6*

8 Twinkle, twinkle, little bat!
   How I wonder what you're at!   THE HATTER   *Ib, Ch. 7*

9 Up above the world you fly,
   Like a tea-tray in the sky.   THE HATTER   *Ib, Ch. 7*

10 'Take some more tea,' the March Hare said to Alice, very earnestly.
   'I've had nothing yet,' Alice replied in an offended tone, 'so I can't take
   more.'
   'You mean you can't take *less*,' said the Hatter: 'it's very easy to take *more*
   than nothing.'   *Ib, Ch. 7*

11 The Queen was in a furious passion, and went stamping about, and shouting
'Off with his head!' or 'Off with her head!' about once in a minute. *Ib, Ch. 8*

12 Everything's got a moral, if only you can find it.   THE DUCHESS   *Ib, Ch. 9*

13 Take care of the sense, and the sounds will take care of themselves.
   THE DUCHESS   *Ib, Ch. 9*

14 'Why did you call him Tortoise, if he wasn't one?' Alice asked.
   'We called him Tortoise because he taught us,' said the Mock Turtle
   angrily: 'really you are very dull!'   *Ib, Ch. 9*

15 'Reeling and Writhing, of course, to begin with,' the Mock Turtle replied;
   'and then the different branches of Arithmetic—Ambition, Distraction,
   Uglification, and Derision.'   *Ib, Ch. 9*

1 'That's the reason they're called lessons,' the Gryphon remarked: 'because
they lessen from day to day.'   *Alice's Adventures in Wonderland, Ch. 9*

2 'Will you walk a little faster?' said a whiting to a snail.
'There's a porpoise close behind us, and he's treading on my tail.'
                                        THE MOCK TURTLE   *Ib, Ch. 10*

3 Will you, won't you, will you, won't you, will you join the dance?
                                        THE MOCK TURTLE   *Ib, Ch. 10*

4 'Tis the voice of the Lobster; I heard him declare,
'You have baked me too brown, I must sugar my hair.'   ALICE
                                                               Ib, Ch. 10

5 Soup of the evening, beautiful Soup!   THE MOCK TURTLE   *Ib, Ch. 10*

6 'The Queen of Hearts, she made some tarts,
      All on a summer day:
The Knave of Hearts, he stole those tarts,
      And took them quite away!'   THE WHITE RABBIT (reading)
                                                               Ib, Ch. 11

7 They told me you had been to her,
      And mentioned me to him:
She gave me a good character,
      But said I could not swim.   THE WHITE RABBIT (reading)
                                                               Ib, Ch. 12

8 'No, no!' said the Queen. 'Sentence first—verdict afterwards.'
'Stuff and nonsense!' said Alice loudly.   *Ib, Ch. 12*

9 'Twas brillig, and the slithy toves
      Did gyre and gimble in the wabe;
All mimsy were the borogoves,
      And the mome raths outgrabe.   ALICE (reading)
                                        Through the Looking-Glass, Ch. 1

10 One, two! One, two! And through and through
      The vorpal blade went snicker-snack!
He left it dead, and with its head
      He went galumphing back.   ALICE (reading)   *Ib, Ch. 1*

11 'And hast thou slain the Jabberwock?
      Come to my arms, my beamish boy!
O frabjous day! Callooh! Callay!'
      He chortled in his joy.   ALICE (reading)   *Ib, Ch. 1*

12 Now, *here*, you see, it takes all the running *you* can do, to keep in the same
place. If you want to get somewhere else, you must run at least twice as
fast as that!   THE QUEEN   *Ib, Ch. 2*

13 'If you think we're wax-works,' he said, 'you ought to pay, you know.
Wax-works weren't made to be looked at for nothing. Nohow!'
                                        TWEEDLEDUM   *Ib, Ch. 4*

14 Tweedledum and Tweedledee
      Agreed to have a battle;
For Tweedledum said Tweedledee
      Had spoiled his nice new rattle.   ALICE   *Ib, Ch. 4*

15 'Contrariwise,' continued Tweedledee, 'if it was so, it might be; and if it
were so, it would be: but as it isn't, it ain't. That's logic.'   *Ib, Ch. 4*

16 The sun was shining on the sea,
      Shining with all his might:
He did his very best to make

The billows smooth and bright—
And this was odd, because it was
The middle of the night.   TWEEDLEDEE (reciting *The Walrus and The Carpenter*) *Through the Looking-Glass, Ch. 4*

1 'It's very rude of him,' she said,
'To come and spoil the fun!'   TWEEDLEDEE   *Ib, Ch. 4*

2 The Walrus and the Carpenter
Were walking close at hand;
They wept like anything to see
Such quantities of sand:
'If this were only cleared away,'
They said, 'it *would* be grand!'   TWEEDLEDEE   *Ib, Ch. 4*

3 'If seven maids with seven mops
Swept it for half a year,
Do you suppose,' the Walrus said,
'That they could get it clear?'
'I doubt it,' said the Carpenter,
And shed a bitter tear.   TWEEDLEDEE   *Ib, Ch. 4*

4 'The time has come,' the Walrus said,
'To talk of many things:
Of shoes—and ships—and sealing-wax—
Of cabbages—and kings—
And why the sea is boiling hot—
And whether pigs have wings.'   TWEEDLEDEE   *Ib, Ch. 4*

5 'I weep for you,' the Walrus said:
'I deeply sympathize.'
With sobs and tears he sorted out
Those of the largest size,
Holding his pocket-handkerchief
Before his streaming eyes.   TWEEDLEDEE   *Ib, Ch. 4*

6 'O Oysters,' said the Carpenter,
'You've had a pleasant run!
Shall we be trotting home again?'
But answer came there none—
And this was scarcely odd, because
They'd eaten every one.   TWEEDLEDEE   *Ib, Ch. 4*

7 The rule is, jam to-morrow and jam yesterday—but never jam to-day.
THE QUEEN   *Ib, Ch. 5*

8 Humpty Dumpty sat on a wall:
Humpty Dumpty had a great fall.
All the King's horses and all the King's men
Couldn't put Humpty Dumpty in his place again.   ALICE   *Ib, Ch. 6*

9 'They gave it me,' Humpty Dumpty continued thoughtfully, . . . 'for an un-birthday present.'   *Ib, Ch. 6*

10 'When *I* use a word,' Humpty Dumpty said in rather a scornful tone, 'it means just what I choose it to mean—neither more nor less.'   *Ib, Ch. 6*

11 In winter, when the fields are white,
I sing this song for your delight—   HUMPTY DUMPTY   *Ib, Ch. 6*

12 In spring, when woods are getting green,
I'll try and tell you what I mean.   HUMPTY DUMPTY   *Ib, Ch. 6*

1 I sent a message to the fish:
   I told them 'This is what I wish.'   HUMPTY DUMPTY *Through the Looking-*
                                                         Glass, Ch. 6

2 The little fishes of the sea,
   They sent an answer back to me.
   The little fishes' answer was
   'We cannot do it, Sir, because—'.   HUMPTY DUMPTY   *Ib, Ch. 6*

3 I said it very loud and clear;
   I went and shouted in his ear.   HUMPTY DUMPTY   *Ib, Ch. 6*

4 He's an Anglo-Saxon Messenger—and those are Anglo-Saxon attitudes.
                                         THE KING   *Ib, Ch. 7*

5 It's as large as life, and twice as natural!   HAIGHA   *Ib, Ch. 7*

6 The Lion looked at Alice wearily. 'Are you animal—or vegetable—or
   mineral?' he said, yawning at every other word.   *Ib, Ch. 7*

7 I'll tell thee everything I can;
   There's little to relate.
   I saw an aged aged man,
   A-sitting on a gate.   THE KNIGHT   *Ib, Ch. 8*

8 'Speak when you're spoken to!' the Red Queen sharply interrupted her.
                                                              Ib, Ch. 9

9 No admittance till the week after next!   CREATURE WITH A LONG BEAK
                                                              Ib, Ch. 9

10 'You look a little shy; let me introduce you to that leg of mutton,' said the
   Red Queen. 'Alice—Mutton; Mutton—Alice.'   *Ib, Ch. 9*

CARY, Phoebe, 1824–1871
11 And though hard be the task,
   'Keep a stiff upper lip.'   *Keep a Stiff Upper Lip*

CASTLING, Harry, 19th century
12 Let's all go down the Strand.   *Title of Song*

CATO, Marcus Porcius, 234–149 B.C.
13 *Delenda est Carthago.* Carthage must be destroyed.   *Plutarch, Life of Cato*

CATULLUS, Gaius Valerius, 87–54? B.C.
14 *Vivamus, mea Lesbia, atque amemus*
   Rumoresque senum severiorum
   Omnes unius aestimemus assis.
   Let us live, my Lesbia, and love, and pay no heed to all the talk of censorious
   old men.   *Carmina, 5*

15 *Da mi basia mille.*
   Give me a thousand kisses.   *Ib*

16 *Odi et amo. Quare id faciam, fortasse requiris.*
   Nescio, sed fieri sentio et excrucior.
   I hate and love. Why I do so, perhaps you ask.
   I do not know, but I feel it and am in torment.   *Ib, 85*

17 *Atque in perpetuum, frater, ave atque vale.*
   And for ever, brother, hail and farewell!   *Ib, 101*

CAVELL, Edith, 1865–1915

1 I realise that patriotism is not enough. I must have no hatred or bitterness towards anyone. *Last Words*

CERVANTES, Miguel de, 1547–1616

2 The knight of the sorrowful countenance. *Don Quixote, Part 1, Ch. 19*

3 Every man is as Heaven made him, and sometimes a great deal worse.
Ib, Part 2, Ch. 4

4 There are only two families in the world, my old grandmother used to say, The *Haves* and the *Have-Nots*. *Ib, Ch. 20*

5 A private sin is not so prejudicial in the world as a public indecency.
Ib, Ch. 22

6 Tell me what company thou keepest, and I'll tell thee what thou art.
Ib, Ch. 23

CHAMBERLAIN, Joseph, 1836–1914

7 Provided that the City of London remains as at present, the Clearing-house of the World. *Speech, Guildhall, London, 19 Jan. 1904*

8 The day of small nations has long passed away. The day of Empires has come. *Speech, Birmingham, 12 May 1904*

CHAMBERLAIN, Neville, 1869–1940

9 In war, whichever side may call itself the victor, there are no winners, but all are losers. *Speech, Kettering, 3 July 1938*

10 I believe it is peace for our time . . . peace with honour. *Broadcast after Munich Agreement, 1 Oct. 1938*

11 Hitler has missed the bus. *Speech, House of Commons, 4 April 1940*

CHANDLER, John, 1806–1876

12 Conquering kings their titles take
From the foes they captive make:
Jesu, by a nobler deed
From the thousands He hath freed. *Conquering Kings their Titles Take*

CHARLES I of Great Britain, 1600–1649

13 Never make a defence or apology before you be accused. *Letter to Lord Wentworth, 3 Sept. 1636*

CHARLES II of Great Britain, 1630–1685

14 He had been, he said, a most unconscionable time dying; but he hoped that they would excuse it. *Macaulay, History of England, Vol. 1, Ch. 4*

15 Not a religion for gentlemen. [*Presbyterianism*] *Burnet, History of My Own Time, Vol. 1, Bk. 2, Ch. 2*

16 Let not poor Nelly starve. [*Said on his death-bed*] *Ib, Vol. 2, Bk. 3, Ch. 17*

17 Better than a play. *On House of Lords Debate on Divorce Bill, 1670*

CHARLES V, Holy Roman Emperor, 1500–1558

18 I speak Spanish to God, Italian to women, French to men, and German to my horse. *Attributed*

CHARLES, Hughie, see PARKER, Ross

CHAUCER, Geoffrey, 1340 ?–1400

1 Whan that Aprille with his shoures sote
   The droghte of Marche hath perced to the rote.   *The Canterbury Tales,*
                                                       Prologue, 1

2 He was a verray parfit gentil knight.   *Ib, 72*

3 He was as fresh as is the month of May.   *Ib, 92 (Squire)*

4 And Frensh she spak ful faire and fetisly,
   After the scole of Stratford atte Bowe,
   For Frensh of Paris was to hir unknowe.   *Ib, 124 (Prioress)*

5 He yaf nat of that text a pulled hen,
   That seith, that hunters been nat holy men.   *Ib, 177 (Monk)*

6 What sholde he studie, and make himselven wood,
   Upon a book in cloistre alwey to poure,
   Or swinken with his handes, and laboure,
   As Austin bit? How shal the world be served?
   Lat Austin have his swink to him reserved.   *Ib, 184 (Monk)*

7 A Clerk ther was of Oxenford also,
   That un-to logik hadde longe y-go.   *Ib, 285*

8 As lene was his hors as is a rake.   *Ib, 287 (Clerk)*

9 For him was lever have at his beddes heed
   Twenty bokes, clad in blak or reed,
   Of Aristotle and his philosophye,
   Than robes riche, or fithele, or gay sautrye.
   But all be that he was a philosophre,
   Yet hadde he but litel gold in cofre.   *Ib, 293 (Clerk)*

10 Souninge in moral vertu was his speche,
   And gladly wolde he lerne, and gladly teche.   *Ib, 307 (Clerk)*

11 No-wher so bisy a man as he ther nas,
   And yet he semed bisier than he was.   *Ib, 321 (Man of Law)*

12 It snewed in his hous of mete and drinke.   *Ib, 345 (Franklin)*

13 His studie was but litel on the bible.   *Ib, 438 (Doctor)*

14 For gold in phisik is a cordial,
   Therfore he lovede gold in special.   *Ib, 443 (Doctor)*

15 She was a worthy womman al hir lyve,
   Housbondes at chirche-dore she hadde fyve,
   Withouten other companye in youthe.   *Ib, 459 (Wife of Bath)*

16 This noble ensample to his sheep he yaf,
   That first he wroghte, and afterward he taughte. *Ib, 496 (Parson)*

17 If gold ruste, what shal iren do?   *Ib, 500 (Parson)*

18 But Cristes lore, and his apostles twelve,
   He taughte, and first he folwed it himselve.   *Ib, 527 (Parson)*

19 His walet lay biforn him in his lappe,
   Bret-ful of pardoun come from Rome al hoot.   *Ib, 686 (Pardoner)*

20 The smyler with the knyf under the cloke.   *Ib, The Knight's Tale, 1141*

21 This world nis but a thurghfare ful of wo,
   And we ben pilgrimes, passinge to and fro;
   Deeth is an ende of every worldly sore.   *Ib, Ib, 1989*

22 So was hir joly whistle wel y-wet.   *Ib, The Reve's Tale, 235*

1 Tragedie is to seyn a certeyn storie,
As olde bokes maken us memorie,
Of him that stood in greet prosperitee
And is y-fallen out of heigh degree
Into miserie, and endeth wrecchedly. *The Canterbury Tales, The Monk's*
Prologue, 85

2 Mordre wol out, that see we day by day. *Ib, The Nun's Priest's Tale, 232*

3 My sone, keep wel thy tonge and keep thy freend.
Ib, The Maunciple's Tale, 319

4 The lyf so short, the craft so long to lerne,
Th'assay so hard, so sharp the conquering. *The Parlement of Foules, 1*

5 For of fortunes sharp adversitee
The worst kinde of infortune is this,
A man to have ben in prosperitee,
And it remembren, whan it passed is. *Troilus and Criseyde, 3, 1625*

6 Go, litel book, go litel myn tragedie. *Ib, 5, 1786*

7 O moral Gower, this book I directe
To thee. *Ib, 5, 1856*

CHESTERFIELD, Philip Dormer Stanhope, 4th Earl of, 1694-1773

8 Be wiser than other people if you can, but do not tell them so.
Letter to his Son, 19 Nov. 1745

9 Whatever is worth doing at all is worth doing well. *Ib, 10 March 1746*

10 An injury is much sooner forgotten than an insult. *Ib, 9 Oct. 1746*

11 Take the tone of the company you are in. *Ib, 9 Oct. 1747*

12 Advice is seldom welcome; and those who want it the most always like it
the least. *Ib, 29 Jan. 1748*

13 In my mind, there is nothing so illiberal and so ill-bred, as audible laughter.
Ib, 9 Mar. 1748

14 A man of sense only trifles with them [*women*], plays with them, humours
and flatters them, as he does with a sprightly and forward child; but he
neither consults them about, nor trusts them with, serious matters.
Ib, 5 Sept. 1748

15 Idleness is only the refuge of weak minds. *Ib, 20 July 1749*

16 Women are much more like each other than men: they have, in truth, but
two passions, vanity and love; these are their universal characteristics.
Ib, 19 Dec. 1749

17 Every woman is infallibly to be gained by every sort of flattery, and every
man by one sort or other. *Ib, 16 March 1752*

18 Unlike my subject will I frame my song,
It shall be witty and it shan't be long.
Epigram on 'Long' Sir Thomas Robinson

19 Give Dayrolles a chair. *Last words*

CHESTERTON, Gilbert Keith, 1874-1936

20 The strangest whim has seized me . . . After all
I think I will not hang myself to-day. *A Ballade of Suicide*

1 When fishes flew and forests walked
    And figs grew upon thorn,
  Some moment when the moon was blood
    Then surely I was born.   *The Donkey*

2 The devil's walking parody
    On all four-footed things.   *Ib*

3 Fools! For I also had my hour;
    One far fierce hour and sweet;
  There was a shout about my ears,
    And palms before my feet.   *Ib*

4 White founts falling in the Courts of the sun,
  And the Soldan of Byzantium is smiling as they run.   *Lepanto*

5 Strong gongs groaning as the guns boom far,
  Don John of Austria is going to the war.   *Ib*

6 Before the Roman came to Rye or out to Severn strode,
  The rolling English drunkard made the rolling English road.
                                    The Rolling English Road

7 The night we went to Birmingham by way of Beachy Head.   *Ib*

8 For there is good news yet to hear and fine things to be seen,
  Before we go to Paradise by way of Kensal Green.   *Ib*

9 Smile at us, pay us, pass us, but do not quite forget,
  For we are the people of England, that never have spoken yet.
                                        The Secret People

10 God made the wicked Grocer
   For a mystery and a sign,
   That men might shun the awful shops
   And go to inns to dine.   *The Song Against Grocers*

11 And Noah he often said to his wife when he sat down to dine,
   'I don't care where the water goes if it doesn't get into the wine'.
                                        Wine and Water

12 The human race, to which so many of my readers belong.
      The Napoleon of Notting Hill, Bk. 1, Ch. 1, Opening Words

CHEVALIER, Albert, 1861–1923

13   'Wot cher!' all the neighbours cried,
        'Who're yer goin' to meet Bill?
      Have yer bought the street Bill?'
   Laugh! I thought I should have died,
   Knock'd 'em in the Old Kent Road.   *Knock'd 'em in the Old Kent Road*

14 We've been together now for forty years,
   An' it don't seem a day too much;
   There ain't a lady livin' in the land
   As I'd 'swop' for my dear old Dutch!   *My Old Dutch*

CHEVALIER, Maurice, 1888—

15 I prefer old age to the alternative.   *Remark, 1962*

CHURCHILL, Charles, 1731–1764

1   Be England what she will,
With all her faults, she is my country still.   *The Farewell, 27*

2 The danger chiefly lies in acting well;
No crime's so great as daring to excel.   *Epistle to William Hogarth*

3 He for subscribers baits his hook,
And takes your cash, but where's the book?
No matter where; wise fear, you know,
Forbids the robbing of a foe;
But what, to serve our private ends,
Forbids the cheating of our friends?   *[Dr Johnson and his Dictionary]*
       The Ghost, 3, 801

CHURCHILL, Lord Randolph Spencer, 1849–1894

4 The old gang. *[Members of the Conservative Government]*
       Speech, House of Commons, 7 March 1878

5 An old man in a hurry. *[Gladstone]*   *Speech, June 1886*

6 I never could make out what those damned dots meant. *[The decimal point]*
       Quoted in Winston Churchill's Biography

CHURCHILL, Sir Winston Leonard Spencer, 1874–1965

7 It cannot in the opinion of His Majesty's Government be classified as slavery in the extreme acceptance of the word without some risk of terminological inexactitude.   *Speech, House of Commons, 22 Feb. 1906*

8 The maxim of the British people is 'Business as usual'.
       Speech, Guildhall, London, 9 Nov. 1914

9 The German dictator, instead of snatching the victuals from the table, has been content to have them served to him course by course.
       Speech, House of Commons, 5 Oct. 1938

10 I cannot forecast to you the action of Russia. It is a riddle wrapped in a mystery inside an enigma.   *Broadcast, 1 Oct. 1939*

11 I would say to the House, as I said to those who have joined the Government: 'I have nothing to offer but blood, toil, tears and sweat.'
       Speech, House of Commons, 13 May 1940

12 Victory at all costs, victory in spite of all terror, victory however long and hard the road may be; for without victory there is no survival.   *Ib*

13 We shall not flag or fail. We shall fight in France, we shall fight on the seas and oceans, we shall fight with growing confidence and growing strength in the air, we shall defend our island, whatever the cost may be, we shall fight on the beaches, we shall fight on the landing grounds, we shall fight in the fields and in the streets, we shall fight in the hills; we shall never surrender.   *Speech, House of Commons, 4 June 1940*

14 Let us therefore brace ourselves to our duties, and so bear ourselves that, if the British Empire and its Commonwealth last for a thousand years, men will still say, 'This was their finest hour'.   *Speech, House of Commons,
18 June 1940*

15 Never in the field of human conflict was so much owed by so many to so few.   *Speech, House of Commons, 20 Aug. 1940
on R.A.F. in Battle of Britain*

1 *Nous attendons l'invasion promise de longue date. Les poissons aussi.*
   We are waiting for the long-promised invasion. So are the fishes.
   Broadcast to the French People, 21 Oct. 1940

2 Here is the answer which I will give to President Roosevelt. . . . Give us the
   tools, and we will finish the job.   *Broadcast, 9 Feb. 1941*

3 What kind of a people do they [*the Japanese*] think we are ?
   Speech, U.S. Congress, 26 Dec. 1941

4 When I warned them [*the French Government*] that Britain would fight on
   alone whatever they did, their generals told their Prime Minister and his
   divided Cabinet: 'In three weeks England will have her neck wrung like a
   chicken.' Some chicken! Some neck!   *Speech, Canadian Parliament,
                                                      30 Dec. 1941*

5 This is not the end. It is not even the beginning of the end. But it is, perhaps,
   the end of the beginning.   *Speech, Mansion House, London, 10 Nov. 1942*

6 Let me, however, make this clear, in case there should be any mistake about
   it in any quarter. We mean to hold our own. I have not become the King's
   First Minister in order to preside over the liquidation of the British Empire.
                                                                         Ib

7 The soft under-belly of the Axis.   *Speech, House of Commons,
                                                      11 Nov. 1942*

8 The problems of victory are more agreeable than those of defeat, but they
   are no less difficult.   *Ib*

9 There is no finer investment for any community than putting milk into
   babies. Healthy citizens are the greatest asset any country can have.
   Broadcast: A Four Years' Plan, 21 March 1943

10 I view with profound misgivings the retreat of the American Army to our
   line of occupation in the central sector, thus bringing Soviet power into the
   heart of Western Europe and the descent of an iron curtain between us and
   everything to the eastward.   *Cable to President Truman, 4 June 1945
   Quoted in The Second World War, Vol. 6, Triumph and Tragedy, 1954,
                                                      p. 523*

11 From Stettin in the Baltic to Trieste in the Adriatic, an iron curtain has
   descended across the Continent.   *Speech, Westminster College, Fulton,
                                                      U.S.A., 5 March 1946*

12 This is the sort of English up with which I will not put.   *Attributed
   Marginal comment on document, quoted by Sir Ernest Gowers in
                                          Plain Words, 1948, p. 74*

13 In War: Resolution. In Defeat: Defiance. In Victory: Magnanimity. In
   Peace: Goodwill.   *The Second World War, Vol. 1, The Gathering Storm,
                                          1948, Moral of the Work*

14 I have never accepted what many people have kindly said, namely that I
   inspired the nation. It was the nation and the race dwelling all round the
   globe that had the lion heart. I had the luck to be called upon to give the
   roar.   *Speech on 80th birthday, Westminster Hall, 30 Nov. 1954*

CIBBER, Colley, 1671-1757

15 One had as good be out of the world, as out of the fashion.
                                                Love's Last Shift, Act 2

16 Stolen sweets are best.   *The Rival Fools, Act 1*

CICERO, Marcus Tullius, 106–43 B.C.

1 *Nihil tam absurde dici potest, quod non dicatur, ab alique philosophorum.* There is nothing so absurd but some philosopher has said it. *De Divinatione, 2, 58*

2 *Salus populi suprema est lex.* The good of the people is the chief law.
De Legibus, 3, 3, 8

3 *Summum bonum.* The greatest good. *De Officiis, 1, 2*

4 *Cedant arma togae, concedant laurea laudi.* Let wars give way to peace, laurels to paeans. *Ib, 1, 22*

5 *Mens cuiusque is est quisque.* The mind of each man is the man himself.
De Republica, 6, 26

6 *O tempora! O mores!* What times! What customs! *In Catilinam, 1, 1*

7 *Civis Romanus sum.* I am a Roman citizen. *In Verrem, 5, 57, 147*

8 *O fortunatam natam me consule Romam!* O happy Rome, born when I was consul. *Quoted in Juvenal, 10, 22*

CLAY, Henry, 1777–1852

9 I had rather be right than be President. *Speech, 1850*

CLEMENS, Samuel Langhorne, see TWAIN, Mark

CLEVELAND, Stephen Grover, 1837–1908

10 However plenty silver dollars may become, they will not be distributed as gifts among the people. *First Annual Message as President of U.S.A., 8 Dec. 1885*

CLIVE, Lord Robert, 1725–1774

11 By God, Mr. Chairman, at this moment I stand astonished at my own moderation! *Reply during Parliamentary Inquiry, 1773*

CLOUGH, Arthur Hugh, 1819–1861

12 A world where nothing is had for nothing.
The Bothie of Tober-na-Vuolich, 8, 5

13 How pleasant it is to have money. *Dipsychus, Part 1, Scene 4*

14 And almost every one when age,
   Disease, or sorrows strike him,
Inclines to think there is a God,
   Or something very like Him. *Ib, Part 1, Scene 5*

15 Thou shalt have one God only; who
Would be at the expense of two? *The Latest Decalogue, 1*

16 Thou shalt not kill; but needst not strive
Officiously to keep alive. *Ib, 11*

17 Thou shalt not covet; but tradition
Approves all forms of competition. *Ib, 19*

18 'Tis better to have fought and lost,
Than never to have fought at all. *Peschiera*

1 Say not the struggle naught availeth,
  The labour and the wounds are vain,
The enemy faints not, nor faileth,
  And as things have been, things remain.   *Say not the struggle naught*
                                                           availeth

2 For while the tired waves, vainly breaking,
  Seem here no painful inch to gain,
Far back through creeks and inlets making
  Comes silent, flooding in, the main.   *Ib*

3 And not by eastern windows only,
  When daylight comes, comes in the light,
In front the sun climbs slow, how slowly,
  But westward, look, the land is bright.   *Ib*

COBBETT, William, 1762–1835

4 To be poor and independent is very nearly an impossibility.   *Advice to*
                                                           Young Men

5 But what is to be the fate of the great wen [*London*] of all?   *Rural Rides*

COBORN, Charles, 1852–1945

6 Two lovely black eyes,
  Oh, what a surprise!
Only for telling a man he was wrong,
  Two lovely black eyes!   *Two Lovely Black Eyes*

COKE, Sir Edward, 1552–1634

7 How long soever it hath continued, if it be against reason, it is of no force
  in law.   *First Institute*

8 A man's house is his castle.   *Third Institute*

9 Six hours in sleep, in law's grave study six,
  Four spend in prayer, the rest on Nature fix.   *Pandects*

COLERIDGE, Hartley, 1796–1849

10 She is not fair to outward view
  As many maidens be;
Her loveliness I never knew
  Until she smiled on me.   *Song, She is not Fair*

COLERIDGE, Samuel Taylor, 1772–1834

11 It is an ancient Mariner,
  And he stoppeth one of three.
'By thy long grey beard and glittering eye,
  Now wherefore stopp'st thou me?'   *The Rime of the Ancient Mariner,*
                                                     Pt. 1, 1

12 He holds him with his glittering eye.   *Ib, 1, 13*

13 The Sun came up upon the left,
  Out of the sea came he!
And he shone bright, and on the right
  Went down into the sea.   *Ib, 1, 25*

1 The bride hath paced into the hall,
   Red as a rose is she.   *The Rime of the Ancient Mariner, Pt. 1, 33*

2 The ice was here, the ice was there,
   The ice was all around:
   It cracked and growled, and roared and howled,
   Like noises in a swound!   *Ib, 1, 59*

3   With my cross-bow
   I shot the albatross.   *Ib, 1, 81*

4 The fair breeze blew, the white foam flew,
   The furrow followed free;
   We were the first that ever burst
   Into that silent sea.   *Ib, Pt. 2, 103*

5 As idle as a painted ship
   Upon a painted ocean.   *Ib, 2, 117*

6 Water, water, every where,
   And all the boards did shrink;
   Water, water, every where,
   Nor any drop to drink.   *Ib, 2, 119*

7 I bit my arm, I sucked the blood,
   And cried, A sail! a sail!   *Ib, Pt. 3, 160*

8 Her lips were red, her looks were free,
   Her locks were yellow as gold:
   Her skin was as white as leprosy,
   The Night-mare Life-in-Death was she,
   Who thicks man's blood with cold.   *Ib, 3, 190*

9 I fear thee, ancient Mariner!
   I fear thy skinny hand!   *Ib, Pt. 4, 224*

10 Alone, alone, all, all alone,
   Alone on a wide wide sea!
   And never a saint took pity on
   My soul in agony.   *Ib, 4, 232*

11 The many men, so beautiful!
   And they all dead did lie:
   And a thousand thousand slimy things
   Lived on; and so did I.   *Ib, 4, 236*

12 The moving Moon went up the sky,
   And no where did abide:
   Softly she was going up,
   And a star or two beside.   *Ib, 4, 263*

13 Oh sleep! it is a gentle thing,
   Beloved from pole to pole!   *Ib, Pt. 5, 292*

14 We were a ghastly crew.   *Ib, 5, 340*

15 Quoth he, 'The man hath penance done,
   And penance more will do.'   *Ib, 5, 408*

16 Like one, that on a lonesome road
   Doth walk in fear and dread,
   And having once turned round walks on,
   And turns no more his head;
   Because he knows, a frightful fiend
   Doth close behind him tread.   *Ib, Pt. 6, 446*

1 No voice; but oh! the silence sank
  Like music on my heart.   *The Rime of the Ancient Mariner, Pt. 6, 498*

2 O Wedding-Guest! this soul hath been
  Alone on a wide wide sea:
  So lonely 'twas, that God himself
  Scarce seemed there to be.   *Ib, Pt. 7, 597*

3 He prayeth well, who loveth well
  Both man and bird and beast.   *Ib, 7, 612*

4 He prayeth best, who loveth best
  All things both great and small;
  For the dear God who loveth us,
  He made and loveth all.   *Ib, 7, 614*

5 A sadder and a wiser man,
  He rose the morrow morn.   *Ib, 7, 624*

6 A sight to dream of, not to tell!   *Christabel, 1, 253*

7 And constancy lives in realms above;
  And life is thorny; and youth is vain;
  And to be wroth with one we love
  Doth work like madness in the brain.   *Ib, 2, 410*

8 I see, not feel, how beautiful they are!   *Dejection: An Ode, 38*

9 I may not hope from outward forms to win
  The passion and the life, whose fountains are within.   *Ib, 45*

10 Swans sing before they die—'twere no bad thing
   Should certain persons die before they sing.
                                  Epigram on a Volunteer Singer

11 In Xanadu did Kubla Khan
   A stately pleasure-dome decree:
   Where Alph, the sacred river, ran
   Through caverns measureless to man
      Down to a sunless sea.   *Kubla Khan, 1*

12 A savage place! as holy and enchanted
   As e'er beneath a waning moon was haunted
   By woman wailing for her demon-lover!   *Ib, 14*

13 Through wood and dale the sacred river ran,
   Then reached the caverns measureless to man.   *Ib, 26*

14 And 'mid this tumult Kubla heard from far
   Ancestral voices prophesying war!   *Ib, 29*

15 It was a miracle of rare device,
   A sunny pleasure-dome with caves of ice!   *Ib, 35*

16 Weave a circle round him thrice,
   And close your eyes with holy dread,
   For he on honey-dew hath fed,
   And drunk the milk of Paradise.   *Ib, 51*

17 This Lime-tree Bower my Prison!   *Title of Poem*

18 Tranquillity! thou better name
   Than all the family of Fame!   *Ode to Tranquillity*

19 That willing suspension of disbelief for the moment, which constitutes
   poetic faith.   *Biographia Literaria, Ch. 14*

1 Our myriad-minded Shakespeare. *Biographia Literaria, Ch. 15*

2 Summer has set in with its usual severity.
Remark quoted in C. Lamb's letter to V. Novello, 9 May 1826

3 I wish our clever young poets would remember my homely definitions of prose and poetry; that is, prose = words in their best order;—poetry = the best words in the best order. *Table Talk, 12 July 1827*

4 No mind is thoroughly well organized that is deficient in a sense of humour.
Table Talk

5 What comes from the heart, goes to the heart. *Ib*

COLLINGS, Jesse, 1831–1921
6 Three acres and a cow. *Slogan for Land Reform, 1885*

COLLINS, Mortimer, 1827–1876
7 A man is as old as he's feeling,
A woman as old as she looks. *The Unknown Quantity*

COLLINS, William, 1721–1759
8 To fair Fidele's grassy tomb
Soft maids, and village kinds shall bring
Each op'ning sweet, of earliest bloom,
And rifle all the breathing Spring. *Dirge in Cymbeline, 1*

9 Hamlets brown, and dim-discover'd spires. *Ode to Evening, 37*

10 How sleep the brave, who sink to rest,
By all their country's wishes blest! *Ode written in the Year 1746, 1*

11 By fairy hands their knell is rung,
By forms unseen their dirge is sung;
There Honour comes, a Pilgrim grey,
To bless the turf that wraps their clay,
And Freedom shall a-while repair,
To dwell a weeping hermit there! *Ib, 7*

12 When Music, heavenly maid, was young. *The Passions, An Ode for Music, 1*

13 With eyes up-rais'd, as one inspir'd,
Pale Melancholy sate retir'd. *Ib, 57*

14 O Music, sphere-descended Maid,
Friend of Pleasure, Wisdom's aid. *Ib, 95*

COLMAN, George, 1762–1836
15 Mum's the word. *The Battle of Hexham, Act 2, Scene 1*

16 When taken
To be well shaken. *Newcastle Apothecary*

COLTON, Charles Caleb, 1780?–1832
17 Men will wrangle for religion; write for it; fight for it; anything but—live for it. *Lacon, 1, No. 25*

18 When you have nothing to say, say nothing. *Ib, No. 183*

19 Imitation is the sincerest form of flattery. *Ib, No. 217*

20 Examinations are formidable even to the best prepared, for the greatest fool may ask more than the wisest man can answer. *Ib, No. 322*

1 The debt which cancels all others.   *Lacon, 2, No. 66*

CONFUCIUS, 551-479 B.C.

2 Men's natures are alike; it is their habits that carry them far apart.
                                                      Analects

3 Study the past, if you would divine the future.   *Ib*

4 Learning without thought is labour lost; thought without learning is
perilous.   *Ib*

CONGREVE, William, 1670-1729

5 Music has charms to soothe a savage breast,
  To soften rocks, or bend a knotted oak.   ALMERIA
                                      The Mourning Bride, Act 1

6 Heaven has no rage like love to hatred turned,
  Nor hell a fury like a woman scorned.   ZARA   *Ib, Act 3*

7 They come together like the coroner's inquest, to sit upon the murdered
  reputations of the week.   FAINALL   *The Way of the World,*
                                                      Act 1, Scene 1

8 'Tis for the honour of England, that all Europe should know that we have
  blockheads of all ages.   FAINALL   *Ib, Act 1, Scene 5*

9 A wit should no more be sincere, than a woman constant; one argues a
  decay of parts, as t'other of beauty.   WITWOUD   *Ib, Act 1, Scene 6*

10 Here she comes i' faith full sail, with her fan spread and streamers out, and
   a shoal of fools for tenders.   MIRABELL   *Ib, Act 2, Scene 5*

11 I am persecuted with letters—I hate letters—nobody knows how to write
   letters; and yet one has 'em, one does not know why.—They serve one to
   pin up one's hair.   MRS MILLAMENT   *Ib*

12 MRS MILLAMENT: I believe I gave you some pain.
      MIRABELL: Does that please you?
   MRS MILLAMENT: Infinitely; I love to give pain.   *Ib*

13 Lord, what is a lover, that it can give? Why, one makes lovers as fast as one
   pleases, and they live as long as one pleases, and they die as soon as one
   pleases: and then if one pleases one makes more.   MRS MILLAMENT   *Ib*

14 Love's but the frailty of the mind,
   When 'tis not with ambition join'd.   SONG   *Ib, Act 3, Scene 12*

15 O, nothing is more alluring than a levee from a couch in some confusion.
                          LADY WISHFORT   *Ib, Act 4, Scene 1*

16 I nauseate walking; 'tis a country diversion, I loathe the country and everything that relates to it.   MRS MILLAMENT   *Ib, Act 4, Scene 4*

17 Let us never visit together, nor go to a play together, but let us be very
   strange and wellbred: let us be as strange as if we had been married a great
   while; and as wellbred as if we were not married at all.   MRS MILLAMENT
                                                      Ib, Act 4, Scene 5

18 These articles subscribed, if I continue to endure you a little longer, I may
   by degrees dwindle into a wife.   MRS MILLAMENT   *Ib*

1 I hope you do not think me prone to any iteration of nuptials.
LADY WISHFORT *The Way of the World, Act 4, Scene 12*

2 O, she is the antidote to desire.　WAITWELL　*Ib, Act 4, Scene 14*

CONNELL, James, 1852–1929

3 Then raise the scarlet standard high!
Beneath its shade we'll live and die!
Though cowards flinch, and traitors jeer,
We'll keep the Red Flag flying here!　*The Red Flag*

CONNOLLY, Cyril, 1903—

4 As repressed sadists are supposed to become policemen or butchers so those with irrational fear of life become publishers.　*Enemies of Promise*

CONNOR, T. W., 19th century

5 She was one of the early birds,
And I was one of the worms.　*She was a Dear Little Dickie-Bird*

CONRAD, Joseph, 1857–1924

6 You shall judge of a man by his foes as well as by his friends.
Lord Jim, Ch. 34

7 A work that aspires, however humbly, to the condition of art should carry its justification in every line.　*The Nigger of the Narcissus, Preface*

8 The sea never changes and its works, for all the talk of men, are wrapped in mystery.　*Typhoon, Ch. 2*

9 The belief in a supernatural source of evil is not necessary; men alone are quite capable of every wickedness.　*Under Western Eyes, Part 2*

COOLIDGE, Calvin, 1872–1933

10 There is no right to strike against the public safety by anybody, anywhere, any time.　*On the Boston police strike, 14 Sept. 1919*

11 He said he was against it.　*When asked what a clergyman had said in a sermon on sin*

COOPER, James Fenimore, 1789–1851

12 The Last of the Mohicans.　*Title of Novel*

CORBUSIER, Le, 1887—

13 *Une maison est une machine-à-habiter.* A house is a machine for living in.
Vers une architecture, 1923

CORNEILLE, Pierre, 1606–1684

14 *À vaincre sans péril, on triomphe sans gloire.* We triumph without glory when we conquer without danger.　DON GOMÈS　*Le Cid, Act 2, Scene 2*

15 *Faites votre devoir, et laissez faire aux dieux.* Do your duty and leave the rest to the Gods.　LE VIEIL HORACE　*Horace, Act 2, Scene 8*

CORNFORD, Frances Crofts, 1886–1960

16 O why do you walk through the fields in gloves.
Missing so much and so much?

O fat white woman whom nobody loves
Why do you walk through the fields in gloves
When the grass is as soft as the breast of doves
And shivering-sweet to the touch?   *To a Fat Lady Seen from a Train*

CORNUEL, Anne Bigot de, 1605–1694

1 *Il n'y a pas de héros pour son valet de chambre.* No man is a hero to his valet.
Lettres de Mlle. Aissé, 13 Aug. 1728

COUBERTIN, Baron Pierre de, 1863–1937

2 *L'important dans ces olympiades, c'est moins d'y gagner que d'y prendre part.*
... L'important dans la vie ce n'est point le triomphe mais le combat.
The most important thing in the Olympic Games is not winning but taking
part. ... The essential thing in life is not conquering but fighting well.
Speech at Banquet to Officials of Olympic Games, London, 24 July 1908

COUÉ, Émile, 1857–1926

3 *Tous les jours, à tous points de vue, je vais de mieux en mieux.* Every day, in
every way, I am getting better and better.   *Formula for his cures by*
auto-suggestion

COUSIN, Victor, 1792–1867

4 *L'art pour l'art.* Art for art's sake.   *Lecture at Sorbonne, 1818*

COWARD, Noel, 1899—

5 The Stately Homes of England
How beautiful they stand,
To prove the upper classes
Have still the upper hand.   *Operette, Act 1, Scene 7, The Stately Homes*
of England

6 And tho' if the Van Dycks have to go
And we pawn the Bechstein Grand,
We'll stand by the Stately Homes of England.   *Ib*

7 A room with a view—and you
And no one to worry us
No one to hurry us.   *This Year of Grace, Act 1, A Room with a View*

8 At twelve noon the natives swoon
And no further work is done.
But mad dogs and Englishmen
Go out in the midday sun.   *Words and Music, Mad Dogs and Englishmen*

9 Don't let's be Beastly to the Germans.   *Title of song*

10 Don't put your Daughter on the Stage, Mrs. Worthington.   *Title of song*

11 Poor Little Rich Girl.   *Title of song*

COWLEY, Abraham, 1618–1667

12 God the first garden made, and the first city Cain.   *The Garden*

13 This only grant me, that my means may lie
Too low for envy, for contempt too high.   *Of Myself*

COWLEY, Hannah, 1743–1809

14 But what is woman?—only one of Nature's agreeable blunders.
DOILEY   *Who's the Dupe? Act 2, Scene 2*

COWPER, William, 1731–1800

1 Hark! the Gaul is at her gates! *Boadicea*

2 Regions Caesar never knew
    Thy posterity shall sway,
Where his eagles never flew,
    None invincible as they. *Ib*

3 He found it inconvenient to be poor. *Charity, 189*

4 A moral, sensible, and well-bred man
Will not affront me, and no other can. *Conversation, 193*

5 Pernicious weed! whose scent the fair annoys,
Unfriendly to society's chief joys,
Thy worst effect is banishing for hours
The sex whose presence civilises ours. *Ib, 251*

6 John Gilpin was a citizen
    Of credit and renown,
A train-band captain eke was he,
    Of famous London town. *John Gilpin, 1*

7 Tomorrow is our wedding day
    And we will then repair
Unto the Bell at Edmonton
    All in a chaise and pair. *Ib, 2*

8 O'erjoyed was he to find
    That, though on pleasure she was bent,
    She had a frugal mind. *Ib, 8*

9 Away went Gilpin—who but he?
    His fame soon spread around;
He carries weight! he rides a race,
    'Tis for a thousand pound! *Ib, 29*

10 The dinner waits, and we are tired:
    Said Gilpin, So am I! *Ib, 37*

11 Said John, 'It is my wedding-day,
    And all the world would stare,
If wife should dine at Edmonton,
    And I should dine at Ware.' *Ib, 49*

12 'Twas for your pleasure you came here,
    You shall go back for mine. *Ib, 50*

13 Now let us sing, Long live the King,
    And Gilpin long live he;
And when he next doth ride abroad,
    May I be there to see! *Ib, 63*

14 What peaceful hours I once enjoyed!
    How sweet their memory still!
But they have left an aching void,
    The world can never fill. *Olney Hymns, 1*

15 God moves in a mysterious way,
    His wonders to perform;
He plants His footsteps in the sea,
    And rides upon the storm. *Ib, 35*

1 Toll for the brave,
   The brave that are no more:
   All sunk beneath the wave,
   Fast by their native shore. *On the Loss of the Royal George*

2 How much a dunce that has been sent to roam
   Excels a dunce that has been kept at home. *Progress of Error, 415*

3 Thou god of our idolatry, the press. *Ib, 461*

4 Absence of occupation is not rest,
   A mind quite vacant is a mind distressed. *Retirement, 623*

5 I sing the Sofa. *The Task, 1, The Sofa, 1*

6 God made the country, and man made the town. *Ib, 1, 749*

7 England, with all thy faults, I love thee still,
   My country. *Ib, 2, The Timepiece, 206*

8 Variety's the very spice of life
   That gives it all its flavour. *Ib, 2, 606*

9   Detested sport,
   That owes its pleasure to another's pain. *Ib, 3, The Garden, 326*

10 Now stir the fire, and close the shutters fast,
   Let fall the curtains, wheel the sofa round,
   And, while the bubbling and loud-hissing urn
   Throws up a steamy column, and the cups,
   That cheer but not inebriate, wait on each,
   So let us welcome peaceful evening in. *Ib, 4, The Winter Evening, 36*

11 Nature is but a name for an effect
   Whose cause is God. *Ib, 6, The Winter Walk at Noon, 223*

12 I would not enter on my list of friends
   (Though graced with polished manners and fine sense,
   Yet wanting sensibility) the man
   Who needlessly sets foot upon a worm. *Ib, 6, 560*

13 The twentieth year is well-nigh past,
   Since first our sky was overcast:
   Ah, would that this might be the last
          My Mary! *To Mary*

14 I am monarch of all I survey
   My right there is none to dispute. *Verses supposed to be written by Alexander Selkirk*

15 O Solitude! Where are the charms
   That sages have seen in thy face?
   Better dwell in the midst of alarms
   Than reign in this horrible place. *Ib*

CRABBE, George, 1754–1832

16 Habit with him was all the test of truth,
   'It must be right: I've done it from my youth.' *The Borough, Letter 3, The Vicar, 138*

17 Books cannot always please, however good;
   Minds are not ever craving for their food. *Ib, Letter 24, Schools, 402*

18 A master-passion is the love of news. *The Newspaper, 279*

1 Secrets with girls, like loaded guns with boys,
  Are never valued till they make a noise.
  *Tales of the Hall, 11, The
  Maid's Story, 84*

CRASHAW, Richard, 1612?–1649

2 I would be married but I'd have no wife,
  I would be married to a single life.
  On Marriage

3 Whoe'er she be,
  That not impossible she
  That shall command my heart and me.
  Wishes to his Supposed Mistress

CREIGHTON, Mandell, 1843–1901

4 No people do so much harm as those who go about doing good.
  Life, 1904

CROKER, John Wilson, 1780–1857

5 A game which a sharper once played with a dupe, entitled 'Heads I win,
  tails you lose.'
  Croker Papers

6 We now are, as we always have been, decidedly and conscientiously attached
  to what is called the Tory, and which might with more propriety be called
  the Conservative, party.
  Quarterly Review, Jan, 1830

CROMWELL, Oliver, 1599–1658

7 I beseech you, in the bowels of Christ, think it possible you may be mistaken.
  Letter to the General Assembly of the Church of Scotland, 3 Aug. 1650

8 What shall we do with this bauble? There, take it away.
  Speech dismissing Parliament, 20 April 1653

9 It is not fit that you should sit here any longer! . . . you shall now give place
  to better men.
  Speech to the Rump Parliament, 22 Jan. 1654

10 Mr. Lely, I desire you would use all your skill to paint my picture truly like
   me, and not flatter me at all; but remark all these roughnesses, pimples,
   warts, and everything as you see me, otherwise I will never pay a farthing
   for it.
   Horace Walpole's Anecdotes of Painting, Ch. 12

CUMBERLAND, Bishop Richard, 1631–1718

11 It is better to wear out than to rust out.
   *Quoted in G. Horne, The Duty
   of Contending for the Faith*

CUMMINGS, Edward Estlin, 1894–1962

12 a politician is an arse upon
   which everyone has sat except a man.
   a politician

13 anyone lived in a pretty how town
   (with up so floating many bells down)
   spring summer autumn winter
   he sang his didn't he danced his did.
   anyone lived in a pretty how town

14 Humanity i love you because
   when you're hard up you pawn your
   intelligence to buy a drink.
   humanity i love you

CUNNINGHAM, Allan, 1784–1842

1 A wet sheet and a flowing sea,
   A wind that follows fast,
   And fills the white and rustling sail,
   And bends the gallant mast.   *A Wet Sheet and a Flowing Sea*

2 It's hame and it's hame, hame fain wad I be,
   O, hame, hame, hame to my ain countree!   *It's Hame and It's Hame*

CURRAN, John Philpot, 1750–1817

3 The condition upon which God hath given liberty to man is eternal vigilance.
   Speech on the Right of Election of Lord Mayor of Dublin, 10 July 1790

DACRE, Harry, 19th century

4 Daisy, Daisy, give me your answer, do!
   I'm half crazy, all for the love of you!
     It won't be a stylish marriage,
     I can't afford a carriage,
   But you'll look sweet upon the seat
   Of a bicycle made for two!   *Daisy Bell*

DANA, Charles Anderson, 1819–1897

5 When a dog bites a man that is not news, but when a man bites a dog, that
   is news.   *What is News? The New York Sun, 1882*

DANTE, Alighieri, 1265–1321

6 *Lasciate ogni speranza voi ch'entrate.* Abandon hope, all ye who enter here.
   Divine Comedy, Inferno, 3, 9

7   *Nessun maggior dolore,*
   Che ricordarsi del tempo felice
   Nella miseria.
   There is no greater sorrow than to recall a time of happiness when in misery.
   Ib, 5, 121

8 *L'amor che muove il sole e l'altre stelle.* The love that moves the sun and the
   other stars.   *Ib, Paradiso, 33, 145*

DANTON, Georges Jaques, 1759–1794

9 *De l'audace, encore de l'audace, et toujours de l'audace!* Boldness, and again
   boldness, and always boldness!   *Speech, French Legislative Committee,*
   2 Sept. 1792

DARWIN, Charles Robert, 1809–1882

10 Man with all his noble qualities ... still bears in his bodily frame the
   indelible stamp of his lowly origin.   *The Descent of Man, Last Words*

11 I have called this principle, by which each slight variation, if useful, is
   preserved, by the term of Natural Selection.   *The Origin of Species, Ch. 3*

12 The expression often used by Mr. Herbert Spencer of the Survival of the
   Fittest is more accurate, and is sometimes equally convenient.   *Ib, Ch. 3*

DAVENANT, Sir William, 1606–1668

13 I shall sleep like a top.   CELANIA   *The Rivals, Act 3*

SLEEP LIKE A ROCK

1 Awake, awake! the morn will never rise,
  Till she can dress her beauty at your eyes. *Song*

DAVIES, William Henry, 1871–1940

2 What is this life if, full of care,
  We have no time to stand and stare? *Leisure*

3 Sweet Stay-at-Home, sweet Well-content. *Sweet Stay-at-Home*

DAVIS, Jefferson, 1808–1889

4 All we ask is to be let alone. *Attributed remark, Inaugural Address as*
President of Confederated States of America, 1861

DAY LEWIS, Cecil, 1904—

5 Nothing so sharply reminds a man he is mortal
  As leaving a place
  In a winter morning's dark, the air on his face
  Unkind as the touch of sweating metal. *Departure in the Dark*

6 Tempt me no more; for I
  Have known the lightning's hour,
  The poet's inward pride,
  The certainty of power. *Tempt me no more*

DECATUR, Stephen, 1779–1820

7 Our country! In her intercourse with foreign nations, may she always be in
  the right; but our country, right or wrong. *Speech, Norfolk, Virginia*
April 1816

DEFOE, Daniel, 1660?–1731

8 I takes my man Friday with me. *Robinson Crusoe, Pt. 1*

9 Wherever God erects a house of prayer,
  The Devil always builds a chapel there;
  And 'twill be found, upon examination,
  The latter has the largest congregation. *The True-Born Englishman, Pt. 1, 1*

10 And of all plagues with which mankind are curst,
   Ecclesiastic tyranny's the worst. *Ib, Pt. 2, 299*

DEKKER, Thomas, 1570?–1641?

11 Golden slumbers kiss your eyes,
   Smiles awake you when you rise. *Patient Grissil, Act 4, Scene 2*

12 Brave shoemakers, all gentlemen of the gentle craft. *The Shoemaker's*
Holiday, Act 3, Scene 1

DE LA MARE, Walter, 1873–1956

13 Look thy last on all things lovely,
   Every hour. *Farewell*

14 'Is there anybody there?' said the Traveller,
   Knocking on the moonlit door. *The Listeners*

15 'Tell them I came, and no one answered,
   That I kept my word,' he said. *Ib*

1 Softly along the road of evening,
  In a twilight dim with rose,
  Wrinkled with age, and drenched with dew,
  Old Nod, the shepherd, goes.   *Nod*

2 Three jolly Farmers
  Once bet a pound
  Each dance the others would
  Off the ground.   *Off the Ground*

3 Slowly, silently, now the moon
  Walks the night in her silver shoon.   *Silver*

DENMAN, Thomas, 1st Baron, 1779–1854

4 Trial by jury itself, instead of being a security to persons who are accused,
  will be a delusion, a mockery, and a snare.   *Judgment in O'Connell v.*
                                                       The Queen, 4 Sept. 1844

DENNIS, John, 1657–1734

5 A man who could make so vile a pun would not scruple to pick a pocket.
                                                The Gentleman's Magazine, 1781

DE QUINCEY, Thomas, 1785–1859

6 Murder considered as one of the Fine Arts.   *Title of Essay*

DESCARTES, René, 1596–1650

7 *Cogito, ergo sum.* I think, therefore I am.   *Le Discours de la Méthode*

DICKENS, Charles, 1812–1870

8 'There are strings', said Mr. Tappertit, 'in the human heart that had better
  not be wibrated.'   *Barnaby Rudge, Ch. 22*

9 This is a London particular . . . A fog, miss.   *Bleak House, Ch. 3*

10 I expect a judgment. Shortly.   MISS FLITE   *Ib*

11 It is a melancholy truth that even great men have their poor relations.
                                                                   Ib, Ch. 28

12 'God bless us every one!' said Tiny Tim, the last of all.   *A Christmas Carol,*
                                                                    Stave 3

13 'I am a lone lorn creetur',' were Mrs. Gummidge's words . . . 'and every-
   think goes contrairy with me.'   *David Copperfield, Ch. 3*

14 Barkis is willin'.   BARKIS   *Ib, Ch. 5*

15 I have known him [*Mr. Micawber*] come home to supper with a flood of
   tears, and a declaration that nothing was now left but a jail; and go to bed
   making a calculation of the expense of putting bow-windows to the house,
   'in case anything turned up,' which was his favourite expression. *Ib, Ch. 11*

16 Annual income twenty pounds, annual expenditure nineteen nineteen six,
   result happiness. Annual income twenty pounds, annual expenditure twenty
   pounds ought and six, result misery.   MR MICAWBER   *Ib, Ch. 12*

17 We are so very 'umble.   URIAH HEEP   *Ib, Ch. 17*

18 I only ask for information.   ROSA DARTLE   *Ib, Ch. 20*

19 'It was as true', said Mr. Barkis, 'as taxes is. And nothing's truer than them.'
                                                                   Ib, Ch. 21

1 Accidents will occur in the best-regulated families.   MR MICAWBER
David Copperfield, Ch. 28

2 I'm Gormed—and I can't say no fairer than that.   MR PEGGOTTY
Ib, Ch. 63

3 When found, make a note of.   CAPTAIN CUTTLE   *Dombey and Son,*
Ch. 15

4 Whatever was required to be done, the Circumlocution Office was before-
hand with all the public departments in the art of perceiving—HOW NOT
TO DO IT.   *Little Dorrit, Bk. 1, Ch. 10*

5 Let us be moral. Let us contemplate existence.   MR PECKSNIFF
Martin Chuzzlewit, Ch. 10

6 Here's the rule for bargains: 'Do other men, for they would do you.' That's
the true business precept.   JONAS CHUZZLEWIT   *Ib, Ch. 11*

7 He'd make a lovely corpse.   MRS GAMP   *Ib, Ch. 25*

8 Oh Sairey, Sairey, little do we know what lays afore us!   MRS GAMP
Ib, Ch. 40

9 At Mr. Wackford Squeers' Academy, Dotheboys Hall . . . Youth are
boarded, clothed, booked, furnished with pocket-money, provided with all
necessaries, instructed in all languages living and dead . . . No extras, no
vacations, and diet unparalleled.   *Nicholas Nickleby, Ch. 3*

10 Every baby born into the world is a finer one than the last.   *Ib, Ch. 36*

11 My life is one demd horrid grind!   MR MANTALINI   *Ib, Ch. 64*

12 Oliver Twist has asked for more.   BUMBLE   *Oliver Twist, Ch. 2*

13 Known by the *sobriquet* of 'The artful Dodger.'   *Ib, Ch. 8*

14 I only know two sorts of boys. Mealy boys, and beef-faced boys.
MR GRIMWIG   *Ib, Ch. 14*

15 'If the law supposes that,' said Mr. Bumble . . . , 'the law is a ass—a idiot.'
Ib, Ch. 51

16 The question about everything was, would it bring a blush to the cheek of
a young person?   *Our Mutual Friend, 1, 11*

17 Not presume to dictate, but broiled fowl and mushrooms—capital thing!
JINGLE   *Pickwick Papers, Ch. 2*

18 Kent, sir—everybody knows Kent—apples, cherries, hops and women.
JINGLE   *Ib*

19 I wants to make your flesh creep.   JOE, THE FAT BOY   *Ib, Ch. 8*

20 'It's always best on these occasions to do what the mob do.'
'But suppose there are two mobs?' suggested Mr. Snodgrass.
'Shout with the largest,' replied Mr. Pickwick.   *Ib, Ch. 13*

21 Can I unmoved see thee dying
On a log,
Expiring frog!   MRS LEO HUNTER   *Ib, Ch. 15*

22 'Sir,' said Mr. Tupman, 'you're a fellow.' 'Sir,' said Mr. Pickwick, 'you're
another!'   *Ib*

23 Mr. Weller's knowledge of London was extensive and peculiar.   *Ib, Ch. 20*

24 Take example by your father, my boy, and be very careful o' vidders all
your life, specially if they've kept a public house, Sammy.   MR WELLER
Ib

1 Poverty and oysters always seem to go together.   SAM WELLER
Pickwick Papers, Ch. 22

2 Wery glad to see you indeed and hope our acquaintance may be a long 'un,
as the gen'l'm'n said to the fi' pun' note.   SAM WELLER   *Ib, Ch. 25*

3 Wen you're a married man, Samivel, you'll understand a good many things
as you don't understand now; but vether it's worth goin' through so much,
to learn so little, as the charity-boy said ven he got to the end of the alphabet,
is a matter o' taste.   MR WELLER   *Ib, Ch. 27*

4 A double glass o' the inwariable.   MR WELLER   *Ib, Ch. 33*

5 Poetry's unnat'ral; no man ever talked poetry 'cept a beadle on boxin' day.
MR WELLER   *Ib*

6 It's my opinion, sir, that this meeting is drunk.   STIGGINS   *Ib*

7 Chops and Tomata sauce. Yours, Pickwick.   *Ib, Ch. 34*

8 Put it down a we, my lord, put it down a we!   MR WELLER   *Ib*

9 Oh Sammy, Sammy vy worn't there a alleybi!   MR WELLER   *Ib*

10 Anythin' for a quiet life, as the man said wen he took the sitivation at the
lighthouse.   SAM WELLER   *Ib, Ch. 43*

11 A smattering of everything, and a knowledge of nothing.
Sketches by Boz, Tales, Ch. 3, Sentiment, Minerva House

12 It is a far, far, better thing that I do, than I have ever done; it is a far, far,
better rest that I go to, than I have ever known.   SIDNEY CARTON
A Tale of Two Cities, Ch. 15

DICKINSON, Emily, 1830–1886

13 Success is counted sweetest
By those who ne'er succeed.   *Poems, Part 1, Life*

14 How dreary to be somebody!
How public, like a frog
To tell your name the livelong day
To an admiring bog!   *Ib*

15 Parting is all we know of heaven,
And all we need of hell.   *Ib*

16 There's a certain slant of light,
On winter afternoons,
That oppresses, like the weight
Of Cathedral tunes.   *Ib, Part 2, Nature*

17 Because I could not stop for Death,
He kindly stopped for me;
The carriage held but just ourselves
And Immortality.   *Ib, Part 4, Time and Eternity*

18 If I shouldn't be alive
When the robins come,
Give the one in red cravat
A memorial crumb.   *Ib*

DIOGENES, 412?–323? B.C.

19 Stand a little less between me and the sun.   *Plutarch, Life of Alexander, 14*

DIONYSIUS of Halicarnassus, 40?–8 B.C.

1 History is philosophy teaching by examples.   *Ars rhetorica, 11, 2*

DISRAELI, Benjamin, 1st Earl of Beaconsfield, 1804–1881

2 I will sit down now, but the time will come when you will hear me.
     Maiden Speech, House of Commons, 7 Dec. 1837

3 The right honourable gentleman [*Sir Robert Peel*] caught the Whigs bathing, and walked away with their clothes.   *Speech, House of Commons, 28 Feb. 1845*

4 A Conservative government is an organised hypocrisy.   *Ib, 17 Mar. 1845*

5 The question is this: Is man an ape or an angel? I, my lord, am on the side of the angels.   *Speech, 25 Nov. 1864*

6 An author who speaks about his own books is almost as bad as a mother who talks about her own children.   *Speech, Glasgow, 19 Nov. 1873*

7 Lord Salisbury and myself have brought you back peace—but a peace I hope with honour.   *Speech, House of Commons, 16 July 1878*

8 A sophistical rhetorician [*Gladstone*] inebriated with the exuberance of his own verbosity.   *Speech, 27 July, 1878*

9 Youth is a blunder; manhood a struggle; old age a regret.   SIDONIA
     Coningsby, Bk. 3, Ch. 1

10 Every woman should marry—and no man.   HUGO BOHUN
     Lothair, Ch. 30

11 To be conscious that you are ignorant is a great step to knowledge.
     Sybil, Bk. 1, Ch. 5

12 I was told that the Privileged and the People formed Two Nations.
     Ib, Bk. 4, Ch. 8

13 Variety is the mother of enjoyment.   *Vivian Grey, Bk. 5, Ch. 4*

14 She is an excellent creature, but she never can remember which came first, the Greeks or the Romans. [*Of his wife*]   *Attributed*

15 When I want to read a novel I write one.   *Attributed*

DODGSON, Charles Lutwidge, see CARROLL, Lewis

DONNE, John, 1573–1631

16 And new Philosophy calls all in doubt,
     The Element of fire is quite put out;
     The Sun is lost, and th' earth, and no man's wit
     Can well direct him where to look for it.   *An Anatomy of the World, 205*

17 Come live with me, and be my love,
     And we will some new pleasures prove
     Of golden sands, and crystal brooks,
     With silken lines, and silver hooks.   *The Bait*

18 Reason is our Soul's left hand, Faith her right,
     By these we reach divinity.   *To the Countess of Bedford, 1*

19 Love built on beauty, soon as beauty, dies.
     Elegies, No. 2, The Anagram, 27

1 No Spring, nor Summer beauty hath such grace,
  As I have seen in one Autumnal face.   *Elegies, No. 9, The Autumnal, 1*

2 Whoever loves, if he do not propose
  The right true end of love, he's one that goes
  To sea for nothing but to make him sick.   *Ib, No. 18, Love's Progress, 1*

3 Licence my roving hands, and let them go,
  Before, behind, between, above, below.
  O my America! my new-found-land,
  My Kingdom, safeliest when with one man man'd.
                                  Ib, No. 19, Going To Bed, 25

4 Death be not proud, though some have called thee
  Mighty and dreadful, for, thou art not so,
  For, those, whom thou think'st, thou dost overthrow,
  Die not, poor death.   *Holy Sonnets, 10*

5 Go, and catch a falling star,
  Get with child a mandrake root,
  Tell me, where all past years are,
  Or who cleft the Devil's foot.   *Song, Go and Catch a Falling Star*

6 But I do nothing upon myself, and yet I am mine own Executioner.
                                                Devotions, 12

7 No man is an Island, entire of itself; every man is a piece of the Continent,
  a part of the main.   *Ib, 17*

8 Any man's death diminishes me, because I am involved in Mankind; And
  therefore never send to know for whom the bell tolls; it tolls for thee.   *Ib, 17*

DONNELLY, Ignatius, 1831–1901

9 The Democratic Party is like a mule—without pride of ancestry or hope of
  posterity.   *Speech, Minnesota Legislature*

DOUGLAS, William, 1672–1748

10 And for bonnie Annie Laurie
   I'll lay me down and dee.   *Annie Laurie*

DOWSON, Ernest Christopher, 1867–1900

11 I have been faithful to thee, Cynara! in my fashion.
                                        Non Sum Qualis Eram

DOYLE, Sir Arthur Conan, 1859–1930

12 It has long been an axiom of mine that the little things are infinitely the
   most important.   *The Adventures of Sherlock Holmes,*
                                               A Case of Identity

13 It is quite a three-pipe problem.   *Ib, The Red-Headed League*

14 You know my methods, Watson.   *The Memoirs of Sherlock Holmes,*
                                                  The Crooked Man

15 'Excellent!' I [*Dr. Watson*] cried. 'Elementary,' said he [*Holmes*].   *Ib*

16 He [*Professor Moriarty*] is the Napoleon of crime.   *Ib, The Final Problem*

1 'Is there any point to which you would wish to draw my attention?'
  'To the curious incident of the dog in the night-time.'
  'The dog did nothing in the night-time.'
  'That was the curious incident,' remarked Sherlock Holmes.
  　　　　　　　The Memoirs of Sherlock Holmes, Silver Blaze

2 An experience of women which extends over many nations and three
  continents.　　　　　　　*The Sign of Four*

3 When you have eliminated the impossible, whatever remains, however
  improbable, must be the truth.　　　　　　　*Ib*

4 The Baker Street irregulars.　　　　　　　*Ib*

5 London, that great cesspool into which all the loungers of the Empire are
  irresistibly drained.　　　　　　　*A Study in Scarlet*

6 The vocabulary of 'Bradshaw' is nervous and terse, but limited.　　　*Ib*

DRAKE, Sir Francis, 1540?–1596

7 I have singed the Spanish king's beard.　*After destroying on 19 April 1587,*
  　　　　　　　a vast amount of shipping in the Harbour of Cadiz

8 There is plenty of time to win this game, and to thrash the Spaniards too.
  　　　　20 July 1588, while playing bowls, when the Armada was sighted

DRAYTON, Michael, 1563–1631

9 Fair stood the wind for France
  When we our sails advance.　　　　　　　*Agincourt*

10 Ill news hath wings, and with the wind doth go,
   Comfort's a cripple and comes ever slow.　　　*The Barrons' Wars, 2*

11 Neat Marlowe, bathed in the Thespian springs,
   Had in him those brave translunary things
   That the first poets had.　　　　　　　*Of Poets and Poesy*

12 Since there's no help, come let us kiss and part—
   Nay, I have done, you get no more of me;
   And I am glad, yea glad with all my heart
   That thus so cleanly I myself can free.　　*Sonnets, 61, The Parting*

DRUMMOND, Thomas, 1797–1840

13 Property has its duties as well as its rights.　*Letter to the Earl of Donough-*
   　　　　　　　more, 22 May, 1838

DRYDEN, John, 1631–1700

14 In pious times, e'r Priest-craft did begin,
   Before Polygamy was made a Sin.　*Absalom and Achitophel, Pt. 1,*

15 What e'r he did was done with so much ease,
   In him alone, 'twas Natural to please.　　　*Ib, 1, 2*

16 Of these the false Achitophel was first,
   A Name to all succeeding Ages curst.
   For close Designs and crooked Counsels fit,
   Sagacious, Bold, and Turbulent of wit.　　　*Ib, 1, 15*

17 A fiery Soul, which working out its way,
   Fretted the Pigmy Body to decay:

And o'r informed the Tenement of Clay.
A daring Pilot in extremity;
Pleas'd with the Danger, when the Waves went high
He sought the Storms; but, for a Calm unfit,
Would Steer too nigh the Sands to boast his Wit.
Great Wits are sure to Madness near alli'd
And thin Partitions do their Bounds divide. *Absalom and Achitophel, 1, 156*

1 Bankrupt of Life, yet Prodigal of Ease.   *Ib, 1, 168*

2 For Politicians neither love nor hate.   *Ib, 1, 223*

3 But far more numerous was the Herd of such,
Who think too little, and who talk too much.   *Ib, 1, 533*

4 A man so various, that he seem'd to be
Not one, but all Mankind's Epitome.
Stiff in Opinions, always in the wrong;
Was Everything by starts, and Nothing long:
But, in the course of one revolving Moon,
Was Chymist, Fidler, States-man, and Buffoon.   *Ib, 1, 545*

5 So over Violent, or over Civil,
That every Man, with him, was God or Devil.
In squandring Wealth was his peculiar Art:
Nothing went unrewarded, but Desert.   *Ib, 1, 557*

6 Did wisely from Expensive Sins refrain,
And never broke the Sabbath, but for Gain.   *Ib, 1, 587*

7 During his Office, Treason was no Crime.
The Sons of Belial had a Glorious Time:
For Shimei, though not prodigal of pelf,
Yet lov'd his wicked Neighbour as himself.   *Ib, 1, 597*

8 Nor is the Peoples Judgment always true:
The Most may err as grosly as the Few.   *Ib, 1, 781*

9 Beware the Fury of a Patient Man.   *Ib, 1, 1005*

10 The Midwife laid her hand on his Thick Skull,
With this Prophetick blessing—Be thou Dull.   *Ib, Pt. 2, 476*

11 The lovely Thais by his side,
Sate like a blooming Eastern Bride.   *Alexander's Feast, 9*

12 None but the Brave deserves the Fair.   *Ib, 15*

13 Sound the Trumpets; beat the Drums.   *Ib, 50*

14 Bacchus Blessings are a Treasure;
Drinking is the Soldiers Pleasure;
        Rich the Treasure;
        Sweet the Pleasure;
Sweet is Pleasure after Pain.   *Ib, 56*

15 Let old Timotheus yield the Prize,
        Or both divide the Crown:
He rais'd a Mortal to the Skies;
        She drew an Angel down.   *Ib, 167*

16 Errors, like Straws, upon the surface flow;
He who would search for Pearls must dive below.   *All for Love, Prologue*

1 Men are but children of a larger growth.   DOLABELLA   *All for Love,*
Act 4, Scene 1

2 Her Poverty was glad; her Heart content,
Nor knew she what the Spleen or Vapors meant.
The Cock and the Fox, 29

3 He [*Shakespeare*] was the man who of all modern, and perhaps ancient
poets, had the largest and most comprehensive soul.
Essay of Dramatic Poesy

4 He was naturally learned; he needed not the spectacles of books to read
nature; he looked inwards, and found her there.   *Ib*

5 Here lies my wife: here let her lie!
Now she's at rest, and so am I.   *Epitaph intended for Dryden's Wife*

6 For truth has such a face and such a meen
As to be lov'd needs only to be seen.   *The Hind and the Panther, 1, 33*

7 Of all the Tyrannies on humane kind
The worst is that which Persecutes the mind.
Let us but weigh at what offence we strike,
'Tis but because we cannot think alike.   *Ib, 1, 239*

8 And love's the noblest frailty of the mind.   CORTEZ   *The Indian*
Emperor, Act 2, Scene 2

9 For all the happiness mankind can gain
Is not in pleasure, but in rest from pain.   CORTEZ   *Ib, Act 4, Scene 1*

10 All heiresses are beautiful.   ALBANACT   *King Arthur, Act 1, Scene 2*

11 Three Poets, in three distant Ages born,
Greece, Italy, and England did adorn.
The first in Loftiness of Thought surpass'd,
The next in Majesty, in both the last:
The Force of Nature could no farther go;
To make a third she join'd the former two.   *Lines under Portrait of Milton*

12 Cousin Swift, you will never be a poet.
Quoted in Johnson's Lives of the Poets, Swift

13 All humane things are subject to decay,
And, when Fate summons, Monarchs must obey:
This Fleckno found, who, like Augustus, young
Was call'd to Empire and had govern'd long:
In Prose and Verse was own'd, without dispute
Through all the realms of Non-sense, absolute.   *Mac Flecknoe, 1*

14 Shadwell alone my perfect image bears,
Mature in dullness from his tender years;
Shadwell alone of all my Sons is he
Who stands confirm'd in full stupidity.
The rest to some faint meaning make pretence,
But Shadwell never deviates into sense.   *Ib, 15*

15 For I am young, a Novice in the Trade,
The Fool of Love, unpractis'd to persuade.   *Palamon and Arcite, 3, 325*

16 Happy the Man, and happy he alone,
    He who can call to-day his own:
    He who, secure within, can say,
To-morrow do thy worst, for I have liv'd to-day.
Translation of Horace, 3, 65

1 Arms, and the man I sing, who, forced by fate,
 And haughty Juno's unrelenting hate.   *Translation of Virgil,*
                                                            Aeneid, 1, 1

DUFFIELD, George, 1818–1888
2 Stand up! Stand up for Jesus!   *Hymn*

DUMAS, Alexandre, 1803–1870
3 *Tous pour un, un pour tous.* All for one, and one for all.
                                                        The Three Musketeers

DUNBAR, William, 1460?–1520?
4 London, thou art the flower of Cities all!   *In honour of the City of London*
5 *Timor mortis conturbat me.*   *Lament for the Makaris*

DYER, Sir Edward, 1540–1607
6 My mind to me a kingdom is.   *Title of poem*

DYER, John, 18th century
7 And he that will this health deny,
 Down among the dead men let him lie!   *Here's a Health to the King*

EDISON, Thomas Alva, 1847–1931
8 Genius is one per cent inspiration and ninety-nine per cent perspiration.
                                                        Newspaper interview

EDWARD III of England, 1312–1377
9 Let the boy win his spurs.   *Of the Black Prince at Crécy, 1345*

EDWARD VIII of Great Britain, 1894—
10 I have found it impossible to carry the heavy burden of responsibility and
 to discharge my duties as King as I would wish to do without the help and
 support of the woman I love.   *Broadcast, 11 Dec. 1936*

EDWARDS, Oliver, 1711–1791
11 I have tried too in my time to be a philosopher; but, I don't know how,
 cheerfulness was always breaking in.   *Boswell's Johnson, 17 April 1778*

EINSTEIN, Albert, 1879–1955
12 I never think of the future. It comes soon enough.   *Interview, 1930*

ELIOT, George (Mary Ann Evans), 1819–1880
13 A prophetess? Yea, I say unto you, and more than a prophetess—a uncommon pretty young woman.   *Adam Bede, Ch. 1.*
14 It's but little good you'll do a-watering the last year's crop.   *Ib, Ch. 18*
15 The happiest women, like the happiest nations, have no history.
                                            The Mill on the Floss, Bk. 6, Ch. 3
16 Animals are such agreeable friends—they ask no questions, they pass no
 criticisms.   *Scenes of Clerical Life, Mr. Gilfil's Love Story, Ch. 7*

ELIOT, Thomas Stearns, 1888–1965

1 Because I do not hope to turn again
  Because I do not hope
  Because I do not hope to turn.   *Ash-Wednesday*

2 The readers of the Boston Evening Transcript
  Sway in the wind like a field of ripe corn.   *The Boston Evening Transcript*

3 Time present and time past
  Are both perhaps present in time future,
  And time future contained in time past.   *Burnt Norton*

4   Human kind
  Cannot bear very much reality.   *Ib*

5 Here I am, an old man in a dry month,
  Being read to by a boy, waiting for rain.   *Gerontion*

6 Thoughts of a dry brain in a dry season.   *Ib*

7 We are the hollow men
  We are the stuffed men
  Leaning together
  Headpiece filled with straw.   *The Hollow Men*

8 Between the idea
  And the reality
  Between the motion
  And the act
  Falls the Shadow.   *Ib*

9 This is the way the world ends
  Not with a bang but a whimper.   *Ib*

10 Ash on an old man's sleeve
  Is all the ash the burnt roses leave.
  Dust in the air suspended
  Marks the place where a story ended.   *Little Gidding*

11 Let us go then, you and I,
  When the evening is spread out against the sky
  Like a patient etherised upon a table.   *The Love Song of J. Alfred Prufrock*

12 In the room the women come and go
  Talking of Michelangelo.   *Ib*

13 The yellow fog that rubs its back upon the window panes.   *Ib*

14 I have measured out my life with coffee spoons.   *Ib*

15 I grow old . . . I grow old . . .
  I shall wear the bottoms of my trousers rolled.   *Ib*

16 Shall I part my hair behind? Do I dare to eat a peach?
  I shall wear white flannel trousers, and walk upon the beach.
  I have heard the mermaids singing, each to each.   *Ib*

17 I do not think that they will sing to me.   *Ib*

18 Macavity, Macavity, there's no one like Macavity.
                                        Macavity: The Mystery Cat

19 The winter evening settles down
  With smell of steaks in passageways.   *Preludes, I*

1 And the wind shall say 'Here were decent godless people;
   Their only monument the asphalt road
   And a thousand lost golf balls.'   *The Rock*

2 Birth, and copulation, and death.
   That's all the facts when you come to brass tacks.   *Sweeney Agonistes,*
                                         Fragment of an Agon

3 April is the cruellest month, breeding
   Lilacs out of the dead land, mixing
   Memory and desire, stirring
   Dull roots with spring rain.   *The Waste Land, The Burial of the Dead, 1*

4 I read, much of the night, and go south in the winter.   *Ib, 18*

5 When lovely woman stoops to folly and
   Paces about her room again, alone,
   She smoothes her hair with automatic hand,
   And puts a record on the gramophone.   *Ib, The Fire Sermon, 253*

6 Webster was much possessed by death
   And saw the skull beneath the skin.   *Whispers of Immortality*

7 You've missed the point completely, Julia:
   There were no tigers. That was the point.   ALEX
                        The Cocktail Party, Act 1, Scene 1

8 You shouldn't interrupt my interruptions:
   That's really worse than interrupting.   JULIA   *Ib, Act 3*

9 Yet we have gone on living,
   Living and partly living.   CHORUS   *Murder in the Cathedral, Act 1*

10 The last temptation is the greatest treason:
   To do the right deed for the wrong reason.   THOMAS   *Ib*

11 However certain our expectation
   The moment foreseen may be unexpected
   When it arrives.   THOMAS   *Ib, Act 2*

ELIZABETH I of England, 1533–1603

12 I will make you shorter by a head.   *Chamberlin, Sayings of Queen Elizabeth*

13 I know I have the body of a weak and feeble woman, but I have the heart
   and stomach of a King, and of a King of England too.   *Speech at Tilbury*
                       on the Approach of the Spanish Armada

14 Though God hath raised me high, yet this I count the glory of my crown:
   that I have reigned with your loves.   *The Golden Speech, 1601*

15 All my possessions for a moment of time.   *Last words*

ELLERTON, John, 1826–1893

16 Now the labourer's task is o'er;
     Now the battle day is past;
   Now upon the farther shore
     Lands the voyager at last.   *Now the Labourer's Task*

17 The day thou gavest, Lord, is ended,
   The darkness falls at thy behest.   *The Day Thou Gavest*

ELLIOTT, Ebenezer, 1781–1849

18 What is a communist? One who has yearnings
   For equal division of unequal earnings.   *Epigram*

EMERSON, Ralph Waldo, 1803–1882

1 Art is a jealous mistress.   *Conduct of Life, Wealth*

2 The louder he talked of his honour, the faster we counted our spoons.
                    Ib, Worship

3 Nothing great was ever achieved without enthusiasm.   *Essays, Circles*

4 A Friend may well be reckoned the masterpiece of Nature.   *Ib, Friendship*

5 The only reward of virtue is virtue; the only way to have a friend is to be one.   *Ib*

6 There is properly no history; only biography.   *Ib, History*

7 All mankind love a lover.   *Ib, Love*

8 The reward of a thing well done is to have done it.
                    Ib, New England Reformers

9 Every man is wanted, and no man is wanted much.
                    Ib, Nominalist and Realist

10 In skating over thin ice, our safety is in our speed.   *Ib, Prudence*

11 Whoso would be a man must be a nonconformist.   *Ib, Self-Reliance*

12 To be great is to be misunderstood.   *Ib*

13 Nothing can bring you peace but yourself.   *Ib*

14 Next to the originator of a good sentence is the first quoter of it.
                    Letters and Social Arms, Quotation and Originality

15 By necessity, by proclivity, and by delight, we all quote.   *Ib*

16 Every hero becomes a bore at last.   *Representative Men,*
                    Uses of Great Men

17 Never read any book that is not a year old.   *Society and Solitude, Books*

18 Hitch your wagon to a star.   *Ib, Civilization*

19 Poverty consists in feeling poor.   *Ib, Domestic Life*

20 We boil at different degrees.   *Ib, Eloquence*

21 America is a country of young men.   *Ib, Old Age*

22 Can anybody remember when the times were not hard, and money not scarce?   *Ib, Works and Days*

23 If a man write a better book, preach a better sermon, or make a better mouse-trap than his neighbour, though he build his house in the woods, the world will make a beaten path to his door.   *Attributed*

EMPSON, William, 1906—

24 Seven Types of Ambiguity.   *Title of book*

ESTIENNE, Henri, 1531–1598

25 *Si jeunesse savait; si vieillesse pouvait.* If only youth knew; if only age could.
                    Les Prémices

EUCLID, c. 300 B.C.

26 *Quod erat demonstrandum.* Which was to be proved.
                    Translated from the Greek

27 There is no royal road to geometry.   *Said to Ptolemy 1*

EUWER, Anthony Henderson, 1877—

1 As a beauty I'm not a great star,
   There are others more handsome by far;
         But my face—I don't mind it
         Because I'm behind it;
   It's the folks out in front that I jar.   *Limerick*

EVELYN, John, 1620–1706

2 I saw Hamlet Prince of Denmark played, but now the old plays begin to
   disgust this refined age.   *Diary, 26 Nov. 1661*

FARQUHAR, George, 1678–1707

3 There's no scandal like rags, nor any crime so shameful as poverty.
                    ARCHER   *The Beaux Strategem, Act 1, Scene 1*

4 How a little love and good company improves a woman.   MRS SULLEN
                    Ib, Act 4, Scene 1

5 Spare all I have, and take my life.   SCRUB   *Ib, Act 5, Scene 2*

FERDINAND I, Holy Roman Emperor, 1503–1568

6 *Fiat justitia, et pereat mundus.* Let justice be done, though the world perish.
                    Attributed

FIELDING, Henry, 1707–1754

7 When widows exclaim loudly against second marriage, I would always lay
   a wager that the man, if not the wedding-day, is absolutely fixed on.
                    Amelia, Bk. 6, Ch. 10

8 I am as sober as a Judge.   *Don Quixote in England, 3, 14*

9 Oh! the roast beef of England,
   And old England's roast beef.   *The Grub Street Opera, 3, 3*

10 Public schools are the nurseries of all vice and immorality.
                    Joseph Andrews, Bk. 3, Ch. 5

11 Thwackum was for doing justice, and leaving mercy to heaven.
                    Tom Jones, Bk. 3, Ch. 10

FISHER, John Arbuthnot, 1st Baron, 1841–1920

12 Sack the lot!   *Letter to The Times, 2 Sept. 1919*

FITZGERALD, Edward, 1809–1883

13 Awake! for Morning in the Bowl of Night
   Has flung the Stone that puts the Stars to Flight:
         And Lo! the Hunter of the East has caught
   The Sultan's Turret in a Noose of Light.   *Rubáiyát of Omar Khayyám*
                    (1st ed.) Verse 1

14 Come, fill the Cup, and in the Fire of Spring
   The Winter Garment of Repentance fling:
         The Bird of Time has but a little way
   To fly—and Lo! the Bird is on the Wing.   *Ib, 7*

15 Here with a Loaf of Bread beneath the Bough,
   A Flask of Wine, a Book of Verse—and Thou
         Beside me singing in the Wilderness—
   And Wilderness is Paradise enow.   *Ib, 11*

1 The Worldly Hope men set their Hearts upon
  Turns Ashes—or it prospers; and anon,
     Like snow upon the Desert's dusty Face
  Lighting a little Hour or two—is gone.   *Rubáiyát of Omar Khayyám,*
                                                                 Verse 14

2 Ah, my Belovéd, fill the Cup that clears
  TO-DAY of past Regrets and future Fears:
     To-morrow !—Why, To-morrow I may be
  Myself with Yesterday's Sev'n Thousand Years.   *Ib, 20*

3 Ah, make the most of what we yet may spend,
  Before we too into the Dust descend;
     Dust into Dust, and under Dust, to lie,
  Sans Wine, sans Song, sans Singer, and—sans End!   *Ib, 23*

4   One thing is certain, that Life flies;
     One thing is certain, and the Rest is Lies;
  The Flower that once has blown for ever dies.   *Ib, 26*

5 I came like Water, and like Wind I go.   *Ib, 28*

6 There was a Door to which I found no key:
  There was a Veil past which I could not see.   *Ib, 32*

7 Ah, fill the Cup:—what boots it to repeat
  How Time is slipping underneath our Feet:
     Unborn TO-MORROW, and dead YESTERDAY,
  Why fret about them if TO-DAY be sweet!   *Ib, 37*

8   Better be merry with the fruitful Grape
  Than sadden after none, or bitter, Fruit.   *Ib, 39*

9 You know, my Friends, how long since in my House
  For a new Marriage I did make Carouse:
     Divorced old barren Reason from my Bed,
  And took the Daughter of the Vine to Spouse.   *Ib, 40*

10 The Grape that can with Logic absolute
  The Two-and-Seventy jarring Sects confute.   *Ib, 43*

11 'Tis all a Chequer-board of Nights and Days
  Where Destiny with Men for Pieces plays:
     Hither and thither moves, and mates, and slays,
  And one by one back in the Closet lays.   *Ib, 49*

12 The Moving Finger writes; and, having writ,
  Moves on: nor all thy Piety nor Wit
     Shall lure it back to cancel half a Line,
  Nor all thy Tears wash out a Word of it.   *Ib, 51*

13 And that inverted Bowl we call The Sky,
  Whereunder crawling coop't we live and die,
     Lift not thy hands to *It* for help—for It
  Rolls impotently on as Thou or I.   *Ib, 52*

14 Who *is* the Potter, pray, and who the Pot?   *Ib, 60*

15 Indeed the Idols I have loved so long
  Have done my Credit in Men's Eye much wrong:
     Have drown'd my Honour in a shallow Cup,
  And sold my Reputation for a Song.   *Ib, 69*

1 And when Thyself with shining Foot shall pass
 Among the Guests Star-scattered on the Grass,
   And in thy joyous Errand reach the Spot
 Where I made one—turn down an empty Glass!   *Rubáiyát of Omar*
                                                    Khayyám, Verse 75

FLECKER, James Elroy, 1884–1915

2 For lust of knowing what should not be known,
 We take the Golden Road to Samarkand.   *Hassan, 5, 2*

3 I have seen old ships sail like swans asleep,
 Beyond the village which men still call Tyre.   *The Old Ships*

FLETCHER, John, see BEAUMONT, Francis

FLORIO, John, 1553?–1625

4 England is the paradise of women, the purgatory of men, and the hell of
 horses.   *Second Fruits*

FOCH, Ferdinand, Marshal, 1851–1929

5 *Mon centre cède, ma droite recule, situation excellente. J'attaque.* My centre is
 giving way, my right is retreating. Situation excellent. I shall attack.
                                                    Message to Joffre, Sept. 1914

FONTAINE, Jean de la, 1621–1695

6 *Elle alla crier famine*
 Chez la fourmi sa voisine.
 She went to cry famine at her neighbour's the ant's.   *Fables, 1, 1,*
                                                    La Cigale et la Fourmi

7 *Aide-toi, le ciel t'aidera.*
 Help yourself and heaven will help you.   *Ib, 6, 18, Le Chartier Embourbé*

FOOTE, Samuel, 1720–1777

8 He is not only dull in himself, but the cause of dullness in others.
                                                    Boswell's Life of Johnson

FORD, Henry, 1863–1947

9 History is bunk.   *In court, during libel action against Chicago Tribune, 1919*

FORD, John, 1586–1639?

10 He hath shook hands with time.   BASSANES
                                          The Broken Heart, Act 5, Scene 2

11 'Tis Pity She's a Whore.   *Title of Play*

FORD, Lena Guilbert, ?–1916?

12 Keep the home fires burning, while your hearts are yearning,
    Though your lads are far away they dream of home;
 There's a silver lining through the dark cloud shining,
    Turn the dark cloud inside out, till the boys come home.
                                                    Keep the Home Fires Burning

FORGY, Howell Maurice, 1908—

13 Praise the Lord and pass the ammunition.   *Said at Pearl Harbour,*
                                                    7 Dec. 1941

FORSTER, Edward Morgan, 1879—

1 It will be generally admitted that Beethoven's Fifth Symphony is the most sublime noise that has ever penetrated into the ear of man.   *Howards End, Ch. 5*

2 Two Cheers for Democracy.   *Title of Book*

FOSTER, Sir George Eulas, 1847–1931

3 In these somewhat troublesome days when the great Mother Empire stands splendidly isolated in Europe.   *Speech, Canadian House of Commons, 16 Jan. 1896*

FOSTER, Stephen Collins, 1826–1864

4 Gwine to run all night!
Gwine to run all day!
I bet my money on de bob-tail nag,
Somebody bet on de bay.   *Camptown Races*

5 I dream of Jeanie with the light brown hair.
Jeanie with the Light Brown Hair

6 Down in de cornfield
Hear dat mournful sound!
All de darkies am a weeping
Massa's in de cold, cold ground.   *Massa's in de Cold, Cold Ground*

7 Weep no more, my lady,
Oh! weep no more to-day!
We will sing one song for the old Kentucky Home,
For the old Kentucky Home far away.   *My Old Kentucky Home*

8 'Way down upon de Swanee Ribber.   *Old Folks at Home*

9 All de world am sad and dreary,
Ev'ry-where I roam.
O darkies, how my heart grows weary,
Far from de old folks at home.   *Ib*

10 Gone are the days when my heart was young and gay,
Gone are my friends from the cotton fields away,
Gone from the earth to a better land I know.   *Poor old Joe*

11 I'm coming, I'm coming,
For my head is bending low,
I hear the gentle voices calling
'Poor old Joe.'   *Ib*

12 Dere's no more hard work for poor old Ned,
He's gone whar de good niggers go.   *Uncle Ned*

FRANKLIN, Benjamin, 1706–1790

13 Remember that time is money.   *Advice to a Young Tradesman*

14 No nation was ever ruined by trade.   *Essays, Thoughts on Commercial Subjects*

15 Be in general virtuous, and you will be happy.   *Ib, On Early Marriages*

16 Here Skugg lies snug
As a bug in a rug.
Letter to Miss G. Shipley, 26 Sept. 1772

1 We must indeed all hang together, or, most assuredly, we shall all hang separately. *Remark at signing of Declaration of Independence, 4 July 1776*

2 There never was a good war or a bad peace. *Letter to Josiah Quincy, 11 Sept. 1783*

3 Our Constitution is in actual operation; everything appears to promise that it will last; but in this world nothing is certain but death and taxes. *Letter to Jean-Baptiste Leroy, 13 Nov. 1789*

4 Man is a tool-making animal. *Boswell's Life of Johnson, 1778*

FREDERICK THE GREAT of Prussia, 1712–1786

5 You rogues, do you want to live for ever? *When the Guards hesitated at Kolin, 1757*

6 My people and I have come to an agreement which satisfies us both. They are to say what they please, and I am to do what I please. *Attributed*

FROHMAN, Charles, 1860–1915

7 Why fear death? It is the most beautiful adventure in life. *Last words before going down in the Lusitania*

FROST, Robert, 1875–1963

8   Earth's the right place for love:
I don't know where it's likely to go better. *Birches*

9 Most of the change we think we see in life
Is due to truths being in and out of favour. *The Black Cottage*

10 And nothing to look backward to with pride,
And nothing to look forward to with hope. *The Death of the Hired Man*

11 Home is the place where, when you have to go there,
They have to take you in. *Ib*

12 Some say the world will end in fire,
Some say in ice,
From what I've tasted of desire
I hold with those who favour fire. *Fire and Ice*

13 My apple trees will never get across
And eat the cones under his pines, I tell him.
He only says, 'Good fences make good neighbours.' *Mending Wall*

14 Something there is that doesn't love a wall,
That wants it down. *Ib*

15 Happiness makes up in Height for what it Lacks in Length. *Title of poem*

16 Like a piece of ice on a hot stove, a poem must ride on its own melting. A poem may be worked over once it is in being but may not be worried into being. *Preface, Collected Poems*

FRY, Christopher, 1907—

17 Why so shy, my pretty Thomasina?
Thomasin, O Thomasin,
Once you were so promising. IST GUARD, singing.
The Dark is Light Enough, Act 2

1   I travel light; as light
That is, as a man can travel who will
Still carry his body around because
Of its sentimental value.   THOMAS   *The Lady's Not For Burning, Act 1*

2   What after all
Is a halo? It's only one more thing to keep clean.   THOMAS   *Ib*

3   What is official
Is incontestable. It undercuts
The problematical world and sells us life
At a discount.   HUMPHREY   *Ib*

4 Where in this small-talking world can I find
A longitude with no platitude?   THOMAS   *Ib, Act 3*

5   The best
Thing we can do is to make wherever we're lost in
Look as much like home as we can.   NICHOLAS   *Ib*

6 Try thinking of love, or something.
Amor vincit insomnia.   PRIVATE PETER ABLE   *A Sleep of Prisoners*

FULLER, Thomas, 1608-1661

7 There is a great difference between painting a face and not washing it.
Church History, Book 7

8 A proverb is much matter decorated into few words.   *The History of the*
Worthies of England, Ch. 2

9 He knows little who will tell his wife all he knows.   *The Holy State and*
the Profane State, The Good Husband

10 Learning hath gained most by those books by which the printers have lost.
Ib, Of Books

FYLEMAN, Rose, 1877-1957

11 There are fairies at the bottom of our garden.   *Fairies*

GALBRAITH, John Kenneth, 1908—

12 The Affluent Society.   *Title of book*

13 Wealth is not without its advantages and the case to the contrary, although
it has often been made, has never proved widely persuasive.
The Affluent Society, Ch. 1

GALILEO, 1564-1643

14 *Eppur si muove.* But it does move.   *Attributed*

GARBO, Greta, 1905—

15 I want to be alone.   *Attributed*

GARDNER, Augustus P., 1865-1918

16 Wake up, America.   *Speech, 16 Oct. 1916*

GARRICK, David, 1717-1779

17 For physic and farces
His equal there scarce is;

His farces are physic,
His physic a farce is.   *Epigram, Written soon after Dr Hill's farce called*
                                          'The Rout' was acted

1 Come, cheer up, my lads, 'tis to glory we steer,
  To add something more to this wonderful year;
  To honour we call you, as free-men, not slaves,
  For who are so free as the sons of the waves?
      Heart of oak are our ships,
      Jolly tars are our men.
      We always are ready,
      Steady, boys, steady;
  We'll fight and we'll conquer again and again.   *Heart of Oak*

2 Here lies Nolly Goldsmith, for shortness called Noll,
  Who wrote like an angel, but talked like poor Poll.   *Impromptu Epitaph*
                                                                on Goldsmith

GAVARNI, Paul, 1801–1866

3 *Les enfants terribles.* The embarrassing young.   *Title of series of prints*

GAY, John, 1685–1732

4 O ruddier than the cherry
  O sweeter than the berry.   *Acis and Galatea, 2*

5 Do you think your mother and I should have liv'd comfortably so long
  together, if ever we had been married?   PEACHUM   *The Beggar's Opera,*
                                                        Act 1, Scene 8

6 MACHEATH: If with me you'd fondly stray
  POLLY PEACHUM: Over the hills and far away.   *Ib, Scene 13*

7 How happy could I be with either,
  Were t'other dear charmer away!   MACHEATH   *Ib, Act 2, Scene 13*

8 She who has never loved has never lived.   ASTARBE   *The Captives, 2, 2*

9 Whence is thy learning? Hath thy toil
  O'er books consumed the midnight oil?   *Fables, Introduction*

10 Where yet was ever found a mother,
   Who'd give her booby for another?   *Ib, Part 1, No. 3*

11 Those who in quarrels interpose,
   Must often wipe a bloody nose.   *Ib, No. 34*

12 'Tis a gross error held in schools,
   That fortune always favours fools.   *Ib, Part 2, No. 12*

13 Life is a jest; and all things show it.
   I thought so once; but now I know it.   *My Own Epitaph*

GEORGE II of Great Britain, 1683–1760

14 Oh! he is mad, is he? Then I wish he would *bite* some other of my generals.
                                                        Of General Wolfe

GEORGE V of Great Britain, 1865–1936

15 Wake up, England.   *Title of reprinted speech*

16 How is the Empire?   *Last Words*

GIBBON, Edward, 1737–1794

1 To the University of Oxford I acknowledge no obligation; and she will as willingly renounce me for a son, as I am willing to disclaim her for a mother. I spent fourteen months at Magdalen College; they proved the fourteen months the most idle and unprofitable of my whole life. *Autobiography*

2 Crowds without company, and dissipation without pleasure. [*London*] *Ib*

3 History, which is, indeed, little more than the register of the crimes, follies, and misfortunes of mankind. *Decline and Fall of the Roman Empire, Ch. 3*

4 All that is human must retrograde if it does not advance. *Ib, Ch. 71*

GIBBONS, Stella, 1902–

5 Something nasty in the woodshed. *Cold Comfort Farm*

GILBERT, Sir William Schwenk, 1836–1911

6 In enterprise of martial kind,
    When there was any fighting,
He led his regiment from behind—
    He found it less exciting. DUKE OF PLAZA-TORO *The Gondoliers, Act 1*

7   That celebrated,
    Cultivated,
    Underrated,
    Nobleman,
The Duke of Plaza-Toro! DUKE OF PLAZA-TORO *Ib*

8 I stole the Prince, and I brought him here,
    And left him gaily prattling
With a highly respectable gondolier. DON ALHAMBRA etc. *Ib*

9 Of that there is no manner of doubt—
No probable, possible shadow of doubt—
    No possible doubt whatever. DON ALHAMBRA etc. *Ib*

10 A taste for drink, combined with gout,
    Had doubled him up for ever. DON ALHAMBRA etc. *Ib*

11 When a merry maiden marries,
Sorrow goes and pleasure tarries. TESSA *Ib*

12 Rising early in the morning,
    We proceed to light the fire,
Then our Majesty adorning
    In its workaday attire,
        We embark without delay
        On the duties of the day. GIUSEPPE *Ib, Act 2*

13   But the privilege and pleasure
    That we treasure beyond measure
Is to run on little errands for the Ministers of State. GIUSEPPE *Ib*

14 Take a pair of sparkling eyes. MARCO *Ib*

15 When every one is somebodee,
    Then no one's anybody! DON ALHAMBRA *Ib*

16 Tripping hither, tripping thither,
    Nobody knows why or whither. CHORUS OF FAIRIES *Iolanthe, Act 1*

1 Bow, bow, ye lower middle classes!
  Bow, bow, ye tradesmen, bow, ye masses!   CHORUS OF PEERS   *Iolanthe,*
                                                                Act 1

2 The Law is the true embodiment
  Of everything that's excellent.
  It has no kind of fault or flaw,
  And I, my Lords, embody the Law.   LORD CHANCELLOR   *Ib*

3 A pleasant occupation for
  A rather susceptible Chancellor!   LORD CHANCELLOR   *Ib*

4 When I went to the Bar as a very young man,
      (Said I to myself—said I).   LORD CHANCELLOR   *Ib*

5 My learned profession I'll never disgrace
  By taking a fee with a grin on my face,
  When I haven't been there to attend to the case.   LORD CHANCELLOR   *Ib*

6 When all night long a chap remains
      On sentry-go, to chase monotony
  He exercises of his brains,
      That is, assuming that he's got any.   PRIVATE WILLIS   *Ib, Act 2*

7 I am an intellectual chap,
      And think of things that would astonish you.   PRIVATE WILLIS   *Ib*

8 I often think it's comical
  How Nature always does contrive
      That every boy and every gal
          That's born into the world alive
      Is either a little Liberal
          Or else a little Conservative!   PRIVATE WILLIS   *Ib*

9 When in that House M.P.'s divide,
      If they've a brain and cerebellum, too,
  They've got to leave that brain outside,
      And vote just as their leaders tell 'em to.   PRIVATE WILLIS   *Ib*

10 Yet Britain won her proudest bays
       In good Queen Bess's glorious days!   LORD MOUNTARARAT   *Ib*

11 The House of Peers, throughout the war,
       Did nothing in particular,
       And did it very well.   LORD MOUNTARARAT   *Ib*

12 When you're lying awake with a dismal headache, and repose is taboo'd by
       anxiety,
   I conceive you may use any language you choose to indulge in, without
       impropriety.   LORD CHANCELLOR   *Ib*

13 For you dream you are crossing the Channel, and tossing about in a steamer
       from Harwich—
   Which is something between a large bathing machine and a very small
       second-class carriage.   LORD CHANCELLOR   *Ib*

14 Pooh-Bah (Lord High Everything Else)   *The Mikado, Dramatis Personae*

15 If you want to know who we are,
       We are gentlemen of Japan.   CHORUS OF NOBLES   *Ib, Act 1*

16 A wandering minstrel I—
       A thing of shreds and patches,
       Of ballads, songs and snatches,
   And dreamy lullaby!   NANKI-POO   *Ib*

1 But if patriotic sentiment is wanted,
   I've patriotic ballads cut and dried.   NANKI-POO   *The Mikado, Act 1*

2 I can trace my ancestry back to a protoplasmal primordial atomic globule.
                                              POOH-BAH   *Ib*

3 Taken from the county jail
   By a set of curious chances.   KO-KO   *Ib*

4 As some day it may happen that a victim must be found,
   I've got a little list—I've got a little list
   Of society offenders who might well be underground,
      And who never would be missed—who never would be missed!
   There's the pestilential nuisances who write for autographs—
   All people who have flabby hands and irritating laughs.   KO-KO   *Ib*

5 The idiot who praises, with enthusiastic tone,
   All centuries but this, and every country but his own.   KO-KO   *Ib*

6 Three little maids from school are we,
   Pert as a school-girl well can be,
   Filled to the brim with girlish glee.   YUM-YUM, PEEP-BO AND PITTI-SING
                                                             Ib

7 To sit in solemn silence in a dull, dark dock,
   In a pestilential prison, with a life-long lock,
   Awaiting the sensation of a short sharp shock,
   From a cheap and chippy chopper on a big black block!
                         KO-KO, POOH-BAH AND PISH-TUSH   *Ib*

8 Brightly dawns our wedding day;
   Joyous hour, we give thee greeting!   YUM-YUM, PITTI-SING, NANKI-POO
                                              AND PISH-TUSH   *Ib, Act 2*

9 Here's a how-de-do!
      If I marry you,
   When your time has come to perish,
   Then the maiden whom you cherish
         Must be slaughtered, too!
      Here's a how-de-do!   YUM-YUM   *Ib*

10 My object all sublime
   I shall achieve in time—
   To let the punishment fit the crime—
      The punishment fit the crime.   MIKADO   *Ib*

11 A source of innocent merriment!   MIKADO   *Ib*

12 On a cloth untrue,
      With a twisted cue
   And elliptical billiard balls!   MIKADO   *Ib*

13 I have a left shoulder-blade that is a miracle of loveliness. People come
   miles to see it. My right elbow has a fascination that few can resist.
                                              KATISHA   *Ib*

14 Something lingering, with boiling oil in it, I fancy.   MIKADO   *Ib*

15 The flowers that bloom in the spring,
            Tra la,
   Have nothing to do with the case.
   I've got to take under my wing,
            Tra la,

A most unattractive old thing,
        Tra la,
    With a caricature of a face.   KO-KO   *The Mikado, Act 2*

1 On a tree by a river a little tom-tit
        Sang 'Willow, titwillow, titwillow!'   KO-KO   *Ib*

2 Twenty love-sick maidens we,
    Love-sick all against our will.   CHORUS   *Patience, Act 1*

3 Now is not this ridiculous—and is not this preposterous?
    A thorough-paced absurdity—explain it if you can.
                                        CHORUS OF DRAGOONS   *Ib*

4 If this young man expresses himself in terms too deep for *me*,
    Why, what a very singularly deep young man this deep young man must be!
                                        BUNTHORNE   *Ib*

5 An attachment *à la* Plato for a bashful young potato, or a not-too-French
    French bean!   BUNTHORNE   *Ib*

6 Prithee, pretty maiden, will you marry me?
    (Hey, but I'm hopeful, willow willow waly!)   GROSVENOR   *Ib*

7 A greenery-yallery, Grosvenor Gallery,
    Foot-in-the-grave young man!   BUNTHORNE   *Ib, Act 2*

8 We sail the ocean blue,
    And our saucy ship's a beauty.   CHORUS   *H.M.S. Pinafore, Act 1*

9 For I'm called Little Buttercup—dear Little Buttercup,
        Though I could never tell why,
    But still I'm called Buttercup—poor Little Buttercup,
        Sweet Little Buttercup I!   LITTLE BUTTERCUP   *Ib*

10 CAPTAIN CORCORAN: I am the Captain of the *Pinafore*;
                    ALL: And a right good captain, too!   *Ib*

11 CAPTAIN: I'm never, never sick at sea!
        ALL: What, never?
    CAPTAIN: No, never!
        ALL: What, *never*?
    CAPTAIN: Hardly ever!   *Ib*

12 Though 'Bother it' I may
        Occasionally say,
    I never use a big, big D.   CAPTAIN CORCORAN   *Ib*

13 Then give three cheers, and one cheer more,
    For the well-bred Captain of the *Pinafore*!   CREW   *Ib*

14 And so do his sisters, and his cousins, and his aunts!   CHORUS   *Ib*

15 When I was a lad I served a term
    As office boy to an Attorney's firm.
    I cleaned the windows and I swept the floor,
    And I polished up the handle of the big front door.
        I polished up that handle so carefullee
        That now I am the Ruler of the Queen's Navee!   SIR JOSEPH PORTER
                                                              Ib

16 I grew so rich that I was sent
    By a pocket borough into Parliament.
    I always voted at my party's call,
    And I never thought of thinking for myself at all.
        I thought so little, they rewarded me
        By making me the Ruler of the Queen's Navee!   SIR JOSEPH PORTER   *Ib*

1 Never mind the why and wherefore. CAPTAIN CORCORAN *H.M.S. Pinafore, Act 2*

2 For he himself has said it,
     And it's greatly to his credit,
   That he is an Englishman!   BOATSWAIN   *Ib*

3 For he might have been a Roosian,
   A French, or Turk, or Proosian,
   Or perhaps Itali-an!   BOATSWAIN   *Ib*

4 I am the very model of a modern Major-General,
   I've information vegetable, animal, and mineral,
   I know the kings of England, and I quote the fights historical,
   From Marathon to Waterloo, in order categorical.
              MAJOR-GENERAL STANLEY   *The Pirates of Penzance, Act 1*

5 When the foeman bares his steel,
              Tarantara! tarantara!
   We uncomfortable feel.   SERGEANT   *Ib, Act 2*

6 When constabulary duty's to be done—
   A policeman's lot is not a happy one.   SERGEANT   *Ib*

7 When the enterprising burglar's not a-burgling—
   When the cut-throat isn't occupied in crime—
   He loves to hear the little brook a-gurgling—
   And listen to the merry village chime.   SERGEANT   *Ib*

8 Politics we bar,
     They are not our bent;
   On the whole we are
     Not intelligent.   ARAC   *Princess Ida, Act 1*

9 We will hang you, never fear,
     Most politely, most politely!   HILDEBRAND   *Ib*

10 Man's a ribald—Man's a rake,
   Man is Nature's sole mistake!   LADY PSYCHE   *Ib, Act 2*

11 While Darwinian Man, though well-behaved,
   At best is only a monkey shaved!   LADY PSYCHE   *Ib*

12 Hunger, I beg to state,
   Is highly indelicate.   LADY BLANCHE   *Ib*

13 Oh, don't the days seem lank and long
   When all goes right and nothing goes wrong,
   And isn't your life extremely flat
   With nothing whatever to grumble at!   GAMA   *Ib, Act 3*

14 Some word that teems with hidden meaning—like 'Basingstoke'.
                          MAD MARGARET *Ruddigore, Act 2*

15 She may very well pass for forty-three
     In the dusk, with a light behind her!   JUDGE   *Trial by Jury*

16 The screw may twist and the rack may turn,
   And men may bleed and men may burn.   DAME CARRUTHERS
                                   The Yeomen of the Guard, Act 1

17 Is life a boon?
     If so, it must befall
     That Death, whene'er he call,
   Must call too soon.   FAIRFAX   *Ib*

1 POINT: I have a song to sing, O!
    ELSIE: Sing me your song, O!
    POINT: It is sung to the moon
               By a love-lorn loon.   *The Yeomen of the Guard, Act 1*

2 It's a song of a merryman, moping mum,
    Whose soul was sad, and whose glance was glum,
    Who sipped no sup, and who craved no crumb,
    As he sighed for the love of a ladye.   POINT   *Ib*

3 For he who'd make his fellow-creatures wise
    Should always gild the philosophic pill!   POINT   *Ib*

4   Were I thy bride,
  Then all the world beside
       Were not too wide
           To hold my wealth of love—
       Were I thy bride!   PHOEBE   *Ib*

5 Oh! a private buffoon is a light-hearted loon,
    If you listen to popular rumour.   POINT   *Ib, Act 2*

6 It is purely a matter of skill,
    Which all may attain if they will:
       But every Jack,
       He must study the knack
       If he wants to make sure of his Jill!   ELSIE, PHOEBE AND FAIRFAX   *Ib*

GLADSTONE, William Ewart, 1809–1898

7 You cannot fight against the future. Time is on our side.   *Speech on*
Reform Bill, 1866

8 [*The Turks*] one and all, bag and baggage, shall, I hope, clear out from the
    province they have desolated and profaned.   *Speech, House of Commons,*
7 May 1877

9 All the world over, I will back the masses against the classes.   *Speech,*
Liverpool, 28 June 1886

10 We are part of the community of Europe, and we must do our duty as such.
Speech, Carnarvon, 10 April 1888

GLASSE, Hannah, 18th century

11 Take your hare when it is cased.   *Art of Cookery (Often misquoted as*
'First catch your hare' and wrongly attributed to Mrs. Beeton)

GLENN, Colonel John Herschel, 1921—

12 It was hot in there.   *Remark after return from orbit, 20 Feb. 1962*

GLOUCESTER, William Henry, Duke of, 1743–1805

13 Another damned, thick, square book! Always scribble, scribble, scribble!
    Eh! Mr. Gibbon?   *Attributed*

GLOVER-KIND, John A., ?–1918

14 I do Like to be Beside the Seaside.   *Title of Song*

GOERING, Hermann, 1893–1946

1 Guns will make us powerful; butter will only make us fat. *Broadcast, 1936*

GOETHE, Johann Wolfgang von, 1749–1832

2 *Ein unnütz Leben ist ein früher Tod.* A useless life is an early death.
Iphigenie, 1, 2

3 *Mehr Licht !* More light!   *Last words, attributed*

GOLDSMITH, Oliver, 1728?–1774

4 Sweet Auburn! loveliest village of the plain.   *The Deserted Village, 1*

5 Ill fares the land, to hastening ills a prey,
  Where wealth accumulates, and men decay.   *Ib, 51*

6 A time there was, ere England's griefs began
  When every rood of ground maintained its man.   *Ib, 57*

7 How happy he who crowns in shades like these,
  A youth of labour with an age of ease.   *Ib, 99*

8 The watchdog's voice that bayed the whispering wind,
  And the loud laugh that spoke the vacant mind.   *Ib, 121*

9 A man he was to all the country dear,
  And passing rich with forty pounds a year.   *Ib, 141*

10 Truth from his lips prevailed with double sway,
   And fools, who came to scoff, remained to pray.   *Ib, 179*

11 The village master taught his little school;
   A man severe he was, and stern to view;
   I knew him well, and every truant knew;
   Well had the boding tremblers learned to trace
   The day's disasters in his morning face.   *Ib, 196*

12 And still they gazed, and still the wonder grew,
   That one small head could carry all he knew.   *Ib, 215*

13 The chest contrived a double debt to pay,
   A bed by night, a chest of drawers by day.   *Ib, 229*

14 In all the silent manliness of grief.   *Ib, 384*

15 Man wants but little here below,
   Nor wants that little long.   *Edwin and Angelina, 31*

16 The King himself has followed her,—
   When she has walked before.   *Elegy on Mrs. Mary Blaize, 19*

17 The doctors found, when she was dead,—
   Her last disorder mortal.   *Ib, 23*

18 Good people all, of every sort,
   Give ear unto my song;
   And if you find it wond'rous short,
   It cannot hold you long.   *Elegy on the Death of a Mad Dog, 1*

19 The dog, to gain some private ends,
   Went mad and bit the man.   *Ib, 19*

20 The man recovered of the bite,
   The dog it was that died.   *Ib, 31*

1 Here lies our good Edmund, whose genius was such,
We scarcely can praise it, or blame it too much;
Who, born for the Universe, narrowed his mind,
And to party gave up what was meant for mankind.　*[Edmund Burke]*
Retaliation, 29

2 Too nice for a statesman, too proud for a wit:
For a patriot, too cool; for a drudge, disobedient;
And too fond of the *right* to pursue the *expedient*.　*[Edmund Burke] Ib, 38*

3 Here lies David Garrick, describe me, who can,
An abridgement of all that was pleasant in man.　*Ib, 93*

4 As a wit, if not first, in the very first line.　*[Garrick] Ib, 96*

5 On the stage he was natural, simple, affecting;
'Twas only that when he was off he was acting.　*[Garrick] Ib, 101*

6 I love everything that's old: old friends, old times, old manners, old books,
old wine.　HARDCASTLE　*She Stoops to Conquer, Act 1, Scene 2*

7 It's a damned long, dark, boggy, dirty, dangerous way.　TONY LUMPKIN
Ib, Act 1, Scene 2

8 This is Liberty Hall, gentlemen.　HARDCASTLE　*Ib, Act 2*

9 We are the boys
That fear no noise
Where the thundering cannons roar.　TONY LUMPKIN　*Ib*

10 Ask me no questions, and I'll tell you no fibs.　TONY LUMPKIN
Ib, Act 3

11 Women and music should never be dated.　MISS HARDCASTLE　*Ib*

12 Remote, unfriended, melancholy, slow.　*The Traveller, 1*

13 Where'er I roam, whatever realms to see,
My heart untravelled fondly turns to thee.　*Ib, 7*

14 Such is the patriot's boast, where'er we roam,
His first, best country ever is, at home.　*Ib, 73*

15 Where wealth and freedom reign, contentment fails,
And honour sinks where commerce long prevails.　*Ib, 91*

16 Laws grind the poor, and rich men rule the law.　*Ib, 386*

17 Still to ourselves in every place consigned,
Our own felicity we make or find.　*Ib, 431*

18 A book may be amusing with numerous errors, or it may be very dull
without a single absurdity.　*The Vicar of Wakefield, Preface*

19 I was ever of opinion that the honest man who married and brought up a
large family, did more service than he who continued single and only
talked of population.　*Ib, Ch. 1*

20 I . . . chose my wife, as she did her wedding gown, not for a fine glossy
surface, but such qualities as would wear well.　*Ib, Ch. 1*

21 Let us draw upon content for the deficiencies of fortune.　*Ib, Ch. 3*

22 I find you want me to furnish you with argument and intellects, too.
Ib, Ch. 7

23 They would talk of nothing but high life, and high-lived company, with
other fashionable topics, such as pictures, taste, Shakespeare, and the
musical glasses.　*Ib, Ch. 9*

1 When lovely woman stoops to folly,
      And finds too late that men betray,
What charm can soothe her melancholy,
      What art can wash her guilt away? *The Vicar of Wakefield, Song,*
                                              Ch. 9

2 There is no arguing with Johnson: for if his pistol misses fire, he knocks
you down with the butt end of it.   *1769, Boswell's Life of Johnson*

3 [*To Dr. Johnson*] If you were to make little fishes talk, they would talk like
whales.   *1773, Ib*

GOLDWYN, Samuel, 1882—

4 In two words: im - possible.   *Quoted in Alva Johnson, The Great Goldwyn*

5 Include me out.   *Attributed*

GORDON, Adam Lindsay, 1833–1870

6 Life is mostly froth and bubble,
    Two things stand like stone,
Kindness in another's trouble,
    Courage in your own.   *Ye Wearie Wayfarer*

GOSCHEN, George Joachim, 1st Viscount, 1831–1907

7 We have stood alone in what is called isolation—our splendid isolation, as
one of our Colonial friends was good enough to call it.   *Speech, Lewes,*
                              26 Feb. 1896 (see Sir George Foster)

GRAHAM, Harry, 1874–1936

8 'There's been an accident,' they said,
'Your servant's cut in half; he's dead!'
'Indeed!' said Mr. Jones, 'and please,
Send me the half that's got my keys.'   *Ruthless Rhymes, Mr. Jones*

9 I had written to Aunt Maud,
Who was on a trip abroad,
When I heard she'd died of cramp
Just too late to save the stamp.   *Ib, Waste*

10 Billy, in one of his nice new sashes,
Fell in the fire and was burned to ashes;
Now, although the room grows chilly,
I haven't the heart to poke poor Billy.   *Ib, Billy*

11 Weep not for little Leonie,
Abducted by a French *Marquis*!
Though loss of honour was a wrench,
Just think how it's improved her French.   *Compensation*

GRAHAME, Kenneth, 1859–1932

12 There is nothing—absolutely nothing—half so much worth doing as simply
messing about in boats.   WATER RAT   *The Wind in the Willows, Ch. 1*

13 The clever men at Oxford
    Know all that there is to be knowed.
But they none of them know one half as much
    As intelligent Mr. Toad.   TOAD   *Ib, Ch. 10*

GRANT, Ulysses Simpson, 1822–1885

1 No terms except an unconditional and immediate surrender can be accepted.
To General Buckner, 16 Feb. 1862

2 I know no method to secure the repeal of bad or obnoxious laws so effective
as their stringent execution. *Inaugural Address, 4 Mar. 1869*

GRANVILLE, George, 1st Baron Lansdowne, 1667–1735

3 Of all the plagues with which the world is curst,
Of every ill, a woman is the worst. AMADIS *The British Enchanters, Act 2*

GRAVES, Alfred Perceval, 1846–1931

4 Of priests we can offer a charmin' variety,
Far renowned for larnin' and piety. *Father O'Flynn*

5 Checkin' the crazy ones, coaxin' unaisy ones,
Liftin' the lazy ones on wid the stick. *Ib*

GRAVES, John Woodcock, 1795–1886

6 D'ye ken John Peel with his coat so gay,
D'ye ken John Peel at the break of the day
D'ye ken John Peel when he's far, far away
With his hounds and his horn in the morning?

For the sound of his horn brought me from my bed,
And the cry of his hounds which he oft-times led;
Peel's view halloo would a-waken the dead,
Or a fox from his lair in the morning. *John Peel*

GRAVES, Robert, 1895—

7 Goodbye to All That. *Title of Book*

8 As you are woman, so be lovely:
As you are lovely, so be various,
Merciful as constant, constant as various,
So be mine, as I yours for ever. *Pygmalion to Galatea*

GRAY, Thomas, 1716–1771

9 'Twas on a lofty vase's side,
Where China's gayest art had dy'd
The azure flowers, that blow. *Ode on the Death of a Favourite Cat, 1*

10 What female heart can gold despise?
What Cat's averse to fish? *Ib, 23*

11 A Fav'rite has no friend! *Ib, 36*

12 Not all that tempts your wand'ring eyes
And heedless hearts, is lawful prize;
Nor all, that glisters, gold. *Ib, 40*

13 Where once my careless childhood stray'd,
A stranger yet to pain! *Ode on a Distant Prospect of Eton College, 13*

1 They hear a voice in every wind,
 And snatch a fearful joy. *Ode on a Distant Prospect of Eton College, 39*

2   Where ignorance is bliss,
 'Tis folly to be wise. *Ib, 99*

3 The Curfew tolls the knell of parting day,
 The lowing herd winds slowly o'er the lea,
 The plowman homeward plods his weary way,
 And leaves the world to darkness and to me.
      Elegy written in a Country Church-Yard, 1

4 Now fades the glimmering landscape on the sight,
 And all the air a solemn stillness holds,
 Save where the beetle wheels his droning flight,
 And drowsy tinklings lull the distant folds. *Ib, 5*

5 Save that from yonder ivy-mantled tow'r
 The moping owl does to the moon complain. *Ib, 9*

6 The rude Forefathers of the hamlet sleep. *Ib, 16*

7 Let not Ambition mock their useful toil,
 Their homely joys, and destiny obscure;
 Nor Grandeur hear with a disdainful smile,
 The short and simple annals of the poor. *Ib, 29*

8 The boast of heraldry, the pomp of pow'r. *Ib, 33*

9 The paths of glory lead but to the grave. *Ib, 36*

10 Full many a gem of purest ray serene,
 The dark unfathom'd caves of ocean bear:
 Full many a flower is born to blush unseen,
 And waste its sweetness on the desert air. *Ib, 53*

11 Some village-Hampden, that with dauntless breast
 The little Tyrant of his fields withstood;
 Some mute inglorious Milton here may rest,
 Some Cromwell guiltless of his country's blood. *Ib, 57*

12 Far from the madding crowd's ignoble strife. *Ib, 73*

13 Here rests his head upon the lap of Earth
 A Youth to Fortune and to Fame unknown.
 Fair Science frown'd not on his humble birth,
 And Melancholy mark'd him for her own. *Ib, The Epitaph, 117*

14 Large was his bounty, and his soul sincere,
 Heav'n did a recompence as largely send:
 He gave to Mis'ry all he had, a tear,
 He gain'd from Heav'n ('twas all he wish'd) a friend. *Ib, 121*

15 No farther seek his merits to disclose,
 Or draw his frailties from their dread abode,
 (There they alike in trembling hope repose,)
 The bosom of his Father and his God. *Ib, 125*

16 Daughter of Jove, relentless Power,
 Thou Tamer of the human breast,
 Whose iron scourge and tort'ring hour,
 The Bad affright, afflict the Best! *Hymn to Adversity, 1*

1   Far from the sun and summer-gale,
    In thy green lap was Nature's Darling laid.   [*Shakespeare*]
                                        The Progress of Poesy, 83

2 Yet shall he mount, and keep his distant way
   Beyond the limits of a vulgar fate,
   Beneath the Good how far—but far above the Great.   [*Milton*]   *Ib, 121*

3 Too poor for a bribe, and too proud to importune,
   He had not the method of making a fortune.   *Sketch of his own Character*

GREELEY, Horace, 1811–1872

4 Go West, young man, and grow up with the country.   *Hints toward Reform*

GREENE, Robert, 1560?–1592

5 Weep not, my wanton, smile upon my knee;
   When thou art old there's grief enough for thee.   *Sephestia's Song*

6 For there is an upstart crow, beautified with our feathers, that with his
   tiger's heart wrapped in a player's hide, supposes he is as well able to
   bumbast out a blank verse as the best of you; and being an absolute *Iohannes
   fac totum* is in his own conceit the only shake-scene in a country. [*Reference
   probably to Shakespeare*]   *A Groatsworth of Wit*

GREGORY 1, Pope, 540–604

7 *Non Angli, sed Angeli.* Not Angles, but angels.   *Attributed (on seeing a
                                        group of English captives on sale at Rome)*

GREY OF FALLODON, Edward, 1st Viscount, 1862–1933

8 The lamps are going out all over Europe; we shall not see them lit again in
   our Lifetime.   *On the eve of war, 3 Aug. 1914*

GROSSMITH, George, 1847–1912, and GROSSMITH, Walter Weedon, 1854–1919

9 What's the good of a home, if you are never in it?   *The Diary of a
                                        Nobody, Ch. 1*

GUINAN, Texas, 1884–1933

10 Fifty million Frenchmen can't be wrong.   *Attributed*

HALE, Sarah Josepha, 1788–1879

11 Mary had a little lamb,
    Its fleece was white as snow;
    And everywhere that Mary went
        The lamb was sure to go.   *Mary's Little Lamb*

HALIFAX, George Savile, 1st Marquis of, 1633–1695

12 Men are not hanged for stealing horses, but that horses may not be stolen.
                    Political Thoughts and Reflections of Punishment

HALL, Charles Sprague, 19th century

13 John Brown's body lies a mould'ring in the grave,
    His soul is marching on!   *John Brown's Body*

HAMMERSTEIN, Oscar, 1895–1960

1 The last time I saw Paris, her heart was young and gay,
I heard the laughter of her heart in every street café.

The Last Time I saw Paris

2 Ol' man river, dat ol' man river,
He must know sumpin', but don't say nothin',
He just keeps rollin', he keeps on rollin' along. *Ol' Man River*

HANDLEY, Thomas Reginald (Tommy), see KAVANAGH, Ted

HANFF, Minny Maud, c. 1900

3 Since then they called him Sunny Jim. *Advertisement for Force, a
breakfast food*

HANKEY, Katherine, 1834–1911

4 Tell me the old, old story,
Of unseen things above. *Hymn*

HARCOURT, Sir William, 1827–1904

5 We are all Socialists now. *Speech*

HARDY, E. J., 1849–1910

6 How to be Happy though Married. *Title of book, 1910*

HARDY, Thomas, 1840–1928

7 My argument is that War makes rattling good history; but Peace is poor
reading. *The Dynasts, Pt. 1*

8 A lover without indiscretion is no lover at all. *The Hand of Ethelberta,
Ch. 20*

9 Good, but not religious-good. *Under the Greenwood Tree, Ch. 2*

10 This is the weather the cuckoo likes,
And so do I. *Weathers*

HARE, Maurice Evan, 1886—

11 There once was a man who said, 'Damn!
It is borne in upon me I am
An engine that moves
In determinate grooves,
I'm not even a bus but a tram.' *Limerick*

HARGREAVES, William, 1846–1919

12 I'm Burlington Bertie:
I rise at ten-thirty. *Burlington Bertie*

HARINGTON, Sir John, 1561–1612

13 Treason doth never prosper: what's the reason?
For if it prosper, none dare call it treason. *Epigrams, Of Treason*

HARRIS, Charles K., 1865–1930

1 Many a heart is aching, if you could read them all,
Many the hopes that have vanished, after the ball.   *After the Ball*

HARTE, Francis Bret, 1836–1902

2 And on that grave where English oak and holly
And laurel wreaths entwine
Deem it not all a too presumptuous folly,—
This spray of Western pine!   *Dickens in Camp*

3 He smiled a kind of sickly smile, and curled up on the floor,
And the subsequent proceedings interested him no more.   *The Society
upon the Stanislaus*

HAWKER, Robert Stephen, 1803–1875

4 And have they fixed the where and when?
And shall Trelawny die?
Here's twenty thousand Cornish men
Will know the reason why!   *Song of the Western Men*

HAY, Ian (John Hay Beith), 1876–1952

5 Funny peculiar, or funny ha-ha?   'BUTTON' FARINGDON   *Housemaster,
Act 3*

HAYES, J. Milton, 1884–1940

6 There's a one-eyed yellow idol to the north of Khatmandu,
There's a little marble cross below the town,
There's a broken-hearted woman tends the grave of Mad Carew,
And the yellow god forever gazes down.   *The Green Eye of the Yellow
God*

HAZLITT, William, 1778–1830

7 His sayings are generally like women's letters; all the pith is in the post-script. [*Charles Lamb*]   *Conversations of Northcote, Boswell Redivivus*

8 He [*Coleridge*] talked on for ever; and you wished him to talk on for ever.
Lectures on the English Poets, 8

9 The English (it must be owned) are rather a foul-mouthed nation.
On Criticism

10 No young man believes he shall ever die.
On the Feeling of Immortality in Youth, 1

11 One of the pleasantest things in the world is going a journey; but I like to
go by myself.   *On Going a Journey*

12 There is not a more mean, stupid, dastardly, pitiful, selfish, spiteful,
envious, ungrateful animal than the public. It is the greatest of cowards,
for it is afraid of itself.   *On Living to Oneself*

13 The art of pleasing consists in being pleased.   *On Manner*

14 A nickname is the heaviest stone that the devil can throw at a man.
On Nicknames

15 We never do anything well till we cease to think about the manner of
doing it.   *On Prejudice*

HEBER, Bishop Reginald, 1783–1826

1 From Greenland's icy mountains,
   From India's coral strand,
   Where Afric's sunny fountains,
   Roll down their golden sand.   *From Greenland's Icy Mountains*

2 Though every prospect pleases,
   And only man is vile.   *Ib*

3 Holy, Holy, Holy! all the Saints adore Thee.   *Holy, Holy, Holy!*

HEMANS, Felicia Dorothea, 1793–1835

4 The boy stood on the burning deck,
   Whence all but he had fled.   *Casabianca*

5 The stately homes of England!
   How beautiful they stand,
   Amidst their tall ancestral trees,
   O'er all the pleasant land.   *The Homes of England*

HEMINGWAY, Ernest, 1898–1961

6 A Farewell to Arms.   *Title of novel*

7 Bullfighting is the only art in which the artist is in danger of death and in
   which the degree of brilliance in the performance is left to the fighter's
   honour.   *Death in the Afternoon, Ch. 9*

HENLEY, William Ernest, 1849–1903

8 Out of the night that covers me,
   Black as the pit from pole to pole,
   I thank whatever gods may be
   For my unconquerable soul.   *Invictus*

9 Under the bludgeonings of chance
   My head is bloody, but unbowed.   *Ib*

10 I am the master of my fate:
   I am the captain of my soul.   *Ib*

11 What have I done for you,
   England, my England?
   What is there I would not do,
   England, my own?   *Rhymes and Rhythms, 25, For England's Sake*

HENRI IV of France, 1553–1610

12 *Paris vaut bien une messe.* Paris is well worth a mass.   *Attributed*

13 The wisest fool in Christendom. [*James I*]   *Attributed*

HENRY II of England, 1133–1189

14 Will no one free me of this turbulent priest? [*Becket*]   *Attributed*

HENRY, Matthew, 1662–1714

15 They that die by famine die by inches.   *Commentaries, Psalms, 59, 15*

16 All this and heaven too.   *Life of Philip Henry*

HENRY, O. (William Sydney Porter), 1862–1910

1 Life is made up of sobs, sniffles, and smiles, with sniffles predominating.
Gift of the Magi

2 If men knew how women pass the time when they are alone, they'd never
marry. *Memoirs of a Yellow Dog*

3 Turn up the lights; I don't want to go home in the dark. *Last words*

HENRY, Patrick, 1736–1799

4 I know not what course others may take; but as for me, give me liberty or
give me death. *Speech in the Virginia Convention, 23 Mar. 1775*

HERBERT, Sir Alan Patrick, 1890—

5 Not huffy or stuffy, nor tiny or tall,
But fluffy, just fluffy, with no brains at all. *I Like them Fluffy*

6 This high official, all allow,
Is grossly overpaid,
There wasn't any board; and now
There isn't any trade. *On the President of the Board of Trade*

7 The Englishman never enjoys himself except for a noble purpose.
Uncommon Law

8 Holy Deadlock. *Title of novel*

HERBERT, George, 1593–1633

9 Dare to be true: nothing can need a lie;
A fault, which needs it most, grows two thereby.
The Temple, The Church Porch

10 Love bade me welcome; yet my soul drew back,
    Guilty of dust and sin. *Ib, Love*

11 'You must sit down,' says Love, 'and taste My meat,'
    So I did sit and eat. *Ib*

12 Sweet day, so cool, so calm, so bright,
The bridal of the earth and sky. *Ib, Virtue*

HERRICK, Robert, 1591–1674

13 Cherry ripe, ripe, ripe, I cry,
Full and fair ones; come and buy:
If so be, you ask me where
They do grow? I answer, there
Where my Julia's lips do smile;
There's the land, or cherry-isle. *Hesperides, Cherry Ripe*

14 A sweet disorder in the dress
Kindles in clothes a wantonness. *Ib, Delight in Disorder, 2*

15 A careless shoe-string, in whose tie
I see a wild civility:
Do more bewitch me, than when art
Is too precise in every part. *Ib*

1 Fair daffodils, we weep to see
   You haste away so soon:
   As yet the early-rising sun
   Has not attain'd his noon.   *Hesperides, To Daffodils*

2 I dare not ask a kiss;
   I dare not beg a smile;
   Lest having that, or this,
   I might grow proud the while.   *Ib, To Electra*

3 You say, to me-wards your affection's strong;
   Pray love me little, so you love me long.   *Ib, Love me little, love me long*

4 Night makes no difference 'twixt the Priest and Clerk;
   Joan as my Lady is as good i' th' dark.   *Ib, No difference i' th' dark*

5 Attempt the end, and never stand to doubt;
   Nothing's so hard, but search will find it out.   *Ib, Seek and find*

6 Whenas in silks my Julia goes,
   Then, then (methinks) how sweetly flows
   That liquefaction of her clothes.   *Ib, Upon Julia's Clothes*

7 Gather ye rosebuds while ye may,
   Old time is still a-flying:
   And this same flower that smiles to-day
   To-morrow will be dying.   *Ib, To the Virgins, to make much of Time*

8 Then be not coy, but use your time;
   And while ye may, go marry:
   For having lost but once your prime,
   You may for ever tarry.   *Ib*

HEYWOOD, Thomas, 1574?-1641

9 Seven cities warred for Homer, being dead,
   Who, living, had no roof to shroud his head.
                                   Hierarchy of the Blessed Angels

10 A Woman Killed with Kindness.   *Title of play*

HICKSON, William Edward, 1803-1870

11 If at first you don't succeed,
   Try, try again.   *Try and Try Again*

HILL, Rowland, 1744-1833

12 He did not see any good reasons why the devil should have all the good
   tunes.   *E. W. Broome, Rev. Rowland Hill*

HIPPOCRATES, 460?-377? B.C.

13 *Ars longa, vita brevis.* Art is long, but life is short.   *The Latin version of*
                                                      the Greek original

HITLER, Adolf, 1889-1945

14 The Sudetenland is the last territorial claim I have to make in Europe.
                                           Speech, 26 Sept. 1938

1 Germany will be either a world power or will not be at all.   *Mein Kampf*

HOBBES, Thomas, 1588–1679

2 The condition of man . . . is a condition of war of everyone against everyone.
Leviathan, Pt. 1, Ch. 4

3 No arts; no letters; no society; and which is worst of all, continual fear and
danger of violent death; and the life of man, solitary, poor, nasty, brutish,
and short.   *Ib, Ch. 13*

4 I am about to take my last voyage, a great leap in the dark.   *Last words*

HOCH, Edward Wallis, 1849–1925

5 There is so much good in the worst of us,
And so much bad in the best of us,
That it hardly becomes any of us
To talk about the rest of us.   *Good and Bad*

HODGSON, Ralph, 1871–1962

6 Time, you old gypsy man,
    Will you not stay,
Put up your caravan
    Just for one day?   *Time, you old Gypsy Man*

HOFFMANN, August Heinrich, von Fallersleben, 1798–1874

7 *Deutschland, Deutschland, über alles.* Germany, Germany above all.   *Song*

HOFFMANN, Heinrich, 1809–1874

8 But one day, one cold winter's day,
He screamed out, 'Take the soup away!'   *Struwwelpeter, Augustus*

9 Here is cruel Frederick, see!
A horrid wicked boy was he.   *Ib, Cruel Frederick*

10 Look at little Johnny there,
Little Johnny Head-in-Air.   *Ib, Johnny Head-In-Air*

11 Anything to me is sweeter
Than to see Shock-headed Peter.   *Ib, Shock-headed Peter*

HOLMES, Oliver Wendell, 1809–1894

12 When the last reader reads no more.   *The Last Reader*

13 And silence, like a poultice, comes
To heal the blows of sound.   *The Music Grinders*

14 Wisdom has taught us to be calm and meek,
To take one blow, and turn the other cheek;
It is not written what a man shall do
If the rude caitiff smite the other too.   *Non-Resistance*

1 Ay, tear her tattered ensign down!
  Long has it waved on high,
  And many an eye has danced to see
  That banner in the sky.   *Old Ironsides*

2 Man wants but little drink below,
  But wants that little strong.   *A Song of other Days*
                                          (Parody on Goldsmith, see 122:15)

3 Man has his will,—but woman has her way.
                              The Autocrat of the Breakfast Table, Prologue

4 A thought is often original, though you have uttered it a hundred times.
                                                          Ib, Ch. 1

5 Build thee more stately mansions, O my soul,
      As the swift seasons roll!
      Leave thy low-vaulted past!   *Ib, Ch. 4,*
                                                The Chambered Nautilus

6 The world's great men have not commonly been great scholars, nor great
  scholars great men.   *Ib, Ch. 6*

7 To be seventy years young is sometimes far more cheerful and hopeful than
  to be forty years old.   *On the Seventieth Birthday of Julia Ward Howe*

HOMER, c. 900 B.C.

8 As the generation of leaves, so also is that of men.   *Iliad, 6, 146*

9 Always to be best and distinguished above others.   *Ib, 6, 208*

HOOD, Thomas, 1799–1845

10 One more Unfortunate,
   Weary of breath,
   Rashly importunate,
   Gone to her death!

   Take her up tenderly,
   Lift her with care;
   Fashion'd so slenderly,
   Young, and so fair!   *The Bridge of Sighs*

11 Ben Battle was a soldier bold,
       And used to war's alarms;
   But a cannon-ball took off his legs,
       So he laid down his arms!   *Faithless Nelly Gray*

12 For here I leave my second leg,
       And the Forty-second Foot!   *Ib*

13 His death, which happen'd in his berth,
       At forty-odd befell:
   They went and told the sexton, and
       The sexton toll'd the bell.   *Faithless Sally Brown*

14 I remember, I remember,
   The house where I was born,
   The little window where the sun
   Came peeping in at morn.   *I Remember, I Remember*

15 I remember, I remember,
   The fir trees dark and high;

I used to think their slender tops
Were close against the sky.   *I Remember, I Remember*

1 But evil is wrought by want of Thought,
   As well as want of Heart!   *The Lady's Dream*

2 When Eve upon the first of Men
      The apple press'd with specious cant
   Oh! what a thousand pities then
      That Adam was not Adamant!   *A Reflection*

3 With fingers weary and worn,
      With eyelids heavy and red,
   A woman sat, in unwomanly rags,
      Plying her needle and thread—
         Stitch! stitch! stitch!
   In poverty, hunger, and dirt.   *The Song of the Shirt*

4 Oh! God! that bread should be so dear,
   And flesh and blood so cheap.   *Ib*

HOOVER, Herbert Clark, 1874–1964

5 The American system of rugged individualism. *Speech, New York,*
                                                22 Oct. 1928

HOPKINS, Gerard Manley, 1844–1889

6 The world is charged with the grandeur of God.   *God's Grandeur*

7 Glory be to God for dappled things—
      For skies of couple-colour as a brinded cow;
      For rose-moles all in stipple upon trout that swim.   *Pied Beauty*

HORACE, Quintus Horatius Flaccus, 65–8 B.C.

8   *Brevis esse laboro,*
   Obscurus fio.
   I struggle to be brief, and become obscure.   *Ars Poetica, 25*

9 *Grammatici certant et adhuc sub iudice lis est.*
   Scholars dispute, and the case is still before the courts.   *Ib, 78*

10 *Indignor, quandoque bonus dormitat Homerus.*
   I think it shame when the worthy Homer nods.   *Ib, 359*

11 *Si possis recte, si non, quocumque modo rem.*
   By honest means, if you can, but by any means make money.   *Epistles,*
                                                I, 1, 66

12 *Pallida Mors aequo pulsat pede pauperum tabernas Regumque turris.*
   Pale Death with impartial foot knocks at the doors of poor men's hovels and
   of King's palaces.   *Odes I, 4, 13*

13 *Carpe diem, quam minimum credula postero.*
   Seize the present day, trusting the morrow as little as you can.   *Ib, I, 11, 8*

14 *Integer vitae scelerisque purus.*
   The man of upright life unstained by guilt.   *Ib, I, 22, 1*

15 *Eheu fugaces, Postume, Postume,*
   Labuntur anni.
   Alas, Postumus, Postumus, the fleeting years are slipping by.   *Ib, 2, 14, 1*

1 *Dulce et decorum est pro patria mori.*
It is a sweet and seemly thing to die for one's country.   *Odes, 3, 2, 13*

HORNE, Kenneth, see MURDOCH, Richard

HOUSMAN, Alfred Edward, 1859–1936

2 The Grizzly Bear is huge and wild;
He has devoured the infant child.
The infant child is not aware
He has been eaten by the bear.   *Infant Innocence*

3 We'll to the woods no more,
The laurels all are cut.   *Last Poems*

4 And naked to the hangman's noose
The morning clocks will ring
A neck God made for other use
Than strangling in a string.   *A Shropshire Lad, 9*

5 When I was one-and-twenty
I heard a wise man say,
'Give crowns and pounds and guineas
But not your heart away.'   *Ib, 13*

6 Here of a Sunday morning
My love and I would lie,
And see the coloured counties,
And hear the larks so high
About us in the sky.   *Ib, 21*

7 From far, from eve and morning
And yon twelve-winded sky,
The stuff of life to knit me
Blew hither: here am I.   *Ib, 32*

8 With rue my heart is laden
For golden friends I had,
For many a rose-lipt maiden
And many a lightfoot lad.   *Ib, 54*

9   Malt does more than Milton can
To justify God's ways to man.   *Ib, 62*

HOWITT, Mary, 1799–1888

10 'Will you walk into my parlour?' said a spider to a fly;
"Tis the prettiest little parlour that ever you did spy.'
            The Spider and the Fly

HOYLE, Edmond, 1672–1769

11 When in doubt, win the trick.   *Hoyle's Games, Whist, Twenty-four Short*
            Rules for Learners

HUBBARD, Elbert, 1856–1915

12 Life is just one damned thing after another.   *A Thousand and One*
            Epigrams

HUGHES, Thomas, 1822–1896

13 Life isn't all beer and skittles.   *Tom Brown's Schooldays, Pt. 1, Ch. 2*

HUME, David, 1711-1776

1 Avarice, the spur of industry.   *Essays, Of Civil Liberty*

2 Custom, then, is the great guide of human life.   *Inquiry Concerning
Human Understanding, 5, 1*

HUNGERFORD, Margaret, 1855?-1897

3 Beauty is altogether in the eye of the beholder.   *Molly Bawn*

HUNT, George William, 1825-1904

4 We don't want to fight, but by jingo if we do,
We've got the ships, we've got the men, we've got the money too.
Music-Hall Song, 1878

HUNT, James Henry Leigh, 1784-1859

5 Abou Ben Adhem (may his tribe increase!)
Awoke one night from a deep dream of peace.   *Abou Ben Adhem and the
Angel*

6 Write me as one that loves his fellow-men.   *Ib*

7 Jenny kissed me when we met,
Jumping from the chair she sat in.   *Rondeau*

HUXLEY, Aldous Leonard, 1894-1963

8 The time of our Ford.   *Brave New World, Ch. 3*

9 Ending is better than mending.   *Ib*

10 The Ideal man is the non-attached man.   *Ends and Means, Ch. 1*

11 I can sympathise with people's pains, but not with their pleasures. There
is something curiously boring about somebody else's happiness.
Limbo, Cynthia

12 There are not enough *bons mots* in existence to provide any industrious
conversationalist with a new stock for every social occasion.
Point Counter Point, Ch. 7

13 A bad book is as much a labour to write as a good one; it comes as sincerely
from the author's soul.   *Ib, Ch. 13*

14 A million million spermatozoa,
All of them alive:
Out of their cataclysm but one poor Noah
Dare hope to survive,
And among that billion minus one
Might have chanced to be
Shakespeare, another Newton, a new Donne—
But the One was Me.   *The Fifth Philosopher's Song*

15   But when the wearied Band
Swoons to a waltz, I take her hand,
And there we sit in peaceful calm,
Quietly sweating palm to palm.   *Frascati's*

HUXLEY, Thomas Henry, 1825–1895

1 It is the customary fate of new truths to begin as heresies and to end as superstitions.   *The Coming of Age of the Origin of Species*

IBSEN, Henrik, 1828–1906

2 In that moment it burst upon me that I had been living here these eight years with a strange man, and had borne him three children. NORA HELMER
A Doll's House, Act 3

3 The majority never has right on its side. Never I say! That is one of the social lies that a free, thinking man is bound to rebel against. Who makes up the majority in any given country? Is it the wise men or the fools? I think we must agree that the fools are in a terrible, overwhelming majority, all the wide world over.   DR STOCKMANN   *An Enemy of the People,*
Act 4

4 A man should never put on his best trousers when he goes out to battle for freedom and truth.   DR STOCKMANN   *Ib, Act 5*

5 Mother, give me the sun.   OSWALD ALVING   *Ghosts, Act 3*

6 What's a man's first duty? The answer's brief: To be himself.   PEER GYNT
Peer Gynt, Act 4, Scene 1

INGE, William Ralph, 1860–1954

7 Literature flourishes best when it is half a trade and half an art.
The Victorian Age

8 The nations which have put mankind and posterity most in their debt have been small states—Israel, Athens, Florence, Elizabethan England.
Marchant, Wit and Wisdom of Dean Inge

INGERSOLL, Robert Green, 1833–1899

9 An honest God is the noblest work of man.   *Gods, Part 1 (see also 203:8)*

IRVING, Washington, 1783–1859

10 Whenever a man's friends begin to compliment him about looking young, he may be sure that they think he is growing old.   *Bracebridge Hall,*
Bachelors

11 A woman's whole history is a history of the affections.   *The Sketch Book,*
The Broken Heart

12 A sharp tongue is the only edged tool that grows keener with constant use.
Ib, Rip Van Winkle

13 The almighty dollar, that great object of universal devotion throughout our land, seems to have no genuine devotees in these peculiar villages.
Wolfert's Roost, The Creole Village

JAMES I of England, 1566–1625

14 A custom loathsome to the eye, hateful to the nose, harmful to the brain, dangerous to the lungs, and in the black, stinking fume thereof nearest resembling the horrible Stygian smoke of the pit that is bottomless.
A Counterblast to Tobacco

15 Dr. Donne's verses are like the peace of God: they pass all understanding.
Attributed

1 No bishop, no King.   *Attributed*

JAMES, Henry, 1843–1916

2 The deep well of unconscious cerebration.   *The American, Preface*

3 The only obligation to which in advance we may hold a novel without incurring the accusation of being arbitrary, is that it be interesting.
The Art of Fiction, Partial Portraits

4 It takes a great deal of history to produce a little literature.   *Life of Nathaniel Hawthorne, Ch. 1*

5 He [*Thoreau*] was unperfect, unfinished, inartistic; he was worse than provincial—he was parochial.   *Ib, Ch. 4*

JEFFERSON, Thomas, 1743–1826

6 We hold these truths to be self-evident: that all men are created equal; that they are endowed by their Creator with certain unalienable rights; that among these are life, liberty, and the pursuit of happiness.
Declaration of American Independence, 4 July 1776

7 We mutually pledge to each other our lives, our fortunes, and our sacred honour.   *Ib*

8 Error of opinion may be tolerated when reason is left free to combat it.
First Inaugural Address, 4 Mar. 1801

9 Peace, commerce, and honest friendship with all nations, entangling alliances with none.   *Ib*

10 The care of human life and happiness, and not their destruction, is the first and only legitimate object of good government.
To the Republican citizens of Washington County, Maryland, 1809

11 Resistance to tyrants is obedience to God.   *Epigrams*

12 Ignorance is preferable to error; and he is less remote from the truth who believes nothing, than he who believes what is wrong.
Notes on the state of Virginia

13 I tremble for my country when I reflect that God is just.   *Ib*

JEROME, Jerome Klapka, 1859–1927

14 Love is like the measles; we all have to go through with it.   *Idle Thoughts of an Idle Fellow, On Being in Love*

15 It always does seem to me that I am doing more work than I should do. It is not that I object to the work, mind you; I like work; it fascinates me. I can sit and look at it for hours. I love to keep it by me; the idea of getting rid of it nearly breaks my heart.   *Three Men in a Boat, Ch. 15*

16 The Passing of the Third Floor Back.   *Title of Play*

JERROLD, Douglas William, 1803–1857

17 Religion's in the heart, not in the knees.   *The Devil's Ducat, 1*

18 The best thing I know between France and England is the sea.   *Wit and opinions of Douglas Jerrold*

JOAD, Cyril Edwin Mitchinson, 1891–1953

19 It all depends what you mean by . . .   *B.B.C. Brains Trust, 1942 to 1948*

JOHNSON, Samuel, 1709–1784

1 When I took the first survey of my undertaking, I found our speech copious without order, and energetic without rules.   *Dictionary of the English Language, Preface*

2 I am not yet so lost in lexicography, as to forget that words are the daughters of earth, and that things are the sons of heaven.   *Ib*

3 Every quotation contributes something to the stability or enlargement of the language.   *Ib*

4 I have protracted my work till most of those whom I wished to please have sunk into the grave, and success and miscarriage are empty sounds; I therefore dismiss it with frigid tranquillity, having little to fear or hope from censure or from praise.   *Ib*

5 *Cricket.*—A sport, at which the contenders drive a ball with sticks in opposition to each other.   *Ib, Definitions*

6 *Grubstreet.*—Originally the name of a street near Moorfields in London much inhabited by writers of small histories, dictionaries, and temporary poems.   *Ib*

7 *Lexicographer.*—A harmless drudge.   *Ib*

8 *Network.*—Any thing reticulated or decussated, at equal distances, with interstices between the intersections.   *Ib*

9 *Oats.*—A grain, which in England is generally given to horses, but in Scotland supports the people.   *Ib*

10 *Patron.*—Commonly a wretch who supports with insolence, and is paid with flattery.   *Ib*

11 *Pension.*—An allowance made to any one without an equivalent. In England it is generally understood to mean pay given to a state hireling for treason to his country.   *Ib*

12 When two Englishmen meet, their first talk is of the weather.   *The Idler, 11*

13 Condemned to hope's delusive mine.   *On the Death of Mr. Levet*

14 Officious, innocent, sincere,
　　Of every friendless name the friend.   *Ib*

15 Of all the griefs that harrass the distressed,
　Sure the most bitter is a scornful jest.   *London*

16 This mournful truth is ev'rywhere confessed
　Slow rises worth, by poverty depressed.   *Ib*

17 If the man who turnips cries,
　Cry not when his father dies,
　'Tis a proof that he had rather
　Have a turnip than his father.   *Burlesque of lines by Lope De Vega*

18 Long expected, one-and-twenty,
　Lingering year, at length is flown.   *One-and-twenty*

19 When learning's triumph o'er her barb'rous foes
　First rear'd the stage, immortal Shakspear rose;
　Each change of many-colour'd life he drew,
　Exhausted worlds, and then imagin'd new:
　Existence saw him spurn her bounded reign,
　And panting time toil'd after him in vain.   *Prologue at the Opening of the Theatre in Drury Lane, 1747*

1 For we that live to please, must please to live.   *Prologue at the Opening*
  of the Theatre in Drury Lane, 1747

2 No place affords a more striking conviction of the vanity of human hopes,
  than a public library.   *The Rambler, 23 March 1751*

3 Ye who listen with credulity to the whispers of fancy, and pursue with
  eagerness the phantoms of hope; who expect that age will perform the
  promises of youth, and that the deficiencies of the present day will be
  supplied by the morrow; attend to the history of Rasselas, prince of
  Abyssinia.   *Rasselas, Ch. 1*

4 Some desire is necessary to keep life in motion, and he whose real wants are
  supplied, must admit those of fancy.   *Ib, Ch. 8*

5 The business of a poet, said Imlac, is to examine, not the individual, but
  the species; to remark general properties and large appearances: he does
  not number the streaks of the tulip, or describe the different shades in the
  verdure of the forest.   *Ib, Ch. 10*

6 Human life is every where a state in which much is to be endured, and little
  to be enjoyed.   *Ib, Ch. 11*

7 The life of a solitary man will be certainly miserable, but not certainly
  devout.   *Ib, Ch. 21*

8 To live without feeling or exciting sympathy, to be fortunate without adding to the felicity of others, or afflicted without tasting the balm of pity, is
  a state more gloomy than solitude: it is not retreat but exclusion from mankind. Marriage has many pains, but celibacy has no pleasures.   *Ib, Ch. 26*

9 Let observation with extensive view,
  Survey mankind from China to Peru;
  Remark each anxious toil, each eager strife,
  And watch the busy scenes of crowded life.   *The Vanity of Human Wishes*

10 There mark what ills the scholar's life assail,
   Toil, envy, want, the patron, and the jail.   *Ib*

11 He left the name, at which the world grew pale,
   To point a moral, or adorn a tale.   *Ib*

12 Hides from himself his state, and shuns to know
   That life protracted is protracted woe.   *Ib*

13 Still raise for good the supplicating voice,
   But leave to Heaven the measure and the choice.   *Ib*

14 JOHNSON: I had no notion that I was wrong or irreverent to my tutor.
   BOSWELL: That, Sir, was great fortitude of mind.
   JOHNSON: No, Sir, stark insensibility.   *Boswell's Life of Johnson, 1728*

15 If you call a dog Hervey, I shall love him.   *Ib, 1737*

16 When asked how he felt upon the ill success of his tragedy [*Irene*], he replied,
   'Like the Monument'.   *Ib, 1750*

17 Johnson scolded him [*Langton*] for 'leaving his social friends to go and sit
   with a set of wretched un-idea'd girls'.   *Ib, 1752*

18 This man [*Lord Chesterfield*] I thought had been a Lord among wits; but, I
   find, he is only a wit among Lords!   *Ib, 1754*

19 They teach the morals of a whore, and the manners of a dancing-master.
   [*Lord Chesterfield's Letters*]   *Ib*

1 Is not a Patron, my Lord, one who looks with unconcern on a man struggling for life in the water, and, when he has reached ground, encumbers him with help? The notice which you have been pleased to take of my labours, had it been early, had been kind; but it has been delayed till I am indifferent, and cannot enjoy it; till I am solitary, and cannot impart it; till I am known, and do not want it. *Boswell's Life of Johnson, Letter to Lord Chesterfield,*
7 Feb. 1755

2 When the messenger who carried the last sheet [*of Johnson's Dictionary*] to Millar returned, Johnson asked him, 'Well, what did he say?'—'Sir, (answered the messenger) he said, thank God I have done with him.' 'I am glad (replied Johnson, with a smile,) that he thanks God for any thing.'
Ib, 1755

3 I respect Millar, Sir; he has raised the price of literature. *Ib*

4 Ignorance, Madam, pure ignorance. [*When asked why, in his Dictionary, he defined 'Pastern' as the 'knee of a horse'*] *Ib*

5 If a man does not make new acquaintances as he advances through life, he will soon find himself left alone. A man, Sir, should keep his friendship in constant repair. *Ib*

6 BOSWELL: I do indeed come from Scotland, but I cannot help it . . .
JOHNSON: That, Sir, I find, is what a very great many of your countrymen cannot help. *Ib, 1763*

7 The morality of an action depends on the motive from which we act. If I fling half a crown to a beggar with intention to break his head, and he picks it up and buys victuals with it, the physical effect is good; but, with respect to me, the action is very wrong. *Ib*

8 The noblest prospect which a Scotchman ever sees, is the high road that leads him to England. *Ib*

9 A man ought to read just as inclination leads him; for what he reads as a task will do him little good. *Ib*

10 In civilized society, personal merit will not serve you so much as money will. Sir, you may make the experiment. Go into the street, and give one man a lecture on morality, and another a shilling, and see which will respect you most. *Ib*

11 It is a sad reflection but a true one, that I knew almost as much at eighteen as I do now. *Ib*

12 Your levellers wish to level down as far as themselves; but they cannot bear levelling up to themselves. They would all have some people under them; why not then have some people above them? *Ib*

13 A woman's preaching is like a dog's walking on his hind legs. It is not done well; but you are surprised to find it done at all. *Ib*

14 I mind my belly very studiously, and very carefully; for I look upon it, that he who does not mind his belly, will hardly mind any thing else. *Ib*

15 This was a good dinner enough, to be sure; but it was not a dinner to ask a man to. *Ib*

16 A very unclubbable man. [*Sir John Hawkins*] *Ib, 1764*

17 The longer we live, and the more we think, the higher value we learn to put on the friendship and tenderness of parents and of friends. Parents we can have but once; and he promises himself too much, who enters life with the expectation of finding many friends. *Ib, 1766*

1 I cannot see that lectures can do so much good as reading the books from which the lectures are taken.   *Boswell's Life of Johnson, 1766*

2 So far is it from being true that men are naturally equal, that no two people can be half an hour together, but one shall acquire an evident superiority over the other.   *Ib*

3 JOHNSON: Well, we had good talk.
BOSWELL: Yes, Sir, you tossed and gored several persons.   *Ib, 1768*

4 It matters not how a man dies, but how he lives.   *Ib, 1769*

5 Now that you are going to marry, do not expect more from life, than life will afford.   *Ib*

6 A gentleman who had been very unhappy in marriage, married immediately after his wife died: Johnson said, it was the triumph of hope over experience.
                                                                Ib, 1770

7 I would not give half a guinea to live under one form of Government rather than another. It is of no moment to the happiness of an individual.
                                                                Ib, 1772

8 The mass of every people must be barbarous where there is no printing. *Ib*

9 Much may be made of a Scotchman, if he be caught young.   *Ib*

10 People seldom read a book which is given to them; and few are given. The way to spread a work is to sell it at a low price. No man will send to buy a thing that costs even sixpence, without an intention to read it.   *Ib, 1773*

11 The Irish are not in a conspiracy to cheat the world by false representations of the merits of their countrymen. No, Sir; the Irish are a fair people;—they never speak well of one another.   *Ib, 1775*

12 They [*the Americans*] are a race of convicts, and ought to be thankful for any thing we allow them short of hanging.   *Ib*

13 There are few ways in which a man can be more innocently employed than in getting money.   *Ib*

14 Fleet-street has a very animated appearance; but I think the full tide of human existence is at Charing-Cross.   *Ib*

15 There may be other reasons for a man's not speaking in publick than want of resolution: he may have nothing to say.   *Ib*

16 The greatest part of a writer's time is spent in reading, in order to write; a man will turn over half a library to make one book.   *Ib*

17 Patriotism is the last refuge of a scoundrel.   *Ib*

18 Being pressed upon this subject, and asked if he really was of opinion, that though, in general, happiness was very rare in human life, a man was not sometimes happy in the moment that was present, he answered, 'Never, but when he is drunk.'   *Ib*

19 Knowledge is of two kinds. We know a subject ourselves, or we know where we can find information upon it.   *Ib*

20 There is now less flogging in our great schools than formerly, but then less is learned there; so that what the boys get at one end they lose at the other.
                                                                    Ib

21 A ship is worse than a gaol. There is, in a gaol, better air, better company, better conveniency of every kind; and a ship has the additional disadvantage of being in danger. When men come to like a sea-life, they are not fit to live on land.   *Ib, 1776*

1 There is no private house, (said he) in which people can enjoy themselves so well, as at a capital tavern.   *Boswell's Life of Johnson, 1776*

2 Marriage is the best state for a man in general; and every man is a worse man, in proportion as he is unfit for the married state.   *Ib*

3 It is commonly a weak man, who marries for love.   *Ib*

4 Melancholy, indeed, should be diverted by every means but drinking.   *Ib*

5 No man but a blockhead ever wrote, except for money.   *Ib*

6 A man who has not been in Italy, is always conscious of an inferiority.   *Ib*

7 If I had no duties, and no reference to futurity, I would spend my life in driving briskly in a post-chaise with a pretty woman.   *Ib, 1777*

8 Depend upon it, Sir, when a man knows he is to be hanged in a fortnight, it concentrates his mind wonderfully.   *Ib*

9 You find no man, at all intellectual, who is willing to leave London. No, Sir, when a man is tired of London, he is tired of life; for there is in London all that life can afford.   *Ib*

10 I am willing to love all mankind, except an American.   *Ib, 1778*

11 It is better to live rich than to die rich.   *Ib*

12 I have always said, the first Whig was the Devil.   *Ib*

13 Wine gives great pleasure; and every pleasure is of itself a good. It is a good, unless counterbalanced by evil.   *Ib*

14 What I gained by being in France was, learning to be better satisfied with my own country.   *Ib*

15 Claret is the liquor for boys; port for men; but he who aspires to be a hero must drink brandy.   *Ib, 1779*

16 BOSWELL: Is not the Giant's-Causeway worth seeing?
JOHNSON: Worth seeing? Yes; but not worth going to see.   *Ib*

17 Sir, I have two very cogent reasons for not printing any list of subscribers;—one, that I have lost all the names,—the other, that I have spent all the money.   *Ib, 1781*

18 Clear your mind of cant. You may talk as other people do: you may say to a man, 'Sir, I am your most humble servant.' You are *not* his most humble servant.   *Ib, 1783*

19 Let your imports be more than your exports, and you'll never go far wrong.   *Ib*

20 No man is a hypocrite in his pleasures.   *Ib, 1784*

21 I look upon every day to be lost, in which I do not make a new acquaintance.   *Ib*

22 *Nullum quod tetigit non ornavit*—He touched nothing that he did not adorn.   *Epitaph on Goldsmith*

23 There is no tracing the connection of ancient nations, but by language; and therefore I am always sorry when any language is lost, because languages are the pedigree of nations.   *Boswell's Journal of a Tour to the Hebrides*

24 Difficult do you call it, Sir? I wish it were impossible. [*Of a violinist's performance*]   *Anecdotes by William Seward*

25 What is written without effort is in general read without pleasure.   *Ib*

26 The great source of pleasure is variety.   *Lives of the English Poets, Butler*

1 But what are the hopes of man! I am disappointed by that stroke of death, which has eclipsed the gaiety of nations and impoverished the public stock of harmless pleasure. [*Garrick's death*]   *Lives of the English Poets,* Edmund Smith

2 I have heard him assert, that a tavern chair was the throne of human felicity.
Hawkin's Life of Johnson

3 A man is in general better pleased when he has a good dinner upon his table, than when his wife talks Greek.   *Johnsonian Miscellanies*

4 You could not stand five minutes with that man [*Edmund Burke*] beneath a shed, while it rained, but you must be convinced you had been standing with the greatest man you had ever yet seen.   *Attributed by Mrs Piozzi*

JONSON, Ben, 1573–1637

5 Our scene is London, 'cause we would make known,
No country's mirth is better than our own.   *The Alchemist, Prologue*

6 Zeal-of-the-Land Busy.   *Bartholomew Fair, name of character*

7 Drink to me only with thine eyes
And I will pledge with mine;
Or leave a kiss but in the cup
And I'll not look for wine.   *To Celia*

8 Queen and Huntress, chaste and fair,
Now the sun is laid to sleep,
Seated in thy silver chair,
State in wonted manner keep:
  Hesperus entreats thy light,
  Goddess, excellently bright.   HESPERUS   *Cynthia's Revels,
Act 5, Scene 3*

9 Still to be neat, still to be drest,
As you were going to a feast.   SONG   *Epicoene, Act 1, Scene 1*

10 Such sweet neglect more taketh me,
Than all the adulteries of art;
They strike mine eyes, but not my heart.   SONG   *Ib*

11   Soul of the Age!
The applause! delight! the wonder of our Stage.
To the Memory of William Shakespeare

12 Thou art a monument, without a tomb.   *Ib*

13   How far thou didst our Lyly out-shine
Or sporting Kyd, or Marlowe's mighty line.   *Ib*

14 Thou hadst small Latin, and less Greek.   *Ib*

15 He was not of an age, but for all time!   *Ib*

16 Sweet Swan of Avon!   *Ib*

17 Good morning to the day: and, next, my gold!—
Open the shrine, that I may see my saint.   VOLPONE
Volpone, Act 1, Scene 1

18 O, health! health! the blessing of the rich! the riches of the poor! who can buy thee at too dear a rate, since there is no enjoying the world without thee?   VOLPONE   *Ib, Act 2, Scene 1*

1 Come, my Celia, let us prove,
While we can, the sports of love,
Time will not be ours for ever,
He, at length, our good will sever.   VOLPONE   *Volpone, Act 3, Scene 6*

2 O rare Ben Jonson.   *Epitaph in Westminster Abbey*

JORDAN, Dorothea, 1762–1816

3 'Oh! where, and Oh! where is your Highland Laddie gone?'
'He's gone to fight the French, for King George upon the throne,
And it's Oh! in my heart, how I wish him safe at home!'
       The Blue Bells of Scotland

JOYCE, James, 1882–1941

4 A Portrait of the Artist as a Young Man.   *Title of Book*

JUDGE, Jack, see WILLIAMS, Harry

JUNIUS, 18th century

5 The Liberty of the press is the *Palladium* of all the civil, political and
religious rights of an Englishman.   *Letters, Dedication*

6 To be acquainted with the merit of a ministry, we need only observe the
condition of the people.   *Letter 1, 21 Jan. 1769*

7 There is a holy, mistaken zeal in politics, as well as religion. By persuading
others we convince ourselves.   *Letter 35, 19 Dec. 1769*

JUVENAL, 60–130? A.D.

8 *Nemo repente fuit turpissimus.* No one ever became thoroughly bad in one
step.   *Satires, 2, 83*

9   *Quis custodiet ipsos*
Custodes?
Who is to guard the guards themselves?   *Ib, 6, 347*

10   *Tenet insanabile multos*
Scribendi cacoethes et aegro in corde senescit.
An inveterate and incurable itch for writing besets many and grows old
with their sick hearts.   *Ib, 7, 51*

11 *Orandum est ut sit mens sana in corpore sano.*
Your prayer must be for a sound mind in a sound body.   *Ib, 10, 356*

KARR, Alphonse, 1808–1890

12 *Plus ça change, plus c'est la même chose.* The more things change, the more
they are the same.   *Les Guêpes, Jan. 1849*

KAVANAGH, Ted, 1892–1958

13 Can I do you now, sir?   MRS MOP   *Itma, B.B.C. Radio Programme,*
1939–1949, with Tommy Handley (1892–1949)

14 Don't forget the diver.   *Ib*

15 I don't mind if I do.   COLONEL CHINSTRAP   *Ib*

16 It's That Man Again.   *Ib*

17 Wot, me? In my state of health?   CHARLES ATLAS   *Ib*

KEATS, John, 1795-1821

1 Season of mists and mellow fruitfulness,
    Close bosom-friend of the maturing sun;
Conspiring with him how to load and bless
    With fruit the vines that round the thatch-eves run.   *To Autumn*

2   To set budding more,
And still more, later flowers for the bees,
Until they think warm days will never cease,
    For Summer has o'er-brimm'd their clammy cells.   *Ib*

3 Who hath not seen thee oft amid thy store?
    Sometimes whoever seeks abroad may find
Thee sitting careless on a granary floor.   *Ib*

4 Where are the songs of Spring? Ay, where are they?
    Think not of them, thou hast thy music too.   *Ib*

5 The red-breast whistles from a garden-croft;
    And gathering swallows twitter in the skies.   *Ib*

6 Bards of Passion and of Mirth,
Ye have left your souls on earth!
Have ye souls in heaven too,
Double lived in regions new?   *Ode, Written on the blank page before*
                                Beaumont and Fletcher's 'The Fair Maid of the Inn'

7 The imagination of a boy is healthy, and the mature imagination of a man
is healthy; but there is a space of life between, in which the soul is in a
ferment, the character undecided, the way of life uncertain, the ambition
thick-sighted: thence proceeds mawkishness.   *Endymion, Preface*

8 A thing of beauty is a joy for ever:
Its loveliness increases; it will never
Pass into nothingness.   *Ib, Book 1, 1*

9 Pleasure is oft a visitant; but pain
Clings cruelly to us.   *Ib, 906*

10   O Sorrow,
    Why dost borrow
Heart's lightness from the merriment of May?   *Ib, Book 4, 164*

11   It is a flaw
In happiness, to see beyond our bourn,—
It forces us in summer skies to mourn,
It spoils the singing of the Nightingale.
    Epistle to John Hamilton Reynolds, 82

12 St. Agnes' Eve—Ah, bitter chill it was!
The owl, for all his feathers, was a-cold;
The hare limp'd trembling through the frozen grass,
And silent was the flock in woolly fold.   *The Eve of St. Agnes, 1*

13 Upon the honey'd middle of the night.   *Ib, 6*

14 And they are gone: aye, ages long ago
These lovers fled away into the storm.   *Ib, 42*

15   The Beadsman, after thousand aves told,
For aye unsought for slept among his ashes cold.   *Ib*

1 Fanatics have their dreams, wherewith they weave
  A paradise for a sect.   *The Fall of Hyperion, Book 1, 1*

2 The poet and the dreamer are distinct,
  Diverse, sheer opposite, antipodes.
  The one pours out a balm upon the World,
  The other vexes it.   *Ib, 199*

3 Ever let the fancy roam,
  Pleasure never is at home.   *Fancy, 1*

4 Deep in the shady sadness of a vale
  Far sunken from the healthy breath of morn,
  Far from the fiery noon, and eve's one star,
  Sat gray-hair'd Saturn, quiet as a stone.   *Hyperion, Book 1, 1*

5   No stir of air was there,
  Not so much life as on a summer's day
  Robs not one light seed from the feather'd grass,
  But where the dead leaf fell, there did it rest.   *Ib, 7*

6   As when, upon a tranced summer-night,
  Those green-rob'd senators of mighty woods,
  Tall oaks, branch-charmed by the earnest stars,
  Dream, and so dream all night without a stir.   *Ib, 72*

7 For as in theatres of crowded men
  Hubbub increases more they call out 'Hush!'   *Ib, 253*

8   For 'tis the eternal law
  That first in beauty should be first in might.   *Ib, Book 2, 228*

9 Knowledge enormous makes a God of me.   *Ib, Book 3, 113*

10 Parting they seem'd to tread upon the air,
  Twin roses by the zephyr blown apart
  Only to meet again more close, and share
  The inward fragrance of each other's heart.   *Isabella, 10*

11 But, for the general award of love,
  The little sweet doth kill much bitterness.   *Ib, 13*

12 So the two brothers and their murder'd man
  Rode past fair Florence.   *Ib, 27*

13   O cruelty,
  To steal my Basil-pot away from me!   *Ib, 63*

14 Ah, what can ail thee, wretched wight,
  Alone and palely loitering;
  The sedge is wither'd from the lake,
  And no birds sing.   *La Belle Dame Sans Merci, 1*

15 I met a lady in the meads
  Full beautiful, a faery's child;
  Her hair was long, her foot was light,
  And her eyes were wild.   *Ib, 4*

16 She look'd at me as she did love,
  And made sweet moan.   *Ib, 6*

17 And sure in language strange she said,
  I love thee true.   *Ib, 7*

1 Love in a hut, with water and a crust,
  Is—Love, forgive us!—cinders, ashes, dust;
Love in a palace is perhaps at last
More grievous torment than a hermit's fast.   *Lamia, Part 2, 1*

2   Do not all charms fly
  At the mere touch of cold philosophy?   *Ib, 229*

3 Philosophy will clip an Angel's wings.   *Ib, 234*

4 Souls of Poets dead and gone,
What Elysium have ye known,
Happy field or mossy cavern,
Choicer than the Mermaid Tavern?
Have ye tippled drink more fine
Than mine host's Canary wine?   *Lines on the Mermaid Tavern, 1*

5 Ah! dearest love, sweet home of all my fears,
  And hopes, and joys, and panting miseries.   *Ode to Fanny, 2*

6 Thou still unravish'd bride of quietness,
  Thou foster-child of silence and slow time.   *Ode on a Grecian Urn, 1*

7 Heard melodies are sweet, but those unheard
  Are sweeter; therefore, ye soft pipes, play on;
Not to the sensual ear, but, more endear'd,
Pipe to the spirit ditties of no tone.   *Ib, 2*

8 She cannot fade, though thou hast not thy bliss,
  For ever wilt thou love, and she be fair!   *Ib*

9 For ever piping songs for ever new.   *Ib, 3*

10 'Beauty is truth, truth beauty,'—that is all
  Ye know on earth, and all ye need to know.   *Ib, 5*

11 No, no, go not to Lethe, neither twist
  Wolf's-bane, tight-rooted, for its poisonous wine. *Ode on Melancholy, 1*

12 She dwells with Beauty—Beauty that must die;
  And Joy, whose hand is ever at his lips
Bidding adieu.   *Ib, 3*

13 My heart aches, and a drowsy numbness pains
  My sense, as though of hemlock I had drunk.   *Ode to a Nightingale, 1*

14 O for a beaker full of the warm South,
  Full of the true, the blushful Hippocrene,
    With beaded bubbles winking at the brim,
      And purple-stained mouth;
That I might drink, and leave the world unseen,
  And with thee fade away into the forest dim.   *Ib, 2*

15 Where youth grows pale, and spectre-thin, and dies;
  Where but to think is to be full of sorrow
    And leaden-eyed despairs.   *Ib, 3*

16 Away! away! for I will fly to thee,
  Not charioted by Bacchus and his pards,
But on the viewless wings of Poesy,
  Though the dull brain perplexes and retards:
Already with thee! tender is the night,
  And haply the Queen-Moon is on her throne,   *Ib, 4*

1 I cannot see what flowers are at my feet,
   Nor what soft incense hangs upon the boughs.   *Ode to a Nightingale, 5*

2 The murmurous haunt of flies on summer eves.   *Ib*

3 Darkling I listen; and, for many a time
   I have been half in love with easeful Death,
Call'd him soft names in many a mused rhyme,
   To take into the air my quiet breath;
Now more than ever seems it rich to die,
   To cease upon the midnight with no pain,
     While thou art pouring forth thy soul abroad
      In such an ecstasy!   *Ib, 6*

4 Thou wast not born for death, immortal Bird!
   No hungry generations tread thee down;
The voice I hear this passing night was heard
   In ancient days by emperor and clown:
Perhaps the self-same song that found a path
   Through the sad heart of Ruth, when, sick for home,
     She stood in tears amid the alien corn;
      The same that oft-times hath
Charm'd magic casements, opening on the foam
   Of perilous seas, in faery lands forlorn.   *Ib, 7*

5 Forlorn! the very word is like a bell
   To toll me back from thee to my sole self!   *Ib, 8*

6 Was it a vision, or a waking dream?
   Fled is that music:—Do I wake or sleep?   *Ib*

7 A bright torch, and a casement ope at night,
   To let the warm Love in!   *Ode to Psyche, 66*

8 What is more gentle than a wind in summer?   *Sleep and Poetry, 1*

9 Stop and consider! life is but a day;
A fragile dew-drop on its perilous way
From a tree's summit.   *Ib, 85*

10 O for ten years, that I may overwhelm
Myself in poesy; so I may do the deed
That my own soul has to itself decreed.   *Ib, 96*

11 And can I ever bid these joys farewell?
Yes, I must pass them for a nobler life,
Where I may find the agonies, the strife
Of human hearts.   *Ib, 122*

12   A drainless shower
Of light is poesy; 'tis the supreme of power;
'Tis might half slumb'ring on its own right arm.   *Ib, 235*

13   The great end
Of poesy, that it should be a friend
To sooth the cares, and lift the thoughts of man.   *Ib, 245*

14 Much have I travell'd in the realms of gold,
   And many goodly states and kingdoms seen.
         Sonnet, On First Looking into Chapman's Homer

15 Then felt I like some watcher of the skies
   When a new planet swims into his ken;

Or like stout Cortez when with eagle eyes
    He star'd at the Pacific—and all his men
Look'd at each other with a wild surmise—
    Silent, upon a peak in Darien.   *Sonnet, On First Looking into*
                                          Chapman's Homer

1 The poetry of earth is never dead:
    When all the birds are faint with the hot sun,
    And hide in cooling trees, a voice will run
From hedge to hedge about the new-mown mead.
                                          Sonnet, On the Grasshopper and Cricket

2 Happy is England! I could be content
    To see no other verdure than its own.   *Sonnet, Happy is England*

3 Happy is England, sweet her artless daughters;
    Enough their simple loveliness for me.   *Ib*

4 Four seasons fill the measure of the year;
    There are four seasons in the mind of man. *Sonnet, The Human Seasons*

5 Glory and loveliness have pass'd away.   *Sonnet, To Leigh Hunt*

6 To one who has been long in city pent,
    'Tis very sweet to look into the fair
    And open face of heaven.   *Sonnet, To one who has been long in*
                                          City pent

7 When I have fears that I may cease to be
    Before my pen has glean'd my teeming brain.
                                          Sonnet, When I have fears

8   Then on the shore
Of the wide world I stand alone, and think
Till love and fame to nothingness do sink.   *Ib*

9 I am certain of nothing but of the holiness of the Heart's affections and the
    truth of Imagination—What the imagination seizes as Beauty must be
    truth—whether it existed before or not.   *Letter to Benjamin Bailey,*
                                          22 Nov. 1817

10 O for a Life of Sensations rather than of Thoughts!   *Ib*

11 Negative Capability, that is, when a man is capable of being in uncertain-
    ties, mysteries, doubts, without any irritable reaching after fact and reason.
                                Letter to George and Thomas Keats, 28 Dec. 1817

12 I am quite perplexed in a world of doubts and fancies—there is nothing
    stable in the world; uproar's your only music.
                                Letter to George and Thomas Keats, 13 Jan. 1818

13 Poetry should be great and unobtrusive, a thing which enters into one's
    soul, and does not startle it or amaze it with itself, but with its subject.
                                          Letter to J. H. Reynolds, 3 Feb. 1818

14 Poetry should surprise by a fine excess and not by Singularity—it should
    strike the Reader as a wording of his own highest thoughts, and appear
    almost a Remembrance.   *Letter to John Taylor, 27 Feb. 1818*

15 If Poetry comes not as naturally as the Leaves to a tree it had better not
    come at all.   *Ib*

16 Scenery is fine—but human nature is finer.   *Letter to Benjamin Bailey,*
                                          13 March 1818

1 I have not the slightest feel of humility towards the Public—or to anything in existence,—but the eternal Being, the Principle of Beauty, and the Memory of great Men. *Letter to J. H. Reynolds, 9 April 1818*

2 I find that I can have no enjoyment in the World but continual drinking of Knowledge. *Letter to John Taylor, 24 April 1818*

3 I compare human life to a large Mansion of Many Apartments, two of which I can only describe, the doors of the rest being as yet shut upon me. *Letter to J. H. Reynolds, 3 May 1818*

4 I would sooner fail than not be among the greatest. *Letter to J. A. Hessey, 9 Oct. 1818*

5 I think I shall be among the English Poets after my death. *Letter to George and Georgiana Keats, Oct. 1818*

6 Though the most beautiful Creature were waiting for me at the end of a Journey or a Walk . . . my Happiness would not be so fine, as my Solitude is sublime. Then instead of what I have described, there is a Sublimity to welcome me home. The roaring of the wind is my wife and the Stars through the window pane are my children. The mighty abstract Idea I have of Beauty in all things stifles the more divided and minute domestic happiness. *Ib*

7 A Man's life of any worth is a continual allegory, and very few eyes can see the Mystery of his life—a life like the scriptures, figurative—which such people can no more make out than they can the hebrew Bible. Lord Byron cuts a figure—but he is not figurative—Shakespeare led a life of Allegory: his works are the comments on it. *Letter to George and Georgiana Keats, 14 Feb. 1819*

8 I have two luxuries to brood over in my walks, your Loveliness and the hour of my death. O that I could have possession of them both in the same minute. *Letter to Fanny Brawne, 25 July 1819*

9 I equally dislike the favour of the public with the love of a woman—they are both a cloying treacle to the wings of independence. *Letter to John Taylor, 24 Aug. 1819*

10 Love is my religion—I could die for that. *Letter to Fanny Brawne, 13 Oct. 1819*

11 'If I should die,' said I to myself, 'I have left no immortal work behind me—nothing to make my friends proud of my memory—but I have lov'd the principle of beauty in all things, and if I had had time I would have made myself remember'd.' *Letter to Fanny Brawne, Feb. 1820*

12 You, I am sure, will forgive me for sincerely remarking that you might curb your magnanimity, and be more of an artist, and load every rift of your subject with ore. *Letter to P. B. Shelley, Aug. 1820*

13 Here lies one whose name was writ in water. *Epitaph*

KEMPIS, Thomas À, 1380–1471

14 Man proposes but God disposes. *The Imitation of Christ, 1, 19*

15 *Sic transit gloria mundi.* Thus the glory of the world passes away. *Ib, 3, 6*

16 It is much safer to obey than to rule. *Ib, 9, 1*

KENNEDY, John Fitzgerald, 1917–1963

1 Let the word go forth from this time and place, to friend and foe alike, that the torch has been passed to a new generation of Americans—born in this century, tempered by war, disciplined by a hard and bitter peace, proud of our ancient heritage.   *Inaugural address, 20 Jan. 1961*

2 My fellow Americans, ask not what your country can do for you—ask what you can do for your country. My fellow citizens of the world: ask not what America will do for you, but what together we can do for the freedom of man.   *Ib*

KESSELRING, Joseph, 1902—

3 Arsenic and Old Lace.   *Title of play*

KETHE, William, ?–1608

4 All people that on earth do dwell
    Sing to the Lord with cheerful voice.   *All People that on Earth do Dwell*

5 For why, the Lord our God is good:
    His mercy is for ever sure;
    His truth at all times firmly stood,
        And shall from age to age endure.   *Ib*

KEY, Francis Scott, 1780–1843

6 O! say can you see, by the dawn's early light,
    What so proudly we hailed at the twilight's last gleaming,
    Whose broad stripes and bright stars, through the perilous fight,
    O'er the ramparts we watched, were so gallantly streaming.
                                            The Star-Spangled Banner

7 'Tis the star-spangled banner! O long may it wave,
    O'er the land of the free, and the home of the brave.   *Ib*

KHAYYÁM, Omar, see FITZGERALD, Edward

KILMER, Joyce, 1886–1918

8 I think that I shall never see
    A poem lovely as a tree.

    A tree whose hungry mouth is pressed
    Against the earth's sweet flowing breast.   *Trees*

9 Poems are made by fools like me
    But only God can make a tree.   *Ib*

KING, Benjamin Franklin, 1857–1894

10 Nothing to do but work,
    Nothing to eat but food,
    Nothing to wear but clothes,
    To keep one from going nude.   *The Pessimist*

KING, Stoddard, 1889–1933

11 There's a long, long trail a-winding
    Into the land of my dreams.   *The Long, Long Trail*

KINGSLEY, Charles, 1819–1875

1 Airly Beacon, Airly Beacon;
　　Oh the pleasant sight to see
　Shires and towns from Airly Beacon,
　　While my love climbed up to me. *Airly Beacon*

2 Be good, sweet maid, and let who will be clever;
　　Do noble things, not dream them, all day long:
　And so make life, death, and that vast for-ever
　　One grand, sweet song. *A Farewell, To C.E.G.*

3 For men must work, and women must weep,
　And the sooner it's over, the sooner to sleep. *The Three Fishers*

4 When all the world is young, lad,
　　And all the trees are green. *Songs from the Water Babies, Young and Old*

5 Young blood must have its course, lad,
　　And every dog its day. *Ib*

6 He did not know that a keeper is only a poacher turned outside in, and a poacher is a keeper turned inside out. *The Water Babies, Ch. 1*

7 More ways of killing a cat than choking her with cream. *Westward Ho!* *Ch. 20*

KIPLING, Rudyard, 1865–1936

8 Oh, East is East, and West is West, and never the twain shall meet.
　　The Ballad of East and West

9 Four things greater than all things are,—
　Women and Horses and Power and War. *Ballad of the King's Jest*

10 And a woman is only a woman, but a good cigar is a smoke. *The Betrothed*

11 Boots—boots—boots—boots—movin' up an' down again! *Boots*

12 But the Devil whoops, as he whooped of old:
　'It's clever, but is it art?' *The Conundrum of the Workshops*

13 And what should they know of England who only England know?
　　The English Flag

14 For the female of the species is more deadly than the male.
　　The Female of the Species

15 Gentlemen-rankers out on the spree,
　Damned from here to Eternity. *Gentlemen Rankers*

16 You're a better man than I am, Gunga Din. *Gunga Din*

17 If you can keep your head when all about you
　　Are losing theirs and blaming it on you. *If*

18 If you can dream—and not make dreams your master. *Ib*

19 If you can meet with Triumph and Disaster
　　And treat those two impostors just the same. *Ib*

20 If you can fill the unforgiving minute
　　With sixty seconds' worth of distance run,
　Yours is the Earth and everything that's in it,
　　And—which is more—you'll be a Man, my son! *Ib*

21 Now this is the Law of the Jungle—as old and true as the sky.
　　The Law of the Jungle

1 On the road to Mandalay
  Where the flyin'-fishes play.   *Mandalay*

2 Ship me somewhere East of Suez, where the best is like the worst,
  Where there aren't no Ten Commandments, an' a man can raise a thirst.
                                                                      Ib

3 The tumult and the shouting dies—
  The captains and the kings depart.   *Recessional*

4 Lest we forget, lest we forget!   *Ib*

5 Oh, it's Tommy this, an' Tommy that, an' 'Tommy, go away';
  But it's 'Thank you, Mister Atkins,' when the band begins to play.
                                                                   Tommy

6 Take up the White Man's Burden.   *The White Man's Burden*

7 This is too butch for be.   *Just-so Stories, The Elephant's Child*

8 Led go! You are hurtig be!   *Ib*

9 The camel's hump is an ugly lump
  Which well you may see at the Zoo;
  But uglier yet is the hump we get
  From having too little to do.   *Ib, How the Camel got his Hump*

10 A man of infinite—resource—and—sagacity.
                                        Ib, How the Whale got his Throat

11 The Light that Failed.   *Title of novel*

KLINGER, Friedrich von, 1752–1831

12 *Sturm und Drang*. Storm and stress.   *Title of play*

KNOX, John, 1505–1572

13 The First Blast of the Trumpet Against the Monstrous Regiment of Women.
                                          Title of Pamphlet, 1558

KNOX, Ronald Arbuthnot, 1888–1957

14 There once was a man who said, 'God
    Must think it exceedingly odd
      If he finds that this tree
      Continues to be
    When there's no one about in the Quad.'   *Limerick*

15 A loud noise at one end and no sense of responsibility at the other.
                                                   Definition of a Baby

KYD, Thomas, 1558?–1594?

16 In time the savage bull sustains the yoke,
   In time all haggard hawks will stoop to lure,
   In time small wedges cleave the hardest oak,
   In time the flint is pierced with softest shower.   LORENZO   *The Spanish
                                                       Tragedy, Act 2, Scene 1*

LABOUCHÈRE, Henry, 1831–1912

17 He [*Labouchère*] did not object, he once said, to Gladstone's always having
   the ace of trumps up his sleeve, but only to his pretence that God had put
   it there.   *Quoted in Dictionary of National Biography, 1912–1921*

LAMB, Lady Caroline, 1785–1828

1 Mad, bad, and dangerous to know. [*Byron*]   *Journal*

LAMB, Charles, 1775–1834

2 The human species, according to the best theory I can form of it, is composed of two distinct races, the men who borrow, and the men who lend.
Essays of Elia, The Two Races of Men

3 Borrowers of books—those mutilators of collections, spoilers of the symmetry of shelves, and creators of odd volumes.   *Ib*

4 'A clear fire, a clean hearth, and the rigour of the game.' This was the celebrated wish of old Sarah Battle (now with God) who, next to her devotions, loved a good game of whist.   *Ib, Mrs. Battle's Opinions on Whist*

5 'Presents,' I often say, 'endear Absents.'
Ib, A Dissertation upon Roast Pig

6 I love to lose myself in other men's minds. When I am not walking, I am reading; I cannot sit and think. Books think for me.
Last Essays of Elia, Detached Thoughts on Books and Reading

7 To be strong-backed and neat-bound is the desideratum of a volume. Magnificence comes after.   *Ib*

8 Newspapers always excite curiosity. No one ever lays one down without a feeling of disappointment.   *Ib*

9 I have had playmates, I have had companions,
In my days of childhood, in my joyful schooldays—
All, all are gone, the old familiar faces.   *The Old Familiar Faces*

LANDOR, Walter Savage, 1775–1864

10 George the First was always reckoned
Vile, but viler George the Second;
And what mortal ever heard
Any good of George the Third?
When from earth the Fourth descended
God be praised, the Georges ended.   *Epigram*

11 I strove with none; for none was worth my strife;
Nature I loved and, next to Nature, Art:
I warmed both hands before the fire of life;
It sinks, and I am ready to depart.   *Finis*

12 I loved him not; and yet now he is gone,
I feel I am alone.
I check'd him while he spoke: yet, could he speak,
Alas! I would not check.   *The Maid's Lament*

13 Ah, what avails the sceptred race!
Ah, what the form divine!   *Rose Aylmer*

LANE, George Martin, 1823–1897

14 The waiter roars it through the hall:
'We don't give bread with one fish-ball!'   *One Fish-ball*

LANGBRIDGE, Frederick, 1849–1923

15 Two men look out through the same bars:
One sees the mud, and one the stars.   *A Cluster of Quiet Thoughts*

LANGLAND, William, 1330?–1400?

  1 In a somer seson, when soft was the sonne.   *A Vision of William concerning Piers the Plowman, B Text, Prologue, 1*

LATIMER, Bishop Hugh, 1485?–1555

  2 Be of good comfort, Master Ridley, and play the man; we shall this day light such a candle by God's grace in England, as I trust shall never be put out.   *16 Oct. 1555, while Latimer and Ridley were being burned at the stake for heresy*

LAUDER, Sir Harry, 1870–1950

  3 I love a lassie.   *Song*

  4 Just a wee doch-an'-dorris
Before we gang awa' . . .
If you can say, 'It's a braw, bricht, moonlicht nicht'
Ye're a' richt.   *Song*

  5 Keep right on to the end of the road,
Keep right on to the end.
'Though you're tired and weary still journey on.   *Song*

  6 O! it's nice to get up in the mornin'
But it's nicer to lie in bed.   *Song*

  7 Roamin' in the gloamin'.   *Song*

LAWRENCE, David Herbert, 1885–1930

  8 How beastly the bourgeois is
especially the male of the species.   *How Beastly the Bourgeois is*

  9 Nicely groomed, like a mushroom
Standing there so sleek and erect and eyeable—
and like a fungus, living on the remains of bygone life
sucking his life out of the dead leaves of greater life than his own.   *Ib*

 10 My love lies underground
With her face upturned to mine,
And her mouth unclosed in a last long kiss
That ended her life and mine.   *Hymn to Priapus*

 11 When I read Shakespeare I am struck with wonder
That such trivial people should muse and thunder
In such lovely language.   *When I Read Shakespeare, 1*

LEACOCK, Stephen Butler, 1869–1944

 12 If every day in the life of a school could be the last day but one, there would be little fault to find with it.   *College Days, Memories and Miseries of a Schoolmaster*

 13 Lord Ronald said nothing; he flung himself from the room, flung himself upon his horse and rode madly off in all directions.   *Nonsense Novels, Gertrude the Governess*

 14 Golf may be played on Sunday, not being a game within the view of the law, but being a form of moral effort.   *Other Fancies, Why I refuse to play Golf*

 15 The general idea, of course, in any first-class laundry is to see that no shirt or collar ever comes back twice.   *Winnowed Wisdom, Ch. 6*

LEAR, Edward, 1812–1888

1 Who, or why, or which, or *what*, is the Akond of Swat?

The Akond of Swat

2 On the Coast of Coromandel
   Where the early pumpkins blow,
 In the middle of the woods
   Lived the Yonghy-Bonghy-Bò.

The Courtship of the Yonghy-Bonghy-Bò

3   The Dong!—the Dong!
 The wandering Dong through the forest goes!
   The Dong!—the Dong!
 The Dong with a luminous Nose!   *The Dong with a Luminous Nose*

4 They went to sea in a sieve, they did
   In a sieve they went to sea.   *The Jumblies*

5 Far and few, far and few,
 Are the lands where the Jumblies live;
 Their heads are green, and their hands are blue,
 And they went to sea in a sieve.   *Ib*

6 'How pleasant to know Mr. Lear!'
 Who has written such volumes of stuff!
 Some think him ill-tempered and queer,
 But a few think him pleasant enough.   *Nonsense Songs, Preface*

7 The Owl and the Pussy-Cat went to sea
   In a beautiful pea-green boat,
 They took some honey, and plenty of money,
   Wrapped up in a five-pound note.   *The Owl and the Pussy-Cat*

8 They sailed away for a year and a day,
   To the land where the Bong-tree grows,
 And there in a wood a Piggy-wig stood,
   With a ring at the end of his nose.   *Ib*

9 They dined on mince and slices of quince,
   Which they ate with a runcible spoon;
 And hand in hand, on the edge of the sand
   They danced by the light of the moon.   *Ib*

10 He has gone to fish, for his Aunt Jobiska's
 Runcible Cat with crimson whiskers.   *The Pobble who has no Toes*

11 Two old Bachelors were living in one house;
 One caught a Muffin, the other caught a Mouse.   *The Two Old Bachelors*

12 There was an Old Man who said, 'Hush!
 I perceive a young bird in this bush!'
   When they said, 'Is it small?'
   He replied, 'Not at all!
 It is four times as big as the bush!'   *The Old Man Who said 'Hush!'*

13 There was an Old Man with a beard,
 Who said, 'It is just as I feared!—
   Two Owls and a Hen,
   Four Larks and a Wren,
 Have all built their nests in my beard!'   *The Old Man With a Beard*

LEE, Nathaniel, 1655?–1692

1 When Greeks joined Greeks, then was the tug of war.   CLYTUS
The Rival Queens, Act 4, Scene 2

LELAND, Charles Godfrey, 1824–1903

2 Hans Breitmann gife a barty—
Where ish dat barty now ?   *Hans Breitmann's Barty*

LENIN, Nikolai, 1870–1924

3 It is true that liberty is precious—so precious that it must be rationed.
Attributed

LÉVIS, Duc de, 1764–1830

4 *Noblesse oblige.* Nobility imposes its own obligations.   *Maximes et Réflexions*

LEYBOURNE, George, ?–1884

5 O, he flies through the air with the greatest of ease,
This daring young man on the flying trapeze.   *The Man on the Flying
Trapeze*

LINCOLN, Abraham, 1809–1865

6 If the good people in their wisdom shall see fit to keep me in the back-
ground, I have been too familiar with disappointments to be very much
chagrined.   *Speech, 9 March 1832*

7 No man is good enough to govern another man without that other's consent.
Speech, 1854

8 The ballot is stronger than the bullet.   *Speech, 19 May 1856*

9 We cannot be free men if this is, by our national choice, to be a land of
slavery. Those who deny freedom to others, deserve it not for themselves.
Ib

10 That is the issue that will continue in this country when these poor tongues
of Judge Douglas and myself shall be silent. It is the eternal struggle
between these two principles—right and wrong—throughout the world.
They are the two principles that have stood face to face from the beginning
of time, and will ever continue to struggle.   *Speech, 15 Oct. 1858*

11 What is conservatism ? Is it not adherence to the old and tried, against the
new and untried ?   *Speech, 27 Feb. 1860*

12 I intend no modification of my oft-expressed personal wish that all men
everywhere could be free.   *Letter to Horace Greeley, 22 Aug. 1862*

13 That this nation, under God, shall have a new birth of freedom; and that
government of the people, by the people, and for the people, shall not
perish from the earth.   *Address at Dedication of National Cemetery,
Gettysburg, 19 Nov. 1863*

14 An old Dutch farmer, who remarked to a companion once that it was not
best to swap horses in mid-stream.   *Speech, 9 June 1864*

15 With malice toward none; with charity for all; with firmness in the right,
as God gives us to see the right,—let us strive on to finish the work we are
in: to bind up the nation's wounds; to care for him who shall have borne
the battle, and for his widow and his orphan; to do all which may achieve
and cherish a just and lasting peace among ourselves, and with all nations.
Second Inaugural Address, 1865

1 You can fool some of the people all the time and all the people some of the time; but you can't fool all the people all the time. *Attributed*

2 People who like this sort of thing will find this is the sort of thing they like.
Criticism of book

LITVINOV, Maxim, 1876–1951

3 Peace is indivisible. *Speech, Geneva, 1 July 1936*

LIVY, 59 B.C.–A.D. 17

4 *Vae victis.* Woe to the vanquished. *History, 5, 48*

LLOYD, Marie, 1870–1922

5 A little of what you fancy does you good. *Song*

6 I'm one of the ruins that Cromwell knocked about a bit. *Song*

7 Oh, mister porter, what shall I do?
I wanted to go to Birmingham, but they've carried me on to Crewe.
Song, words by Thomas Le Brunn

LLOYD, Robert, 1733–1764

8 Slow and steady wins the race. *The Hare and the Tortoise*

LLOYD GEORGE, David, 1st Earl, 1863–1945

9 What is our task? To make Britain a fit country for heroes to live in.
Speech, 24 Nov. 1918

LONGFELLOW, Henry Wadsworth, 1807–1882

10 I shot an arrow into the air,
It fell to earth I knew not where. *The Arrow and the Song*

11 Thou, too, sail on, O Ship of State!
Sail on, O Union, strong and great!
Humanity with all its fears,
With all the hopes of future years
Is hanging breathless on thy fate! *The Building of the Ship*

12 The shades of night were falling fast,
As through an Alpine village passed
A youth, who bore, 'mid snow and ice,
A banner with the strange device,
Excelsior! *Excelsior*

13 A traveller, by the faithful hound,
Half-buried in the snow was found. *Ib*

14 Tell me not, in mournful numbers,
Life is but an empty dream!
For the soul is dead that slumbers,
And things are not what they seem.

Life is real! Life is earnest!
And the grave is not its goal;
Dust thou art, to dust returnest,
Was not spoken of the soul. *A Psalm of Life*

15 Art is long, and Time is fleeting,
And our hearts, though stout and brave,
Still, like muffled drums, are beating
Funeral marches to the grave. *Ib*

1 Lives of great men all remind us
    We can make our lives sublime,
And, departing, leave behind us
    Footprints on the sands of time.   *A Psalm of Life*

2 Let us, then, be up and doing,
    With a heart for any fate,
Still achieving, still pursuing,
    Learn to labour and to wait.   *Ib*

3 Though the mills of God grind slowly,
        yet they grind exceeding small;
Though with patience He stands waiting,
        with exactness grinds He all.   *Retribution*
                                    (*translation from von Logau*)

4 'Wouldst thou'—so the helmsman answered,—
    'Learn the secret of the sea?
Only those who brave its dangers
    Comprehend its mystery.'   *The Secret of the Sea*

5 From the waterfall he named her,
Minnehaha, Laughing Water.   *The Song of Hiawatha, 4*

6 As unto the bow the cord is,
So unto the man is woman,
Though she bends him, she obeys him,
Though she draws him, yet she follows,
Useless each without the other!   *Ib, 10*

7 Ships that pass in the night, and speak each other in passing,
Only a signal shown and a distant voice in the darkness;
So on the ocean of life we pass and speak one another,
Only a look and a voice, then darkness again and a silence.
            Tales of a Wayside Inn, 3, The Theologian's Tale

8 There was a little girl
Who had a little curl
Right in the middle of her forehead,
And when she was good
She was very, very good,
But when she was bad she was horrid.   *There was a Little Girl*

9 Under a spreading chestnut-tree
    The village smithy stands;
The smith, a mighty man is he,
    With large and sinewy hands.   *The Village Blacksmith*

10   He earns whate'er he can,
And looks the whole world in the face,
    For he owes not any man.   *Ib*

11 Something attempted, something done
    Has earned a night's repose.   *Ib*

12 It was the schooner Hesperus,
    That sailed the wintry sea;
And the skipper had taken his little daughter,
    To bear him company.   *The Wreck of the Hesperus*

LOOS, Anita, 1893—

13 Gentlemen Prefer Blondes.   *Title of Book*

1 Kissing your hand may make you feel very very good but a diamond and safire bracelet lasts forever. *Gentlemen Prefer Blondes, Ch. 4*

LOUIS XIV of France, 1638–1715

2 *L'État c'est moi.* I am the State. *Attributed*

3 *Il n'y a plus de Pyrénées.* The Pyrenees no longer exist. *Attributed*

LOUIS XVIII of France, 1755–1824

4 *L'exactitude est la politesse des rois.* Punctuality is the politeness of kings. *Attributed*

LOVELACE, Richard, 1618–1658

5 Stone walls do not a prison make,
Nor iron bars a cage. *To Althea, from Prison*

6 Tell me not, sweet, I am unkind,
     That from the nunnery
Of thy chaste breast, and quiet mind,
     To war and arms I fly. *To Lucasta, Going to the Wars*

7 I could not love thee, Dear, so much,
     Loved I not Honour more. *Ib*

LOVELL, Maria Anne, 1803–1877

8 Two souls with but a single thought,
Two hearts that beat as one. *Ingomar the Barbarian (translated from German)*

LOVER, Samuel, 1797–1868

9 When once the itch of literature comes over a man, nothing can cure it but the scratching of a pen. *Handy Andy, Ch. 36*

LOWELL, James Russell, 1819–1891

10 An' you've got to get up airly
     Ef you want to take in God. *The Biglow Papers, 1st series, No. 1*

11 I *don't* believe in princerple,
     But O, I *du* in interest. *Ib, No. 6*

12 No man is born into the world, whose work
Is not born with him; there is always work,
And tools to work withal, for those who will:
And blessed are the horny hands of toil! *A Glance Behind the Curtain, 201*

13 The birch, most shy and ladylike of trees. *An Indian Summer Reverie*

14 Once to every man and nation comes the moment to decide,
In the strife of Truth with Falsehood, for the good or evil side. *The Present Crisis*

15 And what is so rare as a day in June?
     Then, if ever, come perfect days;
Then Heaven tries earth if it be in tune,
     And over it softly her warm ear lays. *The Vision of Sir Launfal, Part 1, Prelude*

16 A wise scepticism is the first attribute of a good critic. *Among My Books, Shakespeare Once More*

1 There is no good in arguing with the inevitable. The only argument available with an east wind is to put on your overcoat. *Democracy and Addresses*

LUTHER, Martin, 1483–1546

2 *Wer nicht liebt Wein, Weib und Gesang,*
Der bleibt ein Narr sein Lebelang.
Who loves not wine, woman and song,
Remains a fool his whole life long.   *Attributed*

LYLY, John, 1554?–1606

3 Cupid and my Campaspe play'd
At cards for kisses—Cupid paid.   *Campaspe, 3, 5*

4 O Love! has she done this to thee?
What shall, alas! become of me?   *Ib*

LYTE, Henry Francis, 1793–1847

5 Abide with me; fast falls the eventide;
The darkness deepens; Lord, with me abide!
When other helpers fail, and comforts flee,
Help of the helpless, O abide with me.   *Abide with Me*

6 Change and decay in all around I see;
O thou who changest not, abide with me.   *Ib*

7 I fear no foe with thee at hand to bless;
Ills have no weight, and tears no bitterness.
Where is death's sting? where, grave, thy victory?
I triumph still, if thou abide with me.   *Ib*

8 Praise, my soul, the King of heaven;
To his feet thy tribute bring.   *Praise, my soul, the King of Heaven*

LYTTON, 1st Earl of, see MEREDITH, Owen

MACAULAY, Thomas Babington, 1st Baron, 1800–1859

9 Lars Porsena of Clusium
By the Nine Gods he swore
That the great house of Tarquin
Would suffer wrong no more.   *Lays of Ancient Rome, Horatius, 1*

10 And how can man die better
Than facing fearful odds,
For the ashes of his fathers,
And the temples of his Gods?   *Ib, 27*

11 Now who will stand on either hand,
And keep the bridge with me?   *Ib, 29*

12 Then none was for a party;
Then all were for the state.   *Ib, 32*

13 But those behind cried 'Forward!'
And those before cried 'Back!'   *Ib, 50*

14 Oh, Tiber! father Tiber!
To whom the Romans pray,
A Roman's life, a Roman's arms,
Take thou in charge this day!   *Ib, 59*

1 And even the ranks of Tuscany
Could scarce forbear to cheer. *Lays of Ancient Rome, Horatius, 60*

2 Every schoolboy knows who imprisoned Montezuma, and who strangled
Atahualpa. *Essay in Edinburgh Review, Lord Clive*

3 The English Bible, a book which, if everything else in our language should
perish, would alone suffice to show the whole extent of its beauty and power.
Ib, On John Dryden

4 The gallery in which the reporters sit has become a fourth estate of the
realm. *Ib, Hallam's Constitutional History*

5 The history of England is emphatically the history of progress.
Ib, Sir J. Mackintosh's History of the Revolution

6 We know of no spectacle so ridiculous as the British public in one of its
periodical fits of morality. *Ib, Moore's Life of Lord Byron*

7 The Puritan hated bear-baiting, not because it gave pain to the bear, but
because it gave pleasure to the spectators. *History of England, Ch. 2*

McCRAE, John, 1872–1918

8 In Flanders fields the poppies blow
Between the crosses, row on row. *In Flanders Fields*

9 If ye break faith with us who die
We shall not sleep, though poppies grow
In Flanders fields. *Ib*

MACDONALD, George, 1824–1905

10 Here lie I, Martin Elginbrodde:
Hae mercy o' my soul, Lord God;
As I wad do, were I Lord God,
And ye were Martin Elginbrodde. *David Elginbrod, Book 1, Ch. 13*

MACMAHON, Maurice de, 1808–1893

11 *J'y suis, j'y reste.* Here I am, and here I stay. *Attributed at taking of*
Malakoff, 1855

MACMILLAN, Harold, 1894—

12 Most of our people have never had it so good. Go around the country—go
to the industrial towns, go to the farms—and you will see a state of prosperity
such as we have never had in my lifetime, or indeed ever in the history of
this country. *Speech, Bedford Football Ground, 20 July 1957*

13 The wind of change is blowing through the continent. Whether we like it
or not, this growth of national consciousness is a political fact.
Speech, South African Parliament, Cape Town, 3 Feb. 1960

MACNEICE, Louis, 1907–1963

14 It's no go the merrygoround, it's no go the rickshaw,
All we want is a limousine and a ticket for the peepshow. *Bagpipe Music*

15 It's no go my honey love, it's no go my poppet;
Work your hands from day to day, the winds will blow the profit.
The glass is falling hour by hour, the glass will fall for ever,
But if you break the bloody glass you won't hold up the weather. *Ib*

1 Between the enormous fluted Ionic columns
There seeps from heavily jowled or hawk-like foreign faces
The guttural sorrow of the refugees.   *The British Museum Reading Room*

2 Time was away and somewhere else,
There were two glasses and two chairs
And two people with one pulse
(Somebody stopped the moving stairs):
Time was away and somewhere else.   *Meeting Point*

MAISTRE, Joseph de, 1754–1821

3 *Toute nation a le gouvernement qu'elle mérite.* Every nation has the government it deserves.   *Letter about Russia, 1811*

MALLET, David, 1705?–1765

4 O grant me, Heaven, a middle state,
Neither too humble nor too great;
More than enough, for nature's ends,
With something left to treat my friends.   *Imitation of Horace*

MANDALE, W. R., 19th century

5 Up and down the City Road,
In and out the Eagle,
That's the way the money goes—
Pop goes the weasel!   *Pop Goes the Weasel*

MANNERS, Lord John, see RUTLAND, 7th Duke of

MARIE-ANTOINETTE, Queen of France, 1755–1793

6 *Qu'ils mangent de la brioche.* Let them eat cake.   *Attributed (Similar phrases date back to thirteenth century)*

MARLOWE, Christopher, 1564–1593

7 What doctrine call you this, *Che sera, sera,*
What will be, shall be?   FAUSTUS   *Doctor Faustus*

8 Was this the face that launch'd a thousand ships
And burnt the topless towers of Ilium?
Sweet Helen, make me immortal with a kiss.
Her lips suck forth my soul: see, where it flies!
Come, Helen, come, give me my soul again.
Here will I dwell, for heaven is in these lips,
And all is dross that is not Helena.   FAUSTUS   *Ib*

9 O, thou art fairer than the evening air
Clad in the beauty of a thousand stars.   FAUSTUS   *Ib*

10 Now hast thou but one bare hour to live,
And then thou must be damn'd perpetually!
Stand still, you ever-moving spheres of heaven,
That time may cease, and midnight never come.   FAUSTUS   *Ib*

11 Ugly hell, gape not! come not, Lucifer!
I'll burn my books!   FAUSTUS   *Ib*

1 Cut is the branch that might have grown full straight,
  And burned is Apollo's laurel-bough,
  That sometime grew within this learned man.   CHORUS   *Doctor Faustus*

2 My men, like satyrs grazing on the lawns,
  Shall with their goat-feet dance an antic hay.   GAVESTON
                                                            Edward the Second

3 I count religion but a childish toy,
  And hold there is no sin but ignorance.   MACHIAVEL   *The Jew of Malta,*
                                                                Prologue

4 And, as their wealth increaseth, so inclose
  Infinite riches in a little room.   BARABAS   *Ib, Act 1*

5 FRIAR BARNARDINE: Thou hast committed—
          BARABAS: Fornication: but that was in another country;
                    And beside the wench is dead.   *Ib, Act 4*

6 Jigging veins of rhyming mother-wits.   *Tamburlaine the Great, Pt. 1,*
                                                                Prologue

7 Zenocrate, lovelier than the love of Jove,
  Brighter than is the silver Rhodope,
  Fairer than whitest snow on Scythian hills.   TAMBURLAINE
                                                            Ib, Act 1, Scene 2

8 Accurs'd be he that first invented war.   MYCETES   *Ib, Act 2, Scene 4*

9 Is it not passing brave to be a king,
  And ride in triumph through Persepolis?   TAMBURLAINE
                                                            Ib, Act 2, Scene 5

10 Nature, that fram'd us of four elements
   Warring within our breasts for regiment,
   Doth teach us all to have aspiring minds:
   Our souls, whose faculties can comprehend
   The wondrous architecture of the world,
   And measure every wandering planet's course,
   Still climbing after knowledge infinite,
   And always moving as the restless spheres,
   Will us to wear ourselves, and never rest,
   Until we reach the ripest fruit of all,
   That perfect bliss and sole felicity,
   The sweet fruition of an earthly crown.   TAMBURLAINE
                                                            Ib, Act 2, Scene 7

11 Ah, fair Zenocrate!—divine Zenocrate!
   Fair is too foul an epithet for thee.   TAMBURLAINE   *Ib, Act 5, Scene 1*

12 Holla, ye pamper'd jades of Asia!
   What, can ye draw but twenty miles a-day?   TAMBURLAINE
                                                            Ib, Pt. 2, Act 4, Scene 3

13 Tamburlaine, the scourge of God, must die.   TAMBURLAINE
                                                            Ib, Act 5, Scene 3

14 It lies not in our power to love or hate,
   For will in us is over-rul'd by fate.   *Hero and Leander*

15 Where both deliberate, the love is slight:
   Who ever lov'd, that lov'd not at first sight?   *Ib*

1 Come live with me, and be my love;
  And we will all the pleasures prove
  That hills and valleys, dales and fields,
  Woods or steepy mountain yields.   *The Passionate Shepherd to his Love*

MARQUIS, Donald Robert, 1878–1937

2 its cheerio
  my deario that
  pulls a lady through   *archy and mehitabel, cheerio my deario*

3 toujours gai archy
  toujours gai   *Ib*

4   so unlucky
  that he runs into accidents
  which started out to happen
  to somebody else   *archy's life of mehitabel, archy says*

MARRYAT, Frederick, 1792–1848

5 If you please, ma'am, it was a very little one. [*Of her illegitimate baby*]
    Midshipman Easy, Ch. 3

6 I never knows the children. It's just six of one and half-a-dozen of the other.
    The Pirate, Ch. 4

7 Every man paddle his own canoe.   *Settlers in Canada, Ch. 8*

MARVELL, Andrew, 1621–1678

8 Where the remote Bermudas ride,
  In the ocean's bosom unespied.   *Bermudas, 1*

9 Echo beyond the Mexique Bay.   *Ib, 36*

10 And all the way, to guide their chime,
  With falling oars they kept the time.   *Ib, 39*

11 Had we but world enough, and time,
  This coyness, lady, were no crime.   *To His Coy Mistress, 1*

12 My vegetable love should grow
  Vaster than empires and more slow.   *Ib, 11*

13 But at my back I always hear
  Time's winged chariot hurrying near;
  And yonder all before us lie
  Deserts of vast eternity.   *Ib, 21*

14 The grave's a fine and private place,
  But none, I think, do there embrace.   *Ib, 31*

15 Thus, though we cannot make our sun
  Stand still, yet we will make him run.   *Ib, 45*

16 My Love is of a birth as rare
  As 'tis, for object, strange and high;
  It was begotten by Despair
  Upon Impossibility.   *The Definition of Love, 1*

17 Therefore the love which us doth bind,
  But fate so enviously debars,
  Is the conjunction of the mind,
  And opposition of the stars.   *Ib, 29*

1 Annihilating all that's made
  To a green thought in a green shade.   *The Garden, 47*

2 Casting the body's vest aside,
  My soul into the boughs does glide.   *Ib, 51*

3 So restless Cromwell could not cease
  In the inglorious arts of peace.   *An Horatian Ode upon Cromwell's Return*
                                                              from Ireland, 9

4 He nothing common did or mean,
  Upon that memorable scene.
      But with his keener eye
      The axe's edge did try.   [*Charles 1*]   *Ib, 57*

5 Who can foretell for what high cause
  This darling of the Gods was born?   *The Picture of Little T.C. in a*
                                          Prospect of Flowers, 9

6 Gather the flowers, but spare the buds.   *Ib, 35*

MARX, Karl, 1818–1883

7 From each according to his abilities, to each according to his needs.
                                   Criticism of the Gotha Programme

8 Religion . . . is the opium of the people.   *Criticism of the Hegelian*
                                        Philosophy of Right, Introduction

9 The ruling ideas of each age have ever been the ideas of its ruling class.
                                   Manifesto of the Communist Party, 2

10 The workers have nothing to lose but their chains. They have a world to
   gain. Workers of the world, unite.   *Ib, 4*

MARY TUDOR, Queen of England, 1516–1558

11 When I am dead and opened, you shall find 'Calais' lying in my heart.
                                   Holinshed's Chronicles, 3, 1160

MASEFIELD, John, 1878—

12 But the loveliest things of beauty God ever has showed to me,
   Are her voice, and her hair, and eyes, and the dear red curve of her lips.
                                                              Beauty

13 Quinquireme of Nineveh from distant Ophir
   Rowing home to haven in sunny Palestine,
   With a cargo of ivory,
   And apes and peacocks,
   Sandalwood, cedarwood, and sweet white wine.   *Cargoes*

14 Dirty British coaster with a salt-caked smoke-stack
   Butting through the Channel in the mad March days.   *Ib*

15 I must down to the seas again, to the lonely sea and the sky,
   And all I ask is a tall ship and a star to steer her by. *Sea Fever*

16 I must down to the seas again, for the call of the running tide
   Is a wild call and a clear call that may not be denied.   *Ib*

17 I must down to the seas again, to the vagrant gypsy life,
   To the gull's way and the whale's way where the wind's like a whetted knife;
   And all I ask is a merry yarn from a laughing fellow-rover,
   And quiet sleep and a sweet dream when the long trick's over. *Ib*

1 It is good to be out on the road, and going one knows not where,
Going through meadow and village, one knows not whither nor why.

Tewkesbury Road

MASSINGER, Philip, 1583–1640

2 He that would govern others, first should be
The master of himself. *The Bondman, Act 1, Scene 3*

3 A New Way to Pay Old Debts. *Title of Play*

MAUGHAM, William Somerset, 1874—

4 People ask you for criticism, but they only want praise.

Of Human Bondage, Ch. 50

5 Impropriety is the soul of wit. *The Moon and Sixpence, Ch. 4*

6 I would sooner read a time-table or a catalogue than nothing at all. They
are much more entertaining than half the novels that are written.

The Summing Up

7 Life is too short to do anything for oneself that one can pay others to do for
one. *Ib*

MEARNS, Hughes, 1875—

8 As I was going up the stair
I met a man who wasn't there.
He wasn't there again today.
I wish, I wish he'd stay away. *The Psychoed*

MELBOURNE, William Lamb, 2nd Viscount, 1779–1848

9 I like the Garter; there is no damned merit in it.

On the Order of the Garter

10 Things have come to a pretty pass when religion is allowed to invade the
sphere of private life. *Attributed*

11 I wish that I was as cocksure of anything as Tom Macaulay is of everything.

Attributed

MENCKEN, Henry Louis, 1880–1956

12 All successful newspapers are ceaselessly querulous and bellicose. They
never defend anyone or anything if they can help it; if the job is forced
upon them, they tackle it by denouncing someone or something else.

Prejudices, First Series

13 The average schoolmaster is and always must be essentially an ass, for how
can one imagine an intelligent man engaging in so puerile an avocation?

Ib, Third Series

14 I've made it a rule never to drink by daylight and never to refuse a drink
after dark. *Quoted in New York Post, 18 Sept. 1945*

MEREDITH, George, 1828–1909

15 Cynicism is intellectual dandyism. *The Egoist, Ch. 7*

16 The actors are, it seems, the usual three:
Husband, and wife, and lover. *Modern Love, Stanza 25*

1   We'll sit contentedly
And eat our pot of honey on the grave.   *Modern Love, Stanza 29*

2 Ah, what a dusty answer gets the soul
When hot for certainties in this our life!   *Ib, Stanza 50*

3 I expect that Woman will be the last thing civilized by Man.
      The Ordeal of Richard Feverel, Ch. 1

4 Kissing don't last: cookery do!   *Ib, Ch. 28*

MEREDITH, Owen (Earl of Lytton), 1831–1891

5 Genius does what it must, and Talent does what it can.   *Last Words of a*
      Sensitive Second-Rate Poet

MERRITT, Dixon Lanier, 1879–1954

6 A wonderful bird is the pelican,
His beak holds more than his belican.
     He can take in his beak
     Enough food for a week,
But I'm damned if I know how the helican!   *The Pelican*

MIKES, George, 1912—

7 On the Continent people have good food; in England people have good
table manners.   *How to be an Alien*

8 Continental people have sex life; the English have hot-water bottles.   *Ib*

9 An Englishman, even if he is alone, forms an orderly queue of one.   *Ib*

MILL, John Stuart, 1806–1873

10 All good things which exist are the fruits of originality.   *On Liberty, Ch. 3*

11 The worth of a State in the long run is the worth of the individuals composing it.   *Ib*

12 That so few now dare to be eccentric marks the chief danger of the time.
      Ib

MILLAY, Edna St. Vincent, 1892–1950

13 My candle burns at both ends;
     It will not last the night;
But, oh, my foes, and oh, my friends—
     It gives a lovely light.   *Figs from Thistles, First Fig*

14 What lips my lips have kissed, and where, and why,
I have forgotten, and what arms have lain
Under my head till morning; but the rain
Is full of ghosts tonight, that tap and sigh
Upon the glass and listen for reply.   *Sonnet, What Lips My Lips Have*
      Kissed

15 I only know that summer sang in me
A little while, that in me sings no more.   *Ib*

MILLIGAN, Spike, 1918—

16 'Do you come here often?'
     'Only in the mating season.'   *B.B.C. programme, The Goon Show, with*
     Spike Milligan, Harry Secombe and Peter Sellers

MILNE, Alan Alexander, 1882–1956

1 The more it snows
        (Tiddely pom),
   The more it goes
        (Tiddely pom),
   The more it goes
        (Tiddely pom),
     On snowing.
   And nobody knows
        (Tiddely pom),
   How cold my toes
        (Tiddely pom),
   How cold my toes
        (Tiddely pom),
     Are growing.   POOH   *The House at Pooh Corner, Ch. 1*

2 Tiggers don't like honey.   TIGGER   *Ib, Ch. 2*

3 'Climbing trees is what they do best,' said Tigger. 'Much better than Poohs.'
                                                          Ib, Ch. 4

4 King John was not a good man—
        He had his little ways.   *Now We Are Six, King John's Christmas*

5 No one can tell me,
     Nobody knows,
   Where the wind comes from,
     Where the wind goes.   *Ib. Wind on the Hill*

6 They're changing guard at Buckingham Palace—
   Christopher Robin went down with Alice.
   Alice is marrying one of the guard.
   'A soldier's life is terrible hard,'
                        Says Alice.   *When We Were Very Young,*
                                        Buckingham Palace

7 'Do you think the King knows all about me?'
   'Sure to, dear, but it's time for tea,'
                        Says Alice.   *Ib*

8 James James
   Morrison Morrison
   Weatherby George Dupree
   Took great
   Care of his Mother,
   Though he was only three.   *Ib, Disobedience*

9 You must never go down to the end of the town, if you don't go down with
     me.   *Ib*

10 *What* is the matter with Mary Jane?
   I've promised her sweets and a ride in the train,
   And I've begged her to stop for a bit and explain—
   What *is* the matter with Mary Jane?   *Ib, Rice Pudding*

11 The King asked
    The Queen, and
    The Queen asked
    The Dairymaid:
    'Could we have some butter for
    The Royal slice of bread?'   *Ib, The King's Breakfast*

1 I do like a little bit of butter to my bread!　　*When We Were Very Young,*
　　　　　　　　　　　　　　　　　　　　　　　The King's Breakfast

2 Little Boy kneels at the foot of the bed,
　Droops on the little hands little gold head.
　Hush! Hush! Whisper who dares!
　Christopher Robin is saying his prayers.　　　　　　*Ib, Vespers*

3 Isn't it funny
　How a bear likes honey?
　Buzz! Buzz! Buzz!
　I wonder why he does?　　　　　　　　　　*Winnie-the-Pooh, Ch. 1*

4 'Well', said Owl, 'the customary procedure in such cases is as follows.'
　'What does Crustimoney Proseedcake mean?' said Pooh. 'For I am a Bear
　of Very Little Brain, and long words Bother me.'　　　　　*Ib, Ch. 4*

5 Eeyore, the old grey Donkey, stood by the side of the stream, and looked
　at himself in the water.
　'Pathetic,' he said. 'That's wat it is, Pathetic.'　　　　　*Ib, Ch. 6*

6 Cottleston, Cottleston, Cottleston Pie.
　A fly can't bird, but a bird can fly.
　Ask me a riddle and I reply:
　'Cottleston, Cottleston, Cottleston Pie.'　　POOH　　　　　*Ib*

7 Time for a little something.　　POOH　　　　　　　　　　*Ib*

8 My spelling is Wobbly. It's good spelling but it Wobbles, and letters get in
　the wrong places.　　POOH　　　　　　　　　　　　*Ib*

9 A Useful Pot to put things in.　　POOH　　　　　　　　*Ib*

10 Sing Ho! for the life of a Bear.　　POOH　　　　　*Ib, Ch. 8*

11 3 Cheers for Pooh!
　(For Who?)
　For Pooh—
　(Why What did he do?)
　I thought you knew;
　He saved his friend from a wetting.　　ANXIOUS POOH SONG　　*Ib, Ch. 10*

MILTON, John, 1608–1674

12 Blest pair of Sirens, pledges of Heaven's joy,
　Sphere-born harmonious sisters, Voice and Verse.　　*At a Solemn Music, 1*

13 Before the starry threshold of Jove's court
　My mansion is.　　ATTENDANT SPIRIT　　　　　　*Comus: A Mask, 1*

14 Above the smoke and stir of this dim spot
　Which men call Earth.　　ATTENDANT SPIRIT　　　　　*Ib, 5*

15 What hath night to do with sleep?　　COMUS　　　　　*Ib, 122*

16 Come, knit hands, and beat the ground
　In a light fantastic round.　　COMUS　　　　　　　*Ib, 143*

17 'Tis chastity, my brother, chastity:
　She that has that, is clad in complete steel.　　ELDER BROTHER　　*Ib, 420*

18 How charming is divine Philosophy!
　Not harsh and crabbed, as dull fools suppose.
　But musical as is Apollo's lute,
　And a perpetual feast of nectared sweets,
　Where no crude surfeit reigns.　　SECOND BROTHER　　　*Ib, 476*

1   That power
  Which erring men call Chance.   ELDER BROTHER   *Comus: A Mask, 587*

2 Beauty is Nature's coin; must not be hoarded,
   But must be current.   COMUS   *Ib, 739*

3 Sabrina fair,
       Listen where thou art sitting
   Under the glassy, cool, translucent wave,
       In twisted braids of lilies knitting
   The loose train of thy amber-dropping hair.   ATTENDANT SPIRIT *Ib, 859*

4   Mortals, that would follow me,
   Love Virtue, she alone is free.
   She can teach ye how to climb
   Higher than the sphery chime;
   Or, if Virtue feeble were,
   Heaven itself would stoop to her.   ATTENDANT SPIRIT   *Ib, 1018*

5 Hence, vain deluding Joys,
       The brood of Folly without father bred!   *Il Penseroso, 1*

6 But, hail! thou Goddess sage and holy
   Hail, divinest Melancholy!   *Ib, 11*

7 Thy rapt soul sitting in thine eyes.   *Ib, 40*

8 Sweet bird, that shunn'st the noise of folly,
   Most musical, most melancholy!   *Ib, 61*

9 Where glowing embers through the room
   Teach light to counterfeit a gloom,
   Far from all resort of mirth,
   Save the cricket on the hearth.   *Ib, 79*

10 Where more is meant than meets the ear.   *Ib, 120*

11 And storied windows richly dight,
   Casting a dim religious light.   *Ib, 159*

12 Till old experience do attain
   To something like prophetic strain.   *Ib, 173*

13 These pleasures, Melancholy, give;
   And I with thee will choose to live.   *Ib, 175*

14 Hence, loathed Melancholy,
       Of Cerberus and blackest Midnight born
   In Stygian cave forlorn
       'Mongst horrid shapes, and shrieks, and sights unholy!   *L'Allegro, 1*

15 So buxom, blithe, and debonair.   *Ib, 24*

16 Haste thee, Nymph, and bring with thee
   Jest, and youthful Jollity,
   Quips and Cranks and wanton Wiles,
   Nods and Becks and wreathed Smiles.   *Ib, 25*

17 Sport that wrinkled Care derides,
   And Laughter holding both his sides.
   Come, and trip it as you go
   On the light fantastic toe.   *Ib, 31*

18 The mountain-nymph, sweet Liberty.   *Ib, 36*

1 And, if I give thee honour due,
  Mirth, admit me of thy crew,
  To live with her, and live with thee,
  In unreproved pleasures free.   *L'Allegro, 37*

2 To hear the lark begin his flight,
  And, singing, startle the dull night,
  From his watch-tower in the skies,
  Till the dappled dawn doth rise;
  Then to come, in spite of sorrow,
  And at my window bid good morrow,
  Through the sweet-briar or the vine,
  Or the twisted eglantine.   *Ib, 41*

3 While the ploughman, near at hand,
  Whistles o'er the furrowed land,
  And the milkmaid singeth blithe,
  And the mower whets his scythe,
  And every shepherd tells his tale
  Under the hawthorn in the dale.   *Ib, 63*

4 Then to the spicy nut-brown ale.   *Ib, 100*

5 Towered cities please us then,
  And the busy hum of men.   *Ib, 117*

6   Store of ladies, whose bright eyes
  Rain influence, and judge the prize
  Of wit or arms.   *Ib, 121*

7 Such sights as youthful poets dream
  On summer eves by haunted stream.   *Ib, 129*

8 Or sweetest Shakespeare, Fancy's child,
  Warble his native wood-notes wild.   *Ib, 133*

9 Untwisting all the chains that tie
  The hidden soul of harmony.   *Ib, 143*

10 Such strains as would have won the ear
  Of Pluto, to have quite set free
  His half-regained Eurydice.   *Ib, 148*

11   These delights if thou canst give,
  Mirth, with thee I mean to live.   *Ib, 151*

12 Yet once more, O ye laurels, and once more,
  Ye myrtles brown, with ivy never sere,
  I come to pluck your berries harsh and crude,
  And with forced fingers rude
  Shatter your leaves before the mellowing year.   *Lycidas, 1*

13   He knew
  Himself to sing, and build the lofty rhyme.   *Ib, 10*

14   But, oh! the heavy change, now thou art gone,
  Now thou art gone, and never must return!   *Ib, 37*

15   Alas! what boots it with incessant care
  To tend the homely, slighted, shepherd's trade,
  And strictly meditate the thankless Muse?   *Ib, 64*

16 To sport with Amaryllis in the shade,
  Or with the tangles of Neaera's hair?   *Ib, 68*

1 Fame is the spur that the clear spirit doth raise
(That last infirmity of noble mind)
To scorn delights, and live laborious days.   *Lycidas, 70*

2 Fame is no plant that grows on mortal soil.   *Ib, 78*

3 Blind mouths! that scarce themselves know how to hold
A sheep-hook.   *Ib, 119*

4 And, when they list, their lean and flashy songs
Grate on their scrannel pipes of wretched straw;
The hungry sheep look up, and are not fed,
But, swoln with wind and the rank mist they draw,
Rot inwardly, and foul contagion spread.   *Ib, 123*

5 Bring the rathe primrose that forsaken dies.   *Ib, 142*

6 At last he rose, and twitched his mantle blue:
To-morrow to fresh woods, and pastures new.   *Ib, 192*

7 This is the month, and this the happy morn.   *On the Morning of*
                                                       Christ's Nativity, 1

8 It was the winter wild,
While the Heaven-born Child
All meanly wrapt in the rude manger lies.   *Ib, 29*

9 Time will run back and fetch the age of gold.   *Ib, 135*

10 So when the sun in bed,
Curtained with cloudy red,
Pillows his chin upon an orient wave.   *Ib, 229*

11 What needs my Shakespeare for his honoured bones,
The labour of an age in piled stones?   *On Shakespeare, 1*

12 Dear son of memory, great heir of fame,
What need'st thou such weak witness of thy name?   *Ib, 5*

13 Kings for such a tomb would wish to die.   *Ib, 16*

14 Rhyme being no necessary adjunct or true ornament of poem or good verse,
in longer works especially, but the invention of a barbarous age, to set off
wretched matter and lame metre.   *Paradise Lost, Preface, The Verse*

15 Of Man's first disobedience, and the fruit
Of that forbidden tree, whose mortal taste
Brought death into the World, and all our woe,
With loss of Eden, till one greater Man
Restore us, and regain the blissful seat,
Sing, Heavenly Muse.   *Ib, Book 1, 1*

16 Things unattempted yet in prose or rhyme.   *Ib, 1, 16*

17   What in me is dark
Illumine, what is low raise and support;
That, to the height of this great argument,
I may assert Eternal Providence,
And justify the ways of God to men.   *Ib, 1, 22*

18   What though the field be lost?
All is not lost—the unconquerable will,
And study of revenge, immortal hate,
And courage never to submit or yield:
And what is else not to be overcome?   *Ib, 1, 105*

1   To be weak is miserable,
Doing or suffering.   *Paradise Lost, Book, 1, 157*

2 And out of good still to find means of evil.   *Ib, 1, 165*

3 What reinforcement we may gain from hope,
If not, what resolution from despair.   *Ib, 1, 190*

4   Farewell, happy fields,
Where joy for ever dwells! Hail, horrors! hail.   *Ib, 1, 249*

5 A mind not to be changed by place or time.
The mind is its own place, and in itself
Can make a Heaven of Hell, a Hell of Heaven.   *Ib, 1, 253*

6 To reign is worth ambition, though in Hell:
Better to reign in Hell than serve in Heaven.   *Ib, 1, 262*

7 Awake, arise, or be for ever fallen!   *Ib, 1, 330*

8   And when night
Darkens the streets, then wander forth the sons
Of Belial, flown with insolence and wine.   *Ib, 1, 500*

9 Th' imperial ensign; which, full high advanced,
Shone like a meteor streaming to the wind.   *Ib, 1, 536*

10 A shout that tore Hell's concave, and beyond
Frighted the reign of Chaos and old Night.   *Ib, 1, 542*

11   His form had yet not lost
All her original brightness, nor appeared
Less than Archangel ruined, and the excess
Of glory obscured.   *Ib, 1, 591*

12 Tears, such as Angels weep, burst forth.   *Ib, 1, 620*

13   Who overcomes
By force hath overcome but half his foe.   *Ib, 1, 648*

14   From morn
To noon he fell, from noon to dewy eve,
A summer's day, and with the setting sun
Dropped from the zenith, like a falling star.   *Ib, 1, 742*

15 High on a throne of royal state, which far
Outshone the wealth of Ormus and of Ind,
Or where the gorgeous East with richest hand
Showers on her kings barbaric pearl and gold,
Satan exalted sat, by merit raised
To that bad eminence.   *Ib, Book 2, 1*

16 My sentence is for open war. Of wiles,
More unexpert, I boast not.   *Ib, 2, 51*

17   In our proper motion we ascend
Up to our native seat; descent and fall
To us is adverse.   *Ib, 2, 75*

18   Though his tongue
Dropped manna, and could make the worse appear
The better reason.   *Ib, 2, 112*

19   For who would lose,
Though full of pain, this intellectual being,
Those thoughts that wander through eternity,

To perish rather, swallowed up and lost
In the wide womb of uncreated Night,
Devoid of sense and motion?   *Paradise Lost, Book, 2, 146*

1 Unrespited, unpitied, unreprieved,
   Ages of hopeless end.   *Ib, 2, 185*

2 Our torments also may, in length of time,
   Become our elements.   *Ib, 2, 274*

3   With grave
   Aspect he rose, and in his rising seemed
   A pillar of state; deep on his front engraven
   Deliberation sat, and public care;
   And princely counsel in his face yet shone,
   Majestic, though in ruin.   *Ib, 2, 300*

4   Another World, the happy seat
   Of some new race, called Man, about this time
   To be created like to us, though less
   In power and excellence.   *Ib, 2, 347*

5   Long is the way
   And hard that out of Hell leads up to light.   *Ib, 2, 432*

6 Others apart sat on a hill retired,
   In thoughts more elevate, and reasoned high
   Of Providence, Foreknowledge, Will, and Fate—
   Fixed fate, free will, foreknowledge absolute—
   And found no end, in wandering mazes lost.   *Ib, 2, 557*

7   The other Shape—
   If shape it might be called that shape had none.   *Ib, 2, 666*

8 For Hot, Cold, Moist, and Dry, four champions fierce,
   Strive here for mastery.   *Ib, 2, 898*

9 Hail, holy Light, offspring of Heaven first-born!   *Ib, Book 3, 1*

10   Thus with the year
    Seasons return; but not to me returns
    Day, or the sweet approach of even or morn,
    Or sight of vernal bloom, or summer's rose,
    Or flocks, or herds, or human face divine;
    But cloud instead and ever-during dark
    Surrounds me.   *Ib, 3, 40*

11 Into a Limbo large and broad, since called
    The Paradise of Fools; to few unknown.   *Ib, 3, 495*

12   At whose sight all the stars
    Hide their diminished heads.   *Ib, Book 4, 34*

13 Me miserable! which way shall I fly
    Infinite wrath and infinite despair?
    Which way I fly is Hell; myself am Hell;
    And, in the lowest deep, a lower deep
    Still threat'ning to devour me opens wide,
    To which the Hell I suffer seems a Heaven.   *Ib, 4, 73*

14 So farewell hope, and, with hope, farewell fear,
    Farewell remorse! All good to me is lost;
    Evil, be thou my Good.   *Ib, 4, 108*

1 Thence up he flew, and on the Tree of Life,
The middle tree and highest there that grew,
Sat like a cormorant. *Paradise Lost, Book 4, 194*

2 A Heaven on Earth. *Ib, 4, 208*

3 For contemplation he and valour formed,
For softness she and sweet attractive grace;
He for God only, she for God in him. *Ib, 4, 297*

4 Adam, the goodliest man of men since born
His sons; the fairest of her daughters Eve. *Ib, 4, 323*

5 Imparadised in one another's arms. *Ib, 4, 506*

6 Now came still Evening on, and Twilight grey
Had in her sober livery all things clad. *Ib, 4, 598*

7 God is thy law, thou mine: to know no more
Is woman's happiest knowledge, and her praise.
With thee conversing, I forget all time. *Ib, 4, 637*

8 Hail, wedded Love, mysterious law, true source
Of human offspring. *Ib, 4, 750*

9 Not to know me argues yourselves unknown. *Ib, 4, 830*

10 Abashed the Devil stood,
And felt how awful goodness is, and saw
Virtue in her shape how lovely. *Ib, 4, 846*

11 But wherefore thou alone? Wherefore with thee
Came not all Hell broke loose? *Ib, 4, 917*

12 Now Morn, her rosy steps in th' eastern clime
Advancing, sowed the earth with orient pearl. *Ib, Book 5, 1*

13 Good, the more
Communicated, more abundant grows. *Ib, 5, 71*

14 Best image of myself, and dearer half. *Ib, 5, 95*

15 Him first, him last, him midst, and without end. *Ib, 5, 165*

16 Nor jealousy
Was understood, the injured lover's hell. *Ib, 5, 449*

17 Midnight brought on the dusky hour
Friendliest to sleep and silence. *Ib, 5, 667*

18 Among the faithless, faithful only he. *Ib, 5, 897*

19 Servant of God, well done! Well hast thou fought
The better fight, who single hast maintained
Against revolted multitudes the cause
Of truth, in word mightier than they in arms. *Ib, Book 6, 29*

20 More safe I sing with mortal voice, unchanged
To hoarse or mute, though fallen on evil days,
On evil days though fallen, and evil tongues;
In darkness, and with dangers compassed round,
And solitude. *Ib, Book 7, 24*

21 God saw the light was good;
And light from darkness by the hemisphere
Divided: light the Day, and darkness Night,
He named. *Ib, 7, 249*

1 The Angel ended, and in Adam's ear
  So charming left his voice that he a while
  Thought him still speaking, still stood fixed to hear. *Paradise Lost, Book 8, 1*

2   To know
  That which before us lies in daily life,
  Is the prime wisdom.   *Ib, 8, 192*

3   In solitude
  What happiness ? who can enjoy alone,
  Or, all enjoying, what contentment find ?   *Ib, 8, 364*

4 Accuse not Nature! she hath done her part;
  Do thou but thine.   *Ib, 8, 561*

5 My unpremeditated verse.   *Ib, Book 9, 24*

6 Since first this subject for heroic song
  Pleased me, long choosing and beginning late.   *Ib, 9, 25*

7   Revenge, at first though sweet,
  Bitter ere long back on itself recoils.   *Ib, 9, 171*

8 For solitude sometimes is best society,
  And short retirement urges sweet return.   *Ib, 9, 249*

9 As one who, long in populous city pent,
  Where houses thick and sewers annoy the air.   *Ib, 9, 445*

10 O fairest of creation, last and best
   Of all God's works, creature in whom excelled
   Whatever can to sight or thought be formed,
   Holy, divine, good, amiable, or sweet!
   How art thou lost! how on a sudden lost,
   Defaced, deflowered, and now to death devote!   *Ib, 9, 896*

11   Yet I shall temper so
   Justice with mercy as may illustrate most
   Them fully satisfied, and thee appease.   *Ib, Book 10, 77*

12 A dismal universal hiss, the sound
   Of public scorn.   *Ib, 10, 508*

13 Demoniac frenzy, moping melancholy,
   And moon-struck madness.   *Ib, Book 11, 485*

14 Nor love thy life, nor hate; but what thou liv'st
   Live well; how long or short permit to Heaven.   *Ib, 11, 553*

15 A bevy of fair women, richly gay
   In gems and wanton dress.   *Ib, 11, 582*

16 An olive-leaf he brings, pacific sign.   *Ib, 11, 860*

17 In me is no delay; with thee to go
   Is to stay here; without thee here to stay
   Is to go hence unwilling; thou to me
   Art all things under Heaven, all places thou,
   Who for my wilful crime art banished hence.   *Ib, Book 12, 615*

18 The world was all before them, where to choose
   Their place of rest, and Providence their guide:
   They, hand in hand, with wandering steps and slow,
   Through Eden took their solitary way.   *Ib, 12, 646*

1   Most men admire
Virtue who follow not her lore.   *Paradise Regained, Book 1, 482*

2   Beauty stands
In the admiration only of weak minds
Led captive.   *Ib, Book 2, 220*

3   The childhood shows the man,
As morning shows the day.   *Ib, Book 4, 220*

4 The first and wisest of them all professed
To know this only, that he nothing knew.   *Ib, 4, 293*

5 Deep-versed in books and shallow in himself.   *Ib, 4, 327*

6   He, unobserved,
Home to his mother's house private returned.   *Ib, 4, 638*

7 Let us with a gladsome mind,
Praise the Lord, for He is kind,
    For His mercies ay endure,
    Ever faithful, ever sure.   *Psalm 136*

8 A little onward lend thy guiding hand
To these dark steps, a little further on.   SAMSON   *Samson Agonistes, 1*

9 Ask for this great deliverer now, and find him
Eyeless in Gaza at the mill with slaves.   SAMSON   *Ib, 40*

10 O dark, dark, dark, amid the blaze of noon,
Irrecoverably dark, total eclipse,
Without all hope of day!   SAMSON   *Ib, 80*

11 The Sun to me is dark
And silent as the Moon,
When she deserts the night,
Hid in her vacant interlunar cave.   SAMSON   *Ib, 86*

12   Wisest men
Have erred, and by bad women been deceived.   CHORUS   *Ib, 210*

13 Just are the ways of God,
And justifiable to men,
Unless there be who think not God at all.   CHORUS   *Ib, 293*

14   Let me here,
As I deserve, pay on my punishment,
And expiate, if possible, my crime,
Shameful garrulity.   SAMSON   *Ib, 488*

15   But who is this, what thing of sea or land?
Female of sex it seems,
That, so bedecked, ornate, and gay,
Comes this way sailing,
Like a stately ship
Of Tarsus, bound for th' isles
Of Javan or Gadire,
With all her bravery on, and tackle trim,
Sails filled, and streamers waving,
Courted by all the winds that hold them play.   CHORUS   *Ib, 710*

16 Out, out, hyaena! These are thy wonted arts,
And arts of every woman false like thee.   SAMSON   *Ib, 748*

1   Weakness is thy excuse,
And I believe it; weakness to resist
Philistian gold.   SAMSON   *Samson Agonistes, 829*

2   At length, that grounded maxim,
So rife and celebrated in the mouths
Of wisest men, that to the public good
Private respects must yield, with grave authority
Took full possession of me, and prevailed.   DALILA   *Ib, 865*

3 In argument with men a woman ever
Goes by the worse, whatever be her cause.   DALILA   *Ib, 903*

4 Fame, if not double-faced, is double-mouthed,
And with contrary blast proclaims most deeds.   DALILA   *Ib, 971*

5 Yet beauty, though injurious, hath strange power,
After offence returning, to regain
Love once possessed.   CHORUS   *Ib, 1003*

6 He's gone, and who knows how he may report
Thy words by adding fuel to the flame?   CHORUS   *Ib, 1350*

7 All is best, though we oft doubt
What th' unsearchable dispose
Of Highest Wisdom brings about.   CHORUS   *Ib, 1745*

8 His servants he, with new acquist
Of true experience from this great event,
With peace and consolation hath dismissed,
And calm of mind, all passion spent.   CHORUS   *Ib, 1755*

9 How soon hath Time, the subtle thief of youth,
    Stolen on his wing my three-and-twentieth year!   *Sonnet, On being
                                    arrived at the age of twenty-three*

10 When I consider how my light is spent,
Ere half my days in this dark world and wide,
And that one talent which is death to hide
Lodged with me useless.   *Sonnet, On his Blindness*

11   God doth not need
Either man's work or his own gifts. Who best
Bear his mild yoke, they serve him best: his state
Is kingly: thousands at his bidding speed,
And post o'er land and ocean without rest;
They also serve who only stand and wait.   *Ib*

12 New Presbyter is but old Priest writ large.   *Sonnet, On the new Forcers
                                    of Conscience under the Long Parliament*

13   Peace hath her victories
No less renowned than War.   *Sonnet, To the Lord General Cromwell,
                                                        May 1652*

14 For what can war but endless war still breed?   *Sonnet, On the Lord
                                                    General Fairfax*

15 Fly envious Time, till thou run out thy race,
Call on the lazy, leaden-stepping hours.   *Sonnet, On Time*

16 Methought I saw my late espoused saint.   *Sonnet, On his deceased wife*

1 He who would not be frustrate of his hope to write well hereafter in laudable things ought himself to be a true poem.   *Apology for Smectymnuus*

2 Who kills a man kills a reasonable creature, God's image; but he who destroys a good book, kills reason itself, kills the image of God, as it were in the eye.   *Areopagitica*

3 A good book is the precious life-blood of a master spirit, embalmed and treasured up on purpose to a life beyond life.   *Ib*

4 I cannot praise a fugitive and cloistered virtue, unexercised and unbreathed, that never sallies out and sees her adversary, but slinks out of the race, where that immortal garland is to be run for, not without dust and heat. *Ib*

5 Our sage and serious poet Spenser, whom I dare be known to think a better teacher than Scotus or Aquinas.   *Ib*

6 God sure esteems the growth and completing of one virtuous person more than the restraint of ten vicious.   *Ib*

7 God is decreeing to begin some new and great period in His Church, even to the reforming of Reformation itself: what does He then but reveal Himself to His servants, and as His manner is, first to His Englishmen? *Ib*

8 Methinks I see in my mind a noble and puissant nation rousing herself like a strong man after sleep, and shaking her invincible locks. Methinks I see her as an eagle mewing her mighty youth, and kindling her undazzled eyes at the full midday beam.   *Ib*

9 Give me the liberty to know, to utter, and to argue freely according to conscience, above all liberties.   *Ib*

10 Let her and Falsehood grapple; who ever knew Truth put to the worse, in a free and open encounter?   *Ib*

11 None can love freedom heartily, but good men; the rest love not freedom, but licence.   *Tenure of Kings and Magistrates*

MIRABEAU, Comte de, 1749–1791

12 *La guerre est l'industrie nationale de la Prusse.* War is the national industry of Prussia.   *Attributed*

MOLIÈRE (Jean Baptiste Poquelin), 1622–1673

13 *Par ma foi! il y a plus de quarante ans que je dis de la prose sans que j'en susse rien.* M. JOURDAIN
Good heavens! I have been talking prose for over forty years without realizing it.   *Le Bourgeois Gentilhomme, Act 2, Scene 4*

14 *C'est une folie à nulle autre seconde,*
De vouloir se mêler à corriger le monde.   PHILINTE
It is a stupidity second to none, to want to busy oneself with the correction of the world.   *Le Misanthrope, Act 1, Scene 1*

15 *Ah! pour être dévot, je n'en suis pas moins homme!*   TARTUFFE
Oh, I may be devout, but I am human all the same.   *Tartuffe, Act 3, Scene 3*

16 *La scandale du monde est ce qui fait l'offense,*
Et ce n'est pas pécher que pécher en silence.   TARTUFFE
It is a public scandal that gives offence, and it is no sin to sin in secret.
                        Ib, Act 4, Scene 5

MONKHOUSE, William Cosmo, 1840–1901

1 There was an old party of Lyme,
  Who married three wives at one time.
      When asked, 'Why the third?'
      He replied, 'One's absurd,
  And bigamy, sir, is a crime!'   *Limerick*

MONSELL, John Samuel Bewley, 1811–1875

2 Fight the good fight with all thy might,
  Christ is thy strength, and Christ thy right;
  Lay hold on life, and it shall be
  Thy joy and crown eternally.   *Fight the Good Fight*

MONTAIGNE, Michel de, 1533–1592

3 The greatest thing in the world is to know how to be self-sufficient.
                                    Essays, 1, 39

4 When I play with my cat, who knows whether she is not amusing herself
  with me more than I with her.   *Ib, 2, 12*

5 Marriage is like a cage; one sees the birds outside desperate to get in, and
  those inside equally desperate to get out.   *Ib, 3, 5*

6 It might well be said of me that here I have merely made up a bunch of
  other men's flowers, and provided nothing of my own but the string to tie
  them together.   *Ib, 3, 12*

MONTGOMERY, Bernard Law, 1st Viscount, 1887—

7 Anyone who votes Labour ought to be locked up.   *Speech, Woodford,*
                                   Essex, 1959

MONTROSE, Percy, 19th century

8 In a cavern, in a canyon,
  Excavating for a mine,
  Dwelt a miner, Forty-niner,
    And his daughter Clementine.
  Oh my darling, oh my darling, oh my darling Clementine!
  Thou art lost and gone for ever, dreadful sorry, Clementine.   *Clementine*

9 Light she was and like a fairy,
  And her shoes were number nine;
  Herring boxes, without topses,
    Sandals were for Clementine.   *Ib*

10 How I missed her, how I missed her,
  How I missed my Clementine!
  But I kissed her little sister,
    And forgot my Clementine.   *Ib*

MOORE, Thomas, 1779–1852

11 The harp that once through Tara's halls
    The soul of music shed,
  Now hangs as mute on Tara's walls,
    As if that soul were fled.   *Irish Melodies, The Harp that once through*
                                      Tara's Halls

1 'Tis the last rose of summer
   Left blooming alone;
   All her lovely companions
      Are faded and gone.   *Irish Melodies, The Last Rose of Summer*

2 The Minstrel Boy to the war is gone,
      In the ranks of death you'll find him;
   His father's sword he has girded on,
      And his wild harp slung behind him.   *Ib, The Minstrel Boy*

3 'Come, Come,' said Tom's father, 'at your time of life,
      There's no longer excuse for thus playing the rake—
   It is time you should think, boy, of taking a wife'—
      'Why, so it is, father—whose wife shall I take?'   *A Joke Versified*

MORE, Sir Thomas, 1478–1535

4 I pray you, Master Lieutenant, see me safe up, and for coming down let me
   shift for myself. [*On mounting the scaffold*]   *Roper, Life of Sir Thomas
   More*

5 Pluck up thy spirits, man, and be not afraid to do thine office; my neck is
   very short; take heed therefore thou strike not awry, for saving of thine
   honesty. [*To the executioner*]   *Ib*

MORELL, Thomas, 1703–1784

6 See, the conquering hero comes!
   Sound the trumpets, beat the drums!   *Joshua, Pt. 3*

MORGAN, Augustus de, 1806–1871

7 Great fleas have little fleas upon their backs to bite 'em,
   And little fleas have lesser fleas, and so *ad infinitum*.
                                        A Budget of Paradoxes

MORLEY, Christopher Darlington, 1890–1957

8 The man who never in his life
   Has washed the dishes with his wife
   Or polished up the silver plate—
   He still is largely celibate.   *Washing the Dishes*

MORRIS, William, 1834–1896

9 Dreamer of dreams, born out of my due time,
      Why should I strive to set the crooked straight?   *The Earthly Paradise,
                                                                An Apology*

10 Love is enough: though the world be a-waning,
   And the woods have no voice but the voice of complaining.
                                        Love is Enough, 1

MOTLEY, John Lothrop, 1814–1877

11 Give us the luxuries of life, and we will dispense with its necessities.
      O. W. Holmes, The Autocrat of the Breakfast Table, Ch. 6

MOTTEUX, Peter Anthony, 1660–1718

1 The devil was sick, the devil a monk wou'd be;
The devil was well, and the devil a monk he'd be. *Translation of Rabelais,*
Gargantua and Pantagruel, Bk. 4, Ch. 24

MUNRO, Hector Hugh, see 'SAKI'

MUNSTER, Ernst Friedrich Herbert, 1766–1839

2 Absolutism tempered by assassination.   [*The Russian Constitution*]
Letter

MURDOCH, Richard, 1907–, and HORNE, Kenneth, 1900–

3 Have you read any good books lately?   *Much Binding in the Marsh,*
B.B.C. Radio Programme, 1945 to 1954

MURPHY, C. W., 19th century

4 Has anybody here seen Kelly?
Kelly from the Isle of Man?   *Has Anybody Here Seen Kelly?*

MUSSET, Alfred de, 1810–1857

5 *Il faut qu'une porte soit ouverte ou fermée.* A door must be either open or shut.
Title of Play

6 *On ne badine pas avec l'amour.* One must not trifle with love. *Title of Play*

NAIRNE, Lady Carolina, 1766–1845

7 Charlie is my darling, my darling, my darling,
Charlie is my darling, the young Chevalier.   *Charlie is my Darling*

8 Better lo'ed ye canna be,
Will ye no come back again?   *Will ye no come back again?*

NAPIER, Sir Charles James, 1782–1853

9 *Peccavi.* [I have Sind].   *Despatch after victory of Hyderabad in Sind,*
1843

NAPOLEON, Bonaparte, 1769–1821

10 *Soldats, songez que, du haut de ces pyramides, quarante siècles vous contemplent.*
—Think of it, soldiers, from the summit of these pyramids, forty centuries
look down upon you.   *Speech before Battle of the Pyramids, 1798*

11 *Du sublime au ridicule il n'y a qu'un pas.*—It is only a step from the sublime
to the ridiculous.   *After the retreat from Moscow, 1812*

12 *L'Angleterre est une nation de boutiquiers.*—England is a nation of shop-
keepers.   *Attributed, See Adam Smith*

13 *Tout soldat français porte dans sa giberne le bâton de maréchal de France.*—
Every French soldier carries in his cartridge-pouch the baton of a marshal
of France.   *Attributed*

14 An army marches on its stomach.   *Attributed*

NASH, Ogden, 1902—

1 A girl whose cheeks are covered with paint
Has an advantage with me over one whose ain't.   *Biological Reflection*

2 One would be in less danger
From the wiles of the stranger
If one's own kin and kith
Were more fun to be with.   *Family Court*

3 Home is heaven and orgies are vile
But you need an orgy, once in a while.   *Home, 99 44/100% Sweet Home*

4 Beneath this slab
John Brown is stowed.
He watched the ads
And not the road.   *Lather as You Go*

5 I have a bone to pick with fate,
Come here and tell me, girlie,
Do you think my mind is maturing late,
Or simply rotted early?   *Lines on Facing Forty*

6 Children aren't happy with nothing to ignore,
And that's what parents were created for.   *The Parent*

7 A bit of talcum
Is always walcum.   *Reflection on Babies*

8 Candy
is dandy
But liquor
is quicker.   *Reflection on Ice-Breaking*

9 I test my bath before I sit,
And I'm always moved to wonderment
That what chills the finger not a bit
Is so frigid upon the fundament.   *Samson Agonistes*

10 I think that I shall never see
A billboard lovely as a tree.
Perhaps unless the billboards fall,
I'll never see a tree at all.   *Song of the Open Road*

11 The turtle lives 'twixt plated decks
Which practically conceal its sex.
I think it clever of the turtle
In such a fix to be so fertile.   *The Turtle*

NASHE, Thomas, 1567-1601

12 Brightness falls from the air;
Queens have died young and fair;
Dust hath closed Helen's eye.   *In Time of Pestilence*

NEALE, John Mason, 1818-1866

13 Brief Life is here our portion;
Brief sorrow, short-lived care.   *Brief Life is Here*

14 Good Christian men, rejoice
With heart, and soul, and voice.   *Good Christian Men*

1 Good King Wenceslas looked out
   On the Feast of Stephen;
   When the snow lay round about,
      Deep and crisp and even.   *Good King Wenceslas*

2 Bring me flesh and bring me wine,
   Bring me pine logs hither.   *Ib*

3 In his master's steps he trod
   Where the snow lay dinted.   *Ib*

NELSON, Horatio, 1st Viscount, 1758–1805

4 Westminster Abbey or victory.   *Remark at Battle of Cape St. Vincent*

5 England expects every man will do his duty.   *Battle of Trafalgar*

6 Thank God, I have done my duty.   *Ib*

7 Kiss me, Hardy.   *Ib*

NERO (Nero Claudius Caesar), A.D. 37–68

8 *Qualis artifex pereo!* What an artist dies with me!   *Last words, attributed*

NEWBOLT, Sir Henry John, 1862–1938

9 Drake he's in his hammock till the great Armadas come.
   (Capten, art tha sleepin' there below?)
   Slung atween the round shot, listenin' for the drum,
      An' dreamin' arl the time o' Plymouth Hoe.   *Drake's Drum*

10 Where the old trade's plying an' the old flag flyin'
   They shall find him ware an' wakin', as they found him long ago!   *Ib*

11 There's a breathless hush in the Close to-night—
   Ten to make and the match to win—
   A bumping pitch and a blinding light,
      An hour to play and the last man in.   *Vitai Lampada*

12 But his captain's hand on his shoulder smote—
   'Play up! play up! and play the game!'   *Ib*

NEWMAN, John Henry, Cardinal, 1801–1890

13 It is almost a definition of a gentleman to say that he is one who never
   inflicts pain.   *The Idea of a University, Knowledge and Religious Duty*

14 Lead, Kindly Light, amid the encircling gloom,
      Lead thou me on;
   The night is dark, and I am far from home,
      Lead thou me on.   *Lead Kindly Light*

NICHOLAS I of Russia, 1796–1855

15 Russia has two generals in whom she can confide—Generals Janvier and
   Février.   *Punch, 10 March 1853*

NORTH, Christopher (John Wilson), 1785–1854

16 His Majesty's dominions, on which the sun never sets.
                           Noctes Ambrosianae, No. 20, April 1829

17 Laws were made to be broken.   *Ib, No. 24, May 1830*

NOYES, Alfred, 1880–1958

1 Go down to Kew in lilac-time, in lilac-time, in lilac-time,
  Go down to Kew in lilac-time (it isn't far from London!)
And you shall wander hand in hand with love in summer's wonderland;
  Go down to Kew in lilac-time (it isn't far from London!)

The Barrel Organ

2   Look for me by moonlight;
        Watch for me by moonlight;
    I'll come to thee by moonlight, though hell should bar the way!

The Highwayman

NURSERY RHYMES

The Oxford Dictionary of Nursery Rhymes, edited by Iona and Peter Opie, gives
the sources of over 500 nursery rhymes.
In many cases nursery rhymes have changed considerably since they first
appeared in print. It seemed most useful, in the selection of familiar nursery
rhymes below, to give the version most commonly in use to-day, together with
title and date of the first known publication.

3 As I was going to St. Ives,
  I met a man with seven wives.   *Mother Goose's Quarto, c. 1825*

4 Baa, baa, black sheep,
    Have you any wool?
  Yes, sir, yes, sir,
    Three bags full;
  One for the master,
    And one for the dame,
  And one for the little boy
    Who lives down the lane.   *Tommy Thumb's Pretty Song Book, c. 1744*

5 Bobby Shafto's gone to sea,
    Silver buckles at his knee;
  He'll come back and marry me,
    Bonny Bobby Shafto!   *Songs for the Nursery, 1805*

6 Boys and girls come out to play,
  The moon doth shine as bright as day.   *Useful Transactions in Philosophy,*
                                          William King, 1708–9

7 Cock a doodle doo!
  My dame has lost her shoe,
  My master's lost his fiddlestick,
  And knows not what to do.   *The Most Cruel and Bloody Murder, 1606*

8 Curly locks, Curly locks,
    Wilt thou be mine?
  Thou shalt not wash dishes
    Nor yet feed the swine,
  But sit on a cushion
    And sew a fine seam,
  And feed upon strawberries,
    Sugar and cream.   *Infant Institutes, 1797*

9 Ding, dong, bell,
    Pussy's in the well.
  Who put her in?

Little Johnny Green.
Who pulled her out?
Little Tommy Stout.   *Mother Goose's Melody, c. 1765*

1 Eena, meena, mina, mo,
  Catch a nigger by his toe;
  If he squeals, let him go,
  Eena, meena, mina, mo.   *Games and Songs of American Children,*
                                              Newell, 1883

2 A frog he would a-wooing go,
     Heigh ho! says Rowley,
  A frog he would a-wooing go,
  Whether his mother would let him or no.
     With a rowley, powley, gammon and spinach,
     Heigh ho! says Anthony Rowley. *Melismata, Thomas Ravenscroft, 1611*

3 Georgie Porgie, pudding and pie,
  Kissed the girls and made them cry;
  When the boys came out to play,
  Georgie Porgie ran away.   *Nursery Rhymes, J. O. Halliwell, 1844*

4 Goosey, goosey gander,
     Whither shall I wander?
  Upstairs and downstairs
     And in my lady's chamber.   *Gammer Gurton's Garland, 1784*

5 Hey diddle diddle,
  The cat and the fiddle,
  The cow jumped over the moon;
  The little dog laughed
  To see such sport,
  And the dish ran away with the spoon. *Mother Goose's Melody, c. 1765*

6 Hickory, dickory, dock,
  The mouse ran up the clock.
     The clock struck one,
     The mouse ran down,
  Hickory, dickory, dock.   *Tommy Thumb's Pretty Song Book, c. 1744*

7 Hot cross buns!
  Hot cross buns!
  One a penny, two a penny,
  Hot cross buns!   *Christmas Box, 1797*

8 How many miles to Babylon?
  Three score miles and ten.
  Can I get there by candle-light?
  Yes, and back again.
  If your heels are nimble and light,
  You may get there by candle-light.   *Songs for the Nursery, 1805*

9 Humpty Dumpty sat on a wall,
  Humpty Dumpty had a great fall.
     All the king's horses,
     And all the king's men,
  Couldn't put Humpty together again.   *Gammer Gurton's Garland, 1810*

10 Hush-a-bye, baby, on the tree top,
   When the wind blows the cradle will rock;
   When the bough breaks the cradle will fall,
   Down will come baby, cradle, and all.   *Mother Goose's Melody, c. 1765*

1 I had a little nut tree,
   Nothing would it bear
But a silver nutmeg
   And a golden pear;
The King of Spain's daughter
   Came to visit me,
And all for the sake
   Of my little nut tree.   *Newest Christmas Box, c. 1797*

2 I love sixpence, jolly little sixpence,
   I love sixpence better than my life;
I spent a penny of it, I lent a penny of it,
   And I took fourpence home to my wife.   *Gammer Gurton's Garland,*
                                                1810

3 I'm the king of the castle,
   Get down you dirty rascal.   *Brand's Popular Antiquities, 1870*

4 I saw three ships come sailing by,
   Come sailing by, come sailing by,
I saw three ships come sailing by,
   On Christmas day in the morning.   *Bishoprick Garland,*
                                            Sir Cuthbert Sharp, 1834

5 I see the moon,
   And the moon sees me;
God bless the moon,
   And God bless me.   *Gammer Gurton's Garland, 1784*

6 Jack and Jill went up the hill
   To fetch a pail of water;
Jack fell down and broke his crown,
   And Jill came tumbling after.   *Mother Goose's Melody, c. 1765*

7 Jack Sprat could eat no fat,
   His wife could eat no lean,
And so between them both, you see,
   They licked the platter clean.   *Paroemiologia Anglo-Latina,*
                                            John Clarke, 1639

8 Ladybird, ladybird,
   Fly away home,
Your house is on fire
   And your children all gone.   *Tommy Thumb's Pretty Song Book, c. 1744*

9 The lion and the unicorn
   Were fighting for the crown;
The lion beat the unicorn
   All round about the town.

Some gave them white bread,
   And some gave them brown;
Some gave them plum cake
   And drummed them out of town.   *Useful Transactions in Philosophy,*
                                            William King, 1708-9

10 Little Bo-peep has lost her sheep,
   And can't tell where to find them;
Leave them alone, and they'll come home,
   And bring their tails behind them.   *Gammer Gurton's Garland, 1810*

1 Little Boy Blue,
      Come blow your horn,
   The sheep's in the meadow,
         The cow's in the corn.   *Famous Tommy Thumb's Little Story Book,*
                                                              c. 1760

2 Little Jack Horner
   Sat in the corner,
   Eating a Christmas pie;
   He put in his thumb,
   And pulled out a plum,
   And said, What a good boy am I!   *Namby Pamby, Henry Carey, 1725*

3 Little Miss Muffet
   Sat on a tuffet,
   Eating her curds and whey;
   There came a big spider,
   Who sat down beside her
   And frightened Miss Muffet away.   *Songs for the Nursery, 1805*

4 Little Tommy Tucker,
      Sings for his supper:
   What shall we give him?
      White bread and butter.
   How shall he cut it
      Without a knife?
   How will he be married
      Without a wife?   *Tommy Thumb's Pretty Song Book, c. 1744*

5 London Bridge is broken down,
      My fair lady.   *Namby Pamby, Henry Carey, 1725*

6   The man in the moon
      Came down too soon,
   And asked his way to Norwich;
      He went by the south,
      And burnt his mouth
   With supping cold plum porridge.   *Gammer Gurton's Garland, 1784*

7 Mary, Mary, quite contrary,
      How does your garden grow?
   With silver bells and cockle shells,
      And pretty maids all in a row.   *Tommy Thumb's Pretty Song Book, c. 1744*

8 Monday's child is fair of face,
   Tuesday's child is full of grace,
   Wednesday's child is full of woe,
   Thursday's child has far to go,
   Friday's child is loving and giving,
   Saturday's child works hard for his living,
   And the child that is born on the Sabbath day
   Is bonny and blithe, and good and gay.   *Traditions of Devonshire,*
                                                         A. E. Bray, 1838

9 My mother said that I never should
   Play with the gypsies in the wood;
   If I did, she would say,
   Naughty girl to disobey.   *Come Hither, Walter de la Mare, 1922*

1   Old King Cole
     Was a merry old soul,
And a merry old soul was he;
    He called for his pipe,
    And he called for his bowl,
And he called for his fiddlers three.   *Useful Transactions in Philosophy,*
William King, 1708–9

2   Old Mother Hubbard
     Went to the cupboard,
To fetch her poor dog a bone;
    But when she got there
    The cupboard was bare
And so the poor dog had none.   *The Comic Adventures of Old Mother*
Hubbard and Her Dog, 1805

3 One, two,
  Buckle my shoe;
Three, four,
  Knock at the door.   *Songs for the Nursery, 1805*

4   Oranges and lemons,
     Say the bells of St. Clement's.

     You owe me five farthings,
     Say the bells of St. Martin's.

     When will you pay me?
     Say the bells of Old Bailey.

     When I grow rich,
     Say the bells of Shoreditch.

     When will that be?
     Say the bells of Stepney.

     I'm sure I don't know,
     Says the great bell at Bow.

Here comes a candle to light you to bed,
Here comes a chopper to chop off your head.   *Tommy Thumb's Pretty*
Song Book, c. 1744

5 Pat-a-cake, pat-a-cake, baker's man,
  Bake me a cake as fast as you can;
  Pat it and prick it, and mark it with B,
  Put it in the oven for baby and me.   *The Campaigners, Tom D'Urfey,*
1698

6 Peter Piper picked a peck of pickled pepper;
  A peck of pickled pepper Peter Piper picked;
  If Peter Piper picked a peck of pickled pepper,
  Where's the peck of pickled pepper Peter Piper picked?
    Peter Piper's Practical Principles of Plain and Perfect Pronunciation, 1819

7 Pussy cat, pussy cat, where have you been?
  I've been to London to look at the queen.
  Pussy cat, pussy cat, what did you there?
  I frightened a little mouse under her chair.   *Songs for the Nursery, 180*

8   The Queen of Hearts
     She made some tarts,

All on a summer's day;
  The Knave of Hearts
  He stole the tarts,
And took them clean away.   *The European Magazine, April, 1782*

1 Ride a cock-horse to Banbury Cross,
  To see a fine lady upon a white horse;
  Rings on her fingers and bells on her toes,
  And she shall have music wherever she goes.   *Gammer Gurton's Garland,*
                                                              1784

2 Ring-a-ring o' roses,
  A pocket full of posies,
    A-tishoo! A-tishoo!
  We all fall down.   *Mother Goose, Kate Greenaway, 1881*

3 See-saw, Margery Daw,
  Jacky shall have a new master;
  Jacky shall have but a penny a day,
  Because he can't work any faster.   *Mother Goose's Melody, c. 1765*

4 Simple Simon met a pieman,
    Going to the fair;
  Says Simple Simon to the pieman,
    Let me taste your ware.
  Says the pieman to Simple Simon,
    Show me first your penny;
  Says Simple Simon to the pieman,
    Indeed I have not any.   *Simple Simon (Chapbook Advertisement), 1764*

5 Sing a song of sixpence,
    A pocket full of rye;
  Four and twenty blackbirds,
    Baked in a pie.

  When the pie was opened,
    The birds began to sing;
  Was not that a dainty dish,
    To set before the king?

  The king was in his counting-house,
    Counting out his money;
  The queen was in the parlour,
    Eating bread and honey.

  The maid was in the garden,
    Hanging out the clothes,
  There came a little blackbird,
    And snapped off her nose.   *Tommy Thumb's Pretty Song Book, c. 1744*

6 Solomon Grundy,
  Born on a Monday,
  Christened on Tuesday,
  Married on Wednesday,
  Took ill on Thursday,
  Worse on Friday,
  Died on Saturday,
  Buried on Sunday.
  This is the end
  Of Solomon Grundy.   *Nursery Rhymes, J. O. Halliwell, 1842*

1 The first day of Christmas,
  My true love sent to me
  A partridge in a pear tree.   *Mirth without Mischief, c. 1780*

2 The twelfth day of Christmas,
  My true love sent to me
  Twelve lords a-leaping,
  Eleven ladies dancing,
  Ten pipers piping,
  Nine drummers drumming,
  Eight maids a-milking,
  Seven swans a-swimming,
  Six geese a-laying,
  Five gold rings,
  Four colly birds,
  Three French hens,
  Two turtle doves, and
  A partridge in a pear tree.   *Ib*

3 There was a crooked man, and he walked a crooked mile,
  He found a crooked sixpence against a crooked stile:
  He bought a crooked cat, which caught a crooked mouse,
  And they all lived together in a little crooked house.   *Nursery Rhymes,*
                                                          J. O. Halliwell, 1842

4 There was an old woman
    Lived under a hill,

  And if she's not gone
    She lives there still.   *Academy of Complements, 1714*

5 There was an old woman who lived in a shoe,
  She had so many children she didn't know what to do;
  She gave them some broth without any bread;
  She whipped them all soundly and put them to bed.   *Gammer Gurton's*
                                                       Garland, 1784

6 Thirty days hath September,
  April, June, and November;
  All the rest have thirty-one,
  Excepting February alone
  And that has twenty-eight days clear
  And twenty-nine in each leap year.   *Abridgement of the Chronicles of*
                                        England, Richard Grafton, 1570

7 This little pig went to market,
  This little pig stayed at home,
  This little pig had roast beef,
  This little pig had none,
  And this little pig cried, Wee-wee-wee-wee-wee,
    I can't find my way home.   *The Famous Tommy Thumb's Little Story*
                                 Book, c. 1760

8 This is the farmer sowing his corn,
  That kept the cock that crowed in the morn,
  That waked the priest all shaven and shorn,
  That married the man all tattered and torn,
  That kissed the maiden all forlorn,

That milked the cow with the crumpled horn,
That tossed the dog,
That worried the cat,
That killed the rat,
That ate the malt,
That lay in the house that Jack built.   *Nurse Truelove's New-Year's-Gift,*
1755

1 Three blind mice, see how they run!
They all run after the farmer's wife,
Who cut off their tails with a carving knife,
Did you ever see such a thing in your life,
   As three blind mice?   *Deuteromelia, Thomas Ravenscroft, 1609*

2 Tinker,
   Tailor,
Soldier,
   Sailor,
Rich man,
   Poor man,
Beggarman,
   Thief.   *Popular Rhymes and Nursery Tales, J. O. Halliwell, 1849*

3 Tom, he was a piper's son,
He learnt to play when he was young,
And all the tune that he could play
Was 'Over the hills and far away'.   *Tom, The Piper's Son, c. 1795*

4 Tom, Tom, the piper's son,
Stole a pig and away he run;
   The pig was eat
   And Tom was beat,
And Tom went howling down the street.   *Ib*

5 Two little dicky birds,
Sitting on a wall;
One named Peter,
The other named Paul.
Fly away, Peter!
Fly away, Paul!
Come back, Peter!
Come back, Paul!   *Mother Goose's Melody, c. 1765*

6 What are little boys made of?
What are little boys made of?
   Frogs and snails
   And puppy-dogs' tails,
That's what little boys are made of.
What are little girls made of?
What are little girls made of?
   Sugar and spice
   And all that's nice,
That's what little girls are made of.   *Nursery Rhymes, J. O. Halliwell,*
1844

7 Where are you going to, my pretty maid?
I'm going a-milking, sir, she said.   *Archaeologia Cornu-Britannica,*
William Pryce, 1790

1 What is your fortune, my pretty maid?
My face is my fortune, sir, she said.

Then I can't marry you, my pretty maid.
Nobody asked you, sir, she said. *Archaeologia Cornu-Britannica,*
William Pryce, 1790

2 Who killed Cock Robin?
I, said the Sparrow,
With my bow and arrow,
I killed Cock Robin.

Who saw him die?
I, said the Fly,
With my little eye,
I saw him die. *Tommy Thumb's Pretty Song Book, c. 1744*

3 All the birds of the air
Fell a-sighing and a-sobbing,
When they heard the bell toll
For poor Cock Robin. *Ib*

4 Yankee Doodle came to town,
Riding on a pony;
He stuck a feather in his cap
And called it macaroni. *Gammer Gurton's Garland, 1810*

For other nursery rhymes, see Thomas Ady (9:13), S. J. Hale (127:11), and Jane Taylor (311:5).

OAKELEY, Frederick, 1802–1880

5 O come, all ye faithful,
Joyful and triumphant,
O come ye, O come ye to Bethlehem. *Hymn translated from Latin,*
Adeste Fideles

6 Sing, choirs of Angels,
Sing in exultation,
Sing, all ye citizens of heaven above. *Ib*

OATES, Lawrence Edward Grace, 1880–1912

7 I am just going outside, and may be some time. *Last words. Recorded in*
Captain R. F. Scott's Antarctic Diary, 16 March 1912

O'CASEY, Sean, 1884—

8 The whole worl's in a state o' chassis. BOYLE *Juno and the Paycock*
Act 1

OCHS, Adolph S., 1858–1935

9 All the news that's fit to print. *Motto of New York Times*

O'KEEFE, Patrick, 1872–1934

10 Say it with flowers. *Slogan for Society of American Florists*

OPIE, John, 1761–1807

11 I mix them with my brains, sir. *When asked with what he mixed his colours.*
Quoted in Samuel Smiles, Self Help, Ch.

ORWELL, George, (Eric Blair) 1903–1950

1 All animals are equal but some animals are more equal than others.
Animal Farm, Ch. 10

2 It was a bright cold day in April, and the clocks were striking thirteen.
Nineteen Eighty-Four, Pt. 1, Ch. 1

3 Big Brother is watching you. *Ib*

4 War is Peace, Freedom is Slavery, Ignorance is Strength. *Ib*

5 Down with Big Brother. *Ib*

6 Doublethink means the power of holding two contradictory beliefs in one's mind simultaneously, and accepting both of them. *Ib, Pt. 2, Ch. 9*

OSBORNE, John, 1929 —

7 But I have a go, lady, don't I ? I 'ave a go. ARCHIE RICE
The Entertainer, No. 7

8 Don't clap too hard—it's a very old building. ARCHIE RICE *Ib*

9 Yes, thank God we're normal,
Yes, this was our finest shower! ARCHIE RICE *Ib*

10 How I long for a little ordinary human enthusiasm. Just enthusiasm—that's all. I want to hear a warm, thrilling voice cry out Hallelujah! Hallelujah! I'm alive! JIMMY PORTER *Look Back in Anger, Act 1*

11 His knowledge of life and ordinary human beings is so hazy, he really deserves some sort of decoration for it—a medal inscribed 'For Vaguery in the Field'. JIMMY PORTER *Ib*

12 I don't think one 'comes down' from Jimmy's university. According to him, it's not even red brick, but white tile. ALISON PORTER *Ib, Act 2, Scene 1*

OTIS, James, 1725–1783

13 Taxation without representation is tyranny. *Watchword of the American Revolution*

OVID (Publius Ovidius Naso), 43 B.C.–17 A.D.

14 *Quae dant, quaeque negant, gaudent tamen esse rogatae.* Whether they give or refuse, women are glad to have been asked. *Ars Amatoria, 1*

15 *Inopem me copia fecit.* Plenty makes me poor. *Metamorphoses, 3*

16 *Tempus edax rerum.* Time, the devourer of things. *Ib, 15*

OWEN, Robert, 1771–1858

17 All the world is queer save thee and me, and even thou art a little queer.
Of his business partner, William Allen, 1828

PAINE, Thomas, 1737–1809

18 The sublime and the ridiculous are often so nearly related that it is difficult to class them separately. One step above the sublime makes the ridiculous; and one step above the ridiculous makes the sublime again.
The Age of Reason, Part 2

19 Government, even in its best state, is but a necessary evil; in its worst state, an intolerable one. *Common Sense, Ch. 1*

PALMERSTON, Henry John Temple, 3rd Viscount, 1784–1865

1 Die, my dear Doctor, that's the last thing I shall do! *Last words, attributed*

PARKER, Dorothy, 1893—

2 Men seldom make passes
  At girls who wear glasses.   *News Item*

3 Guns aren't lawful;
  Nooses give;
  Gas smells awful;
  You might as well live.   *Résumé*

PARKER, Ross, 1914—, and CHARLES, Hughie, 1907—

4 There'll always be an England
    While there's a country lane,
  Wherever there's a cottage small
    Beside a field of grain.   *There'll Always be an England*

PARKINSON, Cyril Northcote, 1909—

5 Work expands so as to fill the time available for its completion. General
  recognition of this fact is shown in the proverbial phrase 'It is the busiest
  man who has time to spare.'   *Parkinson's Law*

6 The Law of Triviality. Briefly stated, it means that the time spent on any
  item of the agenda will be in inverse proportion to the sum involved.
                            Ib, High Finance or the Point of Vanishing Interest

PASCAL, Blaise, 1623–1662

7 *Le nez de Cléopâtre: s'il eût été plus court, toute la face de la terre aurait
  changé.*—Had Cleopatra's nose been shorter, the whole history of the world
  would have been different.   *Pensées, 2, 162*

8 *Le cœur a ses raisons que la raison ne connaît point.*—The heart has its reasons
  which reason does not know.   *Ib, 4, 277*

PATER, Walter Horatio, 1839–1894

9 To burn always with this hard, gem-like flame, to maintain this ecstasy, is
  success in life.   *The Renaissance, Conclusion*

PATERSON, Andrew, 1864–1941

10 Once a jolly swagman camped by a billabong,
     Under the shade of a coolibah tree,
   And he sang as he sat and waited till his billy boiled,
     'You'll come a-waltzing, Matilda, with me.'   *Waltzing Matilda*

PATMORE, Coventry Kersey Dighton, 1823–1896

11 'I saw you take his kiss!' 'Tis true,'
   'O, modesty!' 'Twas strictly kept:
   He thought me asleep; at least, I knew
   He thought I thought he thought I slept.'
                                          The Angel in the House, Bk. 2,

12 A woman is a foreign land,
     Of which, though there he settle young,
   A man will ne'er quite understand
     The customs, politics, and tongue.   *Ib, Bk. 2,*

PAUL, Leslie Allen, 1905—

1 Angry Young Man. *Title of Book, 1951*

PAYNE, John Howard, 1791–1852

2 Mid pleasures and palaces though we may roam,
  Be it ever so humble, there's no place like home.
Clari, The Maid of Milan, Home, Sweet Home

PEACOCK, Thomas Love, 1785–1866

3 Respectable means rich, and decent means poor. I should die if I heard my family called decent.   LADY CLARINDA   *Crotchet Castle, Ch. 3*

4 A book that furnishes no quotations is, *me judice*, no book—it is a plaything.
Ib, Ch. 9

5 There are two reasons for drinking: one is, when you are thirsty, to cure it; the other, when you are not thirsty, to prevent it . . . Prevention is better than cure.   MR PORTPIPE   *Melincourt, Ch. 16*

6 The mountain sheep are sweeter,
  But the valley sheep are fatter;
  We therefore deemed it meeter
  To carry off the latter.   *The Misfortunes of Elphin, Ch. 11, The War Song of Dinas Vawr*

PENN, William, 1644–1718

7 Men are generally more careful of the breed of their horses and dogs than of their children.   *Reflexions and Maxims, Pt. 1, 85*

PEPYS, Samuel, 1633–1703

8 And so to bed.   *Diary, 6 May 1660 and passim*

9 A silk suit, which cost me much money, and I pray God to make me able to pay for it.   *Ib, 1 July 1660*

10 Strange to say what delight we married people have to see these poor fools decoyed into our condition.   *Ib, 25 Dec. 1665*

11 Music and women I cannot but give way to, whatever my business is.
Ib, 9 Mar. 1666

12 To church; and with my mourning, very handsome, and new periwig, make a great show.   *Ib, 31 Mar. 1667*

13 And so I betake myself to that course, which is almost as much as to see myself go into my grave; for which, and all the discomforts that will accompany my being blind, the good God prepare me!
Ib, 31 May 1669 (final entry)

PERRAULT, Charles, 1628–1703

14 She [*Cinderella*] was as good as she was beautiful.   *Histoires ou Contes du Temps Passé, 1697. First English Translation by Robert Samber*

15 Sister Anne, sister Anne, do you see anyone coming?   BLUE BEARD   *Ib*

PÉTAIN, Marshal Henri Phillipe, 1856–1951

16 *Ils ne passeront pas.* They shall not pass.   *Verdun, Feb. 1916*

PETRONIUS, ?–66? A.D.

1 *Cave canem.*—Beware of the dog. *Satyricon, 29, 1*

PHELPS, Edward John, 1822–1900

2 The man who makes no mistakes does not usually make anything.
Speech, Mansion House, London, 24 Jan. 1899

PHILLIPS, Wendell, 1811–1884

3 One on God's side is a majority. *Speech, Brooklyn, 1 Nov. 1859*

4 Every man meets his Waterloo at last. *Ib*

PINDAR, 522?–442? B.C.

5 Water is best. *Olympian Odes, 1*

PITT, William, 1st Earl of Chatham, 1708–1778

6 The atrocious crime of being a young man . . . I shall neither attempt to palliate nor deny. *Speech, House of Commons, 27 Jan. 1741*

7 Unlimited power is apt to corrupt the minds of those who possess it.
Speech, House of Lords, 9 Jan. 1770

PITT, William, 1759–1806

8 Necessity is the plea for every infringement of human freedom. It is the argument of tyrants; it is the creed of slaves. *Speech, House of Commons, 18 Nov. 1783*

9 England has saved herself by her exertions, and will, as I trust, save Europe by her example. *Speech, Guildhall, 1805*

10 Roll up that map; it will not be wanted these ten years. *On hearing of Napoleon's victory at the Battle of Austerlitz*

11 I think I could eat one of Bellamy's veal pies. *Last words, attributed*

12 Oh, my country! How I leave my country! [Or 'love' for 'leave']
Last words, attributed

PLATO, 429?–347? B.C.

13 The good is the beautiful. *Lysis*

14 Our object in the construction of the state is the greatest happiness of the whole, and not that of any one class. *Republic, 4*

PLAUTUS, 254–184 B.C.

15 *Miles gloriosus.*—The Boastful Soldier. *Title of Play*

PLINY, The Elder, 23–79 A.D.

16 *Ex Africa semper aliquid novi.* There is always something new out of Africa
Natural History, 2, 8, 4

17 *In vino veritas.* Truth comes out in wine. *Ib, 14, 14*

POE, Edgar Allan, 1809–1849

18 The glory that was Greece
And the grandeur that was Rome. *To Helen*

19 Take thy beak from out my heart, and take thy form from off my door!
Quoth the Raven, 'Nevermore.' *The Raven*

POMPADOUR, Madame de, 1721–1764

  1 *Après nous le déluge.* After us the deluge.   *After Battle of Rossbach, 1757*

POPE, Alexander, 1688–1744

  2 A wit with dunces, and a dunce with wits.   *The Dunciad, 4, 90*

  3 The right divine of kings to govern wrong.   *Ib, 4, 188*

  4 O Grave! where is thy Victory?
    O Death! where is thy Sting?   *The Dying Christian to his Soul*

  5 What beckoning ghost along the moonlight shade
    Invites my steps, and points to yonder glade.   *Elegy to the Memory of an Unfortunate Lady, 1*

  6 Is it, in heav'n, a crime to love too well?   *Ib, 6*

  7 Ambition first sprung from your blest abodes,
    The glorious fault of angels and of gods.   *Ib, 13*

  8 Love, free as air, at sight of human ties,
    Spreads his light wings, and in a moment flies.   *Eloisa to Abelard, 75*

  9 How happy is the blameless vestal's lot!
    The world forgetting, by the world forgot.   *Ib, 207*

  10 Shut, shut the door, good John! fatigued, I said;
    Tie up the knocker, say I'm sick, I'm dead.   *Epistle to Dr. Arbuthnot, 1*

  11 Is there a parson much bemused in beer,
    A maudlin poetess, a rhyming peer,
    A clerk, foredoom'd his father's soul to cross,
    Who pens a stanza, when he should engross?   *Ib, 15*

  12 No creature smarts so little as a fool.   *Ib, 84*

  13 Why did I write? whose sin to me unknown
    Dipt me in ink, my parents', or my own?
    As yet a child, nor yet a fool to fame,
    I lisp'd in numbers, for the numbers came.   *Ib, 125*

  14 The Muse but serv'd to ease some friend, not Wife,
    To help me through this long disease, my Life.   *Ib, 131*

  15 And He, whose fustian's so sublimely bad,
    It is not Poetry, but prose run mad.   *Ib, 187*

  16 Damn with faint praise, assent with civil leer,
    And, without sneering, teach the rest to sneer.   *Ib, 201*

  17 Who but must laugh, if such a man there be?
    Who would not weep, if Atticus were he?   *Ib, 213*

  18 Curst be the verse, how well so'er it flow,
    That tends to make one worthy man my foe.   *Ib, 283*

  19 Wit that can creep, and pride that licks the dust.   *Ib, 333*

  20 Unlearn'd, he knew no schoolman's subtle art,
    No language but the language of the heart.   *Ib, 398*

  21 Nature and Nature's Laws lay hid in Night:
    God said, Let Newton be! and all was Light.   *Epitaph, intended for Sir Isaac Newton*

  22 In wit a man: simplicity a child.   *Epitaph on Mr. Gay*

1 'Tis hard to say, if greater want of skill
  Appear in writing or in judging ill.   *An Essay on Criticism, 1*

2 'Tis with our judgments as our watches, none
  Go just alike, yet each believes his own.   *Ib, 9*

3 First follow Nature, and your judgment frame
  By her just standard, which is still the same:
  Unerring Nature, still divinely bright,
  One clear, unchang'd, and universal light,
  Life, force, and beauty, must to all impart,
  At once the source, and end, and test of Art.   *Ib, 58*

4 Of all the causes which conspire to blind
  Man's erring judgment, and misguide the mind,
  What the weak head with strongest bias rules,
  Is Pride, the never-failing vice of fools.   *Ib, 201*

5 A little learning is a dangerous thing;
  Drink deep, or taste not the Pierian spring:
  There shallow draughts intoxicate the brain,
  And drinking largely sobers us again.   *Ib, 215*

6 A perfect judge will read each work of Wit
  With the same spirit that its author writ.   *Ib, 233*

7 Whoever thinks a faultless piece to see,
  Thinks what ne'er was, nor is, nor e'er shall be.   *Ib, 253*

8 True wit is nature to advantage dress'd;
  What oft was thought, but ne'er so well express'd.   *Ib, 297*

9   As some to church repair,
  Not for the doctrine, but the music there.   *Ib, 342*

10 True ease in writing comes from art, not chance,
  As those move easiest who have learn'd to dance.
  'Tis not enough no harshness gives offence,
  The sound must seem an echo to the sense.   *Ib, 362*

11 Yet let not each gay turn thy rapture move,
  For fools admire, but men of sense approve.   *Ib, 390*

12 Some praise at morning what they blame at night,
  But always think the last opinion right.   *Ib, 430*

13 Fondly we think we honour merit then,
  When we but praise ourselves in other men.   *Ib, 454*

14 To err is human, to forgive, divine.   *Ib, 525*

15 The bookful blockhead, ignorantly read,
  With loads of learned lumber in his head.   *Ib, 612*

16 For fools rush in where angels fear to tread.   *Ib, 625*

17 Awake, my St. John! leave all meaner things
  To low ambition, and the pride of kings.
  Let us (since life can little more supply
  Than just to look about us and to die)
  Expatiate free o'er all this scene of man;
  A mighty maze! but not without a plan.   *An Essay on Man, Epistle 1, 1*

18 Laugh where we must, be candid where we can;
  But vindicate the ways of God to Man.   *Ib, 1, 15*

1 Hope springs eternal in the human breast;
  Man never is, but always to be blest.   *An Essay on Man, Epistle 1, 95*

2 Why has not man a microscopic eye?
  For this plain reason, man is not a fly.   *Ib, 1, 193*

3 All are but parts of one stupendous whole,
  Whose body Nature is, and God the soul.   *Ib, 1, 267*

4 All nature is but art, unknown to thee;
  All chance, direction which thou canst not see;
  All discord, harmony not understood;
  All partial evil, universal good:
  And, spite of pride, in erring reason's spite,
  One truth is clear, whatever is, is right.   *Ib, 1, 289*

5 Know then thyself, presume not God to scan,
  The proper study of Mankind is Man.   *Ib, Epistle 2, 1*

6 Vice is a master of so frightful mien,
  As to be hated needs but to be seen;
  Yet seen too oft, familiar with her face,
  We first endure, then pity, then embrace.   *Ib, 2, 217*

7 O happiness! our being's end and aim!
  Good, pleasure, ease, content! whate'er thy name:
  That something still which prompts th' eternal sigh,
  For which we bear to live, or dare to die.   *Ib, Epistle 4, 1*

8 An honest Man's the noblest work of God.   *Ib, 4, 248*

9 If parts allure thee, think how Bacon shined,
  The wisest, brightest, meanest of mankind:
  Or, ravished with the whistling of a name,
  See Cromwell, damned to everlasting fame.   *Ib, 4, 281*

10 Formed by thy converse happily to steer
   From grave to gay, from lively to severe.   *Ib, 4, 379*

11 Thou wert my guide, philosopher, and friend.   *Ib, 4, 390*

12 That true self-love and social are the same;
   That virtue only makes our bliss below;
   And all our knowledge is, ourselves to know.   *Ib, 4, 396*

13 To observations which ourselves we make,
   We grow more partial for th' observer's sake. *Moral Essays, Epistle 1, 11*

14 'Tis education forms the common mind,
   Just as the twig is bent, the tree's inclined.   *Ib, 1, 149*

15 Men, some to business, some to pleasure take;
   But every woman is at heart a rake.   *Ib, Epistle 2, 215*

16 See how the world its veterans rewards!
   A youth of frolics, an old age of cards.   *Ib, 2, 243*

17 And mistress of herself, though China fall.   *Ib, 2, 268*

18 Woman's at best a contradiction still.   *Ib, 2, 270*

19 The ruling passion, be it what it will,
   The ruling passion conquers reason still.   *Ib, Epistle 3, 153*

20 Happy the man, whose wish and care
   A few paternal acres bound,
   Content to breathe his native air,
       In his own ground.   *Ode on Solitude*

1 Thus let me live, unseen, unknown,
   Thus unlamented let me die,
Steal from the world, and not a stone
   Tell where I lie.   *Ode on Solitude*

2 I am His Highness' dog at Kew;
   Pray tell me sir, whose dog are you?   *On the collar of a dog given to*
                        His Royal Highness, Frederick, Prince of Wales

3 I know the thing that's most uncommon;
   (Envy, be silent and attend!)
I know a reasonable woman,
   Handsome and witty, yet a friend.   *On a Certain Lady at Court*

4 Where'er you walk, cool gales shall fan the glade.
Trees where you sit shall crowd into a shade:
Where'er you tread, the blushing flowers shall rise,
And all things flourish where you turn your eyes.   *Pastorals, Summer, 73*

5 What dire offence from am'rous causes springs,
What mighty contests rise from trivial things.   *The Rape of the Lock,*
                                         Canto 1, 1

6 If to her share some female errors fall,
Look on her face, and you'll forget 'em all.   *Ib, Canto 2, 17*

7 Fair tresses man's imperial race insnare,
And beauty draws us with a single hair.   *Ib, 2, 27*

8 At ev'ry word a reputation dies.   *Ib, Canto 3, 16*

9 The hungry judges soon the sentence sign,
And wretches hang that jury-men may dine.   *Ib, 3, 21*

10 Coffee, which makes the politician wise,
And see through all things with his half-shut eyes.   *Ib, 3, 117*

11 Charms strike the sight, but merit wins the soul.   *Ib, Canto 5, 34*

PORSON, Richard, 1759–1808

12 When Dido found Aeneas would not come,
She mourn'd in silence, and was Di-do-dum.   *Epigram on Latin Gerunds*

13 I went to Frankfort, and got drunk
With that most learned professor, Brunck;
I went to Worts, and got more drunken
With that more learn'd professor, Ruhnken.   *Facetiae Cantabrigienses*

PORTER, William Sydney, see HENRY, O.

POTTER, Beatrix, 1866–1943

14 They [*the rabbits*] did not awake because the lettuces had been so soporific.
                                       The Tale of the Flopsy Bunnies

POTTER, Stephen, 1900—

15 Gamesmanship or The Art of Winning Games Without Actually Cheating
                                       Title of book

16 *How to be one up*—how to make the other man feel that something has gone
wrong, however slightly.   *Lifemanship, Introduction*

17 We work from half a dozen centres co-ordinated, of course, from our
'H.Q.' at Station Road, Yeovil.   *Ib*

1 'Yes, but not in the South', with slight adjustments will do for any argument about any place, if not about any person. *Lifemanship, The Canterbury Block*

POUND, Ezra Loomis, 1885—

2 Winter is icummen in,
Lhude sing Goddamm,
Raineth drop and staineth slop
And how the wind doth ramm!
Sing: Goddamm. *Ancient Music*

3 Bah! I have sung women in three cities,
But it is all the same;
And I will sing of the sun. *Cino*

PRESCOTT, William, 1726–1795

4 Don't fire until you see the whites of their eyes. *Bunker Hill, 1775*
(Also attributed to Israel Putnam, 1718–1790)

PRIOR, Matthew, 1664–1721

5 Be to her virtues very kind;
Be to her faults a little blind;
Let all her ways be unconfined;
And clap your padlock on her mind. *An English Padlock, 78*

6 The merchant to secure his treasure,
Conveys it in a borrowed name;
Euphelia serves to grace my measure;
But Chloe is my real flame. *Ode, The Merchant to Secure his Treasure*

7 From ignorance our comfort flows,
The only wretched are the wise. *To the Hon. C. Montague*

PROVERBS

In this selection of familiar proverbs mainly in the English language, the name and publication date of the Dictionary in which the proverb was first included has been given, or the century of the first recorded use of the proverb in literature. Most proverbs were obviously in common use for many years before they were included in a dictionary.

The abbreviations shown opposite proverbs refer to the following Dictionaries:

Bohn	*H. G. Bohn, A Handbook of Proverbs, 1855.*
Camden	*W. Camden, Remains Concerning Britain, 1614 or later edition.*
Clarke	*J. Clarke, Parœmiologia Anglo-Latina, 1639.*
Draxe	*T. Draxe, Bibliotheca Scholastica, 1616 or later edition.*
Fergusson	*D. Fergusson, Scottish Proverbs, 1641.*
Fuller	*T. Fuller, Gnomologia, 1732.*
Herbert	*G. Herbert, Outlandish Proverbs, 1640 or later edition.*
Heywood	*J. Heywood, A Dialogue containing . . . the Proverbs in the English Tongue, 1546 or later edition.*
Howell	*J. Howell, Proverbs, 1659.*
Kelly	*J. Kelly, A Complete Collection of Scottish Proverbs, 1721.*
Lean	*V. S. Lean, Collectanea, 1902–4.*
Ray	*J. Ray, A Collection of English Proverbs, 1670, 1678 or later edition.*

8 Absence sharpens love, presence strengthens it. *Fuller, 1732*

9 Absent are always in the wrong, The. *Herbert, 1640*

1	Abundance of money ruins youth, The.	*Ray, 1670*
2	Accidents will happen in the best-regulated families.	*19th c.*
3	Accounting for tastes, There is no.	*Latin*
4	Actions speak louder than words.	*20th c.*
5	Adversity makes a man wise, not rich.	*Ray, 1678*
6	Adversity, Many can bear/ but few contempt.	*Fuller, 1732*
7	Advise none to marry or go to war.	*Herbert, 1640*
8	After a storm comes a calm.	*16th c.*
9	Agree, for the law is costly.	*Camden, 1623*
10	All in the day's work, It is.	*18th c.*
11	All is fair in love and war.	*17th c.*
12	All is not gold that glitters.	*Latin*
13	All is over bar (but) the shouting.	*19th c.*
14	All is well that ends well.	*14th c.*
15	All my eye and Betty Martin.	*18th c.*
16	All sorts to make a world, It takes.	*17th c.*
17	Any port in a storm.	*18th c.*
18	Anything for a quiet life.	*17th c.*
19	Apple a day keeps the doctor away, An.	*19th c.*
20	Apple-cart, To upset the.	*18th c.*
21	Archer is not known by his arrows, but his aim, A good.	*16th c.*
22	Art has no enemy except ignorance.	*Latin*
23	Art lies in concealing art.	*Latin*
24	Ask no questions and you will be told no lies.	*18th c.*
25	Ask thy purse what thou shouldst buy.	*Fuller, 1732*
26	Ass of oneself, To make an.	*19th c.*
27	*Audi alteram partem*—Hear the other side.	*Latin*
28	Aunt had been a man, If my/ she'd have been my uncle.	*Ray, 1813*
29	*Autres temps, autres moeurs*—Other times, other manners.	*French*
30	Axe to grind, To have an.	*19th c.*
31	Bachelors' fare: bread and cheese, and kisses.	*18th c.*
32	Back again, like a bad penny.	*19th c.*
33	Bad excuse is better than none, A.	*16th c.*
34	Bad workman quarrels with his tools, A.	*Herbert, 1640*
35	Bald as a coot, As.	*15th c.*
36	Bald heads are soon shaven.	*Ray, 1678*
37	Barber shaves so close but another finds work, No.	*Herbert, 1640*
38	Bark at the moon, To.	*15th c.*
39	Bark is worse than his bite, His.	*17th c.*
40	Bark up the wrong tree, To.	*19th c.*

1	Barking dogs seldom bite.	*16th c.*
2	Bats in the belfry, To have.	*20th c.*
3	Be sure before you marry of a house wherein to tarry.	*Italian*
4	Bear wealth, poverty will bear itself.	*Fergusson, 1641*
5	Beat about the bush, To.	*16th c.*
6	Beauty is but skin-deep.	*17th c.*
7	Beauty is potent, but money is omnipotent.	*Ray, 1670*
8	Beauty will buy no beef.	*Fuller, 1732*
9	Bee in one's bonnet, To have a.	*19th c.*
10	Before one can say Jack Robinson.	*18th c.*
11	Beggar can never be bankrupt, A.	*Clarke, 1639*
12	Beggars cannot be choosers.	*Heywood, 1546*
13	Believe, He does not/ that does not live according to his belief.	*Fuller, 1732*
14	Beloved, To be/ is above all bargains.	*Herbert, 1640*
15	Best foot forward, To put one's.	*16th c.*
16	Best of a bad job, To make the.	*16th c.*
17	Better a lean peace than a fat victory.	*17th c.*
18	Better an egg to-day than a hen to-morrow.	*Italian*
19	Better an open enemy than a false friend.	*17th c.*
20	Better be alone than in bad company.	*15th c.*
21	Better be born lucky than rich.	*Clarke, 1639*
22	Better be envied than pitied.	*Greek*
23	Better be happy than wise.	*Heywood, 1546*
24	Better be sure (safe) than sorry.	*19th c.*
25	Better be the head of a dog than the tail of a lion.	*16th c.*
26	Better buy than borrow.	*Fergusson, 1641*
27	Better die a beggar than live a beggar.	*Ray, 1670*
28	Better give a shilling than lend a half-crown.	*Howell, 1659*
29	Better go to heaven in rags than to hell in embroidery.	*Fuller, 1732*
30	Better late than never.	*Latin*
31	Better luck next time.	*19th c.*
32	Better never begin than never make an end.	*16th c.*
33	Better some of a pudding than none of a pie.	*Ray, 1670*
34	Better suffer ill than do ill.	*Clarke, 1639*
35	Better the devil you know than the devil you don't know.	*19th c.*
36	Better untaught than ill-taught.	*Ray, 1678*
37	Better wear out shoes than sheets.	*17th c.*
38	Between Scylla and Charybdis.	*Greek*
39	Between two stools one falls to the ground.	*Latin*
40	Between you and me and the (gate) post.	*19th c.*
41	Bird in hand is worth two in the bush, A.	*Latin*

1 Birds of a feather flock together. *16th c.*

2 Bitter to endure may be sweet to remember, That which was. *Latin*

3 Black as ink. *16th c.*

4 Black as soot. *15th c.*

5 Black as the devil. *14th c.*

6 Black sheep in every flock, There are. *19th c.*

7 Blessings are not valued till they are gone. *Fuller, 1732*

8 Blind as a bat, As. *16th c.*

9 Blind as those who won't see, None so. *Heywood, 1546*

10 Blind in their own cause, Men are. *Heywood, 1546*

11 Blind man will not thank you for a looking-glass, A. *Fuller, 1732*

12 Blind, In the land of the/ the one-eyed man is king. *Greek*

13 Blood is thicker than water. *17th c.*

14 Blow one's own trumpet, To. *16th c.*

15 Bone in one's leg, To have a. *Greek*

16 Book that is shut is but a block, A. *Fuller, 1732*

17 Books and friends should be few and good. *Spanish*

18 Books, To be in a person's good (or bad). *19th c.*

19 Boot is on the other leg, The. *19th c.*

20 Born on the wrong side of the blanket. *18th c.*

21 Born to be hanged, He that is/ shall never be drowned. *16th c.*

22 Born with a silver spoon in his mouth, He was. *Clarke, 1639*

23 Born within the sound of Bow Bells, To be. *16th c.*

24 Born yesterday, I was not. *19th c.*

25 Both ends meet, To make. *Clarke, 1639*

26 Bow at all, If you/ bow low. *Chinese*

27 Boys will be boys. *17th c.*

28 Boys will be men. *17th c.*

29 Bread is buttered on both sides, His. *Ray, 1678*

30 Bull in a china shop, A. *19th c.*

31 Bulls the cow must keep the calf, He that. *16th c.*

32 Bully is always a coward, A. *19th c.*

33 Burn one's boats, To. *19th c.*

34 Burn the candle at both ends, To. *Ray, 1678*

35 Burn the midnight oil, To. *17th c.*

36 Bury the hatchet, To. *18th c.*

37 Busiest men have the most leisure, The. *19th c.*

38 Business is business. *18th c.*

39 Business before pleasure. *19th c.*

40 Busy, Who is more/ than he that hath least to do? *Draxe, 1616*

41 Butter would not melt in his mouth. *Heywood, 1546*

1	Buy a pig in a poke, To.	*Heywood, 1546*
2	Buy and sell, and live by the loss, To.	*Draxe, 1616*
3	Bygones be bygones, Let.	*Heywood, 1546*
4	Calf love, half love; old love, cold love.	*19th c.*
5	Call a spade a spade, To.	*Latin*
6	Cap fits, If the/ wear it.	*18th c.*
7	Care killed a cat.	*16th c.*
8	Carry coals to Newcastle, To.	*16th c.*
9	Cart before the horse, To put the.	*Latin*
10	Cast ne'er a clout till May be out.	*Fuller, 1732*
11	Castles in Spain, To build.	*14th c.*
12	Castles in the air, To build.	*Latin*
13	Cat has nine lives, A.	*Heywood, 1546*
14	Cat jumps, To see which way the.	*19th c.*
15	Cat on hot bricks, Like a.	*17th c.*
16	*Caveat emptor*—Let the buyer beware.	*Latin*
17	Chalk and cheese.	*14th c.*
18	Chanceth in an hour, It/ that happeneth not in seven years.	*Heywood, 1546*
19	Charity begins at home.	*14th c.*
20	*Che sera, sera*—Whatever will be, will be.	*Italian*
21	Children should be seen and not heard.	*19th c.*
22	Chip of the old block, A.	*17th c.*
23	Choose a horse made, and a wife to make.	*Herbert, 1640*
24	Choose a wife rather by your ear than your eye.	*Fuller, 1732*
25	Choose neither a woman nor linen by candle-light.	*16th c.*
26	Chop and change, To.	*16th c.*
27	Christmas comes but once a year / But when it comes it brings good cheer.	*16th c.*
28	Circumstances alter cases.	*19th c.*
29	Civility costs nothing.	*19th c.*
30	Clean as a whistle, As.	*19th c.*
31	Clean breast, To make a.	*18th c.*
32	Cleanliness is next to godliness.	*Hebrew*
33	Close mouth catcheth no flies, A.	*Italian*
34	Cloud has a silver lining, Every.	*19th c.*
35	Cloud, To be under a.	*16th c.*
36	Coast is clear, The.	*17th c.*
37	Cock-a-hoop, To be.	*17th c.*
38	Cock-and-bull story, A.	*17th c.*
39	Cold as charity.	*14th c.*

1 Cold comfort. *16th c.*

2 Cold hand and a warm heart, A. *Lean, 1902*

3 Cold shoulder, To give the. *19th c.*

4 Company makes the feast, The. *17th c.*

5 Comparisons are odious. *15th c.*

6 Confession is good for the soul. *Kelly, 1721*

7 Constant guest is never welcome, A. *Fuller, 1732*

8 Cook one's goose, To. *19th c.*

9 Cook that cannot lick his own fingers, He is an ill. *Heywood, 1546*

10 Cool one's heels, To. *17th c.*

11 Costs more to do ill than to do well, It. *Herbert, 1640*

12 Counsel be good, If the/ no matter who gave it. *Fuller, 1732*

13 Count one's chickens before they are hatched, To. *16th c.*

14 Couple is not a pair, Every. *19th c.*

15 Courtesy on one side only lasts not long. *Herbert, 1640*

16 Coventry, To send to. *17th c.*

17 Creditors have better memories than debtors. *Howell, 1659*

18 Crocodile tears. *16th c.*

19 Crooked by nature is never made straight by education. *Fuller, 1732*

20 Cross the bridge till you get to it, Don't. *19th c.*

21 Crowd is not company, A. *17th c.*

22 Cry for the moon, To. *19th c.*

23 Cry 'Wolf', To. *17th c.*

24 Crying over spilt milk, It is no use. *Howell, 1659*

25 Cupboard love. *17th c.*

26 Curate's egg, good in parts, Like the. (*See Punch, 232:4*) *19th c.*

27 Curses are like chickens; they come home to roost. *14th c.*

28 Custom without reason is but ancient error. *16th c.*

29 Cut off one's nose to spite one's face, To. *13th c.*

30 Cut off with a shilling, To. *18th c.*

31 Cut the grass from under a person's feet, To. *16th c.*

32 Cut your coat according to your cloth. *Heywood, 1546*

33 Dally not with money or women. *Herbert, 1640*

34 Daughter win, He that would the/must with the mother first begin.
Ray, 1670

35 Day is short and the work is long, The. *15th c.*

36 *De gustibus non est disputandum*—There is no disputing about tastes.
Latin

37 *De mortuis nil nisi bonum*—Concerning the dead (say) nothing but good.
Latin

38 Dead as a door-nail, As. *14th c.*

1 Dead men don't bite. *Greek*

2 Dead men tell no tales. *17th c.*

3 Deaf as a post. *16th c.*

4 Deaf as those who won't hear, None so. *Heywood, 1546*

5 Death devours lambs as well as sheep. *17th c.*

6 Death is the grand leveller. *Fuller, 1732*

7 Death pays all debts. *17th c.*

8 Debt is the worst poverty. *Fuller, 1732*

9 Deceives me once, If a man/ shame on him; if he deceives me twice, shame on me. *Italian*

10 Deceive oneself is very easy, To. *Herbert, 1640*

11 Deeds are males, and words are females. *16th c.*

12 Deepest water is the best fishing, In the. *Draxe, 1616*

13 Delays are dangerous. *14th c.*

14 Deserves not the sweet that will not taste the sour, He. *Latin*

15 Desires honour, He that/ is not worthy of honour. *17th c.*

16 Desperate diseases must have desperate remedies. *Latin*

17 Devil and the deep sea, Between the. *17th c.*

18 Devil is not so black as he is painted, The. *16th c.*

19 Devil take the hindmost, The. *17th c.*

20 Discreet women have neither eyes nor ears. *Herbert, 1640*

21 Discretion is the better part of valour. *16th c.*

22 *Divide et impera*—Divide and rule. *Latin*

23 Divine grace was never slow. *Herbert, 1640*

24 Do as you would be done by. *14th c.*

25 Do as you're bidden and you'll never bear blame. *Ray, 1678*

26 Dog does not eat dog. *18th c.*

27 Dog has his day, Every. *Heywood, 1546*

28 Dog will not howl if you beat him with a bone, A. *Howell, 1659*

29 Dogs that bark at a distance never bite. *Camden, 1623*

30 Done by night appears by day, What is. *14th c.*

31 Done cannot be undone, Things. *Heywood, 1546*

32 Door may be shut but death's door, Every. *Italian*

33 Draw the line somewhere, One must. *19th c.*

34 Drink wine, and have the gout; drink no wine, and have the gout too. *16th c.*

35 Drowning man will catch at a straw, A. *17th c.*

36 Drunk as a fish, As. *17th c.*

37 Drunk as a lord, As. *17th c.*

38 Drunk as a mouse, As. *14th c.*

39 Drunk as a wheelbarrow, As. *Ray, 1678*

40 Drunken folks seldom take harm. *17th c.*

1 Drunken night makes a cloudy morning, A.	*Fuller, 1732*
2 Dry as dust, As.	*16th c.*
3 Ducks and drakes of, To make.	*16th c.*
4 Dull as ditchwater, As.	*18th c.*
5 Dumb men get no lands.	*14th c.*
6 Dying duck in a thunderstorm, Like a.	*18th c.*
7 Ears burn, If your/ someone is talking about you.	*Heywood, 1546*
8 Early bird catches the worm, The.	*Camden, 1636*
9 Early to bed and early to rise, Makes a man healthy, wealthy and wise.	*Clarke, 1639*
10 Easier said than done.	*15th c.*
11 East or west, home is best.	*Bohn, 1855*
12 Easy come, easy go.	*19th c.*
13 Easy to be wise after the event, It is.	*17th c.*
14 Eat, and welcome; fast, and heartily welcome.	*Ray, 1678*
15 Eat one's words, To.	*16th c.*
16 Eat to live, but do not live to eat.	*Latin*
17 Eat your cake and have it, You cannot.	*Heywood, 1546*
18 Education begins a gentleman, conversation completes him.	*Fuller, 1732*
19 Eggs in one basket, Do not put all your.	*18th c.*
20 Eleventh Commandment: The/ thou shalt not be found out.	*19th c.*
21 Empty purse that is full of other men's money, That is but an.	*Ray, 1678*
22 Empty vessels make the most noise.	*16th c.*
23 End justifies the means, The.	*17th c.*
24 England is the paradise of women, the hell of horses, and the purgatory of servants.	*16th c.*
25 English never know when they are beaten, The.	*19th c.*
26 Englishman's house (home) is his castle, An.	*17th c.*
27 Enough is as good as a feast.	*15th c.*
28 Enough is enough.	*Heywood, 1546*
29 Evening crowns the day, The.	*17th c.*
30 Every little helps.	*18th c.*
31 Every man for himself, and God for us all.	*Heywood, 1562*
32 Every man has his faults.	*16th c.*
33 Every man is best known to himself.	*Draxe, 1616*
34 Every man to his taste.	*16th c.*
35 Everybody's business is nobody's business.	*17th c.*
36 Everything comes to him who waits.	*16th c.*
37 Everything hath an end, and a pudding hath two.	*16th c.*
38 Everything is the worse for wearing.	*Clarke, 1639*
39 Everything must have a beginning.	*14th c.*

1 Evils, Of two/ choose the least.   *14th c.*

2 Example is better than precept.   *Latin*

3 Exception proves the rule, The.   *17th c.*

4 Experience is good, if not bought too dear.   *Kelly, 1721*

5 *Experientia docet*—Experience teaches.   *Latin*

6 Extremes meet.   *18th c.*

7 Eye sees not, What the/ the heart rues not.   *Heywood, 1546*

8 Failing to trust everybody, It is an equal/ and to trust nobody.   *Fuller, 1732*

9 Faint heart never won fair lady.   *16th c.*

10 Fair and softly goes far.   *14th c.*

11 Fair exchange is no robbery, A.   *16th c.*

12 Fair face and a foul heart, A.   *Howell, 1659*

13 Fair face is half a fortune, A.   *Draxe, 1616*

14 Fair play's a jewel.   *19th c.*

15 Fairer the hostess, the fouler the reckoning, The.   *Howell, 1659*

16 Familiarity breeds contempt.   *Latin*

17 Far from eye, far from heart.   *14th c.*

18 Fast bind, fast find.   *Heywood, 1546*

19 Fat is in the fire, The.   *Heywood, 1546*

20 Faults are theirs that commit them, The first/ the second theirs that permit them.   *Fuller, 1732*

21 Faults are thick where love is thin.   *Howell, 1659*

22 Few lawyers die well, few physicians live well.   *16th c.*

23 Few words are best.   *Ray, 1678*

24 *Fiat justitia, ruat coelum*—Let justice be done, though heaven fall.   *Latin*

25 Fiddle while Rome is burning, To.   *17th c.*

26 Finding's keeping.   *19th c.*

27 Finger in the pie, To have a.   *17th c.*

28 Fire is a good servant but a bad master.   *17th c.*

29 First blow is half the battle, The.   *18th c.*

30 First catch your hare and then cook it.   *18th c.*

31 First come, first served.   *16th c.*

32 First impressions are most lasting.   *19th c.*

33 First think, and then speak.   *Clarke, 1639*

34 Fish out of water, Like a.   *Latin*

35 Fish to fry, I have other.   *17th c.*

36 Fit as a fiddle, As.   *17th c.*

37 Flat as a pancake, As.   *16th c.*

38 Fling dirt enough, and some will stick.   *Latin*

39 Flog a dead horse, To.   *19th c.*

 1 Follow the river and you'll get to the sea. *Fuller, 1732*
 2 Fool and his money are soon parted, A. *16th c.*
 3 Fool like an old fool, No. *Heywood, 1546*
 4 Fool that forgets himself, He is a. *14th c.*
 5 Fool that is not melancholy once a day, He is a. *Ray, 1678*
 6 Fool to the market, Send a/ and a fool he'll return. *16th c.*
 7 Fool wanders, The/ the wise man travels. *Fuller, 1732*
 8 Fools went not to market, If/ bad wares would not be sold. *Herbert, 1640*
 9 Forewarned, forearmed. *Latin*
10 Forgive and forget. *Heywood, 1546*
11 Fortune favours fools. *Latin*
12 Fortune is blind. *16th c.*
13 Fortune knocks, When/open the door. *17th c.*
14 Foul water will quench fire. *Heywood, 1546*
15 Four eyes see more than two. *Latin*
16 Fox knows much, The/ but more he that catcheth him. *Herbert, 1640*
17 Friend at court, A. *17th c.*
18 Friend in need is a friend indeed, A. *Latin*
19 Friend to thyself, Be a/ and others will befriend thee. *Kelly, 1721*
20 Friend to everybody is a friend to nobody, A. *17th c.*
21 Friends are thieves of time. *17th c.*
22 Friends both in heaven and hell, It is good to have some. *Herbert, 1640*
23 Friends (The best of friends) must part. *17th c.*
24 Friends, Have but few/ though many acquaintances. *Howell, 1659*
25 Friendship should not be all on one side. *17th c.*
26 Frying-pan into the fire, Out of the. *Heywood, 1546*
27 Full of courtesy, full of craft. *16th c.*

28 Game is not worth the candle, The. *17th c.*
29 Geese are swans, All his. *16th c.*
30 Gift horse in the mouth, Look not a. *Latin*
31 Give a dog a bad name and hang him. *Kelly, 1721*
32 Give him an inch and he'll take an ell. *Heywood, 1546*
33 Give the devil his due. *16th c.*
34 Gives to all, denies all, Who. *Herbert, 1640*
35 Gives twice who gives quickly, He. *Latin*
36 Giving much to the poor doth increase a man's store. *Herbert, 1640*
37 Glass houses, People who live in/ should never throw stones. *Herbert, 1640*
38 Gluttony kills more than the sword. *16th c.*
39 Go down the ladder when thou marriest a wife; go up when thou choosest a friend. *Ray, 1678*
40 Go farther and fare worse. *Heywood, 1546*

1 Go to bed with the lamb, and rise with the lark. *16th c.*

2 God comes at last when we think he is furthest off. *Italian*

3 God defend me from my friends; from my enemies I can defend myself. *17th c.*

4 God heals, and the doctor takes the fee. *Herbert, 1640*

5 God help the poor, for the rich can help themselves. *Kelly, 1721*

6 God help the rich, the poor can beg. *Howell, 1659*

7 God helps them that help themselves. *Herbert, 1640*

8 God send me a friend that will tell me of my faults. *Fuller, 1732*

9 God send you joy, for sorrow will come fast enough. *Draxe, 1616*

10 God sends fortune to fools. *Heywood, 1546*

11 God tempers the wind to the shorn lamb. *French*

12 God's mill grinds slow but sure. *Greek*

13 Good against evil, Set. *Herbert, 1640*

14 Good and quickly seldom meet. *Herbert, 1640*

15 Good beginning makes a good ending, A. *14th c.*

16 Good example is the best sermon, A. *Fuller, 1732*

17 Good face needs no paint, A. *Fuller, 1732*

18 Good judgement that relieth not wholly on his own, He hath a. *Fuller, 1732*

19 Good life is the only religion, A. *Fuller, 1732*

20 Good to want and to have, It is not. *Fergusson, 1641*

21 Good turn deserves another, One. *15th c.*

22 Good wife and health are a man's best wealth, A. *Fuller, 1732*

23 Good wife makes a good husband, A. *Heywood, 1546*

24 Good wine needs no bush. *16th c.*

25 Good workmen are seldom rich. *Herbert, 1640*

26 Grasp all, lose all. *14th c.*

27 Great minds think alike. *20th c.*

28 Great ones if there were no little ones, There would be no. *Herbert, 1640*

29 Great talkers are great liars. *French*

30 Great trees are good for nothing but shade. *Herbert, 1640*

31 Greater the truth, The/ the greater the libel. *18th c.*

32 Greatest hate springs from the greatest love, The. *16th c.*

33 Greek to me, It is. *16th c.*

34 Grist to the mill, To bring. *16th c.*

35 Hail fellow well met, To be. *16th c.*

36 Half a loaf is better than no bread. *Heywood, 1546*

37 Half the world knows not how the other half lives. *Herbert, 1640*

38 Half-seas over, To be. *18th c.*

39 Halves, Never do things by. *18th c.*

40 Hand and glove. *17th c.*

1 Handful of good life is better than a bushel of learning, A.   *Herbert, 1640*

2 Hands, Many/ make light work.   *Latin*

3 Handsome at twenty, He that is not/ nor strong at thirty, nor rich at forty, nor wise at fifty, will never be handsome, strong, rich or wise. *Herbert, 1640*

4 Handsome is that handsome does.   *Ray, 1670*

5 Hanged for a sheep as a lamb, As good be.   *Ray, 1678*

6 Hanging and wiving go by destiny.   *Heywood, 1546*

7 Happiness takes no account of time.   *18th c.*

8 Happy is he that is happy in his children.   *Fuller, 1732*

9 Happy is the country which has no history.   *19th c.*

10 Happy is the child whose father goes to the devil.   *16th c.*

11 Hard as a Flint (stone), As.   *14th c.*

12 Hard cases make bad law.   *Lean, 1902*

13 Hard cheese.   *19th c.*

14 Hard nut to crack, A.   *16th c.*

15 Haste, The more/ the less speed.   *Heywood, 1546*

16 Hatred is blind, as well as love.   *Fuller, 1732*

17 Hatch, match and despatch.   *19th c.*

18 Haul over the coals, To.   *16th c.*

19 Head, He that hath no/ needs no hat.   *Herbert, 1640*

20 Heads I win, tails you lose.   *17th c.*

21 Health is better than wealth.   *16th c.*

22 Health is not valued till sickness come.   *Fuller, 1732*

23 Hear all parties.   *15th c.*

24 Hear twice before you speak once.   *19th c.*

25 Heard a pin drop, You might have.   *19th c.*

26 Heart is in his mouth, His.   *16th c.*

27 Heavy purse makes a light heart, A.   *17th c.*

28 Hell and Chancery are always open.   *Fuller, 1732*

29 Hell is paved with good intentions. (The road to)   *18th c.*

30 Hell, Hull and Halifax, From/ good Lord deliver us.   *16th c.*

31 Higher up, The/ the greater the fall.   *16th c.*

32 History repeats itself.   *19th c.*

33 Hit the nail on the head, To.   *16th c.*

34 Hobson's choice.   *17th c.*

35 Hoist with his own petard.   *17th c.*

36 Hold a candle to the devil, To.   *15th c.*

37 Honest man's word is as good as his bond, An.   *17th c.*

38 Honest men marry soon, wise ones not at all.   *Ray, 1670*

39 Honesty is the best policy.   *16th c.*

40 *Honi soit qui mal y pense*—Evil be to him who evil thinks.   *French*

1 Honour among thieves, There is.	*18th c.*
2 Hook or by crook, By.	*14th c.*
3 Hope for the best and prepare for the worst.	*16th c.*
4 Hope is as cheap as despair.	*Fuller, 1732*
5 Hot love is soon cold.	*16th c.*
6 Hour in the morning is worth two in the evening, An.	*19th c.*
7 Hour of pain is as long as a day of pleasure, An.	*Fuller, 1732*
8 Hour to-day, One/ is worth two to-morrow.	*Fuller, 1732*
9 Hour's sleep before midnight, One/ is worth three after.	*Herbert, 1640*
10 House on fire, Like a.	*19th c.*
11 *Humanum est errare*—To err is human.	*Latin*
12 Hypocrisy is a homage that vice pays to virtue.	*Fuller, 1732*
13 Idle that might be better employed, He is.	*Fuller, 1732*
14 If Ifs and Ans were pots and pans There'd be no trade for tinkers.	*19th c.*
15 *Il faut reculer pour mieux sauter*—One must draw back in order to leap better.	*French*
16 Ill doers are ill thinkers.	*16th c.*
17 Ill gotten, ill spent.	*Latin*
18 Ill news comes too soon.	*16th c.*
19 Ill wind that blows nobody good, It is an.	*Heywood, 1546*
20 In at one ear and out at the other.	*14th c.*
21 In for a penny, in for a pound.	*17th c.*
22 Insult to injury, To add.	*Latin*
23 Iron entered his soul, The.	*Latin*
24 Iron hand in a velvet glove, An.	*French*
25 Irons in the fire, To have many.	*16th c.*
26 Jack has his Jill, Every.	*17th c.*
27 Jack of all trades and master of none.	*18th c.*
28 Joan is as good as my lady, in the dark.	*17th c.*
29 Jolly (happy) as a sandboy, As.	*19th c.*
30 Judge from appearances, Never.	*16th c.*
31 Keep a dog and bark yourself, Do not.	*16th c.*
32 Keep a thing seven years and you will find a use for it.	*17th c.*
33 Keep one's tongue between one's teeth, To.	*17th c.*
34 Keep up with the Joneses, To.	*20th c.*
35 Keep your eyes wide open before marriage and half shut afterwards.	*18th c.*
36 Keep your mouth shut and your eyes open.	*18th c.*
37 Kill not the goose that lays the golden eggs.	*15th c.*
38 Kill two birds with one stone, To.	*17th c.*

1 King can do no wrong, The. *17th c.*
2 King never dies, The. *Latin*
3 King's favour is no inheritance, The. *Fuller, 1732*
4 Kiss and be friends. *14th c.*
5 Kiss the mistress, If you can/ never kiss the maid. *Ray, 1670*
6 Knaves and fools divide the world. *Ray, 1670*
7 Knocked me down with a feather, You might have. *19th c.*
8 Know on which side one's bread is buttered, To. *Heywood, 1546*
9 Know the ropes, To. *19th c.*
10 Know the worth of water till the well is dry, We never. *Kelly, 1721*
11 Know which way the wind blows, To. *Heywood, 1546*
12 Knowledge is power. *17th c.*
13 Knows how many beans make nine, He. *19th c.*
14 Knows little, He that/ soon repeats it. *18th c.*
15 Knows nothing, He that/ doubts nothing. *Herbert, 1640*

16 *Laborare est orare*—To work is to pray. *Latin*
17 Large as life, As. *18th c.*
18 Last but not least. *16th c.*
19 Last legs, To be on one's. *16th c.*
20 Last straw breaks the camel's back, The. *17th c.*
21 Laughs best who laughs last, He. *18th c.*
22 Law is a bottomless pit. *18th c.*
23 Law for the rich, One/ and another for the poor. *19th c.*
24 Law makers should not be law breakers. *14th c.*
25 Laws, The more/ the more offenders. *Latin*
26 Lawyers' houses are built on the heads of fools. *Herbert, 1640*
27 Lay it on with a trowel, To. *16th c.*
28 Lead a horse to the water, A man may/ but he cannot make him drink.
   Heywood, 1546
29 Lean as a rake, As. *14th c.*
30 Learning makes a good man better and an ill man worse. *17th c.*
31 Least foolish is wise, The. *Herbert, 1640*
32 Least said, soonest mended. *15th c.*
33 Leave in the lurch, To. *16th c.*
34 Leave no stone unturned, To. *Greek*
35 Lend I am a friend, When I/ when I ask I am a foe. *16th c.*
36 Lend your money and lose your friend. *17th c.*
37 Let sleeping dogs lie. *14th c.*
38 Let the cat out of the bag, To. *18th c.*
39 Liar is not believed when he speaks the truth, A. *Latin*
40 Liars should have good memories. *Latin*

1 Lick into shape, To. *15th c.*

2 Lie begets a lie, A. *Fuller, 1732*

3 Lies upon the ground, He that/ can fall no lower. *Latin*

4 Life is half spent before we know what it is. *Herbert, 1640*

5 Life is sweet. *14th c.*

6 Life, While there is/ there is hope. *Latin*

7 Lifeless that is faultless, He is. *Heywood, 1546*

8 Light cares speak, great ones are dumb. *Latin*

9 Light purse makes a heavy heart, A. *16th c.*

10 Lightly come, lightly go. *16th c.*

11 Like father, like son. *Latin*

12 Like it, If you don't/ you can (may) lump it. *19th c.*

13 Like master, like man. *Latin*

14 Line one's pockets, To. *16th c.*

15 Lion is not so fierce as he is painted, The. *17th c.*

16 Listeners hear no good of themselves. *17th c.*

17 Little and often fills the purse. *17th c.*

18 Little things please little minds. *Latin*

19 Live and learn. *Clarke, 1639*

20 Live and let live. *Dutch*

21 Live without our friends, We can/ but not without our neighbours.
Kelly, 1721

22 Lock, stock, and barrel. *19th c.*

23 Lombard Street to a China orange, All. *18th c.*

24 Long absent, soon forgotten. *Draxe, 1616*

25 Long spoon, He should have a/ that sups with the devil. *14th c.*

26 Longest day must have an end, The. *17th c.*

27 Look before you leap. *14th c.*

28 Look (at) on the bright side. *19th c.*

29 Lookers-on see most of the game. *16th c.*

30 Losers are always in the wrong. *Spanish*

31 Losers seekers, finders keepers. *19th c.*

32 Lost his taste, To him that has/ sweet is sour. *Draxe, 1616*

33 Love and a cough cannot be hid. *Latin*

34 Love and business teach eloquence. *Herbert, 1640*

35 Love begets love. *Latin*

36 Love best, Whom we/ to them we can say least. *16th c.*

37 Love comes in at the window and goes out at the door. *Camden, 1614*

38 Love is blind. *14th c.*

39 Love is sweet in the beginning but sour in the ending. *Draxe, 1616*

40 Love lives in cottages as well as in courts. *16th c.*

1	Love makes one fit for any work.	*Herbert, 1640*
2	Love makes the world go round.	*17th c.*
3	Love me little, love me long.	*Heywood, 1546*
4	Love me, love my dog.	*Latin*
5	Love of money and the love of learning rarely meet, The.	*Herbert, 1651*
6	Love too much that die for love, They.	*17th c.*
7	Love will find a way.	*16th c.*
8	Mad as a hatter.	*19th c.*
9	Mad as a March hare, As.	*14th c.*
10	Maidens should be meek until they be married.	*Fergusson, 1641*
11	Main chance, Have an eye to the.	*16th c.*
12	Make hay while the sun shines.	*Heywood, 1546*
13	Man can only die once, A.	*16th c.*
14	Man in the moon.	*14th c.*
15	Man in the street, The.	*19th c.*
16	Man loveth his fetters, No/ be they made of gold.	*Heywood, 1546*
17	Man is as old as he feels, and a woman as old as she looks, A.	*20th c.*
18	Man is known by the company he keeps, A.	*17th c.*
19	Man lives, As a/ so shall he die.	*16th c.*
20	Man or mouse.	*16th c.*
21	Man proposes, God disposes.	*Latin*
22	Many a little makes a mickle.	*13th c.*
23	March comes in like a lion and goes out like a lamb.	*Ray, 1670*
24	Mare's nest, To find a.	*16th c.*
25	Marriage is a lottery.	*17th c.*
26	Marriages are made in heaven.	*16th c.*
27	Marries for wealth, He that/ sells his liberty.	*Herbert, 1640*
28	Marries late, He that/ marries ill.	*16th c.*
29	Marrieth for love without money, Who/ hath good nights and sorry days.	*Ray, 1670*
30	Marry first and love will follow.	*17th c.*
31	Marry in haste and repent at leisure.	*16th c.*
32	Marry late or never, It is good to.	*Clarke, 1639*
33	Marry your daughters betimes, lest they marry themselves.	*16th c.*
34	Marry your son when you will, your daughter when you can.	*Herbert, 1640*
35	Measure in all things, There is a.	*14th c.*
36	Measure thrice before you cut once.	*Italian*
37	Meat, One man's/ is another man's poison.	*Latin*
38	Meet troubles half-way, Don't.	*16th c.*
39	Men who make a city, It is the.	*Greek*

1 Meekness of Moses is better than the strength of Samson, The.

Fuller, 1732

2 Merry as a cricket, As. *Heywood, 1546*

3 Might is right. *14th c.*

4 Mind your own business. *Clarke, 1639*

5 Mirror, The best/ is an old friend. *Herbert, 1640*

6 Misfortunes never come singly. *14th c.*

7 Miss is as good as a mile, A. *19th c.*

8 Mob has many heads, but no brains, The. *Fuller, 1732*

9 Money be not thy servant, If/ it will be thy master. *17th c.*

10 Money begets money. *Italian*

11 Money is a good servant, but a bad master. *17th c.*

12 Money makes marriage. *Fuller, 1732*

13 Money makes the man. *Greek*

14 Money or your life! Your. *19th c.*

15 Money talks. *17th c.*

16 More the merrier, The/ the fewer the better cheer. *Heywood, 1546*

17 Mother, Like/ like daughter. *16th c.*

18 Mother-in-law remembers not that she was a daughter-in-law, The.

Howell, 1659

19 Mountain out of a molehill, To make a. *16th c.*

20 Much law, but little justice. *Fuller, 1732*

21 Murder will out. *14th c.*

22 Natural folly is bad enough, but learned folly is intolerable. *Fuller, 1732*

23 Necessity hath no law. *Latin*

24 Necessity is the mother of invention. *16th c.*

25 Neck or nothing. *Ray, 1678*

26 Need makes the old wife trot. *15th c.*

27 Needle in a haystack, To look for a. *15th c.*

28 Needs must when the devil drives. *15th c.*

29 Never a bad day that hath a good night, It is. *17th c.*

30 Never ask pardon before you are accused. *Bohn, 1855*

31 Never put off till to-morrow what may be done to-day. *14th c.*

32 Never refuse a good offer. *Ray, 1670*

33 Never say die. *19th c.*

34 Never too late to mend, It is. *17th c.*

35 Never too old to learn. *17th c.*

36 Never trouble trouble till trouble troubles you. *19th c.*

37 New broom sweeps clean, A. *Heywood, 1546*

38 No fire without some smoke. *Heywood, 1546*

39 No man's religion ever survives his morals. *Fuller, 1732*

1 No mischief but a woman or a priest is at the bottom of it.	*Latin*
2 No money, no swiss.	*17th c.*
3 No names, no pack drill.	*20th c.*
4 No news is good news.	*Italian*
5 No pleasure without pain.	*16th c.*
6 No rose without a thorn.	*15th c.*
7 No smoke without some fire.	*15th c.*
8 No sunshine but has some shadow.	*Ray, 1678*
9 No taxation without representation.	*18th c.*
10 Nose to the grindstone, To keep one's.	*16th c.*
11 Nothing costs so much as what is given us.	*Fuller, 1732*
12 Nothing for nothing.	*18th c.*
13 Nothing is certain but uncertainty.	*Latin*
14 Nothing is ours, but time.	*Fuller, 1732*
15 Nothing questioneth, He that/ nothing learneth.	*16th c.*
16 Nothing seek, nothing find.	*16th c.*
17 Nothing succeeds like success.	*French*
18 Nothing that is violent is permanent.	*16th c.*
19 Nothing venture, nothing win.	*15th c.*
20 Nowadays truth is the greatest news.	*Fuller, 1732*
21 Obedience is much more seen in little things than in great.	*Fuller, 1732*
22 Oil upon the waters, To pour.	*19th c.*
23 Old as the hills, As.	*19th c.*
24 Old friends and old wine are best.	*Herbert, 1640*
25 Old head on young shoulders, An.	*Clarke, 1639*
26 Old poacher makes a good game-keeper, An.	*14th c.*
27 Once bitten, twice shy.	*19th c.*
28 One foot in the grave, To have.	*16th c.*
29 Opportunity makes the thief.	*13th c.*
30 Ounce of discretion is worth a pound of learning, An.	*17th c.*
31 Out of sight, out of mind.	*13th c.*
32 P's and Q's, To mind one's.	*17th c.*
33 Painters and poets have leave to lie.	*16th c.*
34 Past cure, past care.	*16th c.*
35 Patience is a flower that grows not in everyone's garden.	*Ray, 1670*
36 Patience, money and time bring all things to pass.	*Herbert, 1640*
37 Pay a person in his own coin, To.	*16th c.*
38 Pay through the nose, To.	*17th c.*
39 Pays the piper may call the tune, He who.	*17th c.*
40 Peace makes plenty.	*15th c.*

He who calls the tune must pay the piper. Too

1 Penny and penny laid up will be many.	*Clarke, 1639*
2 Penny for your thoughts, A.	*Heywood, 1546*
3 Penny wise, pound foolish.	*17th c.*
4 Pension never enriched a young man.	*Herbert, 1640*
5 Pigs might fly, but they are very unlikely birds.	*19th c.*
6 Pillar to post, From.	*15th c.*
7 Plain as a pike-staff, As.	*16th c.*
8 Play first (or second) fiddle, To.	*19th c.*
9 Plays best (well) that wins, He.	*Heywood, 1555*
10 Pleased as Punch, As.	*19th c.*
11 Pleased ourselves, When we are/ we begin to please others.	*Fuller, 1732*
12 Pleasure, There is more/ in loving than in being loved.	*Fuller, 1732*
13 Pleasure, To overcome/ is the greatest pleasure.	*Fuller, 1732*
14 Pleasure of what we enjoy is lost by coveting more, The.	*Fuller, 1732*
15 Poor as Job, As.	*14th c.*
16 Poor heart that never rejoices, It is a.	*19th c.*
17 Possession is nine points of the law.	*Draxe, 1616*
18 Pot calls the kettle black, The.	*17th c.*
19 Poverty breeds strife.	*Ray, 1678*
20 Poverty is no sin.	*Herbert, 1640*
21 Poverty is not a shame, but the being ashamed of it is.	*Fuller, 1732*
22 Practice makes perfect.	*Latin*
23 Practise what you preach.	*14th c.*
24 Praise makes good men better and bad men worse.	*Fuller, 1732*
25 Preaches well that lives well, He.	*17th c.*
26 Prevention is better than cure.	*Latin*
27 Pride will have a fall.	*16th c.*
28 Promises too much, He that/ means nothing.	*Draxe, 1616*
29 Proof of the pudding is in the eating, The.	*Camden, 1623*
30 Prospect is often better than possession.	*Fuller, 1732*
31 Prosperity has damned more souls than all the devils together.	*Fuller, 1732*
32 Proud as Lucifer, As.	*14th c.*
33 Proud as a peacock, As.	*14th c.*
34 Put on one's thinking cap, To.	*17th c.*
35 Pull down than to build, It is easier to.	*16th c.*
36 Purse-strings are the most common ties of friendship, The.	*Fuller, 1732*
37 Put that in your pipe and smoke it.	*19th c.*
38 Put your shoulder to the wheel.	*17th c.*
39 Queen Anne is dead.	*18th c.*
40 *Quos Deus vult perdere, prius dementat*—Whom God wishes to destroy, he first makes mad.	*Latin*

1 Rain before seven: fine before eleven. *19th c.*

2 Rain, rain, go to Spain: fair weather come again. *Howell, 1659*

3 Rains but it pours, It never. *18th c.*

4 Rainy day, Lay it up for a. *16th c.*

5 Rats desert a sinking ship. *17th c.*

6 Red as a rose, As. *14th c.*

7 Red rag to a bull, Like a. *16th c.*

8 Redemption from hell, There is no. *17th c.*

9 Religion an ill man is of, It matters not what. *Fuller, 1732*

10 Religion is the best armour in the world, but the worst cloak. *Fuller, 1732*

11 Remedy for all things but death, There is a. *16th c.*

12 Repentance comes too late. *15th c.*

13 Resolves to deal with none but honest men, He that/ must leave off dealing. *Fuller, 1732*

14 Respects not is not respected, He that. *Herbert, 1640*

15 Revenge is sweet. *16th c.*

16 Revenge never repairs an injury. *Fuller, 1732*

17 Rich men have no faults. *Fuller, 1732*

18 Rich that is satisfied, He is. *Fuller, 1732*

19 Riches of the mind only that make a man rich and happy, It is. *Fuller, 1732*

20 Ridicule than commend, It is easier to. *Fuller, 1732*

21 Right as rain, As. *19th c.*

22 Roads lead to Rome, All. *14th c.*

23 Roar like a bull, To. *16th c.*

24 Rob Peter to pay Paul, To. *14th c.*

25 Rod for his own back, He makes a. *14th c.*

26 Rolling stone gathers no moss, A. *Heywood, 1546*

27 Rome was not built in a day. *Latin*

28 Room to swing a cat, Not. *18th c.*

29 Rope enough and he'll hang himself, Give a thief. *Ray, 1670*

30 Rough with the smooth, Take the. *15th c.*

31 Rule the roast (roost), To. *15th c.*

32 Rule youth well, for age will rule itself. *Fergusson, 1641*

33 Run with the hare and hunt with the hounds, To. *Heywood, 1546*

34 Sadness and gladness succeed each other. *Clarke, 1639*

35 Sail near the wind, To. *19th c.*

36 Same boat, To be all in the. *16th c.*

37 Sauce for the goose is sauce for the gander, What is. *Ray, 1670*

38 Save one's bacon, To. *17th c.*

39 Say Bo(o) to a goose, He cannot. *16th c.*

40 Say no ill of the year till it be past. *Herbert, 1640*

1 Saying is one thing and doing another.	*Heywood, 1550*
2 Scot-free, To go.	*16th c.*
3 Scratch, To come up to (the).	*19th c.*
4 Scratch my back and I'll scratch yours, You.	*17th c.*
5 Screw loose somewhere, There is a.	*19th c.*
6 Second thoughts are best.	*Latin*
7 See Naples and die.	*Italian*
8 See the wood for the trees, You cannot.	*Heywood, 1546*
9 See what we shall see, We shall.	*19th c.*
10 Seeing is believing.	*Clarke, 1639*
11 Seeks trouble, He that/ never misses.	*Herbert, 1640*
12 Self-praise is no recommendation.	*17th c.*
13 Self-preservation is the first law of nature.	*17th c.*
14 Set the Thames on fire, To.	*18th c.*
15 Share and share alike.	*17th c.*
16 Shoe pinches, To know where the.	*14th c.*
17 Short and sweet.	*16th c.*
18 Shortest answer is doing, The.	*Herbert, 1640*
19 Short life and a merry one, A.	*17th c.*
20 Short pleasure, long lament.	*15th c.*
21 Sickness is better than sadness.	*Fuller, 1732*
22 Sight for sore eyes, A.	*19th c.*
23 Silence gives consent.	*14th c.*
24 Silk purse out of a sow's ear, You cannot make a.	*16th c.*
25 Six hours' sleep for a man, seven for a woman, and eight for a fool.	*18th c.*
26 Six of one and half a dozen of the other.	*19th c.*
27 Sixes and sevens, To be at.	*14th c.*
28 Skin of one's teeth, By the.	*16th c.*
29 Slept well, He hath/ that remembers not he hath slept ill.	*Fuller, 1732*
30 Slippery as an eel, As.	*15th c.*
31 Slow but sure.	*Clarke, 1639*
32 Small profits and quick returns.	*19th c.*
33 Smell a rat, To.	*16th c.*
34 Snake in the grass, There is a.	*Latin*
35 Sneezed at, Not to be.	*19th c.*
36 So far, so good.	*Kelly, 1721*
37 Soberness conceals, What/ drunkenness reveals.	*Latin*
38 Some are wise and some are otherwise.	*Howell, 1659*
39 Soon as a man is born he begins to die, As.	*Latin*
40 Soon got, soon spent.	*Heywood, 1546*
41 Soon hot, soon cold.	*15th c.*

1 Soon ripe, soon rotten. *Latin*

2 Sorrow comes unsent for. *Latin*

3 Soup and love, Of/ the first is the best. *Spanish*

4 Sour grapes can ne'er make sweet wine. *Fuller, 1732*

5 Speak not of my debts unless you mean to pay them. *Herbert, 1640*

6 Speak well of your friend, of your enemy say nothing. *18th c.*

7 Speak when you are spoken to. *16th c.*

8 Speaks ill of his wife, He that/ dishonours himself. *Fuller, 1732*

9 Speech is silver, silence is golden. *Persian*

10 Spick and span. *16th c.*

11 Split hairs, To. *16th c.*

12 Spoke in one's wheel, To put a. *17th c.*

13 Sprat to catch a mackerel (whale), To throw a. *19th c.*

14 Spur a free horse, Do not. *Latin*

15 Spur of the moment, On the. *19th c.*

16 Stepmother, Take heed of a/ the very name of her sufficeth. *Herbert, 1651*

17 Stew (fry) in one's own juice (grease), To. *14th c.*

18 Sticks and stones may break my bones, but words will never hurt me.

19th c.

19 Stiff as a poker. *18th c.*

20 Stiff upper lip, To keep a. *19th c.*

21 Still waters run deep. *14th c.*

22 Sting is in the tail, The. *16th c.*

23 Sting of a reproach is the truth of it, The. *Fuller, 1732*

24 Stir up a hornets' nest, To. *Latin*

25 Stitch in time saves nine, A. *Fuller, 1732*

26 Stone that lieth not in your way need not offend you, The. *Fuller, 1732*

27 Storm in a tea-cup, A. *19th c.*

28 Straight trees have crooked roots. *16th c.*

29 Strike while the iron is hot. *14th c.*

30 Subtlety is better than force. *Draxe, 1616*

31 Sun shines upon all alike, The. *16th c.*

32 Sure as eggs is eggs, As. *17th c.*

33 Swallow, One/ does not make a summer. *Greek*

34 Sweet discourse makes short days and nights. *Herbert, 1640*

35 Sweet tooth, To have a. *16th c.*

36 Swine, women, and bees cannot be turned. *Ray, 1678*

37 Take a farthing away from a thousand pounds, it will be a thousand pounds no longer. *18th c.*

38 Take a leaf out of one's book, To. *19th c.*

39 Take away my good name and take away my life. *Ray, 1670*

1 Take care of the pence and the pounds will take care of themselves. *18th c.*

2 Take one down a peg or two, To. *16th c.*

3 Take the bull by the horns, To. *19th c.*

4 Take the gilt off the gingerbread, To. *19th c.*

5 Take the law into one's own hands, To. *17th c.*

6 Take the wind out of one's sails, To. *19th c.*

7 Take things as you find them. *Lean, 1902*

8 Tales out of school, To tell. *16th c.*

9 Talk the hind leg off a donkey, To. *19th c.*

10 Talk of the devil, and he is sure to appear. *17th c.*

11 Talk without thinking, To/ is to shoot without aiming. *Fuller, 1732*

12 Talkers, The greatest/ are (always) the least doers. *16th c.*

13 Talks to himself, He that/ speaks to a fool. *Kelly, 1721*

14 Tarred with the same brush, All. *19th c.*

15 Taste of the kitchen is better than the smell, The. *19th c.*

16 Teach an old dog tricks, It is hard to. *16th c.*

17 Teach your grandmother to suck eggs. *18th c.*

18 Teacheth ill, He/ who teacheth all. *Howell, 1659*

19 Tell that to the Marines. *19th c.*

20 Tell the truth and shame the devil. *16th c.*

21 Tells his wife news, He that/ is but newly married. *Herbert, 1640*

22 *Tempus fugit*—Time flies. *Latin*

23 Tenterhooks, To be on. *18th c.*

24 There's many a slip 'twixt the cup and the lip. *Greek*

25 Thick as thieves, As. *19th c.*

26 Thief to catch a thief, Set a. *Ray, 1670*

27 Thin end of the wedge is to be feared, The. *19th c.*

28 Things are difficult before they are easy, All. *Fuller, 1732*

29 Things at the worst will mend. *17th c.*

30 Think today and speak tomorrow. *Bohn, 1855*

31 Think well of all men. *Howell, 1659*

32 Think with the wise, but talk with the vulgar. *Greek*

33 Thinking is very far from knowing. *18th c.*

34 Though I say it that should not. *16th c.*

35 Thought is free. *14th c.*

36 Thousand pounds of law, In a/ there's not an ounce of love. *Ray, 1670*

37 Threadneedle Street, The old lady of. *19th c.*

38 Threatened men live long. *16th c.*

39 Three may keep counsel if two be away. *Heywood, 1546*

40 Three women and a goose make a market. *Italian*

41 Throw good money after bad, To. *19th c.*

1 Time and thinking tame the strongest grief.   *Ray, 1670*

2 Time and tide wait for no man.   *16th c.*

3 Time for all things, There is a.   *14th c.*

4 Time like the present, No.   *18th c.*

5 To-day, One/ is worth two to-morrows.   *17th c.*

6 Tomorrow never comes.   *Ray, 1678*

7 Tomorrow is a new day.   *16th c.*

8 Tongue, One/ is enough for a woman.   *Ray, 1678*

9 Tongue is not steel, yet it cuts, The.   *Heywood, 1546*

10 Tongue of idle people is never idle, The.   *Fuller, 1732*

11 Too big for one's boots, To be.   *19th c.*

12 Too clever by half.   *19th c.*

13 Too many cooks spoil the broth.   *16th c.*

14 Touch him with a pair of tongs, I would not.   *Ray, 1670*

15 Touch wood.   *20th c.*

16 *Tout passe, tout casse, tout lasse.* Everything passes, everything perishes, everything palls.   *French*

17 Translators, traitors.   *Italian*

18 Travels far, He that/ knows much.   *Clarke, 1639*

19 Tread on a worm and it will turn.   *Heywood, 1546*

20 Tree is known by its fruit, A.   *14th c.*

21 True blue will never stain.   *Howell, 1659*

22 True word is spoken in jest, Many a.   *14th c.*

23 Trust not a new friend nor an old enemy.   *Kelly, 1721*

24 Truth fears no colours.   *Ray, 1678*

25 Truth is stranger than fiction.   *19th c.*

26 Truth is the daughter of God.   *Fuller, 1732*

27 Truth never grows old.   *Fuller, 1732*

28 Truth, The/ the whole truth, and nothing but the truth.   *17th c.*

29 Turn an honest penny, To.   *Heywood, 1546*

30 Turn in his grave, To make a person.   *19th c.*

31 Turn over a new leaf, To.   *Heywood, 1546*

32 Turn the tables, To.   *17th c.*

33 Turn up one's nose, To.   *16th c.*

34 Turn up trumps, To.   *17th c.*

35 Twist round one's little finger, To.   *19th c.*

36 Two bites of a cherry, To make.   *French*

37 Two blacks do not make a white.   *Kelly, 1721*

38 Two can play at that game.   *19th c.*

39 Two dogs strive for a bone, and a third runs away with it.   *16th c.*

1 Two heads are better than one.   *Heywood, 1546*

2 Two is company, three is none.   *19th c.*

3 Two negatives make an affirmative.   *16th c.*

4 Two sides to every question, There are.   *19th c.*

5 Two strings to one's bow, To have.   *15th c.*

6 Two to make a quarrel, It takes.   *19th c.*

7 Two wrongs don't make a right.   *19th c.*

8 Ugly as sin, As.   *19th c.*

9 Uncertainty of the law, The glorious.   *19th c.*

10 Under the blanket the black one is as good as the white.   *Fuller, 1732*

11 Unforeseen (unexpected) that always happens, It is the.   *Latin*

12 Unity is strength.   *French*

13 Variety is pleasing.   *Greek*

14 Vengeance, The noblest/is to forgive.   *16th c.*

15 Venom to that of the tongue, There is no.   *Howell, 1659*

16 *Verbum sapienti sat est*—A word is enough to the wise.   *Latin*

17 Virtue dwells not in the tongue but in the heart.   *Fuller, 1732*

18 Virtue is its own reward.   *Latin*

19 Virtue never grows old.   *Herbert, 1640*

20 Virtue of necessity, Make a.   *Latin*

21 Vows made in storms are forgotten in calm.   *Fuller, 1732*

22 Wait and see.   *19th c.*

23 Walls have ears.   *17th c.*

24 Want a thing well done, If you/ do it yourself.   *Draxe, 1616*

25 Want of wit is worse than want of wealth.   *Kelly, 1721*

26 War begins, When/ hell opens.   *Herbert, 1651*

27 Wars bring scars.   *Clarke, 1639*

28 Warm the cockles of the heart, To.   *17th c.*

29 Wash dirty linen in public, To.   *19th c.*

30 Wash your hands often, your feet seldom, and your head never. *Ray, 1670*

31 Waste not, want not.   *18th c.*

32 Watched pot never boils, A.   *19th c.*

33 Water in a sieve, To carry.   *Latin*

34 Water off a duck's back, Like.   *19th c.*

35 Water (blood) out of a stone, To get.   *Latin*

36 Way to an Englishman's heart is through his stomach, The.   *19th c.*

37 Way to be safe is never to be secure, The.   *Fuller, 1732*

38 Weakest goes to the wall, The.   *16th c.*

39 Wealth, The greatest/ is contentment with a little.   *Ray, 1670*

1 Wear one's heart on one's sleeve, To. *17th c.*

2 Wear the breeches (pants), To. *15th c.*

3 Wedlock is a padlock. *Ray, 1678*

4 Welcome is the best cheer. *Greek*

5 Well begun is half done. *Latin*

6 Wet one's whistle, To. *14th c.*

7 What can't be cured must be endured. *14th c.*

8 What is worth doing is worth doing well. *18th c.*

9 What's yours is mine, and what's mine is my own. *18th c.*

10 Wheels within wheels, There are. *17th c.*

11 When in doubt, leave out. *20th c.*

12 When the cat is away the mice will play. *16th c.*

13 Whispering, Where there is/ there is lying. *Ray, 1678*

14 Widows are always rich. *Ray, 1678*

15 Wife, He that has a/ has a master. *Kelly, 1721*

16 Wild oats, To sow one's. *16th c.*

17 Will, Where there's a/ there's a way. *Herbert, 1640*

18 Will, Where there's a/ there's trouble. *20th c.*

19 Wine and wenches empty men's purses. *Clarke, 1639*

20 Wine in the bottle does not quench thirst, The. *Herbert, 1640*

21 Wine in, truth out. *16th c.*

22 Wisdom like silence, No. *Greek*

23 Wise child that knows its own father, It is a. *16th c.*

24 Wise man, He is not a/ who cannot play the fool on occasion. *16th c.*

25 Wise men learn by other men's mistakes; fools by their own. *Latin*

26 Wish is father to the thought, The. *Latin*

27 Wive and thrive both in a year, It is hard to. *15th c.*

28 Wives must be had, be they good or bad. *Clarke, 1639*

29 Wolf from the door, To keep the. *Heywood, 1546*

30 Woman conceals what she knows not, A. *16th c.*

31 Woman's work is never done, A. *16th c.*

32 Women and geese, Where there are/ there wants no noise. *Draxe, 1616*

33 Women are always in extremes. *Clarke, 1639*

34 Women are necessary evils. *16th c.*

35 Women look in their glass, The more/ the less they look to their house. *Herbert, 1640*

36 Women must have their wills while they live, because they make none when they die. *17th c.*

37 Women must have the last word. *16th c.*

38 Wonders will never cease. *18th c.*

39 Wool over a person's eyes, To pull the. *19th c.*

40 Work and no play makes Jack a dull boy, All. *Ray, 1670*

1 World and his wife, All the.   *18th c.*

2 Worse things happen at sea.   *19th c.*

3 Worth his weight in gold, He is.   *16th c.*

4 Worth of a thing is best known by the want, The.   *17th c.*

5 Wrong never comes right.   *19th c.*

6 Young man should not marry yet, A/ an old man not at all.   *16th c.*

7 Young men may die, old men must.   *16th c.*

8 Young men think old men fools, and old men know young men to be so.
                                                                 16th c.

9 Young saint, old devil.   *15th c.*

10 Youth and age will never agree.   *16th c.*

11 Youth will be served.   *19th c.*

12 Youth will have its course (or swing, or fling).   *16th c.*

13 Zeal is fit only for wise men, but is found mostly·in fools.   *Fuller, 1732*

14 Zeal, when it is a virtue, is a dangerous one.   *Fuller, 1732*

15 Zeal without knowledge is fire without light.   *Fuller, 1732*

PUDNEY, John, 1909—

16 Do not despair
   For Johnny head-in-air;
   He sleeps as sound
   As Johnny underground.   *For Johnny*

PUNCH

17 Advice to persons about to marry.—'Don't.'   *Vol. 8, Page 1, 1845*

18 You pays your money and you takes your choice.   *Vol. 10, 16, 1846*

19 What is better than Presence of Mind·in a Railway accident ?—Absence of
   Body.   *Vol. 16, 231, 1849*

20 Never do today what you can put off till tomorrow. *Vol. 17, 241, 1849*

21 What is Matter ?—Never Mind.
   What is Mind ?—No Matter.   *Vol. 29, 19, 1855*

22 Why are Trafalgar Square fountains like Government Clerks ?—Because
   they play from 10 till 4.   *Vol. 35, 21, 1858*

23 Mun, a had no' been the-erre abune two hours when—bang—went sax-
   pence!!!   *Vol. 55, 235, 1868*

24 Nothink for nothink 'ere, and precious little for sixpence.
                                                       Vol. 57, 152, 1869

25 Go directly—see what she's doing, and tell her she mustn't. *Vol. 63, 202,*
                                                                        1872

26 Here was an old owl liv'd in an oak,
   The more he heard the less he spoke:
   The less he spoke, the more he heard,
   O, if men were all like that wise bird.   *Vol. 68, 155, 1875*

1 I never read books—I *write* them.   *Vol. 74, 210, 1878*

2 I used your soap two years ago: since then I have used no other.
                                                         Vol. 86, 197, 1884

3 Nearly all our best men are dead! Carlyle, Tennyson, Browning, George Eliot! I'm not feeling very well myself!   *Vol. 104, 210, 1893*

4 I'm afraid you've got a bad egg, Mr. Jones.
Oh no, my Lord, I assure you! Parts of it are excellent.
                                                         Vol. 109, 222, 1895

5 Look here, Steward, if this is coffee, I want tea; but if this is tea, then I wish for coffee.   *Vol. 123, 44, 1902*

QUESNAY, François, 1694–1774

6 *Laissez faire, laissez passer.*—No interference, and complete freedom of movement.   *[Of Government interference] Attributed*

RABELAIS, François, 1494?–1553?

7 *L'appétit vient en mangeant.* Appetite comes with eating.   *Gargantua, 1, 5*

8 *Tirez le rideau, la farce est jouée.* Ring down the curtain, the farce is over.
                                                         Last words, attributed

9 *Je m'en vais chercher un grand peut-être.* I am going in search of a great perhaps.   *Last words, attributed*

RACINE, Jean, 1639–1699

10 *Elle flotte, elle hésite; en un mot, elle est femme.* She wavers, she hesitates; in a word, she is a woman.   MATHAN   *Athalie, Act 3, Scene 3*

RALEIGH, Sir Walter, 1552?–1618

11 Even such is Time, that takes in trust
       Our youth, our joys, our all we have,
And pays us but with age and dust;
       Who in the dark and silent grave,
When we have wandered all our ways,
Shuts up the story of our days;
But from this earth, this grave, this dust,
My God shall raise me up, I trust.   *Written the night before his death*

12 Give me my scallop-shell of quiet,
My staff of faith to walk upon,
My scrip of joy, immortal diet,
My bottle of salvation,
My gown of glory, hope's true gage,
And thus I'll take my pilgrimage.   *The Passionate Man's Pilgrimage*

13 So the heart be right, it is no matter which way the head lies.
                                       On laying his head on the block

14 If all the world and love were young,
And truth in every shepherd's tongue,
These pretty pleasures might me move
To live with thee, and be thy love.   *The Nymph's Reply to the Passionate Shepherd*

RALEIGH, Sir Walter Alexander, 1861–1922

1 I wish I loved the Human Race;
  I wish I loved its silly face;
  I wish I liked the way it walks;
  I wish I liked the way it talks;
  And when I'm introduced to one
  I wish I thought *What Jolly Fun!*   *The Wishes of an Elderly Man*

RANKIN, Jeremiah Eames, 1828–1904

2 God be with you till we meet again.   *Hymn*

RANSOME, Arthur, 1884—

3 Grab a chance and you won't be sorry for a might-have-been.
                    COMMANDER WALKER   *We Didn't Mean To Go to Sea*

READE, Charles, 1814–1884

4 *Courage, mon ami, le diable est mort.* Courage, my friend, the devil is dead.
                                      The Cloister and the Hearth, Ch. 24

5 Make 'em laugh; make 'em cry; make 'em wait.   *Advice to young author*
                                                     on writing novels

REED, Henry, 1914—

6 To-day we have naming of parts. Yesterday,
  We had daily cleaning. And to-morrow morning
  We shall have what to do after firing. But to-day,
  To-day we have naming of parts.   *Naming of Parts*

REMARQUE, Erich Maria, 1898—

7 *Im Westen nichts Neues.* All Quiet on the Western Front.   *Title of Novel*

REYNOLDS, Frederic, 1764–1841

8 [*Taking out his watch*] How goes the *enemy*?   ENNUI   *The Dramatist,*
                                                           Act 1

REYNOLDS, Sir Joshua, 1723–1792

9 If you have great talents, industry will improve them: if you have but
  moderate abilities, industry will supply their deficiency.   *Discourses, 2*

RHODES, Cecil John, 1853–1902

10 So little done, so much to do.   *Last words*

11 Educational relations make the strongest tie.   *Will, endowing Rhodes*
                                                         Scholarships

RICE, Grantland, 1880–1954

12 For when the one Great Scorer comes
       To write against your name,
   He marks—not that you won or lost—
       But how you played the game.   *Alumnus Football*

RIPLEY, Robert Leroy, 1893–1949

13 Believe it or not.   *Title of newspaper feature*

ROCHE, Sir Boyle, 1743–1807

1 My love for England and Ireland is so great that I would have the two sisters embrace like one brother. *Reported in Irish Parliamentary Register, 11, 294*

2 What has posterity done for us? *Speech in Irish Parliament, 1780*

3 Mr Speaker, I smell a rat; I see him forming in the air and darkening the sky; but I'll nip him in the bud. *Attributed*

ROCHEFOUCAULD, Duc de la, 1613–1680

4 We have all enough strength to bear the misfortunes of others.
Les Maximes, 19

5 Everyone complains of his memory, but no one complains of his judgment.
Ib, 89

6 The intellect is always fooled by the heart. *Ib, 102*

7 Hypocrisy is the homage paid by vice to virtue. *Ib, 218*

8 The height of cleverness is to conceal one's cleverness. *Ib, 245*

9 In the misfortunes of our best friends, we find something that is not displeasing. *Maximes supprimées, 583*

ROCHEFOUCAULD-LIANCOURT, Duc de La, 1747–1827

10 LOUIS XVI: *C'est une révolte?* Is it a revolt?
THE DUKE: *Non, sire, c'est une révolution.* No, sire, it is a revolution.
On hearing of the Fall of the Bastille, 1789

ROCHESTER, John Wilmot, 2nd Earl of, 1647–1680

11 Here lies our sovereign lord the King,
 Whose word no man relies on;
 He never said a foolish thing,
 Nor ever did a wise one. *Epitaph on Charles II*

ROGERS, E. W., 1864–1913

12 Ev'ry member of the force
 Has a watch and chain, of course;
 If you want to know the time,
 Ask a P'liceman. *Ask a P'liceman*

ROGERS, Samuel, 1763–1855

13 When a new book is published, read an old one. *Attributed*

14 Think nothing done while aught remains to do. *Human Life, 49*

15 Sheridan was listened to with such attention that you might have heard a pin drop. *Table Talk*

ROLAND, Madame Marie Jeanne Philipon, 1754–1793

16 *O Liberté! O Liberté! que de crimes on commet en ton nom!* O liberty, liberty, what crimes are committed in your name! *Remark from the scaffold, on viewing the Statue of Liberty*

ROOSEVELT, Franklin Delano, 1882–1945

17 I pledge you, I pledge myself, to a new deal for the American people.
Speech accepting nomination for Presidency, Democratic National Convention, Chicago, 2 July 1932

18 The only thing we have to fear is fear itself. *First Inaugural Address, 4 March 1933*

1 In the field of world policy, I would dedicate this nation to the policy of a good neighbour.   *First Inaugural Address, 4 March, 1933*

2 I see one third of a nation ill-housed, ill-clad, ill-nourished.
                               Second Inaugural Address, 20 Jan. 1937

3 A radical is a man with both feet firmly planted in the air.
                                              Broadcast, 26 Oct. 1939

4 We look forward to a world founded upon four essential human freedoms. The first is freedom of speech and expression—everywhere in the world. The second is freedom of every person to worship God in his own way—everywhere in the world. The third is freedom from want ... everywhere in the world. The fourth is freedom from fear ... anywhere in the world.
                                       Speech to Congress, 6 Jan. 1941

5 We all know that books burn—yet we have the greater knowledge that books cannot be killed by fire. People die, but books never die. No man and no force can abolish memory ... In this war, we know, books are weapons.
                Message to American Booksellers Association, 23 April 1942

6 More than an end to war, we want an end to the beginnings of all wars.
           Speech written for broadcast, 13 April 1945 (the day after his death)

ROOSEVELT, Theodore, 1858–1919

7 I wish to preach, not the doctrine of ignoble ease, but the doctrine of the strenuous life.   *Speech, Chicago, 10 April 1899*

8 The first requisite of a good citizen in this Republic of ours is that he shall be able and willing to pull his weight.   *Speech, New York, 11 Nov. 1902*

9 A man who is good enough to shed his blood for his country is good enough to be given a square deal afterwards. More than that no man is entitled to, and less than that no man shall have.   *Speech, Springfield, Illinois,
                                                               4 July 1903*

10 There is no room in this country for hyphenated Americanism.
                                       Speech, New York, 12 Oct. 1915

11 No man is justified in doing evil on the ground of expediency.
                                                    The Strenuous Life

ROSEBERY, Archibald Philip Primrose, 5th Earl of, 1847–1929

12 The Empire is a Commonwealth of Nations.   *Speech, Adelaide,
                                                             18 Jan. 1884*

13 It is beginning to be hinted that we are a nation of amateurs.
                             Rectorial Address, Glasgow, 16 Nov. 1900

ROSS, Alan Strode Campbell, 1907—

14 U and Non-U, An Essay in Sociological Linguistics.   *Title of Essay
                                          included in Noblesse Oblige, 1956*

ROSSETTI, Christina Georgina, 1830–1894

15 In the bleak mid-winter
    Frosty wind made moan,
  Earth stood hard as iron,
    Water like a stone;
  Snow had fallen, snow on snow,
    Snow on snow,
  In the bleak mid-winter,
    Long ago.
                                                          Mid-Winter

1 Remember me when I am gone away,
  Gone far away into the silent land. *Remember*

2 Better by far you should forget and smile
  Than that you should remember and be sad. *Ib*

3 'Does the road wind up-hill all the way ?'
   'Yes, to the very end.'
  'Will the day's journey take the whole long day ?'
   'From morn to night, my friend.' *Up-Hill*

4 When I am dead, my dearest
  Sing no sad songs for me. *When I am Dead*

5 And if thou wilt, remember,
  And if thou wilt, forget. *Ib*

ROSSETTI, Dante Gabriel, 1828–1882

6 A sonnet is a moment's monument,—
  Memorial from the Soul's eternity
  To one dead deathless hour. *The House of Life, Part 1, Introduction*

7 The hour when you too learn that all is vain
  And that Hope sows what Love shall never reap.
  Ib, 44, Cloud and Wind

8   My name is Might-Have-Been;
  I am also called No-More, Too-Late, Farewell. *Ib, Part 2, 97*
  A Superscription

9 Unto the man of yearning, thought
  And aspiration, to do nought
  Is in itself almost an act. *Soothsay*

10 I have been here before.
   But when or how I cannot tell:
  I know the grass beyond the door,
   The sweet keen smell,
  The sighing sound, the lights around the shore. *Sudden Light, 1*

ROUGET DE LISLE, Claude Joseph, 1760–1836

11 *Allons, enfants de la patrie,*
  Le jour de gloire est arrivé.
  Come, children of our native land, the day of glory has arrived.
  La Marseillaise

ROUSSEAU, Jean–Jacques, 1712–1778

12 *L'homme est né libre, et partout il est dans les fers.* Man was born free and
  everywhere he is in chains. *Du Contrat Social, Ch. 1*

ROUTH, Martin Joseph, 1755–1854

13 Always verify your references. *Attributed*

'RED ROWLEY', 20th century

14 Mademoiselle from Armenteers,
  Hasn't been kissed for forty years,
  Hinky dinky, parley-voo. *Mademoiselle from Armentières*

RUNYON, Damon, 1884–1946

15 More than somewhat. *Passim*

RUSKIN, John, 1819–1900

1 All travelling becomes dull in exact proportion to its rapidity.
Modern Painters

2 If a book is worth reading, it is worth buying. *Sesame and Lilies*

3 Remember that the most beautiful things in the world are the most useless; peacocks and lilies for instance. *The Stones of Venice*

4 The purest and most thoughtful minds are those which love colour the most.
Ib

5 Fine art is that in which the hand, the head, and the heart of man go together. *The Two Paths*

6 There is no wealth but life. *Unto this Last*

RUSSELL, John, 1st Earl, 1792–1878

7 If peace cannot be maintained with honour, it is no longer peace.
Speech, Greenock, 19 Sept. 1853

RUSSELL, Bertrand Arthur William, 3rd Earl, 1872–

8 Men are capable, not only of fear and hate, but also of hope and benevolence. If the populations of the world can be brought to see and to realize in imagination the hell to which hate and fear must condemn them on the one hand, and, on the other, the comparative heaven which hope and benevolence can create by means of new skills, the choice should not be difficult, and our self-tormented species should allow itself a life of joy such as the past has never known. *Common Sense and Nuclear Warfare, 1959*

9 Mathematics possesses not only truth, but supreme beauty—a beauty cold and austere, like that of sculpture. *The Study of Mathematics*

RUTLAND, John, 7th Duke of, 1818–1906

10 Let wealth and commerce, laws and learning die,
But leave us still our old nobility. *England's Trust, 3, 227*

'SAKI' (Hector Hugh Munro), 1870–1916

11 He's simply got the instinct for being unhappy highly developed.
Chronicles of Clovis, The Match-Maker

12 The cook was a good cook, as cooks go; and as cooks go she went.
Reginald on Besetting Sins

SALINGER, Jerome David, 1919–

13 If you really want to hear about it, the first thing you'll probably want to know is where I was born, and what my lousy childhood was like, and how my parents were occupied and all before they had me, and all that David Copperfield kind of crap, but I don't feel like going into it.
The Catcher in the Rye, opening words

SALISBURY, Robert Cecil, 3rd Marquis of, 1830–1903

14 By office boys for office boys. *Remark about the Daily Mail*

SALLUST, 86–34 B.C.

15 *Idem velle atque idem nolle, ea demum firma amicitia est.* To like and dislike the same things, that is indeed true friendship. *Catiline, 20*

1 *Pro patria, pro liberis, pro aris atque focis suis.* On behalf of their country, their children, their altars, and their hearths. *Catiline, 59*

SAMUEL, Herbert Louis, 1st Viscount, 1870–1963

2 It takes two to make a marriage a success and only one a failure.
A Book of Quotations

3 A truism is on that account none the less true. *Ib*

SANDBURG, Carl, 1878—

4 The fog comes
on little cat feet.
It sits looking
over the harbor and city
on silent haunches
and then moves on. *Fog*

5 Pile the bodies high at Austerlitz and Waterloo.
Shovel them under and let me work—
    I am the grass; I cover all. *Grass*

6 Look out how you use proud words,
When you let proud words go, it is not easy to call them back.
Primer Lesson

7 Homestead, Braddock, Birmingham, they make their steel with men,
Smoke and blood is the mix of steel. *Smoke and Steel*

SARGENT, Epes, 1813–1880

8 A life on the ocean wave,
    A home on the rolling deep. *A Life on the Ocean Wave*

SASSOON, Siegfried, 1886—

9 And when the war is done and youth stone dead
    I'd toddle safely home and die—in bed. *Base Details*

10 Everyone suddenly burst out singing. *Everyone Sang*

SAYERS, Henry, 1855–1932

11 Ta-ra-ra-boom-de-ay! *Title of song*

SCHILLER, Friedrich von, 1759–1805

12 *Alle Menschen werden Brüder Wo dein sanfter Flügel weilt.* In the shade of your soft wings, all men will be brothers. *An die Freude*

13 *Die Weltgeschichte ist das Weltgericht.* World history is the world's judgment.
Lecture, Jena, 26 May 1789

SCHNECKENBURGER, Max, 1819–1849

14 *Die Wacht am Rhein.* The Watch on the Rhine. *Title of song*

SCOTT, Charles Prestwich, 1846–1932

15 Neither in what it gives, nor in what it does not give, nor in the mode of presentation, must the unclouded face of truth suffer wrong. Comment is free but facts are sacred. *Manchester Guardian, 6 May 1926*

SCOTT, Robert Falcon, 1868–1912

1 Great God! this is an awful place. [*The South Pole*] *Journal, 17 Jan. 1912*

2 For God's sake look after our people.   *Ib, 25 March 1912*

3 Had we lived, I should have had a tale to tell of the hardihood, endurance,
and courage of my companions which would have stirred the hearts of every
Englishman. These rough notes and our dead bodies must tell the tale.
Message to the Public

SCOTT, Sir Walter, 1771–1832

4 Come fill up my cup, come fill up my can,
Come saddle your horses, and call up your men;
Come open the West Port, and let me gang free,
And it's room for the bonnets of Bonny Dundee.
Bonny Dundee, The Doom of Devorgoil, 2, 3

5 But answer came there none.   *Bridal of Triermain, 3, 10*

6 The stag at eve had drunk his fill,
Where danced the moon on Monan's rill.   *The Lady of the Lake, 1, 1*

7 Forward and frolic glee was there,
The will to do, the soul to dare.   *Ib, 1, 21*

8 Yet seem'd that tone, and gesture bland,
Less used to sue than to command.   *Ib*

9 Soldier, rest! thy warfare o'er,
  Sleep the sleep that knows not breaking;
Dream of battled fields no more,
  Days of danger, nights of waking.   *Ib, 1, 31*

10 Like the dew on the mountain,
   Like the foam on the river,
Like the bubble on the fountain,
   Thou art gone, and for ever!   *Ib, 3, 16*

11 The way was long, the wind was cold,
The Minstrel was infirm and old;
His wither'd cheek, and tresses grey,
Seem'd to have known a better day.
The Lay of the Last Minstrel, Introduction, 1

12 If thou would'st view fair Melrose aright,
Go visit it by the pale moonlight.   *Ib, 2, 1*

13 Love rules the court, the camp, the grove,
And men below, and saints above;
For love is heaven, and heaven is love.   *Ib, 3, 2*

14 Call it not vain; they do not err,
   Who say, that when the Poet dies,
Mute Nature mourns her worshipper,
   And celebrates his obsequies.   *Ib, 5, 1*

15 True love's the gift which God has given
To man alone beneath the heaven.   *Ib, 5, 13*

16 Breathes there the man, with soul so dead,
Who never to himself hath said,
   This is my own, my native land!   *Ib, 6, 1*

1 The wretch, concentred all in self,
   Living, shall forfeit fair renown,
   And, doubly dying, shall go down
   To the vile dust, from whence he sprung,
   Unwept, unhonour'd, and unsung. *The Lay of the Last Minstrel, 6, 1*

2 That day of wrath, that dreadful day,
   When heaven and earth shall pass away. *Ib, 6, 31, Hymn for the Dead*

3 November's sky is chill and drear,
   November's leaf is red and sear. *Marmion, 1, Introduction*

4 And come he slow or come he fast,
   It is but Death who comes at last. *Ib, 2, 30*

5 O, young Lochinvar is come out of the west,
   Through all the wide Border his steed was the best. *Ib, 5, 12, Lochinvar*

6 So faithful in love, and so dauntless in war,
   There never was Knight like the young Lochinvar. *Ib*

7   And dar'st thou then
   To beard the lion in his den,
     The Douglas in his hall? *Ib, 6, 14*

8 O what a tangled web we weave,
   When first we practise to deceive! *Ib, 6, 17*

9 O Woman! in our hours of ease,
   Uncertain, coy, and hard to please,
   And variable as the shade,
   By the light quivering aspen made;
   When pain and anguish wring the brow,
   A ministering angel thou! *Ib, 6, 30*

10 He shook the fragment of his blade,
     And shouted 'Victory!
   Charge, Chester, charge! On, Stanley, on!'
   Were the last words of Marmion. *Ib, 6, 32*

11 MRS BERTRAM: That sounds like nonsense, my dear.
     MR BERTRAM: May be so, my dear; but it may be very good law for all that.
   Guy Mannering, Ch. 9

12 The hour is come, but not the man. *The Heart of Midlothian, Ch. 4,*
   Heading

SCOTT, William, 1st Baron Stowell, 1745–1836

13 A dinner lubricates business. *Boswell's Life of Johnson, 1781*

SEARS, Edmund Hamilton, 1810–1876

14 It came upon the midnight clear,
     That glorious song of old. *That Glorious Song of Old*

SEEGER, Alan, 1888–1916

15 I have a rendezvous with Death
     At some disputed barricade. *I have a Rendezvous with Death*

SELDEN, John, 1584–1654

1 Old friends are best. King James used to call for his old shoes; they were easiest for his feet. *Table Talk*

2 There is not anything in the world so much abused as this sentence, Salus populi suprema lex esto. *Ib*

3 Philosophy is nothing but discretion. *Ib*

4 Preachers say, Do as I say, not as I do. *Ib*

5 A king is a thing men have made for their own sakes, for quietness' sake. Just as if in a family one man is appointed to buy the meat. *Ib*

6 Every law is a contract between the king and the people, and therefore to be kept. *Ib*

SELLAR, Walter Carruthers, 1898–1951, and YEATMAN, Robert Julian, 1897—

7 1066 And All That. *Title of Book*

8 The Roman Conquest was, however, a *Good Thing*, since the Britons were only natives at that time. *1066 And All That, Ch. 1*

9 Has it never occurred to you that the Romans *counted backwards*? (Be honest.) *Ib, Test Paper 1*

10 Finding, however, that he was not memorable, he very patriotically abdicated in favour of Henry IV, Part II. *Ib, Ch. 26*

11 Shortly after this the cruel Queen died and a post-mortem examination revealed the word 'CALLOUS' engraved on her heart. *Ib, Ch. 32*

12 Williamanmary: England Ruled by an Orange. *Ib, Heading to Ch. 38*

13 Napoleon's armies always used to march on their stomachs, shouting: 'Vive l'intérieur!' *Ib, Ch. 48*

14 Do not on any account attempt to write on both sides of the paper at once. *Ib, Test Paper 5*

SERVICE, Robert William, 1874–1958

15 This is the Law of the Yukon, that only the strong shall thrive;
That surely the weak shall perish, and only the Fit survive.
The Law of the Yukon

16 When we, the Workers, all demand: 'What are we fighting for?' . . .
Then, then we'll end that stupid crime, that devil's madness—War.
Michael

SEWARD, William Henry, 1801–1872

17 There is a higher law than the Constitution. *Speech, U.S. Senate, 11 March 1850*

SHADWELL, Thomas, 1642?–1692

18 Words may be false and full of art,
Sighs are the natural language of the heart. CUPID *Psyche, Act 3*

19 He's a wise man that marries a harlot; he's on the surest side. Who but an ass would marry an uncertainty? SIR POSITIVE AT-ALL
The Sullen Lovers, Act 5

20 I'll do't instantly, in the twinkling of a bed-staff. SIR SAMUEL HEARTY
The Virtuoso, Act 1

KESPEARE, William, 1564–1616

All's Well that Ends Well

1   Love all, trust a few,
Do wrong to none; be able for thine enemy
Rather in power than use, and keep thy friend
Under thy own life's key; be check'd for silence,
But never tax'd for speech.   COUNTESS OF ROUSILLON   *Act 1, Scene 1,*
Line 57

2 Our remedies oft in ourselves do lie,
Which we ascribe to heaven.   HELENA   *1, 1, 202*

3 My friends were poor, but honest.   HELENA   *1, 3, 186*

4 A young man married is a man that's marr'd.   PAROLLES   *2, 3, 291*

5 No legacy is so rich as honesty.   MARIANA   *3, 5, 12*

6 The web of our life is of a mingled yarn, good and ill together.
2ND LORD   *4, 3, 67*

7   Praising what is lost
Makes the remembrance dear.   KING OF FRANCE   *5, 3, 19*

8 Th' inaudible and noiseless foot of Time.   KING OF FRANCE   *5, 3, 41*

Antony and Cleopatra

9 The triple pillar of the world transform'd
Into a strumpet's fool.   PHILO   *1, 1, 12*

10 There's beggary in the love that can be reckon'd.   ANTONY   *1, 1, 15*

11 The nature of bad news infects the teller.   MESSENGER   *1, 2, 92*

12 Where's my serpent of old Nile?   CLEOPATRA   *1, 5, 25*

13   My salad days,
When I was green in judgment.   CLEOPATRA   *1, 5, 73*

14 The barge she sat in, like a burnish'd throne,
Burn'd on the water. The poop was beaten gold;
Purple the sails, and so perfumed that
The winds were love-sick with them; the oars were silver,
Which to the tune of flutes kept stroke, and made
The water which they beat to follow faster,
As amorous of their strokes. For her own person,
It beggar'd all description.   ENOBARBUS   *2, 2, 195*

15 Age cannot wither her, nor custom stale
Her infinite variety. Other women cloy
The appetites they feed, but she makes hungry
Where most she satisfies.   ENOBARBUS   *2, 2, 239*

16 Though it be honest, it is never good
To bring bad news.   CLEOPATRA   *2, 5, 85*

17 I will praise any man that will praise me.   ENOBARBUS   *2, 6, 88*

18 He will to his Egyptian dish again.   ENOBARBUS   *2, 6, 121*

19 Celerity is never more admir'd
Than by the negligent.   CLEOPATRA   *3, 7, 24*

20   He wears the rose
Of youth upon him.   ANTONY   *3, 13, 20*

1 Let's have one other gaudy night.   ANTONY   *Antony and Cleopatra*
                                                            3, 13, 183

2 To business that we love we rise betime,
  And go to't with delight.   ANTONY   *4, 4, 20*

3 O infinite virtue, com'st thou smiling from
  The world's great snare uncaught?   CLEOPATRA   *4, 8, 18*

4 Unarm, Eros; the long day's task is done,
  And we must sleep.   ANTONY   *4, 14, 35*

5 I am dying, Egypt, dying; only
  I here importune death awhile, until
  Of many thousand kisses the poor last
  I lay upon thy lips.   ANTONY   *4, 15, 18*

6 O, wither'd is the garland of the war,
  The soldier's pole is fall'n! Young boys and girls
  Are level now with men. The odds is gone,
  And there is nothing left remarkable
  Beneath the visiting moon.   CLEOPATRA   *4, 15, 64*

7   The bright day is done,
  And we are for the dark.   IRAS   *5, 2, 192*

8 His biting is immortal; those that do die of it do seldom or never recover.
                                              CLOWN *5, 2, 246*

9 I wish you joy o' th' worm.   CLOWN   *5, 2, 277*

10   I have
   Immortal longings in me.   CLEOPATRA   *5, 2, 278*

11 Dost thou not see my baby at my breast
   That sucks the nurse asleep?   CLEOPATRA   *5, 2, 307*

As You Like It

12 Fleet the time carelessly, as they did in the golden world.   CHARLES
                                                            1, 1, 108

13 Well said; that was laid on with a trowel.   CELIA   *1, 2, 94*

14 Beauty provoketh thieves sooner than gold.   ROSALIND   *1, 3, 106*

15 Sweet are the uses of adversity;
   Which, like the toad, ugly and venomous,
   Wears yet a precious jewel in his head;
   And this our life, exempt from public haunt,
   Finds tongues in trees, books in the running brooks,
   Sermons in stones, and good in everything.   DUKE SENIOR   *2, 1, 12*

16 Sweep on, you fat and greasy citizens.   1ST LORD (quoting Jaques)
                                                            2, 1, 55

17 Unregarded age in corners thrown.   ADAM   *2, 3, 42*

18 Therefore my age is as a lusty winter,
   Frosty, but kindly.   ADAM   *2, 3, 52*

19 O good old man, how well in thee appears
   The constant service of the antique world,
   When service sweat for duty, not for meed!
   Thou art not for the fashion of these times,
   Where none will sweat but for promotion.   ORLANDO   *2, 3, 56*

had rather bear with you than bear you.   TOUCHSTONE   *As You Like It,*
2, 4, 9

2 Ay, now am I in Arden; the more fool I; when I was at home I was in a
better place; but travellers must be content.   TOUCHSTONE   *2, 4, 13*

3 If thou rememb'rest not the slightest folly
That ever love did make thee run into,
Thou hast not lov'd.   SILVIUS   *2, 4, 31*

4   Under the greenwood tree
         Who loves to lie with me,
         And turn his merry note
         Unto the sweet bird's throat,
Come hither, come hither, come hither.
         Here shall he see
         No enemy
But winter and rough weather.   AMIENS   *2, 5, 1*

5 I can suck melancholy out of a song, as a weasel sucks eggs.
                                               JAQUES   *2, 5, 12*

6 Who doth ambition shun,
And loves to live i' th' sun,
Seeking the food he eats,
And pleas'd with what he gets.   AMIENS, ETC.   *2, 5, 34*

7 I'll rail against all the first-born of Egypt.   JAQUES   *2, 5, 56*

8 A fool! I met a fool i' th' forest,
A motley fool.   JAQUES   *2, 7, 12*

9 And so, from hour to hour, we ripe and ripe,
And then, from hour to hour, we rot and rot;
And thereby hangs a tale.   JAQUES   *2, 7, 26*

10   Whate'er you are
That in this desert inaccessible,
Under the shade of melancholy boughs,
Lose and neglect the creeping hours of time.   ORLANDO   *2, 7, 109*

11   All the world's a stage,
And all the men and women merely players;
They have their exits and their entrances;
And one man in his time plays many parts,
His acts being seven ages. At first the infant,
Mewling and puking in the nurse's arms;
Then the whining school-boy, with his satchel
And shining morning face, creeping like snail
Unwillingly to school.   And then the lover,
Sighing like furnace, with a woeful ballad
Made to his mistress' eyebrow. Then a soldier,
Full of strange oaths, and bearded like the pard,
Jealous in honour, sudden and quick in quarrel,
Seeking the bubble reputation
Even in the cannon's mouth. And then the justice,
In fair round belly with good capon lin'd,
With eyes severe and beard of formal cut,
Full of wise saws and modern instances;
And so he plays his part. The sixth age shifts
Into the lean and slipper'd pantaloon,

With spectacles on nose and pouch on side,
His youthful hose, well sav'd, a world too wide
For his shrunk shank; and his big manly voice,
Turning again toward childish treble, pipes
And whistles in his sound. Last scene of all,
That ends this strange eventful history,
Is second childishness and mere oblivion;
Sans teeth, sans eyes, sans taste, sans every thing.   JAQUES *As You Like It*,
2, 7, *139*

1   Blow, blow, thou winter wind,
               Thou art not so unkind
                  As man's ingratitude;
               Thy tooth is not so keen,
               Because thou art not seen,
                  Although thy breath be rude.
Heigh-ho! sing heigh-ho! unto the green holly.
Most friendship is feigning, most loving mere folly.   AMIENS   2, 7, *174*

2 Run, run, Orlando; carve on every tree,
   The fair, the chaste, and unexpressive she.   ORLANDO   3, 2, 9

3 He that wants money, means, and content, is without three good friends.
                                                   CORIN   3, 2, 23

4 Let us make an honourable retreat; though not with bag and baggage, yet
   with scrip and scrippage.   TOUCHSTONE   3, 2, *150*

5 O wonderful, wonderful, and most wonderful wonderful, and yet again
   wonderful, and after that, out of all whooping!   CELIA   3, 2, *177*

6 Do you not know I am a woman? When I think, I must speak.   ROSALIND
                                                              3, 2, *234*

7 I do desire we may be better strangers.   ORLANDO   3, 2, *243*

8 Time travels in divers paces with divers persons. I'll tell you who Time
   ambles withal, who Time trots withal, who Time gallops withal, and who
   he stands still withal.   ROSALIND   3, 2, *290*

9 Truly, I would the gods had made thee poetical.   TOUCHSTONE   3, 3, *13*

10 The truest poetry is the most feigning.   TOUCHSTONE   3, 3, *16*

11 I am not a slut, though I thank the gods I am foul.   AUDREY   3, 3, *34*

12 Men have died from time to time, and worms have eaten them, but not for
    love.   ROSALIND   4, 1, *94*

13 Men are April when they woo, December when they wed: maids are May
    when they are maids, but the sky changes when they are wives.   ROSALIND
                                                                4, 1, *130*

14 No sooner met but they look'd; no sooner look'd but they lov'd; no sooner
    lov'd but they sigh'd; no sooner sigh'd but they ask'd one another the
    reason; no sooner knew the reason but they sought the remedy.
                                                   ROSALIND   5, 2, *29*

15 O, how bitter a thing it is to look into happiness through another man's
    eyes!   ORLANDO   5, 2, *40*

16 It was a lover and his lass,
        With a hey, and a ho, and a hey nonino,
    That o'er the green corn-field did pass
        In the spring time, the only pretty ring time,

When birds do sing, hey ding a ding, ding.
Sweet lovers love the spring.   TWO PAGES   *As You Like It, 5, 3, 14*

1 An ill-favour'd thing, sir, but mine own.   TOUCHSTONE   *5, 4, 55*

2 I will name you the degrees. The first, the Retort Courteous; the second,
the Quip Modest; the third, the Reply Churlish; the fourth, the Reproof
Valiant; the fifth, the Countercheck Quarrelsome; the sixth, the Lie with
Circumstance; the seventh, the Lie Direct.   TOUCHSTONE   *5, 4, 86*

3 Your If is the only peace-maker; much virtue in If.   TOUCHSTONE
5, 4, 97

4 If it be true that good wine needs no bush, 'tis true that a good play needs
no epilogue.   ROSALIND   *Epilogue, 3*

The Comedy of Errors

5 They brought one Pinch, a hungry lean-fac'd villain,
A mere anatomy, a mountebank,
A threadbare juggler, and a fortune-teller,
A needy, hollow-ey'd, sharp-looking wretch,
A living dead man.   ANTIPHOLUS OF EPHESUS   *5, 1, 237*

Coriolanus

6 My gracious silence, hail!   CORIOLANUS   *2, 1, 166*

7   Bid them wash their faces
And keep their teeth clean.   CORIOLANUS   *2, 3, 59*

8   Custom calls me to't.
What custom wills, in all things should we do't,
The dust on antique time would lie unswept,
And mountainous error be too highly heap'd
For truth to o'erpeer.   CORIOLANUS   *2, 3, 114*

9 Hear you this Triton of the minnows? Mark you
His absolute 'shall'?   CORIOLANUS   *3, 1, 89*

10 His nature is too noble for the world:
He would not flatter Neptune for his trident,
Or Jove for's power to thunder. His heart's his mouth;
What his breast forges, that his tongue must vent.   MENENIUS   *3, 1, 255*

11   Like a dull actor now
I have forgot my part and I am out,
Even to a full disgrace.   CORIOLANUS   *5, 3, 40*

12 If you have writ your annals true, 'tis there
That, like an eagle in a dove-cote, I
Flutter'd your Volscians in Corioli.
Alone I did it.   CORIOLANUS   *5, 6, 114*

Cymbeline

13 Hark, hark! the lark at heaven's gate sings,
    And Phoebus 'gins arise,
His steeds to water at those springs
    On chalic'd flow'rs that lies;
And winking Mary-buds begin
    To ope their golden eyes.

With everything that pretty bin,
  My lady sweet, arise;
    Arise, arise!   SONG   *Cymbeline, 2, 3, 19*

1   There be many Caesars
Ere such another Julius. Britain is
A world by itself, and we will nothing pay
For wearing our own noses.   CLOTEN   *3, 1, 11*

2 O for a horse with wings!   IMOGEN   *3, 2, 47*

3   O, this life
Is nobler than attending for a check,
Richer than doing nothing for a bribe,
Prouder than rustling in unpaid-for silk.   BELARIUS   *3, 3, 21*

4 I have not slept one wink.   PISANIO   *3, 4, 99*

5 Hath Britain all the sun that shines?   IMOGEN   *3, 4, 135*

6   Society is no comfort
To one not sociable.   IMOGEN   *4, 2, 12*

7   Though mean and mighty rotting
Together have one dust, yet reverence—
That angel of the world—doth make distinction
Of place 'tween high and low.   BELARIUS   *4, 2, 247*

8 Thersites' body is as good as Ajax',
When neither are alive.   GUIDERIUS   *4, 2, 253*

9 Fear no more the heat o' th' sun
    Nor the furious winter's rages;
Thou thy worldly task hast done,
    Home art gone, and ta'en thy wages.
Golden lads and girls all must,
As chimney-sweepers, come to dust.   GUIDERIUS   *4, 2, 259*

10 All lovers young, all lovers must
    Consign to thee and come to dust.   GUIDERIUS AND ARVIRAGUS   *4, 2, 275*

11 Quiet consummation have,
    And renowned be thy grave!   GUIDERIUS AND ARVIRAGUS   *4, 2, 281*

12 He that sleeps feels not the toothache.   GAOLER   *5, 4, 171*

Hamlet

13 For this relief much thanks. 'Tis bitter cold,
   And I am sick at heart.   FRANCISCO   *1, 1, 8*

14 What, has this thing appear'd again to-night?   HORATIO   *1, 1, 21*

15 We do it wrong, being so majestical,
   To offer it the show of violence.   MARCELLUS   *1, 1, 143*

16 But look, the morn, in russet mantle clad,
   Walks o'er the dew of yon high eastward hill.   HORATIO   *1, 1, 166*

17 The memory be green.   CLAUDIUS   *1, 2, 2*

18 A little more than kin, and less than kind.   HAMLET   *1, 2, 65*

19 Not so, my lord; I am too much in the sun.   HAMLET   *1, 2, 67*

20 Thou know'st 'tis common—all that lives must die,
   Passing through nature to eternity.   GERTRUDE   *1, 2, 72*

1 But I have that within which passes show—
  These but the trappings and the suits of woe.   HAMLET *Hamlet, 1, 2, 85*

2 O, that this too too solid flesh would melt,
  Thaw, and resolve itself into a dew!
  Or that the Everlasting had not fix'd
  His canon 'gainst self-slaughter! O God! God!
  How weary, stale, flat, and unprofitable,
  Seem to me all the uses of this world!   HAMLET   *1, 2, 129*

3 So excellent a king that was to this
  Hyperion to a satyr.   HAMLET   *1, 2, 139*

4   Why, she would hang on him
  As if increase of appetite had grown
  By what it fed on.   HAMLET   *1, 2, 143*

5 Frailty, thy name is woman!   HAMLET   *1, 2, 146*

6 It is not, nor it cannot come to good.   HAMLET   *1, 2, 158*

7 A truant disposition, good my lord.   HORATIO   *1, 2, 169*

8 Thrift, thrift, Horatio! The funeral bak'd-meats
  Did coldly furnish forth the marriage tables.   HAMLET   *1, 2, 180*

9 'A was a man, take him for all in all,
  I shall not look upon his like again.   HAMLET   *1, 2, 187*

10 A countenance more in sorrow than in anger.   HORATIO   *1, 2, 231*

11 Give it an understanding, but no tongue.   HAMLET   *1, 2, 249*

12   All is not well.
  I doubt some foul play.   HAMLET   *1, 2, 254*

13 The chariest maid is prodigal enough
  If she unmask her beauty to the moon.   LAERTES   *1, 3, 36*

14 Do not, as some ungracious pastors do,
  Show me the steep and thorny way to heaven,
  Whiles, like a puff'd and reckless libertine,
  Himself the primrose path of dalliance treads
  And recks not his own rede.   OPHELIA   *1, 3, 47*

15 And these few precepts in thy memory
  Look thou character. Give thy thoughts no tongue,
  Nor any unproportion'd thought his act.
  Be thou familiar, but by no means vulgar.
  Those friends thou hast, and their adoption tried,
  Grapple them to thy soul with hoops of steel.   POLONIUS   *1, 3, 58*

16   Beware
  Of entrance to a quarrel; but, being in,
  Bear't that th' opposed may beware of thee.
  Give every man thy ear, but few thy voice;
  Take each man's censure, but reserve thy judgment.
  Costly thy habit as thy purse can buy,
  But not express'd in fancy; rich, not gaudy;
  For the apparel oft proclaims the man.   POLONIUS   *1, 3, 65*

17 Neither a borrower nor a lender be;
  For loan oft loses both itself and friend,

And borrowing dulls the edge of husbandry.
This above all—to thine own self be true,
And it must follow, as the night the day,
Thou canst not then be false to any man.   POLONIUS   *Hamlet, 1, 3, 75*

1 Be something scanter of your maiden presence.   POLONIUS   *1, 3, 121*

2 But to my mind, though I am native here
And to the manner born, it is a custom
More honour'd in the breach than the observance.   HAMLET   *1, 4, 14*

3 Angels and ministers of grace defend us!
Be thou a spirit of health or goblin damn'd,
Bring with thee airs from heaven or blasts from hell,
Be thy intents wicked or charitable,
Thou com'st in such a questionable shape
That I will speak to thee.   HAMLET   *1, 4, 39*

4 I do not set my life at a pin's fee;
And for my soul, what can it do to that,
Being a thing immortal as itself?   HAMLET   *1, 4, 65*

5 Something is rotten in the state of Denmark.   MARCELLUS   *1, 4, 90*

6   I am thy father's spirit,
Doom'd for a certain term to walk the night.   GHOST   *1, 5, 9*

7   But that I am forbid
To tell the secrets of my prison-house,
I could a tale unfold whose lightest word
Would harrow up thy soul, freeze thy young blood,
Make thy two eyes, like stars, start from their spheres,
Thy knotted and combined locks to part,
And each particular hair to stand on end,
Like quills upon the fretful porpentine.
But this eternal blazon must not be
To ears of flesh and blood. List, list, O, list!   GHOST   *1, 5, 13*

8 Revenge his foul and most unnatural murder.   GHOST   *1, 5, 25*

9 Murder most foul, as in the best it is;
But this most foul, strange, and unnatural.   GHOST   *1, 5, 27*

10 O my prophetic soul! My uncle!   HAMLET   *1, 5, 40*

11 O Hamlet, what a falling off was there.   GHOST   *1, 5, 47*

12 There are more things in heaven and earth, Horatio,
Than are dreamt of in your philosophy.   HAMLET   *1, 5, 166*

13 To put an antic disposition on.   HAMLET   *1, 5, 172*

14 The time is out of joint. O cursed spite,
That ever I was born to set it right!   HAMLET   *1, 5, 189*

15 Brevity is the soul of wit.   POLONIUS   *2, 2, 90*

16 More matter with less art.   GERTRUDE   *2, 2, 95*

17 That he's mad, 'tis true: 'tis true 'tis pity;
And pity 'tis 'tis true.   POLONIUS   *2, 2, 97*

18 POLONIUS: Do you know me, my lord?
    HAMLET: Excellent well; you are a fishmonger.   *2, 2, 172*

1 To be honest, as this world goes, is to be one man pick'd out of ten thousand.
HAMLET   *Hamlet, 2, 2, 177*

2 POLONIUS: What do you read, my Lord?
HAMLET: Words, words, words.   *2, 2, 190*

3 Though this be madness, yet there is method in't.   POLONIUS   *2, 2, 204*

4   HAMLET: What news?
ROSENCRANTZ: None, my lord, but that the world's grown honest.
HAMLET: Then is doomsday near.   *2, 2, 235*

5 There is nothing either good or bad, but thinking makes it so.   HAMLET
2, 2, 248

6 What a piece of work is a man! How noble in reason! how infinite in faculties!
in form and moving, how express and admirable! in action, how like an
angel! in apprehension, how like a god! the beauty of the world! the
paragon of animals! And yet, to me, what is this quintessence of dust? Man
delights not me—no, nor woman neither.   HAMLET   *2, 2, 303*

7 He that plays the king shall be welcome.   HAMLET   *2, 2, 317*

8 I am but mad north-north-west; when the wind is southerly I know a hawk
from a handsaw.   HAMLET   *2, 2, 374*

9 The best actors in the world, either for tragedy, comedy, history, pastoral,
pastoral-comical, historical-pastoral, tragical-historical, tragical-comical-
historical-pastoral, scene individable, or poem unlimited.   POLONIUS
2, 2, 392

10 The play, I remember, pleas'd not the million; 'twas caviare to the general.
HAMLET *2, 2, 429*

11 The mobled queen.   1st PLAYER   *2, 2, 496*

12 Let them be well used; for they are the abstract and brief chronicles of the
time.   HAMLET   *2, 2, 517*

13 Use every man after his desert, and who shall scape whipping?   HAMLET
2, 2, 523

14 O, what a rogue and peasant slave am I!   HAMLET   *2, 2, 543*

15 What's Hecuba to him or he to Hecuba,
That he should weep for her?   HAMLET   *2, 2, 552*

16 A dull and muddy-mettl'd rascal.   HAMLET   *2, 2, 561*

17 But I am pigeon-liver'd and lack gall
To make oppression bitter.   HAMLET   *2, 2, 572*

18   This is most brave,
That I, the son of a dear father murder'd,
Prompted to my revenge by heaven and hell,
Must, like a whore, unpack my heart with words,
And fall a-cursing like a very drab.   HAMLET   *2, 2, 578*

19   The play's the thing
Wherein I'll catch the conscience of the King.   HAMLET   *2, 2, 600*

20 To be, or not to be—that is the question;
Whether 'tis nobler in the mind to suffer
The slings and arrows of outrageous fortune,

Or to take arms against a sea of troubles,
And by opposing end them? To die, to sleep—
No more; and by a sleep to say we end
The heart-ache and the thousand natural shocks
That flesh is heir to. 'Tis a consummation
Devoutly to be wish'd. To die, to sleep;
To sleep, perchance to dream. Ay, there's the rub;
For in that sleep of death what dreams may come,
When we have shuffled off this mortal coil,
Must give us pause. There's the respect
That makes calamity of so long life;
For who would bear the whips and scorns of time,
Th' oppressor's wrong, the proud man's contumely,
The pangs of despis'd love, the law's delay,
The insolence of office, and the spurns
That patient merit of th' unworthy takes,
When he himself might his quietus make
With a bare bodkin? Who would fardels bear,
To grunt and sweat under a weary life,
But that the dread of something after death—
The undiscover'd country, from whose bourn
No traveller returns—puzzles the will,
And makes us rather bear those ills we have
Than fly to others that we know not of?
Thus conscience does make cowards of us all;
And thus the native hue of resolution
Is sicklied o'er with the pale cast of thought,
And enterprises of great pith and moment,
With this regard, their currents turn awry
And lose the name of action.   HAMLET   *Hamlet, 3, 1, 56*

1   For to the noble mind
Rich gifts wax poor when givers prove unkind.   OPHELIA   *3, 1, 100*

2 Get thee to a nunnery.   HAMLET   *3, 1, 121*

3 Be thou as chaste as ice, as pure as snow, thou shalt not escape calumny.
                                                HAMLET   *3, 1, 135*

4 I have heard of your paintings too, well enough; God hath given you one
face, and you make yourselves another.   HAMLET   *3, 1, 142*

5 O, what a noble mind is here o'erthrown!
The courtier's, soldier's, scholar's, eye, tongue, sword;
Th' expectancy and rose of the fair state,
The glass of fashion and the mould of form,
Th' observ'd of all observers—quite, quite down!   OPHELIA   *3, 1, 150*

6 Madness in great ones must not unwatch'd go.   CLAUDIUS   *3, 1, 188*

7 Speak the speech, I pray you, as I pronounc'd it to you, trippingly on the
tongue; but if you mouth it, as many of our players do, I had as lief the
town-crier spoke my lines. Nor do not saw the air too much with your hand,
thus, but use all gently.   HAMLET   *3, 2, 1*

8 It out-herods Herod.   HAMLET   *3, 2, 14*

9 Suit the action to the word, the word to the action; with this special observance, that you o'erstep not the modesty of nature.   HAMLET   *3, 2, 17*

1
                          Give me that man
That is not passion's slave, and I will wear him
In my heart's core, ay, in my heart of heart,
As I do thee.   HAMLET   *Hamlet, 3, 2, 69*

2 Here's metal more attractive.   HAMLET   *3, 2, 106*

3 OPHELIA: 'Tis brief, my lord.
    HAMLET: As woman's love.   *3, 2, 148*

4 The lady doth protest too much, methinks.   GERTRUDE   *3, 2, 225*

5 We that have free souls, it touches us not. Let the galled jade wince, our
withers are unwrung.   HAMLET   *3, 2, 235*

6 The proverb is something musty.   HAMLET   *3, 2, 334*

7 Very like a whale.   POLONIUS   *3, 2, 372*

8 'Tis now the very witching time of night,
When churchyards yawn, and hell itself breathes out
Contagion to this world.   HAMLET   *3, 2, 378*

9 Let me be cruel, not unnatural:
I will speak daggers to her, but use none.   HAMLET   *3, 2, 385*

10 O, my offence is rank, it smells to heaven.   CLAUDIUS   *3, 3, 36*

11 My words fly up, my thoughts remain below.
Words without thoughts never to heaven go.   CLAUDIUS   *3, 3, 97*

12 How now! a rat? Dead, for a ducat, dead!   HAMLET   *3, 4, 23*

13 A king of shreds and patches.   HAMLET   *3, 4, 102*

14 Assume a virtue, if you have it not.   HAMLET   *3, 4, 160*

15 I must be cruel only to be kind.   HAMLET   *3, 4, 178*

16
                   Diseases desperate grown
By desperate appliance are reliev'd,
Or not at all.   CLAUDIUS   *4, 3, 9*

17 How all occasions do inform against me,
And spur my dull revenge! What is a man,
If his chief good and market of his time
Be but to sleep and feed? A beast, no more!   HAMLET   *4, 4, 32*

18
                   Some craven scruple
Of thinking too precisely on th' event.   HAMLET   *4, 4, 40*

19
                   Rightly to be great
Is not to stir without great argument,
But greatly to find quarrel in a straw,
When honour's at the stake.   HAMLET   *4, 4, 53*

20 Come, my coach! Good night, ladies; good night, sweet ladies, good night,
good night.   OPHELIA   *4, 5, 69*

21 When sorrows come, they come not single spies,
But in battalions!   CLAUDIUS   *4, 5, 75*

22 There's such divinity doth hedge a king
That treason can but peep to what it would.   CLAUDIUS   *4, 5, 120*

23 There's rosemary, that's for remembrance; pray you, love, remember.
And there is pansies, that's for thoughts.   OPHELIA   *4, 5, 172*

24 A very riband in the cap of youth.   CLAUDIUS   *4, 7, 77*

1 There is a willow grows aslant the brook
   That shows his hoar leaves in the glassy stream.   GERTRUDE   *Hamlet,*
                                                                    4, 7, 167

2 Alas, poor Yorick! I knew him, Horatio: a fellow of infinite jest, of most
   excellent fancy.   HAMLET   *5, 1, 179*

3   Lay her i' th' earth;
   And from her fair and unpolluted flesh
   May violets spring! I tell thee, churlish priest,
   A minist'ring angel shall my sister be
   When thou liest howling.   LAERTES   *5, 1, 232*

4 Sweets to the sweet; farewell!   GERTRUDE   *5, 1, 237*

5 Let Hercules himself do what he may,
   The cat will mew, and dog will have his day.   HAMLET   *5, 1, 285*

6 There's a divinity that shapes our ends,
   Rough-hew them how we will.   HAMLET   *5, 2, 10*

7 A hit, a very palpable hit.   OSRIC   *5, 2, 273*

8 Report me and my cause aright.   HAMLET   *5, 2, 331*

9 If thou didst ever hold me in thy heart,
   Absent thee from felicity awhile,
   And in this harsh world draw thy breath in pain,
   To tell my story.   HAMLET   *5, 2, 338*

10 The rest is silence.   HAMLET   *5, 2, 350*

11 Now cracks a noble heart. Good night, sweet prince,
   And flights of angels sing thee to thy rest!   HORATIO   *5, 2, 351*

12 For he was likely, had he been put on,
   To have prov'd most royal.   FORTINBRAS   *5, 2, 389*

King Henry the Fourth, Part One

13 So shaken as we are, so wan with care.   HENRY IV   *1, 1, 1*

14 To chase these pagans in those holy fields
   Over whose acres walk'd those blessed feet
   Which fourteen hundred years ago were nail'd
   For our advantage on the bitter cross.   HENRY IV   *1, 1, 24*

15 See riot and dishonour stain the brow
   Of my young Harry.   HENRY IV   *1, 1, 85*

16 Shall there be gallows standing in England when thou art king?
                                                    FALSTAFF   *1, 2, 56*

17 O, thou hast damnable iteration, and art indeed able to corrupt a saint.
                                                    FALSTAFF   *1, 2, 88*

18 Why, Hal, 'tis my vocation, Hal; 'tis no sin for a man to labour in his
   vocation.   FALSTAFF   *1, 2, 101*

19 There's neither honesty, manhood, nor good fellowship in thee.
                                                    FALSTAFF   *1, 2, 133*

20 I know you all, and will awhile uphold
   The unyok'd humour of your idleness.   PRINCE   *1, 2, 188*

21 If all the year were playing holidays,
   To sport would be as tedious as to work.   PRINCE   *1, 2, 197*

1   A certain lord, neat, and trimly dress'd,
Fresh as a bridegroom, and his chin new reap'd
Show'd like a stubble-land at harvest-home.
He was perfumed like a milliner,
And 'twixt his finger and his thumb he held
A pouncet-box, which ever and anon
He gave his nose and took't away again.   HOTSPUR   *Henry the Fourth,
Part One, 1, 3, 33*

2   He made me mad
To see him shine so brisk, and smell so sweet,
And talk so like a waiting-gentlewoman
Of guns, and drums, and wounds—God save the mark!—
And telling me the sovereignest thing on earth
Was parmaceti for an inward bruise.   HOTSPUR   *1, 3, 53*

3   O, the blood more stirs
To rouse a lion than to start a hare!   HOTSPUR   *1, 3, 197*

4 By heaven, methinks it were an easy leap
To pluck bright honour from the pale-fac'd moon;
Or dive into the bottom of the deep,
Where fathom-line could never touch the ground,
And pluck up drowned honour by the locks.   HOTSPUR   *1, 3, 201*

5 I know a trick worth two of that.   FIRST CARRIER   *2, 1, 36*

6 I am bewitch'd with the rogue's company. If the rascal have not given me
medicines to make me love him, I'll be hang'd.   FALSTAFF   *2, 2, 16*

7 Have you any levers to lift me up again, being down?   FALSTAFF   *2, 2, 33*

8 It would be argument for a week, laughter for a month, and a good jest for
ever.   PRINCE   *2, 2, 91*

9   Falstaff sweats to death
And lards the lean earth as he walks along.   PRINCE   *2, 2, 104*

10 Out of this nettle, danger, we pluck this flower, safety.   HOTSPUR   *2, 3, 10*

11   Constant you are,
But yet a woman; and for secrecy,
No lady closer; for I well believe
Thou wilt not utter what thou dost not know.   HOTSPUR   *2, 3, 105*

12 I am not yet of Percy's mind, the Hotspur of the north; he that kills me
some six or seven dozen of Scots at a breakfast, washes his hands, and says
to his wife 'Fie upon this quiet life! I want work'.   PRINCE   *2, 4, 97*

13 A plague of all cowards, I say.   FALSTAFF   *2, 4, 109*

14 There lives not three good men unhang'd in England, and one of them is
fat and grows old.   FALSTAFF   *2, 4, 123*

15 I have pepper'd two of them; two I am sure I have paid—two rogues in
buckram suits. I tell thee what, Hal, if I tell thee a lie, spit in my face, call
me horse. Thou knowest my old ward: here I lay, and thus I bore my point.
Four rogues in buckram let drive at me.   FALSTAFF   *2, 4, 183*

16 O monstrous! eleven buckram men grown out of two!   PRINCE   *2, 4, 212*

17 A plague of sighing and grief! it blows a man up like a bladder.   FALSTAFF
2, 4, 322

1 That reverend vice, that grey iniquity, that father ruffian, that vanity in years.   PRINCE   *Henry the Fourth, Part One,* 2, 4, 437

2 Banish plump Jack, and banish all the world.   FALSTAFF   2, 4, 462

3 O monstrous! but one halfpenny-worth of bread to this intolerable deal of sack!   PRINCE   2, 4, 521

4 I am not in the roll of common men.   GLENDOWER   3, 1, 43

5 GLENDOWER: I can call spirits from the vasty deep.
   HOTSPUR: Why, so can I, or so can any man;
            But will they come when you do call for them?   3, 1, 53

6 I had rather be a kitten and cry mew
Than one of these same metre ballad-mongers.   HOTSPUR   3, 1, 129

7   Mincing poetry.
'Tis like the forc'd gait of a shuffling nag.   HOTSPUR   3, 1, 134

8 I understand thy kisses, and thou mine,
And that's a feeling disputation.   MORTIMER   3, 1, 204

9 Swear me, Kate, like a lady as thou art,
A good mouth-filling oath.   HOTSPUR   3, 1, 254

10 He was but as the cuckoo is in June,
Heard, not regarded.   HENRY IV   3, 2, 75

11 Do I not bate? Do I not dwindle? Why, my skin hangs about me like an old lady's loose gown.   FALSTAFF   3, 3, 2

12 Company, villainous company, hath been the spoil of me.   FALSTAFF
                                            3, 2, 10

13 I have more flesh than another man, and therefore more frailty.
                                FALSTAFF   3, 3, 167

14 Doomsday is near; die all, die merrily.   HOTSPUR   4, 1, 134

15 I have misused the King's press damnably.   FALSTAFF   4, 2, 11

16 The cankers of a calm world and a long peace.   FALSTAFF   4, 2, 30

17 To the latter end of a fray and the beginning of a feast
Fits a dull fighter and a keen guest.   FALSTAFF   4, 2, 77

18 For nothing can seem foul to those that win.   HENRY IV   5, 1, 8

19 Rebellion lay in his way, and he found it.   FALSTAFF   5, 1, 28

20 I would 'twere bed-time, Hal, and all well.   FALSTAFF   5, 1, 125

21 Honour pricks me on. Yea, but how if honour prick me off when I come on? How then? Can honour set to a leg? No. Or an arm? No. Or take away the grief of a wound? No. Honour hath no skill in surgery, then? No. What is honour? A word. What is in that word? Honour. What is that honour? Air. A trim reckoning! Who hath it? He that died o' Wednesday. Doth he feel it? No. Doth he hear it? No. 'Tis insensible, then? Yea, to the dead. But will it not live with the living? No. Why? Detraction will not suffer it. Therefore I'll none of it. Honour is a mere scutcheon. And so ends my catechism.   FALSTAFF   5, 1, 129

22   The time of life is short!
To spend that shortness basely were too long.   HOTSPUR   5, 2, 82

23 Two stars keep not their motion in one sphere.   PRINCE   5, 4, 65

1 But thoughts, the slaves of life, and life, time's fool,
And time, that takes survey of all the world,
Must have a stop.   HOTSPUR   *Henry the Fourth, Part One, 5, 4, 81*

2 What, old acquaintance! Could not all this flesh
Keep in a little life? Poor Jack, farewell!
I could have better spar'd a better man.   PRINCE   *5, 4, 102*

3 The better part of valour is discretion; in the which better part I have saved
my life.   FALSTAFF   *5, 4, 120*

4 Lord, Lord, how this world is given to lying!   FALSTAFF   *5, 4, 143*

5 I'll purge, and leave sack, and live cleanly, as a nobleman should do.
     FALSTAFF   *5, 4, 163*

King Henry the Fourth, Part Two

6   This man's brow, like to a title-leaf,
Foretells the nature of a tragic volume.   NORTHUMBERLAND   *1, 1, 60*

7 Yet the first bringer of unwelcome news
Hath but a losing office, and his tongue
Sounds ever after as a sullen bell,
Rememb'red tolling a departing friend.   NORTHUMBERLAND   *1, 1, 100*

8 The brain of this foolish-compounded clay, man, is not able to invent anything that tends to laughter, more than I invent or is invented on me. I am
not only witty in myself, but the cause that wit is in other men. I do here
walk before thee like a sow that hath overwhelm'd all her litter but one.
     FALSTAFF   *1, 2, 7*

9 My lord, I was born about three of the clock in the afternoon, with a white
head and something a round belly. For my voice—I have lost it with
hallooing and singing of anthems.   FALSTAFF   *1, 2, 176*

10 Well, I cannot last ever; but it was alway yet the trick of our English nation,
if they have a good thing, to make it too common.   FALSTAFF   *1, 2, 200*

11 I would to God my name were not so terrible to the enemy as it is.
     FALSTAFF   *1, 2, 204*

12 I can get no remedy against this consumption of the purse; borrowing only
lingers and lingers it out, but the disease is incurable.   FALSTAFF   *1, 2, 223*

13   O thoughts of men accurs'd!
Past and to come seems best; things present, worst.   ARCHBISHOP
                                            1, 3, 107

14 Away, you scullion! you rampallian! you fustilarian! I'll tickle your catastrophe.   FALSTAFF   *2, 1, 57*

15 He hath eaten me out of house and home.   HOSTESS   *2, 1, 71*

16 Now, the Lord lighten thee! Thou art a great fool.   CHIEF JUSTICE
                                            2, 1, 187

17   He was indeed the glass
Wherein the noble youth did dress themselves.   LADY PERCY   *2, 3, 21*

18 Hollow pamper'd jades of Asia.   PISTOL   *2, 4, 155*

19 Is it not strange that desire should so many years outlive performance?
     POINS   *2, 4, 250*

20 Now comes in the sweetest morsel of the night, and we must hence, and
leave it unpick'd.   FALSTAFF   *2, 4, 354*

1 You see, my good wenches, how men of merit are sought after; the undeserver may sleep, when the man of action is call'd on.   FALSTAFF
Henry the Fourth, Part Two, 2, 4, 361

2 How many thousands of my poorest subjects
Are at this hour asleep! O sleep, O gentle sleep,
Nature's soft nurse, how have I frighted thee,
That thou no more wilt weigh my eyelids down,
And steep my senses in forgetfulness ?   HENRY IV   *3, 1, 4*

3 Canst thou, O partial sleep, give thy repose
To the wet sea-boy in an hour so rude;
And in the calmest and most stillest night,
With all appliances and means to boot,
Deny it to a king ? Then, happy low, lie down!
Uneasy lies the head that wears a crown.   HENRY IV   *3, 1, 26*

4 O God! that one might read the book of fate.   HENRY IV   *3, 1, 45*

5 There is a history in all men's lives,
Figuring the natures of the times deceas'd.   WARWICK   *3, 1, 80*

6 Death, as the Psalmist saith, is certain to all; all shall die. How a good yoke
of bullocks at Stamford fair ?   SHALLOW   *3, 2, 36*

7 We have heard the chimes at midnight.   FALSTAFF   *3, 2, 210*

8 I care not; a man can die but once; we owe God a death.   FEEBLE   *3, 2, 228*

9 Care I for the limb, the thews, the stature, bulk, and big assemblance of a
man! Give me the spirit.   FALSTAFF   *3, 2, 251*

10 Lord, Lord, how subject we old men are to this vice of lying!   FALSTAFF
                                                          3, 2, 294

11 Against ill chances men are ever merry;
But heaviness foreruns the good event.   ARCHBISHOP   *4, 2, 81*

12 A peace is of the nature of a conquest;
For then both parties nobly are subdu'd,
And neither party loser.   ARCHBISHOP   *4, 2, 89*

13 I may justly say with the hook-nos'd fellow of Rome—I came, saw, and
overcame.   FALSTAFF   *4, 3, 40*

14 He hath a tear for pity and a hand
Open as day for melting charity.   HENRY IV   *4, 4, 31*

15 Most subject is the fattest soil to weeds.   HENRY IV   *4, 4, 54*

16 O polish'd perturbation! golden care!
That keep'st the ports of slumber open wide
To many a watchful night!   PRINCE   *4, 5, 23*

17 This sleep is sound indeed; this is a sleep
That from this golden rigol hath divorc'd
So many English kings.   PRINCE   *4, 5, 35*

18 Thy wish was father, Harry, to that thought.   HENRY IV   *4, 5, 93*

19   Commit
The oldest sins the newest kind of ways.   HENRY IV   *4, 5, 126*

20 This is the English, not the Turkish court;
Not Amurath an Amurath succeeds,
But Harry Harry.   HENRY V   *5, 2, 47*

1 Under which king, Bezonian?
Speak, or die.   PISTOL   *Henry the Fourth, Part Two, 5, 3, 112*

2 Let us take any man's horses: the laws of England are at my commandment.
FALSTAFF *5, 3, 134*

3 I know thee not, old man. Fall to thy prayers.
How ill white hairs become a fool and jester!
I have long dreamt of such a kind of man,
So surfeit-swell'd, so old, and so profane.   HENRY V   *5, 5, 48*

4 Master Shallow, I owe you a thousand pound.   FALSTAFF   *5, 5, 74*

King Henry the Fifth

5 O for a Muse of fire, that would ascend
The brightest heaven of invention.   CHORUS   *Prologue, 1*

6   Can this cockpit hold
The vasty fields of France? Or may we cram
Within this wooden O the very casques
That did affright the air at Agincourt?   CHORUS   *Prologue, 11*

7 Turn him to any cause of policy,
The Gordian knot of it he will unloose,
Familiar as his garter; that, when he speaks,
The air, a charter'd libertine, is still.   ARCHBISHOP OF CANTERBURY
1, 1, 45

8   For so work the honey bees,
Creatures that by a rule in nature teach
The act of order to a peopled kingdom.
They have a king, and officers of sorts,
Where some like magistrates correct at home;
Others like merchants venture trade abroad;
Others like soldiers, armed in their stings,
Make boot upon the summer's velvet buds,
Which pillage they with merry march bring home
To the tent-royal of their emperor;
Who, busied in his majesty, surveys
The singing masons building roofs of gold,
The civil citizens kneading up the honey,
The poor mechanic porters crowding in
Their heavy burdens at his narrow gate,
The sad-ey'd justice, with his surly hum,
Delivering o'er to executors pale
The lazy yawning drone.   ARCHBISHOP OF CANTERBURY   *1, 2, 187*

9 Now all the youth of England are on fire,
And silken dalliance in the wardrobe lies;
Now thrive the armourers, and honour's thought
Reigns solely in the breast of every man;
They sell the pasture now to buy the horse,
Following the mirror of all Christian kings
With winged heels, as English Mercuries.
For now sits Expectation in the air.   CHORUS   *2, Prologue, 1*

10 I dare not fight; but I will wink and hold out mine iron.   NYM   *2, 1, 6*

11 Though patience be a tired mare, yet she will plod.   NYM   *2, 1, 24*

1 He's in Arthur's bosom, if ever man went to Arthur's bosom. 'A made a finer end, and went away an it had been any christom child; 'a parted ev'n just between twelve and one, ev'n at the turning o' th' tide. HOSTESS

Henry the Fifth, 2, 3, 9

2 His nose was as sharp as a pen, and 'a babbl'd of green fields. HOSTESS

2, 3, 17

3 Once more unto the breach, dear friends, once more;
Or close the wall up with our English dead.
In peace there's nothing so becomes a man
As modest stillness and humility;
But when the blast of war blows in our ears,
Then imitate the action of the tiger:
Stiffen the sinews, summon up the blood,
Disguise fair nature with hard-favour'd rage. HENRY V   3, 1, 1

4   On, on, you noblest English,
Whose blood is fet from fathers of war-proof. HENRY V   3, 1, 17

5 I see you stand like greyhounds in the slips,
Straining upon the start. The game's afoot:
Follow your spirit; and upon this charge
Cry 'God for Harry, England, and Saint George!' HENRY V   3, 1, 31

6 Men of few words are the best men. BOY   3, 2, 36

7 I know the disciplines of war. FLUELLEN   3, 2, 132

8 Now entertain conjecture of a time
When creeping murmur and the poring dark
Fills the wide vessel of the universe.
From camp to camp, through the foul womb of night,
The hum of either army stilly sounds,
That the fix'd sentinels almost receive
The secret whispers of each other's watch. CHORUS   4, Prologue, 1

9 The King's a bawcock and a heart of gold,
A lad of life, an imp of fame;
Of parents good, of fist most valiant.
I kiss his dirty shoe, and from heart-string
I love the lovely bully. PISTOL   4, 1, 44

10 I think the King is but a man as I am: the violet smells to him as it doth
to me. HENRY V   4, 1, 101

11 Every subject's duty is the King's; but every subject's soul is his own.

HENRY V   4, 1, 175

12   O that we now had here
But one ten thousand of those men in England
That do no work to-day! WESTMORELAND   4, 3, 16

13 If we are mark'd to die, we are enow
To do our country loss; and if to live,
The fewer men, the greater share of honour. HENRY V   4, 3, 20

14 But if it be a sin to covet honour,
I am the most offending soul alive. HENRY V   4, 3, 28

15 This day is call'd the feast of Crispian.
He that outlives this day, and comes safe home,
Will stand a tip-toe when this day is nam'd,
And rouse him at the name of Crispian. HENRY V   4, 3, 40

1 Old men forget; yet all shall be forgot,
  But he'll remember, with advantages,
  What feats he did that day.   HENRY V   *Henry the Fifth, 4, 3, 49*

2 We few, we happy few, we band of brothers;
  For he to-day that sheds his blood with me
  Shall be my brother; be he ne'er so vile,
  This day shall gentle his condition;
  And gentlemen in England now a-bed
  Shall think themselves accurs'd they were not here,
  And hold their manhoods cheap whiles any speaks
  That fought with us upon Saint Crispin's day.   HENRY V   *4, 3, 60*

3 There is occasions and causes why and wherefore in all things.   FLUELLEN
           5, 1, 3

4 For these fellows of infinite tongue, that can rhyme themselves into ladies'
  favours, they do always reason themselves out again.   HENRY V
           5, 2, 157

King Henry the Sixth, Part One

5 Hung be the heavens with black, yield day to night!   BEDFORD   *1, 1, 1*

6   Unbidden guests
  Are often welcomest when they are gone.   BEDFORD   *2, 2, 55*

7 She's beautiful, and therefore to be woo'd;
  She is a woman, therefore to be won.   SUFFOLK   *5, 3, 78*

King Henry the Sixth, Part Two

8 Smooth runs the water where the brook is deep.   SUFFOLK   *3, 1, 53*

9 I will make it felony to drink small beer.   JACK CADE   *4, 2, 64*

10 The first thing we do, let's kill all the lawyers.   DICK   *4, 2, 73*

11 Thou hast most traitorously corrupted the youth of the realm in erecting a
  grammar school; and whereas, before, our forefathers had no other books
  but the score and the tally, thou hast caused printing to be us'd, and,
  contrary to the King, his crown, and dignity, thou hast built a paper-mill.
  It will be proved to thy face that thou hast men about thee that usually
  talk of a noun and a verb, and such abominable words as no Christian ear
  can endure to hear.   JACK CADE   *4, 7, 30*

12 Away with him, away with him! He speaks Latin.   JACK CADE   *4, 7, 54*

King Henry the Sixth, Part Three

13 O God! methinks it were a happy life
  To be no better than a homely swain;
  To sit upon a hill, as I do now,
  To carve out dials quaintly, point by point,
  Thereby to see the minutes how they run—
  How many makes the hour full complete,
  How many hours brings about the day,
  How many days will finish up the year,
  How many years a mortal man may live.   HENRY VI   *2, 5, 21*

14 Gives not the hawthorn bush a sweeter shade
  To shepherds looking on their silly sheep,
  Than doth a rich embroider'd canopy
  To kings that fear their subjects' treachery?   HENRY VI   *2, 5, 42*

1 Suspicion always haunts the guilty mind:
   The thief doth fear each bush an officer.   GLOUCESTER   *Henry the Sixth,*
                                                            Part Three, 5, 6, 11

2 Down, down to hell; and say I sent thee thither.   GLOUCESTER   *5, 6, 67*

King Henry the Eighth

3 Heat not a furnace for your foe so hot
   That it do singe yourself. We may outrun
   By violent swiftness that which we run at,
   And lose by over-running.   NORFOLK   *1, 1, 140*

4 I swear 'tis better to be lowly born
   And range with humble livers in content
   Than to be perk'd up in a glist'ring grief
   And wear a golden sorrow.   ANNE   *2, 3, 19*

5   I would not be a queen
   For all the world.   ANNE   *2, 3, 45*

6 Orpheus with his lute made trees,
   And the mountain tops that freeze,
       Bow themselves when he did sing.   SONG   *3, 1, 3*

7 Heaven is above all yet: there sits a Judge
   That no king can corrupt.   QUEEN KATHARINE   *3, 1, 100*

8 I have touch'd the highest point of all my greatness,
   And from that full meridian of my glory
   I haste now to my setting. I shall fall
   Like a bright exhalation in the evening,
   And no man see me more.   WOLSEY   *3, 2, 223*

9 Farewell, a long farewell, to all my greatness!
   This is the state of man: to-day he puts forth
   The tender leaves of hopes; to-morrow blossoms
   And bears his blushing honours thick upon him;
   The third day comes a frost, a killing frost,
   And when he thinks, good easy man, full surely
   His greatness is a-ripening, nips his root,
   And then he falls, as I do.   WOLSEY   *3, 2, 351*

10 Vain pomp and glory of this world, I hate ye;
   I feel my heart new open'd.   O, how wretched
   Is that poor man that hangs on princes' favours!
   There is betwixt that smile we would aspire to,
   That sweet aspect of princes, and their ruin
   More pangs and fears than wars or women have;
   And when he falls, he falls like Lucifer,
   Never to hope again.   WOLSEY   *3, 2, 365*

11 A peace above all earthly dignities,
   A still and quiet conscience.   WOLSEY   *3, 2, 379*

12 Love thyself last; cherish those hearts that hate thee;
   Corruption wins not more than honesty.   WOLSEY   *3, 2, 443*

13 Had I but serv'd my God with half the zeal
   I serv'd my King, he would not in mine age
   Have left me naked to mine enemies.   WOLSEY   *3, 2, 455*

14 So may he rest; his faults lie gently on him!   KATHARINE   *4, 2, 31*

1 Men's evil manners live in brass: their virtues
  We write in water.   GRIFFITH   *Henry the Eighth, 4, 2, 45*

2 He was a scholar, and a ripe and good one;
  Exceeding wise, fair-spoken, and persuading;
  Lofty and sour to them that lov'd him not,
  But to those men that sought him sweet as summer.   GRIFFITH *4, 2, 51*

3   Love and meekness, lord,
  Become a churchman better than ambition.   CRANMER   *5, 3, 62*

Julius Caesar

4 You blocks, you stones, you worse than senseless things!   MARULLUS
                                                                1, 1, 36

5 Beware the ides of March.   SOOTHSAYER   *1, 2, 18*

6 Well, honour is the subject of my story.
  I cannot tell what you and other men
  Think of this life; but, for my single self,
  I had as lief not be as live to be
  In awe of such a thing as I myself.   CASSIUS   *1, 2, 92*

7   Ye gods! it doth amaze me
  A man of such a feeble temper should
  So get the start of the majestic world,
  And bear the palm alone.   CASSIUS   *1, 2, 128*

8 Why, man, he doth bestride the narrow world
  Like a Colossus, and we petty men
  Walk under his huge legs, and peep about
  To find ourselves dishonourable graves.
  Men at some time are masters of their fates:
  The fault, dear Brutus, is not in our stars,
  But in ourselves, that we are underlings.   CASSIUS   *1, 2, 135*

9 Let me have men about me that are fat;
  Sleek-headed men, and such as sleep o' nights.
  Yond Cassius has a lean and hungry look;
  He thinks too much. Such men are dangerous.   CAESAR   *1, 2, 192*

10 'Tis very like. He hath the falling sickness.   BRUTUS   *1, 2, 253*

11 For mine own part, it was Greek to me.   CASCA   *1, 2, 283*

12 And yesterday the bird of night did sit,
   Even at noon-day, upon the market-place,
   Hooting and shrieking.   CASCA   *1, 3, 26*

13 Between the acting of a dreadful thing
   And the first motion, all the interim is
   Like a phantasma or a hideous dream.
   The Genius and the mortal instruments
   Are then in council; and the state of man,
   Like to a little kingdom, suffers then
   The nature of an insurrection.   BRUTUS   *2, 1, 63*

14 Let's carve him as a dish fit for the gods.   BRUTUS   *2, 1, 173*

15 Cowards die many times before their deaths:
   The valiant never taste of death but once.   CAESAR   *2, 2, 32*

1 How hard it is for women to keep counsel! PORTIA *Julius Caesar, 2, 4, 9*

2 Et tu, Brute? CAESAR 3, 1, 77

3 Why, he that cuts off twenty years of life
Cuts off so many years of fearing death. CASSIUS 3, 1, 102

4   How many ages hence
Shall this our lofty scene be acted over
In states unborn and accents yet unknown! CASSIUS 3, 1, 112

5 O mighty Caesar! dost thou lie so low?
Are all thy conquests, glories, triumphs, spoils,
Shrunk to this little measure? MARK ANTONY 3, 1, 149

6 The choice and master spirits of this age. MARK ANTONY 3, 1, 164

7 O, pardon me, thou bleeding piece of earth,
That I am meek and gentle with these butchers!
Thou art the ruins of the noblest man
That ever lived in the tide of times. MARK ANTONY 3, 1, 255

8 Cry 'Havoc!' and let slip the dogs of war. MARK ANTONY 3, 1, 274

9 Not that I lov'd Caesar less, but that I lov'd Rome more. BRUTUS 3, 2, 20

10 As Caesar lov'd me, I weep for him; as he was fortunate, I rejoice at it; as
he was valiant, I honour him; but—as he was ambitious, I slew him. There
is tears for his love; joy for his fortune; honour for his valour; and death
for his ambition. Who is here so base that would be a bondman? If any,
speak; for him have I offended. BRUTUS 3, 2, 24

11 Friends, Romans, countrymen, lend me your ears;
I come to bury Caesar, not to praise him.
The evil that men do lives after them;
The good is oft interred with their bones. MARK ANTONY 3, 2, 73

12 For Brutus is an honourable man;
So are they all, all honourable men. MARK ANTONY 3, 2, 82

13 Ambition should be made of sterner stuff. MARK ANTONY 3, 2, 92

14 But yesterday the word of Caesar might
Have stood against the world: now lies he there,
And none so poor to do him reverence. MARK ANTONY 3, 2, 118

15 The will, the will! We will hear Caesar's will. PLEBEIANS 3, 2, 139

16 If you have tears, prepare to shed them now. MARK ANTONY 3, 2, 169

17 See what a rent the envious Casca made. MARK ANTONY 3, 2, 175

18 This was the most unkindest cut of all. MARK ANTONY 3, 2, 183

19 O, what a fall was there, my countrymen! MARK ANTONY 3, 2, 190

20 For I have neither wit, nor words, nor worth,
Action, nor utterance, nor the power of speech,
To stir men's blood; I only speak right on. MARK ANTONY 3, 2, 221

21 Tear him for his bad verses, tear him for his bad verses! 4TH PLEBEIAN
3, 3, 30

22   You yourself
Are much condemn'd to have an itching palm. BRUTUS 4, 3, 9

23 I had rather be a dog and bay the moon
Than such a Roman. BRUTUS 4, 3, 27

1 Away, slight man!   BRUTUS   *Julius Caesar, 4, 3, 37*

2 A friend should bear his friend's infirmities,
But Brutus makes mine greater than they are.   CASSIUS   *4, 3, 85*

3 There is a tide in the affairs of men
Which, taken at the flood, leads on to fortune;
Omitted, all the voyage of their life
Is bound in shallows and in miseries.
On such a full sea are we now afloat,
And we must take the current when it serves,
Or lose our ventures.   BRUTUS   *4, 3, 216*

4 For ever and for ever farewell, Cassius!
If we do meet again, why, we shall smile;
If not, why then this parting was well made.   BRUTUS   *5, 1, 116*

5   O that a man might know
The end of this day's business ere it come!   BRUTUS   *5, 1, 122*

6 This was the noblest Roman of them all.
All the conspirators save only he
Did that they did in envy of great Caesar.   MARK ANTONY   *5, 5, 68*

7 His life was gentle; and the elements
So mix'd in him that Nature might stand up
And say to all the world 'This was a man!'   MARK ANTONY   *5, 5, 73*

King John

8 A strange beginning—'borrowed majesty'!   ELINOR   *1, 1, 5*

9 Lord of thy presence and no land beside.   ELINOR   *1, 1, 137*

10 For courage mounteth with occasion.   AUSTRIA   *2, 1, 82*

11 Saint George, that swing'd the dragon, and e'er since
Sits on's horse back at mine hostess' door.   BASTARD   *2, 1, 288*

12 Mad world! mad kings! mad composition!   BASTARD   *2, 1, 561*

13 That smooth-fac'd gentleman, tickling commodity,
Commodity, the bias of the world.   BASTARD   *2, 1, 573*

14 Well, whiles I am a beggar, I will rail
And say there is no sin but to be rich;
And being rich, my virtue then shall be
To say there is no vice but beggary.   BASTARD   *2, 1, 593*

15   Here I and sorrows sit;
Here is my throne, bid kings come bow to it.   CONSTANCE   *3, 1, 73*

16 Bell, book, and candle, shall not drive me back,
When gold and silver becks me to come on.   BASTARD   *3, 3, 12*

17 Life is as tedious as a twice-told tale
Vexing the dull ear of a drowsy man.   LEWIS   *3, 4, 108*

18 Heat me these irons hot.   HUBERT   *4, 1, 1*

19 To gild refined gold, to paint the lily,
To throw a perfume on the violet,
To smooth the ice, or add another hue
Unto the rainbow, or with taper-light
To seek the beauteous eye of heaven to garnish,
Is wasteful and ridiculous excess.   SALISBURY   *4, 2, 11*

1 And oftentimes excusing of a fault
   Doth make the fault the worse by th' excuse.   PEMBROKE   *King John*
                                                                                                4, 2, 30

2 How oft the sight of means to do ill deeds
   Make deeds ill done!   KING JOHN   *4, 2, 219*

3 I beg cold comfort.   KING JOHN   *5, 7, 42*

4 This England never did, nor never shall,
   Lie at the proud foot of a conqueror,
   But when it first did help to wound itself.   BASTARD   *5, 7, 112*

5   Nought shall make us rue,
   If England to itself do rest but true.   BASTARD   *5, 7, 117*

King Lear

6 Nothing will come of nothing. Speak again.   LEAR   *1, 1, 89*

7   LEAR: So young and so untender?
   CORDELIA: So young, my lord, and true.   *1, 1, 105*

8 A still-soliciting eye.   CORDELIA   *1, 1, 231*

9 These late eclipses in the sun and moon portend no good to us.
                                    GLOUCESTER   *1, 2, 99*

10 This is the excellent foppery of the world, that, when we are sick in fortune,
   often the surfeits of our own behaviour, we make guilty of our disasters the
   sun, the moon, and stars.   EDMUND   *1, 2, 112*

11 My cue is villainous melancholy, with a sigh like Tom o' Bedlam.
                                  EDMUND   *1, 2, 129*

12 KENT: You have that in your countenance which I would fain call master.
   LEAR: What's that?
   KENT: Authority.   *1, 4, 28*

13 LEAR: Dost thou call me fool, boy?
   FOOL: All thy other titles thou hast given away; that thou wast born with.
                                                 1, 4, 147

14 Ingratitude, thou marble-hearted fiend,
   More hideous when thou show'st thee in a child
   Than the sea-monster!   LEAR   *1, 4, 259*

15 How sharper than a serpent's tooth it is
   To have a thankless child.   LEAR   *1, 4, 288*

16 Striving to better, oft we mar what's well.   ALBANY   *1, 4, 347*

17 O, let me not be mad, not mad, sweet heaven!
   Keep me in temper; I would not be mad!   LEAR   *1, 5, 43*

18 Thou whoreson zed! thou unnecessary letter!   KENT   *2, 2, 58*

19 I have seen better faces in my time
   Than stands on any shoulder that I see
   Before me at this instant.   KENT   *2, 2, 88*

20 Fortune, good night; smile once more; turn thy wheel.   KENT   *2, 2, 168*

21 Hysterica passio—down, thou climbing sorrow,
   Thy element's below.   LEAR   *2, 4, 56*

22   You are old;
   Nature in you stands on the very verge
   Of her confine.   REGAN   *2, 4, 144*

1   LEAR: I gave you all.
    REGAN: And in good time you gave it.   *King Lear, 2, 4, 248*

2 O, reason not the need! Our basest beggars
  Are in the poorest thing superfluous.
  Allow not nature more than nature needs,
  Man's life is cheap as beast's.   LEAR   2, 4, 263

3 And let not women's weapons, water-drops,
  Stain my man's cheeks!   LEAR   2, 4, 276

4 No, I'll not weep.
  I have full cause of weeping; but this heart
  Shall break into a hundred thousand flaws
  Or ere I'll weep. O fool, I shall go mad!   LEAR   2, 4, 282

5 Who's there, besides foul weather?   KENT   3, 1, 1

6 Blow, winds, and crack your cheeks; rage, blow.
  You cataracts and hurricanoes, spout
  Till you have drench'd our steeples, drown'd the cocks.   LEAR   3, 2, 1

7 Rumble thy bellyful. Spit, fire; spout, rain.
  Nor rain, wind, thunder, fire, are my daughters.
  I tax not you, you elements, with unkindness.   LEAR   3, 2, 14

8   Here I stand, your slave,
  A poor, infirm, weak and despis'd old man.   LEAR   3, 2, 19

9 For there was never yet fair woman but she made mouths in a glass.
                                       FOOL   3, 2, 35

10   Things that love night
  Love not such nights as these.   KENT   3, 2, 42

11   I am a man
  More sinn'd against than sinning.   LEAR   3, 2, 59

12 O, that way madness lies; let me shun that.   LEAR   3, 4, 21

13 Poor naked wretches, wheresoe'er you are,
  That bide the pelting of this pitiless storm,
  How shall your houseless heads and unfed sides,
  Your loop'd and window'd raggedness, defend you
  From seasons such as these?   LEAR   3, 4, 28

14   Take physic, pomp;
  Expose thyself to feel what wretches feel.   LEAR   3, 4, 33

15 'Tis a naughty night to swim in.   FOOL   3, 4, 109

16 Poor Tom's a-cold.   EDGAR   3, 4, 143

17 Child Rowland to the dark tower came,
  His word was still 'Fie, foh, and fum,
  I smell the blood of a British man'.   EDGAR   3, 4, 178

18   Out vile jelly!
  Where is thy lustre now?   CORNWALL   3, 7, 82

19   The worst is not
  So long as we can say 'This is the worst'.   EDGAR   4, 1, 28

20 As flies to wanton boys are we to th' gods—
  They kill us for their sport.   GLOUCESTER   4, 1, 37

21 Wisdom and goodness to the vile seem vile;
  Filths savour but themselves.   ALBANY   4, 2, 38

1   It is the stars,
The stars above us, govern our conditions.   KENT   *King Lear, 4, 3, 32*

2   How fearful
And dizzy 'tis to cast one's eyes so low!
The crows and choughs that wing the mid-way air
Show scarce so gross as beetles.   EDGAR   *4, 6, 11*

3 Ay, every inch a king.   LEAR   *4, 6, 107*

4 The wren goes to't, and the small gilded fly
Does lecher in my sight.   LEAR   *4, 6, 112*

5 Give me an ounce of civet, good apothecary, to sweeten my imagination.
                      LEAR   *4, 6, 129*

6 Through tatter'd clothes small vices do appear;
Robes and furr'd gowns hide all.   LEAR   *4, 6, 164*

7   Get thee glass eyes,
And, like a scurvy politician, seem
To see the things thou dost not.   LEAR   *4, 6, 170*

8 When we are born, we cry that we are come
To this great stage of fools.   LEAR   *4, 6, 183*

9   Mine enemy's dog,
Though he had bit me, should have stood that night
Against my fire.   CORDELIA   *4, 7, 36*

10 Thou art a soul in bliss; but I am bound
Upon a wheel of fire, that mine own tears
Do scald like molten lead.   LEAR   *4, 7, 46*

11 I am a very foolish fond old man,
Fourscore and upward, not an hour more nor less;
And, to deal plainly,
I fear I am not in my perfect mind.   LEAR   *4, 7, 60*

12   Men must endure
Their going hence, even as their coming hither:
Ripeness is all.   EDGAR   *5, 2, 9*

13   Come, let's away to prison.
We two alone will sing like birds i' th' cage;
When thou dost ask me blessing, I'll kneel down
And ask of thee forgiveness; so we'll live,
And pray, and sing, and tell old tales, and laugh
At gilded butterflies, and hear poor rogues
Talk of court news; and we'll talk with them too—
Who loses and who wins; who's in, who's out—
And take upon's the mystery of things
As if we were God's spies.   LEAR   *5, 3, 8*

14 The gods are just, and of our pleasant vices
Make instruments to plague us:
The dark and vicious place where thee he got
Cost him his eyes.   EDGAR   *5, 3, 170*

15 The wheel is come full circle.   EDMUND   *5, 3, 174*

1   But his flaw'd heart—
Alack, too weak the conflict to support!—
'Twixt two extremes of passion, joy and grief,
Burst smilingly.   EDGAR   *King Lear*, 5, 3, 196

2 Howl, howl, howl, howl! O, you are men of stones!
Had I your tongues and eyes, I'd use them so
That heaven's vault should crack.   LEAR   5, 3, 257

3   Her voice was ever soft,
Gentle, and low—an excellent thing in woman.   LEAR   5, 3, 272

4 And my poor fool is hang'd! No, no, no life!
Why should a dog, a horse, a rat have life,
And thou no breath at all? Thou'lt come no more,
Never, never, never, never, never.
Pray you undo this button.   LEAR   5, 3, 305

5 Vex not his ghost. O, let him pass! He hates him
That would upon the rack of this tough world
Stretch him out longer.   KENT   5, 3, 313

Love's Labour's Lost

6 Spite of cormorant devouring Time.   KING   1, 1, 4

7 Why, all delights are vain; but that most vain
Which, with pain purchas'd, doth inherit pain.   BEROWNE   1, 1, 72

8 Small have continual plodders ever won,
Save base authority from others' books.   BEROWNE   1, 1, 86

9 At Christmas I no more desire a rose
Than wish a snow in May's new-fangled shows.   BEROWNE   1, 1, 105

10 Remuneration! O, that's the Latin word for three farthings.   COSTARD
3, 1, 129

11 He hath never fed of the dainties that are bred in a book; he hath not eat
paper, as it were; he hath not drunk ink; his intellect is not replenished.
SIR NATHANIEL   4, 2, 22

12 For where is any author in the world
Teaches such beauty as a woman's eye?
Learning is but an adjunct to ourself.   BEROWNE   4, 3, 308

13 And when Love speaks, the voice of all the gods
Make heaven drowsy with the harmony.   BEROWNE   4, 3, 340

14 From women's eyes this doctrine I derive.
They sparkle still the right Promethean fire;
They are the books, the arts, the academes,
That show, contain, and nourish, all the world.   ROSALINE   4, 3, 346

15 A world-without-end bargain.   PRINCESS   5, 2, 777

16 A jest's prosperity lies in the ear
Of him that hears it, never in the tongue
Of him that makes it.   BEROWNE   5, 2, 849

17 When daisies pied and violets blue
And lady-smocks all silver-white
And cuckoo-buds of yellow hue
Do paint the meadows with delight,

The cuckoo then on every tree
Mocks married men, for thus sings he:
'Cuckoo;
Cuckoo, cuckoo'—O word of fear,
Unpleasing to a married ear!   SPRING   *Love's Labour's Lost, 5, 2, 881*

1 When icicles hang by the wall,
And Dick the shepherd blows his nail,
And Tom bears logs into the hall,
And milk comes frozen home in pail,
When blood is nipp'd, and ways be foul,
Then nightly sings the staring owl:
'Tu-who;
Tu-whit, Tu-who'—A merry note,
While greasy Joan doth keel the pot.

When all aloud the wind doth blow,
And coughing drowns the parson's saw,
And birds sit brooding in the snow,
And Marian's nose looks red and raw,
When roasted crabs hiss in the bowl.   WINTER   *5, 2, 899*

2 The words of Mercury are harsh after the songs of Apollo.   ARMADO
5, 2, 917

Macbeth

3 1ST WITCH: When shall we three meet again?
              In thunder, lightning, or in rain?
  2ND WITCH: When the hurlyburly's done,
              When the battle's lost and won.   *1, 1, 1*

4 Fair is foul, and foul is fair:
Hover through the fog and filthy air.   THREE WITCHES   *1, 1, 10*

5 What bloody man is that?   DUNCAN   *1, 2, 1*

6 So foul and fair a day I have not seen.   MACBETH   *1, 3, 38*

7 What are these,
So wither'd, and so wild in their attire,
That look not like th' inhabitants o' th' earth,
And yet are on't?   BANQUO   *1, 3, 39*

8 If you can look into the seeds of time
And say which grain will grow and which will not,
Speak then to me, who neither beg nor fear
Your favours nor your hate.   BANQUO   *1, 3, 58*

9 This supernatural soliciting
Cannot be ill; cannot be good.   MACBETH   *1, 3, 130*

10 Come what come may,
Time and the hour runs through the roughest day.   MACBETH   *1, 3, 146*

11 Nothing in his life
Became him like the leaving it: he died
As one that had been studied in his death
To throw away the dearest thing he ow'd
As 'twere a careless trifle.   MALCOLM   *1, 4, 7*

12 Stars, hide your fires.   MACBETH   *1, 4, 50*

1 Yet do I fear thy nature;
It is too full o' th' milk of human kindness
To catch the nearest way.   LADY MACBETH   *Macbeth*, *1, 5, 13*

2 Come, thick night,
And pall thee in the dunnest smoke of hell.   LADY MACBETH   *1, 5, 47*

3 O, never
Shall sun that morrow see!
Your face, my thane, is as a book where men
May read strange matters.   LADY MACBETH   *1, 5, 57*

4 If it were done when 'tis done, then 'twere well
It were done quickly.   MACBETH   *1, 7, 1*

5 That but this blow
Might be the be-all and the end-all here—
But here upon this bank and shoal of time—
We'd jump the life to come.   MACBETH   *1, 7, 4*

6 I have no spur
To prick the sides of my intent, but only
Vaulting ambition, which o'er-leaps itself,
And falls on th' other.   MACBETH   *1, 7, 25*

7   MACBETH: If we should fail?
   LADY MACBETH: We fail!
              But screw your courage to the sticking place,
              And we'll not fail.   *1, 7, 59*

8 False face must hide what the false heart doth know.   MACBETH   *1, 7, 82*

9 Is this a dagger which I see before me,
The handle toward my hand?   MACBETH   *2, 1, 33*

10   The bell invites me.
Hear it not, Duncan, for it is a knell
That summons thee to heaven or to hell.   MACBETH   *2, 1, 62*

11 Methought I heard a voice cry 'Sleep no more;
Macbeth does murder sleep'—the innocent sleep,
Sleep that knits up the ravell'd sleave of care,
The death of each day's life, sore labour's bath,
Balm of hurt minds, great nature's second course,
Chief nourisher in life's feast.   MACBETH   *2, 2, 35*

12 Will all great Neptune's ocean wash this blood
Clean from my hand? No; this my hand will rather
The multitudinous seas incarnadine,
Making the green one red.   MACBETH   *2, 2, 60*

13 I had thought to have let in some of all professions that go the primrose way
to th' everlasting bonfire.   PORTER   *2, 3, 18*

14 It provokes the desire, but it takes away the performance. Therefore much
drink may be said to be an equivocator with lechery.   PORTER   *2, 3, 28*

15 Had I but died an hour before this chance,
I had liv'd a blessed time; for, from this instant,
There's nothing serious in mortality—
All is but toys.   MACBETH   *2, 3, 89*

16   Where we are,
There's daggers in men's smiles; the near in blood,
The nearer bloody.   DONALBAIN   *2, 3, 138*

1 Ay, in the catalogue ye go for men;
  As hounds, and greyhounds, mongrels, spaniels, curs,
  Shoughs, water-rugs, and demi-wolves, are clept
  All by the name of dogs.   MACBETH   *Macbeth, 3, 1, 91*

2 I am one, my liege,
  Whom the vile blows and buffets of the world
  Hath so incens'd that I am reckless what
  I do to spite the world.   2ND MURDERER   *3, 1, 107*

3 Nought's had, all's spent,
  Where our desire is got without content.
  'Tis safer to be that which we destroy,
  Than by destruction dwell in doubtful joy.   LADY MACBETH   *3, 2, 4*

4   Duncan is in his grave;
  After life's fitful fever he sleeps well.   MACBETH   *3, 2, 22*

5 Things bad begun make strong themselves by ill.   MACBETH   *3, 2, 55*

6 I had else been perfect,
  Whole as the marble, founded as the rock,
  As broad and general as the casing air,
  But now I am cabin'd, cribb'd, confin'd, bound in
  To saucy doubts and fears.   MACBETH   *3, 4, 21*

7 Now good digestion wait on appetite,
  And health on both!   MACBETH   *3, 4, 38*

8   The time has been
  That when the brains were out the man would die,
  And there an end.   MACBETH   *3, 4, 78*

9 Stand not upon the order of your going,
  But go at once.   LADY MACBETH   *3, 4, 119*

10   I am in blood
  Stepp'd in so far that, should I wade no more,
  Returning were as tedious as go o'er.   MACBETH   *3, 4, 136*

11 Double, double toil and trouble;
  Fire burn, and cauldron bubble.   THREE WITCHES   *4, 1, 10*

12 Ditch-deliver'd by a drab.   3RD WITCH   *4, 1, 31*

13 How now, you secret, black, and midnight hags!   MACBETH   *4, 1, 47*

14 A deed without a name.   THREE WITCHES   *4, 1, 49*

15 Be bloody, bold, and resolute; laugh to scorn
  The pow'r of man, for none of woman born
  Shall harm Macbeth.   SECOND APPARITION   *4, 1, 79*

16 But yet I'll make assurance double sure,
  And take a bond of fate.   MACBETH   *4, 1, 83*

17 What, will the line stretch out to th' crack of doom?   MACBETH   *4, 1, 117*

18 I think our country sinks beneath the yoke;
  It weeps, it bleeds; and each new day a gash
  Is added to her wounds.   MALCOLM   *4, 3, 39*

19 Stands Scotland where it did?   MACDUFF   *4, 3, 164*

1 The night is long that never finds the day.   MALCOLM   *Macbeth, 4, 3, 240*

2 Out, damned spot! out, I say!   LADY MACBETH   *5, 1, 33*

3 Here's the smell of the blood still. All the perfumes of Arabia will not sweeten this little hand.   LADY MACBETH   *5, 1, 48*

4 To bed, to bed; there's knocking at the gate. Come, come, come, come, give me your hand. What's done cannot be undone.   LADY MACBETH   *5, 1, 64*

5 I have liv'd long enough. My way of life
Is fall'n into the sear, the yellow leaf;
And that which should accompany old age,
As honour, love, obedience, troops of friends,
I must not look to have.   MACBETH   *5, 3, 22*

6 Canst thou not minister to a mind diseas'd,
Pluck from the memory a rooted sorrow,
Raze out the written troubles of the brain,
And with some sweet oblivious antidote
Cleanse the stuff'd bosom of that perilous stuff
Which weighs upon the heart?   MACBETH   *5, 3, 40*

7 I will not be afraid of death and bane
Till Birnam Forest come to Dunsinane.   MACBETH   *5, 3, 59*

8 Hang out our banners on the outward walls;
The cry is still 'They come'.   MACBETH   *5, 5, 1*

9 I have supp'd full with horrors.   MACBETH   *5, 5, 13*

10 She should have died hereafter;
There would have been a time for such a word.
To-morrow, and to-morrow, and to-morrow,
Creeps in this petty pace from day to day
To the last syllable of recorded time,
And all our yesterdays have lighted fools
The way to dusty death. Out, out, brief candle!
Life's but a walking shadow, a poor player,
That struts and frets his hour upon the stage,
And then is heard no more; it is a tale
Told by an idiot, full of sound and fury,
Signifying nothing.   MACBETH   *5, 5, 17*

11 I gin to be aweary of the sun,
And wish th' estate o' th' world were now undone.
Ring the alarum bell. Blow wind, come wrack;
At least we'll die with harness on our back.   MACBETH   *5, 5, 49*

12 MACBETH: I bear a charmed life, which must not yield
            To one of woman born.
    MACDUFF: Despair thy charm;
            And let the angel whom thou still hast serv'd
            Tell thee Macduff was from his mother's womb
            Untimely ripp'd.   *5, 8, 12*

13 Live to be the show and gaze o' th' time.   MACDUFF   *5, 8, 24*

14   Lay on, Macduff;
    And damn'd be him that first cries 'Hold, enough!'   MACBETH   *5, 8, 33*

Measure for Measure

1 'Tis one thing to be tempted, Escalus,
   Another thing to fall. I not deny
   The jury, passing on the prisoner's life,
   May in the sworn twelve have a thief or two
   Guiltier than him they try.   ANGELO   *2, 1, 17*

2 Some rise by sin, and some by virtue fall.   ESCALUS   *2, 1, 38*

3 This will last out a night in Russia,
   When nights are longest there.   ANGELO   *2, 1, 128*

4 No ceremony that to great ones longs,
   Not the king's crown nor the deputed sword,
   The marshal's truncheon nor the judge's robe,
   Become them with one half so good a grace
   As mercy does.   ISABELLA   *2, 2, 59*

5 The law hath not been dead, though it hath slept.   ANGELO   *2, 2, 90*

6   O, it is excellent
   To have a giant's strength! But it is tyrannous
   To use it like a giant.   ISABELLA   *2, 2, 107*

7   But man, proud man,
   Dress'd in a little brief authority,
   Most ignorant of what he's most assur'd,
   His glassy essence, like an angry ape,
   Plays such fantastic tricks before high heaven
   As makes the angels weep.   ISABELLA   *2, 2, 117*

8 That in the captain's but a choleric word
   Which in the soldier is flat blasphemy.   ISABELLA   *2, 2, 130*

9 The miserable have no other medicine
   But only hope.   CLAUDIO   *3, 1, 2*

10 Ay, but to die, and go we know not where;
   To lie in cold obstruction, and to rot;
   This sensible warm motion to become
   A kneaded clod; and the delighted spirit
   To bathe in fiery floods or to reside
   In thrilling region of thick-ribbed ice.   CLAUDIO   *3, 1, 119*

11 The weariest and most loathed worldly life
   That age, ache, penury, and imprisonment,
   Can lay on nature is a paradise
   To what we fear of death.   CLAUDIO   *3, 1, 130*

12 Take, O, take those lips away,
      That so sweetly were forsworn;
   And those eyes, the break of day,
      Lights that do mislead the morn;
   But my kisses bring again, bring again;
   Seals of love, but seal'd in vain, seal'd in vain.   SONG   *4, 1, 1*

13 I am a kind of burr; I shall stick.   LUCIO   *4, 3, 173*

14 Haste still pays haste, and leisure answers leisure;
   Like doth quit like, and Measure still for Measure.   DUKE   *5, 1, 408*

15 What's mine is yours, and what is yours is mine.   DUKE   *5, 1, 535*

The Merchant of Venice

1 I hold the world but as the world, Gratiano—
A stage, where every man must play a part,
And mine a sad one.   ANTONIO   *I, I, 77*

2 There are a sort of men whose visages
Do cream and mantle like a standing pond.   GRATIANO   *I, I, 88*

3 As who should say 'I am Sir Oracle,
And when I ope my lips let no dog bark'.   GRATIANO   *I, I, 93*

4 In Belmont is a lady richly left,
And she is fair and, fairer than that word,
Of wondrous virtues.   BASSANIO   *I, I, 161*

5 By my troth, Nerissa, my little body is aweary of this great world.   PORTIA
I, 2, I

6 If to do were as easy as to know what were good to do, chapels had been
churches, and poor men's cottages princes' palaces.   PORTIA   *I, 2, II*

7 How like a fawning publican he looks!
I hate him for he is a Christian;
But more for that in low simplicity
He lends out money gratis, and brings down
The rate of usance here with us in Venice.
If I can catch him once upon the hip,
I will feed fat the ancient grudge I bear him.   SHYLOCK   *I, 3, 36*

8 The devil can cite Scripture for his purpose.   ANTONIO   *I, 3, 93*

9   Many a time and oft
In the Rialto you have rated me.   SHYLOCK   *I, 3, 101*

10 Still have I borne it with a patient shrug,
For suff'rance is the badge of all our tribe;
You call me misbeliever, cut-throat dog,
And spit upon my Jewish gaberdine.   SHYLOCK   *I, 3, 104*

11 I like not fair terms and a villain's mind.   BASSANIO   *I, 3, 174*

12 It is a wise father that knows his own child.   LAUNCELOT GOBBO   *2, 2, 69*

13 There is some ill a-brewing towards my rest,
For I did dream of money-bags to-night.   SHYLOCK   *2, 5, 17*

14 But love is blind, and lovers cannot see
The pretty follies that themselves commit.   JESSICA   *2, 6, 36*

15 The ancient saying is no heresy:
Hanging and wiving goes by destiny.   NERISSA   *2, 9, 82*

16 Let him look to his bond.   SHYLOCK   *3, I, 39*

17 Hath not a Jew eyes? Hath not a Jew hands, organs, dimensions, senses,
affections, passions, fed with the same food, hurt with the same weapons,
subject to the same diseases, healed by the same means, warmed and cooled
by the same winter and summer, as a Christian is? If you prick us, do we
not bleed? If you tickle us, do we not laugh? If you poison us, do we not
die? And if you wrong us, shall we not revenge?   SHYLOCK   *3, I, 49*

18 Tell me where is fancy bred,
Or in the heart or in the head,
How begot, how nourished?   SONG   *3, 2, 63*

1 The quality of mercy is not strain'd;
It droppeth as the gentle rain from heaven
Upon the place beneath. It is twice blest:
It blesseth him that gives and him that takes.
'Tis mightiest in the mightiest; it becomes
The throned monarch better than his crown;
His sceptre shows the force of temporal power,
The attribute to awe and majesty,
Wherein doth sit the dread and fear of kings;
But mercy is above this sceptred sway,
It is enthroned in the hearts of kings,
It is an attribute to God himself;
And earthly power doth then show likest God's
When mercy seasons justice. Therefore, Jew,
Though justice be thy plea, consider this—
That in the course of justice none of us
Should see salvation; we do pray for mercy,
And that same prayer doth teach us all to render
The deeds of mercy.   PORTIA   *The Merchant of Venice, 4, 1, 179*

2 Wrest once the law to your authority;
To do a great right do a little wrong.   BASSANIO   *4, 1, 210*

3 A Daniel come to judgment! Yea, a Daniel!   SHYLOCK   *4, 1, 218*

4 'Tis not in the bond.   SHYLOCK   *4, 1, 257*

5 A pound of that same merchant's flesh is thine.
The court awards it and the law doth give it.   PORTIA   *4, 1, 294*

6 You take my house when you do take the prop
That doth sustain my house; you take my life
When you do take the means whereby I live.   SHYLOCK   *4, 1, 370*

7 He is well paid that is well satisfied.   PORTIA   *4, 1, 410*

8 How sweet the moonlight sleeps upon this bank!
Here will we sit and let the sounds of music
Creep in our ears; soft stillness and the night
Become the touches of sweet harmony.
Sit, Jessica. Look how the floor of heaven
Is thick inlaid with patines of bright gold;
There's not the smallest orb which thou behold'st
But in his motion like an angel sings,
Still quiring to the young-ey'd cherubins;
Such harmony is in immortal souls,
But whilst this muddy vesture of decay
Doth grossly close it in, we cannot hear it.   LORENZO   *5, 1, 54*

9 I am never merry when I hear sweet music.   JESSICA   *5, 1, 69*

10 The man that hath no music in himself,
Nor is not mov'd with concord of sweet sounds,
Is fit for treasons, stratagems, and spoils.   LORENZO   *5, 1, 83*

11 How far that little candle throws his beams!
So shines a good deed in a naughty world.   PORTIA   *5, 1, 90*

12 For a light wife doth make a heavy husband.   PORTIA   *5, 1, 130*

The Merry Wives of Windsor

1 I will make a Star Chamber matter of it.   SHALLOW   *I, I, I*

2 I had rather than forty shillings I had my Book of Songs and Sonnets here.
                                        SLENDER   *I, I, 179*

3 Here will be an old abusing of God's patience and the King's English.
                              MISTRESS QUICKLY   *I, 4, 5*

4 Why, then the world's mine oyster,
   Which I with sword will open.   PISTOL   *2, 2, 4*

5 I cannot tell what the dickens his name is.   MRS PAGE   *3, 2, 15*

6 O, what a world of vile ill-favour'd faults
   Looks handsome in three hundred pounds a year!   ANNE PAGE   *3, 4, 32*

7 I'll no pullet-sperm in my brewage.   FALSTAFF   *3, 5, 27*

8 They say there is divinity in odd numbers, either in nativity, chance, or
   death.   FALSTAFF   *5, I, 3*

A Midsummer Night's Dream

9 To live a barren sister all your life,
   Chanting faint hymns to the cold fruitless moon.   THESEUS   *I, I, 72*

10   For aught that I could ever read,
   Could ever hear by tale or history,
   The course of true love never did run smooth.   LYSANDER   *I, I, 132*

11 O hell! to choose love by another's eyes.   HERMIA   *I, I, 140*

12 Love looks not with the eyes, but with the mind;
   And therefore is wing'd Cupid painted blind.   HELENA   *I, I, 234*

13 'The most Lamentable Comedy and most Cruel Death of Pyramus and
   Thisby.'   QUINCE   *I, 2, 10*

14 A part to tear a cat in, to make all split.   BOTTOM   *I, 2, 24*

15 I am slow of study.   SNUG   *I, 2, 59*

16 Over hill, over dale,
       Thorough bush, thorough brier,
   Over park, over pale,
       Thorough flood, thorough fire.   FAIRY   *2, I, 2*

17 Ill met by moonlight, proud Titania.   OBERON   *2, I, 60*

18 Since once I sat upon a promontory,
   And heard a mermaid on a dolphin's back
   Uttering such dulcet and harmonious breath
   That the rude sea grew civil at her song,
   And certain stars shot madly from their spheres
   To hear the sea-maid's music.   OBERON   *2, I, 149*

19 I'll put a girdle round about the earth
   In forty minutes.   PUCK   *2, I, 175*

20 I know a bank whereon the wild thyme blows,
   Where oxlips and the nodding violet grows,
   Quite over-canopied with luscious woodbine,
   With sweet musk-roses, and with eglantine.   OBERON   *2, I, 249*

21 A lion among ladies is a most dreadful thing; for there is not a more fearful
   wild-fowl than your lion living.   BOTTOM   *3, I, 27*

1 A calendar, a calendar! Look in the almanack; find out moonshine, find out moonshine.   BOTTOM   *A Midsummer Night's Dream*, 3, 1, 46

2 Bless thee, Bottom, bless thee! Thou art translated.   QUINCE   3, 1, 109

3 Lord, what fools these mortals be!   PUCK   3, 2, 115

4 I have a reasonable good ear in music. Let's have the tongs and the bones.   BOTTOM   4, 1, 26

5 The lunatic, the lover, and the poet,
Are of imagination all compact.   THESEUS   5, 1, 7

6 The poet's eye, in a fine frenzy rolling,
Doth glance from heaven to earth, from earth to heaven;
And as imagination bodies forth
The forms of things unknown, the poet's pen
Turns them to shapes, and gives to airy nothing
A local habitation and a name.   THESEUS   5, 1, 12

7 Very tragical mirth.   THESEUS   5, 1, 57

8 The iron tongue of midnight hath told twelve.
Lovers, to bed; 'tis almost fairy time.   THESEUS   5, 1, 352

Much Ado About Nothing

9 A victory is twice itself when the achiever brings home full numbers.   LEONATO   1, 1, 7

10 He wears his faith but as the fashion of his hat.   BEATRICE   1, 1, 62

11 BEATRICE: I wonder that you will still be talking, Signior Benedick; nobody marks you.
BENEDICK: What, my dear Lady Disdain! Are you yet living?   1, 1, 99

12 Would you have me speak after my custom, as being a professed tyrant to their sex?   BENEDICK   1, 1, 144

13 Benedick the married man.   BENEDICK   1, 1, 232

14 What need the bridge much broader than the flood?   DON PEDRO   1, 1, 278

15 Friendship is constant in all other things
Save in the office and affairs of love.   CLAUDIO   2, 1, 154

16 She speaks poniards, and every word stabs.   BENEDICK   2, 1, 220

17 Silence is the perfectest herald of joy: I were but little happy if I could say how much.   CLAUDIO   2, 1, 275

18 DON PEDRO: Will you have me, lady?
BEATRICE: No, my lord, unless I might have another for working-days; your Grace is too costly to wear every day.   2, 1, 293

19 I was born to speak all mirth and no matter.   BEATRICE   2, 1, 297

20 There was a star danc'd, and under that was I born.   BEATRICE   2, 1, 302

21 Sigh no more, ladies, sigh no more,
Men were deceivers ever,
One foot in sea and one on shore,
To one thing constant never.   BALTHASAR   2, 3, 57

22 Doth not the appetite alter? A man loves the meat in his youth that he cannot endure in his age.   BENEDICK   2, 3, 215

1 The world must be peopled. When I said I would die a bachelor, I did not think I should live till I were married.   BENEDICK

Much Ado About Nothing, 2, 3, 219

2 Disdain and scorn ride sparkling in her eyes.   HERO   *3, 1, 51*

3 Are you good men and true?   DOGBERRY   *3, 3, 1*

4 To be a well-favoured man is the gift of fortune; but to write and read comes by nature.   DOGBERRY   *3, 3, 13*

5 You are thought here to be the most senseless and fit man for the constable of the watch.   DOGBERRY   *3, 3, 19*

6 For the watch to babble and to talk is most tolerable and not to be endured.   DOGBERRY   *3, 3, 32*

7 I thank God I am as honest as any man living that is an old man and no honester than I.   VERGES   *3, 5, 13*

8 Comparisons are odorous.   DOGBERRY   *3, 5, 16*

9 A good old man, sir, he will be talking; as they say 'When the age is in the wit is out'.   DOGBERRY   *3, 5, 32*

10 Our watch, sir, have indeed comprehended two aspicious persons.

DOGBERRY   *3, 5, 42*

11 O, what men dare do! What men may do! What men daily do, not knowing what they do!   CLAUDIO   *4, 1, 18*

12   For it so falls out
That what we have we prize not to the worth
Whiles we enjoy it, but being lack'd and lost,
Why, then we rack the value, then we find
The virtue that possession would not show us
Whiles it was ours.   FRIAR FRANCIS   *4, 1, 217*

13 Write down that they hope they serve God; and write God first; for God defend but God should go before such villains!   DOGBERRY   *4, 2, 17*

14 Flat burglary as ever was committed.   DOGBERRY   *4, 2, 46*

15 O villain! thou wilt be condemn'd into everlasting redemption for this.

DOGBERRY   *4, 2, 52*

16 O that he were here to write me down an ass!   DOGBERRY   *4, 2, 70*

17 For there was never yet philosopher
That could endure the toothache patiently.   LEONATO   *5, 1, 35*

18 They have committed false report; moreover, they have spoken untruths; secondarily, they are slanders; sixth and lastly, they have belied a lady; thirdly, they have verified unjust things; and to conclude, they are lying knaves.   DOGBERRY   *5, 1, 204*

19 Done to death by slanderous tongues.   CLAUDIO   *5, 3, 3*

Othello

20 But I will wear my heart upon my sleeve
For daws to peck at.   IAGO   *1, 1, 65*

21   Rude am I in my speech,
And little blest with the soft phrase of peace;
For since these arms of mine had seven years' pith,
Till now some nine moons wasted, they have us'd
Their dearest action in the tented field.   OTHELLO   *1, 3, 81*

1 I will a round unvarnish'd tale deliver
  Of my whole course of love.   OTHELLO   *Othello, I, 3, 90*

2   My story being done,
  She gave me for my pains a world of sighs;
  She swore, in faith, 'twas strange, 'twas passing strange;
  'Twas pitiful, 'twas wondrous pitiful.
  She wish'd she had not heard it; yet she wish'd
  That heaven had made her such a man. She thank'd me;
  And bade me, if I had a friend that lov'd her,
  I should but teach him how to tell my story,
  And that would woo her. Upon this hint I spake;
  She lov'd me for the dangers I had pass'd;
  And I lov'd her that she did pity them.
  This only is the witchcraft I have us'd.   OTHELLO   *I, 3, 158*

3 To mourn a mischief that is past and gone
  Is the next way to draw new mischief on.   DUKE   *I, 3, 204*

4 The robb'd that smiles steals something from the thief.   DUKE   *I, 3, 208*

5 Look to her, Moor, if thou hast eyes to see:
  She has deceiv'd her father, and may thee.   BRABANTIO   *I, 3, 292*

6 Put money in thy purse.   IAGO   *I, 3, 338*

7 For I am nothing if not critical.   IAGO   *2, I, 119*

8 To suckle fools and chronicle small beer.   IAGO   *2, I, 159*

9 But men are men; the best sometimes forget.   IAGO   *2, 3, 233*

10 Reputation, reputation, reputation! O, I have lost my reputation! I have
   lost the immortal part of myself, and what remains is bestial.   CASSIO
                                                              2, 3, 254

11 Good wine is a good familiar creature if it be well us'd.   IAGO   *2, 3, 299*

12 How poor are they that have not patience!
   What wound did ever heal but by degrees?   IAGO   *2, 3, 358*

13 Thereby hangs a tail.   CLOWN   *3, I, 8*

14 Excellent wretch! Perdition catch my soul
   But I do love thee; and when I love thee not
   Chaos is come again.   OTHELLO   *3, 3, 91*

15 Good name in man and woman, dear my lord,
   Is the immediate jewel of their souls:
   Who steals my purse steals trash; 'tis something, nothing;
   'Twas mine, 'tis his, and has been slave to thousands;
   But he that filches from me my good name
   Robs me of that which not enriches him
   And makes me poor indeed.   IAGO   *3, 3, 159*

16 O, beware, my lord, of jealousy;
   It is the green-ey'd monster which doth mock
   The meat it feeds on.   IAGO   *3, 3, 169*

17   O curse of marriage,
   That we can call these delicate creatures ours,
   And not their appetites! I had rather be a toad,
   And live upon the vapour of a dungeon,
   Than keep a corner in the thing I love
   For others' uses.   OTHELLO   *3, 3, 272*

1 He that is robb'd, not wanting what is stol'n,
Let him not know't, and he's not robb'd at all. OTHELLO *Othello, 3, 3, 346*

2   O, now for ever
Farewell the tranquil mind! farewell content!
Farewell the plumed troops, and the big wars
That makes ambition virtue! O, farewell!
Farewell the neighing steed and the shrill trump,
The spirit-stirring drum, th' ear-piercing fife,
The royal banner, and all quality,
Pride, pomp, and circumstance, of glorious war!   OTHELLO   3, 3, 351

3 They are not ever jealous for the cause,
But jealous for they are jealous.   EMILIA   3, 4, 161

4 But yet the pity of it, Iago! O, Iago, the pity of it, Iago!   OTHELLO
                                                                4, 1, 191

5   But, alas, to make me
The fixed figure for the time of scorn
To point his slow unmoving finger at.   OTHELLO   4, 2, 54

6   O thou weed
Who art so lovely fair and smell'st so sweet
That the sense aches at thee!
Would thou had'st never been born!   OTHELLO   4, 2, 67

7 'Tis neither here nor there.   EMILIA   4, 3, 57

8   If Cassio do remain,
He hath a daily beauty in his life
That makes me ugly.   IAGO   5, 1, 18

9   This is the night
That either makes me or fordoes me quite.   IAGO   5, 1, 128

10 It is the cause, it is the cause, my soul—
Let me not name it to you, you chaste stars—
It is the cause.   OTHELLO   5, 2, 1

11 Put out the light, and then put out the light.
If I quench thee, thou flaming minister,
I can again thy former light restore,
Should I repent me; but once put out thy light,
Thou cunning'st pattern of excelling nature,
I know not where is that Promethean heat
That can thy light relume. When I have pluck'd thy rose,
I cannot give it vital growth again.   OTHELLO   5, 2, 7

12 Not Cassio kill'd! Then murder's out of tune,
And sweet revenge grows harsh.   OTHELLO   5, 2, 118

13 Here is my journey's end, here is my butt,
And very sea-mark of my utmost sail.   OTHELLO   5, 2, 270

14 Soft you; a word or two before you go.
I have done the state some service, and they know't—
No more of that. I pray you, in your letters,
When you shall these unlucky deeds relate,
Speak of me as I am; nothing extenuate,
Nor set down aught in malice. Then must you speak
Of one that lov'd not wisely, but too well;
Of one not easily jealous, but, being wrought,

Perplexed in the extreme; of one whose hand,
Like the base Indian, threw a pearl away
Richer than all his tribe; of one whose subdu'd eyes,
Albeit unused to the melting mood,
Drops tears as fast as the Arabian trees
Their med'cinable gum. Set you down this:
And say besides that in Aleppo once,
Where a malignant and a turban'd Turk
Beat a Venetian and traduc'd the state,
I took by th' throat the circumcised dog,
And smote him—thus.   OTHELLO   *Othello,* *5, 2, 341*

1 I kiss'd thee ere I kill'd thee. No way but this—
  Killing my self, to die upon a kiss.   OTHELLO   *5, 2, 361*

Pericles

2 See where she comes, apparell'd like the spring.   PERICLES   *1, 1, 12*

3 Few love to hear the sins they love to act.   PERICLES   *1, 1, 92*

4 Kings are earth's gods; in vice their law's their will.   PERICLES   *1, 1, 103*

5 3RD FISHERMAN: Master, I marvel how the fishes live in the sea.
  1ST FISHERMAN: Why, as men do a-land—the great ones eat up the little
                 ones.   *2, 1, 27*

King Richard the Second

6 Old John of Gaunt, time-honoured Lancaster.   RICHARD II   *1, 1, 1*

7 Let's purge this choler without letting blood.   RICHARD II   *1, 1, 153*

8 The purest treasure mortal times afford
  Is spotless reputation; that away,
  Men are but gilded loam or painted clay.
  A jewel in a ten-times barr'd-up chest
  Is a bold spirit in a loyal breast.
  Mine honour is my life; both grow in one;
  Take honour from me, and my life is done.   MOWBRAY   *1, 1, 177*

9 We were not born to sue, but to command.   RICHARD II   *1, 1, 196*

10 That which in mean men we entitle patience
   Is pale cold cowardice in noble breasts.   DUCHESS OF GLOUCESTER
                                                           1, 2, 33

11   This must my comfort be—
   That sun that warms you here shall shine on me.   BOLINGBROKE
                                                           1, 3, 144

12 How long a time lies in one little word!
   Four lagging winters and four wanton springs
   End in a word: such is the breath of Kings.   BOLINGBROKE   *1, 3, 213*

13 Things sweet to taste prove in digestion sour.   GAUNT   *1, 3, 236*

14 All places that the eye of heaven visits
   Are to a wise man ports and happy havens.
   Teach thy necessity to reason thus:
   There is no virtue like necessity.   GAUNT   *1, 3, 275*

1 O, who can hold a fire in his hand
By thinking on the frosty Caucasus?
Or cloy the hungry edge of appetite
By bare imagination of a feast?
Or wallow naked in December snow
By thinking on fantastic summer's heat?
O, no! the apprehension of the good
Gives but the greater feeling to the worse.   BOLINGBROKE
Richard the Second, *1, 3, 295*

2 Pray God we may make haste, and come too late!   RICHARD II   *1, 4, 64*

3 More are men's ends mark'd than their lives before.
The setting sun, and music at the close,
As the last taste of sweets, is sweetest last,
Writ in remembrance more than things long past.   GAUNT   *2, 1, 11*

4 Methinks I am a prophet new inspir'd,
And thus expiring do foretell of him:
His rash fierce blaze of riot cannot last,
For violent fires soon burn out themselves;
Small showers last long, but sudden storms are short;
He tires betimes that spurs too fast betimes.   GAUNT   *2, 1, 31*

5 This royal throne of kings, this sceptred isle,
This earth of majesty, this seat of Mars,
This other Eden, demi-paradise,
This fortress built by Nature for herself
Against infection and the hand of war,
This happy breed of men, this little world,
This precious stone set in the silver sea,
Which serves it in the office of a wall,
Or as a moat defensive to a house,
Against the envy of less happier lands;
This blessed plot, this earth, this realm, this England,
This nurse, this teeming womb of royal kings,
Fear'd by their breed, and famous by their birth.   GAUNT   *2, 1, 40*

6 England, bound in with the triumphant sea,
Whose rocky shore beats back the envious siege
Of wat'ry Neptune, is now bound in with shame,
With inky blots and rotten parchment bonds;
That England, that was wont to conquer others,
Hath made a shameful conquest of itself.
Ah, would the scandal vanish with my life,
How happy then were my ensuing death!   GAUNT   *2, 1, 61*

7 Can sick men play so nicely with their names?   RICHARD II   *2, 1, 84*

8 I count myself in nothing else so happy
As in a soul rememb'ring my good friends.   BOLINGBROKE   *2, 3, 46*

9 Grace me no grace, nor uncle me no uncle.   YORK   *2, 3, 87*

10 The caterpillars of the commonwealth.   BOLINGBROKE   *2, 3, 166*

11 Things past redress are now with me past care.   YORK   *2, 3, 171*

12 Eating the bitter bread of banishment.   BOLINGBROKE   *3, 1, 21*

1
                  I weep for joy
To stand upon my kingdom once again.
Dear earth, I do salute thee with my hand,
Though rebels wound thee with their horses' hoofs.   RICHARD II

                         Richard the Second, 3, 2, 4

2 Not all the water in the rough rude sea
Can wash the balm off from an anointed king;
The breath of worldly men cannot depose
The deputy elected by the Lord.   RICHARD II   *3, 2, 54*

3 O, call back yesterday, bid time return.   SALISBURY   *3, 2, 69*

4 Cry woe, destruction, ruin, and decay—
The worst is death, and death will have his day.   RICHARD II   *3, 2, 102*

5   Of comfort no man speak.
Let's talk of graves, of worms, and epitaphs;
Make dust our paper, and with rainy eyes
Write sorrow on the bosom of the earth.
Let's choose executors and talk of wills.   RICHARD II   *3, 2, 144*

6 For God's sake let us sit upon the ground
And tell sad stories of the death of kings:
How some have been depos'd, some slain in war,
Some haunted by the ghosts they have depos'd,
Some poison'd by their wives, some sleeping kill'd,
All murder'd—for within the hollow crown
That rounds the mortal temples of a king
Keeps Death his court; and there the antic sits,
Scoffing his state and grinning at his pomp;
Allowing him a breath, a little scene,
To monarchize, be fear'd, and kill with looks;
Infusing him with self and vain conceit,
As if this flesh which walls about our life
Were brass impregnable; and, humour'd thus,
Comes at the last, and with a little pin
Bores through his castle wall, and farewell, king!   RICHARD II   *3, 2, 155*

7 What must the King do now? Must he submit?
The King shall do it. Must he be depos'd?
The King shall be contented. Must he lose
The name of king? A God's name, let it go.
I'll give my jewels for a set of beads,
My gorgeous palace for a hermitage,
My gay apparel for an almsman's gown,
My figur'd goblets for a dish of wood,
My sceptre for a palmer's walking staff,
My subjects for a pair of carved saints,
And my large kingdom for a little grave,
A little little grave, an obscure grave.   RICHARD II   *3, 3, 143*

8 And if you crown him, let me prophesy—
The blood of English shall manure the ground,
And future ages groan for this foul act;
Peace shall go sleep with Turks and infidels.   CARLISLE   *4, 1, 136*

1 Did they not sometime cry 'All hail!' to me?
So Judas did to Christ; but he, in twelve,
Found truth in all but one; I, in twelve thousand, none.
God save the King! Will no man say amen?
Am I both priest and clerk? Well then, amen.   RICHARD II
Richard the Second, 4, 1, 169

2 I give this heavy weight from off my head,
And this unwieldy sceptre from my hand,
The pride of kingly sway from out my heart;
With mine own tears I wash away my balm,
With mine own hands I give away my crown.   RICHARD II   *4, 1, 204*

3 The woe's to come; the children yet unborn
Shall feel this day as sharp to them as thorn.   CARLISLE   *4, 1, 322*

4   I am sworn brother, sweet,
To grim Necessity; and he and I
Will keep a league till death.   RICHARD II   *5, 1, 19*

5 As in a theatre the eyes of men
After a well-grac'd actor leaves the stage
Are idly bent on him that enters next,
Thinking his prattle to be tedious.   YORK   *5, 2, 23*

6 I have been studying how I may compare
This prison where I live unto the world.   RICHARD II   *5, 5, 1*

7   How sour sweet music is
When time is broke and no proportion kept!
So is it in the music of men's lives.   RICHARD II   *5, 5, 42*

King Richard the Third

8 Now is the winter of our discontent
Made glorious summer by this sun of York.   GLOUCESTER   *1, 1, 1*

9 Our stern alarums chang'd to merry meetings,
Our dreadful marches to delightful measures.   GLOUCESTER   *1, 1, 7*

10 Deform'd, unfinish'd, sent before my time
Into this breathing world scarce half made up,
And that so lamely and unfashionable
That dogs bark at me as I halt by them.   GLOUCESTER   *1, 1, 20*

11 In this weak piping time of peace.   GLOUCESTER   *1, 1, 24*

12 I am determined to prove a villain.   GLOUCESTER   *1, 1, 30*

13 Was ever woman in this humour woo'd?
Was ever woman in this humour won?   GLOUCESTER   *1, 2, 227*

14 And thus I clothe my naked villainy
With odd old ends stol'n forth of holy writ,
And seem a saint when most I play the devil.   GLOUCESTER   *1, 3, 336*

15 O, I have pass'd a miserable night,
So full of fearful dreams, of ugly sights,
That, as I am a Christian faithful man,
I would not spend another such a night
Though 'twere to buy a world of happy days—
So full of dismal terror was the time!   CLARENCE   *1, 4, 2*

1 O Lord, methought what pain it was to drown,
   What dreadful noise of waters in my ears,
   What sights of ugly death within my eyes!
   Methoughts I saw a thousand fearful wrecks,
   A thousand men that fishes gnaw'd upon,
   Wedges of gold, great anchors, heaps of pearl,
   Inestimable stones, unvalued jewels,
   All scatt'red in the bottom of the sea;
   Some lay in dead men's skulls, and in the holes
   Where eyes did once inhabit there were crept,
   As 'twere in scorn of eyes, reflecting gems,
   That woo'd the slimy bottom of the deep
   And mock'd the dead bones that lay scatt'red by.   CLARENCE
                                        Richard the Third, 1, 4, 21

2 So wise so young, they say, do never live long.   GLOUCESTER   *3, 1, 79*

3 My lord of Ely, when I was last in Holborn
   I saw good strawberries in your garden there.   GLOUCESTER   *3, 4, 32*

4 Talk'st thou to me of ifs? Thou art a traitor.
   Off with his head!   GLOUCESTER   *3, 4, 77*

5 High-reaching Buckingham grows circumspect.   RICHARD III   *4, 2, 31*

6   But I am in
   So far in blood that sin will pluck on sin.   RICHARD III   *4, 2, 65*

7 I am not in the giving vein to-day.   RICHARD III   *4, 2, 120*

8 Their lips were four red roses on a stalk,
   And in their summer beauty kiss'd each other.   TYRREL   *4, 3, 12*

9 An honest tale speeds best being plainly told.   QUEEN ELIZABETH   *4, 4, 358*

10 Harp not on that string.   RICHARD III   *4, 4, 364*

11 Is the chair empty? Is the sword unsway'd?
   Is the King dead, the empire unpossess'd?   RICHARD III   *4, 4, 470*

12 True hope is swift and flies with swallow's wings;
   Kings it makes gods, and meaner creatures kings.   RICHMOND   *5, 2, 23*

13 The King's name is a tower of strength.   RICHARD III   *5, 3, 12*

14 I have not that alacrity of spirit
   Nor cheer of mind that I was wont to have.   RICHARD III   *5, 3, 73*

15 My conscience hath a thousand several tongues,
   And every tongue brings in a several tale,
   And every tale condemns me for a villain.   RICHARD III   *5, 3, 193*

16 A horse! a horse! my kingdom for a horse!   RICHARD III   *5, 4, 7*

Romeo and Juliet

17 A pair of star-cross'd lovers.   CHORUS   *Prologue, 6*

18 The two hours' traffic of our stage.   CHORUS   *Prologue, 12*

19 Saint-seducing gold.   ROMEO   *1, 1, 213*

20 For I am proverb'd with a grandsire phrase;
   I'll be a candle-holder and look on.   ROMEO   *1, 4, 37*

1 O, then I see Queen Mab hath been with you.
She is the fairies' midwife, and she comes
In shape no bigger than an agate stone
On the fore-finger of an alderman,
Drawn with a team of little atomies
Athwart men's noses as they lie asleep. MERCUTIO *Romeo and Juliet,*
1, 4, 53

2 For you and I are past our dancing days. CAPULET *1, 5, 29*

3 O, she doth teach the torches to burn bright!
It seems she hangs upon the cheek of night
As a rich jewel in an Ethiop's ear—
Beauty too rich for use, for earth too dear! ROMEO *1, 5, 42*

4 For I ne'er saw true beauty till this night. ROMEO *1, 5, 51*

5 My only love sprung from my only hate! JULIET *1, 5, 136*

6 He jests at scars that never felt a wound.
But, soft! What light through yonder window breaks?
It is the east, and Juliet is the sun. ROMEO *2, 2, 1*

7 See how she leans her cheek upon her hand!
O that I were a glove upon that hand,
That I might touch that cheek! ROMEO *2, 2, 23*

8 O Romeo, Romeo! wherefore art thou Romeo? JULIET *2, 2, 33*

9 What's in a name? That which we call a rose
By any other name would smell as sweet. JULIET *2, 2, 43*

10 O, swear not by the moon, th' inconstant moon,
That monthly changes in her circled orb,
Lest that thy love prove likewise variable. JULIET *2, 2, 109*

11 This bud of love, by summer's ripening breath,
May prove a beauteous flow'r when next we meet. JULIET *2, 2, 121*

12 Love goes toward love as school-boys from their books;
But love from love, toward school with heavy looks. ROMEO *2, 2, 156*

13 How silver-sweet sound lovers' tongues by night,
Like softest music to attending ears! ROMEO *2, 2, 166*

14 Good night, good night! Parting is such sweet sorrow
That I shall say good night till it be morrow. JULIET *2, 2, 185*

15 Wisely and slow; they stumble that run fast. FRIAR LAWRENCE *2, 3, 94*

16 O flesh, flesh, how art thou fishified! MERCUTIO *2, 4, 37*

17 I am the very pink of courtesy. MERCUTIO *2, 4, 56*

18 Therefore love moderately: long love doth so;
Too swift arrives as tardy as too slow. FRIAR LAWRENCE *2, 6, 14*

19 A plague o' both your houses!
They have made worms' meat of me. MERCUTIO *3, 1, 103*

20 O, I am fortune's fool! ROMEO *3, 1, 133*

21   Come, civil night,
Thou sober-suited matron, all in black. JULIET *3, 2, 10*

22 Night's candles are burnt out, and jocund day
Stands tiptoe on the misty mountain tops. ROMEO *3, 5, 9*

1 Thank me no thankings, nor proud me no prouds. CAPULET
Romeo and Juliet, 3, 5, 152

2 'Tis an ill cook that cannot lick his own fingers. SERVINGMAN *4, 2, 6*

3   Beauty's ensign yet
Is crimson in thy lips and in thy cheeks,
And death's pale flag is not advanced there. ROMEO *5, 3, 94*

4   O, here
Will I set up my everlasting rest,
And shake the yoke of inauspicious stars
From this world-wearied flesh. Eyes, look your last.
Arms, take your last embrace. ROMEO *5, 3, 109*

The Taming of the Shrew

5 Look in the chronicles: we came in with Richard Conqueror.
CHRISTOPHER SLY *Induction, 1, 4*

6 No profit grows where is no pleasure ta'en;
In brief, sir, study what you most affect. TRANIO *1, 1, 39*

7 There's small choice in rotten apples. HORTENSIO *1, 1, 131*

8 Kiss me, Kate. PETRUCHIO *2, 1, 316*

9 Thereby hangs a tale. GRUMIO *4, 1, 50*

10 This is a way to kill a wife with kindness. PETRUCHIO *4, 1, 192*

11 Our purses shall be proud, our garments poor;
For 'tis the mind that makes the body rich;
And as the sun breaks through the darkest clouds,
So honour peereth in the meanest habit. PETRUCHIO *4, 3, 167*

12 A woman mov'd is like a fountain troubled—
Muddy, ill-seeming, thick, bereft of beauty. KATHERINA *5, 2, 142*

The Tempest

13 He hath no drowning mark upon him; his complexion is perfect gallows.
GONZALO *1, 1, 28*

14 The wills above be done, but I would fain die a dry death. GONZALO
1, 1, 63

15   What seest thou else
In the dark backward and abysm of time? PROSPERO *1, 2, 49*

16 Your tale, sir, would cure deafness. MIRANDA *1, 2, 106*

17   My library
Was dukedom large enough. PROSPERO *1, 2, 109*

18 From the still-vex'd Bermoothes. ARIEL *1, 2, 229*

19 You taught me language, and my profit on't
Is, I know how to curse. The red plague rid you
For learning me your language! CALIBAN *1, 2, 363*

20 Come unto these yellow sands,
And then take hands. ARIEL *1, 2, 375*

1 Full fathom five thy father lies;
　　Of his bones are coral made;
　Those are pearls that were his eyes;
　　Nothing of him that doth fade
　But doth suffer a sea-change
　Into something rich and strange.　ARIEL　　*The Tempest, 1, 2, 396*

2　　　　　　　This swift business
　I must uneasy make, lest too light winning
　Make the prize light.　PROSPERO　　　　　　*1, 2, 450*

3 He receives comfort like cold porridge.　SEBASTIAN　　*2, 1, 10*

4 I' th' commonwealth I would by contraries
　Execute all things.　GONZALO　　　　　　*2, 1, 141*

5 While you here do snoring lie,
　Open-ey'd conspiracy
　　His time doth take.　ARIEL　　　　　　*2, 1, 291*

6 When they will not give a doit to relieve a lame beggar, they will lay out
　ten to see a dead Indian.　TRINCULO　　　　*2, 2, 29*

7 Misery acquaints a man with strange bedfellows.　TRINCULO　　*2, 2, 38*

8 Well, here's my comfort. (*Drinks*)　STEPHANO　　*2, 2, 43*

9 The master, the swabber, the boatswain, and I,
　The gunner, and his mate,
　Lov'd Mall, Meg, and Marian, and Margery,
　But none of us car'd for Kate.　STEPHANO　　*2, 2, 44*

10 'Ban 'Ban, Ca—Caliban,
　Has a new master—Get a new man.　CALIBAN　　*2, 2, 173*

11 They say there's but five upon this isle: we are three of them; if th' other
　two be brain'd like us, the state totters.　TRINCULO　　*3, 2, 4*

12 He that dies pays all debts.　STEPHANO　　　*3, 2, 126*

13 Be not afeard. The isle is full of noises,
　Sounds, and sweet airs, that give delight, and hurt not.　CALIBAN
　　　　　　　　　　　　　　　　　　3, 2, 130

14　　　　　Travellers ne'er did lie,
　Though fools at home condemn 'em.　ANTONIO　　*3, 3, 26*

15　　　　　　You fools! I and my fellows
　Are ministers of Fate; the elements
　Of whom your swords are temper'd may as well
　Wound the loud winds, or with bemock'd-at stabs
　Kill the still-closing waters, as diminish
　One dowle that's in my plume.　ARIEL　　　*3, 3, 60*

16 Our revels now are ended. These our actors,
　As I foretold you, were all spirits, and
　Are melted into air, into thin air;
　And, like the baseless fabric of this vision,
　The cloud-capp'd towers, the gorgeous palaces,
　The solemn temples, the great globe itself,
　Yea, all which it inherit, shall dissolve,
　And, like this insubstantial pageant faded,
　Leave not a rack behind. We are such stuff
　As dreams are made on; and our little life
　Is rounded with a sleep.　PROSPERO　　　*4, 1, 148*

1 Wit shall not go unrewarded while I am king of this country.   STEPHANO
                                          The Tempest, 4, 1, 240

2 With foreheads villainous low.   CALIBAN   *4, 1, 248*

3   The rarer action is
In virtue than in vengeance.   PROSPERO   *5, 1, 27*

4 Ye elves of hills, brooks, standing lakes, and groves;
  And ye that on the sands with printless foot
  Do chase the ebbing Neptune, and do fly him
  When he comes back.   PROSPERO   *5, 1, 33*

5   I'll break my staff,
Bury it certain fathoms in the earth,
And deeper than did ever plummet sound
I'll drown my book.   PROSPERO   *5, 1, 54*

6   Where the bee sucks, there suck I;
      In a cowslip's bell I lie;
      There I couch when owls do cry.
      On the bat's back I do fly
      After summer merrily.
  Merrily, merrily shall I live now
  Under the blossom that hangs on the bough.   ARIEL   *5, 1, 88*

7 How beauteous mankind is! O brave new world
  That has such people in't!   MIRANDA   *5, 1, 183*

8   Retire me to my Milan, where
Every third thought shall be my grave.   PROSPERO   *5, 1, 310*

Timon of Athens

9 'Tis not enough to help the feeble up,
  But to support him after.   TIMON   *1, 1, 110*

10 I wonder men dare trust themselves with men.   APEMANTUS   *1, 2, 42*

11 Uncover, dogs, and lap.   TIMON   *3, 6, 85*

Titus Andronicus

12 Sweet mercy is nobility's true badge.   TAMORA   *1, 1, 119*

13 She is a woman, therefore may be woo'd;
   She is a woman, therefore may be won;
   She is Lavinia, therefore must be lov'd.
   What, man! more water glideth by the mill
   Than wots the miller of; and easy it is
   Of a cut loaf to steal a shive, we know.   DEMETRIUS   *2, 1, 82*

14 If one good deed in all my life I did,
   I do repent it from my very soul.   AARON   *5, 3, 189*

Troilus and Cressida

15   Women are angels, wooing:
   Things won are done; joy's soul lies in the doing.
   That she belov'd knows nought that knows not this:
   Men prize the thing ungain'd more than it is.   CRESSIDA   *1, 2, 278*

1 The heavens themselves, the planets, and this centre,
  Observe degree, priority, and place,
  Insisture, course, proportion, season, form,
  Office, and custom, in all line of order.   ULYSSES   *Troilus and Cressida,*
                                                          1, 3, 85

2   O, when degree is shak'd,
  Which is the ladder of all high designs,
  The enterprise is sick!   ULYSSES   *1, 3, 101*

3 Take but degree away, untune that string,
  And hark what discord follows!   ULYSSES   *1, 3, 109*

4 I would thou didst itch from head to foot and I had the scratching of thee.
                                            THERSITES   *2, 1, 26*

5 To be wise and love
  Exceeds man's might.   CRESSIDA   *3, 2, 152*

6 Time hath, my lord, a wallet at his back,
  Wherein he puts alms for oblivion,
  A great-siz'd monster of ingratitudes.   ULYSSES   *3, 3, 145*

7 One touch of nature makes the whole world kin.   ULYSSES   *3, 3, 175*

8 There's language in her eye, her cheek, her lip,
  Nay, her foot speaks; her wanton spirits look out
  At every joint and motive of her body.   ULYSSES   *4, 5, 55*

9 Lechery, lechery! Still wars and lechery! Nothing else holds fashion.
                                            THERSITES   *5, 2, 193*

Twelfth Night

10 If music be the food of love, play on,
   Give me excess of it, that, surfeiting,
   The appetite may sicken and so die.
   That strain again! It had a dying fall;
   O, it came o'er my ear like the sweet sound
   That breathes upon a bank of violets,
   Stealing and giving odour! Enough, no more;
   'Tis not so sweet now as it was before.   DUKE ORSINO   *1, 1, 1*

11 Speaks three or four languages word for word without book.
                                            SIR TOBY BELCH   *1, 3, 24*

12 Is it a world to hide virtues in?   SIR TOBY BELCH   *1, 3, 123*

13 Many a good hanging prevents a bad marriage.   FESTE   *1, 5, 18*

14 A plague o' these pickle-herring!   SIR TOBY BELCH   *1, 5, 114*

15 Make me a willow cabin at your gate,
   And call upon my soul within the house;
   Write loyal cantons of contemned love
   And sing them loud even in the dead of night;
   Halloo your name to the reverberate hills,
   And make the babbling gossip of the air
   Cry out 'Olivia!'   VIOLA   *1, 5, 252*

16 Farewell, fair cruelty.   VIOLA   *1, 5, 272*

17 Not to be abed after midnight is to be up betimes.   SIR TOBY BELCH   *2, 3, 1*

1 O mistress mine, where are you roaming?
   O, stay and hear; your true love's coming,
   That can sing both high and low.
   Trip no further, pretty sweeting;
   Journeys end in lovers meeting,
   Every wise man's son doth know.   FESTE   *Twelfth Night 2, 3, 38*

2 What is love? 'Tis not hereafter;
   Present mirth hath present laughter;
       What's to come is still unsure.
   In delay there lies no plenty,
   Then come kiss me, sweet and twenty;
       Youth's a stuff will not endure.   FESTE   *2, 3, 46*

3 He does it with a better grace, but I do it more natural.
                           SIR ANDREW AGUECHEEK   *2, 3, 79*

4 Is there no respect of place, persons, nor time, in you?   MALVOLIO
                                                               2, 3, 89

5 Dost thou think, because thou art virtuous, there shall be no more cakes and
   ale?   SIR TOBY BELCH   *2, 3, 109*

6   Come away, come away, death;
   And in sad cypress let me be laid;
       Fly away, fly away, breath,
   I am slain by a fair cruel maid.
   My shroud of white, stuck all with yew,
           O, prepare it!
   My part of death no one so true
           Did share it.   FESTE   *2, 4, 50*

7   She never told her love,
   But let concealment, like a worm i' th' bud,
   Feed on her damask cheek. She pin'd in thought;
   And with a green and yellow melancholy
   She sat like Patience on a monument,
   Smiling at grief.   VIOLA   *2, 4, 109*

8 I am all the daughters of my father's house,
   And all the brothers too.   VIOLA   *2, 4, 119*

9 Some are born great, some achieve greatness, and some have greatness
   thrust upon 'em.   MALVOLIO (reading letter)   *2, 5, 129*

10 Remember who commended thy yellow stockings, and wish'd to see thee
   ever cross-garter'd.   MALVOLIO (reading letter)   *2, 5, 135*

11 O world, how apt the poor are to be proud!   OLIVIA   *3, 1, 124*

12 Love sought is good, but given unsought is better.   OLIVIA   *3, 1, 153*

13 Why, this is very midsummer madness.   OLIVIA   *3, 4, 53*

14 If this were play'd upon a stage now, I could condemn it as an improbable
   fiction.   FABIAN   *3, 4, 121*

15 More matter for a May morning.   FABIAN   *3, 4, 136*

16 Still you keep o' th' windy side of the law.   FABIAN   *3, 4, 156*

17 Out of my lean and low ability
   I'll lend you something.   VIOLA   *3, 4, 328*

1 I hate ingratitude more in a man
 Than lying, vainness, babbling drunkenness,
 Or any taint of vice whose strong corruption
 Inhabits our frail blood.   VIOLA   *Twelfth Night, 3, 4, 338*

2 And thus the whirligig of time brings in his revenges.   FESTE   *5, 1, 363*

3 When that I was and a little tiny boy,
   With hey, ho, the wind and the rain,
 A foolish thing was but a toy,
   For the rain it raineth every day.   FESTE   *5, 1, 375*

The Two Gentlemen of Verona

4 Home-keeping youth have ever homely wits.   VALENTINE   *1, 1, 2*

5 I have no other but a woman's reason:
 I think him so, because I think him so.   LUCETTA   *1, 2, 23*

6 O, how this spring of love resembleth
 The uncertain glory of an April day.   PROTEUS   *1, 3, 84*

7 Dumb jewels often in their silent kind
 More than quick words do move a woman's mind.   VALENTINE   *3, 1, 90*

8 Who is Silvia? What is she,
   That all our swains commend her?
 Holy, fair, and wise is she.   SONG   *4, 2, 38*

9 Is she kind as she is fair?
   For beauty lives with kindness.   SONG   *4, 2, 43*

10 How use doth breed a habit in a man!   VALENTINE   *5, 4, 1*

11   O heaven, were man
 But constant, he were perfect!   PROTEUS   *5, 4, 110*

The Winter's Tale

12 Two lads that thought there was no more behind
 But such a day to-morrow as to-day,
 And to be boy eternal.   POLIXENES   *1, 2, 63*

13 A sad tale's best for winter. I have one
 Of sprites and goblins.   MAMILLIUS   *2, 1, 25*

14   What's gone and what's past help
 Should be past grief.   PAULINA   *3, 2, 219*

15 *Exit, pursued by a bear.*   STAGE DIRECTION   *3, 3, 58*

16 I would there were no age between ten and three and twenty, or that youth
 would sleep out the rest; for there is nothing in the between but getting
 wenches with child, wronging the ancientry, stealing, fighting.   SHEPHERD
 3, 3, 59

17 When daffodils begin to peer,
   With heigh! the doxy over the dale,
 Why, then comes in the sweet o' the year,
   For the red blood reigns in the winter's pale.   AUTOLYCUS   *4, 3, 1*

18 A snapper-up of unconsidered trifles.   AUTOLYCUS   *4, 3, 26*

19 Jog on, jog on, the footpath way,
   And merrily hent the stile-a;
 A merry heart goes all the day,
   Your sad tires in a mile-a.   AUTOLYCUS   *4, 3, 118*

1 For you there's rosemary and rue; these keep
Seeming and savour all the winter long.   PERDITA   *The Winter's Tale,*
4, 4, 74

2   What you do
Still betters what is done. When you speak, sweet,
I'd have you do it ever. When you sing,
I'd have you buy and sell so; so give alms;
Pray so; and, for the ord'ring your affairs,
To sing them too.   FLORIZEL   *4, 4, 135*

3 Lawn as white as driven snow.   AUTOLYCUS   *4, 4, 215*

4 The self-same sun that shines upon his court.   PERDITA   *4, 4, 436*

5 Prosperity's the very bond of love,
Whose fresh complexion and whose heart together
Affliction alters.   CAMILLO   *4, 4, 565*

6 Though I am not naturally honest, I am so sometimes by chance.
AUTOLYCUS *4, 4, 701*

7 Let me have no lying; it becomes none but tradesmen.   AUTOLYCUS
4, 4, 711

8 Though authority be a stubborn bear, yet he is oft led by the nose with
gold.   CLOWN   *4, 4, 790*

Sonnets

9 To the onlie begetter of these insuing sonnets.   *Dedication*

10 From fairest creatures we desire increase,
That thereby beauty's rose might never die.   *Sonnet 1*

11 Look in thy glass, and tell the face thou viewest.   *Sonnet 3*

12 But wherefore do not you a mightier way
Make war upon this bloody tyrant Time?   *Sonnet 16*

13 Shall I compare thee to a summer's day?
Thou art more lovely and more temperate.
Rough winds do shake the darling buds of May,
And summer's lease hath all too short a date.   *Sonnet 18*

14 But thy eternal summer shall not fade.   *Sonnet 18*

15 So long as men can breathe or eyes can see,
So long lives this, and this gives life to thee.   *Sonnet 18*

16 A woman's face, with Nature's own hand painted,
Hast thou, the Master Mistress of my passion.   *Sonnet 20*

17 For thy sweet love rememb'red such wealth brings
That then I scorn to change my state with kings.   *Sonnet 29*

18 When to the sessions of sweet silent thought
I summon up remembrance of things past,
I sigh the lack of many a thing I sought,
And with old woes new wail my dear time's waste.   *Sonnet 30*

19 But if the while I think on thee, dear friend,
All losses are restor'd, and sorrows end.   *Sonnet 30*

20 So true a fool is love that in your will,
Though you do anything, he thinks no ill.   *Sonnet 57*

1 Like as the waves make towards the pebbled shore,
So do our minutes hasten to their end.

Sonnet 60

2 Some glory in their birth, some in their skill,
Some in their wealth, some in their body's force;
Some in their garments, though new-fangled ill;
Some in their hawks and hounds, some in their horse.

Sonnet 91

3 For sweetest things turn sourest by their deeds:
Lilies that fester smell far worse than weeds.

Sonnet 94

4 How like a winter hath my absence been
From thee, the pleasure of the fleeting year!
What freezings have I felt, what dark days seen!

Sonnet 97

5 From you have I been absent in the spring,
When proud-pied April, dress'd in all his trim,
Hath put a spirit of youth in every thing.

Sonnet 98

6 When in the chronicle of wasted time
I see descriptions of the fairest wights.

Sonnet 106

7 For we, which now behold these present days,
Have eyes to wonder, but lack tongues to praise.

Sonnet 106

8 Let me not to the marriage of true minds
Admit impediments. Love is not love
Which alters when it alteration finds,
Or bends with the remover to remove.
O, no! it is an ever-fixed mark,
That looks on tempests and is never shaken.

Sonnet 116

9 Love alters not with his brief hours and weeks,
But bears it out even to the edge of doom.
If this be error, and upon me prov'd,
I never writ, nor no man ever lov'd.

Sonnet 116

10 'Tis better to be vile than vile esteemed,
When not to be receives reproach of being.

Sonnet 121

11 Th' expense of spirit in a waste of shame
Is lust in action; and till action, lust
Is perjur'd, murd'rous, bloody, full of blame,
Savage, extreme, rude, cruel, not to trust;
Enjoy'd no sooner but despised straight.

Sonnet 129

12 All this the world well knows; yet none knows well
To shun the heaven that leads men to this hell.

Sonnet 129

13 My mistress' eyes are nothing like the sun;
Coral is far more red than her lips' red.

Sonnet 130

14 And yet, by heaven, I think my love as rare
As any she belied with false compare.

Sonnet 130

15 When my love swears that she is made of truth,
I do believe her, though I know she lies.

Sonnet 138

16 Two loves I have, of comfort and despair,
Which like two spirits do suggest me still;
The better angel is a man right fair,
The worser spirit a woman colour'd ill.

Sonnet 144

Poems

1 Crabbed age and youth cannot live together:
 Youth is full of pleasance, age is full of care;
 Youth like summer morn, age like winter weather;
 Youth like summer brave, age like winter bare. *The Passionate Pilgrim*
                     12

2 Age, I do abhor thee; youth, I do adore thee. *Ib*

3 The first heire of my invention. *Venus and Adonis, Dedication*

4 Hunting he lov'd, but love he laugh'd to scorn. *Ib, 1, 4*

5 Beauty itself doth of itself persuade
 The eyes of men without an orator. *The Rape of Lucrece, 1, 29*

SHAW, George Bernard, 1856–1950

6 Breakages, Limited, the biggest industrial corporation in the country.
          BALBUS *The Apple Cart, Act 1*

7 You can always tell an old soldier by the inside of his holsters and cartridge
 boxes. The young ones carry pistols and cartridges: the old ones grub.
         BLUNTSCHLI *Arms and the Man, Act 1*

8 You are a very poor soldier: a chocolate cream soldier! RAINA
                  Ib, Act 1

9 It is enough that there *is* a beyond. LILITH *Back to Methuselah,*
                 Part 5, Last words

10 When a stupid man is doing something he is ashamed of, he always declares
 that it is his duty. APOLLODORUS *Caesar and Cleopatra, Act 3*

11 We have no more right to consume happiness without producing it than to
 consume wealth without producing it. MORELL *Candida, Act 1*

12 The overpaying instinct is a generous one: better than the underpaying
 instinct, and not so common. MORELL *Ib, Act 1*

13 Im only a beer teetotaller, not a champagne teetotaller. PROSERPINE
                 Ib, Act 3

14 Martyrdom . . . is the only way in which a man can become famous without
 ability. BURGOYNE *The Devil's Disciple, Act 3*

15 SWINDON: What will History say?
 BURGOYNE: History, sir, will tell lies, as usual. *Ib, Act 3*

16 Stimulate the phagocytes. B. B. *The Doctor's Dilemma, Act 1*

17 Go anywhere in England where there are natural, wholesome, contented,
 and really nice English people; and what do you always find? That the
 stables are the real centre of the house-hold. LADY UTTERWORD
              Heartbreak House, Act 3

18 Tell me all me faults as man to man. I can stand anything but flattery.
        TIM *John Bull's Other Island, Act 1*

19 The more a man knows, and the further he travels, the more likely he is to
 marry a country girl afterwards. KEEGAN *Ib, Act 2*

20 My way of joking is to tell the truth. Its the funniest joke in the world.
             KEEGAN *Ib*

1 I am a Millionaire. That is my religion.   UNDERSHAFT
Major Barbara, Act 2

2 Wot prawce selvytion nah?   BILL WALKER   *Ib*

3 A lifetime of happiness! No man alive could bear it: it would be hell on earth.   TANNER   *Man and Superman*, Act 1

4 There is no love sincerer than the love of food.   TANNER   *Ib*

5 The true artist will let his wife starve, his children go barefoot, his mother drudge for his living at seventy, sooner than work at anything but his art.
TANNER   *Ib*

6 It is a womans business to get married as soon as possible, and a mans to keep unmarried as long as he can.   TANNER   *Ib, Act 2*

7 An Englishman thinks he is moral when he is only uncomfortable.
THE DEVIL   *Ib, Act 3*

8 There are two tragedies in life. One is to lose your hearts desire. The other is to gain it.   MENDOZA   *Ib, Act 4*

9 Any person under the age of thirty, who, having any knowledge of the existing social order, is not a revolutionist, is an inferior.
Ib, The Revolutionist's Handbook, Foreword

10 We learn from history that we learn nothing from history.   *Ib*

11 The golden rule is that there are no golden rules.   *Ib, Maxims for Revolutionists*

12 Liberty means responsibility. That is why most men dread it.   *Ib*

13 He who can, does. He who cannot, teaches.   *Ib*

14 Marriage is popular because it combines the maximum of temptation with the maximum of opportunity.   *Ib*

15 Ladies and gentlemen are permitted to have friends in the kennel, but not in the kitchen.   *Ib*

16 Every man over forty is a scoundrel.   *Ib*

17 There is only one religion, though there are a hundred versions of it.
Plays Pleasant, Preface

18 Remember that you are a human being with a soul and the divine gift of articulate speech: that your native language is the language of Shakespear and Milton and The Bible: and dont sit there crooning like a bilious pigeon.
HIGGINS   *Pygmalion*, Act 1

19 I dont want to talk grammar. I want to talk like a lady.   ELIZA
Ib, Act 2

20 Time enough to think of the future when you havent any future to think of.
HIGGINS   *Ib*

21 Im one of the undeserving poor: thats what I am. Think of what that means to a man. It means that he's up agen middle class morality all the time.   DOOLITTLE   *Ib*

22 My aunt died of influenza: so they said ... But its my belief they done the old woman in.   ELIZA   *Ib, Act 3*

23 Walk! Not bloody likely.   ELIZA   *Ib*

24 No eggs! No eggs!! Thousand thunders, man, what do you mean by no eggs?   ROBERT   *Saint Joan*, Scene 1

1 We want a few mad people now. See where the sane ones have landed us!
                    POULENGEY   *Saint Joan, Scene 1*

2 I hear voices telling me what to do. They come from God.   JOAN   *Ib*

3 A miracle, my friend, is an event which creates faith. That is the purpose
and nature of miracles.   ARCHBISHOP   *Ib, Scene 2*

4 Do not think you can frighten me by telling me that I am alone. France is
alone; and God is alone; and what is my loneliness before the loneliness of
my country and my God?   JOAN   *Ib, Scene 5*

5 THE EXECUTIONER: You have heard the last of her.
          WARWICK: The last of her? Hm! I wonder!   *Ib, Scene 6*

6 All dress is fancy dress, is it not, except our natural skins?   DUNOIS
                                                                   Ib, Epilogue

7 Well, sir, you never can tell. Thats a principle in life with me, sir, if youll
excuse my having such a thing, sir.   WAITER   *You Never Can Tell,*
                                                                        Act 2

8 With the single exception of Homer, there is no eminent writer, not even
Sir Walter Scott, whom I can despise so entirely as I despise Shakespeare
when I measure my mind against his.   *Dramatic Opinions and Essays,*
                                                                      Vol. 2, 52

SHELLEY, Percy Bysshe, 1792–1822

9 I weep for Adonais—he is dead!
  O, weep for Adonais! though our tears
  Thaw not the frost which binds so dear a head!   *Adonais, 1*

10 Ah, woe is me! Winter is come and gone,
   But grief returns with the revolving year.   *Ib, 154*

11 Through wood and stream and field and hill and Ocean
   A quickening life from the Earth's heart has burst
   As it has ever done, with change and motion,
   From the great morning of the world when first
   God dawned on Chaos.   *Ib, 163*

12 Alas! that all we loved of him should be,
   But for our grief, as if it had not been,
   And grief itself be mortal!   *Ib, 181*

13 The Pilgrim of Eternity, whose fame
   Over his living head like Heaven is bent,
   An early but enduring monument.   *Ib, 264*

14 A pardlike Spirit beautiful and swift.   *Ib, 280*

15 Live thou, whose infamy is not thy fame!
   Live! fear no heavier chastisement from me,
   Thou noteless blot on a remembered name!   *Ib, 325*

16 He has outsoared the shadow of our night;
   Envy and calumny and hate and pain,
   And that unrest which men miscall delight,
   Can touch him not and torture not again;
   From the contagion of the world's slow stain
   He is secure, and now can never mourn
   A heart grown cold, a head grown gray in vain.   *Ib, 352*

17 He lives, he wakes—'tis Death is dead, not he.   *Ib, 361*

1 He is a portion of the loveliness
  Which once he made more lovely.   *Adonais, 379*

2 The One remains, the many change and pass;
  Heaven's light forever shines, Earth's shadows fly;
  Life, like a dome of many-coloured glass,
  Stains the white radiance of Eternity.   *Ib, 460*

3   The soul of Adonais, like a star,
  Beacons from the abode where the Eternal are.   *Ib, 494*

4 I bring fresh showers for the thirsting flowers,
    From the seas and the streams.   *The Cloud, 1*

5 I wield the flail of the lashing hail,
    And whiten the green plains under,
  And then again I dissolve it in rain,
    And laugh as I pass in thunder.   *Ib, 9*

6 I am the daughter of Earth and Water,
    And the nursling of the Sky;
  I pass through the pores of the ocean and shores;
    I change, but I cannot die.   *Ib, 73*

7 How wonderful is Death,
  Death and his brother Sleep!   *The Daemon of the World, 1, 1*

8 I never was attached to that great sect,
  Whose doctrine is, that each one should select
  Out of the crowd a mistress or a friend,
  And all the rest, though fair and wise, commend
  To cold oblivion.   *Epipsychidion, 149*

9   True Love in this differs from gold and clay,
  That to divide is not to take away.   *Ib, 160*

10 Good-night? ah! no; the hour is ill
     Which severs those it should unite;
   Let us remain together still,
     Then it will be good night.   *Good-Night, 1*

11 The world's great age begins anew,
     The golden years return,
   The earth doth like a snake renew
     Her winter weeds outworn:
   Heaven smiles, and faiths and empires gleam,
   Like wrecks of a dissolving dream.   *Hellas, 1060*

12 Thou Paradise of exiles, Italy!   *Julian and Maddalo, 57*

13 I met Murder on the way—
   He had a mask like Castlereagh.   *The Mask of Anarchy, 5*

14 Shake your chains to earth like dew
   Which in sleep had fallen on you—
   Ye are many—they are few.   *Ib, 153*

15 Swiftly walk o'er the western wave,
       Spirit of Night!
   Out of the misty eastern cave,
   Where, all the long and lone daylight,
   Thou wovest dreams of joy and fear.   *To Night, 1*

1 I ask of thee, belovèd Night—
   Swift be thine approaching flight,
       Come soon, soon!   *To Night, 33*

2 A glorious people vibrated again
       The lightning of the nations.   *Ode to Liberty, 1*

3 O Wild West Wind, thou breath of Autumn's being,
   Thou, from whose unseen presence the leaves dead
   Are driven, like ghosts from an enchanter fleeing,
   Yellow, and black, and pale, and hectic red,
   Pestilence-stricken multitudes.   *Ode to the West Wind, 1*

4 Wild Spirit, which art moving everywhere;
   Destroyer and preserver; hear, oh, hear! *Ib, 13*

5 Oh, lift me as a wave, a leaf, a cloud!
   I fall upon the thorns of life! I bleed!
   A heavy weight of hours has chained and bowed
   One too like thee: tameless, and swift, and proud. *Ib, 53*

6 Scatter, as from an unextinguished hearth
   Ashes and sparks, my words among mankind!
   Be through my lips to unawakened earth
   The trumpet of a prophecy! O, Wind,
   If Winter comes, can Spring be far behind? *Ib, 66*

7 I met a traveller from an antique land
   Who said: Two vast and trunkless legs of stone
   Stand in the desert.   *Ozymandias, 1*

8 And on the pedestal these words appear:
   'My name is Ozymandias, king of kings:
   Look on my works, ye Mighty, and despair!'
   Nothing beside remains. Round the decay
   Of that colossal wreck, boundless and bare
   The lone and level sands stretch far away. *Ib, 9*

9 Hell is a city much like London—
       A populous and a smoky city. *Peter Bell the Third, Part 3, Hell, 1*

10 Crucified 'twixt a smile and whimper. *Ib, 196*

11 But from these create he can
    Forms more real than living man,
    Nurslings of immortality!   *Prometheus Unbound, 1, 747*

12   Yet all love is sweet,
    Given or returned. Common as light is love,
    And its familiar voice wearies not ever. *Ib, 2, 5, 39*

13 Familiar acts are beautiful through love. *Ib, 4, 403*

14 A Sensitive Plant in a garden grew,
    And the young winds fed it with silver dew,
    And it opened its fan-like leaves to the light,
    And closed them beneath the kisses of Night. *The Sensitive Plant, 1, 1*

15 It is a modest creed, and yet
    Pleasant if one considers it,
    To own that death itself must be,
    Like all the rest, a mockery.   *Ib, Conclusion, 126*

16 For love, and beauty, and delight,
    There is no death nor change.   *Ib, Ib, 134*

1   Hail to thee, blithe Spirit!
      Bird thou never wert,
    That from Heaven, or near it,
      Pourest thy full heart
In profuse strains of unpremeditated art.   *To a Skylark, 1*

2   We look before and after,
      And pine for what is not:
    Our sincerest laughter
      With some pain is fraught;
Our sweetest songs are those that tell of saddest thought.   *Ib, 86*

3   Teach me half the gladness
      That thy brain must know,
    Such harmonious madness
      From my lips would flow
The world should listen then—as I am listening now.   *Ib, 101*

4   Rarely, rarely, comest thou,
      Spirit of Delight!   *Song, Rarely, Rarely, Comest Thou*

5   An old, mad, blind, despised, and dying king.   *Sonnet, England in 1819*

6   Music, when soft voices die,
Vibrates in the memory—
Odours, when sweet violets sicken,
Live within the sense they quicken.
Rose leaves, when the rose is dead,
Are heaped for the belovèd's bed;
And so thy thoughts, when thou art gone,
Love itself shall slumber on.   *To —, Music, When Soft Voices Die*

7   I fear thy kisses, gentle maiden,
      Thou needest not fear mine;
My spirit is too deeply laden
      Ever to burthen thine.   *To —, I Fear Thy Kisses*

8   The desire of the moth for the star,
      Of the night for the morrow,
The devotion to something afar
      From the sphere of our sorrow.   *To —, One Word is too often Profaned*

9   Poetry lifts the veil from the hidden beauty of the world, and makes familiar objects be as if they were not familiar.   *A Defence of Poetry*

10   Poetry is the record of the best and happiest moments of the happiest and best minds.   *Ib*

11   Poets are the unacknowledged legislators of the world.   *Ib*

SHENSTONE, William, 1714–1763

12   Whoe'er has travell'd life's dull round,
    Where'er his stages may have been,
    May sigh to think he still has found
    The warmest welcome, at an inn.   *Written at an Inn at Henley*

SHERIDAN, Philip Henry, 1831–1888

13   The only good Indian is a dead Indian.   *Attributed*

SHERIDAN, Richard Brinsley, 1751–1816

1 Yes, sir, puffing is of various sorts; the principal are, the puff direct, the puff preliminary, the puff collateral, the puff collusive, and the puff oblique, or puff by implication.   PUFF   *The Critic, Act 1, Scene 2*

2 No scandal about Queen Elizabeth I hope.   SNEER   *Ib, Act 2, Scene 1*

3 An oyster may be crossed in love.   TILBURINA   *Ib, Act 3, Scene 1*

4 Thought does not become a young woman.   MRS MALAPROP
The Rivals, Act 1, Scene 2

5 Illiterate him, I say, quite from your memory.   MRS MALAPROP   *Ib*

6 'Tis safest in matrimony to begin with a little aversion.   MRS MALAPROP
Ib

7 A circulating library in a town is as an ever-green tree of diabolical knowledge! It blossoms through the year.   SIR ANTHONY ABSOLUTE   *Ib*

8 A progeny of learning.   MRS MALAPROP   *Ib*

9 A supercilious knowledge in accounts.   MRS MALAPROP   *Ib*

10 If I reprehend any thing in this world it is the use of my oracular tongue, and a nice derangement of epitaphs.   MRS MALAPROP   *Ib, Act 3, Scene 3*

11 As headstrong as an allegory on the banks of the Nile.   MRS MALAPROP
Ib

12 Too civil by half.   ACRES   *Ib, Act 3, Scene 4*

13 You shall see them on a beautiful quarto page, where a neat rivulet of text shall meander through a meadow of margin.   SIR BENJAMIN BACKBITE
School for Scandal, Act 1, Scene 1

14 Though I can't make her love me, there is great satisfaction in quarrelling with her.   SIR PETER TEAZLE   *Ib, Act 2, Scene 1*

15 There is the whole set! a character dead at every word.   SIR PETER TEAZLE
Ib, Act 2, Scene 2

16 I'm called away by particular business. But I leave my character behind me.
SIR PETER TEAZLE   *Ib*

17 Here's to the maiden of bashful fifteen;
     Here's to the widow of fifty;
     Here's to the flaunting extravagant quean,
          And here's to the housewife that's thrifty.
               Let the toast pass,—
               Drink to the lass,
I'll warrant she'll prove an excuse for a glass.   SIR HARRY BUMPER
Ib, Act 3, Scene 3

18 What is principle against the flattery of a handsome, lively young fellow?
SIR PETER TEAZLE   *Ib, Act 4, Scene 2*

19 The Right Honourable gentleman is indebted to his memory for his jests, and to his imagination for his facts.   *Reply to Mr. Dundas,*
House of Commons

SHERMAN, General William Tecumseh, 1820–1891

20 There is many a boy here to-day who looks on war as all glory, but, boys, it is all hell.   *Speech, 1880*

SIDNEY, Algernon, 1622–1683

1 Liars ought to have good memories. *Discourses on Government, Ch. 2, 15*

SIDNEY, Sir Philip, 1554–1586

2 My true love hath my heart, and I have his,
By just exchange one for another given:
I hold his dear, and mine he cannot miss,
There never was a better bargain driven. *The Arcadia, 3*

3 Biting my truant pen, beating myself for spite:
'Fool!' said my Muse to me, 'look in thy heart and write.'
Astrophel and Stella, Sonnet 1

4 With how sad steps, O Moon, thou climb'st the skies!
How silently, and with how wan a face! *Ib, Sonnet 31*

5 With a tale forsooth he cometh unto you, with a tale which holdeth children
from play, and old men from the chimney corner. *The Defence of Poesy*

6 Certainly, I must confess mine own barbarousness, I never heard the old
song of Percy and Douglas, that I found not my heart moved more than with
a trumpet. *Ib*

7 Thy necessity is greater than mine. *On giving his water-bottle to a dying
soldier at Zutphen, 1586*

SIMS, George Robert, 1847–1922

8 It was Christmas Day in the Workhouse. *Christmas Day in the Workhouse*

SITWELL, Edith, 1887—

9 Still falls the Rain—
Dark as the world of man, black as our loss—
Blind as the nineteen hundred and forty nails
Upon the Cross. *Still Falls the Rain*

SITWELL, Sir Osbert, 1892—

10 The British Bourgeoisie
Is not born,
And does not die,
But, if it is ill,
It has a frightened look in its eyes. *At the House of Mrs Kinfoot*

SKELTON, John, 1460?–1529

11 For though my ryme be ragged,
Tattered and jagged,
Rudely rayne beaten,
Rusty and mothe eaten;
If ye take well therwith,
It hath in it some pyth. *Colyn Cloute, 2, 53*

12 With solace and gladness,
Much mirth and no madness,
All good and no badness. *To Mistress Margaret Hussey*

SMART, Christopher, 1722–1771

13 Glorious the northern lights astream;
Glorious the song, when God's the theme;
Glorious the thunder's roar. *Song to David, 85*

1 And now the matchless deed's achieved,
   Determined, dared, and done!   *Song to David, 86*

SMEDLEY, Francis Edward, 1818–1864

2 You are looking as fresh as paint.   *Frank Fairleigh, Ch. 41*

SMITH, Adam, 1723–1790

3 No society can surely be flourishing and happy, of which the far greater part of the members are poor and miserable.   *The Wealth of Nations, 1, 8*

4 To found a great empire for the sole purpose of raising up a people of customers, may at first sight appear a project fit only for a nation of shop-keepers. It is, however, a project altogether unfit for a nation of shopkeepers; but extremely fit for a nation that is governed by shopkeepers.   *Ib, 2, 4*

SMITH, Logan Pearsall, 1865–1946

5 Happiness is a wine of the rarest vintage, and seems insipid to a vulgar taste.
                          Afterthoughts, 1, Life and Human Nature

6 There are few sorrows, however poignant, in which a good income is of no avail.   *Ib*

7 The wretchedness of being rich is that you live with rich people.
                                              Ib, 4, In the World

8 People say that Life is the thing, but I prefer Reading.   *Ib, 6, Myself*

9 Thank heavens, the sun has gone in, and I don't have to go out and enjoy it.
                                                        Last words

SMITH, Samuel Francis, 1808–1895

10 My country, 'tis of thee,
    Sweet land of liberty,
        Of thee I sing.   *America*

SMITH, Sydney, 1771–1845

11 Poverty is no disgrace to a man, but it is confoundedly inconvenient.
                                              His Wit and Wisdom

12 No furniture so charming as books.   *Lady Holland, Memoir, Vol. 1, Ch. 9*

13 How can a bishop marry? How can he flirt? The most he can say is, 'I will see you in the vestry after the service.'   *Ib*

14 As the French say, there are three sexes,—men, women, and clergymen.   *Ib*

15 Praise is the best diet for us, after all.   *Ib*

16 I never read a book before reviewing it; it prejudices a man so.
                          H. Pearson, The Smith of Smiths, Ch. 3

17 I am convinced digestion is the great secret of life.   *Letter to*
                                  Arthur Kinglake, 30 Sept. 1837

18 I have no relish for the country; it is a kind of healthy grave.
                                  Letter to Miss G. Harcourt, 1838

SMOLLETT, Tobias George, 1721–1771

19 Hark ye, Clinker, you are a most notorious offender. You stand convicted of sickness, hunger, wretchedness, and want.   *Humphrey Clinker*

20 Some folk are wise, and some are otherwise.   *Roderick Random, Ch. 6*

1 I consider the world as made for me, not me for the world. It is my maxim therefore to enjoy it while I can, and let futurity shift for itself.

Roderick Random, Ch. 45

2 True patriotism is of no party. *Sir Launcelote Greaves*

3 That great Cham of literature, Samuel Johnson. *Letter to John Wilkes, 16 March 1759, quoted in Boswell's Life of Johnson*

SNAGGE, John, 1904—

4 I can't see who's ahead—it's either Oxford or Cambridge.

B.B.C. Commentary on Boat Race, 1949

SOCRATES, 469–399 B.C.

5 I am a citizen, not of Athens or Greece, but of the world.

Plutarch, De Exilio

6 Other men live to eat, whereas I eat to live. *Plutarch, Moralia*

SOLON, 640?–558? B.C.

7 Call no man happy until he dies; he is at best fortunate.

Herodotus, Histories, 1, 32

SOMERVILLE, William, 1675–1742

8 The chase, the sport of kings;
Image of war, without its guilt. *The Chase, 1, 13*

SOULE, John Babsone Lane, 1815–1891

9 Go west, young man. *Terre Haute Express, Indiana, 1851*

SOUTHEY, Robert, 1774–1843

10 My days among the Dead are past:
    Around me I behold,
    Where'er these casual eyes are cast,
        The mighty minds of old. *My Days among the Dead*

11 Yet leaving here a name, I trust,
That will not perish in the dust. *Ib*

12 It was a summer's evening,
Old Kaspar's work was done. *The Battle of Blenheim*

13 And by him sported on the green
His little grandchild Wilhelmine. *Ib*

14 But what they fought each other for,
I could not well make out. *Ib*

15 'And everybody praised the Duke
Who this great fight did win.'
'But what good came of it at last?'
Quoth little Peterkin.
'Why that I cannot tell,' said he,
'But 'twas a famous victory.' *Ib*

SPENCER, Herbert, 1820–1903

16 Time: that which man is always trying to kill, but which ends in killing him.

Definitions

1 Science is organised knowledge.   *Education, Ch. 2*

2 The Republican form of Government is the highest form of government;
  but because of this it requires the highest type of human nature—a type
  nowhere at present existing.   *Essays, The Americans*

3 Survival of the fittest.   *Principles of Biology*

4 We all decry prejudice, yet are all prejudiced.   *Social Statics, Part 2*

5 Education has for its object the formation of character.   *Ib*

6 Hero-worship is strongest where there is least regard for human freedom.
                                              Ib, Part 3

SPENSER, Edmund, 1552?–1599

7 The woods shall to me answer and my Echo ring.   *Epithalamion, 18*

8 Ah! when will this long weary day have end,
  And lend me leave to come unto my love?   *Ib, 278*

9 Fierce wars and faithful loves shall moralize my song.   *The Faerie Queen,*
                                   Book 1, Introduction, Stanza 1

10 A gentle knight was pricking on the plain.   *Ib, Book 1, Canto 1, 1*

11 Sleep after toil, port after stormy seas,
   Ease after war, death after life does greatly please. *Ib, Book 1, Canto 9, 40*

12 And as she looked about, she did behold,
   How over that same door was likewise writ,
   Be bold, be bold, and everywhere Be bold.   *Ib, Book 3, Canto 11, 54*

13 Dan Chaucer, well of English undefiled,
   On Fame's eternal beadroll worthy to be filed.   *Ib, Book 4, Canto 2, 32*

14 The gentle mind by gentle deeds is known,
   For a man by nothing is so well bewrayed
   As by his manners.   *Ib, Book 6, Canto 3, 1*

15 Calm was the day, and through the trembling air,
   Sweet breathing Zephyrus did softly play.   *Prothalamion, 1*

16 Sweet Thames! run softly, till I end my Song.   *Ib, 18*

17 So now they have made our English tongue a gallimaufry or hodgepodge
   of all other speeches.   *The Shepherd's Calendar, Letter to Gabriel Harvey*

SPOONER, Rev. William Archibald, 1844–1930

18 Kinquering Congs their titles take.   *Announcing the hymn in New College*
                            Chapel, Oxford, 1879 (See 78:12)

19 Sir, you have tasted two whole worms; you have hissed all my mystery
   lectures and been caught fighting a liar in the quad; you will leave by the
   next town drain.   *Attributed*

20 Let us drink to the queer old Dean.   *Attributed*

21 I remember your name perfectly, but I just can't think of your face.
                                              Attributed

SPRING-RICE, Sir Cecil Arthur, 1858–1918

22 I vow to thee, my country—all earthly things above—
   Entire and whole and perfect, the service of my love.
                            I Vow to Thee, My Country

1 I am the Dean of Christ Church, Sir,
  This is my wife—look well at her.
  She is the Broad: I am the High:
  We are the University.   *The Masque of Balliol*

SQUIRE, Sir John Collings, 1884–1958

2 It did not last: the Devil howling 'Ho,
  Let Einstein be,' restored the status quo.   *In Continuation of Pope on*
                                              Newton (see 201:21)

3 But I'm not so think as you drunk I am.   *Ballade of Soporific Absorption*

STANLEY, Sir Henry Morton, 1841–1904

4 Dr. Livingstone, I presume?   *On meeting Livingstone in Ujiji, Central*
                                              Africa, 10 Nov. 1871

STANTON, Frank Lebby, 1857–1927

5 Sweetest li'l feller, everybody knows;
  Dunno what to call him, but he's mighty lak' a rose.   *Mighty Lak' a Rose*

STEELE, Sir Richard, 1672–1729

6 Among all the diseases of the mind there is not one more epidemical or more
  pernicious than the love of flattery.   *The Spectator, No. 238*

7 There are so few who can grow old with a good grace.   *Ib, No. 263*

8 Reading is to the mind what exercise is to the body.   *The Tatler, No. 147*

STEPHEN, James Kenneth, 1859–1892

9 Two voices are there: one is of the deep . . .
  And one is of an old half-witted sheep
  Which bleats articulate monotony
  And indicates that two and one are three.   *Lapsus Calami, Sonnet*
                                      (Parody of Wordsworth, see 333:10)

10 When the Rudyards cease from kipling
  And the Haggards ride no more.   *Ib, To R.K.*

STERNE, Laurence, 1713–1768

11 They order, said I, this matter better in France.   *A Sentimental Journey,*
                                              Opening words

12 As an Englishman does not travel to see Englishmen, I retired to my room.
                                              Ib, Preface

13 I pity the man who can travel from Dan to Beersheba, and cry, 'tis all barren.
                                        Ib, In the Street, Calais

14 There are worse occupations in the world than feeling a woman's pulse.
                                              Ib, The Pulse

15 'God tempers the wind,' said Maria, 'to the shorn lamb.'   *Ib, Maria*

16 So that when I stretched out my hand, I caught hold of the fille de
  chambre's—.   *Ib, Last words*

17 'Our armies swore terribly in Flanders,' cried my Uncle Toby, 'but nothing
  to this.'   *Tristram Shandy, Book 3, Ch. 11*

1 Love, 'an please your honour, is exactly like war in this; that a soldier,
  though he has escaped three weeks complete o' Saturday night,—may
  nevertheless be shot through his heart on Sunday morning.
  Tristram Shandy, Book 8, Ch. 21

2 'L--d!' said my mother, 'what is all this story about?'
  'A Cock and a Bull,' said Yorick.   *Ib, Last words*

STEVENSON, Robert Louis, 1850–1894

3 Sing me a song of a lad that is gone,
    Say, could that lad be I?
  Merry of soul he sailed on a day
    Over the sea to Skye.   *Songs of Travel, 42*

4 Fifteen men on the dead man's chest—
    Yo-ho-ho and a bottle of rum!
  Drink and the devil had done for the rest.   SONG   *Treasure Island, Ch. 1*

5 Many's the long night I've dreamed of cheese—toasted, mostly.
                                              BEN GUNN *Ib, Ch. 15*

6 This be the verse you grave for me:
    'Here he lies where he longed to be;
  Home is the sailor, home from sea,
    And the hunter home from the hill.'   *Underwoods, Book 1, 21, Requiem*

7 Even if we take matrimony at its lowest, even if we regard it as no more
  than a sort of friendship recognised by the police.   *Virginibus Puerisque,*
                                                                Part 1

8 Extreme busyness, whether at school or college, kirk or market, is a symptom
  of deficient vitality.   *Ib, An Apology for Idlers*

9 There is no duty we so much underrate as the duty of being happy.   *Ib*

10 To travel hopefully is a better thing than to arrive, and the true success is
   to labour.   *Ib, El Dorado*

STEVENSON, William, 1530?–1575

11 I cannot eat but little meat
     My stomach is not good;
   But sure I think that I can drink
     With him that wears a hood.   SONG   *Gammer Gurton's Needle, Act 2*

12 I stuff my skin, so full within,
     Of jolly good ale and old.   SONG   *Ib*

STONE, Samuel John, 1839–1900

13 The Church's one foundation
     Is Jesus Christ her Lord;
   She is His new creation
     By water and the Word.   *The Church's One Foundation*

STOWE, Harriet Elizabeth Beecher, 1811–1896

14 'Never had any mother? What do you mean? Where were you born?'
   'Never was born!' persisted Topsy; 'never had no father, nor mother, nor
   nothin'. I was raised by a speculator.'   *Uncle Tom's Cabin, Ch. 20*

1 'Do you know who made you?' 'Nobody, as I knows on,' said the child,
[*Topsy*] with a short laugh . . . 'I 'spect I grow'd. Don't think nobody never
made me.'   *Uncle Tom's Cabin, Ch. 20*

SUCKLING, Sir John, 1609–1642

2 Out upon it, I have loved
   Three whole days together;
And am like to love three more,
   If it prove fair weather.   *A Poem with the Answer*

SUETONIUS, 75?–150? A.D.

3 *Festina lente.* Hasten slowly.   *Augustus, 25*

4 *Ave, Imperator, morituri te salutant.* Hail, Emperor, those about to die salute
you.   *Claudius, 21*

SURTEES, Robert Smith, 1803–1864

5 The only infallible rule we know is, that the man who is always talking about
being a gentleman never is one.   *Ask Mamma, Ch. 1*

6 Hellish dark, and smells of cheese!   *Handley Cross, Ch. 50*

7 Three things I never lends—my 'oss, my wife, and my name.
                                                                Hillingdon Hall, Ch. 33

8 Women never look so well as when one comes in wet and dirty from hunting.
                                                                Mr. Sponge's Sporting Tour, Ch. 21

9 He was a gentleman who was generally spoken of as having nothing a-year,
paid quarterly.   *Ib, Ch. 24*

10 There is no secret so close as that between a rider and his horse.   *Ib, Ch. 31*

SWIFT, Jonathan, 1667–1745

11 The two noblest of things, which are sweetness and light.
                                                                The Battle of the Books, Preface

12 'Tis an old maxim in the schools,
   That flattery's the food of fools;
Yet now and then your men of wit
   Will condescend to take a bit.   *Cadenus and Vanessa*

13 Yet malice never was his aim;
   He lash'd the vice, but spared the name;
No individual could resent,
   Where thousands equally were meant.   *On the Death of Dr. Swift, 512*

14 He put this engine [*a watch*] to our ears, which made an incessant noise like
that of a water-mill; and we conjecture it is either some unknown animal,
or the god that he worships.   *Gulliver's Travels, Voyage to Lilliput, Ch. 2*

15 Big-endians and small-endians.   *Ib, Ch. 4*

16 I cannot but conclude the bulk of your natives to be the most pernicious
race of little odious vermin that nature ever suffered to crawl upon the
surface of the earth.   *Ib, Voyage to Brobdingnag; Ch. 6*

1 Whoever could make two ears of corn or two blades of grass to grow upon a spot of ground where only one grew before would deserve better of mankind and do more essential service to his country than the whole race of politicians put together.   *Gulliver's Travels, Voyage to Brobdingnag, Ch. 7*

2 Proper words in proper places make the true definition of a style.
Letter to a young clergyman, 9 Jan. 1720

3 Hail fellow, well met,
All dirty and wet:
Find out, if you can,
Who's master, who's man.   *My Lady's Lamentation*

4 So, naturalists observe, a flea
Hath smaller fleas that on him prey,
And these have smaller fleas to bite 'em,
And so proceed *ad infinitum*.   *On Poetry, 337*

5 Promises and pie-crust are made to be broken.   *Polite Conversation, 1*

6 The sight of you is good for sore eyes.   *Ib*

7 What though his head be empty, provided his common-place book be full.
A Tale of a Tub, Digression in Praise of Digression

8 We have just enough religion to make us hate, but not enough to make us love one another.   *Thoughts on Various Subjects*

9 Few are qualified to shine in company; but it is in most men's power to be agreeable.   *Ib*

10 A nice man is a man of nasty ideas.   *Ib*

11 *Ubi saeva indignatio ulterius cor lacerare nequit*—Where burning indignation no longer lacerates his heart.   *Swift's Epitaph*

12 I shall be like that tree, I shall die at the top.   *Attributed*

13 Good God! What a genius I had when I wrote that book.
[A Tale of a Tub] Attributed

SWINBURNE, Algernon Charles, 1837–1909

14 When the hounds of spring are on winter's traces,
    The mother of months in meadow or plain
Fills the shadows and windy places
    With lisp of leaves and ripple of rain.   *Atalanta in Calydon*

15 Before the beginning of years
    There came to the making of man
Time, with a gift of tears,
    Grief, with a glass that ran.   *Ib*

16 Shall I strew on thee rose or rue or laurel,
    Brother, on this that was the veil of thee?   *Ave Atque Vale*

17 Could you hurt me, sweet lips, though I hurt you?
    Men touch them, and change in a trice
The lilies and languors of virtue
    For the raptures and roses of vice.   *Dolores*

18 I am tired of tears and laughter,
    And men that laugh and weep;
Of what may come hereafter
    For men that sow to reap.   *The Garden of Proserpine*

1 From too much love of living,
    From hope and fear set free,
We thank with brief thanksgiving
    Whatever gods may be
That no life lives for ever;
That dead men rise up never;
That even the weariest river
    Winds somewhere safe to sea.   *The Garden of Proserpine*

2 Glory to Man in the Highest! for Man is the master of things.   *Hymn of Man*

3 I have lived long enough, having seen one thing, that love hath an end;
Goddess and maiden and queen, be near me now and befriend.
                             Hymn to Proserpine

4 Laurel is green for a season, and love is sweet for a day;
But love grows bitter with treason, and laurel outlives not May.   *Ib*

5 Rise ere the dawn be risen;
    Come, and be all souls fed;
From field and street and prison
    Come, for the feast is spread;
Live, for the truth is living; wake, for night is dead.   *A Marching Song*

6 I will go back to the great sweet mother,
    Mother and lover of men, the sea.
I will go down to her, I and no other,
    Close with her, kiss her and mix her with me.   *The Triumph of Time*

SYNGE, John Millington, 1871–1909

7 When I was writing 'The Shadow of the Glen' I got more aid than any
learning could have given me from a chink in the floor of the old Wicklow
house where I was staying, that let me hear what was being said by the
servant girls in the kitchen.   *The Playboy of the Western World, Preface*

TACITUS, 55?–117? A.D.

8 *Ubi solitudinem faciunt pacem appellant.*—They create desolation and call it
peace.   *Agricola, 30*

9 *Proprium humani ingenii est odisse quem laeseris.*—It is human nature to hate
the man whom you have hurt.   *Ib*

TALLEYRAND, Charles Maurice de, 1754–1838

10 *C'est le commencement de la fin.*—It is the beginning of the end.
                          Remark to Napoleon, 1813

11 *Noir comme le diable,*
Chaud comme l'enfer,
Pur comme un ange,
Doux comme l'amour.

Black as the devil,
Hot as hell,
Pure as an angel,
Sweet as love.   *Recipe for coffee*

12 *Ils n'ont rien appris, ni rien oublié.*—They have learnt nothing, and forgotten
nothing.   *Attributed*

1 *La parole a été donnée à l'homme pour déguiser sa pensée.*—Speech was given
 to man to disguise his thoughts.   *Attributed*

2 *Pas trop de zèle.*—Not too much zeal.   *Attributed*

3 War is much too serious a thing to be left to military men.   *Attributed*

TATE, Nahum, 1652–1715

4 While shepherds watched their flocks by night,
   All seated on the ground,
   The Angel of the Lord came down,
   And glory shone around.

   'Fear not,' said he, for mighty dread
   Had seized their troubled mind;
   'Glad tidings of great joy I bring
   To you and all mankind'.   *While Shepherds Watched*

TAYLOR, Jane, 1783–1827

5 Twinkle, twinkle, little star,
   How I wonder what you are!
   Up above the world so high,
   Like a diamond in the sky.   *The Star*

TENNYSON, Alfred, 1st Baron, 1809–1892

6   O for the touch of a vanish'd hand,
     And the sound of a voice that is still!   *Break, Break, Break*

7 A happy bridesmaid makes a happy bride.   *The Bridesmaid, 4*

8 For men may come and men may go
     But I go on for ever.   *The Brook, 33*

9 Half a league, half a league,
     Half a league onward,
   All in the valley of Death
     Rode the six hundred.   *The Charge of the Light Brigade, 1*

10 'Forward, the Light Brigade!'
    Was there a man dismay'd?   *Ib, 2*

11 Their's not to make reply,
    Their's not to reason why,
    Their's but to do and die.   *Ib, 2*

12 Into the jaws of Death
    Into the mouth of Hell.   *Ib, 3*

13 Sunset and evening star,
       And one clear call for me!
    And may there be no moaning of the bar
       When I put out to sea.   *Crossing the Bar*

14 The spacious times of great Elizabeth
     With sounds that echo still.   *A Dream of Fair Women, 7*

15 A daughter of the gods, divinely tall,
    And most divinely fair.   *Ib, 87*

1 He clasps the crag with crooked hands;
  Close to the sun in lonely lands,
  Ring'd with the azure world, he stands.

  The wrinkled sea beneath him crawls;
  He watches from his mountain walls,
  And like a thunderbolt he falls. *The Eagle*

2 God made the woman for the man,
  And for the good and increase of the world. *Edwin Morris, 43*

3 Then she rode forth, clothed on with chastity. *Godiva, 53*

4 His honour rooted in dishonour stood,
  And faith unfaithful kept him falsely true. *Idylls of the King,*
  Lancelot and Elaine, 871

5 He makes no friend who never made a foe. *Ib, 1082*

6 For men at most differ as Heaven and Earth,
  But women, worst and best, as Heaven and Hell. *Ib, Merlin and Vivien,*
  812

7 　　The days darken round me, and the years,
  Among new men, strange faces, other minds. *Ib, The Passing of Arthur,*
  405

8 　　And slowly answer'd Arthur from the barge:
  'The old order changeth, yielding place to new,
  And God fulfils himself in many ways.' *Ib, 407*

9 Pray for my soul. More things are wrought by prayer
  Than this world dreams of. *Ib, 415*

10 Our little systems have their day;
   They have their day and cease to be. *In Memoriam A.H.H., Prologue*

11 　　Men may rise on stepping-stones
   Of their dead selves to higher things. *Ib, 1*

12 　　For words, like Nature, half reveal
   And half conceal the Soul within. *Ib, 5*

13 I hold it true, whate'er befall;
   I feel it, when I sorrow most;
   'Tis better to have loved and lost
   Than never to have loved at all. *Ib, 27*

14 Be near me when my light is low,
   When the blood creeps, and the nerves prick
   And tingle; and the heart is sick,
   And all the wheels of Being slow. *Ib, 50*

15 Oh yet we trust that somehow good
   Will be the final goal of ill. *Ib, 54*

16 Are God and Nature then at strife
   That Nature lends such evil dreams?
   So careful of the type she seems,
   So careless of the single life. *Ib, 55*

17 Nature, red in tooth and claw. *Ib, 56*

18 　　Fresh from brawling courts
   And dusty purlieus of the law. *Ib, 89*

1   There lives more faith in honest doubt,
     Believe me, than in half the creeds.   *In Memoriam, A.H.H., 96*

2 He seems so near and yet so far.   *Ib, 97*

3 Ring out, wild bells, to the wild sky.   *Ib, 106*

4 Ring out the old, ring in the new,
        Ring, happy bells, across the snow:
        The year is going, let him go;
     Ring out the false, ring in the true.   *Ib, 106*

5 Ring out a slowly dying cause,
        And ancient forms of party strife;
        Ring in the nobler modes of life,
     With sweeter manners, purer laws.   *Ib, 106*

6   Ring out the thousand wars of old,
     Ring in the thousand years of peace.   *Ib, 106*

7 Ring in the valiant man and free,
        The larger heart, the kindlier hand;
        Ring out the darkness of the land,
     Ring in the Christ that is to be.   *Ib, 106*

8 And thus he bore without abuse
        The grand old name of gentleman,
        Defamed by every charlatan,
     And soil'd with all ignoble use.   *Ib, 111*

9   One God, one law, one element,
        And one far-off divine event,
     To which the whole creation moves.   *Ib, 131*

10 Kind hearts are more than coronets,
        And simple faith than Norman blood.   *Lady Clara Vere de Vere*

11 On either side the river lie
     Long fields of barley and of rye,
     That clothe the wold and meet the sky;
     And thro' the field the road runs by
        To many-tower'd Camelot.   *The Lady of Shalott, 1*

12 Willows whiten, aspens quiver,
     Little breezes dusk and shiver.   *Ib*

13 'The curse is come upon me,' cried
        The Lady of Shalott.   *Ib, 3*

14 Comrades, leave me here a little, while as yet 'tis early morn:
     Leave me here, and when you want me, sound upon the bugle-horn.
                                                   Locksley Hall, 1

15 In the Spring a young man's fancy lightly turns to thoughts of love.
                                                   Ib, 20

16 For I dipt into the future, far as human eye could see,
     Saw the Vision of the world, and all the wonder that would be.   *Ib, 116*

17 Till the war-drum throbb'd no longer, and the battle-flags were furl'd
     In the Parliament of man, the Federation of the world.   *Ib, 127*

18 Knowledge comes, but wisdom lingers.   *Ib, 141*

19 Woman is the lesser man, and all thy passions, match'd with mine
     Are as moonlight unto sunlight, and as water unto wine.   *Ib, 151*

1   They came upon a land
    In which it seemed always afternoon.   *The Lotos-Eaters*

2 Music that gentlier on the spirit lies,
  Than tir'd eyelids upon tir'd eyes.   *Ib*

3 Come into the garden, Maud,
    For the black bat, night, has flown,
Come into the garden, Maud,
    I am here at the gate alone.   *Maud, Part 1, 22*

4 There has fallen a splendid tear
    From the passion-flower at the gate.
She is coming, my dove, my dear;
    She is coming, my life, my fate.   *Ib, 22*

5 O that 'twere possible
After long grief and pain
To find the arms of my true love
Round me once again!   *Ib, Part 2, 4*

6 You must wake and call me early, call me early, mother dear.
    The May Queen

7 For I'm to be Queen of the May.   *Ib*

8 Follow the Gleam.   *Merlin and the Gleam*

9 The last great Englishman is low.   *Ode on the Death of the Duke of Wellington, 3*

10 O fall'n at length that tower of strength
  Which stood four-square to all the winds that blew!   *Ib*

11 Not once or twice in our rough island-story,
  The path of duty was the way to glory.   *Ib, 8*

12 With prudes for proctors, dowagers for deans,
  And sweet girl-graduates in their golden hair.   *The Princess, Prologue, 141*

13 Sweet and low, sweet and low,
    Wind of the Western Sea.   *Ib, 3, Song*

14 The splendour falls on castle walls
    And snowy summits old in story.   *Ib, 4, Song*

15 Blow, bugle, blow, set the wild echoes flying,
  Blow, bugle; answer, echoes, dying, dying, dying.   *Ib*

16 Tears, idle tears, I know not what they mean,
  Tears from the depth of some divine despair.   *Ib, 2nd Song*

17 Man is the hunter; woman is his game:
  The sleek and shining creatures of the chase,
  We hunt them for the beauty of their skins.   *Ib, 5, 147*

18 Man for the field and woman for the hearth:
Man for the sword and for the needle she:
Man with the head and woman with the heart:
Man to command and woman to obey:
All else confusion.   *Ib, 5, 427*

19 My strength is as the strength of ten,
    Because my heart is pure.   *Sir Galahad*

TERENCE, 190?–159? B.C.

1 *Hinc illae lacrimae.*—Hence these tears.   *Andria, 126*

2 *Amantium irae amoris integratio est.*—Lovers' quarrels are the renewal of love.   *Ib, 555*

3 *Fortis fortuna adiuvat.*—Fortune favours the brave.   *Phormio, 203*

4 *Quot homines tot sententiae.*—So many men, so many opinions.   *Ib, 454*

THACKERAY, William Makepeace, 1811–1863

5 It is impossible, in our condition of society, not to be sometimes a Snob.
                                           The Book of Snobs, Ch. 3

6 'Tis not the dying for a faith that's so hard, Master Harry—every man of every nation has done that—'tis the living up to it that is difficult.
            RICHARD STEELE   *Henry Esmond, Bk. 1, Ch. 6*

7 'Tis strange what a man may do, and a woman yet think him an angel.
                                                          Ib, Ch. 7

8 The *Pall Mall Gazette* is written by gentlemen for gentlemen.
                                                    Pendennis, Ch. 32

9 A woman with fair opportunities and without a positive hump, may marry whom she likes.   *Vanity Fair, Ch. 4*

10 Whenever he met a great man he grovelled before him and my-lorded him as only a free-born Englishman can do.   *Ib, Ch. 13*

11 Them's my sentiments.   FRED BULLOCK   *Ib, Ch. 21*

12 I think I could be a good woman if I had five thousand a year.
                              BECKY SHARP   *Ib, Ch. 36*

THOMAS, Brandon, 1857–1914

13 I'm Charley's aunt from Brazil, where the nuts come from.
               LORD FANCOURT BABERLEY   *Charley's Aunt, Act 1*

THOMAS, Dylan, 1914–1953

14 And death shall have no dominion.
   Dead men naked they shall be one
   With the man in the wind and the west moon.
                          And Death shall have no Dominion

15 Do not go gentle into that good night,
   Old age should burn and rave at close of day;
   Rage, rage, against the dying of the light.
                          Do not go gentle into that good night

16 The force that through the green fuse drives the flower
   Drives my green age.   *The Force that through the green Fuse drives the
                                                              Flower*

17 The hand that signed the treaty bred a fever,
   And famine grew, and locusts came;
   Great is the hand that holds dominion over
   Man by a scribbled name.   *The Hand that Signed the Paper*

18 Light breaks where no sun shines;
   Where no sea runs, the waters of the heart
   Push in their tides.   *Light Breaks where no Sun Shines*

1 After the first death, there is no other.   *A Refusal to Mourn the Death,*
by Fire, of a Child in London

2 It is spring, moonless night in the small town, starless and bible-black.
FIRST VOICE   *Under Milk Wood*

3 It is night neddying among the snuggeries of babies.   FIRST VOICE   *Ib*

4 You're thinking, you're no better than you should be, Polly, and that's good
enough for me. Oh, isn't life a terrible thing, thank God?   POLLY GARTER
Ib

5 Praise the Lord! We are a musical nation.   REV. ELI JENKINS   *Ib*

6 Organ Morgan, you haven't been listening to a word I said. It's organ organ
all the time with you.   MRS ORGAN MORGAN   *Ib*

THOMPSON, Francis, 1859–1907

7 For the field is full of shades as I near the shadowy coast,
And a ghostly batsman plays to the bowling of a ghost,
And I look through my tears on a soundless-clapping host
     As the run-stealers flicker to and fro,
         To and fro:—
    O my Hornby and my Barlow long ago!   *At Lord's*

8 Nothing begins, and nothing ends,
     That is not paid with moan;
For we are born in other's pain,
     And perish in our own.   *Daisy*

9 I fled Him, down the nights and down the days;
I fled Him, down the arches of the years.   *The Hound of Heaven*

10 'Tis ye, 'tis your estrangèd faces,
That miss the many-splendour'd thing.   *The Kingdom of God*

11 Look for me in the nurseries of Heaven.   *To my Godchild*

THOMSON, James, 1700–1748

12 When Britain first, at Heaven's command,
Arose from out the azure main,
This was the charter of the land,
And guardian angels sung this strain:
'Rule, Britannia, rule the waves;
Britons never will be slaves.'   *Alfred: A Masque, Act 2, Scene 5*

13 An elegant sufficiency, content,
Retirement, rural quiet, friendship, books,
Ease and alternate labour, useful life,
Progressive virtue, and approving Heaven!   *The Seasons, Spring, 1161*

THOMSON, Roy Herbert, 1st Lord, 1894—

14 It is as good as having a Government licence to print money.   *Remark on*
the profitability of commercial television in Great Britain, made during an
interview in Canada

THOREAU, Henry David, 1817–1862

15 The mass of men lead lives of quiet desperation.   *Walden, Economy*

1 Our life is frittered away by detail . . . Simplify, simplify.
Walden, Where I Lived and What I Lived For

2 The government of the world I live in was not framed, like that of Britain, in after-dinner conversations over the wine. *Ib, Conclusion*

3 It takes two to speak the truth,—one to speak, and another to hear.
A Week on the Concord and Merrimack Rivers, Wednesday

4 Not that the story need be long, but it will take a long while to make it short.
Letter

THUCYDIDES, c. 471–c. 400 B.C.

5 It is great glory in a woman to show no more weakness than is natural to her sex, and not to be talked of, either for good or evil by men.
History, 2, 45, 2

THURBER, James, 1894–1961

6 Early to rise and early to bed makes a male healthy and wealthy and dead.
Fables for Our Time, The Shrike and the Chipmunks

7 All right, have it your way—you heard a seal bark. *Title of cartoon*

8 Well, if I called the wrong number, why did you answer the phone?
Title of cartoon

9 The War between Men and Women. *Title of series of cartoons*

TILZER, Harry, 1878–1956

10 Come, Come, Come and have a drink with me
Down at the old 'Bull and Bush'. *Song*

11 Come, Come, Come and make eyes at me. *Ib*

TOBIN, John, 1770–1804

12 The man that lays his hand upon a woman,
Save in the way of kindness, is a wretch
Whom 'twere gross flattery to name a coward. *The Honeymoon, Act 2,
Scene 1*

TOLSTOY, Leo, 1828–1910

13 All happy families resemble one another, each unhappy family is unhappy in its own way. *Anna Karenina, 1, Ch. 1*

14 Pure and complete sorrow is as impossible as pure and complete joy.
War and Peace, 15, Ch. 1

TOPLADY, Augustus Montague, 1740–1778

15 Rock of Ages, cleft for me,
Let me hide myself in Thee. *Rock of Ages*

TRAHERNE, Thomas, 1637?–1674

16 You will never enjoy the world aright, till the sea itself floweth in your veins, till you are clothed with the heavens, and crowned with the stars.
Centuries of Meditation, 1, 29

17 The corn was orient and immortal wheat, which never should be reaped, nor was ever sown. I thought it had stood from everlasting to everlasting.
Ib, 3, 3

TRAPP, Joseph, 1679–1747

1 The King, observing with judicious eyes,
  The state of both his universities,
  To Oxford sent a troop of horse, and why?
  That learned body wanted loyalty;
  To Cambridge books, as very well discerning,
  How much that loyal body wanted learning.   *On George I's donation of a*
                                               library to Cambridge University (For reply, see 60:4)

TROLLOPE, Anthony, 1815–1882

2 It's dogged as does it. It ain't thinking about it.   *Last Chronicle of Barset,*
                                                        Ch. 61

3 Three hours a day will produce as much as a man ought to write.
                                                        Autobiography, Ch. 15

TUER, Andrew White, 1838–1900

4 English as she is Spoke.   *Title of Portuguese-English Conversation Guide*

TUSSER, Thomas, 1524?–1580

5 At Christmas play and make good cheer,
  For Christmas comes but once a year.   *Five Hundred Points of Good*
                                          Husbandry, Ch. 12

TWAIN, Mark (Samuel Langhorne Clemens), 1835–1910

6 There was things which he stretched, but mainly he told the truth.
                                          The Adventures of Huckleberry Finn, Ch. 1

7 *Pilgrim's Progress*, about a man that left his family, it didn't say why. I read
  considerable in it now and then. The statements was interesting but tough.
                                          Ib, Ch. 17

8 Deep down in me I knowed it was a lie, and He knowed it. You can't pray
  a lie—I found that out.   *Ib, Ch. 21*

9 All Kings is mostly rapscallions.   *Ib, Ch. 23*

10 There are three kinds of lies: lies, damned lies, and statistics.   *Autobiography*

11 Soap and education are not as sudden as a massacre, but they are more
   deadly in the long run.   *The Facts concerning the Recent Resignation*

12 I must have a prodigious quantity of mind; it takes me as much as a week,
   sometimes, to make it up.   *The Innocents Abroad, Ch. 7*

13 They spell it Vinci and pronounce it Vinchy; foreigners always spell better
   than they pronounce.   *Ib, Ch. 19*

14 Familiarity breeds contempt—and children.   *Notebooks*

15 Adam was but human—this explains it all. He did not want the apple for
   the apple's sake, he wanted it only because it was forbidden.
                                          Pudd'nhead Wilson's Calendar, Ch. 2

16 Training is everything. The peach was once a bitter almond; cauliflower
   is nothing but cabbage with a college education.   *Ib, Ch. 5*

17 One of the most striking differences between a cat and a lie is that a cat has
   only nine lives.   *Ib, Ch. 7*

18 When angry, count four; when very angry, swear.   *Ib, Ch. 10*

1 Nothing so needs reforming as other people's habits. *Pudd'nhead Wilson's Calendar, Ch. 15*

2 A classic is something that everybody wants to have read and nobody wants to read.   *Speech, The Disappearance of Literature*

3 There ain't-a-going to *be* no core.   *Tom Sawyer Abroad, Ch. 1*

4 Reports of my death are greatly exaggerated.   *Cable to the Associated Press*

UNITED NATIONS

5 WE THE PEOPLES OF THE UNITED NATIONS DETERMINED

to save succeeding generations from the scourge of war, which twice in our lifetime has brought untold sorrow to mankind, and

to reaffirm faith in fundamental human rights, in the dignity and worth of the human person, in the equal rights of men and women and of nations large and small, and

to establish conditions under which justice and respect for the obligations arising from treaties and other sources of international law can be maintained, and

to promote social progress and better standards of life in larger freedom,

AND FOR THESE ENDS

to practise tolerance and live together in peace with one another as good neighbours and

to unite our strength to maintain international peace and security, and to ensure, by the acceptance of principles and the institution of methods, that armed force shall not be used, save in the common interest, and

to employ international machinery for the promotion of the economic and social advancement of all peoples,

HAVE RESOLVED TO COMBINE OUR EFFORTS TO ACCOMPLISH THESE AIMS.
                                          Preamble to United Nations Charter, 1945

UNWIN, Sir Stanley, 1884—

6 Much is written of the power of the Press, a power which may last but a day; by comparison, little is heard of the power of books, which may endure for generations.   *The Truth about Publishing*

UPTON, Ralph R., 20th century

7 Stop; look; listen.   *Notice at American railway crossings, 1912*

USTINOV, Peter, 1921—

8 THE PHOTOGRAPHER: The prisoners have been brought in, Your Excellency.
     THE MARSHAL: Question them, promise them life, and then kill them. Let us have the honour of honourable men. Give them hope before you blacken their world. Lift them high in the air before you drop them.
                                                        The Moment of Truth, Act 3

9 You will find us only on the very best atlases, because we are the smallest country left in Europe . . . a self-respecting country which deserves and sometimes achieves a colour of its own on the map—usually a dyspeptic mint green, which misses the outline of the frontier by a fraction of an inch, so that one can almost hear the printer saying damn.   THE GENERAL
                                                        Romanoff and Juliet, Act 1

1 As for being a General, well, at the age of four with paper hats and wooden swords we're all Generals. Only some of us never grow out of it.
THE GENERAL   *Romanoff and Juliet, Act 1*

2 A diplomat these days is nothing but a head-waiter who's allowed to sit down occasionally.   THE GENERAL   *Ib*

VANBRUGH, Sir John, 1664–1726

3 The want of a thing is perplexing enough, but the possession of it is intolerable.   CLARISSA   *The Confederacy, Act 1, Scene 3*

4 Much of a muchness.   JOHN MOODY   *The Provok'd Husband, Act 1*

VAUGHAN, Henry, 1622–1695

5 They are all gone into the world of light,
And I alone sit lingering here.   *Ascension Hymn*

6 Man is the shuttle, to whose winding quest
And passage through these looms
God order'd motion, but ordain'd no rest.   *Man*

7 My soul, there is a country
Far beyond the stars.   *Peace*

VEGETIUS, 4th century

8 *Qui desiderat pacem, praeparet bellum.*—Let him who desires peace, prepare for war.   *De re mil., 3, Prologue*

VERLAINE, Paul, 1844–1896

9 *Et tout le reste est littérature.*—All the rest is just literature.   *L'Art Poétique*

10 *Il pleure dans mon cœur*
Comme il pleut sur la ville.—Tears fall in my heart like rain on the town.
            Romances sans paroles, 3

VICTORIA, Queen, 1819–1901

11 We are not amused.   *Notebooks of a Spinster Lady, 2 Jan. 1900*

12 He [*Gladstone*] speaks to Me as If I was a public meeting.   *Russell,*
Collections and Recollections, Ch. 14

VIGNY, Alfred de, 1797–1863

13 *Hélas je suis, Seigneur, puissant et solitaire.*—Alas, Lord, I am powerful but alone.   *Moïse*

14 *Seul le silence est grand; tout le reste est faiblesse.*—Only silence is great; all else is weakness.   *La Mort du Loup*

VILLON, François, 1431–1485

15 *Mais où sont les neiges d'antan?*—But where are the snows of yesteryear?
            Ballade des Dames du Temps Jadis

VIRGIL, 70–19 B.C.

16 *Arma virumque cano.* Arms and the man I sing.   *Aeneid, 1, 1*

17 *Furor arma ministrat.* Anger supplies the arms.   *Ib, 1, 150*

1 *Forsan et haec olim meminisse iuvabit.* Perhaps even these things will some day be pleasant to remember. *Aeneid, 1, 203*

2 *Timeo Danaos et dona ferentes.* I fear the Greeks, even when they bring gifts. *Ib, 2, 49*

3   *Varium et mutabile semper*
Femina.
Woman is always fickle and changing. *Ib, 4, 569*

4 *Facilis descensus Averni.* The way down to Hell is easy. *Ib, 6, 126*

5 *Omnia vincit amor, et nos cedamus amori.* Love conquers all, and we too succumb to love. *Ib, 10, 69*

6   *Labor omnia vicit*
Improbus et duris urgens in rebus egestas.
Persistent labour overcame all things, and the stress of need in a hard life. *Georgics, 1, 145*

7 *Felix qui potuit rerum cognoscere causas.* Happy is he who has been able to learn the causes of things. *Ib, 2, 490*

8 *Sed fugit interea, fugit inreparabile tempus.* Meanwhile, time is flying— flying, never to return. *Ib, 3, 284*

VOLTAIRE, François Marie Arouet, 1694–1778

9 *Tout est pour le mieux dans le meilleur des mondes possibles.* All is for the best in the best of possible worlds. *Candide, Ch. 1*

10 *Dans ce pays-ci il est bon de tuer de temps en temps un amiral pour encourager les autres.* In this country [*England*] it is good to kill an admiral from time to time, to encourage the others. *Ib, Ch. 23*

11 *Cela est bien dit, répondit Candide, mais il faut cultiver notre jardin.* 'That is well said,' replied Candide, 'but we must cultivate our garden.' *Ib, Ch. 30*

12 *Ils ne se servent de la pensée que pour autoriser leurs injustices, et n'emploient les paroles que pour déguiser leurs pensées.* Men use thought only to justify their wrong-doing, and words only to conceal their thoughts. *Dialogue 14, Le Chapon et la Poularde*

13 *Le mieux est l'ennemi du bien.* The best is the enemy of the good. *Dictionnaire Philosophique, Art Dramatique*

14 *Si Dieu n'existait pas, il faudrait l'inventer.* If God did not exist, it would be necessary to invent Him. *Épîtres, 96, A L'Auteur du livre des Trois Imposteurs*

15 *L'histoire des grands événements de ce monde n'est guère que l'histoire des crimes.* The history of the great events of this world is scarcely more than the history of crimes. *Essai sur les Mœurs et L'Esprit des Nations, 23*

16 *Ce corps qui s'appelait et qui s'appelle encore le saint empire romain n'était en aucune manière ni saint, ni romain, ni empire.* This agglomeration which was called and which still calls itself the Holy Roman Empire was neither holy, nor Roman, nor an empire. *Ib, 70*

17 *On dit que Dieu est toujours pour les gros bataillons.* It is said that God is always for the big battalions. *Letter to M. le Riche, 1770*

18 I disapprove of what you say, but I will defend to the death your right to say it. *Attributed*

WALLER, Edmund, 1606–1687

1 Go, lovely Rose!
   Tell her that wastes her time and me,
  That now she knows
    When I resemble her to thee,
    How sweet and fair she seems to be.   *Go, Lovely Rose*

2 Poets that lasting marble seek
  Must carve in Latin or in Greek.   *Of English Verse*

WALPOLE, Sir Robert, 1st Earl of Orford, 1676–1745

3 The balance of power.   *Speech, House of Commons, 1741*

4 All those men have their price.   *W. Coxe, Memoirs of Walpole*

5 Anything but history, for history must be false.   *Walpoliana*

WALPOLE, Horace, 4th Earl of Orford, 1717–1797

6 It is charming to totter into vogue.   *Letter to G. A. Selwyn, 1765*

7 The world is a comedy to those who think, a tragedy to those who feel.
       Letter to Sir Horace Mann, 1769

8 Prognostics do not always prove prophecies,—at least the wisest prophets
make sure of the event first.   *Letter to Thomas Walpole, 1785*

WALTON, Izaak, 1593–1683

9 We may say of angling as Dr Boteler said of strawberries, 'Doubtless God
could have made a better berry, but doubtless God never did.'
       The Compleat Angler, Ch. 5

WARD, Artemus (Charles Farrar Browne), 1834–1867

10 My pollertics, like my religion, being of an exceedin' accommodatin'
character.   *Artemus Ward His Book, The Crisis*

11 Did you ever have the measels, and if so how many?   *Ib, The Census*

12 I prefer temperance hotels—although they sell worse kinds of liquor than
any other kind of hotels.   *Artemus Ward's Lecture*

13 Why is this thus? What is the reason of this thusness?   *Ib*

14 I am happiest when I am idle. I could live for months without performing
any kind of labour, and at the expiration of that time I should feel fresh and
vigorous enough to go right on in the same way for numerous more months.
       Pyrotechny

15 Let us all be happy and live within our means, even if we have to borrer the
money to do it with.   *Science and Natural History*

WASHINGTON, George, 1752–1799

16 It is our true policy to steer clear of permanent alliances with any portion
of the foreign world.   *Farewell Address, 17 Sept. 1796*

17 Associate yourself with men of good quality if you esteem your own reputation; for 'tis better to be alone than in bad company.   *Rules of Civility*

18 Father, I cannot tell a lie. I did it with my little hatchet.   *Attributed*

WATTS, Isaac, 1674–1748

1 How doth the little busy bee
   Improve each shining hour,
And gather honey all the day
   From every opening flower.   *Against Idleness*

2 For Satan finds some mischief still
   For idle hands to do.   *Ib*

3 Birds in their little nests agree;
   And 'tis a shameful sight,
When children of one family
   Fall out, and chide, and fight.   *Love between Brothers and Sisters*

4 O God, our help in ages past,
   Our hope for years to come,
Our shelter from the stormy blast,
   And our eternal home.   *O God, our help in ages past*

5 A thousand ages in thy sight
   Are like an evening gone,
Short as the watch that ends the night
   Before the rising sun.   *Ib*

6 Time, like an ever-rolling stream,
   Bears all its sons away;
They fly forgotten, as a dream
   Dies at the opening day.   *Ib*

7 'Tis the voice of the sluggard, I heard him complain:
   'You have waked me too soon, I must slumber again.'   *The Sluggard*

WEBB, Sidney, 1st Baron Passfield, 1859–1947

8 The inevitability of gradualness.   *Presidential Address to Labour Party*
                                              Conference, 1920

WEBSTER, Daniel, 1782–1852

9 Let our object be our country, our whole country and nothing but our
country.   *Speech, Bunker Hill, 17 June 1825*

10 Liberty and Union, now and for ever, one and inseparable.   *Speech,*
                                           26 Jan. 1830

11 I was born an American; I will live an American; I shall die an American.
                                    Speech, 17 July 1850

12 There is always room at the top.   *When advised not to become a lawyer,*
                               as there were already too many

WEBSTER, John, 1580?–1625?

13 I am Duchess of Malfi still.   *The Duchess of Malfi, Act 4, Scene 2*

14 Glories, like glow-worms, afar off shine bright,
   But looked to near, have neither heat nor light.   BOSOLA   *Ib*

15 Other sins only speak; murder shrieks out.   BOSOLA   *Ib*

16 Cover her face: mine eyes dazzle: she died young.   FERDINAND   *Ib*

17 We are merely the stars' tennis balls, struck and bandied
   Which way please them.   BOSOLA   *Ib, Act 5, Scene 4*

1 Is not old wine wholesomest, old pippins toothsomest, old wood burn brightest, old linen wash whitest? Old soldiers, sweethearts, are surest, and old lovers are soundest.   BIRDLIME   *Westward Hoe, Act 2, Scene 2*

2 I saw him even now going the way of all flesh, that is to say towards the kitchen.   BIRDLIME   *Ib*

3 Call for the robin redbreast, and the wren,
Since o'er shady groves they hover,
And with leaves and flowers do cover
The friendless bodies of unburied men.   CORNELIA   *The White Devil, Act 5, Scene 4*

4 My soul, like to a ship in a black storm,
Is driven, I know not whither.   VITTORIA   *Ib, Scene 6*

5   I have caught
An everlasting cold; I have lost my voice
Most irrecoverably.   FLAMINEO   *Ib*

WELLINGTON, Arthur Wellesley, 1st Duke of, 1769–1852

6 Nothing except a battle lost can be half so melancholy as a battle won.
Dispatch, 1815

7 I used to say of him [*Napoleon*] that his presence on the field made the difference of forty thousand men.   *Stanhope, Notes of Conversations with the Duke of Wellington, 2 Nov. 1831*

8 Ours [*our army*] is composed of the scum of the earth.   *Ib, 4 Nov. 1831*

9 Up, Guards, and at 'em.   *Waterloo, 18 June 1815, Attributed*

10 The battle of Waterloo was won on the playing fields of Eton.   *Attributed*

11 Publish and be damned.   *Attributed*

WELLS, Herbert George, 1866–1946

12 He [*Mr. Polly*] broke into a quavering song: Roöötten Beëëastly Silly Hole!
The History of Mr. Polly, Ch. 1, 2

13 'Sesquippledan,' he would say. 'Sesquippledan verboojuice.'   *Ib, Ch. 1, 5*

14 I was thinking jest what a Rum Go everything is.   *Kipps, Bk. 2, Ch. 3, 8*

15 In England we have come to rely upon a comfortable time-lag of fifty years or a century intervening between the perception that something ought to be done and a serious attempt to do it.   *The Work, Wealth and Happiness of Mankind, Ch. 11*

16 The Shape of Things to Come.   *Title of Book*

WESKER, Arnold, 1932–

17 God in heaven, Mother, you live in the country but you got no—no—no majesty. You spend your time among green fields, you grow flowers and you breathe fresh air and you got no majesty. You go on and you go on talking and talking so your mind's cluttered up with nothing and you shut out the world. What kind of life did you give me?   BEATIE BRYANT
Roots, Act 2, Scene 2

18 Education ent only books and music—it's asking questions, all the time. There are millions of us, all over the country and no one, not one of us, is asking questions, we're all taking the easiest way out. Everyone I ever worked with took the easiest way out. We don't fight for anything, we're so mentally lazy we might as well be dead!   BEATIE BRYANT   *Ib, Act 3*

WESLEY, Charles, 1707–1788

1 Gentle Jesus, meek and mild,
   Look upon a little child;
   Pity my simplicity,
   Suffer me to come to thee.   *Gentle Jesus, Meek and Mild*

2 Hark! the herald Angels sing
   Glory to the new-born King;
   Peace on earth and mercy mild,
   God and sinners reconciled.   *Hark! the Herald Angels sing*

3 Love Divine, all loves excelling,
      Joy of heaven, to earth come down,
   Fix in us thy humble dwelling,
      All thy faithful mercies crown.
   Jesu, thou art all compassion,
      Pure unbounded love thou art;
   Visit us with thy salvation,
      Enter every trembling heart.   *Love Divine, All Loves Excelling*

WESLEY, John, 1703–1791

4 I look upon all the world as my parish.   *Journal, 11 June 1739*

WEST, Mae, 1893—

5 Come up and see me sometime.   *Diamond Lil*

WHISTLER, James Abbott McNeill, 1834–1903

6 I am not arguing with you—I am telling you.   *The Gentle Art of Making
                                                    Enemies*

7 OSCAR WILDE: I wish I had said that.
   WHISTLER: You will, Oscar, you will.   *L. C. Ingleby, Oscar Wilde*

WHITE, E. B., 1899—

8 Commuter—one who spends his life
   In riding to and from his wife;
   A man who shaves and takes a train,
   And then rides back to shave again.   *The Commuter*

WHITMAN, Walt, 1819–1892

9 Women sit or move to and fro, some old, some young,
   The young are beautiful—but the old are more beautiful than the young.
                                                    Beautiful Women

10 I hear it was charged against me that I sought to destroy institutions,
   But really I am neither for nor against institutions.
                                              I Hear it was Charged Against Me

11 If anything is sacred the human body is sacred. *I Sing the Body Electric, 8*

12 O Captain! my Captain! our fearful trip is done,
   The ship has weather'd every rack, the prize we sought is won,
   The port is near, the bells I hear, the people all exulting.
                                                    O Captain! My Captain!

13 I celebrate myself, and sing myself,
   And what I assume you shall assume.   *Song of Myself, 1*

1 I loafe and invite my soul. *Song of Myself, 1*

2 I think I could turn and live with animals, they're so placid and self-
   contain'd,
   I stand and look at them long and long. *Ib, 32*

3 Behold, I do not give lectures or a little charity,
   When I give I give myself. *Ib, 40*

4 I have said that the soul is not more than the body,
   And I have said that the body is not more than the soul,
   And nothing, not God, is greater to one than one's self is. *Ib, 48*

5 Do I contradict myself?
   Very well then I contradict myself,
   (I am large, I contain multitudes). *Ib, 51*

WHITTIER, John Greenleaf, 1807-1892

6 Oh, rank is good, and gold is fair,
      And high and low mate ill;
   But love has never known a law
      Beyond its own sweet will! *Amy Wentworth*

7 'Shoot, if you must, this old gray head,
   But spare your country's flag,' she said. *Barbara Frietchie*

8 For all sad words of tongue or pen,
   The saddest are these: 'It might have been!' *Maud Muller*

WILCOX, Ella Wheeler, 1850-1919

9 Laugh, and the world laughs with you;
      Weep, and you weep alone,
   For the sad old earth must borrow its mirth,
      But has trouble enough of its own. *Solitude*

10 Feast, and your halls are crowded;
      Fast, and the world goes by. *Ib*

11 So many gods, so many creeds,
   So many paths that wind and wind,
   When just the art of being kind
   Is all this sad world needs. *The World's Need*

WILDE, Oscar Fingall O'Flahertie Wills, 1856-1900

12 Yet each man kills the thing he loves,
      By each let this be heard,
   Some do it with a bitter look,
      Some with a flattering word.
   The coward does it with a kiss,
      The brave man with a sword! *The Ballad of Reading Gaol, 1, 7*

13 Something was dead in each of us,
      And what was dead was Hope. *Ib, 3, 31*

14 For he who lives more lives than one
      More deaths than one must die. *Ib, 3, 37*

15 I know not whether Laws be right
      Or whether Laws be wrong;
   All that we know who live in gaol

Is that the wall is strong;
And that each day is like a year,
  A year whose days are long.   *The Ballad of Reading Gaol, 5, 1*

1 The man who sees both sides of a question is a man who sees absolutely
  nothing at all.   *The Critic as Artist, Part 2*

2 A little sincerity is a dangerous thing, and a great deal of it is absolutely
  fatal.   *Ib*

3 Ah! don't say you agree with me. When people agree with me I always feel
  that I must be wrong.   *Ib*

4 There is no sin except stupidity.   *Ib*

5 To love oneself is the beginning of a lifelong romance.
                             LORD GORING   *An Ideal Husband, Act 3*

6 Really, if the lower orders don't set us a good example, what on earth is the
  use of them?   ALGERNON   *The Importance of Being Earnest, Act 1*

7 The truth is rarely pure and never simple. Modern life would be very
  tedious if it were either, and modern literature a complete impossibility!
                                            ALGERNON   *Ib, 1*

8 I have invented an invaluable permanent invalid called Bunbury, in order
  that I may be able to go down into the country whenever I choose.
                                            ALGERNON   *Ib, 1*

9 The amount of women in London who flirt with their own husbands is
  perfectly scandalous. It looks so bad. It is simply washing one's clean linen
  in public.   ALGERNON   *Ib, 1*

10 In married life three is company and two is none.   ALGERNON   *Ib, 1*

11 I do not approve of anything that tampers with natural ignorance. Ignorance
   is like a delicate exotic fruit; touch it, and the bloom is gone.
                                            LADY BRACKNELL   *Ib, 1*

12 To lose one parent, Mr. Worthing, may be regarded as a misfortune; to
   lose both looks like carelessness.   LADY BRACKNELL   *Ib, 1*

13   JACK: In a hand-bag.
     LADY BRACKNELL: A hand-bag?
            JACK: Yes, Lady Bracknell. It was in a hand-bag—a somewhat
                  large, black leather hand-bag, with handles to it—an
                  ordinary hand-bag in fact.   *Ib, 1*

14 LADY BRACKNELL: The cloak-room at Victoria Station?
            JACK: Yes. The Brighton line.
   LADY BRACKNELL: The line is immaterial.   *Ib, 1*

15 Memory, my dear Cecily, is the diary we all carry about with us.
                                            MISS PRISM   *Ib, Act 2*

16 I never travel without my diary. One should always have something sensational to read in the train.   GWENDOLEN FAIRFAX   *Ib, 2*

17 No woman should ever be quite accurate about her age. It looks so calculat-
   ing.   LADY BRACKNELL   *Ib, Act 3*

18 It is a terrible thing for a man to find out suddenly that all his life he has
   been speaking nothing but the truth.   JACK   *Ib, 3*

19 Please do not shoot the pianist. He is doing his best.   *Impressions of
                                                                America, Leadville*

1 It is absurd to divide people into good and bad. People are either charming or tedious.   LORD DARLINGTON   *Lady Windermere's Fan, Act 1*

2 I can resist everything except temptation.   LORD DARLINGTON   *Ib, 1*

3 Scandal is gossip made tedious by morality.   CECIL GRAHAM   *Ib, Act 3*

4   CECIL GRAHAM: What is a cynic?
   LORD DARLINGTON: A man who knows the price of everything and the value
                  of nothing.   *Ib, 3*

5 All Art is quite useless.   *The Picture of Dorian Gray, Preface*

6 There is only one thing in the world worse than being talked about, and that is not being talked about.   *Ib, 1*

7 The only way to get rid of a temptation is to yield to it.   *Ib, 2*

8   MRS ALLONBY: They say, Lady Hunstanton, that when good Ameri-
                  cans die they go to Paris.
   LADY HUNSTANTON: Indeed? And when bad Americans die, where do
                  they go?
   LORD ILLINGWORTH: Oh, they go to America.
                           A Woman of No Importance, Act 1

9 The youth of America is their oldest tradition. It has been going on now for three hundred years.   LORD ILLINGWORTH   *Ib, 1*

10 One knows so well the popular idea of health. The English country gentle-man galloping after a fox—the unspeakable in full pursuit of the uneatable.
                           LORD ILLINGWORTH   *Ib, 1*

11 We in the House of Lords are never in touch with public opinion. That makes us a civilised body.   LORD ILLINGWORTH   *Ib, 1*

12 One should never trust a woman who tells one her real age. A woman who would tell one that, would tell one anything.   LORD ILLINGWORTH   *Ib, 1*

13 LORD ILLINGWORTH: People's mothers always bore me to death. All women
                  become like their mothers. That is their tragedy.
   MRS ALLONBY: No man does. That is his.   *Ib, 2*

14 Moderation is a fatal thing, Lady Hunstanton. Nothing succeeds like excess.
                           LORD ILLINGWORTH   *Ib, 3*

15 No woman should have a memory. Memory in a woman is the beginning of dowdiness.   LORD ILLINGWORTH   *Ib, 3*

16 I have nothing to declare except my genius.   *At New York Custom House*

17 I suppose that I shall have to die beyond my means. [*When asked a large fee for an operation*]   *Sherard, Life of Wilde*

18 Work is the curse of the drinking classes.   *Attributed*

WILLIAM III of England, 1650–1702

19 I will die in the last ditch.   *Quoted in Hume's History of England*

20 Every bullet has its billet.   *John Wesley, Journal, 6 June 1765*

WILLIAM OF WYKEHAM, 1324–1404

21 Manners maketh man.   *Motto of his foundations, Winchester College and
                                    New College, Oxford*

WILLIAMS, Harry, 1874–1924, and JUDGE, Jack, 1878–1938

1 It's a long way to Tipperary, it's a long way to go;
It's a long way to Tipperary, to the sweetest girl I know!
Good-bye, Piccadilly, farewell, Leicester Square,
It's a long, long way to Tipperary, but my heart's right there!   *Tipperary*

WILLIAMS, W., 1717–1791

2 Guide me, O thou great Redeemer,
    Pilgrim through this barren land;
I am weak, but thou art mighty,
    Hold me with thy powerful hand:
      Bread of heaven,
Feed me till I want no more.   *Guide me, O thou great Redeemer*

WILLS, William Gorman, 1828–1891

3 I'll sing thee songs of Araby,
    And Tales of fair Cashmere.   *Lalla Rookh*

WILSON, Charles Erwin, 1890–1961

4 I thought what was good for the country was good for General Motors and
vice versa.   *Statement to U.S. Congressional Committee, 23 Jan. 1953*

WILSON, Harriette, 1789–1846

5 I shall not say why and how I became, at the age of fifteen, the mistress of
the Earl of Craven.   *Memoirs, Opening words*

WILSON, John, see NORTH, Christopher

WILSON, Sandy, 1924—

6 I could be happy with you.   *The Boy Friend, Title of Song*

WILSON, Thomas Woodrow, 1856–1924

7 There is such a thing as a man being too proud to fight.
       Speech, 10 May 1915

8 America cannot be an ostrich with its head in the sand.   *Speech, 1 Feb. 1916*

9 The world must be made safe for democracy.   *Speech, 2 April 1917*

WITHER, George, 1588–1667

10 I loved a lass, a fair one,
    As fair as e'er was seen;
She was indeed a rare one,
    Another Sheba Queen.   *I Loved a Lass*

11 Shall I, wasting in despair,
Die because a woman's fair?
Or make pale my cheeks with care,
'Cause another's rosy are?   *The Lover's Resolution*

1 If she love me, this believe,
  I will die ere she shall grieve;
  If she slight me when I woo;
  I can scorn and let her go;
      For if she be not for me,
      What care I for whom she be?   *The Lover's Resolution*

WODEHOUSE, Pelham Grenville, 1881—

2 He spoke with a certain what-is-it in his voice, and I could see that, if not
  actually disgruntled, he was far from being gruntled.   *The Code of the*
                                                                Woosters

WOLFE, Charles, 1791–1823

3 Not a drum was heard, not a funeral note,
      As his corse to the rampart we hurried;
  Not a soldier discharged his farewell shot
      O'er the grave where our hero we buried.   *The Burial of Sir John*
                                                        Moore at Corunna, 1

4 We carved not a line, and we raised not a stone,
      But we left him alone with his glory.   *Ib, 31*

WOLFE, James, 1727–1759

5 I would rather have written that poem, [*Gray's Elegy*], gentlemen, than
  take Quebec.   *The night before he was killed in battle at Quebec*

WOLSEY, Thomas, Cardinal, 1475?–1530

6 Had I but served God as diligently as I have served the king, he would not
  have given me over in my gray hairs.   *To Sir William Kingston*

WOOD, Mrs Henry, 1814–1887

7 Dead! and ... never called me mother.   *East Lynne, dramatized version*

WOOLCOTT, Alexander, 1887–1943

8 I must get out of these wet clothes and into a dry Martini.   *Attributed*
                    (*Also attributed to Robert Benchley and Billy Wilder*)

WOOLF, Virginia, 1882–1941

9 A Room of One's Own.   *Title of Book*

WORDSWORTH, Elizabeth, 1840–1932

10 If all the good people were clever,
      And all clever people were good,
   The world would be wiser than ever
      We thought that it possibly could.
   But somehow 'tis seldom or never
      The two hit it off as they should;
   The good are so harsh to the clever,
      The clever so rude to the good!   *Good and Clever*

WORDSWORTH, William, 1770–1850

11 Give all thou canst; high Heaven rejects the lore
      Of nicely-calculated less or more.   *Ecclesiastical Sonnets, Pt. 3, 43,*
                                                King's College Chapel

1 The light that never was, on sea or land,
 The consecration, and the Poet's dream.   *Elegiac Stanzas suggested by a*
                                                 Picture of Peele Castle in a storm, 15

2 A deep distress hath humanised my Soul.   *Ib, 36*

3 On Man, on Nature, and on Human Life,
 Musing in solitude.   *The Excursion, Preface, 1*

4   Oh, Sir! the good die first,
 And they whose hearts are dry as summer dust
 Burn to the socket.   *Ib, 1, 500*

5 Think you, 'mid all this mighty sum
 Of things for ever speaking,
 That nothing of itself will come,
 But we must still be seeking?   *Expostulation and Reply, 25*

6 I travelled among unknown men,
   In lands beyond the sea;
 Nor, England! did I know till then
   What love I bore to thee.   *I travelled among unknown men*

7 I wandered lonely as a cloud
 That floats on high o'er vales and hills,
 When all at once I saw a crowd,
 A host, of golden daffodils;
 Beside the lake, beneath the trees,
 Fluttering and dancing in the breeze.   *I wandered lonely as a Cloud, 1*

8 Continuous as the stars that shine
 And twinkle on the milky way.   *Ib, 7*

9 Ten thousand saw I at a glance,
 Tossing their heads in sprightly dance.   *Ib, 11*

10 A poet could not but be gay,
 In such a jocund company.   *Ib, 15*

11 For oft, when on my couch I lie
 In vacant or in pensive mood,
 They flash upon that inward eye
 Which is the bliss of solitude.   *Ib, 19*

12 There was a time when meadow, grove, and stream,
 The earth, and every common sight,
          To me did seem
       Apparelled in celestial light,
 The glory and the freshness of a dream.   *Ode, Intimations of Immortality*
                                             from Recollections of Early Childhood, Stanza 1

13 The Rainbow comes and goes,
 And lovely is the Rose.   *Ib, Stanza 2*

14   The sunshine is a glorious birth;
       But yet I know, where'er I go,
 That there hath past away a glory from the earth.   *Ib*

15   While the young lambs bound
 As to the tabor's sound.   *Ib, Stanza 3*

16 Whither is fled the visionary gleam?
 Where is it now, the glory and the dream?   *Ib, Stanza 4*

1 Our birth is but a sleep and a forgetting:
 The Soul that rises with us, our life's Star,
  Hath had elsewhere its setting,
   And cometh from afar:
  Not in entire forgetfulness,
  And not in utter nakedness,
 But trailing clouds of glory do we come
  From God, who is our home:
Heaven lies about us in our infancy!
Shades of the prison-house begin to close
  Upon the growing Boy.   *Ode, Intimations of Immortality from*
             Recollections of Early Childhood, Stanza 5

2 The Youth, who daily farther from the east
  Must travel, still is Nature's Priest,
  And by the vision splendid
   Is on his way attended;
At length the Man perceives it die away,
And fade into the light of common day.   *Ib*

3 Behold the Child among his new-born blisses,
A six years' Darling of a pigmy size!   *Ib, Stanza 7*

4 O joy! that in our embers
Is something that doth live,
That nature yet remembers
What was so fugitive!   *Ib, Stanza 9*

5 And O, ye Fountains, Meadows, Hills, and Groves,
Forebode not any severing of our loves!   *Ib, Stanza 11*

6 To me the meanest flower that blows can give
Thoughts that do often lie too deep for tears.   *Ib*

7 I heard a thousand blended notes,
While in a grove I sate reclined,
In that sweet mood when pleasant thoughts
Bring sad thoughts to the mind.   *Lines written in early Spring, 1*

8 Have I not reason to lament
What man has made of man?   *Ib, 23*

9 I chanced to see at break of day
The solitary child.   *Lucy Gray, 3*

10 The sweetest thing that ever grew
Beside a human door!   *Ib, 7*

11   Meantime Luke began
To slacken in his duty; and, at length,
He in the dissolute city gave himself
To evil courses.   *Michael, 442*

12 There is a comfort in the strength of love;
'Twill make a thing endurable, which else
Would overset the brain, or break the heart.   *Ib, 448*

13 Nuns fret not at their convent's narrow room;
And hermits are contented with their cells. *Miscellaneous Sonnets, Pt. 1, 1*

14   'Twas pastime to be bound
Within the Sonnet's scanty plot of ground.   *Ib*

1 Surprised by joy—impatient as the Wind
  I turned to share the transport.   *Miscellaneous Sonnets, Pt. 1, 27*

2 It is a beauteous evening, calm and free,
  The holy time is quiet as a Nun
  Breathless with adoration.   *Ib, 1, 30*

3 The world is too much with us; late and soon,
  Getting and spending, we lay waste our powers:
  Little we see in Nature that is ours.   *Ib, 1, 33*

4   Great God! I'd rather be
  A Pagan suckled in a creed outworn;
  So might I, standing on this pleasant lea,
  Have glimpses that would make me less forlorn;
  Have sight of Proteus rising from the sea;
  Or hear old Triton blow his wreathèd horn. *Ib*

5 Scorn not the Sonnet; Critic, you have frowned,
  Mindless of its just honours; with this key
  Shakespeare unlocked his heart.   *Ib, Pt. 2, 1*

6 Earth has not anything to show more fair:
  Dull would he be of soul who could pass by
  A sight so touching in its majesty:
  This City now doth, like a garment, wear
  The beauty of the morning; silent, bare,
  Ships, towers, domes, theatres, and temples lie
  Open unto the fields, and to the sky;
  All bright and glittering in the smokeless air. *Ib, 2, 36*

7 Dear God! the very houses seem asleep;
  And all that mighty heart is lying still!   *Ib*

8 My heart leaps up when I behold
  A rainbow in the sky.   *My Heart leaps up*

9 The Child is father of the Man;
  And I could wish my days to be
  Bound each to each by natural piety.   *Ib*

10 Two Voices are there; one is of the sea,
   One of the mountains; each a mighty Voice:
   In both from age to age thou didst rejoice,
   They were thy chosen music, Liberty!   *National Independence and*
        Liberty, Pt. 1, 12, Thought of a Briton on the Subjugation of Switzerland

11 Plain living and high thinking are no more:
   The homely beauty of the good old cause
   Is gone; our peace, our fearful innocence,
   And pure religion breathing household laws. *Ib, 1, 13, Written in*
                                                London, Sept. 1802

12 Milton! thou shouldst be living at this hour:
   England hath need of thee: she is a fen
   Of stagnant waters.   *Ib, 1, 14, London, 1802*

13 Thy soul was like a Star, and dwelt apart;
   Thou hadst a voice whose sound was like the sea:
   Pure as the naked heavens, majestic, free,
   So didst thou travel on life's common way,
   In cheerful godliness; and yet thy heart
   The lowliest duties on herself did lay.   *Ib*

1 We must be free or die, who speak the tongue
That Shakespeare spake; the faith and morals hold
Which Milton held.   *National Independence and Liberty, Pt. 1, 16*

2 Another year!—another deadly blow!
Another mighty Empire overthrown!
And We are left, or shall be left, alone.   *Ib, 1, 27*

3 Stern Daughter of the Voice of God!
O Duty! if that name thou love
Who art a light to guide, a rod
To check the erring, and reprove.   *Ode to Duty, 1*

4 Give unto me, made lowly wise,
The spirit of self-sacrifice.   *Ib, 54*

5 Bliss was it in that dawn to be alive,
But to be young was very Heaven!   *The Prelude, 11, 108*

6   There is
One great society alone on earth:
The noble Living and the noble Dead.   *Ib, 11, 393*

7 There was a roaring in the wind all night;
The rain came heavily and fell in floods.   *Resolution and Independence, 1*

8 I thought of Chatterton, the marvellous Boy,
The sleepless Soul that perished in his pride.   *Ib, 7*

9 Still glides the Stream, and shall for ever glide;
The Form remains, the Function never dies.   *The River Duddon, 34,*
After-Thought

10 Through love, through hope, and faith's transcendent dower,
We feel that we are greater than we know.   *Ib*

11 She dwelt among the untrodden ways
    Beside the springs of Dove,
A Maid whom there were none to praise
    And very few to love.   *She Dwelt among the Untrodden Ways*

12 She was a Phantom of delight
When first she gleamed upon my sight.   *She was a Phantom of Delight, 1*

13 I saw her upon nearer view,
A Spirit, yet a Woman too!   *Ib, 11*

14 A perfect Woman, nobly planned,
To warn, to comfort, and command;
And yet a Spirit still, and bright
With something of angelic light.   *Ib, 27*

15 No motion has she now, no force;
    She neither hears nor sees;
Rolled round in earth's diurnal course,
    With rocks, and stones, and trees.   *A Slumber did my Spirit seal*

16 Behold her, single in the field,
Yon solitary Highland Lass!   *The Solitary Reaper, 1*

17 Will no one tell me what she sings?—
Perhaps the plaintive numbers flow
For old, unhappy, far-off things,
And battles long ago.   *Ib, 17*

1   I listened, motionless and still;
    And, as I mounted up the hill,
    The music in my heart I bore,
    Long after it was heard no more.   *The Solitary Reaper, 29*

2   Strange fits of passion have I known:
    And I will dare to tell.   *Strange Fits of Passion, 1*

3   What fond and wayward thoughts will slide
    Into a Lover's head!
    'O mercy!' to myself I cried,
    'If Lucy should be dead!'   *Ib, 25*

4   Up! up! my Friend, and quit your books;
    Or surely you'll grow double.   *The Tables Turned, 1*

5   Books! 'tis a dull and endless strife:
    Come, hear the woodland linnet,
    How sweet his music! on my life,
    There's more of wisdom in it.   *Ib, 9*

6   Come forth into the light of things,
    Let Nature be your Teacher.   *Ib, 15*

7   One impulse from a vernal wood
    May teach you more of man,
    Of moral evil and of good,
    Than all the sages can.   *Ib, 21*

8   Come forth, and bring with you a heart
    That watches and receives.   *Ib, 31*

9   Three years she grew in sun and shower,
    Then Nature said, 'A lovelier flower
    On earth was never sown;
    This Child I to myself will take;
    She shall be mine, and I will make
    A Lady of my own.'   *Three Years she Grew, 1*

10   That best portion of a good man's life,
    His little, nameless, unremembered, acts
    Of kindness and of love.   *Lines composed a few miles above*
                                                       Tintern Abbey, 33

11   That blessed mood,
    In which the burthen of the mystery,
    In which the heavy and the weary weight
    Of all this unintelligible world,
    Is lightened.   *Ib, 37*

12   We are laid asleep
    In body, and become a living soul:
    While with an eye made quiet by the power
    Of harmony, and the deep power of joy,
    We see into the life of things.   *Ib, 45*

13 How oft, in spirit, have I turned to thee,
    O sylvan Wye!   *Ib, 55*

14   I have learned
    To look on nature, not as in the hour
    Of thoughtless youth; but hearing often-times
    The still, sad music of humanity.   *Ib, 88*

1   Nature never did betray
The heart that loved her. *Lines composed a few miles above Tintern Abbey,*
122

2 O Blithe New-comer! I have heard,
I hear thee and rejoice.
O Cuckoo! shall I call thee Bird,
Or but a wandering Voice? *To the Cuckoo, 1*

3 Thrice welcome, darling of the Spring! *Ib, 13*

4 O blessèd Bird! the earth we pace
Again appears to be
An unsubstantial, faery place;
That is fit home for Thee! *Ib, 29*

5 'And where are they? I pray you tell.'
She answered, 'Seven are we;
And two of us at Conway dwell,
And two are gone to sea.' *We are Seven, 17*

6 'You run about, my little Maid,
Your limbs they are alive;
If two are in the church-yard laid,
Then ye are only five.' *Ib, 33*

7 Poetry is the spontaneous overflow of powerful feelings: it takes its origin
from emotion recollected in tranquillity. *Lyrical Ballads, Preface*

WORK, Henry Clay, 1832–1884

8 But it stopped short—never to go again—
When the old man died. *Grandfather's Clock*

9 Bring the good old bugle, boys, we'll sing another song:
Sing it with a spirit that will start the world along,
Sing it as we used to sing it—fifty thousand strong,
    As we were marching through Georgia. *Marching through Georgia*

10 'Hurrah! hurrah! we bring the Jubilee!
Hurrah! hurrah! the flag that makes you free!'
So they sang the chorus from Atlanta to the sea
    As we were marching through Georgia. *Ib, Chorus*

WOTTON, Sir Henry, 1568–1639

11 An Ambassador is an honest man sent to lie abroad for his country.
Written in Mr. Christopher Fleckamore's Album

12 He first deceased; she for a little tried
To live without him, liked it not, and died. *Upon the Death of Sir*
Albertus Morton's wife

13 How happy is he born and taught,
    That serveth not another's will;
Whose armour is his honest thought,
    And simple truth his utmost skill! *The Character of a Happy Life*

WREN, Sir Christopher, 1632–1723

1 *Si monumentum requiris, circumspice.* If you seek my monument, look around
you.   *Inscription in St. Paul's Cathedral, London, written
by his son*

WYKEHAM, William of, see WILLIAM OF WYKEHAM

XENOPHON, 435?–354? B.C.

2 The sea! the sea!   *Anabasis, 4, 7*

YEATMAN, Robert Julian, see SELLAR, Walter Carruthers

YEATS, William Butler, 1865–1939

3   When I was young,
   I had not given a penny for a song
   Did not the poet sing it with such airs
   That one believed he had a sword upstairs.   *All Things can Tempt Me*

4 I will arise and go now, and go to Innisfree,
   And a small cabin build there, of clay and wattles made;
   Nine bean rows will I have there, a hive for the honey bee,
   And live alone in the bee-loud glade.   *The Lake Isle of Innisfree*

5 And I shall have some peace there, for peace comes dropping slow,
   Dropping from the veils of the morning to where the cricket sings.   *Ib*

6   The land of faery,
   Where nobody gets old and godly and grave,
   Where nobody gets old and crafty and wise,
   Where nobody gets old and bitter of tongue.   *The Land of Heart's Desire*

7 All things uncomely and broken, all things worn out and old,
   The cry of a child by the roadway, the creak of a lumbering cart,
   The heavy steps of the ploughman, splashing the wintry mould,
   Are wronging your image that blossoms a rose in the deeps of my heart.
                                        The Lover Tells of the Rose in his Heart

8 When I was a boy with never a crack in my heart.
                                        The Meditation of the Old Fisherman

9 A pity beyond all telling
   Is hid in the heart of love.   *The Pity of Love*

10 When you are old and grey and full of sleep
   And, nodding by the fire, take down this book,
   And slowly read, and dream of the soft look
   Your eyes had once, and of their shadows deep.   *When You are Old*

YOUNG, Edward, 1683–1765

11 Some for renown, on scraps of learning dote,
   And think they grow immortal as they quote.   *Love of Fame, 1, 89*

12   Be wise with speed,
   A fool at forty is a fool indeed.   *Ib, 2, 281*

13 Be wise today; 'tis madness to defer.   *Night Thoughts, Night 1, 390*

14 Procrastination is the thief of time.   *Ib, 393*

1 At thirty man suspects himself a fool;
  Knows it at forty, and reforms his plan;
  At fifty chides his infamous delay,
  Pushes his prudent purpose to resolve:
  In all the magnanimity of thought
  Resolves; and re-resolves; then dies the same.   *Night Thoughts, Night 1,*
                                                                        417

2 Man wants but little, nor that little, long.   *Ib, Night 4, 118*

ZOLA, Émile, 1840–1902

3 *J'accuse.* I accuse.   *Title of open letter to French President about Dreyfus*
                                                                Case, 1898

Index

The overriding aims in compiling the index have been to refresh memories by providing fingerposts to half-remembered quotations, and to furnish useful quotations related to given subjects. This being so, in many cases brief and pregnant passages have received particularly thorough analysis.

'A' and 'the' have frequently been omitted from the beginnings of quoted phrases when their presence did not seem essential. The object has been to quote what are, in each case, the most informative words in a phrase. 'Your', 'yours', 'would', 'could', 'should' are the principal abbreviated words; any other isolated abbreviations have been made only when they are unmistakable.

References in the index after a quotation are to the page and to the place on the page. Thus 95:6 after a quotation refers to page 95, quotation 6.

Index

Alone *(continued)*
    leave them a., and they'll come home
        190:10
    left him a. with his glory   330:4
    not good that the man shd. be a.   30:7
    we are left, or shall be left, a.   334:2
    we two a. will sing like birds   267:13
    weep, and you weep a.   326:9
    who can enjoy a. ?   179:3
Alph the sacred river ran   87:11
Alpha: I am A. and Omega   50:15
Alphabet: got to the end of the a.   99:3
Alpine: through an A. village passed   160:12
Altars: on behalf of ... their a. ... their hearths
    238:1
Alteration: alters when it a. finds   294:8
Alternative: prefer old age to the a.   81:15
Alters: a. when it alteration finds   294:8
    love a. not   294:9
Always (Alway): I am with you a.   45:4
    it seemed a. afternoon   314:1
Am: by the grace of God I a. what I a.   48:12
    here I a., and here I stay   164:11
    I a. that I a.   31:19
    I think, therefore I a.   97:7
Amami: Friday night is A. night   11:3
Amaryllis: sport with A. in the shade   174:16
Amateurs: hinted that we are a nation of a.
    235:13
Amaze: Ye gods! it doth a. me   262:7
Ambassador: an a. is an honest man sent to lie
    336:11
Ambiguity: Seven Types of A.   108:24
Ambition: a. first sprung from yr. blest
    abodes 201:7
    a. shd. be made of sterner stuff   263:13
    a. thick-sighted   147:7
    become a churchman better than a.   262:3
    death for his a.   263:10
    let not a. mock   126:7
    love ... not with a. join'd   89:14
    meaner things to low a.   202:17
    to reign is worth a.   176:6
    vaulting a. which o'erleaps itself   270:6
    wars that makes a. virtue   280:2
    who doth a. shun   244:6
Ambitious: as he was a., I slew him   263:10
Amen: will no man say a. ?   284:1
America: A. cannot be an ostrich   329:8
    A. ... country of young men   108:21
    A.! God shed His grace   253:4
    ask not what A. will do for you   153:2
    O my A.!, my new-found-land   101:3
    Oh, they go to A.   328:8
    the youth of A.   328:9
    wake up, A.   114:16
American: a new deal for the A. people
    234:17
    A. system of rugged individualism   135:5
    born an A.; I will live an A.   323:11
    love all mankind, except an A.   144:10
    retreat of the A. Army to our line   83:10
Americanism: no room ... for hyphenated A.
    235:10
Americans: a new generation of A.   153:1
    my fellow A., ask not   153:2
    when good A. die   328:8
Amiral: tuer de temps en temps un a.   321:10
Ammunition: Praise the Lord and pass the a.
    111:13

Amor: a. che muove il sole   95:8
    a. vincit insomnia   114:6
    omnia vincit a.   321:5
Amoris: amantium irae a. integratio est   315:2
Amorous: water ... a. of their strokes   242:14
Amour: absence est à l'a.   67:13
    doux comme l'a.   310:11
    on ne badine pas avec l'a.   185:6
Amurath: not A. an A. succeeds   257:20
Amused: we are not a.   320:11
Amusing herself [my cat] more with me
    183:4
Anatomy: a mere a., a mountebank   246:5
Ancestral voices prophesying war   87:14
Ancestry: I can trace my a. back   118:2
    mule without pride of a.   101:9
Anchors: great a., heaps of pearl   285:1
Ancient: a. nobility ... act of time   22:7
    a. of days   42:6
    did those feet in a. time   55:8
    fear thee, a. Mariner   86:9
    from a. melody have ceased   56:13
    have you left the a. love   56:14
    it is an a. mariner   85:11
Ancientry: wronging the a., stealing   292:16
Anderson: John A. my jo   66:5
Ange: pur comme un a.   310:11
Angel: a beautiful and ineffectual a.   19:9
    a minist'ring a. ... my sister be   253:3
    a ministering a. thou   240:9
    A. of the Lord came down   311:4
    a. whom thou still hast serv'd   272:12
    clip an A.'s wings   149:3
    in action, how like an a.!   250:6
    is man an ape or an a. ?   100:5
    like an a. sings   275:8
    reverence—that a. of the world   247:7
    she drew an a. down.   103:15
    sword of an a. king   55:5
    the A. ended   179:1
    the A. of Death has been abroad   58:8
    the better a. is a man   294:16
    who wrote like an a.   115:2
    woman yet think him an a.   315:7
Angelic: something of a light   334:14
Angels: a. and ministers of grace defend us
    249:3
    a band of a. coming   17:1
    fantastic tricks ... as makes the a. weep
    273:7
    flights of a. sing thee to thy rest   253:11
    guardian a. sung this strain   316:12
    I ... am on the side of the a.   100:5
    made him a little lower than the a.   35:19
    sing, choirs of A.   196:5
    tears, such as A. weep   176:12
    the glorious fault of a.   201:7
    the herald a. sing   325:2
    where a. fear to tread   202:16
    women are a., wooing   289:15
Anger: a. supplies the arms   320:17
    more in sorrow than in a.   248:10
Angles: not A. but Angels   127:7
Angleterre est une nation de boutiquiers   185:12
Angli: non A. sed Angeli   127:7
Angling: ... say of a. as Dr. Boteler said of
    strawberries 322:9
Anglo-Saxon: he's an A. Messenger   77:4
    those are A. attitudes   77:4
Angry: a. for the gourd   42:20

Arcadia (*continued*)
  I too am in A. 17:12
Archangel: nor appeared less than A. ruined
  176:11
Arches: fled Him down the a. of the years
  316:9
Architecture: the wondrous a. of the world
  166:10
Arden: am in A.; the more fool I 244:2
Arguing: I am not a. ... I am telling 325:6
  no a. with Johnson 124:2
  no good in a. with the inevitable 163:1
Argument: any a. about any place 205:1
  a. for a week 254:8
  furnish ... a. and intellects 123:22
  height of this great a. 175:17
  in a. with men a woman 181:3
  not to stir without great a. 252:19
  Tories ... no a. but force 60:4
  Whigs ... no force but a. 60:4
Arise: I will a. and go now 337:4
  my lady sweet, a. 246–7:13
Aristotle: bokes ... of A. and his philosophye
  79:9
Arithmetic: branches of A.—Ambition, Dis-
  traction 74:15
Ark: a. rested in the seventh month 30:21
  unto Noah into the a. 30:20
Arm: human on my faithless a. 20:2
  I bit my a., I sucked the blood 86:7
Arma: a. virumque cano 320:16
  cedant a. togae ... laurea laudi 84:4
Armadas: till the great A. come 187:9
Armageddon: a place called ... A. 50:27
Armies: our a. swore terribly 306:17
Armour: put on ... a. of God 48:26
  religion is the best a. 224:10
  whose a. is his honest thought 336:13
Armourers: now thrive the a. 258:9
Arms: anger supplies the a. 320:17
  a. against a sea of troubles 250–51:20
  a. and the man I sing 105:1, 320:16
  a. of mine had seven years' pith 278:21
  a., take your last embrace 287:4
  imparadised in one another's a. 178:5
  so he laid down his a. 134:11
  the a. of my true love 314:5
  underneath are the everlasting a. .33:9
  what a. ... under my head 170:14
Army: an a. marches on its stomach 185:14
  hum of either a. stilly sounds 259:8
  noble a. of Martyrs 52:15
  terrible as an a. with banners 40:13
Arrive: a better thing than to a. 307:10
Arrow: an a. from the Almighty's bow 55:5
  I shot an a. into the air 160:10
  the a. that flieth by day 36:26
Arrows: my a. of desire 55:8
Ars longa, vita brevis 132:13
Arse upon which everyone has sat 94:12
Arsenic and Old Lace 153:3
Art: all a. is quite useless 328:5
  all nature is but a. 203:4
  all the adulteries of a. 145:10
  a. for a.'s sake 91:4
  a. has no enemy except ignorance 206:22
  a. is a jealous mistress 108:1
  A. is long, and Time is fleeting 160:15
  a. is long, but l. is short 132:13
  a. is too precise in every part 131:15

Art (*continued*)
  a. lies in concealing a. 206:23
  a. of being kind 326:11
  a. of drawing sufficient conclusions 68:6
  a. pour l'a. 91:4
  aspires ... to the condition of a. 90:7
  China's gayest a. had dyed 125:9
  clever, but is it a.? 154:12
  fine a. ... hand ... head ... heart 237:5
  half a trade and half an a. 138:7
  more matter with less a. 249:16
  nature is the a. of God 59:13
  next to Nature, A. 156:11
  source, and end, and test, of A. 202:3
  squandering ... his peculiar a. 103:5
  strains of unpremeditated a. 300:1
  true ease in writing ... a., not chance 202:10
  what a. can wash her guilt 124:1
Arthur: he's in A.'s bosom 259:1
  slowly answered A. from the barge 312:8
Article: snuff'd out by an a. 70:6
  these a. subscribed ... I may ... dwindle into
  a wife 89:18
Artifex: qualis a. pereo! 187:8
Artificial: all things are a. 59:13
Artisan: merchant, and a., without ... meddling
  9:6
  to give employment to the a. 27:6
Artist: a. is in danger of death 130:7
  be more of an a. 152:12
  true a. will let his wife starve 296:5
  what an a. dies with me! 187:8
Arts: a. of every woman false 180:16
  in the inglorious a. of peace 168:3
  the books, the a., the academes 268:14
Ash on an old man's sleeve 106:10
Ashamed: naked ... and were not a. 30:10
  she that maketh a. 38:12
Ashes: a. and sparks, my words among mankind
  299:6
  a. to a., dust to dust 53:30
  for the a. of his fathers 163:10
  man ... splendid in a. 60:3
  slept among his a. cold 147:15
  to give ... beauty for a. 41:11
Asia: hollow pamper'd jades of A. 256:18
  ye pamper'd jades of A.! 166:12
Ask: we a. and a. 19:2
Asked: nobody a. you, sir, she said 196:1
  women are glad to have been a. 197:14
Askelon: in the streets of A. 34:10
Asleep: he thought me a. 198:11
  old ships sail like swans a. 111:3
  the very houses seem a. 333:7
  we are laid a. in body 335:12
Aspect: meet in her a. and her eyes 71:2
  sweet of princes 261:10
  with grave a. he rose 177:3
Aspen: shade ... light quivering a. made 240:9
Aspens: willows whiten, a. quiver 313:12
Aspicious: comprehended two a. persons
  278:10
Ass: an a. wd. marry an uncertainty 241:19
  a. [knoweth] his master's crib 40:16
  average schoolmaster ... essentially an a.
  169:13
  bridle for ... a., a rod for the fool's back
  38:30
  make an a. of oneself 206:26
  write me down an a. 278:16

Assassination: absolutism tempered with a. 185:2
Assay: th' a. so hard 80:4
Assert: I may a. Eternal Providence 175:17
Asset: healthy citizens are the greatest a. 83:9
Assume: a. a virtue, if you have it not 252:14
what I a. you shall a. 325:13
Assuming that he's got any [brains] 117:6
Assurance: I'll make a. double sure 271:16
Assured: most ignorant of what he's most a. 273:7
Astonish: things that wd a. you 117:7
Astonished: a. at my own moderation 84:11
a. Mayor and Corporation 62:2
Asunder: let no man put a. 53:25
Atahualpa: knows ... who strangled A. 164:2
Atheism: a little philosophy inclineth ... to a. 22:11
Athens: a citizen, not of A. 304:5
Israel, A., Florence 138:8
maid of A. 71:1
Atkins: it's Thank You, Mr. A. 155:5
Atlanta: from A. to the sea 336:10
Atlases: only on the very best a. 319:9
Atomies: drawn with a team of little a. 286:1
Attached: decidedly and conscientiously a. 94:6
Attachment à la Plato 119:5
Attack: dared a. my Chesterton 27:12
situation excellent. I shall a. 111:5
Attempt: serious a. to do it 324:15
Attempted: something a., something done 161:11
Attentions: these pleasing a. 21:1
Attic: beauty crieth in an a. 68:9
mellow glory of the A. stage 18:14
Atticus: if A. were he! 201:17
Attire: in its workaday a. 116:12
so wild in their a. 269:7
Attitudes: Anglo-Saxon a. 77:4
Attorney: office boy to an A.'s firm 119:15
Attraction and repulsion 56:15
Attribute: an a. to God himself 275:1
a. to awe and majesty 275:1
grandest moral a. of a Scotsman 25:1
Auburn: sweet A.! loveliest village 122:4
Audace: de l'a., ... toujours de l'a. 95:9
Audi alteram partem 206:27
Audible: illiberal ... ill-bred as a. laughter 80:13
August: to recommence [winter] in A. 70:8
Augustus: Fleckno ... like A., young was called 104:13
Auld: a. acquaintance 65:12
a. lang syne 65:13
the a. wife sat 71:16
Aunt: if my a. had been a man 206:28
I'm Charley's a. from Brazil 315:13
my a. died of influenza 296:22
written to A. Maud 124:9
Aunts: his cousins and his a. 119:14
Austerlitz: pile the bodies high at A. 238:5
Austin: laboure, as A. bit 79:6
let A. have his swink 79:6
Austria: Don John of A. is going to the war 81:5
Author: as sincerely from the a.'s soul 137:13
a. ... of all good things 53:6
a. who speaks about his own books 100:6
where is any a. in the world 268:12

Authority: a man under a. 44:10
a. be a stubborn bear 293:8
base a. from others' books 268:8
dress'd in a little brief a. 273:7
in your countenance ... a. 265:12
nothing destroys a. so much 22:15
wrest ... the law to your a. 275:2
Autographs: nuisances who write for a. 118:4
Autres temps, autres moeurs 206:29
Autumn: thou breath of A.'s being 299:3
Autumnal: grace ... in one a. face 101:1
Availeth: say not the struggle naught a. 85:1
Avails: what a. the sceptred race! 156:13
Avarice, the spur of industry 137:1
Ave: a. in perpetuum ... a. atque vale 77:17
Averni: facilis descensus A. 321:4
Aversion: in matrimony to begin with a little a. 301:6
Aves: after thousand a. told 147:15
Avocation: engaging in so puerile an a. 169:13
Avon: sweet Swan of A. 145:16
Awake: a.! for Morning in the Bowl of Night 109:13
a. my heart, to be loved 58:3
a., my St. John! 202:17
lying a. with a dismal headache 117:12
smiles a. you 96:11
Award: general a. of love 148:11
Aware: England bore, shaped, made a. 59:6
Away: a.! a.! for I will fly to thee 149:16
a. with him! He speaks Latin 260:12
a., you rolling river 16:9
come, dear children, let us a. 18:11
I wish, I wish he'd stay a. 169:8
spotless reputation; that a. 281:8
the little less, and what worlds a. 60:15
to bear my soul a. 9:13
were t'other dear charmer a. 115:7
Awe: attribute to a. and majesty 275:1
in a. of such a thing as I 262:6
Awful: felt how a. goodness is 178:10
nothing ... nobody ... it's a.! 25:11
that men might shun the a. shops 81:10
Awoke: I a. ... and found myself famous 71:7
so I a., and behold ... a dream 63:12
Awry: their currents turn a. 250–1:20
Axe: an a. to grind 206:30
Lizzie Borden took an a. 14:3
the a.'s edge did try 168:4
Axiom: long been an a. of mine 101:12
Axis: soft under-belly of the A. 83:7
Azure: arose from out the a. main 316:12
ring'd with the a. world 312:1
robes the mountain in ... a. hue 72:9
the a. flowers that blow 125:9

Baa, b., black sheep 188:4
Babble: watch to b. and to talk 278:6
Babbled: a' b. of green fields 259:2
Babe: find the b. ... in a manger 45:21
Babel: name of it called B. 30:27
Babes: out of the mouth of b. 35:17
Babies: bit the b. in the cradles 61:17
putting milk into b. 83:9
the snuggeries of b. 316:3
Baby: a Mother laid her B. 10:6
b., cradle, and all 189:10
every b. born ... finer than the last 98:10

Basingstoke: word ... like B. 120:14
Basket: all yr. eggs in one b. 212:19
Bat: black b., night, has flown **314**:3
  blind as a b. 208:8
  twinkle, twinkle, little b. 74:8
Bataillons: Dieu est ... pour les gros b. 321:17
Bate: do I not B. ? ... dwindle ? 255:11
Bath: I test my b. before I sit 186:9
  sore labour's b. 270:11
Bathe: spirit to b. in fiery floods 273:10
Bathing: caught the Whigs b. 100:3
Bathing machine: between a large b. 117:13
Baton of a marshal of France 185:13
Bats: have b. in the belfry 207:2
  suspicions ... like b. amongst birds 22:24
Batsman: a ghostly b. plays 316:7
Battalions: God is ... for the big b. 321:17
  not single spies, but in b. 252:21
Battle: agreed to have a b. 75:14
  b. [is not] to the strong 39:23
  b. of Waterloo was won 324:10
  Ben B. was a soldier bold 134:11
  care for him who shall have borne the b.
    159:15
  first blow is half the b. 213:29
  melancholy as a b. won 324:6
  nothing except a b. lost 324:6
  the b. and the breeze 72:10
  the b. day is past 107:16
  to b. for freedom and truth 138:4
  when the b.'s lost and won 269:3
Battle-flags: till ... the b. were furl'd 313:17
Battles long ago 53:17
Bauble: what shall we do with this b. ? 94:8
Bays: Britain won her proudest b. 117:10
Bay-tree: flourishing like a green b. 36:10
Be: ain't-a-going to b. no core 319:3
  b. not solitary, b. not idle 67:12
  b. strong and of a good courage 33:10
  fears that I may cease to b. 151:7
  Germany ... will not b. at all 133:1
  God said, Let Newton b.! 201:21
  Ho, let Einstein b.! 306:12
  lest we shd. b. by and by 10:3
  ne'er was, nor is, nor e'er shall b. 202:7
  nobody is healthy ... nobody can b. 20:8
  this tree continues to b. 155:14
  to b. or not to b. 250:20
  what will b., shall b. 165:7
  whatever will b., will b. 209:20
  when will that b. ? say the bells 192:4
  ye shall b. as gods 30:11
Be-all and the end-all 270:5
Beach: I shall ... walk upon the b. 106:16
Beaches: we shall fight on the b. 82:13
Beachy Head: to Birmingham by way of B.
  81:7
Beacons from the abode ... Eternal are 298:3
Beadle: a b. on boxin' day 99:5
Beads: jewels for a set of b. 283:7
Beadsman: the B., after thousand aves 147:15
Beak: b. holds more than his belican 170:6
  take thy b. from out my heart 200:19
Beaker full of the warm South 149:14
Beale: Miss B. and Miss Buss 14:4
Beam: at the full midday b. 182:8
Beamish: my b. boy! 75:11
Beams: little candle throws his b.! 275:11
Bean: home of the b. and the cod 57:10
  nine b. rows 337:4

Bean (*continued*)
  not-too-French French b. 119:5
Beans: how many b. make nine 218:13
Bear: a B. of Very Little Brain 172:4
  authority be a stubborn b. 293:8
  b. those lies we have 250–1:20
  because it gave pain to the b. 164:7
  exit, pursued by a b. 292:15
  funny how a b. likes honey ? 172:3
  grizzly b. is huge and wild 136:2
  he has been eaten by the b. 136:2
  nothing wd. it b. 190:1
  rather b. with you than b. you 244:1
  sing Ho! for the life of a b. 172:10
Bear-baiting: the Puritan hated b. 164:7
Beard: b. of formal cut 244:11
  b. the lion in his den 240:7
  by thy long grey b. 85:11
  Old Man with a b. 158:13
  singed the Spanish king's b. 102:7
Bearded like the pard 244:11
Bears it out ... to the edge of doom 294:9
Beast: a b., but a just b. 13:6
  a b., no more! 252:17
  a wild b. or a god 22:21
  both man and bird and b. 87:3
  man's life is cheap as b.'s 266:2
  wee ... cow'rin', tim'rous [beastie] 66:10
  when people call this b. to mind 27:1
Beastly: don't let's be B. to the Germans 91:9
  how b. the bourgeois is 157:8
Beasts: brute b. that have no understanding
  53:19
Beat: b. him when he sneezes 74:6, 7
  lion b. the unicorn 190:9
  shall b. ... swords into plowshares 40:18
  to b. about the bush 207:5
  Tom was b. 195:4
  ye b. my people to pieces 40:19
Beaten: English never know when ... b.
  212:25
Beating: almost hear the b. of his wings 58:8
  b. myself for spite 302:3
Beats: truth ... with bad intent b. all the lies
  54:14
Beauteous: a b. evening, calm and free
  333:2
Beautified with our feathers 127:6
Beautiful: all heiresses are b. 104:10
  as good as she was b. 199:14
  b. Soup! 75:5
  full b., a faery's child 148:15
  how b. upon the mountains 41:4
  most b. things ... are the most useless
  237:3
  old are more b. than the young 325:9
  see, not feel, how b. 87:8
  she's b. and ... to be woo'd 260:7
  stately homes ... how b. they stand 130:5
  the good is the b. 200:13
  the many men, so b. 86:11
Beauty: a b. cold and austere 237:9
  a daily b. in his life 280:8
  a thing of b. is a joy for ever 147:8
  abstract Idea ... of B. 152:6
  as a b. I'm not a ... star 109:1
  as b. must be truth 151:9
  b. crieth in an attic 68:9
  b. draws us with a single hair 204:7
  b. is but skin-deep 207:6

Better (*continued*)
no b. than you shd. be, Polly 316:4
open rebuke is b. than secret love 39:2
poetry ... had b. not come at all 151:15
seen b. faces in my time 265:19
striving to b. ... mar what's well 265:16
thy love is b. than wine 40:2
to a b. land I know 112:10
wd. deserve b. of mankind 309:1
you shall now give place to b. men 94:9
Betters: order myself lowly ... to all my b. 53:13
still b. what is done 293:2
Between: no age b. ten and three and twenty 292:16
Bevy: a b. of fair women 179:15
Beware: b. the fury of a patient man 103:9
b. the Ides of March 262:5
Bewitched with the rogue's company 254:6
Beyond: enough that there *is* a b. 295:9
Bezonian: under which king, B. ? 258:1
Bias: commodity, the b. of the world 264:13
what the weak head with ... b. rules 202:4
Bible: his studie was but litel on the b. 79:13
make out ... the hebrew B. 152:7
the English B. ... wd. alone suffice 164:3
Bible-black: starless and b. 316:2
Bicycle made for two 95:4
Bigamy, sir, is a crime! 183:1
Billet: every bullet has its b. 328:20
Billiard balls: and elliptical b. 118:12
Billion: among that b. minus one 137:14
Billows: make the b. smooth and bright 75–6:16
Bills: inflammation of his weekly b. 69:20
Billy: B. in one of his nice new sashes 124:10
poke poor B. 124:10
waited till his b. boiled 198:10
Bind: fast b., fast find 213:18
Biographies: history ... essence of innumerable b. 73:10
Biography: B. is about chaps 29:2
b. is different from Geography 29:2
history ... is but the b. of great men 73:8
there is ... no history: only b. 108:6
Birch, most shy and ladylike 162:13
Bird: a b. in hand ... two in the bush 207:41
a young b. in this bush 158:12
all like that wise b. 231:26
b. of night did sit 262:12
B., or but a wandering voice 336:2
b. thou never wert 300:1
both man and b. and beast 87:3
early b. catches the worm 212:8
fly can't b., but a b. can fly 172:6
not born for death, immortal B.! 150:4
O, blessèd B.! the earth we pace 336:4
speed ... like a b. on the wing 57:12
sweet b. that shunn'st the noise 173:8
the B. of Time has ... little way to fly 109:14
unto the sweet b.'s throat 244:4
Birds: all the b. are faint 151:1
all the b. of the air fell a-sighing 196:3
b. began to sing 193:5
b. in their little nests agree 323:3
b. in their ... nests agree with Chinamen 27:11
b. of a feather flock together 208:1

Birds (*continued*)
b. outside desperate to get in 183:5
b. sit brooding in the snow 269:1
four colly b. 194:2
how can ye chant, ye little b. ? 67:5
kill two b. with one stone 217:38
pigs ... are very unlikely b. 223:5
sedge is wither'd ... no b. sing 148:14
she was one of the early b. 90:5
suspicions ... like bats amongst b. 22:24
two little dicky b. 195:5
will sing like b. i' th' cage 267:13
words that frightened the b. 12:11
Birmingham: I wanted to go to B. 160:7
to B. by way of Beachy Head 81:7
Birnam: ... till B. Forest come to Dunsinane 272:7
Birth: b., and copulation, and death 107:2
my love is of a b. as rare 167:16
our b. ... a sleep and a forgetting 332:1
royal kings ... famous by their b. 282:5
some glory in their b. 294:2
sunshine is a glorious b. 331:14
Birthright: sold his b. unto Jacob 31:6
Bishop: b. and abbot and prior 24:4
how can a b. marry ? 303:13
no b., no King 139:1
Bit: b. the babies in their cradles 61:17
condescend to take a b. 308:12
I b. my arm, I sucked the blood 86:7
mine enemy's dog, though he had b. me 267:9
went mad and b. the man 122:19
Bite: bark at a distance never b. 211:29
bark worse than his b. 206:39
b. some other of my generals 115:14
b. the hand that fed them 64:16
dead men don't b. 211:1
smaller fleas to b. 'em 309:4
the man recovered of the b. 122:20
upon their backs to b. 'em 184:7
Bites: make two b. of a cherry 228:36
Biting: his b. is immortal 243:8
Bitten: once b., twice shy 222:27
Bitter: and shed a b. tear 76:3
b. groan of a martyr's woe 55:5
b. ... on itself [revenge] recoils 179:7
b. to endure ... sweet to remember 208:2
children ... make misfortunes more b. 21:18
eating the b. bread of banishment 282:12
lack gall to make oppression b. 250:17
love grows b. with treason 310:4
old and b. of tongue 337:6
peach was once a b. almond 318:16
sadden after none or b. fruit 110:8
Bitterness: ills have no weight, and tears no b. 163:7
little sweet doth kill much b. 148:11
no hatred or b. towards anyone 78:1
Black: b. as ink 208:3
b. as soot 208:4
b. as the devil 208:5
b. as the devil, hot as hell 310:11
b. as the pit from pole to pole 130:8
b. one ... good as the white 229:10
b. sheep in every flock 208:6
dark as the world ... b. as our loss 302:9
hung be the heavens with b. 260:5
I am b. but comely 40:3

Black (*continued*)
I am b. ... my soul is white   56:10
not so b. as he is painted   211:18
one b., and one white, and two khaki   13:2
pot calls the kettle b.   223:18
ravens ... as b. as they might be   11:15
secret, b., and midnight hags!   271:13
ship in a b. storm   324:4
sober-suited matron all in b.   286:21
two lovely b. eyes   85:6
Blackbird: there came a little b.   193:5
Blackbirds: four-and-twenty b.   193:5
Bladder: blows a man up like a b.   254:17
Blade: shook the fragment of his b.   240:10
vorpal b. went snicker-snack!   75:10
Blame: murd'rous, bloody, full of b.   294:11
poor wot gets the b.   16:13
scarcely can ... b. it too much   123:1
what they b. at night   202:12
Blanket: under the b. the black ... as good
229:10
wrong side of the b.   208:20
Blasphemy: in the soldier is flat b.   273:8
Blast: our shelter from the stormy b.   323:4
with contrary b. proclaims most deeds
181:4
Blaze: his rash fierce b. of riot cannot last
282:4
Blazon: this eternal b. must not be   249:7
Bleats articulate monotony   306:9
Bleed: if you prick us, do we not b.?   274:17
upon the thorns of life! I b.!   299:5
Bleeding: thou b. piece of earth   263:7
Bleeds: our country ... weeps it b.   271:18
Bless: b. the turf that wraps their clay   88:11
God b. the moon and God b. me   190:5
'God b. us every one!' said Tiny Tim
97:12
with thee at hand to b.   163:7
Blessed: b. are the horny hands of toil   162:12
judge none b. before his death   51:21
more b. to give   47:8
Blesseth: it b. him that gives ... that takes
275:1
Blessing: a boon and a b. to men   11:8
b. of the Old Testament   21:13
God bless—no harm in b.   68:15
prophetick b.—Be thou dull   103:10
set before you ... b. and cursing   33:5
when thou dost ask me   267:13
Blessings: all the b. of this life   53:1
b. are not valued till ... gone   208:7
Blest: always to be b.   203:1
thou art b. compared with me   66:13
Blind: be to her faults a little b.   205:5
b. as a bat   208:8
b. as the nineteen hundred and forty nails
302:9
b., despised, and dying king   300:5
b. man will not thank you   208:11
b. mouths! that scarce ... know how   175:3
Cupid painted b.   276:12
discomforts ... accompany my being b.
199:13
hatred is b.   216:16
if the b. lead the b.   44:15
in the land of the b.   208:12
love is b.   219:38, 274:14
men are b. in their own cause   208:10
none so b. as those who won't see   208:9

Blind (*continued*)
the maimed, and the halt, and the b.   46:1
three b. mice   195:1
Blindly: never lov'd so b.   65:10
Bliss: b. was it in that dawn to be alive   334:5
inward eye ... the b. of solitude   331:11
perfect b. and sole felicity   166:10
thou art a soul in b.   267:10
though thou hast not thy b.   149:8
virtue only makes our b. below   203:12
where ignorance is b.   126:2
Blisses: child among his new-born b.   332:3
Blithe: no lark more b. than he   54:1
O b. Newcomer ... O Cuckoo!   336:2
Block: a chip of the old b.   209:22
big black b.   118:7
he was ... the old b. itself   64:9
Blockhead: bookful b., ignorantly read
202:15
no man but a b. ever wrote   144:5
Blockheads of all ages   89:8
Blocks: you b., you stones!   262:4
Blood: all great Neptune's ocean wash this b.
270:12
b. and iron   54:8
b. is fet from fathers of war-proof   259:4
b. is nipp'd and ways be foul   269:11
b. is thicker than water   208:13
b. of English shall manure the ground
283:8
b. of this just person   45:3
b. out of a stone   229:35
by man shall his b. be shed   30:24
corruption inhabits our frail b.   292:1
freeze thy young b.   249:7
guiltless of his country's b.   126:11
here's the smell of the b. still   272:3
he today that sheds his b. with me   260:2
I am in b. stepp'd in so far   271:10
I smell the b. of a British man   266:17
I sucked the b.   86:7
in so far in b. that sin will pluck   285:6
nothing to offer but b., toil, tears and sweat
82:11
O, the b. more stirs   254:3
purge this choler without letting b.   281:7
red b. reigns ... winter's pale   292:17
simple faith than Norman b.   313:10
smoke and b. is the mix of steel   238:7
some moment when the moon was b.   81:1
speech to stir men's b.   263:20
summon up the b.   259:3
sunset ran one glorious b.-red   61:4
the b. of Jesus whispers peace   54:4
the near in b. the nearer bloody   270:16
who thicks man's b. with cold   86:8
whoso sheddeth man's b.   30:24
young b. must have its course   154:5
Bloody: be b., bold and resolute   271:15
if you break the b. glass   164:15
my head is b. but unbowed   130:9
often wipe a b. nose   115:11
walk! not b. likely   296:23
what b. man is that?   269:5
wrong with our b. ships   25:6
Bloom: how can ye b. sae fresh and fair?   67:5
you seize the flow'r, its b. is shed   67:4
Blooming: last rose ... left b. alone   184:1
like a b. Eastern bride   103:11
Blossom that hangs on the bough   289:6

Blot: noteless b. on a remembered name 297:15

Blots: inky b. and rotten parchment bonds 282:6

Blow: another deadly b.! 334:2
b., b., thou winter wind 245:1
b., bugle, b., set ... echoes flying 314:15
b. out, you bugles, over the rich Dead 59:1
b. wind, come wrack 272:11
b. your pipe ... till you burst 62:5
hear old Triton b. his wreathed horn 333:4
liberty's in every b. 67:2
that but this b. might be the be-all 270:5
to take one b. and turn 133:14

Blows: heal the b. of sound 133:13
the wild thyme b. 276:20

Bludgeonings: under the b. of chance 130:9

Blue: Little Boy B. 191:1
their hands are b. 158:5
true b. will never stain 228:21

Blunder: wonder at so grotesque a b. 29:6
youth is a b. 100:9

Blunders: one of Nature's agreeable b. 91:14

Blush: wd. it bring a b.? 98:16

Blushing: bears his b. honours 261:9

Blut und Eisen 54:8

Board: wasn't any b. ... isn't any trade 131:6

Boards: all the b. did shrink 86:6

Boast of heraldry ... pomp of power 126:7

Boasts two soul-sides 61:14

Boat: all in the same b. 224:36
beautiful pea-green b. 158:7

Boatman do not tarry 72:8

Boats: burn one's b. 208:33
messing about in b. 124:12

Boatswain and I, the gunner and his mate 288:9

Bobby Shafto: bonny B. 188:5

Bodies: friendless b. of unburied men 324:3
pile the b. high 238:5
rough notes and our dead b. 239:3
their b. are buried in peace 52:8

Bodkin: quietus make with a bare b. 250–1:20

Body: absent in b., ... present in spirit 47:33
asleep in b., ... become a living soul 335:12
b. is not more than the soul 326:4
b. of a ... feeble woman 107:13
carry ... b. around ... its sentimental value 114:1
every joint and motive of her b. 290:8
fretted the pigmy b. to decay 102:17
gin a b. meet a b. 65:15
mind that makes the b. rich 287:11
my little b. is aweary 274:5
need a b. cry? 65:15
perfect little b., without fault 58:6
Presence of Mind ... Absence of B. 231:19
reading is to ... mind what exercise ... to the b. 306:8
some in their b.'s force 294:2
soul not more than the b. 326:4
sound mind in a sound b. 146:11
that learned b. wanted loyalty 318:1
the corruptible b. 51:13
Thersites' b. is as good as Ajax' 247:8
we ... are one b. in Christ 47:22
we therefore commit his b. 53:30
with my b. I thee worship 53:24

Bog: tell your name ... to an admiring b. 99:14

Boil: we b. at different degrees 108:20

Bold: be bloody, b. and resolute 271:15
be b., be b., ... everywhere Be b. 305:12

Boldness, and again b., and always b. 95:9

Bond: let him look to his b. 274:16
take a b. of fate 271:16
'tis not in the b. 275:4
the very b. of love 293:5
word is as good as his b. 216:37

Bondage: out of the house of b. 31:29

Bondman: so base that wd. be a b.? 263:10

Bonds: inky blots and rotten parchment b. 282:6

Bone: a b. to pick with fate 186:5
beat him with a b. 211:28
b. of my bones 30:9
fetch her poor dog a b. 192:2
have a b. in one's leg 208:15
two dogs strive for a b. 228:39

Bones: as rottenness in his b. 38:12
good ... interred with their b. 263:11
let's have the tongs and the b. 277:4
mock'd the dead b. ... scatt'red by 285:1
my Shakespeare for his honoured b. 175:11
o ye dry b., hear the word 41:23
of his b. are coral made 288:1

Bonfire: primrose way to th' everlasting b. 270:13

Bong-tree: land where the B. grows 158:8

Bonnet: a bee in one's b. 207:9

Bonnets: the b. of Bonny Dundee 239:4

Bonnie (Bonny): b., b. banks o' Loch Lomon' 16:10
braes o' b. Doon 67:5
bring back my B. 16:2
for b. Annie Laurie 101:10
is b. and blithe and good 191:8
my B. is over the ocean 16:2

Bons mots: not enough b. in existence 137:12

Bonum: Summum b. 84:3

Bo(o): cannot say B. to a goose 224:39

Booby: give her b. for another 115:10

Book: a bad b. is as much labour 137:13
a b. ... amusing with numerous errors 123:18
a b.'s a b. although 70:12
a good b. is the precious life-blood 182:3
a leaf out of one's b. 226:38
bell, b. and candle shall not drive me back 264:16
b. ... shut is but a block 208:16
b. that furnishes no quotations 199:4
but where's the b.? 82:3
dainties ... bred in a b. 268:11
damned, thick, square b.! 121:13
do not throw this b. about 26:14
go, litel b. 80:6
half a library to make one b. 143:16
he who destroys a good b. 182:2
his common-place b. ... full 309:7
if a b. is worth reading ... worth buying 237:2
I'll drown my b. 289:5
is no b.—it is a plaything 199:4
my B. of Songs and Sonnets 276:2
never read a b. before reviewing 303:16
never read ... b. ... not a year old 108:17
seldom read a b. ... given to them 143:10
take down this b. 337:10
that one might read the b. of fate! 257:4
upon a b. in cloistre ... to poure 79:6

Book (*continued*)
  use of a b. without pictures ?   73:14
  what genius ... when I wrote that b.   309:13
  when a new b. is published   234:13
  word for word without b.   290:11
  write a better b.   108:23
  your face, my thane, is as a b.   270:3
Books: as school-boys from their b.   286:12
  at his beddes heed twenty b.   79:9
  author who speaks about his own b.   100:6
  base authority from others' b.   268:8
  b. and friends ... few and good   208:17
  b. cannot always please   93:17
  b. cannot be killed by fire   235:5
  b. from which the lectures are taken   143:1
  b. in the running brooks   243:15
  b. think for me   156:6
  b.! 'tis a dull and endless strife   335:5
  borrowers of b.   156:3
  deep-versed in b. and shallow   180:5
  his sins ... scarlet ... his b. ... read   27:5
  I keep my b. at the British Museum   68:4
  I never read b.—I *write* them   232:1
  I'll burn my b.!   165:11
  in a person's bad [good] b.   208:18
  in this war, ... b. are weapons   235:5
  learning ... gained most by those b.   114:10
  needed not the spectacles of b.   104:4
  no furniture so charming as b.   303:12
  of making many b. ... is no end   39:28
  old b. maken us memorie   80:1
  old b., old wine   213:6
  quit your b.   335:4
  read any good b. lately ?   185:3
  read of in b., or dreamt of   24:5
  rural quiet, friendship, b.   316:13
  some b. are to be tasted   23:7
  the b., the arts, the academes   268:14
  to Cambridge b.   318:1
  to Cambridge b. he sent   60:4
  true University ... collection of b.   73:9
  we all know that b. burn   235:5
Boom: strong gongs groaning ... guns b. far
  81:5
Boon: a b. and a blessing to men   11:8
  is life a b. ?   120:17
Boot: b. is on the other leg   208:19
  make b. upon the summer's ... buds   258:8
Boots: b., b., b.   154:11
  too big for one's b.   228:11
  what b. it with incessant care ?   174:15
Bo-peep has lost her sheep   190:10
Border: through all the wide B.   240:5
Bore: every hero ... a b. at last   108:16
  people's mothers ... b. me   328:13
Bored: two mighty tribes, the *Bores* and *B.*
  70:9
Boring: something ... b. about somebody else's
  happiness   137:11
Born: a sucker b. every minute   24:10
  better to be lowly b.   261:4
  b., bred, and hanged ... same parish   12:5
  b. for the Universe   123:1
  b. out of my due time   184:9
  b. to be hanged   208:21
  b. to speak all mirth   277:19
  b. with silver spoon   208:22
  b. within the sound of Bow Bells   208:23
  b. ... wrong side of the blanket   208:20
  I was b. about three of the clock   256:9

Born (*continued*)
  I was not b. yesterday   208:24
  is not b., and does not die   302:10
  man that is b. of a woman   53:28
  native here, and to the manner b.   249:2
  'Never was b.!' persisted Topsy   307:14
  none of woman b. shall harm Macbeth
  271:15
  not b. to sue, but to command   281:9
  one b. out of due time   48:11
  powerless to be b.   18:15
  some are b. great   291:9
  that ever I was b. to set it right   249:14
  then surely I was b.   81:1
  under that [star] I was b.   277:20
  we are b. in other's pain   316:8
  when we are b. we cry   267:8
  who are b. of thee   28:10
  wd. thou had'st never been b.   280:6
  ye must be b. again   46:19
  yield to one of woman b.   272:12
Borne it with a patient shrug   274:10
Borogoves: mimsy were the b.   75:9
Borrow: better buy than b.   207:26
  earth must b. its mirth   326:9
  even if we have to b.   322:15
  Sorrow, why dost b. ?   147:10
  the men who b.   156:2
Borrower: neither a b. nor a lender be   248:17
Borrowers of books—those mutilators   156:3
Borrowing: beggar by banqueting upon b.
  51:23
  b. dulls the edge of husbandry   248–9:17
  b. only ... lingers it out   256:12
Bosom: b. of his Father and his God   126:15
  cleanse the stuff'd b.   272:6
Bosom-friend: close b. of the maturing sun
  147:1
Bosoms: to men's business, and b.   21:7
Boston: and this is good old B.   57:10
  readers of the B. Evening Transcript   106:2
Boteler: as Dr. B. said of strawberries   322:9
Both: money ... life; women require b.   68:13
  much might be said on b. sides   9:8
  to lose b. [parents] ... carelessness   327:12
Bottle: my b. of salvation   232:12
  she found a little b. on it   73:11
Bottles: new wine into old b.   45:25
Bottom: bless thee, B. ... thou art translated
  277:2
Bottomless: the b. pit   50:24
Bough: blossom that hangs on the b.   289:6
  when the b. breaks   189:10
Boughs: incense hangs upon the b.   150:1
  lowest b. and the brushwood sheaf   61:1
  my soul into the b. does glide   168:2
  shade of melancholy b.   244:10
Bought: until she has b. her wedding clothes
  9:10
Boulogne: a young man of B.   12:11
Bound upon a wheel of fire   267:10
Bounty: large was his b.   126:14
Bourgeois: how beastly the b. is   157:8
Bourgeoisie: British B. is not born   302:10
Bourn: from whose b. no traveller returns
  250–1:20
  to see beyond our b.   147:11
Boutiquiers: une nation de b.   185:12
Bow: arrow from the Almighty's b.   55:5
  as unto the b. the cord is   161:6

Bow (continued)
b., b., ye lower middle classes! 117:1
b. themselves when he did sing 261:5
bring me my b. of burning gold 55:8
if you b. ... b. low 208:26
my throne, bid kings come b. 264:15
says the great bell at B. 192:4
set my b. in the cloud 30:25
two strings to one's b. 229:5
with my b. and arrow 196:2
Bow Bells: within the sound of B. 208:23
Bowed: b. himself with all his might 33:22
I have not ... b. to its idolatries 69:5
Bowels: beseech you, in the b. of Christ 94:7
his b. of compassion 50:11
Bower: Lime-tree B. my prison 87:17
Bowl: crabs hiss in the b. 269:1
fill the flowing b. 14:14
he called for his b. 192:1
inverted b. we call the sky 110:13
love in a golden b. 55:2
Box: worth a guinea a b. 11:10
Boy: a horrid, wicked b. was he 133:9
and to be b. eternal 292:12
being read to by a b. 106:5
b. stood on the burning deck 130:4
b. who lives down the lane 188:4
b. with never a crack in my heart 337:8
boys when I was a b. 28:4
Chatterton, the marvellous b. 334:8
every b. and every gal 117:8
imagination of a b. is healthy 147:7
let the b. win his spurs 105:9
little B. Blue 191:1
my beamish b.! 75:11
said, what a good b. am I 191:2
shades ... close upon the growing b. 332:1
speak roughly to your little b. 74:6
was and a little tiny b. 292:3
Boys: all the little b. and girls 62:6
as flies to wanton b. 266:20
b. and girls come out to play 188:6
b. will be b. 208:27
b. will be men 208:28
by office b. for office b. 237:14
Christian b. I can scarcely ... make 19:13
claret is the liquor for b. 144:15
guns with b., are never valued 94:1
mealy b., and beef-faced b. 98:14
men that were b. when I was 28:4
only know two sorts of b. 98:14
till the b. come home 111:12
we are the b. that fear no noise 123:9
what are little b. made of? 195:6
when the b. came out to play 189:3
young b. ... are level now with men 243:6
Brace: let us ... b. ourselves to our duties 82:14
Braces: damn b. Bless relaxes 57:4
Bradshaw: the vocabulary of B. is nervous 102:6
Brain: b. [begins] to think again 58:15
b. of ... man is not able 256:8
dull b. perplexes and retards 149:16
gladness ... thy b. must know 300:3
glean'd my teeming b. 151:7
got to leave that b. outside 117:9
I feared it might injure the b. 74:3
let my b. lie also 61:13
like madness in the b. 87:7

Brain (continued)
overset thy b. or break the heart 332:12
shallow draughts intoxicate the b. 202:5
written troubles of the b. 272:6
Brains: fluffy, with no b. at all 131:5
he exercises of his b. 117:6
I mix them with my b., sir 196:11
mob has ... heads but no b. 221:8
when the b. were out the man would die 271:8
Brand plucked out of the fire 43:2
Brandy: some are fou o' b. 66:4
to be a hero must drink b. 144:15
Brass: as if this flesh ... were b. impregnable 283:6
asked ... where he carried his b. 28:9
men's evil manners live in b. 262:1
Brave: b. that are no more 93:1
b. who sink to rest 88:10
fortune favours the b. 315:3
is it not passing b. to be a king? 166:9
none but the b. deserves the fair 103:12
O b. new world! 289:7
sons of the prophet were b. 16:15
toll for the b. 93:1
Bravery: all her b. on and tackle trim 180:15
Bravest: the b. by far in the ranks 16:15
Bray: I will be the Vicar of B. 15:13
Brazil, where the nuts come from 315:13
Breach: more honoured in the b. 249:2
once more unto the b. 259:3
Bread: a Loaf of B. beneath the Bough 109:15
bitter b. of banishment 282:12
b. and cheese and kisses 206:31
b. eaten in secret is pleasant 38:7
b. is buttered on both sides 208:29
b. of heaven, feed me 329:2
b. which the Lord hath given 31:28
b. with one fish-ball 156:14
but one halfpenny-worth of b. 255:3
cast thy b. upon the waters 39:24
did eat b. to the full 31:27
God! that b. shd. be so dear 135:4
in the sweat ... shalt thou eat b. 30:13
looked to government for b. 64:16
man doth not live by b. only 32:23
neither yet b. to the wise 39:23
nor his seed begging b. 36:9
not live by b. alone 43:13
some gave them white b. 190:9
thine enemy ... give him b. 38:28
this day our daily b. 43:24
to eat the b. of sorrows 37:20
trees were b. and cheese 14:1
which side one's b. is buttered 218:8
white b. and butter 191:4
Break: never doubted clouds wd. b. 60:12
Breakages Ltd., the biggest ... corporation 295:6
Breakfast: b., dinner, lunch and tea 27:4
b., supper, dinner, luncheon 62:4
hope is a good b. 23:13
kills me ... Scots at a b. 254:12
where shall we our b. take? 11:15
Breaking: sleep that knows not b. 239:9
Breast: bold spirit in a loyal b. 281:8
charms to soothe a savage b. 89:5
earth's sweet flowing b. 153:8
make a clean b. 209:31
nunnery of thy chaste b. 162:6

Breast (*continued*)
  one who ... marched b. forward   60:12
  panic's in thy b. [breastie]   66:10
  safe ... on Abraham's b.   12:6
  Tamer of the human b.   126:16
  that with dauntless b.   126:11
  what his b. forges ... tongue must vent
    246:10
Breasts: cowardice in noble b.   281:10
Breath: allowing him a b., a little scene   283:6
  although thy b. be rude   245:1
  and thou no b. at all ?   268:4
  b. of worldly men   283:2
  draw thy b. in pain   253:9
  fly away, b.   291:6
  not flatter'd its rank b.   69:5
  such dulcet and harmonious b.   276:18
  such is the b. of kings   281:12
  summer's ripening b.   286:11
  take into the air my quiet b.   150:3
  thou b. of Autumn's being   299:3
Breathe: so long as men can b. or eyes can see
    293:15
Breathes: b. ... man, with soul so dead   239:16
  b. upon a bank of violets   290:10
Breathing: rifle all the b. spring   88:8
Breathless: a nun b. with adoration   333:2
  hanging b. on thy fate!   160:11
Bred: where is fancy b.   274:18
Breeches: to wear the b.   230:2
Breed: b. of their horses and dogs   199:7
  fear'd by their b.   282:5
  this happy b. of men, this little world
    282:5
Breeding lilacs out of the dead land   107:3
Breeze: fair b. blew, the white foam flew   86:4
  fluttering and dancing in the b.   331:7
  the battle and the b.   72:10
Breezes: little b. dusk and shiver   313:12
Brent: yr. bonnie brow was b.   66:5
Brethren: b. to dwell together in unity   37:21
  least of these my b.   44:30
Brevis esse laboro, obscurus fio   135:8
Brevity is the soul of wit   249:15
Brewage: no pullet-sperm in my b.   276:7
Brewery: O take me to a b.   15:9
Bribe: doing nothing for a b.   247:3
  too poor for a b.   127:3
Bribes: how many b. he had taken   29:7
Brick: straw to make b.   31:20
Bricks: a cat on hot b.   209:15
Bridal: the b. of the earth and sky   131:12
Bride: b. hath paced into the hall   86:1
  happy bridesmaid ... happy b.   311:7
  Jerusalem ... as a b. adorned   51:2
  sate like a blooming Eastern b.   103:11
  still unravish'd b. of quietness   149:6
  were I thy b.!   121:4
Bridegroom: fresh as a b.   254:1
Bridesmaid: happy b., happy bride   311:7
Bridge: don't cross the b. till you get to it
    210:20
  keep the b. with me   163:11
  on the bridge at midnight   16:12
  on the B. of Sighs   69:6
  what need the b. much broader ?   277:14
  women, and champagne and b.   27:7
Brief: b. life is here our portion   186:13
  b., my lord, as woman's love   252:3
  dress'd in a little b. authority   273:7

Brief (*continued*)
  I struggle to be b., and become obscure
    135:8
  out, out, b. candle!   272:10
Brigands demand ... women require   68:13
Bright: all things b. and beautiful   10:4
  best of dark and b.   71:2
  goddess, excellently b.   145:8
  look, the land is b.   85:3
  moon be still as b.   71:3
  Sun came up ... and he shone b.   85:13
  young lady named B.   63:1
Brightness: all her original b.   176:11
  b. falls from the air   186:12
Brighton: yes, the B. line   327:14
Brilliance: degree of b. ... left to fighter's
    honour   130:7
Brillig: 'twas b. and the slithy toves   75:9
Bring: b. back my Bonnie to me   16:2
  b. me flesh and b. me wine   187:2
  b. me my bow ... arrows ... spear   55:8
  b. the good old bugle, boys   336:9
Bringer: first b. of unwelcome news   256:7
Brioche: qu'ils mangent de la b.   165:6
Britain: B. a fit country for heroes   160:9
  B. is a world by itself   247:1
  B. won her proudest bays   117:10
  government ... framed, like that of B.   317:2
  hath B. all the sun ?   247:5
  that B. would fight on alone   83:4
  when B. first, at Heaven's command
    316:12
British: B. Bourgeoisie ... if it is ill   302:10
  B. Empire ... last for a thousand years
    82:14
  dirty B. coaster   168:14
  I keep my books at the B. Museum   68:4
  liquidation of the B. Empire   83:6
  maxim of the B. ... 'Business as usual'
    82:8
  no spectacle so ridiculous as the B.   164:6
  smell the blood of a B. man   266:17
  tow, ... row, row, for the B. Grenadier
    16:14
Britons: B. never will be slaves   316:12
  B. were only natives   241:8
Broad: she is the B.: I am the High   306:1
Broken: a b. spirit: a b. ... contrite heart   36:15
  laws were made to be b.   187:17
Broken-hearted: half b. to sever for years   71:5
  we had ne'er been b.   65:10
Brood of Folly without father bred   173:5
Brook: a willow grows aslant the b.   253:1
  hear the little b. a-gurgling   120:7
  where the b. is deep   260:8
Brooks: books in the running b.   243:15
  golden sands, and crystal b.   100:17
Broom: new b. sweeps clean   221:37
Broth: gave them ... b. without any bread
    194:5
  too many cooks spoil the b.   228:13
Brother: am I my b.'s keeper ?   30:16
  be my b.; be he ne'er so vile   260:2
  Big B. is watching you   197:3
  Death and his B. Sleep   298:7
  down with Big B.   197:5
  sworn b. ... to grim Necessity   284:4
  two sisters embrace like one b.   234:1
Brotherhood: crown thy good with b.   25:4
Brotherly: let b. love continue   49:23

Brothers: all men will be b. 238:12
and all the b. too 291:8
two b. and their murder'd man 148:12
Brow: b. like to a title-leaf 256:6
on Ida's shady b. 56:13
yr. bonnie b. was brent 66:5
Brown: baked me too b. 75:4
Bruce: Scots whom B. has ... led 67:1
Brüder: alle Menschen werden B. 238:12
Bruise: parmaceti for an inward b. 254:2
Brunck: most learned professor, B. 204:13
Brush: all tarred with the same b. 227:14
Brute beasts that have no understanding
53:19
Brute: et tu, B. ? 71:14, 263:2
Brutish: life ... nasty, b., and short 133:3
Brutus: for B. is an honourable man 263:12
the fault, dear B. 262:8
you too, B. ? 71:14
Bubble: fire burn and cauldron b. 271 :11
like the b. on the fountain 239:10
seeking the b. reputation 244:11
Bubbles: beaded b. winking 149:14
Bucket: nations are as a drop of a b. 41:1
Buckingham Palace: changing the guard at B.
171:6
high-reaching B. grows circumspect 285:5
Buckram: rogues in b. 254:15
Bud: concealment, like a worm i' th' b.
291:7
this b. of love 286:11
Buds: gather the flowers, but spare the b.
168:6
shake the darling b. of May 293:13
Buffets: blows and b. of the world 271:2
Buffoon: a private b. 121:5
statesman and b. 103:4
Bugle: blow, b.; answer, echoes 314:15
bring the good old b., boys 336:9
Bugles: blow out, you b., over the rich Dead
59:1
Build: easier to pull down than to b. 223:35
except the Lord b. the house 37:19
on this rock ... b. my church 44:16
Building: don't clap too hard ... very old b.
197:8
Built: houses are b. to live in 23:3
Rome was not b. in a day 224:27
Bulbul: Abdul the B. Amir 16:15
Bull: b. in a china shop 208:30
in time the savage b. 155:16
red rag to a b. 224:7
roar like a b. 224:23
take the b. by the horns 227:3
Bull and Bush: down at the old B. 317:10
Bullet: ballot is stronger than the b. 159:8
every b. has its billet 328:20
Bullfighting is the only art in which 130:7
Bullocks: good yoke of b. at Stamford
257:6
he ... whose talk is of b. 52:4
Bulls the cow must keep the calf 208:31
Bully: I love the lovely b. 259:9
Bumbast out a blank verse 127:6
Bunbury: a ... permanent invalid called B.
327:8
Bunk: Gert's poems are b. 13:4
history is b. 111:9
Buns: hot cross b.! 189:7
Burden: take up the White Man's B. 155:6

Burdens: bear ye one another's b. 48:22
heavy b. at his narrow gate 258:8
Burglar: enterprising b.'s not a-burgling
120:7
Burglary: flat b. as ever was committed
278:14
Buried: half-b. in the snow was found 160:13
the old Adam ... so b. 53:10
Burlington: I'm B. Bertie 128:12
Burn: better to marry than to b. 48:3
b. ... candle at both ends 208:34
b. one's boats 208:33
b. the midnight oil 208:35
hearts are dry ... b. to the socket 331:4
I'll b. my books! 165:11
old age shd. b. and rave 315:15
violent fires soon b. out 282:4
we all know that books b. 235:5
Burned: bush b. with fire 31:17
Burning: b. indignation no longer lacerates
309:11
my bow of b. gold 55:8
stood on the b. deck 130:4
tiger, tiger, b. bright 56:5
where is. Sappho loved and sung 69:21
Burnt: ash the b. roses leave 106:10
Burr: a kind of b., I shall stick 273:13
Burst: blow your pipe ... till you b. 62:5
his flaw'd heart ... b. smilingly 268:1
she b. while drinking 12:4
the first that ... b. into that ... sea 86:4
Burthen: b. of the mystery 335:11
spirit ... too ... laden ever to b. thine 300:7
Bury: I come to bury C. 263:11
to b. the hatchet 208:36
Bus: a b. bound for Ealing 13:3
Hitler has missed the b. 78:11
I'm not even a b. but a tram 128:11
Bush: beat about the b. 207:5
b. burned with fire 31:17
fear each b. an officer 261:1
four times as big as the b. 158:12
good wine needs no b. 215:24
true that good wine needs no b. 246:4
two in the b. 207:41
Busier: semed b. than he was 79:11
Business: a dinner lubricates b. 240:13
b. before pleasure 208:39
b. is b. 208:38
b. ... may bring money 20:10
b. of consequence, *do it yourself* 24:3
called away by particular b. 301:16
do b. in great waters 37:4
everybody's b. is nobody's b. 212:35
if everybody minded their own b. 74:5
it is the b. of the wealthy man 27:6
love and b. teach eloquence 219:34
men, some to b., some to pleasure 203:15
mind yr. own b. 221:4
servants of b. 22:2
that's the true b. precept 98:6
the end of this day's b. 264:5
the maxim ... is 'B. as usual' 82:8
to b. that we love we rise 243:2
to men's b. and bosoms 21:7
Buss: Miss B. and Miss Beale 14:4
Busy: b. ... hath least to do 208:40
no–wher so b. a man 79:11
Busyness: extreme b. ... deficient vitality
307:8

Child (*continued*)
Heaven-born C. all meanly wrapt　175:8
Jesus Christ her little c.　10:6
Monday's c. is fair of face　191:8
more hideous ... in a c.　265:14
on a cloud I saw a c.　56:7
the cry of a c. by the roadway　337:7
the old Adam in this c.　53:10
this c. I to myself will take　335:9
to have a thankless c.　265:15
train up a c. in the way　38:27
unto us a c. is born　40:23
wise c. ... knows its own father　230:23
wise father ... knows his own c.　274:12
with that the wretched c. expires　27:4
Childhood: companions, in my days of c.
156:9
my careless c. stray'd　125:13
the c. shows the man　180:3
what my lousy c. was like　237:13
Childishness: second c. and mere oblivion
244–5:11
Children: artist will let ... his c. go barefoot
296:5
as c. fear ... the dark　21:9
become as little c.　44:19
c., dear, was it yesterday?　18:12
c. of one family fall out　323:3
c. of this world ... wiser ... c. of light　46:6
c. shd. be seen and not heard　209:21
c.'s teeth are set on edge　41:16
c. sweeten labours　21:18
c. ... with nothing to ignore　186:6
c. yet unborn shall feel this day　284:3
come, c. of our native land　236:11
come, dear c., let us away　18:11
do you hear the c. weeping?　60:7
familiarity breeds ... c.　318:14
father pitieth his c.　36:28
had borne him three c.　138:2
happy ... that is happy in his c.　216:8
he that hath wife and c.　21:19
men ... c. of a larger growth　104:1
more careful of ... dogs than ... c.　199:7
Rachel weeping for her c.　43:9
she had so many c.　194:5
stars ... are my c.　152:6
tale which holdeth c. from play　302:5
voices of c. are heard on the green　56:11
your c. all gone　190:8
Chill: Ah, bitter c. it was　147:12
Chills the finger not a bit　186:9
Chilly: although the room grows c.　124:10
Chime: higher than the sphery c.　173:4
merry village c.　120:7
Chimes: heard the c. at midnight　257:7
Chimney: old men from the c. corner　302:5
Chimney-sweepers: as c., come to dust
247:9
Chin: his c. new reap'd　254:1
his c. upon an orient wave　175:10
China: bull in a c. shop　208:30
C.'s gayest art had dyed　125:9
mistress of herself, though C. fall　203:17
China orange: Lombard Street to a C.　219:23
Chinamen: birds in ... nests agree with C.
27:11
Chink: aid ... from a c. in the floor　310:7
Chip: a c. of the old block　209:22
not merely a c. of the old block　64:9

Chirche-dore: housbondes at c.　79:15
Chivalry: age of c. is gone　64:11
her Beauty and her C.　69:3
Chloe: but C. is my real flame　205:6
Chocolate cream soldier　295:8
Choice: Hobson's c.　216:34
pays yr. money ... takes yr. c.　231:18
small c. in rotten apples　287:7
Choir: sweet singing in the c.　15:8
Choler: purge ... c. without letting blood
281:7
Choleric: in the captain's but a c. word　273:8
Choose: c. life, that ... thy seed may live　33:5
to c. love by another's eyes　276:11
to c. time is to save time　22:19
where to c. their place of rest　179:18
Choosing: subject for ... song ... long c.　179:6
Chop and change　209:26
Chopper: cheap and chippy c.　118:7
here comes a c.　192:4
Chops and Tomata sauce ... Pickwick　99:7
Chortled in his joy　75:11
Chorus: a c.-ending from Euripides　60:13
Chosen: many are called, but few are c.　44:24
Choughs: the crows and c. that wing　267:2
Christ: beseech you, in the bowels of C.　94:7
C. is thy strength ... thy right　183:2
so Judas did to C.　284:1
the C. that is to be　313:7
we ... are one body in C.　47:22
Christ Church: I am the Dean of C., Sir　306:1
Christendom: the wisest fool in C.　130:13
Christian: a C. faithful man　284:15
assume the honourable style of C.　59:12
good C. men, rejoice　186:14
hate him for he is a C.　274:7
if possible ... C. men for C. boys　19:13
in what peace a C. can die　9:12
mirror of all C. kings　258:9
persuadest me to be a C.　47:14
warmed and cooled ... as a C. is　274:17
words ... no C. ear can endure　260:11
Christians: C. awake, salute　68:14
profess and call themselves C.　52:28
Christmas: at C. I no more desire a rose　268:9
C. comes but once a year　209:27, 318:5
C. Day in the Workhouse　302:8
eating a C. pie　191:2
on C. Day in the morning　14:10, 190:4
the first day of C.　194:1
the twelfth day of C.　194:2
Christopher Robin: C. is saying his prayers
172:2
C. went down with Alice　171:6
Chronicle: in the c. of wasted time　294:6
suckle fools and c. small beer　279:8
Chronicles: abstract and brief c.　250:12
look in the c.: we came in　287:5
Church: if at the C. ... give us some ale　56:4
new and great period in His C.　182:7
some to c. repair, ... for ... the music　202:9
the C.'s one foundation　307:13
the C.'s Restoration in 1883　29:11
wish from the C. to stray　56:4
Churches: chapels had been c.　274:6
let yr. women keep silence in the c.　48:9
Churchman: become a c. better than ambition
262:3
Church-yard: if two are in the c. laid　336:6
Churchyards: when c. yawn　252:8

Cloy the hungry edge of appetite 282:1
Clutching the inviolable shade 19:1
Coals: carry c. to Newcastle 209:8
　haul over the c. 216:18
　heap c. of fire 38:28
Coarse: one of them is rather c. 13:11
Coast: the c. is clear 209:36
Coaster: dirty British c. 168:14
Coat: a riband to stick in his c. 61:8
　c. of many colours 31:10
　cut yr. c. according to yr. cloth 210:32
Cock: a C. and a Bull, said Yorick 307:2
　before the c. crow twice 45:17
　C. a doodle doo! 188:7
　c. that crowed in the morn 194:8
Cock Robin: heard the bell toll for poor C.
　196:3
　I killed C. 196:2
Cock-a-hoop: to be c. 209:37
Cock-and-bull story 209:38
Cockles: c. and mussels ... alive O! 15:10
　warm the c. of the heart 229:28
Cockpit: can this c. hold ... fields of France?
　258:6
Cocks: drench'd our steeples, drown'd the c.
　266:6
Cocksure ... as Tom Macaulay 169:11
Cod: home of the bean and the c. 57:10
Coeur: le c. a ses raisons 198:8
Coffee: c. which makes the politicians wise
　204:10
　if this is c., I want tea 232:5
Cogito ergo sum 97:7
Coil: shuffled off this mortal c. 250–1:20
Coin: beauty is nature's c. 173:2
　pay ... in his own c. 222:37
Cold: caught an everlasting c. 324:5
　c. comfort 210:1
　comfort like c. porridge 288:3
　I beg c. comfort 265:3
　pale grew thy cheek and c. 71:5
　poor Tom's a-c. 147:15
　seedtime ... harvest ... c. and heat 30:23
　slept among his ashes c. 147:15
　'tis bitter c. and I am sick at heart 247:13
　to lie in c. obstruction 273:10
　to shelter me from the c. 28:3
　we called a c. a c. 28:6
　who thicks man's blood with c. 86:8
Colder thy kiss 71:5
Coliseum: when falls the C. 69:8
　while stands the C. 69:8
College: I am Master of this C. 26:6
Colossus: bestride the ... world like a C.
　262:8
Colour: a c. of its own on the map 319:9
　purest ... minds ... love c. the most 237:4
Coloured: see the c. counties 136:6
　worser spirit a woman c. ill 294:16
Colours: all c. will agree in the dark 21:11
　coat of many c. 31:10
　truth fears no c. 228:24
Column: urn throws up a steamy c. 93:10
Columns: enormous fluted Ionic c. 165:1
Combine: love and marriage rarely can c.
　69:18
Come: but will they c. when you do call?
　255:5
　c., and trip it as you go 173:17
　c. back, Peter! C. back, Paul! 195:5

Come (*continued*)
　c., c. and have a drink 317:10
　c., c. and make eyes at me 317:11
　c., c., give me yr. nand 272:4
　c. forth into the light of things 335:6
　c. he slow or c. he fast 240:4
　c., Helen, give me my soul 165:8
　c. here often? ... in the mating season
　170:16
　c. into the garden, Maud 314:3
　c., knit hands 172:16
　c., landlord, fill the flowing bowl 14:14
　c., lasses and lads 14:15
　c., let's away to prison 267:13
　c., my coach! 252:20
　c. not, Lucifer! 165:11
　c. up and see me sometime 325:5
　easy c., easy go 212:12
　lightly c., lightly go 219:10
　nothing of itself will c. 331:5
　O c., all ye faithful ... c. ye 196:5
　rise up, my love ... c. away 40:7
　suffer me to c. to thee 325:1
　the cry is still 'They c.' 272:8
　thou'lt c. no more 268:4
　will ye no c. back again? 185:8
Comedies: all c. are ended by a marriage 69:19
Comedy: most Lamentable C. ... of Pyramus
　276:13
　world is a c. to those who think 322:7
Comes: c. from the heart, goes to the heart
　88:5
　c. silent, flooding in, the main 85:2
　here she c. ... full sail ... fan spread 89:10
　knowledge c. but wisdom lingers 313:18
　nobody c., nobody goes 25:11
　repentance c. too late 224:12
　tomorrow never c. 228:6
　when daylight c., c. in the light 85:3
Cometh: behold, this dreamer c. 31:11
Comfort: cold c. 210:1
　c. in the strength of love 332:12
　c. me with apples 40:6
　c.'s a cripple and comes ... slow 102:10
　from ignorance our c. flows 205:7
　here's my c. 288:8
　I beg cold c. 265:3
　no c. to one not sociable 247:6
　of c., no man speak 283:5
　receives c. like cold porridge 288:3
　this must my c. be 281:11
　to warm, to c., and command 334:14
　two loves ... of c. and despair 294:16
Comfortably: liv'd c. so long together 115:5
Comforters: miserable c. are ye all 35:6
Comforts: not without c. and hopes 21:14
Comical: I often think it's c. 117:8
Coming: Campbells are c. 14:13
　c. through the rye 65:15
　I'm c., I'm c. 112:11
　she is c., my dove, my dear 314:4
　their going ... even as their c. 267:12
　thy going out and thy c. in 37:17
Command: less used to sue than to c. 239:8
　man to c. and woman to obey 314:18
　not born to sue but to c. 281:9
　not in mortals to c. success 9:4
　to warm, to comfort, and c. 334:14
Commanded: nature, to be c., must be obeyed
　23:17

Commandment: laws of England are at my c. 258:2

Commandments: aren't no Ten C. 155:2
fear God, and keep his c. 40:1

Commencement de la fin 310:10

Commend: all our swains c. her 292:8
easier to ridicule than c. 224:20

Commended: who c. thy yellow stockings 291:10

Comment is free but facts are sacred 238:15

Commerce: honour sinks where c. ... prevails 123:15

Commit: c. his body to the ground 53:30
pretty follies that themselves c. 274:14

Committed: they have c. false report 278:18

Commodity, the bias of the world 264:13

Common: earth and every c. sight 331:12
fade into the light of c. day 332:2
have a good thing to make it too c. 256:10
more c. where the climate's sultry 69:10
nothing c. did or mean 168:4

Common-place: his c. book be full 309:7

Commonwealth: caterpillars of the c. 282:10
if the ... C. last for a thousand years 82:14
i' th' c. I wd. ... execute 288:4
The Empire is a C. of Nations 235:12

Communicated: good, the more c., more abundant 178:13

Communist: a c.? One who has yearnings 107:18

Community: no finer investment for any c. 83:9
part of the c. of Europe 121:10

Commuter—one who spends his life 325:8

Compact: of imagination all c. 277:5

Companions: I have had c. 156:9
lovely c. are faded and gone 184:1
wives ... c. for middle age 21:20

Company: better ... alone than in bad c. 207:20
c. makes the feast 210:4
c., villainous c. 255:12
crowd is not c. 210:21
crowds without c. 116:2
his little daughter, to bear him c. 161:12
in married life three is c. 327:10
in such a jocund c. 331:10
known by the c. he keeps 220:18
qualified to shine in c. 309:9
take the tone of the c. 80:11
tell me what c. thou keepest 78:6
two is c., three is none 229:2
withouten other c. in youthe 79:15

Compare: belied with false c. 294:14
c. thee to a summer's day? 293:13
how I may c. this prison 284:6

Comparisons: c. are odious 210:5
c. are odorous 278:8

Compassion: shutteth up his bowels of c. 50:11
thou art all c. 325:3

Compassions: his c. fail not ... new every morning 41:19

Competition: tradition approves all forms of c. 84:17

Complain: moping owl ... to the moon c. 126:5
sluggard, I heard him c. 323:7

Complaining: woods have no voice but ... c. 184:10

Complete: let ... death c. the same 62:10

Complexion: his c. is perfect gallows 287:13
that schoolgirl c. 11:6
whose fresh c. and whose heart 293:5

Complies against his will 68:1

Comprehended: our watch ... have indeed c. 278:10

Compromise: All ... founded on c. and barter 64:7

Comrades, leave me here a little 313:14

Conceal: cleverness is to c. one's cleverness 234:8
knowing anything, shd. c. it 20:15
use ... words ... to c. ... thoughts 321:12

Concealment, like a worm i' th' bud 291:7

Conceit: infusing him with self and vain c. 283:6

Conceits: wise in yr. own c. 47:25

Concentrates: it c. his mind wonderfully 144:8

Concessions of the weak, ... c. of fear 64:4

Conclusions: life ... art of drawing ... c. 68:6

Condemn: age shall not weary ... years c. 54:5
travellers ... fools at home c. 'em 288:14

Condemned: much c. to have an itching palm 263:22

Condemns: Johnson c. whatever he disapproves 65:6

Condescend: your men of wit will c. 308:12

Condition: the c. of man ... c. of war 133:2

Conditions: stars above us, govern our c. 267:1

Cones: eat the c. under his pines 113:13

Conference [maketh] a ready man 23:8

Confession is good for the soul 210:6

Confidence: we shall fight with growing c. 82:13

Confident: never glad c. morning again 61:9

Conflict: never in the field of human c. 82:15
too weak the c. to support 268:1

Confound: Lord did ... c. the language 30:27

Confusion: all else, c. 314:18
c. to his enemies 15:6
levee from a couch in some c. 89:15

Congregation: latter has the largest c. 96:9

Conjecture: now entertain c. of a time 259:8
we c. ... animal or ... god 308:14

Conjunction: is the c. of the mind 167:17

Conquer: England ... wont to c. others 282:6
we'll c. again and again 115:1

Conquered: I came, I saw, I c. 71:13
nation ... perpetually to be c. 64:5

Conquering: see the c. hero comes 184:6
so sharp the c. 80:4
went forth c., and to conquer 50:21

Conqueror: came in with Richard C. 287:5
lie at the proud foot of a c. 265:4

Conquers: love c. all and we too succumb 321:5

Conquest: a shameful c. of itself 282:6
peace is of the nature of a c. 257:12

Conquests: all thy c., glories, triumphs, spoils 263:5

Conscience: a still and quiet c. 261:11
argue freely according to c. 182:9
catch the c. of the king 250:19
c. does make cowards of us all 250–1:20
my c. hath a thousand ... tongues 285:15

Consciousness: this growth of national c. 164:13

Covet: thou shalt not c.; but tradition 84:17

Coveting: pleasure ... is lost by c. 223:14

Cow: couple-colour as a brindled c. 135:7
 c. jumped over the moon 189:5
 c.'s in the corn 191:1
 c. with the crumpled horn 194–5:8
 I never saw a Purple C. 64:1
 I wrote the 'Purple C.' 64:2
 three acres and a c. 88:6

Coward: bully is always a c. 208:32
 c. does it with a kiss 326:12
 gross flattery to name a c. 317:12
 no c. soul is mine 58:12

Cowardice: pale cold c. in noble breasts 281:10

Cowards: a plague of all c. 254:13
 conscience does make c. of us all 250–1:20
 c. die many times before ... deaths 262:15
 it [public] is the greatest of c. 129:12
 though c. flinch, and traitors jeer 90:3

Cowslip: in a c.'s bell I lie 289:6

Coy: be not c. but use yr. time 132:8

Coyness: this c., lady, were no crime 167:11

Crabs: roasted c. hiss in the bowl 269:1

Crack: stretch out to th' c. of doom? 271:17
 that heaven's vault shd. c. 268:2
 winds ... c. yr. cheeks 266:6

Cracked: it c. and growled and roared 86:2

Crackling of thorns under a pot 39:19

Cracks: now c. a noble heart 253:11

Cradle: the c. will rock 189:10

Cradles: bit the babies in the c. 61:17

Craft: c. so long to lerne 80:4
 gentlemen of the gentle c. 96:12

Cramp: when I heard she'd died of c. 124:9

Cravat: the one [robin] in red c. 99:18

Crawling: whereunder c. coop't we live 110:13

Crazy: checkin' the c. ones 125:5
 I'm half c. 95:4

Creak of a lumbering cart 337:7

Cream: choking her with c. 154:7
 visages do c. and mantle 274:2

Created: about ... to be c. like to us 177:4
 c. man in his own image 30:3
 God c. the heaven 30:1

Creation: O fairest of c. 179:10
 our c., preservation 53:1
 she is His new c. 307:13
 to which the whole c. moves 313:9

Creature: God's first c., which was light 23:15
 lone lorn c. 97:13
 she is an excellent c., but 100:14
 though the most beautiful C. ... waiting 152:6
 wine is a good familiar c. 279:11

Creatures: all c. great and small 10:4
 call these delicate c. ours 293:17
 from fairest c. we desire 293:10
 the meanest of his c. 61:14
 true hope ... makes ... meaner c. kings 285:12

Credit: citizen of c. and renown 92:6
 my c. in men's eyes 110:15
 stories ... not to thy c. 72:4
 to his c. ... is an Englishman! 120:2

Creditors have better memories 210:17

Creed: a modest c. and yet 299:15

Creeds: honest doubt ... than in half the c. 313:1
 so many gods, so many c. 326:11

Creeds (*continued*)
 vain are the thousand c. 58:13

Creeks: far back through c. and inlets 85:2

Creep: let the sounds of music c. 275:8

Creeping like snail ... to school 244:11

Creeps: when the blood c. ... nerves prick 312:14

Crew: Mirth, admit me of thy c. 174:1
 we were a ghastly c. 86:14

Cricket: c.—a sport at which the contenders 140:5
 merry as a c. 221:2
 save the c. on the hearth 173:9
 to where the c. sings 337:5

Crime: atrocious c. of being ... young 200:6
 bigamy, sir, is a c.! 183:1
 cut-throat isn't occupied in c. 120:7
 for my wilful c. art banished 179:17
 in heaven, a c. to love too well? 201:6
 no c.'s so great as ... to excel 82:2
 nor any c. so shameful as poverty 109:3
 the Napoleon of c. 101:16
 the punishment fit the c. 118:10
 this coyness, lady, were no c. 167:11
 treason was no c. 103:7

Crimes: c., follies and misfortunes of mankind 116:3
 history of the great events ... history of c. 321:15
 l'histoire des c. 321:15
 liberté, que de c. ... en ton nom 234:16
 liberty, what c. ... in yr. name 234:16

Crimson in thy lips and in thy cheeks 287:3

Cripple: comfort's a c. 102:10

Crispian: this day is call'd the feast of Crispian 259:15

Crispin's: this day is call'd the feast of Crispin

Critic: first attribute of a good c. 162:16
 scorn not the sonnet; C., you have frowned 333:5

Critical: I am nothing if not c. 279:7

Criticism: ask ... for c. ... only want praise 169:4
 my own definition of c. 19:8

Criticisms: animals ... pass no c. 105:16

Critics: before you trust in c. 70:14
 c. all are ready made 70:13

Crocodile: c. tears 210:18
 how doth the little c. 73:17

Cromek: O! Mr. C., how do ye do? 56:1

Cromwell: restless C. cd. not cease 168:3
 ruins that C. knocked about 160:6
 see C., damned to everlasting fame 203:9
 some C. guiltless 126:11

Crooked: c. by nature is never ... straight 210:19
 straight trees have c. roots 226:28
 strive to set the c. straight? 184:9
 there was a c. man 194:3

Crop: a-watering the last year's c. 105:14

Cross: a little marble c. below the town 129:6
 blind as the ... nails upon the C. 302:9
 c. the bridge ... get to it 210:20
 e'en though it be a c. 9:3
 for our advantage on the bitter c. 253:14
 one more river to c. 14:9
 with the C. of Jesus 24:9

Cross-bow: with my c. I shot the albatross 86:3

Crosses: between the c., row on row 164:8

Cross-gartered: wished to see thee ever c. 291:10

Crow: there is an upstart c. 127:6
Crowd: all at once I saw a c. 331:7
  c. is not company 210:21
  madding c.'s ignoble strife 126:12
  out of the c. a mistress or a friend 298:8
  trees ... c. into a shade 204:4
Crowded: feast, and yr. halls are c. 326:10
Crowds without company 116:2
Crowed: cock that c. in the morn 194:8
Crown: all thy faithful mercies c. 325:3
  c. thy good with brotherhood 25:4
  fighting for the c. 190:9
  I give away my c. 284:2
  I will give thee a c. of life 50:16
  if you c. him, let me prophesy 283:8
  let us c. ourselves with rosebuds 51:10
  not the king's c. ... deputed sword 273:4
  sweet fruition of an earthly c. 166:10
  the holly bears the c. 15:8
  this I count the glory of my c. 107:14
  throned monarch better than his c. 275:1
  uneasy ... head that wears a c. 257:3
  virtuous woman ... c. to her husband 38:12
  within the ... c. ... keeps Death his court 283:6
Crowns: evening c. the day 212:29
  give c. and pounds and guineas 136:5
  who c. ... a youth of labour 122:7
Crows: the c. and choughs that wing 267:2
Crucified: c. 'twixt a smile and a whimper 299:10
  the dear Lord was c. 10:7
Crucify him 45:18
Cruel: I must be c. only to be kind 252:15
  let me be c., not unnatural 252:9
  more c. the pen is than the sword 67:9
Cruelly: I am c. used 21:2
Cruelty: farewell, fair c. 290:16
  O c., to steal my Basil-pot 148:13
Crumb: a memorial c. 99:18
  who craved no c. 121:2
Crumbs ... from the rich man's table 46:8
Cruse: neither shall the c. of oil fail 34:18
Crustimoney Proseedcake: what does C. mean? 172:4
Cry: c. for the moon 210:22
  c. 'Havoc!' 263:8
  c. not when his father dies 140:17
  c. out 'Olivia!' 290:15
  c. woe, destruction, ruin 283:4
  c. 'Wolf' 210:23
  did they not sometime c. 'All hail'? 284:1
  kissed the girls and made them c. 189:3
  need a body c.? 65:15
  the c. is still 'They come' 272:8
Crying over spilt milk 210:24
Cuckoo: but as the c. is in June 255:10
  c., c.—O word of fear 268–9:17
  lhude sing c. 14:7
  O C., shall I call thee bird? 336:2
  the c. then on every tree 268–9:17
  the weather the c. likes 128:10
Cuckoo-buds of yellow hue 268:17
Cue: my c. is villainous melancholy 265:11
  with a twisted c. 118:12
Cultivate: we must c. our garden 321:11
Cultiver: il faut c. notre jardin 321:11
Culture, the acquainting ourselves with the best 19:11
Cunning: my right hand forget her c. 37:26

Cup: ah, fill the C. 110:7
  C. that clears TO-DAY of past Regrets 110:2
  kiss but in the c. 145:7
  'twixt the c. and the lip 227:24
  we'll tak' a c. o' kindness 65:13
Cupboard: c. love 210:25
  Mother Hubbard went to the c. 192:2
Cupid: C. and my Campaspe 163:3
  C. painted blind 276:12
  C.'s darts do not feel 14:4
Cups that cheer but not inebriate 93:10
Curate: like the C.'s egg 210:26
Curb: you might c. yr. magnanimity 152:12
Curds: eating her c. and whey 191:3
Cure: past c., past care 222:34
  prevention is better than c. 223:26
  there is no c. for this disease 27:3
Cured: can't be c. must be endured 230:7
Curfew tolls the knell of parting day 126:3
Curiosity: newspapers always excite c. 156:8
Curious: that was the c. incident 102:1
  'Curiouser and c.!' cried Alice 73:16
Curled: he ... c. up on the floor 129:3
Curls: rosy cheeks and flaxen c. 62:6
Curly locks, c. 188:8
Current: take the c. when it serves 264:3
Currents: their c. turn awry 250–1:20
Curs: mongrels, spaniels, c. 271:1
Curse: I know how to c. 287:19
  O c. of marriage 279:17
  the c. is come upon me! 313:13
  work ... c. of the drinking classes 328:18
Curses are like chickens 210:27
Cursing: fall a-c. like a very drab 250:18
Curst be the verse 201:18
Curtain: ring down the c., the farce is over 232:8
Curtained with cloudy red 175:10
Curtains: let fall the c., wheel the sofa 93:10
Curve: dear red c. of her lips 168:12
Custodiet: quis c. ipsos custodes? 146:9
Custom: a c. loathsome ... hateful ... harmful 138:14
  c. calls me to't 246:8
  c. without reason ... ancient error 210:28
  what c. wills ... shd. we do 246:8
Customary: said Owl, the c. procedure 172:4
Customers: a people of c. 303:4
Customs: the c., politics, and tongue 198:12
Cut: c. is the branch that might have grown 166:1
  c. it without a knife? 191:4
  easy ... of a c. loaf to steal 289:13
  most unkindest c. of all 263:18
  the flash c. him 11:18
Cuts: he that c. off twenty years 263:3
  tongue is not steel yet it c. 228:9
Cut-throat: call me misbeliever, c. dog 274:10
Cutting all the pictures out 26:14
Cynara: faithful to thee, C.! 101:11
Cynic: what is a c.? 328:4
Cynicism is intellectual dandyism 169:15
Cypress: in sad c. let me be laid 291:6

D: never use a big, big D. 119:12
Dads: get leave of yr. d. 14:15
Daffodils: a host of golden d. 331:7
  fair d., we weep to see 132:1
  when d. begin to peer 292:17

Dead (*continued*)

concerning the d. [say] ... good   210:37
courage ... the devil is d.   233:4
d.! and never called me mother!   330:7
d. as a door-nail   210:38
d. for a ducat, d.!   252:12
dew on the face of the d.   26:10
doctors found when she was d.   122:17
down among the d. men   105:7
faith without works is d.   49:25
great deal to be said for being d.   29:4
healthy and wealthy and d.   317:6
it struck him d.: and serve him right   27:6
just as d. as if he'd been wrong   12:8
little fairy ... falls down d.   24:12
my days among the d.   304:10
nearly all our best men are d.!   232:3
need charity more than the d.   18:8
on stepping-stones of their d. selves   312:11
Queen Anne is d.   223:39
say I'm sick, I'm d.   201:10
something ... d. in each of us   326:13
soul is d. that slumbers   160:14
that d. men rise up never   310:1
the law hath not been d.   273:5
the noble D.   334:6
'tis Death is d., not he   297:17
to see a d. Indian   288:6
two worlds, one d.   18:15
view halloo wd. awaken the d.   125:6
wake, for night is d.   310:5
we might as well be d.   324:18
weep for Adonais, he is d.   297:9
when I am d. and opened   168:11
when I am d., my dearest   236:4
Deadener: habit is a great d.   26:2
Deadlock: Holy D.   131:8
Deadly: soap ... more d. in the long run   318:11
Deaf: d. as a post   211:3
none so d. as those who won't hear   211:4
Deafness: your tale ... wd. cure d.   287:16
Deal: a new d. for the American people   234:17
d. with none but honest men   224:13
good enough to be given a square d.   235:9
Dean: I am the D. of Christ Church   306:1
queer old D.   305:20
Deans: with ... dowagers for d.   314:12
Dear: a man ... to all the country d.   122:9
beauty ... for earth too d.   286:3
d. to me as light and life   66:3
God! that bread shd. be so d.!   135:4
Plato is d. to me   18:7
the d. God who loveth us   87:4
Dearie: flew o'er me and my d.   66:3
Deario: its cheerio my d.   167:2
Death: a rendezvous with D.   240:15
a sunset-touch, a fancy ... some one's d.   60:13
after the first d. ... no other   316:11
all in the valley of D.   311:9
all tragedies are finished by a d.   69:19
and d. complete the same   62:10
and d. shall have no dominion   315:14
and now to d. devote   179:10
Angel of D. has been abroad   58:8
any man's d. diminishes me   101:8
as one that had been studied in his d.   269:11

Death (*continued*)

be thou faithful unto d.   50:16
because I cd. not stop for D.   99:17
birth, and copulation, and d.   107:2
brood over ... the hour of my d.   152:8
come away, d.   291:6
day of d. [is better]   39:18
d. after life does greatly please   305:11
d., as the Psalmist saith, is certain   257:6
d., be not proud   101:4
d. devours lambs as well   211:5
d. for his ambition   263:10
d. hath no more dominion   47:17
d. is an ende of every ... sore   79:21
d. is the grand leveller   211:6
d. ... like all the rest, a mockery   299:15
d. of each day's life   270:11
d. pays all debts   211:7
d.'s pale flag is not advanced   287:3
D., whene'er he call ... too soon   120: 17
die not, poor d.   101:4
die the d. of the righteous   32:20
disappointed by that stroke of d.   145:1
dread of something after d.   250–1:20
every door ... shut but d.'s door   211:32
fear and danger of violent d.   133:3
for love, and beauty ... no d.   299:16
give me liberty or give me d.   131:4
half in love with easeful D.   150:3
happy ... were my ensuing d.   282:6
his d., which happened in his berth   134:13
how wonderful ... D. and ... Sleep!   298:7
I have set before you life and d.   33:5
I here importune d. awhile   243:5
I will not be afraid of d. and bane   272:7
I'll ... condemn you to d.   74:1
if ought but d. part   33:26
in nativity, chance, or d.   276:8
in that sleep of d. what dreams ?   250–1:20
in the hour of d.   52:25
in the ranks of d.   184:2
in their d. ... not divided   34:11
into the jaws of D.   311:12
it is but D. who comes at last   240:4
judge none blessed before his d.   51:21
keep a league till d.   284:4
love is strong as d.   40:14
men fear d., as children ... dark   21:9
midst of life we are in d.   53:29
most cruel d. of Pyramus   276:13
my part of d. no one so true   291:6
never taste of d. but once   262:15
no one till his d. ... unhappy   60:5
nothing is certain but d. and taxes   113:3
O D., where is thy sting ?   48:13, 201:4
pale D. with impartial foot   135:12
pale horse ... that sat on him was D.   50:22
paradise to what we fear of d.   273:11
precious ... the d. of his saints   37:11
rashly importunate, gone to her d.   134:10
remedy for all ... but d.   224:11
reports of my d. ... exaggerated   319:4
sad stories of the d. of kings   283:6
so many years of fearing d.   263:3
the way to dusty d.   272:10
there is d. in the pot   34:24
there shall be no more d.   51:3
thou wast not born for d.   150:4
through envy of the devil came d.   51:11
till d. us do part   53:22

Death (*continued*)
  'tis D. is dead, not he   297:17
  useless life is an early d.   122:2
  valley of the shadow of d.   35:29
  vasty Hall of D.   18:17
  wages of sin is d.   47:18
  we owe God a d.   257:8
  Webster ... much possessed by d.   107:6
  what sights of ugly d.   285:1
  when d. to either shall come   58:7
  where is d.'s sting ?   163:7
  whose mortal taste brought d.   175:15
  within the hollow crown keeps D. his court 283:6
  worst is d. and d. will have his day   283:4
  wd. fain die a dry d.   287:14
Deaths: cowards die many times before ... d.   262:15
  more d. than one must die   326:14
Debate: Rupert of D.   63:2
Debonair: so buxom, blithe and d.   173:15
Debt: contrived a double d. to pay   122:13
  d. is the worst poverty   211:8
  the d. which cancels all others   89:1
Debts: and forgive us our d.   43:24
  death pays all d.   211:7
  he that dies pays all d.   288:12
  speak not of my d. unless   226:5
Decay: be sincere ... argues a d.   89:9
  d. of that colossal wreck   299:8
  energies of our system will d.   23:23
  fretted the ... body to d.   102:17
  this muddy vesture of d.   275:8
  wealth accumulates, and men d.   122:5
Deceased: he first d.; she for a little tried   336:12
Deceive: Oh, don't d. me   15:1
  to d. oneself is very easy   211:10
  when first we practise to d.   240:8
Deceived: by bad women been d.   180:12
  d. her father, and may thee   279:5
Deceivers: men were d. ever   277:21
Deceives me once ... d. me twice   211:9
December: as soon seek roses in D.   70:14
  D. when they are wed   245:13
  wallow naked in D. snow   282:1
Decent: d. godless people   107:1
  d. means poor   199:3
Decently: things done d. and in order   48:10
Deck: boy stood on the burning d.   130:4
Declare: nothing to d. except my genius   328:16
Decoration: deserves some sort of d.   197:11
Decoyed into our condition   199:10
Decreed: soul has to itself d.   150:10
Dee: lived on the river D.   54:1
Deed: a d. without a name   271:14
  a good d. in a naughty world   275:11
  if one good d. ... I did   289:14
  now the matchless d.'s achieved   303:1
  so I may do the d. ... my soul ... decreed   150:10 :
Deeds: d. are males, and words are females   211:11
  means to do ill d. ... d. ill done   265:2
  these unlucky d. relate   280:14
  turn sourest by their d.   294:3
Deep: call spirits from the vasty d.   255:5
  d. and crisp and even   187:1
  in the lowest d., a lower d.   177:13

Deep (*continued*)
  thoughts ... too d. for tears   332:6
  two voices ... one is of the d.   306:9
  very singularly d. young man   119:4
Deeper than did ever plummet sound   289:5
Deer: in the Highlands, a-chasing the d.   66:14
  the running of the d.   15:8
Defaced, deflowered   179:10
Defamed by every charlatan   313:8
Defeat: in D.: Defiance   83:13
  the problems of victory ... of d.   83:8
Defect: chief d. of Henry King   27:2
Defence or apology before ... accused   78:13
Defend: d. ... yr. right to say it   321:18
  from my enemies ... d. myself   215:3
  they [newspapers] never d. anyone   169:12
  we shall d. our island   82:13
Defender: I mean the Faith's D.   68:15
Defiance: in Defeat: D.   83:13
Defied: age will not be d.   22:23
Definition: true d. of a style   309:2
Definitions: homely d. of prose and poetry   88:3
Deflowered: defaced, d.   179:10
Deformed, unfinish'd, sent before my time   284:10
Degree: a d. of delight ... in ... misfortunes   65:1
  O, when d. is shak'd   290:2
  observe d., priority and place   290:1
  people ... a d. or two lower   20:6
  take but d. away   290:3
Degrees: did ever heal but by d. ?   279:12
  we boil at different d.   108:20
Delay: in d. ... lies no plenty   291:2
  in me is no d.   179:17
Delayed till ... I cannot enjoy ... impart it   142:1
Delays are dangerous   211:13
Deliberate: where both d., the love is slight   166:15
Deliberates: woman that d.   9:5
Deliberation: deep on his front engraven d. sat   177:3
Delicate: we can call these d. creatures ours   279:17
Delicately: Agag came ... d.   34:4
Delight: a Phantom of d.   334:12
  d. ... in ... misfortunes ... of others   65:1
  d. ... ornament ... ability   23:5
  energy is eternal d.   56:16
  go to't with d.   243:2
  I sing this song for your d.   76:11
  my d. on a shining night   16:6
  paint the meadows with d.   268:17
  rarely comest ... Spirit of D.   300:4
  sounds ... give d. and hurt not   288:13
  unrest which men miscall d.   297:16
Delights: man d. not me   250:6
  scorn d. and live laborious days   175:1
  these d. if thou canst give   174:11
Deliver: d. me from myself   60:2
  from ... ghosties ... beasties ... d. us   13:7
Delos: where D. rose   69–70:21
Deluge: after us, the d.   201:1
Déluge: après nous le d.   201:1
Delusion: a d., a mockery, and a snare   97:4
Delved: when Adam d.   24:2
Dementat: quos Deus vult perdere ... d.   223:40

de Mille: Cecil B. d. ... was persuaded   29:8
Democracy: d. resumed her reign   27:7
  two cheers for D.   112:2
  world ... made safe for d.   329:9
Democratic Party is like a mule   101:9
Demon-lover: wailing for her d.   87:12
Den: ye have made it a d. of thieves   45:14
Denmark: something is rotten in the state of
  D.   249:5
Denouncing someone or something else   169:12
Deny: he that will this health d.   105:7
  those who d. freedom to others   159:9
  thou shalt d. me thrice   45:17
Departed: minds me o' d. joys   67:6
Depends: it all d. what you mean by
  139:19
Depth in philosophy bringeth ... to religion
  22:11
Deputy elected by the Lord   283:2
Derangement: a nice d. of epitaphs   301:10
Descent and fall to us is adverse   176:17
Descriptions of the fairest wights   294:6
Desert: in this d. inaccessible   244:10
  legs of stone stand in the d.   299:7
  nothing ... unrewarded but d.   103:5
  rats d. a sinking ship   224:5
  use every man after his d.   250:13
  waste its sweetness on the d. air   126:10
Deserts: d. of vast eternity   167:13
  moon when she d. the night   180:11
Deserve: d. not [freedom] for themselves
  159:9
  Sempronius, we'll d. it   9:4
  wd. d. better of mankind   309:1
Deserves: has the government it d.   165:3
Designs: close d. and crooked counsels
  102:16
Desire: d. of the moth for the star   300:8
  d. shd. so ... outlive performance ?   256:19
  few things to d.   22:14
  from what I've tasted of d.   113:12
  provokes the d. ... takes away the performance   270:14
  she is the antidote to d.   90:2
  some d. is necessary   141:4
  universal ... d. ... to live beyond ... income
  68:7
  where our d. is got without content   271:3
Desired: more to be d. ... than gold   35:24
Desires: he who d. but acts not   57:2
Desolation: create. and call it peace   310:8
Despair: a heaven in hell's d.   56:2
  begotten by D. upon Impossibility   167:16
  hope is as cheap as d.   217:4
  look on my works ... and d.   299:8
  loves ... of comfort and d.   294:16
  owner whereof was Giant D.   63:11
  shall I, wasting in d.   329:11
  some divine d.   314:16
  what resolution from d.   176:3
  where Seraphs might d.   68:18
Despairs: leaden-eyed d.   149:15
Desperate: diseases d. grown   252:16
Desperation: lives of quiet d.   316:15
Despise ... as I d. Shakespeare   297:8
Despised: d. and rejected of men   41:5
  enjoy'd no sooner but d.   294:11
Despond: name of the slough was D.   63:7
Destiny: d. with Men for Pieces plays   110:11
  hanging and wiving goes by d.   274:15

Destiny (*continued*)
  homely joys and d. obscure   126:7
Destroy: doth the wingèd life d.   55:4
  I sought to d. institutions   325:10
  'tis safer to be that which we d.   271:3
  whom God wishes to d.   223:40
Destroyer and preserver; hear, oh, hear!
  299:4
Destruction: by d. dwell in doubtful joy
  271:3
  d. that wasteth at noonday   36:27
  pride goeth before d.   38:19
Detail: our life is frittered away by d.   317:1
Determined, dared and done!   303:1
Detest: but they d. at leisure   70:7
Detraction will not suffer it   255:21
Deutschland über alles   133:7
Device: banner with the strange d.   160:12
  miracle of rare d.   87:15
Devil: abashed the D. stood   178:10
  better the d. you know   207:35
  between the d. and the deep sea   211:17
  black as the d.   208:5, 310:11
  courage ... the d. is dead   233:4
  d. ... builds a chapel   96:9
  d. can cite Scripture   274:8
  d., having nothing else to do   27:8
  d. is not so black   211:18
  d. shd. have all the good tunes   132:12
  d.'s walking parody   81:2
  d. take the hindmost   211:19
  d. was sick ... a monk wd. be   185:1
  d. was well ... a monk he'd be   185:1
  d. whoops, as he whooped   154:12
  drink and the d. had done for   307:4
  every man ... god or d.   103:5
  first Whig was the D.   144:12
  give the d. his due   214:33
  he ... that sups with the d.   219:25
  heaviest stone ... d. can throw   129:14
  hold a candle to the d.   216:36
  needs must when the d. drives   221:28
  renounce the d. ... his works   53:11
  resist the d. and he will flee   50:2
  saint when most I play the d.   284:14
  shame the d.   227:20
  talk of the d. ... sure to appear   227:10
  the D., howling Ho!   306:2
  the world, the flesh, and the d.   52:24
  through envy of the d. came death   51:11
  who cleft the d.'s foot   101:5
  young saint, old d.   231:9
  your adversary the d., as a roaring lion
  50:8
Devils: prosperity has damned more ... than
  ... d.   223:31
Devoir: faites votre d. et laissez faire aux dieux
  90:15
Devon, glorious D.   57:11
Dévot: pour être d. ... pas moins homme!
  182:15
Devotion: dollar ... object of universal d.
  138:13
  the d. to something afar   300:8
Devour: threat'ning to d. me opens wide
  177:13
Devout: d. but ... human   182:15
  miserable, but not ... d.   141:7
Dew: d. on the face of the dead   26:10
  foggy, foggy d.   16:4

Dew (*continued*)
hill-side's d.-pearled 62:7
like the d. on the mountain 239:10
resolve itself into a d. 248:2
walks o'er the d. of yon ... hill 247:16
Dew-drop: fragile d. on its perilous way 150:9
Diable: courage ... le d. est mort 233:4
noir comme le d. 310:11
Dials: carve out d. quaintly 260:13
Diamond: d. and safire bracelet lasts 162:1
like a d. in the sky 311:5
Diana of the Ephesians 47:7
Diary: I never travel without my d. 327:16
memory ... is the d. 327:15
Dick the shepherd blows his nail 269:1
Dickens: what the d. his name is 276:5
Dictate: not presume to d., but broiled fowl 98:17
Dictator: the German d., instead of snatching 82:9
Did: d. nothing ... d. it very well 117:11
d. that they d. in envy of great Caesar 264:6
nor ever d. a wiser one 234:11
sang his didn't he danced his d. 94:13
Dido found Aeneas wd. not come 204:12
Di-do-dum: Dido ... was D. 204:12
Die: a man can d. but once 257:8
and shall Trelawny d.? 129:4
appointed unto men once to d. 49:19
as a man lives, so shall he d. 220:19
as natural to d. 21:10
beauty's rose might never d. 293:10
beauty that must d. 149:12
beneath its shade we'll live and d. 90:3
break faith with us who d. 164:9
cowards d. many times 262:15
crawling coop't we live and d. 110:13
d. a dry death 287:14
d. all, d. merrily 255:14
d. and go we know not where 273:10
d. because a woman's fair 329:11
d. beyond my means 328:17
d. in the last ditch 65:3
d. not, poor death 101:4
d. ... the last thing I shall do! 198:1
do d. of it do seldom ... recover 243:8
how can man d. better? 163:10
I shall d. at the top 309:12
I will d. ere she shall grieve 330:1
I will d. in the last ditch 328:19
if I shd. d. think only this 59:5
if we are mark'd to d. 259:13
in what peace a Christian can d. 9:12
lay me down and d. 101:10
leave me there to d. 15:9
let me d. the death of the righteous 32:20
let us do or d. 67:2
look about us and to d. 202:17
love her till I d. 17:2
love too much ... d. for love 220:6
lovers ... d. as soon as one pleases 89:13
man can only d. once 220:13
more deaths than one must d. 326:14
never say d. 221:33
no young man believes he shall ... d. 129:10
Oh, Sir! the good d. first 331:4
people d., but books never d. 235:5
said I wd. d. a bachelor 278:1

Die (*continued*)
see Naples and d. 225:7
seemly ... to d. for one's country 136:1
seems it rich to d. 150:3
shd. certain persons d. before they sing 87:10
soon as ... born, he begins to d. 225:39
swans sing before they d. 87:10
Tamburlaine ... must d. 166:13
the d. is cast 71:12
the Man perceives it d. away 332:2
theirs but to do and d. 311:11
they ... d. by famine, d. by inches 130:15
those about to d. salute you 308:4
to d. ... awfully big adventure 24:13
to d., to sleep 250–1:20
to d. upon a kiss 281:1
toddle ... home and d. in bed 238:9
we must be free or d. 334:1
when good ... bad ... Americans d. 328:8
who wd. wish to d.? 57:8
with my little eye, I saw him d. 196:2
you asked this man to d. 19:16
young men may d., old men must 231:7
Died: d. maintaining his right of way 12:8
d. when his prospects ... brightening 11:18
in the odour of sanctity d. 24:6
laugh! I thought I shd. have d. 81:13
liked it not, and d. 336:12
men have d. ... but not for love 245:12
queens have d. young and fair 186:12
she damned near d. 16:4
she had d. of cramp 124:9
she shd. have d. hereafter 272:10
since Maurice d. 58:5
stopped short ... when the old man d. 336:8
the dog it was that d. 122:20
to the North-west d. away 61:4
who d. to save us all 10:7
wd. God I had d. for thee 34:14
wd. to God we had d. ... in ... Egypt 31:27
Dies: flower ... once has blown for ever d. 110:4
he that d. pays all debts 288:12
light of the bright world d. 57:13
love ... soon as beauty d. 100:19
no man happy until he d. 304:7
not how a man d., but how he lives 143:4
person who either marries or d. 20:9
say that when the Poet d. 239:14
the king never d. 54:9, 218:2
what an artist d. with me! 187:8
Diet: all necessaries ... d. unparalleled 98:9
no ... idiosyncrasy in d. 59:14
praise is the best d. 303:15
Dieu: D. est ... pour les gros bataillons 321:17
si D. n'existait pas 321:14
Differ: men ... d. as Heaven and Earth 312:6
Different: how d. from us, Miss Beale 14:4
Difficult: all things are d. before ... easy 227:28
d. ..., Sir? I wish it were impossible 144:24
problems of victory ... no less d. 83:8
Dig: I cannot d.; to beg I am ashamed 46:5
Digest: mark, learn, and inwardly d. 53:2
Digestion: d. ... great secret of life 303:17
now good d. wait on appetite 271:7
things sweet ... prove in d. sour 281:13
Diggeth: whoso d. a pit shall fall 39:1

Dignities: peace above all earthly d. 261:11

Dignity and worth of the human person 319:5

Diminish one dowle ... in my plume 288:15

Diminished: stars hide their d. heads 177:12

Diminishes: any man's death d. me 101:8

Dimmed: glory of the sun will be d. 23:23

Dine: and go to inns to d. 81:10
　I shd. at Ware 92:11
　if wife shd. d. at Edmonton 92:11
　Noah ... when he sat down to d. 81:11
　'whar shall we ... d. the day?' 11:16

Dined on mince and ... quince 158:9

Ding: d. dong, bell 188:9
　sing hey d. a d. d. 245–6:16

Dinner: a d. lubricates business 240:13
　d. of herbs where love is 38:18
　good d. enough, to be sure 142:13
　good d. upon his table 145:1
　people who want d. do not ring 23:21

Diplomat these days ... a head-waiter 320:2

Direction: all chance, d. 203:4

Directions: rode madly off in all d. 157:13

Dirge: by forms unseen their d. is sung 88:11

Dirt: fling d. enough ... will stick 213:38

Dirty: hail fellow ... all d. and wet 309:3

Disadvantage: ship has ... d. of ... danger 143:21

Disappointments: I have been too familiar with d. 159:6

Disapprove: I d. ... but will defend ... yr. right 321:18

Disapproves: condemns whatever he d. 65:6

Disaster: meet with Triumph and D. 154:19
　valiant ... 'gainst all d. 63:13

Disasters: day's d. in his morning face 122:11
　we make guilty of our d. 265:10

Disbelief: willing suspension of d. 87:19

Disciplines: I know the d. of war 259:7

Discobolus: the D. standeth ... dusty ... maimed 68:9

Discommendeth: he who d. others 59:11

Discontent: winter of our d. 284:8

Discord: all d., harmony not understood 203:4
　hark what d. follows! 290:3

Discount: sells us life at a d. 114:3

Discouragement: no d. shall make him ... relent 63:13

Discover: doth ... d. vice ... d. virtue 21:15

Discretion: an ounce of d. is worth 222:30
　being now come to the years of d. 53:17
　better part of valour is d. 256:3
　d. is the better part of valour 211:21
　fair woman ... without d. 38:11
　philosophy ... nothing but d. 241:3

Disdain: d. and scorn ride sparkling 278:2
　what, my dear Lady D.! 277:11

Disease: d. [consumption of purse] is incurable 256:12
　remedy ... worse than the d. 22:10
　strange d. of modern life 18:21
　'There is no cure for this d.' 27:3
　this long d., my Life 201:14
　when age, d., or sorrows strike him 84:14

Diseases: among all the d. of the mind 306:6
　desperate d. ... desperate remedies 211:16
　d. desperate grown 252:16
　subject to the same d. 274:17

Disgrace: am out, even to a full d. 246:11

Disgrace (continued)
　its private life is a d. 14:6
　my learned profession ... never d. 117:5

Disgruntled: if not ... d., ... far from ... gruntled 330:2

Dish: a d. fit for the gods 262:14
　butter in a lordly d. 33:15
　d. ran away with the spoon 189:5
　goblets for a d. of wood 283:7
　he will to his Egyptian d. 242:18
　was not that a dainty d. 193:5

Dishes: no washing of d. 12:1
　thou shalt not wash d. 188:8
　washed the d. with his wife 184:8

Dishonour: d. stain the brow of my young Harry 253:15
　his honour rooted in d. 312:4

Dishonourable: find ourselves d. graves 262:8

Dislike what I fancy I feel 12:9

Dismay: let nothing you d. 15:3

Dismayed: was there a man d. ? 311:10

Disobedience: of Man's first d. 175:15

Disobedient: for a drudge, d. 123:2
　not d. unto the heavenly vision 47:13

Disobey: naughty girl to d. 191:9

Disorder: a sweet d. in the dress 131:14
　her last d. mortal 122:17

Dispose: unsearchable d. of Highest Wisdom 181:7

Disposes: man proposes, God d. 220:21

Disposition: a truant d. 248:7
　put an antic d. on 249:13

Disputation: a feeling d. 255:8

Dispute: my right there is none to d. 93:14

Dissimulation: let love be without d. 47:23

Dissipation without pleasure 116:2

Dissolute: in the d. city 332:11

Dissolve: all which it inherit shall d. 288:16
　and then ... I d. it in rain 298:5

Distance: d. lends enchantment 72:9
　sixty seconds' worth of d. 154:20

Distinction: reverence ... doth make d. 247:7

Distress: a deep d. hath humanised 331:2

Distressed: mind quite vacant is a mind d. 93:4

Distributed: dollars ... will not be d. 84:10

Ditch: both shall fall into the d. 44:15
　die in the last d. 65:3
　I will die in the last d. 328:19

Ditchwater: as dull as d. 212:4

Ditties of no tone 149:7

Dive into the bottom of the deep 254:4

Diver: don't forget the d. 146:14

Diverse, sheer opposite 148:2

Diversion: walking ... a country d. 89:16

Divide et impera 211:22

Divide: d. and rule 211:22
　d. the living child in two 34:16
　to d. is not to take away 298:9

Divine: depth of some d. despair 314:16
　one far-off d. event 313:9
　study the past ... d. the future 89:3

Divinely tall and most d. fair 311:15

Divinity: by these we reach d. 100:18
　d. in odd numbers 276:8
　d. that shapes our ends 253:6
　such d. doth hedge a king 252:22

Divorced old barren Reason 110:9

Dizzy 'tis to cast one's eyes 267:2

Do: as I wad d., were I Lord God 164:10

Door (*continued*)
　stand at the d., and knock　50:20
　three, four, knock at the d.　192:3
　thy form from off my d.　200:19
Doorkeeper: I had rather be a d.　36:21
Doors: d. ... being as yet shut upon me　152:3
　pale Death ... knocks at the d.　135:12
Dotheboys Hall: at ... D. Youth are boarded
　98:9
Dots: what those damned d. meant　82:6
Double: d., d., toil and trouble　271:11
　surely you'll grow d.　335:4
Double entendre: the horrible d.　12:11
Doubled him up for ever　116:10
Doublethink means ... two contradictory
　beliefs　197:6
Doubt: 'I d. it,' said the Carpenter　76:3
　more faith in honest d.　313:1
　new philosophy calls all in d.　100:16
　no probable ... possible d. whatever　116:9
　when in d., leave out　230:11
　when in d., win the trick　136:11
Doubted: never d. clouds wd. break　60:12
Doubtful: by destruction dwell in d. joy
　271:3
Doubting: a castle called D. Castle　63:11
Doubts: begin with d., ... end in certainties
　23:12
　he shall end in d.　23:12
　knows nothing, d. nothing　218:15
　saucy d. and fears　271:6
Douglas: Judge D. and myself　159:10
　old song of Percy and D.　302:6
　the D. in his hall　240:7
Dove: beside the springs of D.　334:11
　d. came ... in the evening　30:22
　my d., my dear ... my life　314:4
　Oh that I had wings like a d.!　36:16
Dove-cote: like an eagle in a d.　246:12
Doves: grass is as soft as the breast of d.
　90–1:16
Dowagers: with ... d. for deans　314:12
Dowdiness: memory ... beginning of d.
　328:15
Dower: faith's transcendent d.　334:10
Down: d., d. to hell　261:2
　d. will come baby, cradle　189:10
　easier to pull d. than to build　223:35
　get d. you dirty rascal　190:3
　he that is d. ... fear no fall　63:15
　I don't think one 'comes d.'　197:12
　levers to lift me ... being d.　254:7
　never go d. to the end of the town　171:9
　quite, quite d.　251:5
Downstairs: be off, or I'll kick you d.　74:4
Doxy over the dale　292:17
Drab: a-cursing like a very d.　250:18
　ditch-deliver'd by a d.　271:12
Dragon: Saint George, that swing'd the d.
　264:11
Drain: leave by the next town d.　305:19
Drake he's in his hammock　187:9
Draughts: shallow d. intoxicate the brain
　202:5
Draw: d. back ... to leap better　217:15
　d. but twenty miles a-day?　166:12
　must d. the line somewhere　211:33
Drawers: hewers of wood and d. of water
　33:11
Dread: close your eyes with holy d.　87:16

Dread (*continued*)
　doth walk in fear and d.　86:16
　d. and fear of kings　275:1
　d. of something after death　250–1:20
Dreadful: dancing? Oh, d.　65:4
　death ... mighty and d.　101:4
　O! d. is the check　58:15
　the acting of a d. thing　262:13
Dream: a sight to d. of　87:6
　a vision or a waking d.?　150:6
　and slowly read, and d.　337:10
　awoke ... from a deep d. of peace　137:5
　behold it was a d.　63:12
　consecration, and the poet's d.　331:1
　d. of battled fields no more　239:9
　d. of money-bags to-night　274:13
　d. you are crossing the Channel　117:13
　fly, forgotten, as a d. dies　323:6
　glory and the freshness of a d.　331:12
　if you can d.　154:18
　life is but an empty d.　160:14
　lust of fame was but a d.　58:14
　not d. them, all day long　154:2
　oaks ... d., and so d. all night　148:6
　old men shall d. dreams　42:13
　perchance to d. Ay, there's the rub
　250–1:20
　phantasma or a hideous d.　262:13
　the glory and the d.　331:16
　they d. of home　111:12
　wrecks of a dissolving d.　298:11
Dreamed: d. of cheese—toasted, mostly　307:5
　I d. that Greece might ... be free　70:1
Dreamer: behold, this d. cometh　31:11
　d. of dreams　184:9
　poet and the d.　148:2
Dreaming: city with her d. spires　19:4
　d. arl the time o' Plymouth Hoe　187:9
Dreams: fanatics have their d.　148:1
　into the land of my d.　153:11
　more things ... than this world d.　312:9
　nature lends such evil d.　312:16
　not make d. yr. master　154:18
　read of ... or dreamt of in d.　24:5
　so full of fearful d.　284:15
　such stuff as d. are made on　288:16
　wovest d. of joy and fear　298:15
Dreamt: d. of in yr. philosophy　249:12
　d. that I dwelt in marble halls　63:4
　I have long d. of such a ... man　258:3
　read of ... or d. of　24:5
Dreary: how d. to be somebody　99:14
　world am sad and d.　112:9
Drenched with dew, Old Nod the shepherd
　97:1
Dress: a sweet disorder in the d.　131:14
　all d. is fancy d.　297:6
　noble youths did d. themselves　256:17
Drill: no names, no pack d.　222:3
Drink: a rule never to d. by daylight
　169:14
　d. and the devil had done for the rest　307:4
　d. 'a pinta milka day　11:2
　d. deep, or taste not the Pierian spring
　202:5
　'D. ME' beautifully printed　73:15
　d. no longer water　49:12
　d. to me only with thine eyes　145:7
　d. with him that wears a hood　307:11
　five reasons we shd. d.　10:3

Drink (*continued*)
lead a horse ... cannot make him d. 218:28
man wants but little d. 134:2
much d. ... equivocator with lechery 270:14
nor any drop to d. 86:6
shall sit and d. with me 28:4
taste for d., combined with gout 116:10
that I might d., and leave the world 149:14
what shd. we do for d.? 14:1
Drinking: continual d. of Knowledge 152:2
diverted by every means but d. 144:4
d. Cheltenham waters 11:17
d. is the soldier's pleasure 103:14
d. largely sobers us again 202:5
d. the blude red wine 11:13
there are two reasons for d. 199:5
Drinks his wine 'mid laughter free 17:3
Driven: soul ... d., I know not whither 324:4
Drives the flower .. d. my green age 315:16
Driving: d. of Jehu ... he driveth furiously 34:25
spend my life in d. briskly 144:7
Drone: the lazy, yawning d. 258:8
Drop: every d. of the Thames 65:7
nor any d. to drink 86:6
raineth d. and staineth slop 205:2
Drops: little d. of water 73:13
women's weapons, water-d. 266:3
Dross: all is d. that is not Helena 165:8
Drought of Marche hath perced 79:1
Drown: I'll d. my book 289:5
what pain ... to d. 285:1
Drowned: drench'd our steeples, d. the cocks 266:6
d. in the depth of the sea 44:20
d. my Honour in a shallow Cup 110:15
pluck up d. Honour by the locks 254:4
Drowning: d. man ... catch at a straw 211:35
no d. mark upon him 287:13
Drowns things weighty and solid 23:10
Drudge: for a d., disobedient 123:2
lexicographer—a harmless d. 140:7
Drum: listenin' for the d. 187:9
not a d. was heard 330:3
the spirit-stirring d. 280:2
war-d. throbbed no longer 313:17
Drummed them out of town 190:9
Drummers: nine d. drumming 194:2
Drums: hearts ... like muffled d. are beating 160:15
sound the trumpets, beat the d. 103:13
Drunk: d. as a fish 211:36
d. as a lord 211:37
d. as a mouse 211:38
d. as a wheelbarrow 211:39
d. the milk of Paradise 87:16
man ... must get d. 69:15
never [happy] but when he is d. 143:18
not so think as you d. 306:3
stag at eve had d. his fill 239:6
this meeting is d. 99:6
Drunkard: the rolling English d. made the rolling English road 81:6
Drunken: do with the d. sailor 17:7
d. folks seldom take harm 211:40
d. night ... cloudy morning 212:1
went to Worts and got more d. 204:13
Drunkenness: babbling d. 292:1

Dry: a d. brain in a d. season 106:6
as d. as dust 212:2
but oh, I am so d. 15:9
die a d. death 287:14
hearts ... d. as summer dust 331:4
old man in a d. month 106:5
Dublin: in D.'s fair city 15:10
Duchess: I am D. of Malfi still 323:13
the D.! Oh, my dear paws! 74:2
the D. said, in a hoarse growl 74:5
Duck: dying d. in a thunderstorm 212:6
water off a d.'s back 229:34
Duckling: The Ugly D. 10:11
Ducks and drakes: to make d. of 212:3
Due: give the devil his d. 214:33
one born out of d. time 48:11
Duke: became a most important d. 28:1
everybody praised the D. 304:15
Dukedom: library was d. large enough 287:17
Dulce et decorum est pro patria mori 136:1
Dull: as d. as ditchwater 212:4
d. in himself, ... cause of dullness 11:8
d. wd. he be of soul 333:6
prophetick blessing—Be thou d. 103:10
Dullness: Shadwell ... mature in d. 104:14
Dumb: d. men get no lands 212:5
great [cares] are d. 219:8
Duncan is in his grave 271:4
Dunce: a d. ... kept at home 93:2
a d. ... sent to roam 93:2
a d. with wits 201:2
Dundee: bonnets of Bonny D. 239:4
Dunfermline: king sits in D. town 11:13
Dungeon: live upon the vapour of a d. 279:17
Dunsinane: till Birnam Forest come to D. 272:7
Dusk: in the d. ... light behind her 120:15
little breezes d. and shiver 313:12
Dust: a d. whom England bore 59:6
all lovers must ... come to d. 247:10
as chimney-sweepers, come to d. 247:9
as dry as d. 212:2
ashes to ashes, d. to d. 53:30
before we too into the D. descend 110:3
cinders, ashes, d. 149:1
d. hath closed Helen's eye 186:12
d. in the air suspended 106:10
D. into D., and under D. to lie 110:3
d. on antique time wd. lie unswept 246:8
d. thou art, and unto d. 30:14
d. thou art, to d. returnest 160:14
guilty of d. and sin 131:10
hearts are dry as summer d. 331:4
make d. our paper 283:5
name ... not perish in the d. 304:11
not without d. and heat 182:4
pays us but with age and d. 232:11
pride that licks the d. 201:19
rotting together have one d. 247:7
vile d. from whence he sprung 240:1
what is the quintessence of d.? 250:6
Dust-heap: great d. called history 54:6
Dusty: d. cobweb-covered, maimed 68:9
the way to d. death 272:10
what a d. answer gets the soul 170:2
Dutch: my dear old D. 81:14
Duties: embark ... on the d. of the day 116:12
let us ... brace ourselves to our d. 82:14
lowliest d. on herself did lay 333:13
property has its d. 102:13

Empire (*continued*)
　　another mighty E. overthrown!　334:2
　　how is the E. ?　115:16
　　if the British E. ... last for a thousand years
　　　82:14
　　King dead, the e. unpossess'd ?　285:11
　　Mother E. stands splendidly isolated　112:3
　　neither holy, nor Roman, nor an e.　321:16
　　preside over the liquidation of the British
　　　E.　83:6
　　the E. is a Commonwealth of Nations
　　　235:12
　　to found a great e.　303:4
　　young was called to E.　104:13
Empires: day of E. has come　78:8
　　vaster than e. and more slow　167:12
Employment: give e. to the artisan　27:6
　　the pleasantness of an e.　21:3
Empty vessels make the most noise　212:22
Enchanted: as holy and e.　87:12
Enchanter: ghosts from an e. fleeing　299:3
Enchantment: lends e. to the view　72:9
Encourage: kill an admiral ... to e. the others
　　321:10
Encourager: pour e. les autres　321:10
Encumbers: Patron ... e. him with help　142:1
End: a loud noise at one e.　155:15
　　'a made a finer e.　259:1
　　ages of hopeless e.　177:1
　　attempt the e.　132:5
　　beginning of the e.　310:10
　　big e.-ians and small e.-ians　308:15
　　boys get at one e. ... lose at the other　143:20
　　e. justifies the means　212:23
　　everything hath an e.　212:37
　　found no e., in wandering mazes lost　177:6
　　four ... winters ... springs e. in a word
　　　281:12
　　he shall e. in certainties　23:12
　　long weary day have e.　305:8
　　longest day must have an e.　219:26
　　Lord, make me to know mine e.　36:11
　　more than an e. to war, we want　235:6
　　my last e. be like his!　32:20
　　not even the beginning of the e. ... but ... the
　　　e. of the beginning　83:5
　　our minutes hasten to their e.　294:1
　　seen one thing, that love hath an e.　310:3
　　the e. of this day's business　264:5
　　the man would die ... and there an e.　271:8
　　the right true e. of love　101:2
　　Sans Wine ... Song ... E.!　110:3
　　vegetate and wish ... an e.　65:5
　　yes, to the very e.　236:3
Endeavour: a disinterested e. to learn　19:8
Ending: e. is better than mending　137:9
　　love is ... sour in the e.　219:39
Endowed by their Creator with ... rights.
　　139:6
Ends: divinity that shapes our e.　253:6
　　dog, to gain some private e.　122:19
　　make both e. meet　208:25
　　odd old e. stol'n forth of holy writ　284:14
　　to serve our private e.　82:3
Endurable: love [will] make a thing e.　332:12
Endure: cannot e. in his age　277:22
　　cd. e. the toothache patiently　278:17
　　first e., then pity, then embrace　203:6
　　from age to age e.　153:5
　　youth's a stuff will not e.　291:2

Endured: can't be cured, must be e.　230:7
　　much is to be e.　141:6
　　tolerable and not to be e.　278:6
Enemies: confusion to his e.　15:6
　　left me naked to mine e.　261:13
　　love your e.　43:20
Enemy: best ... e. of the good　321:13
　　better an open e.　207:19
　　here shall he see no e.　244:4
　　how goes the *e.* ?　233:8
　　if thine e. be hungry　38:28
　　mine e.'s dog　267:9
　　my name ... terrible to the e.　256:11
　　of yr e. say nothing　226:6
　　the e. faints not　85:1
　　trust not ... an old e.　228:23
Energetic: our speech ... e. without rules
　　140:1
Energies of our system will decay　23:23
Energy: e. is eternal delight　56:16
　　reason and e., love and hate　56:15
Enfants: les e. terribles　115:3
Enfer: chaud comme l'e.　310:11
Engine: e. that moves in determinate grooves
　　128:11
　　put this e. to our ears　308:14
England: a body of E.'s, breathing English air
　　59:6
　　a dust whom E. bore　59:6
　　a time there was, ere E.'s griefs　122:6
　　be E. what she will　82:1
　　between France and E. is the sea　139:18
　　E., bound in with the triumphant sea
　　　282:6
　　E. expects every man　187:5
　　E. has saved herself ... save Europe　200:9
　　E. hath need of thee　333:12
　　E. ... hell for horses　67:10, 212:24
　　E. is a nation of shop-keepers　185:12
　　E. is the mother of parliaments　58:9
　　E. is the paradise of women　67:10, 111:4,
　　　212:24
　　E., my E. ? E. my own　130:11
　　E.'s green and pleasant land　55:8
　　E. will have her neck wrung　83:4
　　E., with all thy faults　93:7
　　E. ... wont to conquer others　282:6
　　Florence, Elizabethan E.　138:8
　　for E.'s the one land　59:3
　　foreign field ... forever E.　59:5
　　gallows standing in E. when thou art king ?
　　　253:16
　　gentlemen in E., now abed　260:2
　　Happy is E.! I cd. be content　151:2
　　heart and stomach of ... King of E.
　　　107:13
　　high road that leads him to E.　142:8
　　history of E. is ... history of progress　164:5
　　I know the kings of E.　120:4
　　if E. to itself do rest but true　265:5
　　in E.—now!　61:1
　　in E. we ... rely on ... time-lag　324:15
　　know of E. who only E. know ?　154:13
　　laws of E. are at my commandment　258:2
　　light such a candle ... in E.　157:2
　　men in E. that do no work today　259:12
　　my love for E. and Ireland　234:1
　　nor, E., did I know till then　331:6
　　not three good men unhang'd in E.　254:14
　　Oats.—... in E. ... given to horses　140:9

England (*continued*)
Oh, to be in E. 61:1
on E.'s pleasant pastures seen 55:8
people of E. that never have spoken yet 81:9
roast beef of E. 109:9
Stately Homes of E. 91:5,6
stately homes of E.! 130:5
there'll always be an E. 198:4
this earth, this realm, this E. 282:5
this E. never did ... lie at the ... foot 265:4
'Tis for the honour of E. 89:8
wake up, E. 115:15
walk upon E.'s mountains 55:8
ye mariners of E. 72:10
youth of E. are on fire 258:9
English: a body of England's, breathing E. air
59:6
be among the E. Poets after my death
152:5
blood of E. shall manure the ground
283:8
Chaucer, well of E. undefiled 305:13
E. are ... the least ... pure philosophers
23:20
E. as she is Spoke 318:4
E. never know when ... beaten 212:25
E. winter—ending in July 70:8
grave where E. oak and holly 129:2
on, on, you noblest E. 259:4
our E. tongue a gallimaufry 305:17
principle of the E. constitution 54:10
the E. ... a foul-mouthed nation 129:9
the E. country gentleman 328:10
the E. have hot-water bottles 170:8
the rolling E. drunkard made the rolling E.
road 81:6
the sort of E. up with which 83:12
trick of our E. nation 256:10
under an E. heaven 59:7
wholesome ... really nice E. people 295:17
winged heels, as E. Mercuries 258:9
with our E. dead 259:3
Englishman: an E., even ... alone, forms a
... queue 170:9
an E. thinks he is moral 296:7
E. does not travel to see Englishmen
306:12
E. ... enjoys himself ... for a noble purpose
131:7
E.'s home is his castle 212:26
my-lorded as only a free-born E. can
315:10
rights of an E. 146:5
stirred the hearts of every E. 239:3
the last great E. is low 314:9
to his credit ... an E.! 120:2
way to an E.'s heart 229:36
Englishmen: mad dogs and E. 91:8
reveal Himself ... first to his E. 182:7
when two E. meet ... talk of the weather
140:12
Engross: pens a stanza when he shd. e. 201:11
Enigma: a riddle wrapped in a mystery inside
an e. 82:10
Enjoy: can thoroughly e. the pepper 74:7
e. themselves so well, as at ... tavern 144:1
prize not ... whiles we e. it 278:12
who can e. alone? 179:3
you will never e. the world 317:16
Enjoyed: e. no sooner but despised 294:11

Enjoyed (*continued*)
human life ... little to be e. 141:6
that bards of old e. 56:14
to have e. the sun 18:10
what peaceful hours I once e. 92:14
Enjoyment: variety is the mother of e. 100:13
Enjoys: the Englishman never e. himself
131:7
Enough: e. is as good as a feast 54:3, 212:28
e. is e. 212:28
e. that there *is* a beyond 295:9
grant me ... more than e. 165:4
wore e. for modesty 62:13
Enriched: pension never e. a young man
223:4
Enriches: robs me ... not e. him 279:15
Ense: calamus saevior e. patet 67:9
Ensign: beauty's e. yet is crimson 287:3
tear her tattered e. down 134:1
th' imperial e. ... high advanced 176:9
Enter: abandon hope all ye who e. 95:6
e. ye in at ... strait gate 44:8
ye shall not e. into ... Kingdom 44:19
Enterprise: the e. is sick 290:2
Enterprises: e. of great pith and moment
250–1:20
impediments to great e. 21:19
Entertaining: more e. than half the novels
169:6
Enthroned in the hearts of kings 275:1
Enthusiasm: considering that e. moves the
world 24:1
long for a little ordinary e. 197:10
nothing great ... without e. 108:3
Enthusiasts: so few e. ... speak the truth 24:1
Entire and whole and perfect 305:22
Entrance: beware of e. to a quarrel 248:16
Entrances: have their exits and their e. 244:11
Envied: better be e. than pitied 207:22
Envious: rent the e. Casca made 263:17
Envy: e. and calumny and hate and pain
297:16
e., hatred, and malice 52:23
in e. of great Caesar 264:6
means ... too low for e. 91:13
the e. of less happier lands 282:5
Ephesians: Diana of the E. 47:7
Epilogue: a good play needs no e. 246:4
Epitaph: believe a woman or an e. 70:14
Epitaphs: a nice derangement of e. 301:10
graves and worms and e. 283:5
Epithet: fair is too foul an e. for thee 166:11
Epitome: all mankind's e. 103:4
Eppur si muove 114:13
Epsom Salts: had we but stuck to E. 11:17
Equal: all animals are e. but some are more
e. 197:1
e. division of unequal earnings 107:18
far from ... true ... naturally e. 143:2
inferiors revolt ... be e. 18:6
that all men are created e. 139:6
Equals [revolt] that they may be superior
18:6
Eros: unarm, E.; the ... task is done 243:4
Err: better to e. with Pope 70:15
not e., who say ... when the Poet dies 239:14
the most may e. as grossly 103:8
to e. is human 217:11
to e. is human, to forgive divine 202:14
Errand: in thy joyous e. reach the spot 111:1

Errands for the Ministers of State   116:13
Erred: we have e. and strayed   52:12
Erring: a rod to check the e.   334:3
Error: custom without reason ... ancient e.
   210:28
   e. of opinion may be tolerated   139:8
   gross e. held in schools   115:12
   if this be e. and upon me prov'd   294:9
   ignorance is preferable to e.   139:12
   mountainous e. ... highly heap'd   246:8
Errors: amusing with numerous e. [book]
   123:18
   e., like straws, upon the surface   103:16
   if to her share some female e.   204:6
Esau: E. my brother ... a hairy man   31:7
   the hands of E.   31:8
Escape: e. me ?—never   61:7
   thou shalt not e. calumny   251:3
   who shall e. whipping ?   250:13
Essence: his glassy e., like an angry ape   273:7
Estate: become a fourth e. of the realm
   164:4
   ordered their e.   10:5
Esteem: riches I hold in light e.   58:14
Esteemed: better to be vile than vile e.   294:10
Esther: loved E. above all ... women   34:27
État: l'É. c'est moi   162:2
Eternal: abode where the E. are   298:3
   condition ... liberty ... e. vigilance   95:3
   energy is e. delight   56:16
   e. summer gilds them yet   69–70:21
   on Fame's e. beadroll   305:13
   thought ... to be boy e.   292:12
Eternity: damned from here to E.   154:15
   deserts of vast e.   167:13
   e. in an hour   54:12
   lives in e.'s sunrise   55:4
   make the mighty ages of e.   73:13
   memorial from the soul's e.   236:6
   passing through nature to e.   247:20
   stains the white radiance of E.   298:2
   thoughts that wander through e.   176:19
Etherised: evening is spread out ... like a
   patient e.   106:11
Ethiop: a rich jewel in an E.'s ear   286:3
Ethiopian: can the E. change his skin ?   41:14
Eton: Waterloo ... won on the playing fields of
   E.   324:10
Euphelia serves to grace my measure   205:6
Euripides: a chorus-ending from E.   60:13
Europe: all E. shd. know that we have block-
   heads   89:8
   glory of E. is extinguished   64:11
   lamps are going out all over E.   127:8
   last territorial claim ... in E.   132:14
   part of the community of E.   121:10
   save E. by her example   200:9
   Soviet power into heart of Western E.
   83:10
   splendidly isolated in E.   112:3
   we are ... smallest country left in E.   319:9
Eurydice: half-regained E.   174:10
Eve: fairest of her daughters E.   178:4
   from noon to dewy e.   176:14
   when Adam delved and E. span   24:2
   when E. upon the first of Men   135:2
Even: contrive to write so e.   20:19
Événements: l'histoire des grands é.   321:15
Evening: bright exhalation in the e.   261:8
   e. crowns the day   212:29

Evening (continued)
   e. is spread out against the sky   106:11
   I light my lamp in the e.   28:2
   it is a beauteous e.   33:2
   It was a summer's e.   304:12
   like an e. gone   323:5
   now came still e. on   178:6
   shadows of the e. steal   24:8
   the winter e. settles down   106:19
   who turns as I, this e.   61:5
Event: heaviness foreruns the good e.   257:11
   one far-off divine e.   313:9
   wise after the e.   212:13
   wisest prophets make sure of the e.   322:8
Ever: but I go on for e.   311:8
   do nothing for e. and e.   12:1
   for e. and for e. farewell, Cassius !   264:4
   for e. hold his peace   53:20
   if for e., still for e.   70:16
   left lonely for e.   18:13
   that no life lives for e.   310:1
   thou art gone, and for e.   239:10
   what, never ? Hardly e.!   119:11
   wished him to talk on for e.   129:8
Everlasting: caught an e. cold   324:5
   condemn'd into e. redemption   278:15
   had stood [wheat] from e. to e.   317:17
   primrose way to th' e. bonfire   270:13
   that the E. had not fix'd   248:2
Everybody: e. praised the Duke   304:15
   e. wants to have read   319:2
   friend to e. ... friend to nobody   214:20
Everyman, I will go with thee   13:5
Everyone: e. ... put his whole wit   25:7
   e. suddenly burst out singing   238:10
   war of e. against e.   133:2
Everything: a smattering of e.   99:11
   can resist e. except temptation   328:2
   e. by starts and nothing long   103:4
   e.'s got a moral   74:12
   God saw e. ... he had made   30:5
   sans taste, sans e.   244–5:11
   sermons in stones, and good in e.   243:15
   with e. that pretty bin   246–7:13
Everywhere: e. be bold   305:12
   e. that Mary went   127:11
   water, water e.   86:6
Eves: on summer e. by haunted stream   174:7
Evidence of things not seen   49:21
Evil: abhor that which is e.   47:23
   all partial e., universal good   203:4
   be not overcome of e.   47:27
   care not whether ... good or e.   55:7
   decide ... for the good or e. side   162:14
   deliver us from e.   43:24
   doing e. on the ground of expediency
   235:11
   E., be thou my Good   177:14
   e. be to him who e. thinks   216:40
   e. is wrought by want of Thought   135:1
   e. that men do lives after them   263:11
   e. which I wd. not, that I do   47:19
   government ... a necessary e.   197:19
   I will fear no e.   35:29
   knowing good and e.   30:11
   love of money ... root of all e.   49:14
   loved darkness ... their deeds were e.   46:22
   Luke ... gave himself to e. courses   332:11
   maketh ... sun to rise on the e.   43:21
   nature lends such e. dreams   312:16

Evil (*continued*)
of moral e. and of good 335:7
on e. days ... fallen, and e. tongues 178:20
out of good ... find means of e. 176:2
overcome e. with good 47:27
purer eyes than to behold e. 42:25
resist not e. 43:19
root of all e. The want of money 68:3
set good against e. 215:13
supernatural source of e. 90:9
the tongue ... is an unruly e. 50:1
them that call e. good 40:20
Evils: he ... must expect new e. 22:18
of two e. choose the least 213:1
women are necessary e. 230:34
Exact: an e. man 23:8
Exactitude ... politesse des rois 162:4
Exactness: with e. grinds he all 161:3
Exaggerated: reports of my death ... e. 319:4
Exalteth: righteousness e. a nation 38:15
Examination: post-mortem e. revealed ...
'Callous' 241:11
Examinations are formidable even to the
best 88:20
Example: e. is better than precept 213:2
e. is the school of mankind 64:15
good e. is the best sermon 215:16
Excavating for a mine 183:8
Exceed: reach shd. e. his grasp 60:11
Excel: daring to e. 82:2
unstable ... thou shalt not e. 31:14
Excellent: an e. thing in woman 268:3
embodiment of everything ... e. 117:2
e. to have a giant's strength 273:6
Excels: how much a dunce ... e 93:2
Excelsior: the strange device, E.! 160:12
Exception proves the rule 213:3
Excess: e. leads to wisdom 57:1
e. of glory obscured 176:11
give me e. of it 290:10
in charity there is no e. 22:5
nothing in e. 17:10
nothing succeeds like e. 328:14
surprise by a fine e. 151:14
wasteful and ridiculous e. 264:19
Exchange: by just e. one for another given
302:2
fair e. is no robbery 213:11
novels gain by the e. 70:10
Exciting: he found it less e. 116:2
Exclamation: 'fifty thousand!' was the e. 62:2
Excommunicate: unbaptized, or e. 53:27
Excuse: a bad e. is better than none 206:33
make the fault the worse by the e. 265:1
no longer e. for ... playing the rake 184:3
she'll prove an e. for a glass 301:17
Execution: their [of laws] stringent e. 125:2
Executioner: I am mine own e. 101:6
Executors: delivering o'er to e. pale 258:8
let's choose e. and talk of wills 283:5
Exercise: dancing ? ... a barbarian e. 65:4
what e. is to the body 306:8
Exhalation: I shall fall like some bright e.
261:8
Exhausted worlds ... imagin'd new 140:19
Exiles: thou Paradise of e., Italy 298:12
Exist: if God did not e. 321:14
Existence: contraries ... are necessary to ... e.
56:15
E. saw him spurn her ... reign 140:19

Existence (*continued*)
love ... 'tis woman's whole e. 69:14
Exits: they have their e. and their entrances
244:11
Expands: work e. ... to fill the time available
198:5
Expatiate free o'er all this scene of man
202:17
Expectancy and rose of the fair state 251:5
Expectation: however certain our e. 107:11
now sits E. in the air 258:9
Expediency: doing evil on the ground of e.
235:11
Expedient: all things ... lawful ... but ... not e.
48:2
too fond of the *right* to pursue the *e.* 123:2
Expense: at the e. of two [Gods] 84:15
Expensive: did ... from e. sins refrain 103:6
Experience: an e. of women which extends
102:2
e. ... if not bought too dear 213:4
e. teaches 213:5
till old e. do attain ... prophetic 173:12
travel ... part of e. 22:13
triumph of hope over e. 143:6
true e. from this great event 181:8
Experientia docet 213:5
Expires: with that the Wretched Child e. 27:4
Expiring: thus e. do foretell of him 282:4
Expose thyself to feel what wretches feel
266:14
Expressed: oft was thought, but ne'er so well
e. 202:8
Expresses himself in terms too deep 119:4
Extensive: knowledge of London ... e. and
peculiar 98:23
Extent of [our language's] beauty and power
164:3
Extenuate: speak ... as I am; nothing e.
280:14
Extinguished: glory of Europe is e. 64:11
nature is ... seldom e. 22:26
Extinguishes the small, ... inflames the great
67:13
Extremes: e. meet 213:6
two e. of passion, joy and grief 268:1
women are always in e. 230:33
Extremity: a daring pilot in e. 102–3:17
Exuberance: e. is beauty 57:5
e. of his own verbosity 100:8
Exulting: the people all e. 325:12
Eye: a custom loathsome to the e. 138:14
a still-soliciting e. 265:8
all my e. and Betty Martin 206:15
all places that the e. of heaven visits 281:14
an e. for an e. 43:18
an e. made quiet by ... harmony 335:12
as the apple of his e. 33:6
camel ... through the e. of a needle 44:23
courtier's, soldier's, scholar's e. 251:5
e. for e., tooth for tooth 32:10
e. sees not, ... heart rues not 213:7
e. to the main chance 220:11
far from e., far from heart 213:17
flash upon that inward e. 331:11
has not man a microscopic e. ? 203:2
holds him with his glittering e. 85:12
I backward cast my e. 66:13
if thine e. offend thee 44:21
in the e. of the beholder 137:3

Facing: Mr. F.-both-ways 63:10
Facts: all the f. when ... brass tacks 107:2
   f. are sacred 238:15
   indebted to ... imagination for his f. 301:19
   irritable reaching after f. 151:11
Faculties: our souls, whose f. can comprehend 166:10
Fade: f. away into the forest dim 149:14
   f. into the light of common day 332:2
   old soldiers ... only f. away 16:7
   she cannot f. 149:8
   thy eternal summer shall not f. 293:14
Faded: like this insubstantial pageant f. 288:16
Fades: now f. the glimmering landscape 126:4
Faery: full beautiful, a f.'s child 148:15
   in f. lands forlorn 150:4
   the land of f. 337:6
Faiblesse: tout le reste est f. 320:14
Fail: if we shd. f.? We f.! 270:7
   neither shall ... cruse of oil f. 34:18
   sooner f. than not be among the greatest 152:4
   we shall not flag or f. 82:13
Failed: The Light that F. 155:11
Faileth: enemy faints not, nor f. 85:1
Failing: f. to trust everybody ... nobody 213:8
   true ... she had one f. 66:6
Failure: only one [to make a marriage] a f. 238:2
Faint, yet pursuing 33:17
Faints: the enemy f. not 85:1
Fair: all is f. in love and war 206:11
   brave deserves the f. 103:12
   f. is foul and foul is f. 269:4
   f. is too foul an epithet for thee 166:11
   f. stood the wind for France 102:9
   for ever shalt thou love and she be f. 149:8
   holy, f. and wise is she 292:8
   how sweet and f. she seems to be 322:1
   is she kind as she is f.? 292:9
   like not f. terms and a villain's mind 274:11
   most divinely f. 311:15
   pernicious weed! ... the f. annoys 92:5
   she is f. and, fairer 274:4
   she is not f. to outward view 85:10
   so foul and f. a day 269:6
Fair play's a jewel 213:14
Fairer: and f. than that word 274:4
   I can't say no f. than that 98:2
   thou art f. than the evening air 165:9
Fairest: O, f. of creation 179:10
Fairies: do you believe in f.? 24:14
   f. at the bottom of our garden 114:11
   I don't believe in f. 24:12
   she is the f. midwife 286:1
   that was the beginning of f. 24:11
Fair-spoken and persuading 262:2
Fairy: a little f. ... falls down dead 24:12
   by f. hands their knell is rung 88:11
   light she was and like a f. 183:9
   'tis almost f. time 277:8
Faith: an event which creates f. 297:3
   break f. with us who die 164:9
   f. and morals ... Milton held 334:1
   f. ... as the fashion of his hat 277:10
   f. is ... substance of things 49:21
   f. shines equal, arming me 58:12
   f.'s transcendent dower 334:10

Faith (*continued*)
   f. unfaithful kept him falsely true 312:4
   f. without works is dead 49:25
   fight the good fight of f. 49:15
   I have kept the f. 49:17
   I mean the F.'s Defender 68:15
   just shall live by f. 47:15
   more f. in honest doubt 313:1
   my staff of f. to walk upon 232:12
   reaffirm f. in ... human rights 319:5
   reason ... soul's left hand, f. her right 100:18
   remembering ... yr. work of f. 49:5
   simple f. than Norman blood 313:10
   'tis not the dying for a f. 315:6
   we walk by f., not by sight 48:15
   which constitutes poetic f. 87:19
Faithful: be thou f. unto death 50:16
   ever f., ever sure 180:7
   f. are the wounds of a friend 39:3
   f. only he 178:18
   f. to thee, Cynara! 101:11
   O come, all ye f. 196:5
   so f. in love ... dauntless in war 240:6
Faith-healer of Deal 12:9
Faithless: among the f., faithful only he 178:18
   yr. sleeping head ... on my f. arm 20:2
Faiths: heaven smiles and f. and empires gleam 298:11
Fall: another thing to f. 273:1
   A-tishoo! We all f. down 193:2
   f. out, and chide, and fight 323:3
   haughty spirit [goeth] before a f. 38:19
   he that is down need fear no f. 63:15
   held we f. to rise 60:12
   higher ... the greater the f. 216:31
   Humpty Dumpty had a great f. 76:8, 189:3
   pride will have a f. 223:27
   some by virtue f. 273:2
   that strain ...! It had a dying f. 290:10
   the cradle will f. 189:10
   the glass will f. for ever 164:15
   unless the billboards f. 186:10
   upon the ground, can f. no lower 219:3
   what a f. was there, my countrymen! 263:19
Fallen: awake, ... or be for ever f.! 176:7
   f. out of heigh degree 80:1
   f. ... that tower of strength 314:10
   there has f. a splendid tear 314:4
   though f. on evil days 178:20
   you are f. from grace 48:21
Falling: he hath the f. sickness 262:10
   what a f. off was there 249:11
Falls: between two stools one f. 207:39
   like a thunderbolt he f. 312:1
   nips his root, and then he f. 261:9
   when f. the Coliseum, Rome shall fall 69:8
   when he f., he f. like Lucifer 261:10
False: any other thing that's f. 70:14
   canst not then be f. to any man 248–9:17
   history must be f. 322:5
   prov'd true ... prove f. again 67:17
   ring out the f., ring in the true 313:4
   thou shalt not bear f. witness 32:8
   true to thyself, as ... not f. to others 22:17
   what the f. heart doth know 270:8
Falsehood: let her and F. grapple 182:10
Falstaff sweats to death 254:9

Fame: all the family of F.   87:18
  an imp of f.   259:9
  Cromwell, damned to everlasting f.   203:9
  f. ... is double-mouthed   181:4
  f. is like a river   23:10
  f. is no plant ... on mortal soil   175:2
  f. is the spur   175:1
  his f. soon spread around   92:9
  lust of f.   58:14
  nor yet a fool to f.   201:13
  on F.'s eternal beadroll   305:13
  physicians of the utmost f.   27:3
  servants of f.   22:2
  son of memory, great heir of f.   175:12
  thou, whose infamy is not thy f.   297:15
Familiar: f. acts are beautiful   299:13
  f. as his garter   258:7
  f., but by no means vulgar   248:15
  f. objects as if ... not f.   300:9
  the old f. faces   156:9
  too f. with disappointments   159:6
  wine ... a good f. creature   279:11
Familiarity: f. breeds contempt   213:16
  f. breeds contempt and children   318:14
Families: accidents ... in best-regulated f.   98:1
  all happy f. resemble one another   317:13
  I might ... be useful to their f.   20:6
Family: a man that left his f.   318:7
  all the f. of Fame   87:18
  brought up a large f.   123:19
  if I heard my f. called decent   199:3
  wonderful f. called Stein   13:4
Famine: die by f. die by inches   130:15
  elle alla crier f.   111:12
  f. grew and locusts came   315:17
  she went to cry f.   111:6
Famous: awoke ... and found myself f.   71:7
  but 'twas a f. victory   304:15
  man can become f. without ability   295:14
Fan: she comes ... full sail ... f. spread   89:10
Fanatics have their dreams   148:1
Fancy: a f. from a flower-bell   60:13
  a little of what you f.   160:5
  a young man's f. lightly turns   313:15
  admit those [wants] of f.   141:4
  costly thy habit ... not express'd in f.   248:16
  ever let the f. roam   148:3
  fellow ... of most excellent f.   253:2
  listen ... to the whispers of f.   141:3
  sweetest Shakespeare, F.'s child   174:8
  tell me where is f. bred   274:18
  what I f. I feel   12:9
Fantastic: f. summer's heat   282:1
  on the light f. toe   173:17
Far: a f., f. better thing that I do   99:12
  beneath the good how f.!   127:2
  but f. above the great!   127:2
  fair and softly goes f.   213:10
  f. and few, f. and few   158:5
  f. as human eye cd. see   313:16
  f. back through creeks and inlets   85:2
  f. from de old folks   112:9
  f. from eye, f. from heart   213:17
  f. from the madding crowd's ... strife   126:12
  from f., from eve and morning   136:7
  good news from a f. country   38:29
  John Peel when he's f. f. away   125:6
  old Kentucky Home f. away   112:7

Far (*continued*)
  one f.-off divine event   313:9
  over the hills and f. away   195:3
  so near and yet so f.   313:2
  Thursday's child has f. to go   191:8
Farce: the farce is over   232:8
Farces: for physic and f. his equal ... scarce is   114:17
Fardels: who wd. f. bear   250–1:20
Fare: f. thee well ... for ever f.   70:16
  f. thee well for I must leave thee   17:4
  go farther and f. worse   214:40
Farewell: A F. to Arms   130:6
  bores through his castle wall, and f., king!   283:6
  can I ... bid these joys f. ?   150:11
  discharged his f. shot   303:3
  f., a long f. to all my greatness   261:9
  f., fair cruelty   290:16
  f., happy fields   176:4
  f., Leicester Square   329:1
  f. the plumed troops ... big wars   280:2
  f., the tranquil mind   280:2
  hail and f.   77:17
  saying 'F. blighted love'   16:12
  so f. hope ... f. fear   177:14
  sweets to the sweet; f.   253:4
Farmer: all ran after the f.'s wife   195:1
  an old Dutch f. who remarked   159:14
  this is the f. sowing his corn   194:8
Farmers: three jolly f. once bet a pound   97:2
Farthing: a f. from a thousand pounds   226:37
  I will never pay a f.   94:10
  two mites, which make a f.   45:15
Farthings: the Latin word for three f.   268:10
  you owe me five f.   192:4
Fascination: right elbow has a f.   118:13
Fashion: art not for the f. of these times   243:19
  as out of the f.   83:15
  faith but as the f. of his hat   277:10
  faithful ... Cynara! in my f.   101:11
  nothing else holds f.   290:9
Fashioned so slenderly   134:10
Fast: a hermit's f.   149:1
  f. bind, f. find   213:18
  he tires ... that spurs too f.   282:4
  they stumble that run f.   286:15
Faster: run far f. than the rest   27:14
Fat: f. is in the fire   213:19
  f. of the land   31:13
  feed f. the ancient grudge   274:7
  Jack Sprat cd. eat no f.   190:7
  Jeshurun waxed f.   33:7
  men ado about me that are f.   262:9
  one ... is f. and grows old   254:14
Fate: a bone to pick with f.   186:5
  customary f. of new truths   138:1
  f. so enviously debars   167:17
  fixed f., free will   177:6
  Foreknowledge, Will, and F.   177:6
  hanging breathless on thy f.!   160:11
  I am the master of my f.   130:10
  I and my fellows are ministers of F.   288:15
  limits of a vulgar f.   127:2
  my dear ... my life, my f.   314:4
  take a bond of f.   271:16
  that one might read the book of f.!   257:4
  when F. summons, Monarchs must obey   104:13

Fate (*continued*)
    will in us is over-rul'd by f.   166:14
    with a heart for any f.   161:2
Fates: masters of their f.   262:8
Father: as a f. pitieth his children   36:28
    child whose f. goes to the devil   216:10
    cry not when his f. dies   140:17
    foredoom'd his f.'s soul to cross   201:11
    full fathom five thy f. lies   288:1
    gave her f. forty-one   14:3
    hath the rain a f. ?   35:13
    have we not all one f. ?   43:5
    honour thy f. and thy mother   32:4
    like f., like son   219:11
    my mother groan'd, my f. wept   56:3
    shall a man leave his f. ?   48:25
    she has deceived her f.   279:5
    so were her f. and mother before   15:11
    son of a dear f. murder'd   250:18
    take example by your f.   98:24
    wise child that knows its own f.   230:23
    wise f. that knows his own child   274:12
    wise son maketh a glad f.   38:8
    wish is f. to the thought   230:26
Fathers: blood is fet from f. of war-proof   259:4
    f. have eaten a sour grape   41:16
    iniquity of the f. upon the children   32:1
Fathom: full f. five thy father lies   288:1
Fathom-line cd. never touch the ground   254:4
Fathoms: bury it certain f. in the earth   289:5
Fatigued ... tie up the knocker   201:10
Fatter: valley sheep are f.   199:6
Fault: a f. ... grows two thereby   131:9
    body without f. or stain   58:6
    excusing of a f. ... make f. worse   265:1
    f., dear Brutus, is not in our stars   262:8
    glorious f. of angels and of gods   201:7
Faultless: lifeless that is f.   219:7
Faults: be to her f. a little blind   205:5
    England, with all thy f.   93:7
    every man has his f.   212:32
    f. are theirs that commit ... permit   213:20
    f. are thick ... love is thin   213:21
    friend that will tell me ... f.   215:8
    his f. lie gently on him!   261:14
    rich men have no f.   224:17
    tell me all my f.   295:18
    with all her f., ... my country   82:1
Favour: I hold with those who f. fire   113:12
    king's f. is no inheritance   218:3
    truths in and out of f.   113:9
Favourite: a f. has no friend   125:11
Favours: hangs on princes' f.   261:10
    neither beg ... your f.   269:8
Fawning: how like a f. publican he looks!   274:7
Fear: capable not only of f. and hate   237:8
    concessions of the weak are ... of f.   64:4
    doth walk in f. and dread   86:16
    faith ... arming me from f.   58:12
    f. ... God, ... walk in ... his ways   33:1
    f. no more the heat o' th' sun   247:9
    f. not, said he, for mighty dread   311:4
    for f. of little men   10:9
    freedom from f. ... anywhere   235:4
    from hope and f. set free   310:1
    having little to f. ... from censure   140:4
    I f. the Greeks, even when   321:2

Fear (*continued*)
    I f. thee, ancient Mariner   86:9
    I f. thy kisses, gentle maiden   300:7
    I guess an' f.   66:13
    I'll f. not what men say   63:14
    irrational f. of life   90:4
    many things to f.   22:14
    men f. death, as children f. dark   21:9
    mortality, behold and f.   25:8
    needs f. no fall ... no pride   63:15
    no f. in love   50:13
    O word of f.   268–9:17
    only thing ... to f. is f. itself   234:18
    perfect love casteth out f.   50:13
    quite unaccustomed to f.   16:15
    who neither beg nor f.   269:8
    wise f. ... forbids the robbing   82:3
    with f. and trembling   48:28
    with hope, farewell f.   177:14
    yet do I f. thy nature   270:1
Fearful: a lovely and a f. thing   69:16
    our f. innocence   333:11
    our f. trip is done   325:12
    snatch a f. joy   126:1
    thy f. symmetry   56:5
    'tis melancholy and a f. sign   69:18
Fears: bound in to saucy doubts and f.   271:6
    enough for fifty hopes and f.   60:13
    have f. that I may cease to be   151:7
    humanity with all its f.   160:11
    not without ... f. and distastes   21:14
    past Regrets and future F.   110:2
    so are their griefs and f.   21:17
Feast: as good as a f.   54:3
    as you were going to a f.   145:9
    bare imagination of a f.   282:1
    chief nourisher in life's f.   270:11
    company makes the f.   210:4
    enough is as good as a f.   212:27
    f., and yr. halls are crowded   326:10
    perpetual f. of nectared sweets   172:18
Feather: birds of a f.   208:1
    he stuck a f. in his cap   196:4
    knocked me down with a f.   218:7
Feathers: cover thee with his f.   36:25
    crow, beautified with our f.   127:6
Feats: 'twas one of my f.   70:17
February: excepting F. alone   194:6
Fed: appetite ... grown by what it f. on   248:4
    bite the hand that f. them   64:16
    f. with the same food   274:17
    he on honey-dew hath f.   87:16
    hungry sheep look up and are not f.   175:4
Federation: the F. of the world   313:17
Fee: taking a f. with a grin   117:5
Feeble: not enough to help the f. up   289:9
Feed: f. fat the ancient grudge   274:7
    f. me till I want no more   329:2
    f. me with food convenient   39:6
    f. upon strawberries, sugar and cream   188:8
Feel: I f. it when I sorrow most   312:13
    I f. no pain, dear mother   15:9
    see, not f., how beautiful   87:8
    to f. what wretches f.   266:14
    we uncomfortable f.   120:5
    what I fancy I f.   12:9
    world ... a tragedy to those who f.   322:7
Feels: man is as old as he f.   220:17
Fees: as they took their f.   27:3

Feet: at the f. of Gamaliel 47:10
  chase the ... Hours with flying f. 69:4
  did those f. in ancient time 55:8
  f. of him that bringeth good tidings 41:4
  f. was I to the lame 35:10
  palms before my f. 81:3
  walked those blessed f. 253:14
  what flowers are at my f. 150:1
Feigning: most friendship is f. 245:1
  truest poetry ... most f. 245:10
Felicity: absent thee from f. awhile 253:9
  our own f. we make or find 123:17
  perfect bliss and sole f. 166:10
  tavern chair ... throne of human f. 145:2
Felix qui potuit ... cognoscere causas 321:7
Fell: bowed himself ... and the house f. 33:22
  I do not love thee, Dr. F. 59:9
  it f. to earth, I know not where 160:10
Fellow: hail f., well met 309:3
  you're a f. Sir ..., you're another 98:22
  you threaten us, f. ? 62:5
Fellow-creatures: make his f. wise 121:3
Fellow-men: one that loves his f. 137:6
Fellowship: manhood, nor good f. in thee 253:19
  right hands of f. 48:20
Felony: make it a f. to drink ... beer 260:9
Felt: darkness which may be f. 31:22
Female: f. of sex it seems 180:15
  f. of the species is more deadly 154:14
  into the ark the male and the f. 30:20
  male and f. created he them 30:3
  what f. heart can gold despise ? 125:10
Femina: varium et mutabile semper f. 321:3
Femme: en un mot, elle est f. 232:10
Fen: a f. of stagnant waters 333:12
Fences: good f. make good neighbours 113:13
Ferry: to row us o'er the f. 72:8
Fertile: in such a fix to be so f. 186:11
Fester: lilies that f. 294:3
Festina lente 308:3
Fettered: so f. fast we are! 60:10
Fetters: no man loveth his f. 220:16
Feu: ce qu'est au f. le vent 67:13
Fever: after life's fitful f. he sleeps well 271:4
  bred a f. ... famine grew 315:17
Février: Generals Janvier and F. 187:15
Few: far and f., are the lands 158:5
  let thy words be f. 39:16
  miserable ... to have f. things to desire 22:14
  most may err as grossly as the f. 103:8
  so f. enthusiasts can be trusted 24:1
  some f. [books] to be ... digested 23:7
  the sound is forc'd, the notes are f. 56:14
  we f., we happy f. 260:2
Fewer: the f. men, the greater ... honour 259:13
Fiat justitia, ruat coelum 213:24
Fibs: I'll tell you no f. 123:10
Fickle: woman ... f. and changing 321:3
Fiction: condemn it as an improbable f. 291:14
  truth is stranger than f. 228:25
  truth ... stranger than f. 70:10
Fiddle: f. while Rome is burning 213:25
  fit as a f. 213:36
  play first (or second) f. 223:8
  the cat and the f. 189:5
Fiddler: f. statesman and buffoon 103:4

Fiddler (*continued*)
  the f.'s standing by 14:15
Fiddlers: called for his f. three 192:1
Fiddlestick: my master's lost his f. 188:7
Fidele: to fair F.'s grassy tomb 88:8
Fie upon this quiet life! 254:12
Field: action in the tented f. 278:21
  behold her, single in the f. 334:16
  cottage small beside a f. of grain 198:4
  for the f. is full of shades 316:7
  happy f. or mossy cavern 149:4
  in the f. after the reapers 33:27
  man for the f. 314:18
  never in the f. of human conflict 82:15
  some corner of a foreign f. 59:5
  thro' the f. the road runs by 313:11
  what though the f. be lost ? 175:18
Fields: 'a babbl'd of green f. 259:2
  cockpit hold the vasty f. of France ? 258:6
  dream of battled f. no more 239:9
  f. where joy for ever dwells 176:4
  from the cotton f. away 112:10
  pagans in those holy f. 253:14
  tyrant of his f. withstood 126:11
  walk through the f. in gloves 90–1:16
  we shall fight in the f. 82:13
  your time among green f. 324:17
Fiend: a f. hid in a cloud 56:3
  a frightful f. ... behind him 86:16
  ingratitude, thou marble-hearted f. 265:14
Fierce: lion is not so f. as ... painted 219:15
Fiery: Shadrach ... into the burning f. furnace 41:25
Fife: stirring drum, th'ear-piercing f. 280:2
Fifteen: at ... f., the mistress of the Earl 329:5
  f. men on the dead man's chest 307:4
  the maiden of bashful f. 301:17
Fifth of November: please to remember the f. 14:5
Fifty: care f. times more for a marriage 23:19
  enough for f. hopes and fears 60:13
  f. different sharps and flats 62:1
  here's to the widow of f. 301:17
  in Sodom f. righteous 31:3
  one ?—f. thousand! [guilders] 62:2
  time-lag of f. years 324:15
Fig: they sewed f. leaves together 30:12
Fight: f. in France ... seas ... beaches 82:13
  f. the good f. of faith 49:15
  fought the better f. 178:19
  I dare not f.; but I will wink 258:10
  I have fought a good f. 49:17
  man being too proud to f. 329:7
  not cease from mental f. 55:8
  through the perilous f. 153:6
  warned them the Britain would f. on alone 83:4
  we ... are baffled to f. better 60:12
  we don't f. for anything 324:18
  we don't want to f., but by jingo 137:4
  we'll f. and we'll conquer 115:1
  when the f. begins within himself 60:14
  you cannot f. against the future 121:7
Fighter: fits a dull f. 255:17
Fighting: f. a liar in the quad 305:19
  not conquering but f. well 91:2
  were f. for the crown 190:9
Fights: he that f. and runs away 13:8
  I quote the f. historical 120:4
Figs grew upon thorn 81:1

Flatter: Mr. Lely, f. me not   94:10
Flattered: I have not f. its rank breath   69:5
Flatterer: scoundrel, hypocrite, and f.   55:6
Flattering: talent for f. with delicacy   21:1
Flattery: f.'s the food for fools   308:12
   gained by every sort of f.   80:17
   gross f. to name a coward   317:12
   I can stand anything but f.   295:18
   imitation ... sincerest form of f.   88:19
   pernicious ... love of f.   306:6
   supports with insolence ... paid with f.
   140:10
   what is principle against ... f.   301:18
Flavour: gives it [life] all its f.   93:8
Flaw: it is a f. in happiness   147:11
Flaws: break into a hundred thousand f.   266:4
Flax: smoking f. shall he not quench   41:2
Flea: a f. hath smaller fleas   309:4
Fleas: great f. have little f.   184:7
   little f. have lesser f.   184:7
Fleckno(e) ... who like Augustus   104:13
Fled: I f. Him down the nights   316:9
   whence all but he had f.   130:4
Flee from the wrath to come   43:12
Fleece was white as snow   127:11
Fleet-Street ... very animated appearance
143:14
Flesh: a pound of that same merchant's f.
275:5
   a thorn in the f.   48:18
   all f. is as grass   50:4
   all f. is grass   40:29
   all this f. keep in a little life   256:2
   and f. and blood so cheap   135:4
   bring me f. and bring me wine   187:2
   f., f., how art thou fishified   286:16
   f. is weak   45:2
   f. of my f.   30:9
   f. which walls about our life   283:6
   from her fair and unpolluted f.   253:3
   going the way of all f.   324:2
   I have more f. ... more frailty   255:13
   I wants to make yr. f. creep   98:19
   shocks that f. is heir to   250–1:20
   study a weariness of the f.   39:28
   the f. to feel the chain   58:15
   the soul to feel the f.   58:15
   the Word was made f.   46:17
   the world, the f., and the devil   52:24
   this too too solid f. wd. melt   248:2
   this world-wearied f.   287:4
   two shall be one f.   48:25
   we wrestle not against f.   48:27
   what a change of f.   25:8
Fleshly School of Poetry   62:12
Fleshpots: when we sat by the f.   31:27
Flew: the white foam f.   86:4
Flies: as f. to wanton boys are we   266:20
   close mouth catcheth no f.   209:33
   he f. through the air   159:5
   murmurous haunt of f.   150:2
Flight: beetle wheels his droning f.   126:4
   swift be thy approaching f.   126:4
Flint: f. is pierced with ... shower   155:16
   hard as a f.   216:11
Flirt: how can [a bishop] f.?   303:13
Floats on high o'er vales and hills   331:7
Flock: keeping watch over their f.   45:20
   silent was the f. in woolly fold   147:12
Flocks: watched their f. by night   311:4

Flog a dead horse   213:39
Flogging: less f. in our great schools   143:20
Flood: bridge much broader than the f.
277:14
   taken at the f., leads—God knows where
   70:3
   taken at the f., leads on to fortune   264:3
Flooding: comes silent f. in the main   85:2
Floods: spirit to bathe in fiery f.   273:10
Floor of heaven is thick inlaid   275:8
Florence: F., Elizabethan England   138:8
   rode past fair F.   148:12
Flotte: elle f., elle hésite   232:10
Flourish: all things f. where you turn   204:4
Flourishing like a green bay-tree   36:10
Flow gently, sweet Afton   65:11
Flower: a fancy from a f.-bell   60:13
   a Heaven in a wild f.   54:12
   a lovelier f. ... was never sown   335:9
   as a f. of the field ... he flourisheth   37:1
   force that ... drives the f.   315:16
   honey ... from every opening f.   323:1
   London ... f. of Cities   105:4
   many a f. is born to blush unseen   126:10
   may prove a beauteous f.   286:11
   patience is a f.   222:35
   pluck this f., safety   254:10
   the f. ... once has blown for ever dies   110:4
   this same f. that smiles today   132:7
   to me the meanest f. ... can bring   332:6
Flowers: a bunch of other men's f.   183:6
   f. that bloom in the spring, Tra la   118:15
   fresh showers for the thirsting f.   298:4
   gather the f., but spare the buds   168:6
   gave, once, her f. to love   59:6
   grow f. and ... got no majesty   324:17
   I cannot see what f.   150:1
   late f. for the bees   147:2
   on chalic'd f. that lies   246:13
   say it with f.   196:10
   the azure f. that blow   125:9
   the blushing f. shall rise   204:4
   the f. appear on the earth   40:9
   with leaves and f. do cover   324:3
Flowing with milk and honey   31:18
Flown with insolence and wine   176:8
Fluffy, with no brains at all   131:5
Flügel: wo dein sanfter F. weilt   238:12
Fluttered yr. Volscians in Corioli   246:12
Fluttering and dancing in the breeze   331:7
Fly: a f. can't bird, but a bird can f.   172:6
   f. away Peter ... come back Paul   195:5
   I will f. to thee   149:16
   man is not a f.   203:2
   pigs might f.   223:5
   small gilded f. does lecher   267:4
   they f. forgotten, as a dream   323:6
   up above the world you f.   74:9
   which way I f. is Hell   177:13
Flying-fishes play   155:1
Foam: f. of perilous seas   150:4
   like the f. on the river   239:10
   the white f. flew   86:4
Foe: I fear no f. with thee at hand   163:7
   make one worthy man my f.   201:18
   overcome but half his f.   176:13
   the robbing of a f.   82:3
   when I ask I am a f.   218:35
   who never made a f.   312:5
Foeman bares his steel, tarantara   120:5

Foes: judge a man by his f.   90:6
Fog: a London particular ... A f.   97:9
  f. comes on little cat feet   238:4
  hover through the f. and filthy air   269:4
  yellow f. that rubs its back   106:13
Folds: tinklings lull the distant f.   126:4
Follies: the pretty f. that ... commit   274:14
Follow: f. me, and I will make you fishers   43:14
  f. the Gleam   314:8
  f. the river ... get to the sea   214:1
  f. thy fair sun   72:12
Followed: the furrow f. free   86:4
Follows: though she draws him, yet she f.
  161:6
Folly: all my joys to this are f.   67:8
  brood of F. without father bred   173:5
  deem it not ... presumptuous f.   129:2
  fool returneth to his f.   38:31
  frailty, f., also crime   69:18
  learned f. is intolerable   221:22
  lovely woman stoops to f.   107:5, 124:1
  most loving mere f.   245:1
  natural f. is bad enough   221:22
  rememb'rest not the slightest f.   244:3
  shunn'st the noise of f.   173:8
  where ignorance ... 'tis f. to be wise   126:2
Fond: not over-f. of resisting temptation   26:3
Fonder: absence makes the heart grow f.   14:8,
  25:5
Food: Continent ... good f.; ... England ...
  good ... manners   170:7
  flattery's the f. for fools   308:12
  if music be the f. of love   290:10
  minds are not ever craving ... f.   93:17
  no love sincerer than ... of f.   296:4
  nothing to eat but f.   131:8
  seeking the f. he eats   244:6
Fool: a child, nor yet a f. to fame   201:13
  a f. at forty ... f. indeed   337:12
  a f. his whole life long   163:2
  a f. sees not the same tree   57:3
  a f. the rest of his dull life   25:7
  a wise man or a f.   55:7
  and my poor f. is hang'd !   268:4
  at thirty man suspects himself a f.   338:1
  cannot play the f. on occasion   230:24
  dost thou call me f., boy ?   265:13
  eight [hours' sleep] for a f.   225:25
  even a f. ... is counted wise   38:20
  f. and his money are soon parted   214:2
  f. ... ask more than wisest ... answer   88:20
  f. hath said in his heart   35:20
  f. returneth to his folly   38:31
  f. some of the people   160:1
  f. that forgets himself   214:4
  f. that is not melancholy   214:5
  f. to the market ... f. he'll return   214:6
  f. wanders ... wise man travels   214:7
  how ill white hairs become a f.   258:3
  I am fortune's f.   286:20
  I met a f. i' th' forest   244:8
  laughter of the f.   39:19
  more of the f. than of the wise   22:3
  no creature smarts so little as a f.   201:12
  no f. like an old f.   214:3
  O f., I shall go mad   266:4
  rod for the f.'s back   38:30
  so true a f. is love   293:20
  talks to himself, speaks to a f.   227:13
  the f. of love, unpractis'd   104:15

Fool (*continued*)
  the wisest f. in Christendom   130:13
  thou art a great f.   256:16
  transform'd into a strumpet's f.   242:9
Foolish: a very f., fond old man   267:11
  f. thing was but a toy   292:3
  he never said a f. thing   234:11
  penny wise, pound f.   223:3
Fools: a shoal of f. for tenders   89:10
  all our yesterdays have lighted f.   272:10
  flattery ... food for f.   308:12
  f. admire, but men of sense approve   202:11
  f. are in a terrible ... majority   138:3
  f. are my theme   70:11
  f.! for I also had my hour   81:3
  f. rush in ... angels fear to tread   202:16
  f., who came to scoff   122:10
  fortune always favours f.   115:12
  fortune favours f.   214:11
  God sends fortune to f.   215:10
  if f. went not to market   214:8
  knaves and f. divide the world   218:6
  lawyers' houses ... on the heads of f.   218:26
  never-failing vice of f.   202:4
  not harsh [philosophy] as ... f. suppose
  172:18
  Paradise of F.   177:11
  poems are made by f. like me   153:9
  poor f. decoyed into our condition   199:10.
  suckle f. and chronicle small beer   279:8
  this great stage of f.   267:8
  travellers ... f. at home condemn   288:14
  what f. these mortals be ?   277:3
  ye suffer f. gladly   48:17
  you f.! I and my fellows   288:15
  young men think old men f.   231:8
  zeal ... is found mostly in f.   231:13
Foot: and the Forty-second F.   134:12
  Feeble of f., and rheumatic   57:15
  her f. was light   148:15
  nay, her f. speaks   290:8
  noiseless f. of Time   242:8
  one f. in sea, and one on shore   277:21
  one f. in the grave   222:28
  put one's best f. forward   207:15
  thou shalt give ... f. for f.   32:10
  Thyself with shining F. shall pass   111:1
  who cleft the devil's f.   101:5
  ye that on the sands with printless f.   289:4
Footpath: jog on, the f. way   292:19
Footprint: looking for a man's f.   26:8
Footprints in the sands of time   161:1
Foppery: an excellent f. of the world   265:10
Forbearance ceases to be a virtue   64:10
Forbidden: wanted ... because f.   318:15
Forbids: f. the cheating of our friends   82:3
  f. the robbing of a foe   82:3
Force: admit no f. but argument   60:4
  f. is not a remedy   58:11
  f. that through the green fuse   315:16
  own no argument but f.   60:4
  subtlety is better than f.   226:30
  that armed f. shall not be used   319:5
  use of f. alone ... *temporary*   64:5
  who overcomes by f.   176:13
Ford: the time of our F.   137:8
Fordoes: either makes me or f. me   280:9
Forebode not any severing of our loves   332:5
Forecast: I cannot f. to you the action of Russia
  82:10

Forefathers: rude f. of the hamlet   126:6
  think of yr. f.!   9:2
Fore-finger: on the f. of an alderman   286:1
Forehead: curl ... in the middle of her f.   161:8
Foreheads: with f. villainous low   289:2
Foreign: some corner of a f. field   59:5
Foreigners always spell better   318:13
Foreknowledge absolute   177:6
Forest: a fool i' th' f.   244:8
  fade away into the f. dim   149:14
  Till Birnam F. come to Dunsinane   272:7
Forests: when fishes flew and f. walked   81:1
Foretell: expiring do f. of him   282:4
  who can f. for what high cause?   168:5
Forever: pickets off duty f.   26:10
  that is f. England   59:5
  that vast f.   154:2
Forewarned, forearmed   214:9
Forget: and if thou wilt, f.   236:5
  better ... you shd. f. and smile   236:2
  don't f. the diver   146:14
  forgive and f.   214:10
  lest we f.!   155:4
  look on her face and you'll f.   204:6
  old men f., yet all shall be forgot   260:1
  smile at us, pay us, pass us, but do not quite
    f.   81:9
  the best sometimes f.   279:9
Forgetfulness: sleep my senses in f.   257:2
Forgets: is a fool that f. himself   214:4
Forgetting: our birth is but a sleep and a f.
  332:1
  world f., by the world forgot   201:9
Forgive: Father, f. them   46:13
  f. and forget   214:10
  noblest vengeance is to f.   229:14
  to err is human, to f. divine   202:14
Forgiveness: and ask of thee f.; so we'll live
  267:13
  mutual f. of each vice   55:3
Forgot: shd. auld acquaintance be f.?   65:12
Forgotten: learnt nothing, f. nothing   310:12
  long absent, soon f.   219:24
  they fly, f., as a dream   323:6
Forlorn: f! the very word is like a bell   150:5
  glimpses that wd. make me less f.   333:4
Form: ah, what the f. divine!   156:13
  earth was without f.   30:1
  his f. had not yet lost ... brightness   176:11
  in f. and moving, how ... admirable!   250:6
  the F. remains   334:9
  thy f. from off my door!   200:19
Forms: by f. unseen ... dirge is sung   88:11
  f. more real than living man   299:11
  f. of things unknown   277:6
  hope from outward f. to win   87:9
Fornication: but ... in another country   166:5
Forsake not an old friend   51:20
Fortitude: that was great f. of mind   141:14
Fortress: this f. built by Nature for herself
  282:5
Fortuna: fortis f. adiuvat   315:3
Fortunate: as he was f., I rejoice   263:10
  be f. without adding ... felicity   141:8
Fortune: a youth to f. and to fame unknown
  126:13
  children ... hostages to f.   21:19
  fair face is half a f.   213:13
  f. always favours fools   115:12
  f. favours fools   214:11

Fortune (*continued*)
  f. favours the brave   315:3
  f., good night; smile once more   265:20
  f. is blind   214:12
  God sends f. to fools   215:10
  I am f.'s fool   286:20
  method of making a f.   127:3
  my face is my f., sir   196:1
  of f.'s sharp adversity   80:5
  possession of a f. ... in want of a wife   20:17
  slings and arrows of outrageous f.   250:20
  taken at the flood, leads on to f.   264:3
  well-favoured ... the gift of f.   278:4
  when f. knocks, open   214:13
  when we are sick in f.   265:10
Fortune-teller: threadbare juggler and a f.
  246:5
Forty: every man over f. is a scoundrel   296:16
  fool at f. is a fool indeed   337:12
  f. centuries look down on you   185:10
  f. years on, growing older   57:15
  gave her mother f. whacks   276:19
  girdle round ... earth in f. minutes   276:19
  he that is ... not rich at f.   216:3
  his death ... at f. odd befell   134:13
  I had rather than f. shillings   276:2
  passing rich with f. pounds   122:9
  together now for f. years   81:14
Forty-niner: dwelt a miner, f.   183:8
Forward: f. the Light Brigade!   311:10
  f. tho' I canna see   66:13
  look f. to with hope   113:10
  those behind cried 'F.!'   163:13
Foster-child: thou f. of silence   149:6
Fought: better to have f. and lost   84:18
  but what they f. each other for   304:14
  f. with us upon St. Crispin's day   260:2
Foul: blood is nipp'd and ways be f.   269:6
  fair is f. and f. is fair   269:4
  I doubt some f. play   248:12
  nothing can seem f. to those that win
  255:18
  so f. and fair a day   269:6
  thank the gods I am f.   245:11
Foul-mouthed: the English ... a f. nation
  129:9
Found: half-buried in the snow was f.   160:13
  I have f. it! (Eureka!)   18:4
  thou shalt not be f. out   212:20
  when f., make a note of   98:3
Foundation of morals and legislation   29:1
Fountain: a woman mov'd is like a f. troubled
  287:12
Fountains: and O, ye F., Meadows, Hills
  332:5
  passion ... life, whose f. are within   87:9
Founts: white f. falling in the Courts of the sun
  81:4
Four: founded upon f. essential human freedoms   235:4
  f. angels round my head   9:13
  f. elements warring within our breasts
  166:10
  f. lagging winters and f. wanton springs
  281:12
  f. seasons in the mind   151:14
  f. times as big as the bush   158:12
  the f. pillars of government   22:8
  there are f. classes of Idols   23:16
  they f. had one likeness   41:21

Four (*continued*)
  when angry, count f. 318:18
Four-footed: devil's walking parody on all f.
  things 81:2
Fourpence: took f. home to my wife 190:2
Fourscore and upward, not an hour more
  267:11
Fourteen months ... idle and unprofitable
  116:1
Fowl: broiled f. and mushrooms—capital!
  98:17
Fox: f. from his lair in the morning 125:6
  gentlemen galloping after a f. 328:10
Frabjous day! Callooh! Callay! 75:11
Fragrance: inward f. of each other's heart
  148:10
Frailties: draw his f. from their dread abode
  126:15
Frailty: f. folly, also crime 69:18
  f., thy name is woman 248:5
  love's but the f. of the mind 89:14
  love's the noblest f. 104:8
  more flesh ... and therefore more f. 255:13
Frame: all the human f. requires 27:4
  man ... bears in his bodily f. 95:10
  spangled heavens, a shining f. 9:9
France: bâton de maréchal de F. 185:13
  best thing between F. and England 139:18
  fair stood the wind for F. 102:9
  F. is alone; and God is alone 297:4
  order ... this matter better in F. 306:11
  the vasty fields of F. ? 258:6
  we shall fight in F., we shall fight on the seas
  82:13
  what I gained by being in F. 144:14
Frank, haughty, rash—the Rupert 63:2
Frankfort: I went to F. and got drunk 204:13
Frankie and Johnny 15:2
Fraternity: liberty, equality, f. 17:8
Fray: latter end of a f. 255:17
Frederick: cruel F. 133:9
Free: all men everywhere cd. be f. 159:12
  beauteous evening, calm and f. 333:2
  flag that makes you free 336:10
  her looks were f. 86:8
  love Virtue, she alone is f. 173:4
  man ... born f. ... is in chains 236:12
  mother of the f. 28:10
  o'er the land of the f. 153:7
  others abide our question. Thou art f. 19:2
  pure ..., majestic, f. 333:13
  quite set f. ... Eurydice 174:10
  so cleanly I myself can f. 102:12
  so f. we seem, so fettered ... are 60:10
  that Greece might still be f. 70:1
  the furrow followed f. 86:4
  the valiant man and f. 313:7
  thought is f. 227:35
  we cannot be f. men if 159:9
  we must be f. or die 334:1
  what a f. government is 64:17
Freed: from the thousands He hath f. 78:12
Freedom: a new birth of f. 159:13
  battle for f. and truth 138:4
  can do for the f. of man 153:2
  every infringement of human f. 200:8
  f. and Whisky 65:14
  f. from fear ... anywhere 235:4
  f. from want—everywhere 235:4
  F. is Slavery 197:4

Freedom (*continued*)
  f. of speech and expression 235:4
  F. shall a-while repair 88:11
  f. ... to worship God 235:4
  f. with which Dr. Johnson condemns 65:6
  least regard for human f. 305:6
  love not f., but licence 182:11
  none can love f. ... but good men 182:11
  those who deny f. to others 159:9
  whose service is perfect f. 52:17
  yet, F.! yet thy banner 69:7
Freedoms: world ... upon four essential human
  f. 235:4
Freezings: what f. have I felt 294:4
French: F. are wiser than they seem 22:20
  F. of Paris was to her unknowe 79:4
  F., or Turk, or Proosian 120:3
  F. say, there are three sexes 303:14
  F. she spak ful faire 79:4
  he's gone to fight the F. 146:3
  how it's improved her F. 124:11
  not too F. F. bean 119:5
Frenchmen: fifty million F. can't be wrong
  127:10
Frenzy: demonic f., moping melancholy
  179:13
  poet's eye in a fine f. rolling 277:6
Fresh: bloom sae f. and fair 67:5
  f. as in the month of May 79:3
  I shd. feel f. and vigorous 322:14
  looking as f. as paint 303:2
Freshness: glory and ... f. of a dream 331:12
Fret: nuns f. not 332:13
Frets: that struts and f. his hour 272:10
Fretted the ... body to decay 102:17
Friday: F. night is Amami night 11:3
  F.'s child is loving and giving 191:8
  worse on F. 193:6
Friend: a faithful f. is ... medicine 51:16
  a fav'rite has no f.! 125:11
  a f. ... the masterpiece of Nature 108:4
  (all he wished) a f. 126:14
  best mirror ... old f. 221:5
  faithful are the wounds of a f. 39:3
  forsake not an old f. 51:20
  f. at court 214:17
  f., go up higher 45:30
  f. in need ... f. indeed 214:18
  f. shd. bear his f.'s infirmities 264:2
  f. that will tell ... my faults 215:8
  f. to everybody ... f. to nobody 214:20
  f. to thyself ... others will befriend 214:19
  good wine—a f.—or being dry 10:3
  handsome and witty, yet a f. 204:3
  if I had a f. that loved her 279:2
  keep thy f. under ... life's key 242:1
  keep wel thy tonge ... keep thy f. 80:3
  lend yr. money and lose yr. f. 218:36
  loan ... loses ... itself and f. 248:17
  makes no f. who never made a foe 312:5
  my guide, philosopher and f. 203:11
  of every friendless name the f. 140:14
  only way to have a f. 108:5
  open enemy than a false f. 207:19
  save me from the candid f. 72:16
  speak well of your f. 226:6
  tolling a departed f. 256:7
  trust not a new f. 228:23
  up the ladder ... choosest a f. 214:39
  when I lend I am a f. 218:35

Friends: a soul remembering my good f. 282:8
   animals are such agreeable f. 105:16
   best of f. must part 17:4, 214:23
   can live without our f. 219:21
   expectation of finding many f. 142:17
   f. are thieves of time 214:21
   f. begin to compliment him 138:10
   f. in heaven and in hell 214:22
   f. of the mammon of unrighteousness 46:7
   f., Romans, countrymen 263:11
   f. shd. be few and good 208:17
   God defend me from my f. 215:3
   golden f. I had 136:8
   have but few f. 214:24
   How to Win F. and Influence People 73:12
   I love ... old f., old times 219:21
   in the misfortunes of our best f. 234:9
   judge ... man by his foes as well as ... f.
     90:6
   kiss and be f. 218:4
   laughter learnt of f. 59:7
   lay down his life for his f. 46:31
   leaving his social f. 141:17
   love, obedience, troops of f. 272:5
   marriage of his f. 68:11
   my f. proud of my memory 152:11
   old f. ... wine are best 222:24
   one of our Colonial f. 124:7
   permitted to have f. in the kennel 296:15
   the cheating of our f. 82:3
   those f. thou hast, ... grapple them 248:15
   wealth maketh many f. 38:21
   wd. not enter on my list of f. 93:12
   wounded in the house of ... f. 43:4
Friendship: f. hardly ever [brings money]
   20:10
   f. is constant ... save in ... love 277:15
   f. shd. not be ... one side 214:25
   higher value we ... put on ... f. 142:17
   honest f. with all nations 139:9
   matrimony as a sort of f. 307:7
   most common ties of f. 223:36
   most f. is feigning 245:1
   shd. keep his f. in ... repair 142:5
   that is indeed true f. 237:15
Friendships ... invalidated by marriage 68:11
Frighted: f. the reign of Chaos and old Night
   176:10
   sleep ... how have I f. thee 257:2
Frightened: f. a little mouse under her chair
   192:7
   f. Miss Muffet away..191:3
   words that f. the birds 12:11
Frightful: a f. fiend doth ... tread 86:16
Frigid: so f. upon the fundament 186:9
Frittered away by detail 317:1
Frog: a f. he wd. a-wooing go 189:2
   how public, like a f. 99:14
   on a log, expiring f.! 98:21
Frogs and snails and puppy-dogs' tails 195:6
Frontier: misses the outline of the f. 319:9
Frost: comes a f., a killing f. 261:9
   f. which binds so dear a head 297:9
Frosty: lusty winter, f. but kindly 243:18
Frowned: fair science f. not 126:13
Frugal: she had a f. mind 92:8
Fruit: f. of that forbidden tree 175:15
   ignorance ... like delicate exotic f. 327:11
   sadden after ... bitter f. 110:8
   tree is known by its f. 228:20

Fruit (*continued*)
   until we reach the ripest f. 166:10
Fruitful: be f. and multiply 30:4
Fruitfulness: mists and mellow f. 147:1
Fruition: sweet f. of an earthly crown 166:10
Fruitless: faint hymns to ... f. moon 276:9
Fruits: kindly f. of the earth 52:26
Frustrate their knavish tricks 73:2
Fry in one's own grease 226:17
Frying-pan: out of the f. into the fire 214:26
Fuel: report ... by adding f. to the flame 181:6
Fugitive: nature ... remembers what was so f.
   332:4
Full: f. (fou) of love ... of brandy 66:4
   I wasna f., but just had plenty 65:16
   reading maketh a f. man 23:8
Fume: black, stinking f. thereof [smoking]
   138:14
Fun; I wish I thought *What Jolly F.!* 233:1
   own kin and kith more f. 186:2
   to come and spoil the f. 76:1
Function: the F. never dies 334:9
Fundament: so frigid upon the f. 186:9
Funeral: f. baked meats did coldly furnish
   248:8
   f. marches to the grave 160:15
   not a f. note 330:3
Fungus: like a f. living on ... remains 157:9
Funny: f. peculiar, or f. ha-ha? 129:5
   they do taste kind of f. 13:10
Fur: Oh my f. and whiskers! 74:2
Furnace: f. for your foe so hot 261:3
   into the burning fiery f. 41:25
   the lover, sighing like f. 244:11
Furnish: coldly f. forth the marriage tables
   248:8
   f. you with arguments and intellects 123:22
Furnished: f. and burnish'd by Aldershot sun
   29:12
   rich men f. with ability 52:6
Furniture: no f. so charming as books 303:12
Furor arma ministrat 320:17
Furrow: the f. followed free 86:4
Fury: beware the f. of a patient man 103:9
   civil f. first grew high 67:14
   cunning old F. 74:1
   nor hell a f. like a woman scorned 89:6
   tale ... full of sound and f. 272:10
Fuse: through the green f. drives the flower
   315:16
Fustian: whose f.'s so sublimely bad 201:15
Fustilarian: you f.! 256:14
Future: for I dipt into the f. 313:16
   haven't any f. to think of 296:20
   I never think of the f. 105:12
   if you wd. divine the f. 89:3
   you cannot fight ... the f. 121:7
Futurity: let f. shift for itself 304:1

Gaiety: eclipsed the g. of nations 145:1
Gain: broke the Sabbath but for g. 103:6
   no painful inch to g. 85:2
Gales: cool g. shall fan the glade 204:4
Gallantly streaming 153:6
Gallantry: what men call g. 69:10
Gallery in which the reporters sit 164:4
Gallia ... in partes tres 71:11
Gallimaufry: made our English tongue a g.
   305:17
Galloped: I g., Dirck g., we g. 61:6

Galloping after a fox 328:10

Gallows: his complexion is perfect g. 287:13
shall there be g. standing 253:16

Galumphing: he went g. back 75:10

Gamaliel: brought up ... at the feet of G. 47:10

Game: a rich man's g. 16:11
but how you played the g. 233:12
g. is not worth the candle 214:28
golf ... not being a g. 157:14
lookers-on see most of the g. 219:29
rigour of the g. 156:4
the g.'s afoot 259:5
win this g. ... thrash the Spaniards too 102:8
woman is his g. 314:17

Game-keeper: old poacher ... good g. 222:26

Gamesmanship or ... Winning Games Without ... Cheating 204:15

Gang: the old g. 82:4

Gaol: all ... we know who live in g. 326:15
in a g. better air, better company 143:21

Garden: a g. in her face 72:13
a g. is a lovesome thing 59:10
come into the g., Maud 314:3
dispossessed of the g. hard by Heaven 57:11
fairies at the bottom of our g. 114:11
g. ... purest of human pleasures 23:4
God Almighty first planted a g. 23:4
God the first g. made 91:12
good strawberries in yr. g. 285:3
how does your g. grow? 191:7
patience ... not in everyone's g. 222:35
put him into the g. of Eden 30:6
redbreast whistles from a g. croft 147:5
we must cultivate our g. 321:11

Garland: immortal g. is to be run for 182:4
wither'd is the g. of the war 243:6

Garment: City now doth like a g. wear 333:6
Winter G. of Repentance 109:14

Garments: g. though new-fangled ill 294:2
our purses ... proud, our g. poor 287:11

Garnish: the ... eye of heaven to g. 264:19

Garrick: here lies David G. 123:3

Garrulity: my crime, shameful g. 180:14

Garter: he will unloose, familiar as his g. 258:7
I like the G. ... no damned merit 169:9

Gas smells awful 198:3

Gash: each new day a g. is added 271:18

Gasp: at the last g. 52:10

Gate: aged man, a-sitting on a g. 77:7
at the strait g. 44:8
heavy burdens at his narrow g. 258:8
I am here at the g. alone 314:3
lark at heaven's g. sings 246:13
passion-flower at the g. 314:4
the poor man at his g. 10:5
there's knocking at the g. 272:4
willow cabin at your g. 290:15

Gatepost: you and me and the g. 207:40

Gates: such are the g. of paradise 55:3
the Gaul is at her g.! 92:1

Gath: tell it not in G. 34:10

Gather ye rosebuds while ye may 132:7

Gathering nuts in May 15:7

Gaudeamus igitur 17:13

Gaudy: express'd in fancy; rich, not g. 248:16
one other g. night 243:1

Gaul: G. is divided into three parts 71:11
hark! the G. is at her gates! 92:1

Gave: I g. you all. ... And in good time you g. it 266:1
the Lord g. and ... hath taken away 35:1

Gay: a poet cd. not but be g. 331:10
her heart was young and g. 128:1

Gaza: eyeless in G. 180:9

Gaze: show and g. o' th' time 272:13

Gazed: and still they g. ... the wonder grew 122:12

Gazes: yellow god forever g. down 129:6

Geese: all his g. are swans 214:29
six g. a-laying 194:2
where there are women and g. 230:32

Gem of purest ray serene 126:10

General: as for being a G. 320:1
caviare to the g. 250:10
of a constitution so g. 59:14

Generals: all G. ... some never grow out of it 320:1
bite some of my other g. 115:14
g. are already poring over maps 0:1
Russia has two g. 187:15

Generation: O g. of vipers, who hath warned? 43:12
one g. passeth ... another g. cometh 39:11
unto the third and fourth g. 32:1

Generations: no hungry g. tread thee down 150:4
power of books ... may endure for g. 319:6
save succeeding g. from ... war 319:5

Genius: g. (... capacity of taking trouble) 73:5
g. does what it must 170:5
g. is ... inspiration ... perspiration 105:8
good Edmund, whose g. was such [Burke] 123:1
Good God! what a g. I had 309:13
nothing to declare except my g. 328:16
since when was g. found respectable? 60:6
the G. and the mortal instruments 262:13

Gentle: a g. knight was pricking on the plain 305:10
do not go g. 315:15
his life was g. 264:7
humane and g. virtue 65:2
meek and g. with these butchers 263:7
sleep! it is a g. thing 86:13
the g. mind by g. deeds is known 305:14
this day shall g. his condition 260:2
verray parfit g. knight 79:2

Gentleman: almost a definition of a g. 187:13
always talking about being a g. 308:5
education begins a g., conversation completes 212:18
grand old name of g. 313:8
smooth-fac'd g., tickling commodity 264:13
the English country g. galloping 328:10
who was then the g.? 24:2

Gentlemanly: we must look for ... g. conduct 19:12

Gentlemen: by g. for g. 315:8
g. in England, now abed 260:2
g. of the gentle craft 96:12
G. Prefer Blondes 161:13
g. rankers out on the spree 154:15
God rest you merry, g. 15:3
not a religion for g. 78:15
we are g. of Japan 117:15

Gentleness, in hearts at peace 59:7
Gentlier: music that g. on the spirit lies 314:2
Geography is about maps 29:2
Geometry: no royal road to g. 108:27
George: any good of G. the Third 156:10
    G. the First was ... reckoned vile 156:10
    G. the Third ought never to have occurred
       29:6
    King G. upon the throne 146:3
    viler G. the Second 156:10
Georgia: marching through G. 336:9,10
Georgie Porgie, pudding and pie 189:3
German: I speak ... G. to my horse 78:18
    the G. dictator, instead of snatching 82:9
Germans: Don't let's be Beastly to the G.
    91:9
Germany: G. G. above all 133:7
    G. will be ... world power or will not be
    133:1
Gert and ... Epp and ... Ein 13:4
Get: g. thee glass eyes 267:7
    g. thee to a nunnery 251:2
Getting and spending, we lay waste 333:3
Ghastly: we were a g. crew 86:14
Ghost: plays to the bowling of a g. 316:7
    vex not his g. 268:5
    what beckoning g. ... invites my steps ?
    201:5
Ghosts: g. from an enchanter fleeing 299:3
    haunted by the g. they have depos'd 283:6
    rain is full of g. tonight 170:14
Ghoulies: from g. and ghosties and ... beasties
    13:7
Giant: g.'s strength ... use it like a g. 273:6
    owner whereof was G. Despair 63:11
Giants: there were g. ... in those days 30:19
Giant's-Causeway worth seeing ? 144:16
Gibbon: scribble! Eh, Mr. G. ? 121:13
Gibeon: sun, stand thou still upon G. 33:12
Gift: time with a g. of tears 309:15
Gifts: even when they bring g. 321:2
    man's work or his own g. 181:11
    rich g. wax poor 251:1
Gilded: men are but g. loam 281:8
Gilead: is there no balm in G. ? 41:13
Gilpin: and G. long live he 92:13
    away went G.—who but he ? 92:9
    John G. was a citizen 92:6
    said G., so am I 92:10
Gilt off the gingerbread 227:4
Gimble: gyre and g. in the wabe 75:9
Gingerbread: gilt off the g. 227:4
Girdle: I'll put a g. round ... the earth 276:19
Girl: a g. ... cheeks are covered with paint
    186:1
    little g. who had a little curl 161:8
    marry a country g. afterwards 295:19
    naughty g. to disobey 191:9
    Poor Little Rich G. 91:11
    sweet g.-graduates 314:12
    to the sweetest g. I know 329:1
Girlish: filled ... with g. glee 118:6
Girls: a set of wretched un-idea'd g. 141:17
    all the g. ... so smart 73:3
    passes at g. who wear glasses 198:2
    secrets with g. ... guns with boys 94:1
    servant g. in the kitchen 310:7
    what are little g. made of ? 195:6
    where the g. are so pretty 15:10
Give: better g. a shilling 207:28

Give (continued)
    g. all thou canst 330:11
    g. me an ounce of civet 267:5
    g. me back my legions 71:9
    g. me my soul again 165:8
    g. not thy soul unto a woman 51:19
    g., oh g. me back my heart 71:1
    g. one man a lecture ... another a shilling
    142:10
    g. us the luxuries of life 184:11
    it is more blessed to g. 47:8
    Mother, g. me the sun 138:5
    no more g. the people straw 31:20
    such as I have g. I thee 47:1
    these pleasures, Melancholy, g. 173:13
    when I g., I g. myself 326:3
Given: costs so much as what is g. 222:11
    unto ... one that hath shall be g. 44:28
Giver: a cheerful g. 48:16
Givers: when g. prove unkind 251:1
Gives: blesseth him that g. 275:1
    g. twice who g. quickly 214:35
    who g. to all, denies all 214:34
Giving: g. much to the poor 214:36
    not in the g. vein today 285:7
Glad: and I am g., yea g. 102:12
    never g. confident morning 61:9
Glade: alone in the bee-loud g. 337:4
Gladly wolde he lerne ... teche 79:10
Gladness: sadness and g. succeed each other
    224:34
    teach me half the g. 300:3
Gladsome: let us with a g. mind 180:7
Gladstone's always having the ace of trumps
    155:17
Glance: ten thousand saw I at a g. 331:9
    whose g. was glum 121:2
Glare: maidens ... moths ... caught by a g.
    68:18
Glass: double g. o' the inwariable 99:4
    get thee g. eyes 267:7
    ghosts ... tap and sigh upon the g.
    170:14
    g. is falling hour by hour 164:15
    g. of fashion ... mould of form 251:5
    g. wherein the noble youths 256:17
    grief with a g. that ran 309:15
    look in thy g., and tell 293:11
    made mouths in a g. 266:9
    people who live in g. houses 214:37
    prove an excuse for a g. 301:17
    see through a g. darkly 48:7
    the more women look in their g. 230:35
    turn down an empty g.! 111:1
Glasses: taste, Shakespeare, and the musical g.
    123:23
    there were two g. and two chairs 165:2
Gleam: faiths and empires g. 298:11
    follow the G. 314:8
    the visionary g. 331:16
Gleamed: she g. upon my sight 334:12
Glean: thou shalt not g. thy vineyard 32:15
Gleaned ... after the reapers 33:27
Glee: filled with girlish g. 118:6
    forward and frolic g. was there 239:7
    piping songs of pleasant g. 56:7
Glen: down the rushy g. 10:9
Glides: still g. the Stream 334:9
Glimpses that wd. make me less forlorn
    333:4

God (*continued*)

G. hath given liberty 95:3
G. hath given you one face 251:4
G. heals ... doctor takes the fee 215:4
G. help the poor 215:5
G. help the rich 215:5
G. helps them that help themselves 215:7
G. is alone 297:4
G. is decreeing to begin 182:7
G. is ... for the big battalions 321:17
G. is in heaven and thou upon earth 39:16
G. is love 50:12
G. is no respecter of persons 47:5
G. is not mocked 48:23
G. is our refuge and our strength 36:13
G. is thy law, thou mine 178:7
G. loveth a cheerful giver 48:16
G. made the country 93:6
G. made the wicked Grocer 81:10
G. made the woman for the man 312:2
G. made them, high or lowly 10:5
G. make me able to pay 199:9
G. moves in a mysterious way 92:15
G. must think it ... odd 155:14
g. of our idolatry, the press 93:3
G. order'd motion but ordain'd no rest 320:6
G. our help in ages past 323:4
G. ... put him into ... Eden 30:6
G. rest you merry 15:3
G. said, Let Newton be! 201:21
G. save our Gracious King 73:1
G. save the mark! 254:2
G. saw the light was good 178:21
G. send you joy 215:9
G. shall add unto him 51:4
G. shall wipe away all tears 51:3
G. shed his grace on thee 25:4
G. shd. go before such villains 278:13
G.'s in his heaven 62:7
G.'s mill grinds slow 215:12
'G. tempers the wind,' said Maria 306:15
G. tempers the wind ... shorn lambs 215:11
G. the first garden made 91:12
G., who is our home 332:1
G. who made thee mighty 28:10
hath not one G. created us ? 43:5
he for G. only, she for G. in him 178:3
heavens declare the glory of G. 35:22
honest G. ... noblest work of man 138:9
honest Man's the noblest work of G. 203:8
I am the Lord thy G. 31:29
I reflect that G. is just 139:13
I speak Spanish to G. 78:18
I the Lord your G. am holy 32:14
I ... thy G. am a jealous G. 32:1
if G. be for us 47:21
if G. did not exist 321:14
in apprehension, how like a g.! 250:6
in the beginning G. created 30:2
in the image of G. created He him 30:3
inclines to think there is a G. 84:14
into the hands of the living G. 49:20
isn't life ... terrible ... thank G. ? 316:4
it shall please G. to call me 53:15
just are the ways of G. 180:13
justify the ways of G. to men 175:17
knowledge ... makes a G. of me 148:9
knowledge of G. ... burnt offerings 42:8

God (*continued*)

land which the Lord thy G. giveth 32:4
last and best of all G.'s works 179:10
Lord G. made them all 10:4
love, we are in G.'s hands 60:10
make a joyful noise unto G. 36:19
malt ... to justify G.'s ways to man 136:9
man proposes, G. disposes 220:21
name of the Lord thy G. in vain 32:2
nature is the art of G. 59:13
nearer, my G., to thee 9:3
new Jerusalem, coming ... from G. 51:2
not G. is greater ... than ... self 326:4
O G., O Montreal! 68:9
of such is the kingdom of G. 45:13
Oh! G.! that bread shd. be so dear 135:4
one G., one law, one element 313:9
one on G.'s side is a majority 200:3
only G. can make a tree 153:9
out of the mouth of G. 43:13
peace of G., which passeth 48:31
powers ... ordained of G. 47:28
pray G. we may make haste 282:2
prepare to meet thy G. 42:16
presume not G. to scan 203:5
pretence that G. had put it [ace] there 155:17
pure in heart ... shall see G. 43:16
remember ... the name of the Lord our G. 35:26
resistance ... is obedience to G. 139:11
rib which ... G. had taken 30:8
rich man ... into the kingdom of G. 44:23
sabbath of the Lord thy G. 32:3
Sarah Battle, now with G. 156:4
servant of G., well done! 178:19
serv'd my G. with half the zeal 261:13
shall ... man be more just than G. ? 35:2
shalt love the Lord thy G. 32:22
so G. created man 30:3
so lonely 'twas, that G. himself 87:2
souls ... in the hand of G. 51:12
stern daughter of the voice of G. 334:3
taken at the flood, leads—G. knows 70:3
thank G. we're normal 197:9
the dear G. who loveth us 87:4
the Lord our G. is one Lord 32:21
the Lord thy G. chasteneth thee 32:24
the sacrifices of G. are 36:15
there, but for the grace of G. 58:1
they [voices] come from G. 297:2
this is the finger of G. 31:22
those whom G. hath joined 53:25
thou shalt have one G. only 84:15
though G. hath raised me high 107:14
though the mills of G. grind slowly 161:3
thy G. my G. 33:25
to walk humbly with thy G. 42:24
true love's the gift which G. 239:15
turn to G. to praise 61:5
unto G. the things that are G.'s 44:25
vindicate the ways of G. to Man 202:18
voice of the people is the voice of G. 10:2
was the holy Lamb of G. 55:8
we owe G. a death 257:8
what therefore G. hath joined 45:12
when first G. dawned on Chaos 297:11
who think not G. at all 180:13
whole armour of G. 48:26
whom G. wishes to destroy 223:40

God (*continued*)

whose G. is their belly 48:29

Wonderful, Counsellor, The mighty G. 40:23

wd. G. I had died ... O Absalom 34:14

would to G. we had died 31:27

yellow g. forever gazes down 129:6

youth shows but half; trust G. 62:9

Goddess: g. and maiden and queen 310:3

g. excellently bright 145:8

Godliness: in cheerful g. 333:13

Gods: a daughter of the g. 311:15

as flies ... are we to th' g. 266:20

as g., knowing good and evil 30:11

by the Nine G. he swore 163:9

carve him as a dish fit for the g. 262:14

for the ... temples of his G. 163:10

I thank whatever g. may be 130:8

kings are earth's g. 281:4

kings it makes g. 285:12

leave the rest to G. 90:15

men call gallantry and g. adultery 69:10

no other g. before me 31:30

so many g., so many creeds 326:11

thank the g. I am foul 245:11

the darling of the G. was born 168:5

the g. are just 267:14

voice of all the g. make heaven drowsy 268:13

we thank ... whatever g. may be 310:1

wd. the g. had made thee poetical 245:9

Goest: whither thou g. I will go 33:25

Gog, the land of Magog 41:24

Going: as I was g. to St. Ives 188:3

at the g. down of the sun 54:5

Cross of Jesus g. on before 24:9

g. one knows not where 169:1

I am just g. outside 196:7

I don't feel like g. into it 237:13

men must endure their g. hence 267:12

the Lord shall preserve thy g. 37:17

where are you g. to, my pretty maid ? 195:7

Gold: all is not g. that glitters 206:12

beauty provoketh ... sooner than g. 243:14

building roofs of g. 258:8

fetters, be they made of g. 220:16

floor of heaven ... with patines of bright g. 275:8

g. in phisik is a cordial 79:14

hadde he but litel g. in cofre 79:9

her locks were yellow as g. 86:8

if g. ruste, what shall iren do ? 79:17

king's ... a heart of g. 259:9

led by the nose with g. 293:8

my bow of burning g. 55:8

my g.!—open the shrine 145:17

nor all, that glisters, is g. 125:12

rank is good, and g. is fair 326:6

run back and fetch the age of g. 175:9

saint-seducing g. 285:19

showers ... barbaric pearl and g. 176:15

the poop was beaten g. 242:14

to gild refined g. 264:19

travell'd in the realms of g. 150:14

true love ... differs from g. 298:9

weakness to resist Philistian g. 181:1

wedges of g., great anchors 285:1

what female heart can g. despise ? 125:10

when g. and silver becks me 264:16

worth his weight in g. 231:3

Golden: as they did in the g. world 243:12

from this g. rigol 257:17

girl-graduates in their g. hair 314:12

g. friends I had 136:8

g. lads and girls 247:9

g. rule ... there are no g. rules 296:11

g. slumbers kiss yr. eyes 96:11

love in a g. bowl 55:2

O polished perturbation! g. care! 257:16

silver nutmeg and a g. pear 190:1

the g. years return 298:11

waters of the Nile on every g. scale 73:17

wear a g. sorrow 261:4

Goldsmith: here lies Nolly G. ... called Noll 115:2

Golf may be played on Sunday 157:14

Golf-balls: a thousand lost g. 107:1

Gondolier: a highly respectable g. 116:8

Gone: if she's not g. ... there still 194:4

now thou art g., and never must return 174:14

thou art g., and for ever 239:10

thy thoughts, when thou art g. 300:6

what's g. ... shd. be past grief 292:14

Gongs: strong g. groaning as the guns boom far 81:5

Good: a g., unless counterbalanced by evil 144:13

all g. and no badness 302:12

all g. to me is lost 177:14

all partial evil, universal g. 203:4

all things work together for g. 47:20

and for the g. and increase 312:2

any g. of George the Third ? 156:10

apprehension of the g. gives ... feeling 282:1

are you g. men and true ? 278:3

as gods, knowing g. and evil 30:11

as g. as she was beautiful 199:14

as g. be out of the world 83:15

be g., sweet maid 154:2

behold, it was very g. 30:5

beneath the g. how far 127:2

best is the enemy of the g. 321:13

but what g. came of it ? 304:15

care not whether man is g. or evil 55:7

chief g. and market of his time 252:17

cleave to that which is g. 47:23

Continent ... g. food ... England ... g. table manners 170:7

crown thy g. with brotherhood 25:4

curate's egg, g. in parts 210:26

enough is as g. as a feast 54:3

Evil, be thou my G. 177:14

general g. ... plea of the scoundrel 55:6

giver of all g. things 53:6

go about doing g. 94:4

gone whar de g. niggers go 112:12

g. are so harsh to the clever 330:10

g., but not religious—g. 128:9

g. enough to govern another 159:7

g. enough to shed his blood 235:9

g. fences make g. neighbours 113:13

g. for the country was g. for General Motors 329:4

g. is oft interred with their bones 263:11

g. that I wd. I do not 47:19

g. ... the final goal of ill 312:15

g., the more communicated 178:13

g. to be merry ... honest and true 16:1

Good (*continued*)
g. to be out on the road   169:1
Guinness is g. for you   11:4
he [Time] ... our g. will sever   146:1
he who wd. do g. to another   55:6
hear no g. of themselves   219:16
hold fast that which is g.   49:7
if all the g. people were clever   330:10
ill wind that blows nobody g.   217:19
it is not, nor it cannot come to g.   248:6
Joan is as g. as my lady   217:28
let him do what seemeth him g.   33:29
little of what you fancy does you g.   160:5
money ... not g. unless ... spread   22:9
never g. to bring bad news   242:16
never had it so g.   164:12
not g. that man shd. be alone   30:7
nothing ... g. or bad, but thinking makes
   250:5
Oh, Sir! the g. die first   331:4
only g. Indian is a dead Indian   300:13
out of g. still to find means of evil   176:2
sermons in stones, and g. in everything
   243:15
she was very, very g.   161:8
so much g. in the worst of us   133:5
some said it might do g.   63:5
the g. is the beautiful   200:13
the greatest g.   84:3
to the public g. private respects must yield
   181:2
wives must be had, ... g. or bad   230:28
Good night: fortune, g.   265:20
g. ? ah! no; the hour is ill   298:10
g., g.! Parting is such sweet sorrow   286:14
say g. till it be morrow   286:14
sweet ladies, g.   252:20
Goodbye to All That   125:7
Goodness: felt how awful g. is   178:10
g., what is she a-doin' of?   16:12
Goods: with all my worldly g.   53:24
Goose: g. that lays the golden eggs   217:37
sauce for the g. ... the gander   224:37
say Bo(o) to a g.   224:39
three women and a g.   227:40
Goosey, goosey gander   189:4
Gordian: the G. knot ... he will unloose   258:7
Gormed: I'm G.—I can't say no fairer   98:2
Gossip: babbling g. of the air   290:15
scandal is g. made tedious   328:3
Got: vicious place where thee he g.   267:14
Gourd: to be angry for the g.   42:20
Gout: drink, combined with g.   116:10
wine ... the g.; ... no wine ... the g. too
   211:34
Gouvernement: le g. qu'elle mérite   165:3
Govern: g. another man without that other's
   consent   159:7
he that wd. g. others   169:2
Governed: a nation is not g.   64:5
Government: all g. ... founded on compromise
   64:7
every nation has the g. it deserves   165:3
g. ... a necessary evil   197:19
g. ... framed ... in after-dinner conversations
   317:2
g. of the people, by the people   159:13
g. shall be upon his shoulder   40:23
having looked to g. for bread   64:16
if any ask me what a free g. is   64:17

Government (*continued*)
one form of G. rather than another   143:7
only legitimate object of good g.   139:10
Gower: O moral G.   80:7
Gown: g. of glory, hope's true gage   232:12
like an old lady's loose g.   255:11
Gowns: robes and furr'd g. hide all   267:6
Grace: an inward and spiritual g.   53:16
divine g. was never slow   211:23
God shed his g.   25:4
g. me no g.   282:9
grow old with a good g.   306:7
he does it with a better g.   291:3
he had at least the g.   29:7
my g. is sufficient for thee   48:19
no ... beauty hath such g.   101:1
sweet attractive g.   178:3
Tuesday's child is full of g.   191:8
with one half so good a g.   273:4
ye are fallen from g.   48:21
Graced with polished manners   93:12
Gradualness: the inevitability of g.   323:8
Graduates: sweet girl-g. in their golden hair
   314:12
Grain: which g. will grow ... will not   269:8
Grammar: erecting a g. school   260:11
Grammatici certant ... sub iudice lis est   135:9
Gramophone: puts a record on the g.   107:5
Granary: sitting careless on a g. floor   147:3
Grand: they said, 'it wd. be g.'   76:2
Grandchild: his little g. Wilhelmine   304:13
Grandeur: g. hear with a disdainful smile   126:7
g. that was Rome   200:18
Grandmother: teach yr. g. to suck eggs
   227:17
Grandsire: proverb'd with a g. phrase   285:20
Grape: fathers have eaten a sour g.   41:16
merry with the fruitful g.   110:8
neither shalt thou gather every g.   32:15
the g. that can with Logic absolute   110:10
Grapes: our vines have tender g.   40:10
sour g. can ne'er make sweet wine   226:4
Grapeshot: a whiff of g.   73:6
Grapple them to thy soul   248:15
Grasp: a man's reach shd. exceed his g.   60:11
Grass: a snake in the g.   225:34
all flesh is as g.   50:4
all flesh is g.   40:29
cut the g. from under ... feet   210:31
g. ... as soft as ... breast of doves   90–1:16
Guests star-scattered on the G.   111:1
hare limp'd trembling through the frozen g.
   147:12
his days are as g.   37:1
I am the g.; I cover all   238:5
I know the g. beyond the door   236:10
seed from the feather'd g.   148:5
two blades of g. to grow   309:1
Grate on their scrannel pipes   175:4
Gratis: he lends out money g.   274:7
Grave: a little g., an obscure g.   283:7
body lies a mould'ring in the g.   127:13
country ... a kind of healthy g.   303:18
Duncan is in his g.   271:4
eat our pot of honey on the g.   170:1
every third thought ... my g.   289:8
from g. to gay, from lively to severe   203:10
funeral marches to the g.   160:15
g. is not its goal   160:14
g. of Mike O'Day   12:8

Grave (*continued*)
g. where English oak and holly 129:2
g. where our hero we buried 330:3
g.'s a fine and private place 167:14
in the dark and silent g. 232:11
lead but to the g. 126:9
make ... turn in his g. 228:30
man ... pompous in the g. 60:3
my large kingdom for a little g. 283:7
O g., where is thy victory? 48:13
O G.! where is thy Victory? 201:4
one foot in the g. 222:28
renowned be thy g.! 247:11
see myself go into my g. 199:13
where, g., thy victory? 163:7
Graves: find ourselves dishonourable g. 262:8
talk of g., of ... epitaphs 283:5
Gravity: approach this spot with g.! 12:7
Gravy: rich wot gets the g. 16:13
Sir Humphrey Davy detested g. 29:5
Great: all things both g. and small 87:4
brilliant chief, irregularly g. 63:2
but far above the g. 127:2
even g. men have ... poor relations 97:11
g. is Diana of the Ephesians 47:7
g. is Truth, and mighty 51:6
g. men are almost always bad men 9:1
g. men ... not commonly ... g. scholars 134:6
g. ones eat up the little ones 281:5
madness in g. ones 251:6
rightly to be g. ... g. argument 252:19
rule of men entirely g. 63:3
some are born g., some achieve greatness 291:9
such g. men as these 16:14
to be g. is to be misunderstood 108:12
Great War: what did *you* do in the G.? 11:1
Greater: feel that we are g. than we know 334:10
there is no g. sorrow 95:7
thy necessity is g. than mine 302:7
Greatest: g. happiness of the g. number 29:1
g. talkers ... least doers 227:12
sooner fail than not be among the g. 152:4
Greatness: farewell, to all my g. 261:9
highest point of all my g. 261:8
some achieve g. 291:9
some have g. thrust upon them 291:9
thinks ... his g. is a-ripening 261:9
Greece: citizen not of Athens or G. 304:5
dream'd that G. ... be free 70:1
G., Italy and England did adorn 104:11
the glory that was G. 200:18
the isles of G., the isles of G.! 69:21
Greedy: not g. of filthy lucre 49:9
Greek: it is G. to me 215:33
it was G. to me 262:11
must carve in Latin or in G. 322:2
paid at the G. Kalends 71:10
small Latin and less G. 145:14
when his wife talks G. 145:3
Greeks: G. had a word for it 10:1
I fear the G. 321:2
when G. joined G. 159:1
which came first, the G. or the Romans 100:14
Green: a dyspeptic mint g. 319:9
a g. and yellow melancholy 291:7
and all the trees are g. 154:4

Green (*continued*)
drives my g. age 315:16
flourishing like a g. bay-tree 36:10
g. grow the rashes O 66:11
g. thought in a g. shade 168:1
in England's g. and pleasant land 55:8
laurel is g. for a season 310:4
making the g. one red 270:12
salad days, when I was g. 242:13
the memory be g. 247:17
their heads are g. 158:5
there is a g. hill far away 10:7
through the g. fuse drives the flower 315:16
upon England's mountains g. 55:8
voices of children are heard on the g. 56:11
when woods are getting g. 76:12
whiten the g. plains under 298:5
Greenery-yallery ... young man 119:7
Greenland: from G.'s icy mountains 130:1
Greensleeves: G. was all my joy 15:4
who but Lady G.? 15:4
Greet: how shd. I g. thee? 71:6
Grenadier: for the British G. 16:14
Grew: where only one g. before 309:1
Grey: by thy long g. beard 85:11
lend me yr. g. mare 17:5
that g. iniquity 255:1
Greyhounds: stand like g. in the slips 259:5
Grief: after long g. and pain 314:5
but for our g., as if it had not been 297:12
g. and pain for promis'd joy 66:12
g. itself be mortal 297:12
g. returns with the revolving year 297:10
g., with a glass that ran 309:15
hopeless g. is passionless 60:8
past help shd. be past g. 292:14
silent manliness of g. 122:14
smiling at g. 291:7
time and thinking tame the g. 228:1
when thou art old ... g. enough 127:5
Griefs: of all the g. that harass 140:15
secret ... are their g. and fears 21:17
Grin: g. like a dog, and run about 36:18
taking a fee with a g. 117:5
Grind: my life is one demd horrid g. 98:11
[ye] g. the faces of the poor 40:19
Grinds: with exactness g. he all 161:3
Grindstone: one's nose to the g. 222:10
Grinning: antic sits ... g. at his pomp 283:6
Grist: bring g. to the mill 215:34
Groan: bitter g. of a martyr's woe 55:5
future ages g. for this foul act 283:8
Groaned: my mother g., my father wept 56:3
Groaning: strong gongs g. 81:5
Grocer: God made the wicked G. 81:10
Groomed: nicely g., like a mushroom 157:9
Grosvenor Gallery ... young man 119:7
Grotesque: so g. a blunder 29:6
Ground: betwixt the stirrup and the g. 72:5
blood of English shall manure the g. 283:8
children of Israel ... upon the dry g. 31:26
commit his body to the g. 53:30
fathom-line cd. never touch the g. 254:4
let us sit upon the g. 283:6
massa's in de cold, cold g. 112:6
native air, in his own g. 203:20
upon the g., can fall no lower 219:3
when every rood of g. maintained 122:6
Grovel: souls that g. 72:2
Grovelled: he g. ... and my-lorded 315:10

Groves: o'er shady g. they hover 324:3
Grow: ask me where they do g. 131:13
  g. up with the country 127:4
Growed: I 'spect I g. 308:1
Growled: cracked and g. and roared and howled 86:2
Growth: I cannot give it vital g. again 280:11
Grubstreet ... near Moorfields 140:6
Grudge: feed fat the ancient g. 274:7
Grumble: nothing whatever to g. at 12:13
Grumbling: the g. grew to a ... rumbling 62:3
Grundy: the end of Solomon G. 193:6
Grunt and sweat under a weary life 250–1:20
Gruntled: he was far from being g. 330:2
Gryphon: called lessons, the G. remarked 75:1
Guard: Alice is marrying one of the g. 171:6
  g. the guards themselves ? 146:9
Guards: up, G., and at 'em 324:9
Guerre: la g. ... industrie nationale 182:12
Guess: I g. an' fear 66:13
Guest: constant g. is never welcome 210:7
  dull fighter and a keen g. 255:17
Guests: the G. star-scattered on the Grass 111:1
  unbidden g. ... welcomest when ... gone 260:6
Guide: custom ... the great g. 137:2
  g. me, O thou great Redeemer 329:2
  my g., philosopher and friend 203:11
Guilders: 'will you give me a thousand g.?' 62:2
Guilt: other pens dwell on g. and misery 20:13
  what art can wash her g.? 124:1
Guilty: better that ten g. ... escape 54:11
  my soul ... g. of dust and sin 131:10
  suspicion ... haunts the g. mind 261:1
  we make g. of our disasters the sun 265:10
Guinea: worth a g. a box 11:10
Guinness is good for you 11:4
Gulf: a great g. fixed 46:9
Gull's way and the whale's way 168:17
Gum: Arabian trees their med'cinable g. 280–1:14
Gummidge: Mrs. G.'s words 97:13
Gunga Din 154:16
Gunner and his mate lov'd Mall 288:9
Gunpowder treason and plot 14:5
Guns: g. aren't lawful, nooses give 198:3
  g. will make us powerful; butter ... fat 122:1
  loaded g. with boys 94:1
  strong gongs groaning as the g. boom far 81:5
Gustibus: de g. non est disputandum 210:36
Gypsies: play with the g. in the wood 191:9
Gypsy: Time, you old g. man 133:6
Gyre and gimble in the wabe 75:9

Ha, ha, ha, you and me 15:5
Habit: costly thy h. as thy purse can buy 248:16
  h. is a great deadener 26:2
  h. with him was all the test of truth 93:16
  honour ... in the meanest h. 287:11
Habitation: local h. and a name 277:6
Habits: h. ... carry them far apart 89:2
  needs reforming as other people's h. 319:1
Hackney: see to H. ('A) Marshes 25:3
Haggards ride no more 306:10

Hags: secret, black, and midnight h. 271:13
Hail: h. and farewell 77:17
  h., divinest Melancholy! 173:6
  h., Holy Light 177:9
  h., horrors! h. 176:4
  h., wedded Love 178:8
  my gracious silence, h.! 246:6
  the flail of the lashing h. 298:5
  to be h. fellow well met 215:35
Hailed at the twilight's last gleaming 153:6
Hair: beauty draws us with a single h. 204:7
  each particular h. to stand on end 249:7
  graduates in their golden h. 314:12
  her h. was long, her foot was light 148:15
  I must sugar my h. 75:4
  if a woman have long h. 48:5
  Jeanie with the light brown h. 112:5
  [letters] serve ... to pin up one's h. 89:11
  shall I part my h. behind ? 106:16
  smooths her h. with automatic hand 107:5
  train of thy amber-dropping h. 173:3
Hairs: given me over in my grey h. 330:6
  how ill white h. become a ... jester 258:3
  to split h. 226:11
Hairy: Esau, my brother, is a h. man 31:7
Hal: why, H., 'tis my vocation, H. 253:18
Half: h. a league onward 311:9
  h. a trade and h. an art 138:7
  h. as much as ... Mr. Toad 124:13
  h.-seas over 215:38
  knows not how the other h. lives 215:37
  the h. that's got my keys 124:8
  too civil by h. 301:12
  too clever by h. 228:12
  yr. servant's cut in h. 124:8
  youth shows but h. 62:9
Half-a-crown: if I fling h. to a beggar 142:7
Half-a-dozen of the other 167:6, 225:26
Half-way: don't meet trouble h. 220:38
Halifax: from Hell, Hull and H. ... deliver us 216:30
Hall: bride hath paced into the h. 86:1
  the Douglas in his h. 240:7
  Tom bears logs into the h. 269:1
Hallelujah: h.! I'm alive 197:10
  here lies my wife, h.! 12:2
Hallowed: place of justice is an h. place 23:11
Halo ? ... one more thing to keep clean 114:2
Halt: how long h. ye between two opinions 34:19
Halves: never do things by h. 215:39
Hamelin town's in Brunswick 61:16
Hamlet: I saw H. Prince of Denmark played 109:2
  O H., what a falling off! 249:11
  rude forefathers of the h. 126:6
Hamlets brown, and dim-discover'd spires 88:9
Hammock: Drake he's in his h. 187:9
Hampden: some village H. 126:11
Hand: bite the h. that fed them 64:16
  captain's h. on his shoulder smote 187:12
  cold h. ... warm heart 210:2
  come, give me your h. 272:4
  discern between ... right h. ... left h. 42:21
  earth, I do salute thee with my h. 283:1
  every man's h. against him 31:1
  great is the h. that holds dominion 315:17
  h. and glove 215:40
  h. for h., foot for foot 32:10

Hark: h., h. the lark   246:13
  h.! the herald angels sing   325:2
Harlot: wise man that marries a h.   241:19
Harm: do so much h. ... doing good   94:4
  drunken folk seldom take h.   211:40
  none ... shall h. Macbeth   271:15
  when loyalty no h. meant   15:12
Harmony: all discord, h. not understood 203:4
  heaven drowsy with the h.   268:13
  made quiet by the power of h.   335:12
  such h. is in immortal souls   275:8
  tie the hidden soul of h.   174:9
  touches of sweet h.   275:8
Harness: die with h. on our back   272:11
Harp: David took an h.   34:6
  h. not on that string   285:10
  h. that once through Tara's halls   183:11
  his wild h. slung behind him   184:2
  praise the Lord with h.   36:4
Harps: we hanged our h. upon the willows 37:23
Harrow: lightest word wd. h. up thy soul 249:7
Harry: cry, God for H.!   259:5
  not ... Amurath ... but H., H.   257:20
  stain the brow of my young H.   253:15
Harsh: good are so h. to the clever   330:10
  pluck yr. berries h. and crude   174:12
Harshness: not enough no h. gives offence 202:10
Harvest: like a stubble-land at h. home   254:1
  seedtime and h. and cold and heat   30:23
Harwich: a steamer from H.   117:13
Haste: daffodils ... h. away so soon   132:1
  h. still pays h.   273:14
  h. thee, Nymph   173:16
  marry in h.   220:31
  men love in h.   70:7
  more h. the less speed   216:15
  said in my h., All men are liars   37:10
Hat: faith but ... fashion of his h.   277:10
  hath no head, needs no h.   216:19
Hatch, match and despatch   216:17
Hatchet: bury the h.   208:36
  I did it with my little h.   322:18
Hate: cherish those hearts that h. thee   261:12
  enough religion to make us h.   309:8
  generation of them that h. me   32:1
  greatest h. ... from the greatest love   215:32
  h. him for he is a Christian   274:7
  h. the man ... you have hurt   310:9
  I h. and love ... and am in torment   77:16
  I h. letters   89:11
  Juno's unrelenting h.   105:1
  love and h. are necessary   56:15
  neither beg nor fear ... favours nor ... h. 269:8
  only love sprung from my only h.   286:5
  politicians neither love nor h.   103:2
  pomp ... of this world, I h. ye   261:10
  study of revenge, immortal h.   175:18
Hated: h. wickedness that hinders loving 61:12
  loved well because he h.   61:12
  to be h. needs but to be seen   203:6
Hatred: h., and malice, ... uncharitableness 52:23
  h. is blind   216:16
  h. ... the longest pleasure   70:7
  no h. or bitterness   78:1

Hatred (*continued*)
  no rage like love to h. turned   89:6
  stalled ox and h. therewith   38:18
Hatter: mad as a h.   220:8
Haul over the coals   216:18
Haunches: fog ... sits ... on silent h.   238:4
Haunt: murmurous h. of flies on summer eves 150:2
  our life, exempt from public h.   243:15
Haunted: beneath a waning moon was h. 87:12
  on summers eves by h. stream   174:7
Have: not good to want and to h.   215:20
  to h. and to hold   53:22
  what we h. we prize not   278:12
Havens: ports and happy h.   281:14
Haves: the *H*. and the *Have-Nots*   78:4
Havoc: Cry 'H.!' and let slip the dogs of war 263:8
Hawk: I know a h. from a handsaw   250:8
Hawks: all haggard hawks will stoop   155:16
Hawthorn: gives not the h. bush a sweeter shade?   260:14
  under the h. in the dale   174:3
Hay: dance an antic h.   166:2
  make h. while the sun shines   220:12
Haystack: needle in a h.   221:27
He: every h. has ... a she   14:15
Head: a h. grown gray in vain   297:16
  better be the h. of a dog   207:25
  born about three ... with a white h.   256:9
  four angels round my h.   9:13
  frost which binds so dear a h.   297:9
  hath no h., needs no hat   216:19
  heavy weight from off my h.   284:2
  here rests his h. upon the lap of earth 126:13
  I ... covered up her h.   16:4
  I will make you shorter by a h.   107:12
  if you can keep yr. h. when all about you 154:17
  in the heart or in the h.   274:18
  incessantly stand on your h.   74:3
  lay your sleeping h., my love   20:2
  left it dead and with its h.   75:10
  my h. is bending low   112:11
  my h. is bloody, but unbowed   130:9
  old h. on young shoulders   222:25
  on the ... hands little gold h.   172:2
  one small h. cd. carry all he knew   122:12
  precious jewel in his h.   243:15
  rise up before the hoary h.   32:17
  shoot ... this old gray h.   326:7
  shouting 'Off with his h.!'   74:11
  talked ... after his h. was cut off   14:2
  thou art a traitor. Off with his h.!   285:4
  turns no more his h.   86:16
  uneasy lies the h. that wears a crown   257:3
  wash ... yr. h. never   229:30
  weak h. with strongest bias rules   202:4
  what though his h. be empty   309:7
  which way the h. lies   232:13
  with intention to break his h.   142:7
Headache: awake with a dismal h.   117:12
Heads: bald h. are soon shaven   206:36
  h. I win, tails you lose   94:5, 216:20
  houseless h. and unfed sides   266:13
  mob has many h., but no brains   221:8
  stars hide their diminished h.   177:12
  their h. are green   158:5

Heart (*continued*)
  the Lord looketh on the h. 34:5
  the waters of the h. 315:18
  them that are of a broken h. 36:7
  through the sad h. of Ruth 150:4
  to lose your h.'s desire ... to gain it 296:8
  warm the cockles of the h. 229:28
  way to an Englishman's h. 229:36
  wear him in my h.'s core 252:1
  wear one's h. on one's sleeve 230:1
  what female h. can gold despise ? 125:10
  what the false h. doth know 270:8
  when my h. was young and gay 112:10
  where my h. lies 61:13
  whose ... complexion and whose h. 293:5
  wine that maketh glad the h. 37:2
  with a h. for any fate 161:2
  with h., and soul, and voice 186:14
  with rue my h. is laden 136:8
  woman with the h. 314:18
  word 'Callous' engraved on her h. 241:11
Heart-ache: to say we end the h. 250–1:20
Hearts: agonies, the strife of human h. 150:11
  apply our h. unto wisdom 36:24
  enthroned in the h. of kings 275:1
  grows old with their sick h. 146:10
  h. are dry as summer dust 331:4
  h. at peace, under an English heaven 59:7
  kind h. are more than coronets 313:10
  men with splendid h. 59:3
  our h., though stout and brave 160:15
  thousand creeds ... move men's h. 58:13
  two h. that beat as one 162:8
  wand'ring eyes and heedless h. 125:12
  while yr. h. are yearning 111:12
Heat: fear no more the h. o' th' sun 247:9
  have neither h. nor light 323:14
  h. me these irons hot 264:18
  h. not a furnace for your foe 261:3
  I know not where is that Promethean h. 280:11
  thinking on fantastic summer's h. 282:1
Heath: a wind on the h. 57:8
Heathen: why do the h. rage ? 35:16
Heaven: a h. in a wild flower 54:12
  a H. on Earth 178:2
  a new h. and a new earth 51:1
  all this and h. too 130:16
  brightest h. of invention 258:5
  builds a h. in hell's despair 56:2
  created the h. and the earth 30:1
  differ as H. and earth 312:6
  droppeth as the gentle rain from h. 275:1
  every purpose under the h. 39:14
  fallen from h., O Lucifer 40:25
  fantastic tricks before high h. 273:7
  first h. ... passed away 51:1
  floor of h. is thick inlaid 275:8
  friends ... in h. and hell 214:22
  gain'd from h. ... a friend 126:14
  garden hard by H. 57:11
  God is in h. and thou upon earth 39:16
  God's in his h. 62:7
  h. and earth shall pass away 240:2
  h. has no rage like love to hatred turned 89:6
  h. is in these lips 165:8
  H. itself wd. stoop to her [Virtue] 173:4
  H. lies about us in our infancy 332:1
  H. tries earth if it be in tune 162:15

Heaven (*continued*)
  Hell I suffer seems a H. 177:13
  high H. rejects the lore 330:11
  how long ... permit to H. 179:14
  I see H.'s glories shine 58:12
  in earth ... as it is in h. 43:24
  in the nurseries of H. 316:11
  joy shall be in h. 46:2
  justice be done, though h. fall 213:24
  keys of the kingdom of h. 44:17
  kingdom of h. is at hand 43:10
  leave to H. the measure ... choice 141:13
  love is h. and h. is love 239:13
  make h. drowsy with the harmony 268:13
  marriages are made in h. 220:26
  mind ... can make a H. of Hell 176:5
  more things in h. and earth 249:12
  new Jerusalem ... out of h. 51:2
  not mad, sweet h.! 265:17
  O h., were men but constant 292:11
  open face of h. 151:6
  or what's a h. for ? 60:11
  our conversation is in h. 48:30
  over his living head like H. 297:13
  parting is all we know of h. 99:15
  places that the eye of h. visits 281:14
  praise, my soul, the King of H. 163:8
  progressive virtue, and approving H.! 316:13
  puts all H. in a rage 54:13
  reign in Hell than serve in H. 176:6
  shun the h. that leads men to this hell 294:12
  steep and thorny way to h. 248:14
  summons thee to h. or to hell 270:10
  that from H., or near it 300:1
  that h.'s vault shd. crack 268:2
  there was silence in h. 50:23
  to be young was very H.! 334:5
  to seek the ... eye of h. to garnish 264:19
  top ... reached to h. 31:9
  under an English h. 59:7
  watered h. with their tears 56:6
  when Britain first, at H.'s command 316:12
Heavens: pure as the naked h. 333:13
  spangled h., a shining frame 9:9
  the h. declare the glory of God 35:22
  the h. themselves, the planets ... observe 290:1
  till you are clothed with the h. 317:16
Heaviness foreruns the good event 257:11
Heavy: a light wife doth make a h. husband 275:12
Hebrew: called in the H. tongue Armageddon 50:27
Hector: of H. and Lysander 16:14
Hecuba: what's H. to him or he to H. ? 250:15
Hedge: a voice ... from h. to h. 151:1
Heels: if yr. h. are nimble and light 189:8
  to cool one's h. 210:10
Heigh! the doxy over the dale 292:17
Heigh-ho: h.! says Rowley 189:2
  sing h. unto the green holly 245:1
Height: happiness makes up in h. 113:15
  to the h. of this great argument 175:17
Heir: dear son of memory, great h. of fame 175:12
  first h. of my invention 295:3
Heiresses: all h. are beautiful 104:10

Helen: dust hath closed H.'s eye 186:12
sweet H., make me immortal 165:8
Helena: all is dross that is not H. 165:8
Hell: a shout that tore H.'s concave 176:10
airs from heaven or blasts from h. 249:3
all H. broke loose 178:11
all we need of h. 99:15
and H. followed with him 50:22
better to reign in H. 176:6
boys, it [war] is all h. 301:20
builds a Heaven in H.'s despair 56:2
down to h.; and say I sent thee 261:2
dunnest smoke of h. 270:2
England ... h. for horses 67:10
gates of h. shall not prevail 44:16
go ... to h. in embroidery 207:29
heaven that leads men to this h. 294:12
h. and Chancery are always open 216:28
h. is a city ... like London 299:9
h. itself breathes out contagion 252:8
h. to which hate and fear ... condemn 237:8
into the mouth of H. 311:12
Italy ... h. for women 67:10
jealousy ... injured lover's h. 178:16
lifetime of happiness! ... h. on earth 296:3
make a Heaven of H., a H. of Heaven 176:5
myself am H. 177:13
no redemption from h. 224:8
nor h. a fury like a woman scorned 89:6
prompted ... by heaven and h. 250:18
road to h. is paved ... intentions 216:29
summons thee to heaven or to h. 270:10
the bells of h. go ting-a-ling 14:12
to reign ... though in H. 176:6
though h. shd. bar the way 188:2
ugly h., gape not! come not, Lucifer! 165:11
way down to H. is easy 321:4
way ... that out of H. leads 177:5
when war begins, h. opens 229:26
which way I fly is H. 177:13
women ... as Heaven and H. 312:6
Hellish dark, and smells of cheese! 308:6
Helmsman: so the h. answered 161:4
Help: a very present h. 36:13
H. of the helpless 163:5
h. yourself, heaven will h. you 111:7
hills, from whence cometh my h. 37:15
many of yr. countrymen cannot h. 142:6
not enough to h. the feeble up 289:9
O God, our h. in ages past 323:4
past h. shd. be past grief 292:14
past my h. is past my care 25:9
since there's no h. ... kiss and part 102:12
the rich can h. themselves 215:5
Helpers: when other h. fail 163:5
Helpless: Help of the h., O Abide with me 163:5
h., naked, piping loud 56:3
Hemlock: as though of h. I had drunk 149:13
Hen: two Owls and a H. 158:13
yaf nat of that text a pulled h. 79:5
Henry: the chief defect of H. King 27:2
Henry IV Part II: abdicated in favour of H. 241:10
Hens: three French h. 194:2
Heraldry: the boast of h., the pomp of power 126:8
Herbert Spencer: expression ... used by Mr. H. 95:12

Herbs: dinner of h. where love is 38:18
Hercules: and some of H. 16:14
let H. ... do what he may 253:5
Herd: lowing h. winds slowly 126:3
Here: h. he lies where he longed to be 307:6
h. is my journey's end, h. is my butt 280:13
h. lie I and ... daughters 11:17
h. lies a man who was killed 11:18
h. lies a poor woman 12:1
h. lies ... Mary Ann Lowder 12:4
h. lies my wife ... hallelujee! 12:2
h. lies my wife: h. let her lie! 104:5
h. lies ... Richard Hind 12:3
h. lies Will Smith 12:5
h. we come gathering nuts in May 15:7
I have been h. before 236:10
the ice was h., the ice was there 86:2
'tis neither h. nor there 280:7
we're h. because we're h. 17:6
Hereafter: she shd. have died h. 272:10
what is love ? 'Tis not h. 291:2
what may come h. 309:18
Heresies: begin as h. ... end as superstitions 138:1
Heresy: ancient saying is no h. 274:15
there is no worse h. 9:1
Heretics: Jews, Turks, Infidels, and H. 53:4
Heritage: Americans ... proud of our ancient h. 153:1
Hermit: dwell a weeping h. there! 88:11
Hermitage: my gorgeous palace for a h. 283:7
Hermits are contented with their cells 332:13
Hero: be a h. ... must drink brandy 144:15
every h. becomes a bore 108:16
no man is a h. to his valet 91:1
see the conquering h. comes 184:6
the grave where our h. we buried 330:3
to his ... valet seem'd a h. 68:16
Herod: it out-herods H. 251:8
Heroes: fit country for h. to live in 160:9
Héros: pas de h. pour son valet 91:1
Hero-worship is strongest where 305:6
Herring: h. boxes without topses 183:9
plague o' these pickle h. 290:14
Hervey: if you call a dog H. 141:15
Hesperus: H. entreats thy light 145:8
it was the schooner H. 161:12
Hewers of wood and drawers of water 33:11
Hey: and a h. nonino 245:16
H. diddle diddle 189:5
Hickory, dickory, dock 189:6
Hid: fiend h. in a cloud 56:3
love ... cough cannot be h. 219:33
Hide: let me h. myself in thee 317:15
Hideous: ingratitude ... more h. ... in a child 265:14
Hides from himself his state 141:12
High: h. and low mate ill 326:6
means ... for contempt too h. 91:13
when civil fury first grew h. 67:14
ye'll tak' the h. road 16:10
High churchman: a zealous H. was I 15:12
Highland: my sweet H. Mary 66:3
yon solitary H. Lass! 334:16
your H. Laddie 146:3
Highlands: chieftain to the H. bound 72:8
my heart's in the H. 66:14
Hill: apart sat on a h. retired 177:6
dew of yon high eastward h. 247:16
h. will not come to Mahomet 22:4

Hill (*continued*)
laughing is heard on the h.   56:11
there is a green h. far away   10:7
to sit upon a h. as I do now   260:13
Hills: as old as the h.   222:23
floats on high o'er vales and h.   331:7
halloo yr. name to the reverberate h.   290:15
lift up mine eyes unto the h.   37:15
over the h. and far away   115:6, 195:3
the great h. of the South Country   28:2
we shall fight in the h.   82:13
Him first, h. last, h. midst   178:15
Himself: discommendeth others ... commendeth h.   59:11
man's first duty ? ... To be h.   138:6
none ... liveth ... dieth to h.   47:30
shd. be the master of h.   169:12
so lonely 'twas, that God h.   87:2
Hinder end of the spear   34:13
Hindmost: devil take the h.   211:19
Hinky dinky parley-voo   236:14
Hint: upon this h. I spake   279:2
Hip: catch him once upon the h.   274:7
smote them h. and thigh   33:20
Hippo: Lord H.   27:14
Hippocrene: the blushful H.   149:14
Hireling: pay given to a state h.   140:11
Hiss: a dismal universal h.   179:12
roasted crabs h. in the bowl   269:1
Hissed all my mystery lectures   305:19
Histoire des grands événements ... h. des crimes   321:15
Histories make men wise   23:9
History: attend to the h. of Rasselas   141:3
cd. ever hear by tale or h.   276:10
ends this strange eventful h.   244–5:11
great deal of h. to produce a little literature   139:4
great dust-heap called h.   54:5
happiest women ... have no h.   105:15
happy ... country which has no h.   216:9
h. ... essence of innumerable biographies   73:10
h. is ... biography of great men   73:8
h. is bunk   111:9
h. is philosophy teaching   100:1
h. must be false   322:5
h. of England ... h. of progress   164:5
h. of the great events ... h. of crimes   321:15
h. ... register of the crimes, follies   116:3
h. repeats itself   216:32
H. ... will tell lies, as usual   295:15
no h.; only biography   108:6
Thames is liquid h.   65:7
there is a h. in all men's lives   257:5
war makes rattling good h.   128:7
we learn from h. ... nothing from h.   296:10
woman's ... h. ... h. of the affections   138:11
world h. ... world's judgment   238:13
Hit: a h., a very palpable h.   253:7
h. the nail on the head   216:33
Hitch yr. wagon to a star   108:18
Hither: come h., come h.   244:4
Hitler has missed the bus   78:11
Hive: a h. for the honey bee   337:4
Hoarded: beauty is nature's coin; must not be h.   173:2
Hobson's choice   216:34
Hodgepodge: our ... tongue a gallimaufry or h.   305:17

Hoist with his own petard   216:35
Holborn: when I was last in H.   285:3
Hold: for ever h. his peace   53:20
h. fast that which is good   49:7
to have and to h.   53:22
Hole: a better 'ole   23:22
Roöötten, Beëëastly, Silly H.!   324:12
Holes where eyes did once inhabit   285:1
Holidays: if ... year were playing h.   253:21
Holiness: go! put off H.!   55:7
h. of the Heart's affection   151:9
Hollow: we are the h. men   106:7
Holly: heigh-ho unto the green h.   245:1
the h. and the ivy   15:8
the h. bears the crown   15:8
Holy: an h. and a good thought   52:11
H. Deadlock   131:8
h., divine, good, amiable   179:10
h., fair and wise is she   292:8
h., h., h., all the Saints adore thee   130:3
hunters been nat h. men   79:5
sabbath day—to keep it h.   32:3
savage place! As h. and enchanted   87:12
the h. city, new Jerusalem   51:2
was the h. Lamb of God   55:8
ye shall be h. ... for I the Lord ... am h.   32:14
Holy Roman Empire was neither holy, nor Roman, nor an Empire   321:16
Holy writ: odd old ends ... of h.   284:14
Homage: hypocrisy ... h. paid by vice   234:7
Home: as much like h. as we can   114:5
at h. I was in a better place   244:2
blest by suns of h.   59:6
charity begins at h.   209:19
comin' for to carry me h.   17:1
don't want to go h. in the dark   131:3
dunce that has been kept at h.   93:2
east or west, h. is best   212:11
fools at h. condemn 'em   288:14
God, who is our h.   332:1
his first, best country ... h.   123:14
h. art gone, and ta'en thy wages   247:9
h. is heaven   186:3
h. is the sailor, h. from sea   307:6
h. life of our own dear Queen   13:9
h. of the bean and the cod   57:10
h. on the rolling deep   238:8
h. ... they have to take you in   113:11
hunter h. from the hill   307:6
I am far from h.   187:14
it's h. and it's h. ... fain wad I be   95:2
keep the h. fires burning   111:12
ladybird, ladybird, fly away h.   190:8
leave them alone, and they'll come h.   190:10
man goeth to his long h.   39:27
our eternal h.   323:4
pillage ... with merry march bring h.   258:8
pleasure never is at h.   148:3
returned h. the previous night   63:1
sick for h., she stood in tears   150:4
Sublimity to welcome me h.   152:6
sweet h. of ... fears and hopes and joys   149:5
that is fit h. for thee   336:4
the old Kentucky H.   112:7
there's no place like h.   199:2
they dream of h.   111:12
this little pig stayed at h.   194:7
what's the good of a h. ?   127:9

Homely: home-keeping youth have ... h. wits 292:4

Homer: seven cities warred for H., being dead 132:9

  shame when the worthy H. nods 135:10

  with the single exception of H. 297:8

Homerus: quandoque ... dormitat H. 135:10

Homes: the stately h. of England! 91:5, 130:5

Homestead, Braddock, Birmingham 238:7

Homines: quot h. tot sententiae 315:2

Honest: armour is his h. thought 336:13

  deal with none but h. men 224:13

  good to be h. and true 16:1

  h. God is the noblest work of man 138:9

  h. man sent to lie abroad 336:11

  h. man's the noblest work of God 203:8

  I am not naturally h. 293:6

  she was poor but she was h. 16:11

  the world's grown h. 250:4

  to be h. ... is to be one man pick'd out 250:1

Honesty: corruption wins not more than h. 261:12

  for saving of thine h. 184:5

  h. is the best policy 216:39

  neither h., manhood, nor ... fellowship 253:19

  no legacy is so rich as h. 242:5

Honey: and is there h. still for tea? 59:4

  civil citizens kneading up the h. 258:8

  eat our pot of h. on the grave 170:1

  flowing with milk and h. 31:18

  funny how a bear likes h.? 172:3

  gather h. all the day 323:1

  I always eat peas with h. 13:10

  in the parlour eating bread and h. 193:5

  it's no go my h. love 164:15

  some h., and plenty of money 158:7

  sweeter than h. and the h.-comb 35:24

  Tiggers don't like h. 171:2

Honey-dew: he on h. hath fed 87:16

Honeyed middle of the night 147:13

Honi soit qui mal y pense 216:40

Honour: as h., love, obedience 272:5

  brilliance ... left to the fighter's h. 130:7

  can h. set to a leg? 255:21

  desires h. ... not worthy of h. 211:15

  drown'd my H. in a shallow Cup 110:15

  fewer men, the greater share of h. 259:13

  giving h. unto the wife 50:6

  his h. rooted in dishonour 312:4

  h. a physician with the h. due 52:3

  h. all men ... h. the king 50:5

  H. comes, a pilgrim grey 88:11

  h. for his valour 263:10

  h. hath no skill in surgery 255:21

  h. is a mere scutcheon 255:21

  h. is the subject of my story 262:6

  h. of honourable men 319:8

  h. peereth in the meanest habit 287:11

  h. pricks me on 255:21

  h. sinks where commerce ... prevails 123:15

  h.'s thought reigns solely 258:9

  h. the face of the old man 32:17

  h. thy father and thy mother 32:4

  I believe it is ... peace with h. 78:10

  if I give thee h. due 174:1

  if it be a sin to covet h. 259:14

  if peace cannot be ... with h. 237:7

  jealous in h. 244:11

Honour (*continued*)

  loss of h. was a wrench 124:11

  loved I not H. more 162:7

  mine h. is my life 281:8

  pledge ... our fortunes, and our sacred h. 139:7

  pluck bright h. from the ... moon 254:4

  pluck up drowned h. 254:4

  take h. from me ... life is done 281:8

  the louder he talked of his h. 108:2

  there is h. among thieves 217:1

  'tis for the h. of England 89:8

  to h. we call you 115:1

  what is h.? A word 255:21

  when h.'s at the stake 252:19

Honourable: Brutus is an h. man 263:12

Honoured: more h. in the breach than the observance 249:2

Honours: bears his blushing h. thick upon him 261:9

  mindless of its just h. 333:5

Hood: can drink with him that wears a h. 307:11

Hoofs: wound ... with their horses' h. 283:1

Hook: by h. or by crook 217:2

  draw out leviathan with an h. 35:14

  he for subscribers baits his h. 82:3

Hook-nos'd fellow of Rome 257:13

Hooks: silken lines and silver h. 100:17

Hooting: bird of night ... h. and shrieking 262:12

Hope: abandon h. all ye who enter 95:6

  because I do not h. to turn 106:1

  condemned to h.'s delusive mine 140:13

  from h. and fear set free 310:1

  give ... h. before you blacken ... world 319:8

  h. deferred maketh the heart sick 38:13

  h. for the best 217:3

  h. from outward forms to win 87:9

  h. is a good breakfast 23:13

  H. sows what Love shall never reap 236:7

  h. springs eternal in the human breast 203:1

  in trembling h. repose 126:15

  land of h. and glory 28:10

  like Lucifer, never to h. again 261:10

  look forward to with h. 113:10

  my gown of glory, h.'s true gage 232:12

  no other medicine but only h. 273:9

  nursing the unconquerable h. 19:1

  our h. for years to come 323:4

  pursue ... the phantoms of h. 141:3

  reinforcement we may gain from h. 176:3

  so farewell h. 177:14

  they h. they serve God 278:13

  triumph of h. over experience 143:6

  true h. is swift and flies 285:12

  what was dead was h. 326:13

  while there is life, there is h. 219:6

  worldly H. ... turns Ashes 110:1

Hopeful: hey, but I'm h. 119:6

Hopefully: to travel h. 307:10

Hopeless grief is passionless 60:8

Hopes: all the h. of future years 160:11

  enough for fifty h. and fears 60:13

  many the h. that have vanished 129:1

  the tender leaves of h. 261:9

  vanity of human h., ... public library 141:2

  what are the h. of man! 145:1

Hovel: *prefer* ... a h. to ... marble halls 72:2
Hover through the fog and filthy air 269:4
How: a pretty h. town 94:13
How-de-do: here's a h.! 118:9
Howl, h., h., h., ... men of stones! 268:2
Howled: cracked and growled and roared and
h. 86:2
Howling: churlish priest ... when thou liest h.
253:3
Tom went h. down the street 195:4
Hubbard: old Mother H. 192:2
Hubbub increases more they call out 'Hush!'
148:7
Hue: add another h. unto the rainbow 264:19
native h. of resolution 250–1:20
Huffy: not h. or stuffy, nor tiny 131:5
Hull: from Hell, H. and Halifax ... deliver us
216:30
Hum: busy h. of men 174:5
h. of either army stilly sounds 259:8
sad-ey'd justice, with his surly h. 258:8
Human: a fearful sign of h. frailty 69:18
Adam was but h. 318:15
all h. things are subject to decay 104:13
all that is h. must retrograde 116:4
climax of all h. ills 69:20
dignity and worth of the h. person 319:5
every h. benefit and enjoyment 64:7
full tide of h. existence ... Charing-Cross
143:14
[God] ... does a h. form display 55:1
h. on my faithless arm 20:2
h. kind cannot bear ... much reality 106:4
h. race to which ... readers belong 81:12
I may be devout, but I am h. 182:15
I wish I loved the H. Race 233:1
in h. nature ... more of the fool 22:3
purest of h. pleasures 23:4
requires the highest type of h. nature 305:2
the field of h. conflict 82:15
to err is h. 202:14, 217:11
where ... least regard for h. freedom 305:6
women—one half the h. race 23:19
Human being: remember that you are a h.
296:18
Humane: every h. and gentle virtue 65:2
Humanised: distress hath h. my soul 331:2
Humanity: h. i love you because 94:14
h. with all its fears 160:11
still, sad music of h. 335:14
Humanum est errare 217:11
Humble: neither too h. nor too great 165:4
we are so very h. 97:17
you are *not* his most h. servant 144:18
Humbly: walk h. with thy God 42:24
Humility: h. towards the Public 152:1
modest stillness and h. 259:3
Humour: deficient in a sense of h. 88:4
unyok'd h. of yr. idleness 253:20
was ever woman in this h. woo'd ... won?
284:13
Hump: a woman ... without a positive h. 315:9
camel's h. is an ugly lump 155:9
uglier yet is the h. we get 155:9
Humpty Dumpty: 76:8–10; 189:9
Hundred: about two h. pounds a year 67:17
only one religion ... a h. versions 296:17
uttered it a h. times 134:4
Hunger ... is highly indelicate 120:12
Hungry: if thine enemy be h. 38:28

Hungry (*continued*)
makes h. where most she satisfies 242:15
Hunter: h. home from the hill 307:6
Lo! the H. of the East 109:13
man is the h. 314:17
mighty h. before the Lord 30:26
Hunter Dunn: Miss J. H. 29:12
Hunters: seith ... h. been nat holy men 79:5
Hunting: h. he loved but love he laugh'd to
scorn 295:4
we daren't go a-h. 10:9
wet and dirty from h. 308:8
Huntress: queen and h. chaste and fair 145:8
Hurlyburly: when the h.'s done 269:3
Hurrah! H.! we bring the Jubilee 336:10
Hurricanes: you cataracts and h., spout 266:6
Hurry: an old man in a h. 82:5
sick h., its divided aims 18:21
Hurt: cd. you h. me, sweet lips? 309:17
give delight and h. not 288:13
hate the man whom you have h. 310:9
h. with the same weapons 274:17
Hurtig: you are h. be 155:9
Husband: actors are ... h., and wife and lover
169:16
being a h. ... whole-time job 28:8
good wife makes a good h. 215:23
light wife makes a heavy h. 275:12
Husbands: flirt with their own h. 327:9
h. at chirche-dore she hadde fyve 79:15
why so many h. fail 28:8
Hush: a breathless h. in the Close tonight
187:11
they call out 'H.!' 148:7
Hush-a-bye baby 189:10
Husks that the swine did eat 46:3
Hut: love in a h. 149:1
Hymns: chanting faint h. to ... moon 276:9
Hyperion to a satyr 248:3
Hyphenated Americanism: no room ... for h.
235:10
Hypocrisy: Conservative Government ...
organised 100:4
h. ... homage ... by vice to virtue 234:7
h. ... homage that vice pays 217:12
Hypocrite: no man is a h. in his pleasures
144:20
plea of the scoundrel, h. 55:6
Hysterica passio, down ... sorrow 265:21

I: blew hither: here am I 136:7
I am I, and you are you 61:7
I am the State 162:2
I came, I saw, I conquered 71:13
I galloped, Dirck galloped 61:6
I have a go ... don't I? 197:7
I, said the Fly 196:2
I, said the Sparrow 196:2
'I', says the Quarterly 70:17
the spot where I made one 111:1
whoso turns as I 61:5
Iacta alea est 71:12
Iago: the pity of it, I.! 280:4
Ice: as chaste as i., as pure as snow 251:3
i. in June 70:14
in skating over thin i. 108:10
like ... i. on a hot stove 113:16
pleasure-dome with caves of i. 87:15
some say the world will end in ... i. 113:12
the i. was here, the i. was there 86:2

Ice (*continued*)
  thrilling region of thick-ribbed i. 273:10
  to smooth the i. 264:19
Icicles: when i. hang by the wall 269:1
Ida: on I.'s shady brow 56:13
Idea: abstract I. I have of Beauty 152:6
  between the i. and the reality 106:8
Ideal: the i. man ... non-attached 137:10
Ideas: nice man ... of nasty i. 309:10
  ruling i. ... i. of its ruling class 168:9
Idem velle ... nolle, ... firma amicitia 237:15
Ides of March: beware the i. 262:5
Idiosyncrasy: I have no ... i. in ... humour 59:14
Idiot: it is a tale told by an i. 272:10
  law is an ass—a i. 98:15
  the i. who praises 118:5
Idle: as i. as a painted ship 86:5
  be not solitary, be not i. 67:12
  for i. hands to do 323:2
  happiest when I am i. 322:14
  i. that might be better employed 217:13
  tears, i. tears 314:16
  tongue of i. ... is never i. 228:10
Idleness: i. ... the refuge of weak minds 80:15
  unyok'd humour of yr. i. 253:20
Idol: a one-eyed yellow i. 129:6
Idolatries: to its i. a patient knee 69:5
Idolatry: god of our i., the press 93:3
Idols: the i. I have loved so long 110:15
  there are four classes of I. 23:16
If: i. it wasn't for the 'ouses 25:3
  yr. I. is the only peace-maker 246:3
Ifs: if I. and Ans were pots and pans 217:14
  talk'st thou to me of i. ? 285:4
Ignorance: art has no enemy except i. 206:22
  from i. our comfort flows 205:7
  hold there is no sin but i. 166:3
  i. is like ... exotic fruit 327:11
  i. is preferable to error 139:12
  i., Madam, pure i. 142:4
  where i. is bliss 126:2
Ignorant: conscious that you are i. 100:11
  most i. of what he's most assur'd 273:7
Ignore: aren't happy with nothing to i. 186:6
Ilium: the topless towers of I. 165:8
Ill: a fool is love ... he thinks no i. 293:20
  better suffer i. than do i. 207:34
  costs more to do i. 210:11
  i. doers are i. thinkers 217:16
  i. fares the land, to ... ills a prey 122:5
  i. gotten, i. spent 217:17
  i.-housed, i.-clad, i.-nourished 235:2
  i. met by moonlight 276:17
  love worketh no i. 47:29
  marries late, marries i. 220:28
  means to do i. deeds makes deeds i. done 265:2
  of every i. a woman is the worst 125:3
  religion an i. man is of 224:9
  the final goal of i. 312:15
  things bad begun make strong ... by i. 271:5
Ill-bred: nothing so ... i. as audible laughter 80:13
Illiberal: nothing so i. ... as audible laughter 80:13
Illiterate him ... from your memory 301:5
Ills: bear those i. we have 250–1:20
  climax of all human i. 69:20

Ills (*continued*)
  i. have no weight 163:7
  to hastening i. a prey 122:5
  what i. the scholar's life assail 141:10
Ill-tempered and queer 158:6
Illumine: what in me is dark i. 175:17
Image: any graven i. 31:31
  are wronging your i. 337:7
  best i. of myself, and dearer half 178:14
  i. of war, without its guilt 304:8
  in the i. of God created 30:3
Imagination: as i. bodies forth the forms 277:6
  are of i. all compact 277:5
  by bare i. of a feast 282:1
  certain of ... the truth of I. 151:9
  civet ... to sweeten my i. 267:5
  i. of a boy is healthy 147:7
  [indebted to] ... i. for his facts 301:19
  what the I. seizes as Beauty 151:9
Imagined: exhausted worlds and ... i. new 140:19
Imitate the action of the tiger 259:3
Imitation ... sincerest form of flattery 88:19
Imlac: business of a poet, said I. 141:5
Immanuel: shall call his name I. 40:21
Immaterial: the Brighton line. The line is i. 327:14
Immortal: a thing i. as itself 249:4
  grow i. as they quote 337:11
  Helen, make me i. with a kiss 165:8
  his biting is i. 243:8
  I have left no i. work 152:11
  i. longings in me 243:10
  lost the i. part of myself 279:10
  my scrip of joy, i. diet 232:12
  such harmony is in i. souls 275:8
  what i. hand or eye 56:5
Immortality: just ourselves and I. 99:17
  nurslings of i. 299:11
Imparadised in one another's arms 178:5
Impatient: surprised by joy, i. as the Wind 333:1
Impediment: cause or just i. 53:18
Impediments: marriage of true minds admit i. 294:8
  wife and children ... are i. 21:19
Important: little things ... the most i. 101:12
Imports be more than your exports 144:19
Importunate: rashly i., gone to her death 134:10
Importune: too proud to i. 127:3
Impossibility: begotten by Despair upon I. 167:16
Impossible: I wish it were i. 144:24
  in two words, i. 124:4
  pure and complete sorrow ... i. 317:14
  that not i. she 94:3
  when you have eliminated the i. 102:3
Impostors: treat those two i. just the same 154:19
Impotently: rolls i. on as Thou or I 110:13
Impregnable: as if this flesh ... were brass i. 283:6
Impressions: first i. are most lasting 213:32
Improbable: however i., must be the truth 102:3
Impropriety: i. is the soul of wit 169:5
  use any language ... without i. 117:12
Improve: i. each shining hour 323:1

Improve (*continued*)
i. his shining tail 73:17
Impulse: i. of the moment, or ... study 21:1
one i. from a vernal wood 335:7
In: home ... you are never i. it 127:9
they have to take you i. 113:11
Incarnadine: the multitudinous seas i. 270:12
Incense: soft i. hangs upon the boughs 150:1
Inch: ay, every i. a king 267:3
give ... i. ... take an ell 214:32
no painful i. to gain 85:2
Inches: die by famine die by i. 130:15
Incident: curious i. of the dog in the night 102:1
Inclines to think there is a God 84:14
Include me out 124:5
Income: a good i. is of no avail 303:6
annual i. ... annual expenditure ... misery 97:16
innate desire ... to live beyond ... i. 68:7
Inconstant: swear not by ... th' i. moon 286:10
Incontestable: what is official is i. 114:3
Inconvenient: i. to be poor 92:3
poverty ... is confoundedly i. 303:11
Incorruptible: the seagreen I. 73:7
Increase: from fairest creatures we desire i. 293:10
God gave the i. 47:32
good and i. of the world 312:2
Ind: wealth of Ormus and of I. 176:15
Indebted to his memory for his jests 301:19
Indecency: a public i. 78:5
Independence: treacle to the wings of i. 152:9
Independent: poor and i. ... nearly an impossi-bility 85:4
India's coral strand 130:1
Indian: like the base I., threw a pearl away 280~1:14
only good I. is a dead I. 300:13
Indictment against an whole people 64:6
Indifferent: delayed till I am i. 142:1
Indignatio: ubi saeva i. ... lacerare nequit 309:11
Indignation: burning i. no longer lacerates 309:11
Indiscretion: a lover without i. is no lover 128:8
Individual: no i. cd. resent 308:13
not the i. but the species 141:5
Individualism: American system of rugged i. 135:5
Individuals: worth of the i. composing it 170:11
Indivisible: peace is i. 160:3
Industry: avarice, the spur of i. 137:1
i. will improve them [talents] 233:9
i. will supply their deficiency 233:9
Inebriate: cups that cheer but not i. 93:10
Inebriated with the exuberance of ... verbosity 100:8
Ineffectual: beautiful and i. angel [Shelley] 19:9
remote and i. don 27:12
Inelegance: a continual state of i. 21:4
Inert: the earth, tideless and i. 23:23
Inevitability: the i. of gradualness 323:8
Inevitable: arguing with the i. 163:1
Inexactitude: without some risk of termino-logical i. 82:7

Infamy: thou, whose i. is not thy fame 297:15
Infancy: Heaven lies about us in our i. 332:1
Infant: i., mewling and puking 244:11
the i. child is not aware 136:2
to a little i. ... as painful 21:10
Infection: against i. and the hand of war 282:5
Inferiority: conscious of an i. 144:6
Infidels: peace ... go sleep with Turks and i. 283:8
Turks, I., and Hereticks 53:4
Infinite: everything ... as it is, i. 57:7
how i. in faculties! 250:6
i. wrath and i. despair 177:13
Infinity in the palm of your hand 54:12
Infirmities: bear his friend's i. 264:2
bear the i. of the weak 47:31
wine for ... thine often i. 49:12
Infirmity: last i. of noble mind 175:1
Inflammation of his weekly bills 69:20
Influence: bright eyes rain i. 174:6
How to Win Friends and I. People 73:12
Influenza: call it i. if ye like 28:6
my aunt died of i. 296:22
no i. in my young days 28:6
Inform: occasions do i. against me 252:17
Information: I only ask for i. 97:18
i. vegetable, animal 120:4
know where we can find i. 143:19
Infortune: worst kinde of i. 80:5
Ingenious: neither i., sober, nor kind 12:3
Ingratitude: I hate i. more ... than lying 292:1
i., thou marble-hearted fiend 265:14
unkind as man's i. 245:1
Ingratitudes: great-siz'd monster of i. 290:6
Inhabitants: look not like th' i. o' th' earth 269:7
Inherit: all which it i. shall dissolve 288:16
i. the vasty Hall of Death 18:17
Inheritance: king's favour is no i. 218:3
Inhumanity: man's i. to man 66:8
Iniquity: that reverend vice, that grey i. 255:1
the i. of the fathers 32:1
Injury: i. ... sooner forgotten than an insult 80:10
revenge never repairs an i. 224:16
Ink: all the sea were i. 14:1
black as i. 208:3
he hath not drunk i. 268:11
whose sin ... dipt me in i. ? 201:13
Inlets: far back through creeks and i. 85:2
Inn: do you remember an i., Miranda ? 28:5
no room ... in the i. 45:19
warmest welcome at an i. 300:12
Innisfree: and go to I. 337:4
Innocence: our peace, our fearful i. 333:11
Innocent: better ... guilty ... escape than one i. suffer 54:11
i. of the blood of this just person 45:3
Macbeth doth murder sleep—the i. sleep 270:11
rich shall not be i. 39:4
source of i. merriment 118:11
Innocently employed than in getting money 143:13
Innovator: time is the greatest i. 22:18
Inns: shun the awful shops and go to i. 81:10
Inopem me copia fecit 197:15
Inquest: came together like the coroner's i. 89:7

Ivy: i. never sere   174:12
  the holly and the i.   15:8

Jabberwock: hast thou slain the J.?   75:11
Jack: all work ... makes J. a dull boy   230:40
  banish plump J.   255:2
  every J. has his Jill   217:26
  every J. ... study the knack   121:6
  house that J. built   194–5:8
  J. and Jill went up the hill   190:6
  J. fell down and broke his crown   190:6
  J. of all trades and master of none   217:27
  J. Sprat cd. eat no fat   190:6
  little J. Horner   191:2
  poor J., farewell!   256:2
Jack Robinson: before one can say J.   207:10
Jackdaw sat on the Cardinal's chair   24:4
Jackson standing like a stone wall   26:5
Jacky shall have a new master   193:3
Jacob: J. saw ... corn in Egypt   31:12
  sold his birthright unto J.   31:6
  the voice is J.'s voice   31:8
Jade: let the galled j. wince   252:5
Jades: hollow pampered j. of Asia   256:18
  ye pamper'd j. of Asia!   166:12
Jail: nothing now left but a j.   97:15
  taken from the county j.   118:3
  want, the patron, and the j.   141:10
Jam to-morrow and j. yesterday   76:7
James, J., Morrison Morrison   171:8
Janvier: Generals J. and Février   187:15
Japan: gentlemen of J.   117:15
Jar: folk ... in front that I j.   109:1
Jardin: il faut cultiver notre j.   321:11
Javan or Gadire   180:15
Jaws: into the j. of Death   311:12
Jealous: am a j. God   32:1
  j. for the cause   280:3
  j. for they are j.   280:3
  one not easily j.   280–1:14
Jealousy: beware, my lord, of j.   279:16
  j. is cruel as the grave   40:14
  nor j. ... the injured lover's hell   178:16
Jeanie: I dream of J.   112:5
Jehu: J., the son of Nimshi   34:25
  like the driving of J.   34:25
Jelly: out, vile j.!   266:18
Jenny kissed me when we met   137:7
Jerusalem: black but comely ... ye daughters
  of J.   40:3
  if I forget thee, O J.   37:26
  the holy city, new J.   51:2
  till we have built J.   55:8
Jeshurun waxed fat   33:7
Jessica, look how the floor of heaven   275:8
Jest: a fellow of infinite j.   253:2
  a good j. for ever   254:8
  his whole wit in a j.   25:7
  J. and youthful Jollity   173:16
  j.'s prosperity lies in the ear   268:16
  life is a j. and all things show it   115:13
  most bitter is a scornful j.   140:15
  true word is spoken in j.   228:22
Jesting: what is truth? said j. Pilate   21:8
Jests: indebted to his memory for ... j.   301:19
  j. at scars that never felt a wound   286:6
Jesu: J. by a nobler deed   78:12
  J., thou art all compassion   325:3
Jesus: blood of J. whispers peace   54:4
  Gentle J., meek and mild   325:1

Jesus (continued)
  J. wept   46:28
  stand up for J.!   105:2
  the Cross of J. ... on before   24:9
Jesus Christ: J. her little child   10:6
  J. ... the same yesterday ... for ever   49:24
  the Church's one foundation is J.   307:13
Jeunesse: si j. savait   108:25
Jew: hath not a J. eyes? ... hands   274:17
Jewel: a rich j. in an Ethiop's ear   286:3
  j. ... in a swine's snout   38:11
  j. in a ten-times barred-up chest   281:8
  the immediate j. of their souls   279:15
  wears ... precious j. in his head   243:15
Jewels: dumb j. ... in their silent kind   292:7
  give my j. for a set of beads   283:7
  unvalued j. ... bottom of the sea   285:1
Jewish: spit upon my J. gaberdine   274:10
Jews, Turks, Infidels   53:4
Jigging veins of rhyming mother-wits   166:6
Jill: Jack and J.   190:6
  make sure of his J.   121:6
Jim: they called him Sunny J.   128:3
Jingo: but by j. if we do   137:4
Joan: greasy J. doth keel the pot   269:1
  J. as my Lady is as good   132:4
Job: as poor as J.   223:15
  being a husband ... whole-time j.   28:8
  best of a bad j.   207:16
  give us the tools and we will finish the j.
    83:2
  heard of the patience of J.   50:3
Jobiska: to fish for his Aunt J.'s   158:10
Jocund: be gay in such a j. company   331:10
Joe: 'Poor old J.'   112:11
Jog on, j. on, the footpath way   292:19
John: Don J. of Austria is going to the war
    81:5
  King J. was not a good man   171:4
  Matthew, Mark, Luke, and J.   9:13
  O, no J., no J., no!   16:8
  some said, J., print it   63:5
John Anderson my jo   66:5
John Bradford: there ... goes J.   58:1
John Brown: J.'s body ... a mould'ring   127:13
  J. is filling his last cavity   12:7
  J. is stowed. He watched the ads.   186:4
John of Gaunt: old J., time-honoured Lan-
  caster   281:6
John Peel: d'ye ken J.?   125:6
Johnny: little J. Green   188–9:9
Johnny head-in-air: do not despair for J.
    231:16
  Little J.   133:10
Johnson: Dr. J. condemns   65:6
  glad, replied J., ... that he thanks God   142:2
  great Cham of literature, Samuel J.   304:3
  J. said ... triumph of hope   143:6
  J. scolded him [Langton]   141:17
  no arguing with J.   124:2
Join: will you j. the dance?   75:3
Joined: shall be j. unto his wife   48:25
  what ... God hath j. together   45:12
Joint: every j. and motive of her body   290:8
  time is out of j.   O cursed spite   249:14
Joking: my way of j. ... to tell the truth   295:20
Jolly: hir j. whistle wel y-wet   79:22
  j. good ale   307:12
  j. tars are our men   115:1
  there was a j. miller once   54:1

Jonah: J., doest thou well to be angry? 42:20
  J. was in the belly of the fish 42:19
  lot fell upon J. 42:18
Jonathan: Saul and J. 34:11
Jones: indeed! said Mr. J. 124:8
Joneses: keep up with the J. 217:34
Jonson: O rare Ben J. 146:2
Jordan: I looked over J. 17:1
Journey: here is my j.'s end ... my butt 280:13
  is yr. j. really necessary? 11:5
  one of the pleasantest things ... a j. 129:11
  tired and weary still j. on 157:5
  will the day's j. take ... long day? 236:3
Journeys end in lovers meeting 291:1
Jours: tous les j. ... vais de mieux en mieux 91:3
Jove: daughter of J., relentless Power 126:16
  J. for's power to thunder 246:10
  lovelier than the love of J. 166:7
  while J.'s planet rises yonder 61:5
Jowett: my name is J. 26:6
Joy: a j. for ever 147:8
  and snatch a fearful j. 126:1
  dreams of j. and fear 298:15
  dwell in doubtful j. 271:3
  fields where j. for ever dwells 176:4
  glad tidings of great j. 311:4
  God send you j. 215:9
  grief and pain for promis'd j. 66:12
  he chortled in his j. 75:11
  he who bends himself a J. 55:4
  impossible as pure ... complete j. 317:14
  j. cometh in the morning 36:2
  j. of heaven, to earth come down 325:3
  j. shall be in heaven 46:2
  j.'s soul lies in the doing 289:15
  j. whose hand is ever at his lips 149:12
  kisses the j. as it flies 55:4
  let j. be unconfined 69:4
  man was made for j. and woe 54:15
  my scrip of j. 232:12
  O j.! that in our embers 332:4
  pledges of Heaven's j. 172:12
  shd. allow itself a life of j. 237:8
  sow in tears ... reap in j. 37:18
  surprised by j., ... I turned 333:1
  the deep power of j. 335:12
  the oil of j. for mourning 41:11
  there is ... j. for his fortune 263:10
  thy j. and crown eternally 183:2
  weep for j. to stand upon my kingdom 283:1
  wish you the j. o' th' worm 243:9
Joyful: j. and triumphant 196:5
  make a j. noise unto God 36:19
Joyous hour, we give thee greeting! 118:8
Joys: all my j. to this are folly 67:8
  can I ever bid these j. farewell? 150:11
  hence, vain deluding J. 173:5
  j. of parents are secret 21:17
  minds me o' departed j. 67:6
  our youth, our j., our all we have 232:11
  their homely j. and destiny obscure 126:7
  unfriendly to society's chief j. 92:5
Jubilee: we bring the J. 336:10
Judas: so J. did to Christ 284:1
Judge: a j. ... no king can corrupt 261:7
  a perfect j. will read 202:6
  as sober as a j. 109:8
  I'll be j., I'll be jury 74:1
  j. none blessed before his death 51:21

Judge (*continued*)
  j. not 44:5
  j. of a man by his foes 90:6
  J. of all the earth 31:2
  marshal's truncheon nor the j.'s robe 273:4
  never j. from appearances 217:30
Judg(e)ment: a Daniel come to j. 275:3
  but reserve thy j. 248:16
  causes ... blind man's erring j. 202:4
  good j. ... relieth not ... on his own 215:18
  hour of death, ... day of j. 52:25
  no one complains of his j. 234:5
  nor is the People's j. always true 103:8
  right j. in all things 53:5
  world history is the world's j. 238:13
  wd. not give his j. rashly 9:8
Judges: hungry j. soon the sentence sign 204:9
Judging: want of skill appear ... in j. ill 202:1
Judgments: with our j. as our watches 202:2
Jug: little brown j. 15:5
Juggler: a threadbare j. 246:5
Juice (Grease): stew (fry) in one's own j. 226:17
Julia: where my J.'s lips do smile 131:13
Juliet: it is the east and J. is the sun 286:6
Julius: many Caesars ere such another J. 247:1
July: English winter—ending in J. 70:8
Jumblies: lands where the J. live 158:5
Jump: we'd j. the life to come 270:5
Jumping from the chair 137:7
Jumps: which way the cat j. 209:14
June: cuckoo is in J., heard, not regarded 255:10
  ice in J. 70:14
  rose that's newly sprung in J. 66:15
  she needs not J. 19:4
  so rare as a day in J.? 162:15
Jungle: this is the Law of the J. 154:21
Junk: Epp's statues are j. 13:4
Juno: haughty J.'s unrelenting hate 105:1
Jury: the j., passing on the prisoner's life 273:1
  trial by j. ... will be a delusion 97:4
Jury-men: wretches hang that j. may dine 204:9
Just: a beast, but a j. beast 13:6
  cause or j. impediment 53:18
  j. are the ways of God 180:13
  j. shall live by faith 47:15
  j. wore enough for modesty 62:13
  memory of the j. is blessed 38:9
  ninety and nine j. persons 46:2
  rain it raineth on the j. 57:14
  sendeth rain on the j. 43:21
  the gods are j. 267:14
  unjust steals the j.'s umbrella 57:14
Justice: j. be done, though heaven fall 213:24
  let j. be done 109:6
  much law, but little j. 221:20
  place of j. is ... hallowed 23:11
  religion, j., counsel 22:8
  revenge is a kind of wild j. 21:12
  sad-ey'd j. with his surly hum 258:8
  shall temper so j. with mercy 179:11
  the j. in fair round belly 244:11
  though j. be thy plea 275:1
  Thwackum was for doing j. 109:11
  when mercy seasons j. 275:1

Justification: carry its j. in every line 90:7
Justify: j. the ways of God to men 175:17
    to j. God's ways to man 136:9
    use thought to j. ... wrong-doing 321:12
Justitia: fiat j., et pereat mundus 109:6
J'y suis, j'y reste 164:11

Kalendas: ad K. Graecas 71:10
Kaspar: old K.'s work was done 304:12
Kate: kiss me, K. 287:8
    none of us cared for K. 288:9
Keats: who kill'd John K.? 70:17
Keen: rhy tooth is not so k. 245:1
Keener: grows k. with constant use 138:12
Keep: I k. my books at the British Museum 68:4
    I love to k. it [work] by me 139:15
    if you can k. yr. head 154:17
    k. a thing seven years 217:32
    k. up with the Joneses 217:34
Keeper: a k. is only a poacher 154:6
    am I my brother's k.? 30:16
Kelly: has anybody here seen K.? 185:4
Kennel: permitted to have friends in the k. 296:15
Kensal Green: to Paradise by way of K. 81:8
Kent, sir—everybody knows K. 98:18
Kentucky: the old K. Home 112:7
Kept: that I k. my word, he said 96:15
Kettle: pot calls the k. black 223:18
Kew: go down to K. in lilac-time 188:1
    His Highness' dog at K. 204:2
Key: Door to which I found no k. 110:6
    with this k. Shakespeare unlocked 333:5
Keys: k. of the kingdom of heaven 44:17
    send me the half that's got my k. 124:8
Khaki: one black ... one white ... two k. 13:2
Khatmandu: to the north of K. 129:6
Kick: be off or I'll k. you downstairs 74:4
    hard ... to k. against the pricks 47:4
Kicked: Jeshurun waxed fat and k. 33:7
Kill: good to k. an admiral 321:10
    I'll k. you if you quote it 64:2
    k. a wife with kindness 287:10
    k. the still-closing waters 288:15
    let's k. all the lawyers 260:10
    monarchize ... and k. with looks 283:6
    shalt not k., but needst not strive 84:16
    they k. us for their sport 266:20
    thou shalt not k. 32:5
Killed: books cannot be k. by fire 235:5
    I kiss'd thee ere I k. thee 281:1
    k. by ... Cheltenham waters 11:17
    man who was k. by lightning 11:18
    who k. Cock Robin? 196:2
    who k. John Keats? 70:17
Killing: k. my self, to die upon a kiss 281:1
    k. of a mouse on Sunday 58:2
    more ways of k. a cat 154:7
    time: ... which ends in k. him 304:16
Kills: each man k. the thing he loves 326:12
    gluttony k. more than the sword 214:38
    k. a man k. a reasonable creature 182:2
    k. me some ... dozen of Scots 254:12
    k. reason itself, k. the image of God 182:2
Kin: more than k., and less than kind 247:18
    one's own k. and kith 186:2
    one touch of nature ... whole world k. 290:7
Kind: be to her virtues very k. 205:5

Kind (*continued*)
    cruel only to be k. 252:15
    dumb jewels ... in their silent k. 292:7
    just the art of being k. 326:11
    k. as she is fair 292:9
    k. hearts are more than coronets 313:10
    more than kin and less than k. 247:18
    neither ingenious, sober, nor k. 12:3
    what k. of people do they think we are? 83:3
Kindly: is sure of being k. spoken of 20:9
Kindness: A Woman Killed with K. 132:10
    beauty lives with k. 292:9
    kill a wife with k. 287:10
    k. in another's trouble 124:6
    save in the way of k. 317:12
    tak' a cup o' k. 65:13
    too full o' th' milk of human k. 270:1
    unremembered acts of k., love 335:10
Kinds: soft maids and village k. 88:8
King: a little pin bores ... farewell, k.! 283:6
    a new k. over Egypt 31:15
    all the k.'s horses ... men 76:8, 189:9
    as I have served the k. 330:6
    ay, every inch a k. 267:3
    catch the conscience of the K. 250:19
    dainty dish, to set before the k.? 193:5
    deny it [repose] to a k. 257:3
    discharge my duties as K. 105:10
    divinity doth hedge a k. 252:22
    glory to the new-born K. 325:2
    God save the K.! Will no man say amen? 284:1
    have a k., and officers of sorts 258:8
    he that plays the k. ... be welcome 250:7
    here lies our sovereign lord the k. 234:11
    I'm the k. of the castle 190:3
    is the k. dead, the empire unpossess'd? 285:11
    Judge that no k. can corrupt 261:7
    k. is a thing men have made 241:5
    k. is but a man as I am 259:10
    K., observing with judicious eyes 318:1
    k. of shreds and patches 252:13
    K. shall do it ... shall be contented 283:7
    k.'s name is a tower of strength 285:13
    lad that's born to be k. 57:12
    let us sing, Long live the K. 92:13
    mortal temples of a k. 283:6
    no bishop, no K. 139:1
    Old K. Cole 192:1
    old, mad, blind ... dying k. 300:5
    one-eyed man is k. 208:12
    our Gracious K. ... noble K. 73:1
    passing brave to be a k. 166:9
    so excellent a k. 248:3
    sword of an angel k. 55:5
    the K. asked the Queen and 171:11
    the k. can do no wrong 54:10
    the k. himself has followed her 122:16
    the K. is strongest 51:5
    the k. loved Esther 34:27
    the k. never dies 54:9
    the k.'s a bawcock ... heart of gold 259:9
    the k. sits in Dunfermline 11:13
    the K. to Oxford sent 60:4
    think the K. knows all about me? 171:7
    wash the balm off from an anointed k. 283:2

King (*continued*)
we will go by the k.'s high way   32:19
whatsoever K. shall reign   15:13
who Pretender is, or who is K.   68:15
with half the zeal I serv'd my k.   261:13
King Charles: in good K.'s golden days   15:12
King James ... call for his old shoes   241:1
King of the Jews: he that is born K.   43:8
Kingdom: for thine is the k.   43:24
keys of the k. of heaven   44:17
k. of heaven is at hand   43:10
my k. for a horse!   285:16
my large k. for a little grave   283:7
my mind to me a k. is   105:6
my new-found land, my K.   101:3
of such is the k. of God   45:13
stand upon my k. once again   283:1
state of man, like to a little k.   262:13
teach ... order to a peopled k.   258:8
thy k. come   43:24
thy k. is divided   42:3
Kingdoms: goodly states and k. seen   150:14
Kings: all K. is mostly rapscallions   318:9
captains and the k. depart   155:3
conquering k. their titles take   78:12
divorc'd so many English k.   257:17
dread and fear of k.   275:1
I know the k. of England   120:4
k. for such a tomb wd. ... die   175:13
k. it makes gods, and meaner creatures k.   285:12
k. that fear ... subjects' treachery   260:14
left lonely ... the k. of the sea   18:13
low ambition, and the pride of k.   202:17
mad world! mad k.!   264:12
mirror of all Christian k.   258:9
my throne, bid k. come bow   264:15
of cabbages—and k.   76:4
poor men's hovels ... K.' palaces   135:12
punctuality is the politeness of k.   162:4
sad stories of the death of k.   283:6
scorn to change the my state with k.   293:17
showers on her k. barbaric pearl   176:15
such is the breath of K.   281:12
teeming womb of royal k.   282:5
the chase, the sport of k.   304:8
this royal throne of k.   282:5
King's English: an old abusing of ... the K.   276:3
Kinquering Congs their titles take   305:18
Kipling: when the Rudyards cease from k.   306:10
Kiss: ae fond k., and then we sever!   65:8
come let us k. and part   102:12
coward does it with a k.   326:12
gin a body k. a body   65:15
I dare not ask a k. ... a smile   132:2
I k. his dirty shoe   259:9
I saw you take his k.   198:11
if you can k. the mistress   218:5
k. and be friends   218:4
k. me, Hardy   187:7
k. me, Kate   287:8
k. me, sweet and twenty   291:2
k. me with the kisses of his mouth   40:2
leave a k. but in the cup   145:7
make me immortal with a k.   165:8
pale grew thy cheek ... colder thy k.   71:5
to die upon a k.   281:1
Kissed: but I k. her little sister   183:10

Kissed (*continued*)
hasn't been k. for forty years   236:14
I k. thee ere I kill'd thee   281:1
k. the girls and made them cry   189:3
k. the maiden all forlorn   194:8
Kisses: beneath the k. of Night   299:14
bread and cheese and k.   206:31
but my k. bring again   273:12
give me a thousand k.   77:15
I fear thy k., gentle maiden   300:7
I understand thy k., and thou mine   255:8
k. the joy as it flies   55:4
of many thousand k. the poor last   243:5
play'd at cards for k.   163:3
Kissing: k. don't last: cookery do!   170:4
k. yr. hand may make you feel ... good   162:1
when the k. had to stop   62:11
Kit-bag: troubles in your old k.   19:14
Kitchen: friends in the kennel, but not in the k.   296:15
taste of the k. is better   227:15
way of all flesh ... towards the k.   324:2
Kitten: rather be a k. and cry mew   255:6
Knave: a petty sneaking k. I knew   56:1
K. of Hearts, he stole those tarts   75:6, 192–3:8
Knee: not loved the world ... nor bow'd ... patient k.   69:5
silver buckles at his k.   188:5
Kneels at the foot of the bed   172:2
Knees: religion's ... not in the k.   139:17
spectacles lay on her aproned k.   71:16
Knell: by fairy hands their k. is rung   88:11
curfew tolls the k. of parting day   126:3
hear it not, Duncan, for it is a k.   270:10
Knew: fell to earth, I k. not where   160:10
I k. almost as much at eighteen   152:11
I k. him well, and every truant k.   122:11
men fell out they k. not why   67:14
new king ... which k. not Joseph   31:15
one small head cd. carry all he k.   122:12
Knife: cut it without a k.   191:4
cut off their tails ... carving k.   195:1
honey ... keeps them on the k.   13:10
smyler with the k.   79:20
Knight: a verray parfit gentle k.   79:2
gentle k. was pricking on the plain   305:10
k. of the sorrowful countenance   78:2
Knit: k. hands, and beat the ground   172:16
stuff of life to k. me   136:7
Knits up the ravell'd sleave of care   270:11
Knitting: in twisted braids of lilies k.   173:3
Knocked: k. 'em in the Old Kent Road   81:13
k. me down with a feather   218:7
Knocker: tie up the k., say ... I'm dead   201:10
Knocking: k. at Preferment's door   18:20
k. on the moonlit door   96:14
there's k. at the gate   272:4
Knocks you down with the butt end   124:2
Know: all Europe should k. we have block-heads   89:8
all ye need to k.   149:10
and when this we rightly k.   54:15
believe her, though I k. she lies   294:15
but I k. what I like   26:9
do you k. me, my lord?   249:18
does your mother k. you are out?   24:7
every wise man's son doth k.   291:1
he replied, Yes, I k.   13:1

Know (continued)
I don't k. anything ... really   26:9
I k. a bank ... wild thyme blows   276:20
I k. a reasonable woman   204:3
I k. the kings of England   120:4
I k. thee not, old man   258:3
I k. two things about the horse   13:11
I k. you all, and will ... uphold   253:20
I thought so once; but now I k. it   115:13
k. a subject ... k. where ... information
  143:19
k. all that there is to be knowed   124:13
k. cause, or just impediment   53:18
k. then thyself   203:5
k. where the shoe pinches   225:16
little do we k. what lays afore us!   98:8
mad, bad, and dangerous to k.   156:1
no knowledge but I k. it   26:6
not to k. me ... yourselves unknown   178:9
not utter what thou dost not k.   254:11
O, that a man might k. the end   264:5
ol' man river ... must k. sumpin'   128:2
pleasant to k. Mr. Lear   158:6
she didn't k. what to do   194:5
than the devil you don't k.   207:35
they k. not what they do   46:13
this alone I k. full well   59:9
to k. that which before us lies   179:2
to k. this only, that he nothing knew   180:4
we are greater than we k.   334:10
what I don't k. isn't knowledge   26:6
what shd. they k. of England?   154:13
what the false heart doth k.   270:8
whom truly to k. is everlasting life   53:7
Knoweth: talketh what he k.   21:16
Knowing: as gods, k. good and evil   30:11
k. what shd. not be known   111:2
the misfortune of k. anything   20:15
thinking ... far from k.   227:33
Knowledge: a supercilious k. in accounts
  301:9
all k. to be my province   23:14
all our k. is ourselves to know   203:12
conscious ... ignorant is a great step to k.
  100:11
continual drinking of K.   152:2
darkeneth counsel by words without k.
  35:12
ever-green tree of diabolical k.   301:7
fear of the Lord ... beginning of k.   38:1
having any k. of ... social order   296:9
his k. of life ... so hazy   197:11
increaseth k. increaseth sorrow   39:13
k. comes, but wisdom lingers   313:18
k. enormous makes a God   148:9
k. is of two kinds   143:19
k. is power   218:12
k. of God more than burnt offerings   42:8
night unto night showeth k.   35:23
science is organised   305:1
smattering of everything ... k. of nothing
  99:11
still climbing after k. infinite   166:10
Thou ... art still, out-topping k.   19:2
to know no more is woman's happiest k.
  178:7
Zeal without k. is fire without light   231:15
Known: best that has been k. and said   19:11
best that is k. and thought   19:8
I am k. and do not want [patronage]   142:1

Known (continued)
k. by the company he keeps   220:18
Knows: a woman conceals what she k. not
  230:30
I never k. the children   167:6
if you k. of a better 'ole   23:22
k. nought that k. not this   289:15
no man truly k. another   59:16
nobody k. how to write letters   89:11
the more a man k.   295:19
travels far, k. much   228:18
wise father that k. his own child   274:12
Kubla: in Xanadu did K. Khan   87:11
  K. heard from far ancestral voices   87:14
Kyd: Lyly outshine, or sporting K.   145:13

Labor omnia vicit ... egestas   321:6
Laborare est orare   218:16
Labour: crowns a youth of l.   122:7
ease and alternate l.   316:13
l., and do all thy work   32:3
l. and the wounds are vain   85:1
l. night and day to be a pilgrim   63:14
l. of an age in piled stones   175:11
months without ... any kind of l.   322:14
persistent l. overcame all things   321:6
six days shalt thou l.   32:3
sore l.'s bath   270:11
true success is to l.   307:10
votes L. ought to be locked up   183:7
yr. work of faith ... l. of love   49:5
Labourer: l. is worthy of his hire   45:27
now the l.'s task is o'er   107:16
Labours: children sweeten l.   21:18
Lack: sigh the l. of many a thing   293:18
Lacked: being l. and lost ... rack the value
  278:12
Lacrimae: hinc illae l.   315:1
Lad: and many a lightfoot l.   136:8
cd. that l. be I?   307:3
l. that's born to be king   57:12
song of a l. that is gone   307:3
when I was a l. I served a term   119:15
Ladder: a l. set up on the earth   31:9
down the l. when thou marriest   214:39
l. of all high designs   290:2
wiv a l. and some glasses   25:3
Ladies: a lion among l. ... dreadful   276:21
eleven l. dancing   194:2
good night, sweet l.   252:20
rhyme themselves into l.' favours   260:4
sigh no more, l.   277:21
store of l., whose bright eyes   174:6
Lads: golden l. and girls ... come to dust
  247:9
though yr. l. are far away   111:12
two l. that thought ... to be boy eternal
  292:12
Lady: a l. of a certain age   70:4
a l. sweet and kind   17:2
and in my l.'s chamber   189:4
courting his l. in the spring   58:4
faint heart never won fair l.   213:9
fine l. upon a white horse   193:1
for secrecy, no l. closer   254:11
I met a l. in the meads   148:15
I want to talk like a l.   296:19
make a l. of my own   335:9
my l. sweet, arise   246–7:13
old l. of Threadneedle Street   227:37

Lady (*continued*)
returned ... with the l. inside 12:10
sighed for the love of a l. 121:2
swear ... like a l. as thou art 255:9
the elder unto the elect l. 50:14
the l. doth protest too much 252:4
there ain't a l. livin' 81:14
there was a young l. named Bright 63:1
they have belied a l. 278:18
went ... to tempt My L. Poltagrue 27:8
Lady Disdain! Are you yet living? 277:11
Ladybird, fly away home 190:8
Ladylike: the birch, most ... l. of trees 162:13
Lady-smocks all silver-white 268:17
Lag: in England ... a comfortable time-l.
  324:15
Laid: in sad cypress ... l. 291:6
Laissez faire, laissez passer 232:6
Lake: beside the l., beneath the trees 331:7
Lamb: brought as a l. to the slaughter 41:7
did he who made the L. make thee? 56:6
go to bed with the l. 215:1
little l., who made thee? 56:9
Mary had a little l. 127:11
pipe a song about a l. 56:8
tempers the wind to the shorn l. 215:11,
  306:15
was the holy L. ... on England's ... pastures
  seen? 55:8
wolf ... shall dwell with the l. 40:24
Lambs: death devours l. as well as sheep
  211:5
little hills [skipped] like l. 37:7
while the young l. bound 331:15
Lament: have I not reason to l. 332:8
short pleasure, long l. 225:20
Lamp: I light my l. in the evening 28:2
Lamps: bright the l. shone o'er fair women
  69:3
l. are going out all over Europe 127:8
who will change old l.? 18:1
Land: a traveller from an antique l. 299:7
a woman is a foreign l. 198:12
England's green and pleasant l. 55:8
gone far away into the silent l. 236:1
ill fares the l. 122:5
l. flowing with milk and honey 31:18
l. of hope and glory 28:10
l. of the free ... home of the brave 153:7
l. where the Bong-tree grows 158:8
my America, my new-found l. 101:3
my native L.—Good Night! 69:2
my own, my native l.! 239:16
o'er all the pleasant l. 130:5
ring out the darkness of the l. 313:7
stranger in a strange l. 31:16
sweet l. of liberty 303:10
they are not fit to live on l. 143:21
they came upon a l. ... always afternoon
  314:1
westward, look, the l. is bright 85:3
whistles o'er the furrowed l. 174:3
Landing grounds: we shall fight on the l.
  82:13
Landlord: come, l., fill the ... bowl 14:14
Lands: close to the sun in lonely l. 312:1
l. where the Jumblies live 158:5
Landscape: now fades the glimmering l. on the
  sight 126:4
Lane: an England while ... a country l. 198:4

Lane (*continued*)
little boy who lives down the l. 188:4
Language: if everything else in our l. shd.
  perish 164:3
l. in her eye, her cheek 290:8
Lord did ... confound the l. 30:27
natural l. of the heart 241:18
no l. but the l. of the heart 201:20
no tracing ... but by l. 144:23
plague rid you for learning me yr. l. 287:19
sorry when any l. is lost 144:23
stability or enlargement of the l. 140:3
sure in l. strange she said 148:17
thunder in such lovely l. 157:11
use any l. you choose 117:12
you taught me l., and my profit on't 287:19
yr. ... l. is the l. of Shakespeare 296:18
Languages: all l. living and dead 98:9
three or four l. ... without book 290:11
Languid: the l. strings do scarcely move 56:14
Lap: his head upon the l. of earth 126:13
in thy green l. was Nature's Darling 127:1
Lards the lean earth as he walks 254:9
Large as life, and twice as natural 77:5
Largest: shout with the l. [mob] 98:20
Lark: no l. more blithe than he 54:1
rise with the l. 215:1
the l.'s on the wing 62:7
to hear the l. begin his flight 174:2
Larks: hear the l. so high about us 136:6
two Owls ... four L. and a Wren 158:13
Lars Porsena of Clusium 163:9
Lashed the vice, but spared the name 308:13
Lass: I loved a l., a fair one 329:10
yon solitary Highland L. 334:16
Lasses: come, l. and lads 14:15
he dearly lov'd the l. 66:2
hours ... spent amang the l. 66:1
Last: die ... the l. thing I shall do! 198:1
filling his l. cavity..12:7
heard the l. of her ... I wonder! 297:5
it will not l. the night 170:13
kissing don't l.: cookery do! 170:4
l. but not least 218:18
L. of the Mohicans 90:11
l. out a night in Russia 273:3
l. taste of sweets, is sweetest l. 282:3
might be the l., my Mary! 93:13
of many thousand kisses the poor l. 243:5
rash ... blaze of riot cannot l. 282:4
the l. of life, for wh. the first was made
  62:9
there is no l. nor first 62:8
well, I cannot l. ever 256:10
Late: better l. than never 207:30
good to marry l. or never 220:32
make haste, and come too l. 282:2
marries l., marries ill 220:28
never too l. to mend 221:34
too l. to save the stamp 124:9
Lately: read any good books l.? 185:3
Latin: away with him! He speaks L. 260:12
must carve in L. or in Greek 322:2
small L. and less Greek 145:14
Latter: meeter to carry off the l. 199:6
Laugh: and l. at gilded butterflies 267:13
if I l. at any mortal thing 70:2
l. and the world l. with you 326:9
l. as I pass in thunder 298:5
l. to scorn the pow'r of man 271:15

Laugh (*continued*)
　l. where we must, be candid　202:18
　loud l. that spoke the vacant mind　122:8
　love I l. to scorn　58:14
　make 'em l. ... cry ... wait　233:5
　men that l. and weep　309:18
　the l. broke into ... pieces　24:11
　who but must l. ?　201:17
Laughed: little dog l. to see such sport　189:5
　no man who has ... wholly l.　73:11
　when the first baby l.　24:11
Laughing is heard on the hill　56:11
Laughs: flabby hands and irritating l.　118:4
　he l. best who l. last　218:21
Laughter: drinks his wine 'mid l. free　17:3
　I heard the l. of her heart　128:1
　invent anything that tends to l.　256:8
　it wd. be ... l. for a month　254:8
　L. holding both his sides　173:17
　l., learnt of friends　59:7
　nothing so ... ill-bred as audible l.　80:13
　present mirth hath present l.　291:2
　ran ... after the ... music with ... l.　62:6
　sincerest l. with some pain is fraught　300:2
　so is the l. of the fool　39:19
　tired of tears and l.　309:18
Laundry: general idea ... in any ... l.　157:15
Laurel: burned is Apollo's l.-bough　166:1
　l. is green for a season　310:4
　l. outlives not May　310:4
Laurels: the l. all are cut　136:3
　yet once more, O ye l.　174:12
Lavinia: she is L. ... must be loved　289:13
Law: against reason, ... of no force in l.　85:7
　agree, for the l. is costly　206:9
　and the l. doth give it　275:5
　and this is l. that I'll maintain　15:13
　dusty purlieus of the l.　312:18
　every l. is a contract　241:6
　glorious uncertainty of the l.　229:9
　God is thy l., thou mine　178:7
　good of the people ... chief l.　84:2
　hard cases make bad l.　216:12
　higher l. than the Constitution　241:17
　I ... embody the L.　117:2
　in l.'s grave study　85:9
　in vice their l.'s their will　281:4
　l. is a bottomless pit　218:22
　l. is an ass—a idiot　98:15
　l. makers shd. not be l. breakers　218:24
　love ... fulfilling of the l.　47:29
　love has never known a l.　326:6
　may be ... good l. for all that　240:11
　much l., but little justice　221:20
　nature's l. that man was made to mourn　66:7
　necessity hath no l.　221:23
　one God, one l., one element　313:9
　one l. for the rich　218:23
　other sources of international l.　319:5
　ought l. to weed it out　21:12
　possession is nine points of the l.　223:17
　pounds of l., ... not an ounce of love　227:36
　rich men rule the l.　123:16
　self-preservation is the first l.　225:13
　take the l. into one's own hands　227:5
　the l. hath not been dead　273:5
　the L. is the true embodiment　117:2
　the L. of the Yukon　241:15
　the L. of Triviality　198:6
　the l.'s delay　250–1:20

Law (*continued*)
　the more l., the more offenders　218:25
　these ... a l. unto themselves　47:16
　this is the l. and the prophets　44:7
　this is the L. of the Jungle　154:21
　wedded Love, mysterious l.　178:8
　windy side of the l.　291:16
　wrest once the l. to yr. authority　275:2
Lawn as white as driven snow　293:3
Laws: know not whether l. be right　326:15
　l. grind the poor and rich men rule the law
　　123:16
　l. of England are at my commandment　258:2
　l. of the Persians ... Medes　34:26
　l. were made to be broken　187:17
　let ... l. and learning die　237:10
　Nature's L. lay hid in Night　201:21
　religion breathing household l.　333:11
　repeal of bad or obnoxious l.　125:2
　sweeter manners, purer l.　313:5
Lawyers: few l. die well　213:22
　let's kill all the l.　260:10
Lay on, Macduff　272:14
Lazy: liftin' the l. ones on　125:5
　mentally l. ... as well be dead　324:18
Lead: do scald like molten l.　267:10
　l., Kindly Light ... l. thou me on　187:14
　strange ... the life he makes us l.　60:10
Leaden-eyed despairs　149:15
Leadeth me beside the still waters　35:28
Leaf: fall'n into the sear, the yellow l.　272:5
　lowest boughs ... are in tiny l.　61:1
　November's l. is red　240:3
　take a l. out of one's book　226:38
　turn over a new l.　228:31
　where the dead l. fell ... did it rest　148:5
League: half a l. onward　311:9
　keep a l. till death　284:4
Lean: his wife cd. eat no l.　190:7
　l. and slipper'd pantaloon　244:11
Leap: a great l. in the dark　133:4
　methinks it were an easy l.　254:4
Leaps: morn doth break ... l. in the sky　58:3
　my heart l. up when I behold　333:8
Leapt: into the dangerous world I l.　56:3
Leap-year: twenty-nine in each l.　194:6
Lear: how pleasant to know Mr. L.　158:6
Learn: gladly wolde he l.　79:10
　l. by other men's mistakes　230:25
　l. to labour and to wait　161:2
　live and l.　219:19
　they will l. at no other　64:15
　we l. nothing from history　296:10
Learned: he was naturally l.　104:4
　loads of l. lumber in his head　202:15
　that ... grew within this l. man　166:1
　that l. body wanted loyalty　318:1
Learning: a little l. is a dangerous thing　202:5
　better than a bushel of l.　216:1
　l. is but an adjunct to ourself　268:12
　l. makes ... better ... worse　218:30
　l.'s triumph o'er her barb'rous foes　140:19
　l. without thought ... thought without l.
　　89:4
　love of money and love of l.　220:5
　loyal body wanted l.　318:1
　more aid than any l.　310:7
　on scraps of l. dote　337:11
　whence is thy l. ?　115:9
Learnt nothing, and forgotten nothing　310:12

Lease: summer's l. ... too short a date   293:13

Leave: comrades, l. me here a little   313:14
fare thee well, for I must l. thee   17:4
l. me there to die   15:9
l. this barren spot to me   72:7
l. us nought but grief an' pain   66:12
Oh, never l. me!   15:1

Leaven: a little l. leaveneth ... lump   48:1

Leaves: generation of l. ... is that of men   134:8
his hoar l. in the glassy stream   253:1
l. dead are driven, like ghosts   299:3
life out of the dead l.   157:9
lisp of l.   309:14
puts forth the tender l. of hope   261:9
they sewed fig l. together   30:12
with forced fingers rude shatter your l.   174:12
with l. and flowers do cover   324:3

Leben: unnütz L. ... früher Tod   122:2

Lecher: gilded fly does l. in my sight   267:4

Lechery: an equivocator with l.   270:14
l., l.! still wars and l.!   290:9

Lectures: cannot see that l. can do so much good   143:1
I do not give l. or ... charity   326:3

Led by the nose with gold   293:8

Leer: assent with civil l.   201:16

Left: a lady richly l.   274:4
ah! he l. the thorn with me   67:7
l. for contemplation not what ... used   29:11
l. him alone with his glory   330:4
sun came up upon the l.   85:13
we that are l. grow old   54:5

Leg: can honour set to a l. ?   255:21
have a bone in one's l.   208:15
here I leave my second l.   134:12

Legion: my name is L.   45:9

Legions: give me back my l.   71:9

Legislators: poets are the unacknowledged l.   300:11

Legs: a cannon-ball took off his l.   134:11
on one's last l.   218:19
vast and trunkless l. of stone   299:7
walk under his huge l.   262:8

Leicester Square: farewell, L.   329:1

Leisure: busiest men ... most l.   208:37
detest at l.   70:7
l. answers l.   273:14

Lely: Mr. L., ... paint my picture   94:10

Lend: give a shilling than l. a half-crown   207:28
I'll l. you something   291:17
men who borrow ... men who l.   156:2
when I l. I am a friend   218:35

Lender: neither a borrower nor a l. be   248:17

Lends: he l. out money gratis   274:7
three things I never l.   308:7

Length: what [happiness] lacks in l.   113:15

Leopard: can the ... l. [change] his spots ?   41:14
l. shall lie down with the kid   40:24

Leprosy: her skin was as white as l.   86:8

Lesbia: let us live, my L.   77:14
vivamus, mea L., atque amemus   77:14

Less: I love not man the l.   69:9
l. than [square deal] no man shall have   235:9
one failing, had a woman ever l. ?   66:6
stand ... l. betwn. me and the sun   99:19

Less (*continued*)
the little l., and what worlds away   60:15
you mean you can't take l.   74:10

Lessen: they l. from day to day   75:1

Lessons: reason they're called l.   75:1

Lethe: no, no, go not to L.   149:11

Letter: the l. killeth   48:14
thou unnecessary l.!   265:18

Letters: his sayings ... like women's l.   129:7
I am persecuted with l.   89:11
I pray you, in yr. l.   280:14
l. get in the wrong places   172:8
nobody knows how to write l.   89:11

Lettuces had been so soporific   204:14

Leveller: death is the grand l.   211:6

Levellers: yr. l. wish to level down   142:12

Levers to lift me up ... being down ?   254:7

Leviathan: canst thou draw out l. ?   35:14

Lexicographer.—a harmless drudge   140:7

Lexicography: not yet so lost in l.   140:2

Liar ... when he speaks the truth   218:39

Liars: all men are l.   37:10
great talkers are great l.   215:29
l. ought to [should] have good memories   218:40, 302:1

Libel: greater the truth, the greater the l.   215:31

Liberal: is either a little L.   117:8

Liberté: l., égalité, fraternité   17:8
O L.! que de crimes ... en ton nom !   234:16

Libertine: puff'd and reckless l.   248:14
the air, a charter'd l.   258:7

Liberty: give me l. or ... death   131:4
God hath given l. to man   95:3
L. and Union, now and for ever   323:10
l. cannot long exist   64:19
l., equality, fraternity   17:8
l. is precious ... must be rationed   159:3
l. means responsibility ... men dread it   296:12
l. ... must be limited   64:18
L. of the Press ... the *Palladium*   146:5
l.'s in every blow   67:2
l. to know, to utter   182:9
marries for wealth, sells his l.   220:27
mountain-nymph, sweet L.   173:18
O l., l., what crimes ... in yr. name!   234:16
sweet life of l.   303:10
thy chosen music, L.   333:10

Liberty Hall: this is L.   123:8

Library: a circulating l. in a town   301:7
my l. was dukedom ... enough   287:17
vanity of ... hopes ... public l.   141:2

Libre: l'homme est né l. ... est dans les fers   236:12

Licence: Government l. to print money   316:14
the rest love not freedom, but l.   182:11

Licht: mehr L.!   122:3

Lick: ill cook that cannot l. his own fingers   210:9, 287:2
to l. into shape   219:1

Licked: they l. the platter clean   190:7

Lie: a cat and a l.   318:17
a l. begets a l.   219:2
after all, what is a l. ?   70:5
and they all dead did l.   86:11
Father, I cannot tell a l.   322:18
honest man sent to l. abroad   336:11
I knowed it was a l.   318:8

Lie (*continued*)
not a stone tell where I l.   204:1
nothing can need a l.   131:9
oft when on my couch I l.   331:11
painters and poets have leave to l.   222:33
seventh, the L. Direct   246:2
the L. with Circumstance   246:2
where my heart lies, let my brain l.   61:13
while you here do snoring l.   288:5
who loves to l. with me   244:4
Lied: Heart replied ... but it l.   27:9
Lies: ask no questions ... be told no l.   206:24
beats all the l. you can invent   54:14
believe her, though I know she l.   294:15
one of the social l.   138:3
one thing is certain ... Rest is L.   110:4
three kinds of l.   318:10
where my heart l.   61:13
Life: a daily beauty in his l.   280:8
a handful of good l.   216:1
a keen observer of l.   20:3
a lad of l., an imp of fame   259:9
a l. like the scriptures   152:7
a l. on the ocean wave   238:8
a space of l. between   147:7
a useless l. is an early death   122:2
after l.'s fitful fever he sleeps well   271:4
all his l. ... speaking the truth   327:18
all the blessings of this l.   53:1
all the voyage of their l. is bound   264:3
all this flesh keeps in a little l.   256:2
and l. is thorny   87:7
any practical part of l.   9:6
anything for a quiet l.   99:10, 206:18
art is long, but l. is short   132:13
as large as l.   218:17
bankrupt of l., yet prodigal of ease   103:1
before us lies in daily l.   179:2
best of l. is but intoxication   69:15
best portion of a good man's l.   335:10
brief l. is here our portion   186:13
cannot tell what you ... think of this l.   262:6
care of human l. ... not their destruction   139:10
commuter—one who spends his l.   325:8
compare human l. to ... Mansion   152:3
custom ... great guide of ... l.   137:2
dear ... as light and l.   66:3
death after l. doth greatly please   305:11
digestion is the great secret of l.   303:17
doth the wingèd l. destroy   55:4
each change of many-colour'd l.   140:19
essential thing in l. is not conquering   91:2
expect more from l. than l. will afford   143:5
fie upon this quiet l.!   254:12
giveth his l. for the sheep   46:27
he that cuts off twenty years of l.   263:3
his name out of the book of l.   50:18
I bear a charmed l.   272:12
I do not set my l. at a pin's fee   249:4
I fall upon the thorns of l.   299:5
I will give thee a crown of l.   50:16
in London all that l. can afford   144:9
in the midst of l. we are in death   53:29
is l. a boon?   120:17
isn't l. a terrible thing?   316:4
its private l. is a disgrace   14:6
I've done it all my l.   13:10
large as l. and twice as natural   77:5

Life (*continued*)
last of l. for which the first   62:9
lay hold on l.   183:2
letter killeth ... spirit giveth l.   48:14
l. for l., eye for eye   32:10
l., force and beauty must ... impart   202:3
l. ... is a continual allegory   152:7
l. is a jest   115:13
l. is as tedious as a twice-told tale   264:17
l. is but a day; a ... dew-drop   150:9
l. is but an empty dream   160:14
l. is just one damned thing after another   136:12
l. is mostly froth and bubble   124:6
l. is ... process of getting tired   68:5
L. is real! L. is earnest   160:14
l. is sweet   219:5
l. is the art of drawing ... conclusions   68:6
l. is very sweet, brother   57:8
l. isn't all beer and skittles   136:13
l., liberty, ... pursuit of happiness   139:6
l., like a dome of many-coloured glass   298:2
l. protracted is protracted woe   141:12
l. ... solitary, poor, nasty, brutish   133:3
l., time's fool   256:1
l.'s too short for chess   71:8
live a barren sister all yr. l.   276:9
love is of man's l. a thing apart   69:14
make l., death ... for-ever one ... song   154:2
makes calamity of so long l.   250–1:20
man's l. is cheap as beast's   266:2
married to a single l.   94:2
measured out my l. with coffee spoons   106:14
mine honour is my l.   281:8
modern l. ... tedious, ... and modern literature   327:7
most of the change ... in l.   113:9
no, no, no l.   268:4
nor love thy l., nor hate   179:14
not so much l. as on a summer's day   148:5
nothing in his l. became him   269:11
O for a L. of Sensations!   151:10
on human l., musing in solitude   331:3
on the Tree of L. ... sat   178:1
one good deed in all my l.   289:14
our l., exempt from public haunt   243:15
our l. is frittered away by detail   317:1
our little l. is rounded ... sleep   288:16
my l. is one demd horrid grind   98:11
my way of l. ... the yellow leaf   272:5
pass them for a nobler l.   150:11
people say that L. is the thing   303:8
preach ... doctrine of strenuous l.   235:7
promise them l. and then kill them   319:8
quickening l. from the Earth's heart   297:11
saw l. steadily and ... whole   18:14
sells us l. at a discount   114:3
she is coming, my l., my fate   314:4
short l. and a merry one   225:19
shd. ... have everlasting l.   46:21
so careless of the single l.   312:16
soldier's l. is terrible hard   171:6
spare all I have and take my l.   109:5
spend my l. in driving briskly   144:7
strange disease of modern l.   18:21
stuff of l. to knit me   136:7
sucking his l. out of the dead leaves   157:9
take away my good name ... my l.   226:39

Line (*continued*)
  must draw the l. somewhere 211:33
  the Brighton l. ... the l. is immaterial
   327:14
  to cancel half a l. 110:12
  to l. one's pockets 219:14
  we carved not a l. 330:4
Linen: choose neither ... l. by candle-light
  209:25
  old l. wash whitest 324:1
Lines: with silken l. and silver hooks 100:17
Lingering: something l., with boiling oil
  118:14
Lingers: borrowing only l. and l. it out 256:12
Linguistics: An Essay in Sociological L.
  235:14
Lining: there's a silver l. 111:12
Linnet: a l. courting his lady 58:4
  come, hear the woodland l. 335:5
Lion: a l. among ladies 276:21
  dar'st ... beard the l. ... The Douglas 240:7
  in like a l., ... out like a lamb 220:23
  l. is not so fierce as ... painted 219:15
  nation ... had the l. heart 83:14
  not a more fearful wildfowl than ... l.
  276:21
  rouse a l. than to start a hare 254:3
  the devil, as a roaring l. 50:8
  the l. and the unicorn 190:9
  the l. looked at Alice wearily 77:6
Lions: cast him into the den of l. 42:5
  Saul and Jonathan ... stronger than l. 34:11
Lip: keep a stiff upper l. 77:11, 226:20
Lips: beauty's ensign is crimson in thy l. 287:3
  cd. you hurt me, sweet l. ? 309:17
  dear red curve of her l. 168:12
  her l. suck forth my soul 165:8
  her l. were red, her looks were free 86:8
  take, O, take, those l. away 273:12
  their l. were four red roses 285:8
  through my l. to unawakened earth 299:6
  truth sits upon the l. of dying men 19:3
  what l. my l. have kissed 170:12
  when I ope my l. let no dog bark 274:3
  where my Julia's l. do smile 131:13
Liquefaction of her clothes 132:6
Liquid: Thames is l. history 65:7
Liquidation: preside over the l. of the British
  Empire 83:6
Liquor: l. is quicker 186:8
  they sell worse kinds of l. 322:12
Lisp of leaves and ripple of rain 309:14
List: I've got a little l. 118:4
  I wd. not enter on my l. of friends 93:12
  l., l., O, l.! 249:7
Listen: darkling I l. 150:3
  l. with credulity to ... fancy 141:3
  the world shd. l. then 300:3
Listened: I l., motionless and still 335:1
Listeners hear no good of themselves 219:16
Lit again in our lifetime 127:8
Literature: he has raised the price of l. 142:3
  itch of l. comes over a man 162:9
  l. flourishes best when it is half a trade
  138:7
  that great Cham of l. 304:3
  the rest is just l. 320:9
  to produce a little l. 139:4
Litter: all her l. but one 256:8
Littérature: tout le reste est l. 320:9

Little: a l. of what you fancy 160:5
  a l. still she strove 69:11
  comrades, leave me here a l. 313:14
  every l. helps 212:30
  give according to that l. 51:8
  goin' through so much to learn so l. 99:3
  great ones eat up the l. ones 281:5
  having too l. to do 155:9
  I thought so l. they rewarded me 119:16
  if I'm content with a l. 54:3
  it was a very l. one 167:5
  knows l., soon repeats it 218:14
  knows l. who will tell his wife all 114:9
  l. breezes dusk and shiver 313:12
  l. drops ... l. grains ... l. minutes 73:13
  l. things please l. minds 219:18
  l. things ... the most important 101:12
  l. we see in nature that is ours 333:3
  love me l., love me long 220:3
  man wants but l. drink below 134:2
  man wants but l., nor that l. long 338:2
  many a l. makes a mickle 220:22
  no great ones if ... no l. ones 215:28
  nor wants that l. long 122:15
  obedience is ... seen in l. things 222:21
  so l. done, so much to do 233:10
  such a l. tail behind 27:1
  the l. less, and what worlds away 60:15
  the l. more, and how much 60:15
  think too l. ... talk too much 103:3
  through so much to learn so l. 99:3
  wealth is contentment with a l. 229:39
Live: a bachelor, I l. by myself 16:3
  anything but—l. for it [religion] 88:17
  bear to l. or dare to die 203:7
  better to l. rich 144:11
  but a short time to l. 53:28
  but one bare hour to l. 165:10
  come l. with me and be my love 100:17,
  167:1
  crabbed age and youth cannot l. together
  295:1
  desire ... to l. beyond its income 68:7
  eat to l. ... not l. to eat 212:16
  I had as lief not be as l. 262:6
  I marvel how the fishes l. 281:5
  I with thee will choose to l. 173:13
  in our embers is something that doth l.
  332:4
  let me l. unseen, unknown 204:1
  l. a fool the rest of his dull life 25:7
  l. and learn 219:19
  l. and let l. 219:20
  l., move, and have our being 47:6
  l. as the Romans do 10:10
  l., for the truth is living 310:5
  loves to l. i' th' sun 244:6
  may l. to fight another day 13:8
  Mirth, with thee I mean to l. 174:11
  not l. by bread only 32:23
  not suffer a witch to l. 32:11
  other men l. to eat 304:6
  rogues ... want to l. for ever ? 113:5
  she ... tried to l. without him 336:12
  so we'll l., and pray, and sing 267:13
  so wise, so young, ... never l. long 285:2
  take the means whereby I l. 275:6
  threatened men l. long 227:38
  to l. is like love 68:8
  to l. with her and l. with thee 174:1

Live (*continued*)
  to l. with thee and be thy love   232:14
  we that l. to please   141:1
  what thou liv'st l. well   179:14
  will it not l. with the living ?   255:21
  you might as well l.   198:3
Lived: for I have l. to-day   104:16
  I have l. long enough   310:3
  l. in the odium ... sodium   29:5
  l. on, and so did I   86:11
  who has never loved has never l.   115:8
Liver: open and notorious evil l.   53:9
Livery: in her sober l. all things clad   178:6
Lives: a history in all men's l.   257:5
  all that l. must die   247:20
  as a man l., so shall he die   220:19
  cat has only nine l.   318:17
  constancy l. in realms above   87:7
  he l. ... 'tis Death is dead   297:17
  he preaches well that l. well   223:25
  he who l. more l. than one   326:14
  l. in eternity's sunrise   55:4
  l. of great men all remind us   161:1
  love l. in cottages ... courts   219:40
  men lead l. of quiet desperation   316:15
  not how a man dies, but how he l.   143:4
  one really l. nowhere   65:5
  so long l. this, and this gives life   293:15
  the music of men's l.   284:7
  there l. more faith in ... doubt   313:1
Living: from too much love of l.   310:1
  Homer ... who, l., had no roof   132:9
  Lady Disdain, are you yet l. ?   277:11
  live, for the truth is l.   310:5
  l. ... eight years with a strange man   138:2
  l., shall forfeit fair renown   240:1
  plain l. and high thinking   333:11
  the l. need charity   18:8
  the mother of all l.   30:15
  the noble L.   334:6
  'tis the l. up to [faith]   315:6
  we have gone on l., l. and partly l.   107:9
Livingstone: Dr. L., I presume   306:4
Lizzie Borden took an axe   14:3
Load: how to l. and bless with fruit   147:1
Loaf: half a l. is better   215:36
  of a cut l. to steal a shive   289:13
Loafe: I l. and invite my soul   326:1
Loan oft loses both itself and friend   248:17
Lobster: the voice of the l.   75:4
Lochinvar: never was Knight like ... L.   240:6
  young L. is come out of the west   240:5
Lock: l., stock and barrel   219:22
  prison with a life-long l.   118:7
Locks: her l. were yellow as gold   86:8
  knotted and combined l. to part   249:7
  pluck up ... honour by the l.   254:4
  shaking her invincible l.   182:8
  yr. l. were like the raven   66:5
Locust: years that the l. hath eaten   42:12
Lodge: where thou lodgest, I will l.   33:25
Loftiness: in l. of thought surpass'd   104:11
Lofty and sour to them that lov'd him not   262:2
Log: on a l., expiring frog   98:21
Logic: as it isn't, it ain't. That's l.   75:15
  grape that can with L. absolute   110:10
  l. and rhetoric [make] able to contend   23:9
  un-to l. hadde longe y-go   79:7
Logs: bring me pine l. hither   187:2

Logs (*continued*)
  Tom bears l. into the hall   269:1
Loitering: alone anꞇ palely l.   148:14
Lombard Street to a China orange   219:23
London: a L. particular ... A fog   97:9
  as L. is to Paddington   72:17
  citizen ... of famous L. town   92:6
  hell is ... much like L.   299:9
  it isn't far from L.   188:1
  L., ... flower of Cities all   105:4
  L., that great cesspool   102:5
  L. ... the Clearing-house of the World   78:7
  Mr. Weller's knowledge of L.   98:23
  no man ... willing to leave L.   144:9
  nobody is healthy in L.   20:8
  our scene is L.   145:5
  to L. to look at the queen   192:7
  when a man is tired of L.   144:9
London Bridge is broken down   191:5
Loneliness of my country and my God   297:4
Lonely: close to the sun in l. lands   312:1
  left l. for ever the kings   18:13
  so l. 'twas, that God himself   87:2
  wandered l. as a cloud   331:7
Lonesome: one that on a l. road   86:16
Long: a l., l. trail a-winding   153:11
  a l. way to Tipperary   329:1
  by thy l. grey beard   85:11
  has been l. in city pent   151:6
  he l. lived the pride   24:6
  how l. or short permit to Heaven   179:14
  I have lived l. enough   310:3
  it cannot hold you l.   122:18
  it shall be witty and it shan't be l.   80:18
  l. after it was heard no more   335:1
  l., dark, boggy, dirty ... way   123:7
  l. is the way and hard   177:5
  l. live the king, and Gilpin l. live he   92:13
  look at them l. and l.   326:2
  love me little, so you love me l.   132:3
  man goeth to his l. home   39:27
  nor wants that little l.   122:15
  not that the story need be l.   317:4
  Shenandoah, I l. to hear you   16:9
  star-spangled banner! O l. may it wave   153:7
  the night is l. that never finds the day   272:1
  victory however l. ... the road   82:12
  waiting for the l.-promised invasion   83:1
Longed: lies where he l. to be   307:6
Longest: hatred is by far the l. pleasure   70:7
  Russia, when nights are l. there   273:3
Longings: I have immortal l. in me   243:10
Longitude: a l. with no platitude   114:4
Look: but westward, l., the land is bright   85:3
  Cassius has a lean and hungry l.   262:9
  do it with a bitter l.   326:12
  has a frightened l. in its eye   302:10
  houses are built ... not to l. on   23:3
  I'll be a candle-holder and l. on   285:20
  just to l. about us and to die   202:17
  let him l. to his bond   274:16
  l. at [animals] long and long   326:2
  l. before you leap   219:27
  l. thy last on all things lovely   96:13
  mountains l. on Marathon   70:1
  only a l. and a voice   161:7
  shall not l. upon his like again   248:9

Look (*continued*)

 to l. upon verdure ... perfect refreshment 20:12

 we l. before and after 300:2

Looked: having l. to government for bread 64:16

 no sooner l. but they lov'd 245:14

 she l. at me as she did love 148:16

Lookers-on see most of the game 219:29

Looking-glass: not thank you for a l. 208:11

Looks: her l. were free 86:8

 how like a ... publican he l. 274:7

 l. the whole world in the face 161:10

 love l. not with the eyes 276:12

 toward school with heavy l. 286:12

 woman as old as she l. 88:7

Looms: quest and passage through these l. 320:6

Loon: private buffoon is a light-hearted l. 121:5

 sung ... by a love-lorn l. 121:1

Lord: a ... l., neat, and trimly dress'd 254:1

 bread which the L. hath given 31:28

 deputy elected by the L. 283:2

 foundation is Jesus Christ her L. 307:13

 from ghoulies ... good L. deliver us! 13:7

 I thought ... a L. among wits 141:18

 L. Finchley tried to mend ... light 27:6

 L. Hippo suffered fearful loss 27:14

 L. Lucky, by a curious fluke 28:1

 l. of thy presence and no land 264:9

 now, the L. lighten thee! 256:16

 O L., thou lover of souls 51:14

 one day is with the L. 50:10

 praise the L. for he is kind 180:7

 sing to the L. with cheerful voice 153:4

 speak, L.; for thy servant heareth 33:28

 the Angel of the L. came down 311:4

 the day thou gavest, L. 107:17

 the L. bless thee and keep thee 32:18

 the L. ... chasteneth thee 32:24

 the L. do so to me 33:26

 the L. gave and the L. hath taken 35:1

 the L. hardened Pharaoh's heart 31:24

 the L. is my shepherd 35:27

 the L. ... is one L. 32:21

 the L. lift up his countenance 32:18

 the L. make his face shine 32:18

 the L. our God is good 153:5

 the L. set a mark upon Cain 30:17

 the L., whom ye seek 43:6

 where the dear L. was crucified 10:7

 whom the L. loveth he chasteneth 49:22

Lords: twelve l. a-leaping 194:2

Lose: grasp all, l. all 215:26

 heads I win, tails you l. 94:5, 216:20

 l. and neglect the creeping hours 244:10

 l. by over-running 261:3

 l. myself in other men's minds 156:6

 who wd. l. ... this intellectual being 176:19

Losers: l. are ... in the wrong 219:30

 l. seekers, finders keepers 219:31

Loss: buy and sell, and live by the l. 209:2

 enow to do our country's l. 259:13

 Lord Hippo suffered fearful l. 27:14

 l. of honour was a wrench 124:11

Losses: all l. are restor'd 293:19

Lost: and she l. her maiden name 16:11

 better to have fought and l. 84:18

 better to have loved and l. 68:12, 312:13

Lost (*continued*)

 books by which the printers have l. 114:10

 field be l. ? All is not l. 175:18

 how art thou l.! 179:10

 I have l. all the names 144:17

 I have l. my reputation 279:10

 I look upon every day to be l. 144:21

 learning without thought is labour l. 89:4

 l. causes, forsaken beliefs 19:7

 never to have l. at all 68:12

 praising ... l. makes the remembrance dear 242:7

 sorry when any language is l. 144:23

 thou art l. and gone for ever 183:8

 wherever we're l. in 114:5

 woman that deliberates is l. 9:5

Lot: policeman's l. is not a happy one 120:6

 remember L.'s wife 46:10

 the l. fell upon Jonah 42:18

Lots: so they cast l. 42:18

Lottery: marriage is a l. 220:25

Loud: I said it very l. and clear 77:3

Louder: the l. he talked of his honour 108:12

Loungers: all the l. of the Empire 102:5

Love: a little l. and good company 109:4

 absence sharpens l. 205:8

 ah! dearest l., sweet home of all 149:5

 Alas! the l. of women 69:16

 all is fair in l. and war 206:11

 all l. is sweet 299:12

 all mankind l. a lover 108:7

 all she loves is l. 69:17

 am like to l. three more 308:2

 an oyster may be crossed in l. 301:3

 and when l. speaks 268:13

 as honour, l., obedience 272:5

 be wise and l. exceeds man's might 290:5

 brief ... as woman's l. 252:3

 but l. is blind, and lovers cannot see 274:14

 choose l. by another's eyes 276:11

 comfort in the strength of l. 332:12

 corner in the thing I l. 279:17

 course of true l. never ... smooth 276:10

 cupboard l. 210:25

 dinner of herbs where l. is 38:18

 dislike ... the l. of a woman ... treacle 152:9

 drew them ... with bands of l. 42:10

 earth's the right place for l. 113:8

 familiar acts are beautiful through l. 299:13

 faults are thick where l. is thin 213:21

 fear the Lord ... and to l. him 33:1

 few l. to hear the sins they l. to act 281:3

 folly ... l. did make thee run into 244:3

 for ever wilt thou l. 149:8

 for I am sick of l. 40:6

 for ... them that l. God 47:20

 for thy sweet l. rememb'red 293:17

 friendly l. perfecteth 22:1

 friendship is constant ... save in ... l. 277:15

 from too much l. of living 310:1

 gave, once, her flowers to l. 59:6

 general award of l. 148:11

 God is l. 50:12

 greater l. hath no man 46:31

 greatest hate ... from the greatest l. 215:32

 hail, wedded L. 178:8

 half in l. with easeful Death 150:3

 his banner over me was l. 40:5

 hot l. is soon cold 217:5

 how have you left the ancient l. ? 56:14

Love (*continued*)

I cd. not l. thee, Dear, so much   162:7
I do not l. thee, Dr. Fell   59:9
I hate and l. ... and am in torment   77:16
I l. a lassie   157:3
I l. everything that's old   123:6
I l. not man the less   69:9
I l. sixpence   190:2
I l. thee true   148:17
I never shall l. the snow   58:5
I think my l. as rare   294:14
if music be the food of l.   290:10
is it ... a crime to l. too well ?   201:6
leave to come unto my l.   305:8
lest that thy l. prove variable   286:10
let brotherly l. continue   49:23
let l. be without dissimulation   47:23
lightly turns to thoughts of l.   313:15
little brown jug ... I l. thee   15:5
live with me and be my l.   100:17, 167:1
live with thee and be thy l.   232:14
look'd at me as she did l.   148:16
l. all, trust a few   242:1
l. alters not   294:9
l. and a cough cannot be hid   219:33
l. and business teach eloquence   219:34
l. and fame to nothingness   151:8
l. and hate are necessary   56:15
l. and marriage rarely can combine   69:18
l. and meekness ... become a churchman   262:3
l. bade me welcome; yet my soul drew back   131:10
l. begets l.   219:35
l. built on beauty   100:19
l. but her and l. for ever   65:9
l. ceases to be a pleasure   26:11
l. conquers all   321:5
l. ... differs from gold and clay   298:9
l. Divine, all loves excelling   325:3
L. forgive us!—cinders, ashes   149:1
l., free as air, at sight of ... ties   201:8
l. goes toward l. ... but l. from l.   286:12
l. grows bitter with treason   310:4
l. has never known a law   326:6
l. he laughed to scorn   295:4
l. her till I die   17:2
l. I laugh to scorn   58:14
l. in a golden bowl   55:2
l. in a hut with water   149:1
l. in a palace   149:1
l. is blind   219:38
l. is enough   184:10
l. ... is exactly like war   307:1
l. is heaven and heaven is l.   239:13
l. is like the measles   139:14
l. is my religion—I cd. die   152:10
l. is not l. which alters   294:8
l. is ... sour in the ending   219:39
l. is strong as death   40:14
l. is sweet for a day   310:4
l. is the fulfilling of the law   47:29
l. itself shall slumber on   300:6
l. looks not with the eyes   276:12
l. me little, l. me long   220:3
l. me little, so you l. me long   132:3
l. me, l. my dog   220:4
l. of flattery   306:6
l. of money ... root of all evil   49:14
l. rules the court, the camp   239:13

Love (*continued*)

l.'s but the frailty of the mind   89:14
l. seeketh not itself to please   56:2
l. sought is good   291:12
l.'s the noblest frailty of the mind   104:8
l. that moves the sun   95:8
l. that never told can be   55:10
l. the brotherhood   50:5
l. the Lord ... with all thine heart   32:22
l. thy neighbour as thyself   32:16
l. thyself last   261:12
l. too much that die for l.   220:6
l., we are in God's hand   60:10
l. will find a way   220:7
l. worketh no ill   47:29
l. ye therefore the stranger   33:2
l. you because ... hard up you pawn   94:14
l. your enemies   43:20
lovers' quarrels ... renewal of l.   315:2
loyal cantons of contemned l.   290:15
man's l. ... a thing apart   69:14
many waters cannot quench l.   40:15
marry first and l. will follow   220:30
master-passion ... l. of news   93:18
me and my true l.   16:10
medicines to make me l. him   254:6
men have died ... but not for l.   245:12
men l. in haste ... detest at leisure   70:7
my dear l. sits him down   17:3
my l. and I wd. lie   136:6
my l. climbed up to me   154:1
my l. is like a red red rose   66:15
my l. is like the melodie   66:15
my L. is of a birth as rare   167:16
my l. lies underground   157:10
my only l. sprung from my only hate   286:5
my true l. hath my heart   302:2
my true l. sent to me   194:1,2
my vegetable l. shd. grow   167:12
my whole course of l.   279:1
nameless ... acts of kindness and of l.   335:10
never seek to tell thy l.   55:10
no l. sincerer than the l. of food   296:4
no rage like l. to hatred turned   89:6
none to praise ... few to l.   334:11
nor l. thy life, nor hate   179:14
not enough [religion] to make us l.   309:8
not in our power to l. or hate   166:14
nuptial l. maketh mankind   22:1
O L.! has she done this to thee ?   163:4
of soup and l., the first   226:3
off with the old l.   16:1
office and affairs of l.   277:15
old l., cold l.   209:4
one does not l. a place less   20:16
one must not trifle with l.   185:6
open rebuke is better than secret l.   39:2
passing the l. of women   34:12
perfect l. casteth out fear   50:13
pity ... in the heart of l.   337:9
politicians neither l. nor hate   103:2
pounds of law, not an ounce of l.   227:36
pray you, l., remember   252:23
prosperity's the very bond of l.   293:5
prove ... the sports of l.   146:1
regain l. once possessed   181:5
rise up, my l.   40:7
said that the l. of money is the root   68:3
saying 'Farewell, blighted l.'   16:12

Love (continued)

seals of l., but seal'd in vain   273:12
seen ... that l. hath an end   310:3
she never told her l.   291:7
sighed for the l. of a ladye   121:2
so faithful in l.   240:6
so true a fool is l.   293:20
some are fou o' l. divine   66:4
something ... doesn't l. a wall   113:14
support of the woman I l.   105:10
that true self-l. and social are the same   203:12
that ye l. one another   46:29
the arms of my true l.   314:5
the fool of l., unpractis'd   104:15
the l. that can be reckon'd   242:10
the l. which doth us bind   167:17
the pangs of despis'd l.   250–1:20
the right true end of l.   101:2
the service of my l.   305:22
there is no fear in l.   50:13
there is tears for his l.   263:10
things that l. might   266:10
this bud of l. may prove a ... flower   286:11
this spring of l. resembleth   292:6
though I can't make her l. me   301:14
through l., through hope, and faith's   334:10
thy l. is better than wine   40:2
thy l. to me was wonderful   34:12
tired of l. ... tired of rhyme   27:10
to do justly and to l. mercy   42:24
to hold my wealth of l.   121:4
to let the warm L. in   150:7
to live is like l.   68:8
to l. and to cherish   53:22
to l. oneself ... lifelong romance   327:5
to see her was to l. her   65:9
true l.'s the gift which God has given   239:15
try thinking of l. or something   114:6
unbounded l. thou art   325:3
wanton l. corrupteth   22:1
weak man who marries for l.   144:3
what is l.? 'Tis not hereafter   291:2
what L. shall never reap   236:7
when I l. thee not, chaos is come   279:14
where both deliberate, the l. is slight   166:15
with l. in summer's wonderland   188:1
women ... have ... but two passions, vanity and l.   80:16
work of faith ... labour of l.   49:5
wroth with one we l.   87:7
you must sit down, says L.   131:11
your true l.'s coming   291:1
Loved: Alas! that all we l. of him shd. be   297:12
awake, my heart, to be l.   58:3
better l. ye canna be   185:8
better to have l. and lost   68:12
Dante who l. well   61:12
first he l. her, then he left her   16:11
God so l. the world   46:21
had we never l. so kindly   65:10
he dearly l. the lasses   66:2
he l. gold in special   79:14
I have not l. the world   69:5
I l. a lass, a fair one   329:10
I l. him not, and yet   156:12

Loved (continued)

I never writ, nor no man ever l.   294:9
I wish I l. the Human Race   233:1
Lavinia, therefore must be l.   289:13
l. her that she did pity them   279:2
l. I not Honour more   162:7
l. three whole days together   308:2
l. well because he hated   61:12
men l. darkness   46:22
Nature I l., and ... art   156:11
no sooner l. but they sigh'd   245:14
one that l. not wisely, but too well   280:14
she l. me for the dangers ... pass'd   279:2
sour to them that l. him not   262:2
the king l. Esther   34:27
the time and the place and the l. one   61:11
'tis better to have l. and lost   312:13
to be l. needs only to be seen   104:6
to have l. ... thought ... done   18:10
we l., sir—used to meet   60:16
where burning Sappho l. and sung   69:21
who ever l. that l. not at first sight ?   166:15
who has never l. has never lived   115:8
Lovelier than the love of Jove   166:7
Loveliest: the l. things of beauty   168:12
Loveliness: enough their simple l.   151:3
glory and l. have pass'd   151:5
her l. I never knew until   85:10
l. which once he made more lovely   298:1
your L. and the hour of my death   152:8
Lovely: a billboard l. as a tree   186:10
a l. and a fearful thing   69:16
and l. is the rose   331:13
as you are l., so be various   125:8
go, l. rose   322:1
he'd make a l. corpse   98:7
I love the l. bully   259:9
look thy last on all things l.   96:13
l. and pleasant in their lives   34:11
more l. and more temperate   293:13
so l. fair and smell'st so sweet   280:6
whatsoever things are l.   49:1
Lover: a l. and his lass   245:16
a l. without indiscretion   128:8
all mankind love a l.   108:7
jealousy ... the injured l.'s hell   178:16
mother and l. of men, the sea   310:6
my fause l. stole my rose   67:7
O Lord, thou l. of souls   51:14
the l., sighing like furnace   244:11
the lunatic, the l., and the poet   277:5
thoughts will slide into a l.'s head   335:3
what is a l., that it can give ?   89:13
woman loves her l.   69:17
Lovers: a pair of star-cross'd l.   285:17
all l. young, all l. must   247:10
journeys end in l. meeting   291:1
l. cannot see the pretty follies   274:14
l. fled away into the storm   147:14
l., to bed; 'tis almost fairy time   277:8
old l. are soundest   324:1
one makes l. ... as one pleases   89:13
sweet l. love the spring   245–6:16
Loves: a man l. the meat in his youth   277:22
all she l. is love   69:17
faithful l. ... moralize my song   305:9
fat white woman whom nobody l.   90–1:16
forebode not any severing of our l.   332:5
I have reigned with yr. l.   107:14

Loves (*continued*)
  in her first passion woman l. 69:17
  kills the thing he l. 326:12
  Love Divine, all l. excelling 325:3
  one that l. his fellow-men 137:6
  show a woman when he l. 61:14
  two l. ... of comfort and despair 294:16
  who l. to lie with me 244:4
  whoever l., ... do not propose 101:2
Love-sick all against our will 119:2
Lovesome: garden is a l. thing 59:10
Loveth: God l. a cheerful giver 48:16
  l. him chasteneth him betimes 38:14
  the dear God who l. us 87:4
  whom the Lord l. he chasteneth 49:22
  whom the Lord l. he correcteth 38:2
Loving: Friday's child is l. and giving 191:8
  heart be still as l. 71:3
  more pleasure in l. than ... loved 223:12
  most l. mere folly 245:1
  the night was made for l. 71:4
  wickedness that hinders l. 61:12
Low: happy l., lie down! 257:3
  he that is l. 63:15
  her voice ... l.—an excellent thing 268:3
  I'll tak' the l. road 16:10
  last great Englishman is l. 314:9
  sweet and l. 314:13
  to cast one's eyes so l. 267:2
  too l. for envy 91:13
  what is l. raise and support 175:17
  when my light is l. 312:14
Lowells talk to the Cabots 57:10
Lowest: matrimony at its l. 307:7
Lowly: better to be l. born 261:4
  God made them, high or l. 10:5
  me, made l. wise 334:4
  stood a l. cattle shed 10:6
  to order myself l. ... to all my betters 53:13
Loyal: that l. body wanted learning 318:1
Loyalties: home of ... impossible l. [Oxford] 19:7
Loyalty: that learned body wanted l. 318:1
  when l. no harm meant 15:12
Lucifer: as proud as L. 223:32
  come not, L.! 165:11
  falls like L., never to hope again 261:10
  how art thou fallen ... O L.! 40:25
Luck: better l. next time 207:31
  I had the l. to be called upon 83:14
Lucky: better to be born l. 207:21
  Lord L., by a curious fluke 28:1
Lucy: if L. shd. be dead! 335:3
Luke: L. began to slacken in his duty 332:11
  Matthew, Mark, L. and John 9:13
Lukewarm: because thou art l. 50:19
Lullaby: songs and snatches, and dreamy l. 117:16
Lumber: learned l. in his head 202:15
  stowed away in a Montreal l. room 68:9
Luminous: beating ... his l. wings in vain 19:9
  Dong with a l. Nose 158:3
Lump: don't like it, you can l. it 219:12
Lunatic, the lover, and the poet 277:5
Luncheon: breakfast, supper, dinner, l. 62:4
Lungs: a custom ... dangerous to the l. 138:14
Lurch: leave in the l. 218:33
Lure it back to cancel half a line 110:12
Lust: for l. of knowing 111:2
  l. in action; and till action, l. 294:11

Lust (*continued*)
  l. of fame was but a dream 58:14
Lustre: where is thy l. now? 266:18
Lustres: unrisen l. slake the o'ertaken moon 58:3
Lute: musical as is Apollo's l. 172:18
  Orpheus with his l. 261:5
Luxuries: give us the l. of life 184:11
  two l. to brood over 152:8
Lying: let me have no l. 293:7
  l., vainness, ... drunkenness 292:1
  subject we old men are to ... l. 257:10
  there is whispering, there is l. 230:13
  to conclude, they are l. knaves 278:18
  world is given to l.! 256:4
Lyly: didst our L. outshine 145:13
Lyme: an old party of L. 183:1
Lysander: of Hector and L. 16:14

Mab: I see Queen M. hath been with you 286:1
Macaroni: and called it m. 196:4
Macaulay: as cocksure ... as Tom M. is 169:11
Macavity: no one like M. 106:18
Machine: house is a m. for living in 90:13
  maison est une m.-à-habiter 90:13
Mackerel: sprat to catch a m. 226:13
Mad: but m. north-north-west 250:8
  how sad and bad and m. 60:16
  I wd. not be m.! 265:17
  m. as a hatter 220:8
  m. as a March hare 220:9
  m., bad and dangerous to know 156:1
  m. world! m. kings! m. composition! 264:12
  made me m. to see him shine 254:2
  O, fool, I shall go m.! 266:4
  O, let me not be m. 265:17
  Oh, he is m., is he? 115:14
  that he's m., 'tis true 249:17
  to destroy, he first makes m. 223:40
  we want a few m. people now 297:1
  went m. and bit the man 122:19
Madding crowd's ignoble strife 126:12
Made: did he who m. the Lamb make thee? 56:6
  dost thou know who m. thee? 56:9
  fearfully and wonderfully m. 37:28
  m. and loveth all 87:4
  m. him a coat of many colours 31:10
  nobody never m. me 308:1
Mademoiselle from Armenteers 236:14
Madness: devil's m.—War 241:16
  great wits ... to m. near allied 102–3:17
  m. in great ones ... not unwatch'd 251:6
  m., yet there is method in't 250:3
  melancholy and moon-struck m. 179:13
  much mirth and no m. 302:12
  such harmonious m. from my lips 300:3
  that way m. lies 266:12
  this is ... midsummer m. 291:13
  work like m. in the brain 87:7
Magdalen: fourteen months at M. College 116:1
Magistrates: some like m. correct at home 258:8
Magnanimity: in all his m. of thought 338:1
  in Victory: M. 83:13
  you might curb yr. m. 152:12

Magnificence comes after 156:7
Magnificent: it is m., but it is not war 57:9
Magnifique: c'est m. ... pas la guerre 57:9
Magog: Gog, the land of M. 41:24
Mahomet: hill will not come to M. 22:4
Maid: a fair m. dwellin' 11:12
  be good, seet m. 154:2
  chariest m. is prodigal enough 248:13
  I heard a m. singing 15:1
  m. whom there were none to praise 334:11
  Music, heavenly m., was young 88:12
  O Music, sphere-descended M. 88:14
  slain by a fair cruel m. 291:6
  the m. was in the garden 193:5
  way of a man with a m. 39:7
  where are you going to, my pretty m.? 195:7
  woo a fair young m. 16:3
Maiden: for many a rose-lipt m. 136:8
  kissed the m. all forlorn 194:8
  m. of bashful fifteen 301:17
  m. ... must be slaughtered too 118:9
  prithee, pretty m., will you marry me? 119:6
  use a poor m. so 15:1
  when a merry m. marries 116:11
Maidens: m., like moths, are ever caught 68:18
  twenty lovesick m. we 119:2
Maids: eight m. a-milking 194:2
  m. are May when ... m. 245:13
  pretty m. all in a row 191:7
  seven m. with seven mops 76:3
  three little m. from school 118:6
Maimed and set at naught 68:9
Main: every man ... part of the m. 101:7
Maintaining: died m. his right of way 12:8
Majestic: his face ... m. though in ruin 177:3
Majestical: we do it wrong, being so m. 247:15
Majesty: a strange beginning—'borrowed m.'! 264:8
  attribute to awe and m. 275:1
  busied in his m., surveys 258:8
  sight so touching in its m. 333:6
  the next in M. 104:11
  then our M. adorning 116:12
  this earth of m., this seat of Mars 282:5
  you got no-no-no m. 324:17
Major-General: model of a modern M. 120:4
Majority: m. never has right on its side 138:3
  one on God's side is a m. 200:3
  who makes up the m.? 138:3
Make: m. him an help meet 30:7
  makes no mistakes does not m. anything 200:2
  one of them said to his m. 11:15
Makes: the night that either m. me or fordoes 280:9
Male: into the ark ... m. and ... female 30:20
  m. and female created he them 30:3
  more deadly than the m. 154:14
Males: deeds are m. and words are females 211:11
Malice: m. never was his aim 308:13
  nor set down aught in m. 280:14
  with m. toward none 159:15
Malignant: a m. and a turban'd Turk 280-1:14
Malt: m. does more than Milton can 136:9

Malt (*continued*)
  rat that ate the m. 194-5:8
Mammon: and M. wins his way 68:18
  m. of unrighteousness 46:7
Man: a better m. than I am 154:16
  a Christian faithful m. 284:15
  a good old m. sir 278:9
  a hairy m. ... a smooth m. 31:7
  a living dead m. 246:5
  a m. after his own heart 34:3
  a m. can die but once 257:8
  a m. can raise a thirst 155:2
  a m. leave his father and mother 48:25
  a m. more sinn'd against 266:11
  a m. must serve his time 70:13
  a m. of sorrows 41:5
  a m. of such a feeble temper 262:7
  a m.'s a m. for a' that 65:18
  a m.'s [business] to keep unmarried 296:6
  a m.'s first duty? ... To be himself 138:6
  a m.'s friendships ... are invalidated 68:11
  a m.'s reach should exceed his grasp 60:11
  a m.'s worth something 60:14
  a m. severe he was 122:11
  a m. so various 103:4
  a m. that is young in years 23:1
  a m. that left his family 318:7
  a m. under authority 44:10
  a m. who cd. make so vile a pun 97:5
  a m. who has not been in Italy 144:6
  a m. who said 'God' 155:14
  a m. who shaves and takes a train 325:8
  a m. who's untrue to his wife 20:3
  a m. will ne'er quite understand 198:12
  a moral, sensible and well-bred m. 92:4
  a nice m. ... m. of nasty ideas 309:10
  a ready m. 23:8
  a sadder and a wiser m. 87:5
  a single m. ... a good fortune 20:17
  a strong m. after sleep 182:8
  a stupid m. is doing something 295:10
  a very unclubbable m. 142:16
  'A was a m. 248:5
  a weak m. who marries for love 144:3
  Adam, the goodliest m. 178:4
  all my faults as m. to m. 295:18
  all that was pleasant in m. 123:3
  an aged aged m. 77:7
  an elder m. not at all 21:21
  an exact m. 23:8
  an honest God ... noblest work of m. 138:9
  an old m. and no honester 278:7
  an old m. in a dry month 106:5
  and the last m. in 187:11
  Angry Young M. 199:1
  any m.'s death diminishes me 101:8
  apparel oft proclaims the m. 248:16
  as for m., his days are as grass 37:1
  ash on an old m.'s sleeve 106:10
  at thirty m. suspects 338:1
  away, slight m.! 264:1
  beauty crieth ... no m. regardeth 68:9
  became a m., I put away childish things 48:6
  Benedick the married m. 277:13
  better angel is a m. right fair 294:16
  better spar'd a better m. 256:2
  big assemblance of a m.! 257:9
  both m. and bird and beast 87:3
  brothers and their murder'd m. 148:1

Man (*continued*)

Brutus is an honourable m. 263:12
busiest m. who has time to spare 198:5
business of the wealthy m. 27:6
by courtesy a m. 21:5
by m. shall his blood be shed 30:24
came to the making of m. 309:15
care not whether a m. is good 55:7
caverns measureless to m. 87:11, 87:13
child is father of the m. 333:9
cloud ... like a m.'s hand 34:20
condition of m. ... condition of war 133:2
conference [maketh] a ready m. 23:8
crumbs ... from the rich m.'s table 46:8
daring young m. on the flying trapeze 159:5
Darwinian M. ... well-behaved 120:11
deep young m. 119:4
each m. kills ... thing he loves 326:12
every m. did that which was right 33:24
every m. for himself 212:31
every m. has his faults 212:32
every m. is as Heaven made him 78:3
every m. is best known to himself 212:33
every m. is wanted, no m. ... much 108:9
every m. meets his Waterloo 200:4
every m. must play a part 274:1
every m. over forty 296:16
every m.'s hand against him 31:1
every m. that cometh into ... world 46:15
every m. to his taste 212:34
every m. under his vine 42:22
every m. was ... god or devil 103:5
every woman shd. marry ... no m. 100:10
everyone has sat except a m. 94:12
expects every m. ... do his duty 187:5
face of the old m. 32:17
foolish fond old m. 267:11
foolishly-compounded clay, m. 256:8
foot-in-the-grave young m. 119:7
get a new m. 288:10
glory to M. in the highest! 310:2
God created m. in his own image 30:3
God doth not need ... m.'s work 181:11
God made the woman for the m. 312:2
God took the m. and put him 30:6
good for a m. that he bear the yoke 41:20
good name in m. and woman 279:15
greater love hath no m. 46:31
greatest m. you had ... yet sane 145:4
he thinks, good easy m. 261:9
heaven had made her such a m. 279:2
her m. ... he done her wrong 15:2
honest m. sent to lie abroad 336:11
honest m.'s the noblest work of God 203:8
how use doth breed a habit in a m. 292:10
I hate ingratitude ... in a m. 292:1
I love not m. the less 69:9
ideal m. ... non-attached m. 137:10
if a m. will begin with certainties 23:12
if any m. shall add 51:4
if I ever become a rich m. 28:3
if such a m. there be 201:17
if the m. who turnips cries 140:17
I'm truly sorry m.'s dominion 66:11
in the Parliament of m. 313:17
in the spring a young m.'s fancy 313:15
in wit a m.: simplicity a child 201:22
is m. an ape or an angel? 100:5

Man (*continued*)

it is the number of a m. 50:26
It's That M. Again 146:16
laugh to scorn the pow'r of m. 271:15
let no m. despise thy youth 49:11
let no m. put asunder 53:25
let not m. put asunder 45:12
like master, like m. 219:13
looking for a m.'s footprint 26:8
m. and wife together 53:26
m. ... bears in his bodily frame 95:10
m. being too proud to fight 329:7
m. ... born free ... is in chains 236:12
m. delights not me ... nor woman 250:6
m. for the field ... the sword 314:18
m. goeth to his long home 39:27
m. has his will,—but woman 134:3
m. in the moon 220:14
m. in the street 220:15
m. is a noble animal 60:3
m. is ... a political animal 18:5
m. is ... a religious animal 64:12
m. is a tool-making animal 113:4
m. is born unto trouble 35:3
m. is Nature's sole mistake 120:10
m. is not a fly 203:2
m. is the hunter 314:17
m. is the master of things 310:2
m. is the shuttle 320:6
m. ... killed by lightning 11:18
m. looketh on ... outward appearance 34:5
m. made the town 93:6
m. ... must get drunk 69:15
m. of upright life unstained 135:14
m. or mouse 220:20
m. proposes ... God disposes 152:14, 220:21
m., proud m. 273:7
m.'s a ribald ... a rake 120:10
m.'s inhumanity to m. 66:8
m. shall not live by bread 43:13
m. that is born of a woman 35:5, 53:28
m. that lays his hand upon a woman 317:12
m. to afflict his soul 41:10
m. wants but little 338:2
m. wants but little here below 122:15
m. was made for joy and woe 54:15
m. who knows the price 328:4
m. who sees absolutely nothing 327:1
m. who sees both sides 327:1
m. who ... sets foot upon a worm 93:12
m. with the head ... to command 314:18
manners maketh m. 328:21
met a m. who wasn't there 169:8
met a m. with seven wives 188:3
money makes the m. 221:13
Nature might ... say ... 'This was a m.!' 264:7
new m. ... raised up in him 53:10
no great m. lives in vain 73:8
no m. can serve two masters 44:1
no m. dieth to himself 47:30
no m. does [become like his mother] 328:13
no m. ever talked poetry 99:5
no m., having put ... hand to plough 45:26
no m. is an island 101:7
no m. is good enough to govern 159:7
no m. putteth new wine 45:25
no m. truly knows another 59:16
nor no m. ever loved 294:9

Manners (*continued*)
   men's evil m. live in brass   262:1
   old m., old books, old wine   123:6
   sweeter m., purer laws   313:5
Manservant: nor his m., nor his maidservant
   32:9
Mansion: life ... M. of many Apartments
   152:3
Mansions: build thee more stately m.   134:5
   in my Father's house are many m.   46:30
Mantle: cast his m. upon him   34:22
   cream and m. like a standing pond   274:2
   morn, in russet m. clad   247:16
   twitched his m. blue   175:6
Manure: blood of English shall m. the ground
   283:8
Many: have the measels ? ... how m. ?   322:11
   m. are called, but few are chosen   44:24
   m. things to fear   22:14
   owed by so m. to so few   82:15
   the m. change and pass   298:2
   the m. men, so beautiful   86:11
   ye are m.—they are few   298:14
Many-splendour'd: miss the m. thing   316:10
Maps: generals are already poring over m.   20:1
Mar: oft we m. what's well   265:16
Marathon: from M. to Waterloo   120:4
   M. looks on the sea   70:1
Marble: I dreamt ... I dwelt in m. halls   63:4
   poets that lasting m. seek   322:2
   whole as the m., founded as the rock   271:6
   your dreary m. halls   72:2
March: beware the Ides of M.   262:5
   droghte of M. hath perced   79:1
   M. comes in like a lion   220:23
Marched breast forward   60:12
Marches: dreadful m. to delightful measures
   284:9
   funeral m. to the grave   160:15
Marching: as we were m. through Georgia
   336:9,10
   his soul is m. on!   127:13
   m. as to war   24:9
Mare: lend me yr. grey m.   17:5
   patience ... tired m. ... will plod   258:11
   to find a m.'s nest   220:24
Maréchal: le bâton de m. de France   185:13
Margin: through a meadow of m.   301:12
Marian: Mall, Meg, and M., and Margery
   288:9
   M.'s nose looks red and raw   269:1
Mariner: I fear thee, ancient M.   86:9
   it is an ancient M.   85:11
Mariners: ye m. of England   72:10
Marines: tell that to the M.   227:19
Mark: God save the m.!   254:2
   love ... an ever-fixed m.   294:8
   Matthew, M., Luke, and John   9:13
   no drowning m. upon him   287:13
   read, m., learn   53:2
Market: chief good and m. of his time   252:17
   if fools went not to m.   214:8
   school or college, kirk or m.   307:8
   send a fool to the m.   214:6
   women ... goose make a m.   227:40
Market-place: at noon-day, upon the m.
   262:12
   Idols of the M.   23:16
Marks: Signior Benedick; nobody m. you
   277:11

Marlowe: M.'s mighty line   145:13
   neat M.   102:11
Marmion: last words of M.   240:10
Marquis: abducted by a French m.   124:11
Marred: young man married ... man that's m.
   242:4
Marriage: care ... more for a m. than a ministry
   23:19
   coldly furnish ... m. tables   248:8
   comedies are ended by a m.   69:19
   exclaim ... against second m.   109:7
   eyes wide open before m.   217:35
   friendships are ... invalidated by m.   68:11
   hanging prevents a bad m.   290:13
   happiness in m. ... matter of chance   20:18
   love and m. rarely can combine   69:18
   m. has many pains but celibacy has no
      pleasures   141:8
   m. is a lottery   220:25
   m. is like a cage   183:5
   m. is popular because   296:14
   m. is the best state for a man   144:2
   m. of true minds   294:8
   O curse of m.   279:17
   takes two to make a m. a success   238:2
   won't be a stylish m.   95:4
Married: a woman's business to get m.   296:6
   as wellbred as if ... not m.   89:17
   Benedick the m. man   277:13
   cuckoo ... mocks m. men   268–9:17
   how ... be m. without a wife ?   191:4
   how to be happy though m.   128:6
   if ever we had been m.   115:5
   live till I were m.   278:1
   man who m. ... did more service   123:19
   m. three wives at a time   183:1
   unpleasing to a m. ear   268–9:17
   wen you're a m. man, Samivel   99:3
   what delight we m. people have   199:10
   wd. be m. but I'd have no wife   94:2
   wd. be m. to a single life   94:2
   young man m. is ... marr'd   242:4
Marries: m. late, m. ill   220:28
   person who either m. or dies   20:9
Marry: advise none to m.   206:7
   be sure before you m. of a house   207:3
   better to m. than to burn   48:3
   every woman should m.—and no man   100:10
   he'll come back and m. me   188:5
   honest men m. soon   216:38
   I can't m. you, my pretty maid   196:1
   if men knew ... they'd never m.   131:2
   may m. whom she likes   315:9
   now that you are going to m.   143:5
   to persons about to m.—Don't   231:17
   when a man shd. m.   21:21
   while ye may, go m.   132:8
   young man shd. not m. yet   231:6
Mars: this seat of M.   282:5
Marshal: the m.'s truncheon nor the judge's
   robe   273:4
Martin Elginbrode: here lie I, M.   164:10
Martini: get ... into a dry M.   330:8
Martyr: bitter groan of a m.'s woe   55:5
Martyrdom ... in which ... can become famous
   295:14
Martyrs: noble army of M.   52:15
Marvel: I m. how the fishes live   281:5
   match me such m.   64:3
   they m. more and more   27:1

Meat (*continued*)
　　mock the m. it feeds on 279:16
　　one man's m. ... man's poison 220:37
　　out of the eater came forth m. 33:19
　　sit down, ... and taste My m. 131:11
　　some hae m., and canna eat 67:3
Mechanic: poor m. porters crowding in 258:8
Meddling with any practical part of life 9:6
Medes and Persians: law of the M., which
　　altereth not 42:4
　　thy kingdom ... given to the M. 42:3
Medicinable: their m. gum 280-1:4
Medicine: faithful friend is the m. of life
　　51:16
　　no other m. but only hope 273:9
Medicines: given me m. to make me love him
　　254:6
Meditate: strictly m. the thankless Muse?
　　174:15
Meek: blessed are the m. 43:15
　　I am m. and gentle 263:7
　　m. shall inherit the earth 36:8
　　m. until they be married 220:10
　　taught us to be calm and m. 133:14
Meekness: love and m. ... become a churchman
　　262:3
Meet: extremes m. 213:6
　　God be with you till we m. again 233:2
　　if I shd. m. thee 71:6
　　if we do m. again ... shall smile 264:4
　　m. in her aspect and her eyes 71:2
　　never the twain shall m. 154:8
　　we loved, sir—used to m. 60:16
　　will never m. again ... on ... banks 16:10
Meeter to carry off the latter 199:6
Meeting: journeys end in lovers m. 291:1
　　this m. is drunk 99:6
Meetings: alarums changed to merry m.
　　284:9
Melancholy: bird ... most musical, most m.!
　　173:8
　　green and yellow m. 291:7
　　hail, divinest M.! 173:6
　　hence, loathed M. 173:14
　　m. marked him for her own 126:13
　　m. ... shd. be diverted 144:4
　　moping m. 179:13
　　my cue is villainous m. 265:11
　　naught so sweet as m. 67:8
　　not m. once a day 214:5
　　nothing ... so m. as a battle ... won 324:6
　　pale M. sat retired 88:13
　　suck m. out of a song 244:5
　　these pleasures, M., give 173:13
　　'tis m. and a fearful sign 69:18
　　what charm can soothe her m.? 124:1
Melodies: heard m. are sweet 149:7
Melody: from ancient m. have ceas'd 56:13
　　my love is like the m. 66:15
Melrose: view fair M. aright 239:12
Melted into air, into thin air 288:16
Melts: a moment white, then m. for ever 67:4
Member: ev'ry m. of the force 234:12
Members one of another 47:22
Meminisse: forsan et haec ... m. iuvabit 321:1
Memorable: finding ... he was not m. 241:10
Memorial: m. from the Soul's eternity 236:6
　　some ... that have no m. 52:7
Memories: creditors ... better m. than debtors
　　210:17

Memories (*continued*)
　　liars ought to have good m. 302:1
　　liars shd. have good m. 218:40
Memory: dear son of m., ... heir of fame
　　175:12
　　everyone complains of his m. 234:5
　　m. is the diary we ... carry 327:15
　　m. of the just is blessed 38:9
　　m. ... the beginning of dowdiness 328:15
　　mixing m. and desire 107:3
　　no man ... force can abolish m. 235:5
　　no woman shd. have a m. 328:15
　　peaceful hours ... how sweet their m. 92:14
　　pluck from the m. a rooted sorrow 272:6
　　shorter in wind, as in m. long 57:15
　　the m. be green 247:17
　　the M. of great Men 152:1
　　vibrates in the m. 300:6
Men: a sort of m. whose visages 274:2
　　a tide in the affairs of m. 264:3
　　all sorts and conditions of m. 52:27
　　all things to all m. 48:4
　　among new m., strange faces 312:7
　　appointed unto m. once to die 49:19
　　are you good m. and true? 278:3
　　ay, in the catalogue ye go for m. 271:1
　　best m. are dead 232:3
　　bodies of unburied m. 324:3
　　boon and a blessing to m. 11:8
　　busiest m. ... most leisure 208:37
　　busy hum of m. 174:5
　　but m. are m. ... sometimes forget 279:9
　　common wonder of all m. 59:15
　　daggers in m.'s smiles 270:16
　　dead m. don't bite 211:1
　　dead m. naked shall be one 315:14
　　dead m. rise up never 310:1
　　dead m. tell no tales 211:2
　　deal with none but honest m. 224:13
　　despised and rejected of m. 41:5
　　destiny with m. for pieces plays 110:11
　　down among the dead m. 105:7
　　dumb m. get no lands 212:5
　　England ... purgatory of m. 111:4
　　equal rights of m. and women 319:5
　　Eve upon the first of M. 135:2
　　even great m. have ... poor relations 97:11
　　evil that m. do lives after them 263:11
　　fair women and brave m. 69:3
　　fifteen m. on ... dead man's chest 307:4
　　finds too late that m. betray 124:1
　　for fear of little m. 10:9
　　for m. must work 154:3
　　give place to better m. 94:9
　　glory of young m. is their strength 38:25
　　going to dine with some m. 29:3
　　good will toward m. 45:22
　　great m. are almost always bad m. 9:1
　　great m. are not always wise 35:11
　　great m. ... not commonly ... great scholars
　　134:6
　　have m. about me that are fat 262:9
　　heaven ... leads m. to this hell 294:12
　　histories make m. wise 23:9
　　I said ... All m. are liars 37:10
　　I speak ... French to m. 78:18
　　I will make you fishers of m. 43:14
　　idols which beset m.'s minds 23:16
　　in mean m. we entitle patience 281:10
　　in most m.'s power to be agreeable 309:9

Men (*continued*)

it is the m. who make a city 220:39

jolly tars are our m. 115:1

let us now praise famous m. 52:5

lives not three good m. unhang'd 254:14

m. alone ... capable of every wickedness 90:9

m. and women merely players 244:11

m. are April when they woo 245:13

m. are but gilded loam 281:8

m. are capable ... of ... benevolence 237:8

m. are children of a larger growth 104:1

m. at some time are masters of their fates 262:8

m. below and saints above 239:13

m. ... differ as heaven and earth 312:6

m. fear death as children ... dark 21:9

m. fell out ... knew not why 67:14

m. have died from time to time 245:12

m. in great places are thrice servants 22:2

m. love in haste ... detest at leisure 70:7

m. may bleed and m. may burn 120:16

m. may come and m. may go 311:8

m. may rise on stepping-stones 312:11

m. must endure their going hence 267:12

m. of few words ... best m. 259:6

m. of good quality 322:17

m. prize the thing ungain'd 289:15

m. seldom make passes 198:2

m. that laugh and weep 309:18

m. that sow to reap 309:18

m. that were boys when I was 28:4

m. were deceivers ever 277:21

m. who borrow and m. who lend 156:2

m. will still say ... their finest hour 82:14

m. will wrangle ... write ... fight 88:17

m. with splendid hearts 59:3

m.'s natures are alike 89:2

mocks married m. 268–9:17

mother and lover of m. 310:6

my object ... to form Christian m. 19:13

new m., strange faces, other minds 312:7

nor yet favour to m. of skill 39:23

nor yet riches to m. of understanding 39:23

not as other m. are 46:11

not in the roll of common m. 255:4

old m. shall dream dreams 42:13

praise makes ... bad m. worse 223:24

praise makes good m. better 223:24

quit yourselves like m. 34:1

reputed one of the wise m. 21:21

rich m. furnished with ability 52:6

rich m. have no faults 224:17

rule of m. entirely great 63:3

schemes o' mice an' m. 66:12

sleek-headed m., and such as sleep 262:9

so are they all, all honourable m. 263:12

so long as m. can breathe 293:15

so many m., so many opinions 315:4

sons of the prophet ... brave m. 16:15

such m. are dangerous 262:9

talk of censorious old m. 77:14

that all m. are created equal 139:6

that all m. everywhere cd. be free 159:12

the breath of worldly ... m. 283:2

the clever m. at Oxford 124:13

the many m., so beautiful 86:11

the most mighty m. ... in his army 41:25

The War between M. and Women 317:9

they make their steel with m. 238.7

Men (*continued*)

thousand creeds ... move m.'s hearts 58:13

to m.'s business, and bosoms 21:7

to put confidence in m. 37:12

truth ... on the lips of dying m. 19:3

two m. look out through the same bars 156:15

we are the hollow m. ... the stuffed m. 106:7

we cannot be free m. if ... slavery 159:9

we petty m. walk under his huge legs 262:8

wealth accumulates and m. decay 122:5

what m. call gallantry 69:10

whatsoever ye wd. that m. shd. do 44:7

wisest m. have erred 180:12

wives are ... old m.'s nurses 21:20

wives are young m.'s mistresses 21:20

women are more like each other than m. 80:16

wonder m. dare trust th'selves with m. 289:10

you are m. of stones 268:2

young m. shall see visions 42:13

Mend: tried to m. the electric light 27:6

Mended: least said, soonest m. 218:32

Mene, mene, tekel, upharsin 42:1

Mens: m. cuiusque is est quisque 84:5

ut sit m. sana in corpore sano 146:11

Mentioned: and m. me to him 75:7

Merchant: m. to secure his treasure 205:6

that same m.'s flesh 275:5

Merchants: like m., venture trade abroad 258:8

Mercies: all thy faithful m. crown 325:3

His m. ay endure 180:7

Merciful as constant 125:8

Mercuries: as English M. 258:9

Mercury: words of M. are harsh 269:2

Mercy: desired m., and not sacrifice 42:8

doing justice ... leaving m. to heaven 109:11

half so good a grace as m. 273:4

have m. upon us ... sinners 52:22

his m. is for ever sure 153:4

m. I asked, m. I found 72:5

m. is above this sceptred sway 275:1

m. is nobility's true badge 289:12

'O m.!' to myself I cried 335:3

peace on earth and m. mild 325:2

quality of m. is not strain'd 275:1

render the deeds of m. 275:1

to love m., and to walk humbly 42:24

we do pray for m. 275:1

when m. seasons justice 275:1

Meridian: from that full m. of my glory 261:8

Merit: fondly we think we honour m. 202:13

I like the Garter ... no damned m. 169:9

men of m. are sought after 257:1

m. wins the soul 204:11

Satan exalted sat, by m. raised 176:15

spurns that patient m. ... takes 250–1:20

Merits: seek his m. to disclose 126:15

Mermaid: a m. on a dolphin's back 276:18

choicer than the M. Tavern 149:4

seen, done at the M. 25:7

Mermaids: I have heard the m. singing 106:16

Merrier: the more the m. 221:16

Merrily: m. hent the stile-a 292:19

m , m., shall I live now 289:6

Merrily (continued)
tripping and skipping ran m. 62:6
Merriment: borrow ... from the m. of May
147:10
source of innocent m. 118:11
Merry: against ill chances men are ... m.
257:11
God rest you m., gentlemen 15:3
It is good to be m. and wise 16:1
m. heart ... cheerful countenance 38:17
m. heart goes all the day 292:19
m. of soul he sailed 307:3
m. village chime 120:7
m. with the fruitful grape 110:8
m. yarn from ... fellow-rover 168:17
never m. when I hear sweet music 275:9
playing of the m. organ 15:8
short life and a m. one 225:19
so I piped into m. cheer 56:8
tonight we'll m. be 14:14
Tu-whit, Tu-who—a m. note 269:1
Merrygoround: it's no go the m. 164:14
Merryman: a m. moping mum 121:2
Message: the electric m. came 21:6
Messing: simply m. about in boats 124:12
Met: no sooner m. but they look'd 245:14
Metal: here's m. more attractive 252:2
touch of sweating m. 96:5
Meteor: shone like a m. streaming 176:9
Method: madness, yet there is m. in't 250:3
m. of making a fortune 127:3
Methods: you know my m., Watson 101:14
Methuselah: all the days of M. 30:18
Mew: rather be a kitten and cry m. 255:6
the cat will m. 253:5
Mewling: infant, and puking 244:11
Mexique Bay: Echo beyond the M. 167:9
Micawber, Mr. 97:15,16
Mice: best-laid schemes o' m. and men 66:12
cat is away ... m. will play 230:12
three blind m., see how they run! 195:1
Michelangelo: women come and go talking of
M. 106:12
Microbe is so very small 27:13
Microscopic: has not man a m. eye ? 203:2
Middle: in the m. of the woods ... Yonghy-
Bonghy-Bò 158:2
wives are ... companions for m. age 21:20
Midlands: when I am living in the M. 28:2
Midnight: burn the m. oil 208:35
cease upon the m. with no pain 150:3
consum'd the m. oil 115:9
it came upon the m. clear 240:14
not to be abed after m. 290:17
of Cerberus and blackest M. born 173:14
One hour's sleep before m. 217:9
secret, black, and m. hags 271:13
see her on the bridge at m. 16:12
the iron tongue of m. 277:8
time may cease, and m. never come 165:10
we have heard the chimes at m. 257:7
Midsummer: this is very m. madness 291:13
Midwife: she is the fairies' m. 286:1
the m. laid her hand on ... Skull 103:10
Mid-winter: bleak m., long ago 235:15
Mieux: le m. est l'ennemi du bien 321:13
tout est pour le m. 321:9
Might: first in beauty shd. be first in m. 148:8
m. is right 221:3
saddest [words] ... It m. have been 326:8

Might (continued)
'tis m. half-slumbering 150:12
Might-have-been: my name is M. 236:8
you won't be sorry for a m. 233:3
Mightier: God ... make thee m. yet 28:10
in word m. than they in arms 178:19
Mighties: 'tis m. in the m. 275:1
Mighty: a m. man is he 161:9
death ... some have called the m. 101:4
fear not, said he, for m. dread 311:4
God who made thee m. 28:10
how are the m. fallen! 34:9
I am weak, but thou art m. 329:2
look on my works, ye M., and despair!
299:8
mean and m. rotting together 247:7
m. hunter before the Lord 30:26
this m. sum of things 331:5
Truth ... m. above all things 51:6
Mike O'Day: this is the grave of M. 12:8
Milan: retire me to my M. 289:8
Mile: he walked a crooked m. 194:3
miss is as good as a m. 221:7
yr. sad [heart] tires in a m.-a 292:19
Miles: can ye draw but twenty m. a day ?
166:12
how many m. to Babylon ? 189:8
people come m. to see it 118:13
Miles gloriosus 200:15
Military: war ... too serious ... to be left to m.
men 311:3
Milk: crying over spilt m. 210:24
drunk the m. of Paradise 87:16
flowing with m. and honey 31:18
m. comes frozen home in pail 269:1
no finer investment than ... m. in babies 83:9
too full o' th' m. of human kindness 270:1
Milking: going a-m., sir, she said 195:7
Milkmaid singeth blithe 174:3
Milky way: twinkle on the m. 331:8
Mill: bring grist to the m. 215:34
God's m. grinds slow but sure 215:12
in Gaza at the m. with slaves 180:9
more water glideth by the m. 289:13
Millar: I respect M., Sir 142:3
last sheet [*Johnson's Dictionary*] to M.
142:2
Miller: more water ... than wots ... m. of
289:13
there was a jolly m. once 54:1
Milliner: perfumed like a m. 254:1
Million: a m. m. spermatozoa 137:14
among so many m. of faces 59:15
the play ... pleas'd not the m. 250:10
Millionaire: I am a M. That is my religion
296:1
Millions: there are m. of us 324:18
Mills: the m. of God grind slowly 161:3
Millstone ... hanged about his neck 44:20
Milton: faith and morals ... M. held 334:1
malt does more than M. can 136:9
M.! thou shdst. be living 333:12
some mute inglorious M. 126:11
Mimsy were the borogoves 75:9
Mince: they dined on m. and ... quince 158:9
Mind: a m. not to be changed 176:5
a m. quite vacant is a m. distressed 93:4
a miserable state of m. 22:14
a prodigious quantity of m. 318:12
among all the diseases of the m. 306:6

Mind (*continued*)

better than P. of M.   231:19

blind ... judgment, and misguide the m.
202:4

born for the Universe, narrowed his m.
123:1

chẹer of m. ... I was wont to have   285:14

clap yr. padlock on her m.   205:5

distressed, in m., body, or estate   52:29

dread had seized their troubled m.   311:4

education forms the common m.   203:14

fair terms and a villain's m.   274:11

farewell the tranquil m.   280:2

four seasons in the m. of man   151:4

great hills ... come back into my m.   28:2

he who does not m. his belly   142:14

I don't m. if I do   146:15

incline man's m. to atheism   22:11

it concentrates his m. wonderfully   144:8

last infirmity of noble m.   175:1

loud laugh ... spoke the vacant m.   122:8

love looks ... with the m.   276:12

love's but the frailty of the m.   89:14

love's the noblest frailty of the m.   104:8

m. ... deficient in ... humour   88:4

m. one's P's and Q's   222:32

m. that makes the body rich   287:11

m. yr. own business   221:4

minister to a m. diseased   272:6

my m. to me a kingdom is   105:6

never face so pleased my m.   17:2

no m. is thoroughly well organized   88:4

noble m. is here o'erthrown   251:5

not in my perfect m.   267:11

out of sight, out of m.   222:31

reading is to the m.   306:8

riches of the m. ... make ... rich   224:19

she had a frugal m.   92:8

sound m. in a sound body   146:11

that ... was great fortitude of m.   141:14

the gentle m. by gentle deeds   305:14

the m. is its own place   176:5

think my m. is maturing late ?   186:5

'tis strange the m., that fiery particle   70:6

to the noble m., rich gifts   251:1

what is M. ? No Matter   231:21

when I measure my m. against his [Shaw on
Shakespeare]   297:8

when people call this beast to m.   27:1

whether 'tis nobler in the m.   250:20

with a gladsome m.   180:7

worst [tyranny] ... persecutes the m.   104:7

your m.'s cluttered up   324:17

Minds: balm of hurt m.   270:11

bringeth ... m. about to religion   22:11

great m. think alike   215:27

happiest moments of the ... best m.   300:10

lose myself in other men's m.   156:6

m. are not ever craving ... food   93:17

Nature ... doth teach ... to have aspiring m.
166:10

purest and most thoughtful m.   237:4

strange faces, other m.   312:7

the mighty m. of old   304:10

the refuge of weak m.   80:15

the religion of feeble m.   64:13

to the marriage of true m.   294:8

Mine: be m., as I yours for ever   125:8

Curly locks, wilt thou be m. ?   188:8

hope's delusive m.   140:13

Mine (*continued*)

thou needest not fear m. [kisses]   300:7

'twas m., 'tis his   279:15

what's m. is my own   230:9

what's m. is yours, ... yours is m.   273:15

Miner: dwelt a m., forty-niner   183:8

Minister: canst thou not m. to a mind diseas'd ?
272:6

quench thee, thou flaming m.   280:11

Ministers: angels and m. of grace defend us!
249:3

errands for the M. of State   116:13

my fellows are m. of Fate   288:15

Ministries: *Times* has made many m.   23:18

Ministry: more for a marriage than a m.   23:19

the merit of a m.   146:6

Minnehaha, Laughing Water   161:5

Minnows: Triton of the m.   246:9

Minstrel: a wandering m. I   117:16

the M. Boy to the war is gone   184:2

the M. was infirm and old   239:11

Minute: a sucker born every m.   24:10

fill the unforgiving m.   154:20

must do [good] in m. particulars   55:6

Minutes: our m. hasten to their end   294:1

round ... the earth in forty m.   276:19

see the m. how they run   260:13

Miracle: a m. ... event which creates faith
297:3

a m. of loveliness   118:13

a m. of rare device   87:15

Miranda: do you remember an inn, M. ?   28:5

Mirror: best m. is an old friend   221:5

m. of all Christian kings   258:9

Mirth: all m. and no matter   277:19

bards of passion and of M.   147:6

far from all resort of m.   173:9

M., admit me of thy crew   174:1

M., with thee I mean to live   174:11

much m. and no madness   302:12

no country's m. is better than our own
145:5

old earth must borrow its m.   326:9

present m. hath present laughter   291:2

very tragical m.   277:7

Miscarriage: success and m. are empty   140:4

Mischief: no m. but a woman ... priest is at
the bottom   222:1

Satan finds some m. still   323:2

to draw new m. on   279:3

to mourn a m. ... past   279:3

Miserable: a m. state of mind   22:14

me m.!   177:13

m. have no other medicine   273:9

Miseries: bound in shallows and in m.   264:3

hopes, and joys, and panting m.   149:5

Misery: dwell on guilt and m.   20:13

fallen ... into m. and endeth wrecchedly
80:1

gave to m. all he had, a tear   126:14

man ... is full of m.   53:28

m. acquaints ... with strange bedfellows
288:7

my m., the wormwood ... gall   41:18

recall ... happiness when in m.   95:7

Misfortune: the m. of knowing anything
20:15

to lose one parent ... a m.   327:12

Misfortunes: children ... make m. more bitter
21:18

Misfortunes (*continued*)
m. never come singly 221:6
m. of our best friends ... not displeasing 234:9
strength to bear the m. of others 234:4
Misgivings: I view with profound m. the retreat 83:10
Mislead: lights that do m. the morn 273:12
Miss: and mine [heart] he cannot m. 302:2
m. is as good as a mile 221:7
Missed: how I m. my Clementine! 183:10
society offenders ... who never wd. be m. 118:4
Mist: the rank m. they draw 175:4
Mistake: any m. about it in any quarter 83:6
man is Nature's sole m. 120:10
Mistakes: learn by other men's m. 230:25
the man who makes no m. 200:2
Mistress: art is a jealous m. 108:1
if you can kiss the m. 218:5
Master M. of my passion 293:16
m. of herself, though China fall 203:17
m. of the Earl of Craven 329:5
O m. mine 291:1
select ... a m. or a friend 298:8
Mistresses: wives are young men's m. 21:20
Mists: season of m. and ... fruitfulness 147:1
Misunderstood: to be great is to be m. 108:12
Misused the King's press 255:15
Mix: I m. them with my brains, sir 196:11
Moan: is not paid with m. 316:8
Moaning: no m. at the bar 311:13
Moat: as a m. defensive to a house 282:5
Mob: best ... to do what the m. do 98:20
m. has ... no brains 221:8
Mobled queen 250:11
Mobs: suppose there are two m. ? 98:20
Mock: green-ey'd monster wh. doth m. 279:16
m. on, m. on, Voltaire 55:9
Mock Turtle: said the M. angrily 74:14
the M. replied 74:15
Mocked: be not deceived; God is not m. 48:23
Mockery: death itself ... a m. 299:15
Model of a modern Major-General 120:4
Moderately: love m.; long love doth so 286:18
Moderation: astonished at my own m. 84:11
m. is a fatal thing 328:14
Modes: ring in the nobler m. of life 313:5
Modesty: O m.! 'twas strictly kept 198:11
o'erstep not the m. of nature 251:9
wore enough for m. 62:13
Mohicans: The Last of the M. 90:12
Mole: wilt thou go ask the m. 55:2
Molehill: mountain out of a m. 221:19
Molly Malone 15:10
Mome raths outgrabe 75:9
Moment: all my possessions for a m. of time 107:15
happy in the m. that was present 143:18
m. foreseen may be unexpected 107:11
pleasing attentions ... impulse of the m. 21:1
snow falls ... a m. white then melts 67:4
some m. when the moon was blood 81:1
sonnet is a m.'s monument 236:6
spur of the m. 226:15
to every ... nation comes the m. 162:14

Monan's rill: the moon on M. 239:6
Monarch: becomes the ... m. better than his crown 275:1
I am m. of all I survey 93:14
Monday: hanging ... cat on M. 58:2
M.'s child is fair of face 191:8
Monde: se mêler à corriger le m. 182:14
Mondes: meilleur des m. possibles 321:9
Money: abundance of m. ruins youth 206:1
borrer the m. to do it with 322:15
business ... may bring m. 20:10
by any means make m. 135:11
dally not with m. or women 210:33
did dream of m.-bags to-night 274:13
fool ... m. are soon parted 214:2
Government licence to print m. 316:14
he lends out m. gratis 274:7
he that wants m., means 245:3
I have spent all the m. 144:17
if m. be not thy servant 221:9
innocently employed ... getting m. 143:13
lend yr. m. and lose yr. friend 218:36
love of m. ... root of all evil 49:14
marrieth for love without m. 220:29
merit will not serve ... as m. 142:10
m. begets m. 221:10
m. gives me pleasure 27:10
m. is like muck 22:9
m. makes marriage 221:12
m. talks 221:15
no man ... wrote, except for m. 144:5
no m., no swiss 222:2
pays yr. m. ... takes yr. choice 231:18
purse ... full of other men's m. 212:21
put m. in thy purse 279:6
putting m. on a horse 27:14
remember when ... m. not scarce 108:22
said that love of m. is the root 68:3
some honey, and plenty of m. 158:7
that's the way the m. goes 165:5
the want of m. is so [root of evil] 68:3
throw good m. after bad 227:41
thy m. perish with thee 47:2
your m. or your life 68:13
Mongrels: greyhounds, m., spaniels, curs 271:1
Monk: the devil a m. wd. be 185:1
Monkey: only a m. shaved 120:11
Monotony: bleats articulate m. 306:9
to chase m. 117:6
Monster: great-siz'd m. of ingratitudes 290:6
green-ey'd m. wh. doth mock 279:16
Montezuma: knows who imprisoned M. 164:2
Month: April is the cruellest m. 107:3
ark rested in the seventh m. 30:21
laughter for a m. ... jest for ever 254:8
this is the m. ... the happy morn 175:7
Months: cd. live for m. without ... labour 322:14
go right on ... for numerous more m. 322:14
Montreal: in a M. lumber room 68:9
O God! O M.! 68:9
Montrose: young man of M. 28:9
Monument: a sonnet is a moment's m. 236:6
an early but enduring m. 297:13
he replied, 'Like the M.' 141:16
if you seek my m. 337:1
Patience on a m. 291:7

Monument (*continued*)

their only m. the asphalt road   107:1

thou art a m.   145:12

Monumentum: si m. requiris, circumspice   337:1

Mood: albeit unused to the melting m.
280–1:14

in vacant or in pensive m.   331:11

sweet m. when pleasant thoughts bring sad
332:7

that blessed m.   335:11

Moon: a-roving by the light of the m.   71:4

beneath a waning m. was haunted   87:12

beneath the visiting m.   243:6

course of one revolving m.   103:4

cry for the m.   210:22

danced by the light of the m.   158:9

danced the m. on Monan's Rill   239:6

honour from the pale-fac'd m.   254:4

hymns to the cold fruitless m.   276:9

I see the m. ... m. sees me   190:5

late eclipses in the sun and m.   265:9

lustres slake the o'ertaken m.   58:3

make guilty ... the m.   265:10

man in the m.   220:14

man in the m. ... down too soon   191:6

m. in the valley of Ajalon   33:12

m. when she deserts the night   180:11

moving M. went up the sky   86:12

nor the m. [smite thee] by night   37:16

one with ... the west m.   315:14

Queen–M. is on her throne   149:16

rather be a dog and bay the m.   263:23

slowly, silently, now the m.   97:3

sung to the m. by a ... loon   121:1

swear not by the m., th' inconstant m.
286:10

the cow jumped over the m.   189:5

the m. be still as bright   71:3

the m. doth shine as bright as day   188:6

the m. lies fair   18:9

to bark at the m.   206:38

unmask her beauty to the m.   248:13

with how sad steps, O M.   302:4

Moonlight: ghost along the m. shade   201:5

go visit it by the pale m.   239:12

how sweet the m. sleeps   275:8

I'll come to thee by m.   188:2

ill met by m., proud Titania   276:17

look for me by m.   188:2

passions ... as m. unto sunlight   313:19

Moonlit: knocking on the m. door   96:14

Moons: some nine m. wasted   278:21

Moonshine: look in the almanack; find out m.
277:1

Mops: seven maids with seven m.   76:3

Moral: a m., if only you can find it   74:12

a m., sensible, and well-bred man   92:4

golf ... a form of m. effort   157:14

grandest m. attribute of a Scotsman   25:1

let us be m. ... contemplate existence   98:5

O m. Gower   80:7

point a m. or adorn a tale   141:11

Morality: give ... a lecture on m. ... a shilling
142:10

gossip made tedious by m.   328:3

m. of an action depends   142:7

periodical fits of m.   164:6

up agen middle class m.   296:21

Moralize: faithful loves shall m.   305:9

Morals: foundation of m. and legislation   29:1

Morals (*continued*)

no man's religion ... survives his m.   221:39

teach the m. of a whore   141:19

More: and penance m. will do   86:15

easy to take *m.* than nothing   74:10

enough for modesty—no m.   62:13

m. than somewhat   236:15

Oliver Twist has asked for m.   98:12

you get no m. of me   102:12

Morituri te salutant   308:4

Morn: awake, the m. will never rise   96:1

healthy breath of m.   148:4

lights that do mislead the m.   273:12

now M., her rosy steps   178:12

sang from m. till night   54:1

the m., in russet mantle clad   247:16

this the happy m.   175:7

Morning: beauty of the m.; silent, bare   333:6

day's at the morn. M.'s at seven   62:7

early one m. ... sun was rising   15:1

glad, confident m.   61:9

great m. of the world   297:11

hour in the m. is worth two   217:6

in his m. face   122:11

in the m. we will remember them   54:5

it's nice to get up in the m.   157:6

Lucifer, son of the m.   40:25

M. in the Bowl of Night   109:13

on a cold and frosty m.   15:7

peace ... dropping from the veils of the m.
337:5

sees some m., unaware   61:1

Morrow: good night till it be m.   286:14

never shall sun that m. see   270:3

trusting the m. as little as you can   135:13

Mors: pallida M. aequo ... pede   135:12

Morsel: sweetest m. of the night   256:20

Mortal: he raised a m. to the skies   103:15

her last disorder m.   122:17

reminds a man he is m.   96:5

shall m. man be more just than God?
35:2

Mortality: m., behold and fear   25:8

there's nothing serious in m.   270:15

Mortals: not in m. to command success   9:4

what fools these m. be!   277:3

Mortuis: de m. nil nisi bonum   210:37

Moses: meekness of M. ... strength of Samson
221:1

M. said, ... This is the bread   31:28

persuaded to leave M. out   29:8

Moss: a rolling stone gathers no m.   224:26

Most may err as greatly as the few   103:8

Moth: desire of the m. for the star   300:8

Mother: call me early, m. dear   314:6

dead! and ... never called me m.   330:7

disclaim her for a m.   116:1

does your m. know ... you are out?   24:7

England ... m. of parliaments   58:9

foolish son ... heaviness of his m.   38:8

gave her m. forty whacks   14:3

home to his m.'s house   180:6

I arose a m. in Israel   33:13

I feel no pain, dear m.   15:9

let ... his m. drudge ... at seventy   296:5

like m., like daughter   221:17

Mary was that M. mild   10:6

m. of the free, how shall we extol?   28:10

m., who'd give her booby for another
115:10

Mother (*continued*)
m. who talks about her own children   100:6
my m. bore me in ... wild   56:10
my m. said that I never shd.   191:9
never had any m. ?   307:14
the m. of all living   100:13
the m. of months in meadow   309:14
took great care of his m.   171:8
variety ... m. of enjoyment   100:13
where a M. laid her Baby   10:6
whether his m. wd. let him or no   189:2
with the m. first begin   210:34
Mother-in-law remembers not   221:18
Mothers: all women become like their m.
    328:13
people's m. always bore me   328:13
Moths ... ever caught by glare   68:18
Motion: between the m. and the act   106:8
in his m. like an angel sings   275:8
in our proper m. we ascend   176:17
no m. has she now, no force   334:15
sensible warm m. to become ... clod   273:10
Motive: morality ... depends on the m.   142:7
Motley: a m. fool   244:8
Mould: splashing the wintry m.   337:7
the m. of form   251:5
Mount: yet shall he m.   [Milton]   127:2
Mountain: m. out of a molehill   221:19
robes the m. in its azure hue   72:9
tiptoe on the misty m. tops   286:22
up the airy m.   10:9
Mountains: from Greenland's icy m.   130:1
m. skipped like rams   37:7
the m. look on Marathon   70:1
two voices ... one of the m.   333:10
upon the m. of Ararat   30:21
walk upon England's m. green   55:8
Mountebank: a mere anatomy, a m.   246:5
Mourn: don't m. for me never   12:1
in summer skies to m.   147:11
makes countless thousands m.   66:8
secure, and now can never m.   297:16
that man was made to m.   66:7
to m. a mischief ... past   279:3
Mourning: with my m. very handsome
    199:12
Mouse: caught a crooked m.   194:3
frightened a little m. under her chair   192:7
killing of a m. on Sunday   58:2
man or m.   220:20
the m. ran up the clock   189:6
the other caught a m.   158:11
Mouse-trap: make a better m.   108:23
Mouth: a close m. catcheth no flies   209:33
burnt his m. with ... cold plum porridge
    191:6
gift horse in the m.   214:30
heart is in his m.   216:26
her m. unclosed in ... kiss   157:10
if you m. it as many ... players do   251:7
into the m. of Hell   311:12
lo, in her m. ... an olive leaf   30:22
out of thine own m. ... I judge thee   46:12
purple-stained m.   149:14
set a watch ... before my m.   37:29
spue thee out of my m.   50:19
tree whose hungry m. is pressed   153:8
wd. not melt in his m.   208:41
Mouths: blind m. that scarce ... know how
    175:3

Mouths (*continued*)
have m. but ... speak not   37:8
made m. in a glass   266:9
Moutons: revenons à nos m.   17:9
Move: but it does m.   114:14
do m. a woman's mind   292:7
I will m. the earth   18:3
languid strings do scarcely m.   56:14
Moved: not m. with concord of sweet sounds
    275:10
Moves: and having writ, m. on   110:12
m., and mates, and slays   110:11
m. in determinate grooves   128:11
Moving: always m. as the restless spheres
    166:10
m. Moon went up the sky   86:12
Mower whets his scythe   174:3
Much: missing so m. and so m.   90:16
m. may be made of a Scotchman   143:8
m. of a muchness   320:4
m. ... said on both sides   9:8
so m., to learn so little   99:3
Muck: money is like m.   22:9
Mud: two men look out ... one sees the m.
    156:15
Muddy, ill-seeming, thick, bereft   287:12
Mudie's: I keep my books at ... M.   68:4
Muffet: little Miss M. sat on a tuffet   191:3
Muffin: one caught a m.   158:11
Multiply: be fruitful, and m.   30:4
Multitudes: against revolted m.   178:19
I contain m.   326:5
m. in the valley of decision   42:14
pestilence-stricken m.   299:3
Multitudinous: the m. seas incarnadine
    270:12
Munch on, crunch on   62:4
Murder: foul and most unnatural m.   249:8
I met M. on the way   298:13
m. most foul ... unnatural   249:9
m. ... one of the Fine Arts   97:6
m. shrieks out   323:15
m. will out   80:2, 221:21
then m.'s out of tune   280:12
Murdered: death of kings ... all m.   283:6
two brothers and their m. man   148:12
Murderer: Aram ... thief ... liar ... m.   72:3
Murmur: creeping m. and the poring dark
    259:8
live m. of a summer's day   18:19
Muse: Fool, said my M. to me   302:3
O for a M. of fire   258:5
strictly meditate the thankless M.   174:15
the M. but served to ease   201:14
Mushroom: nicely groomed, like a m.   157:9
Mushrooms: broiled fowl and m.—capital!
    98:17
Music: a reasonable good ear in m.   277:4
and let the sounds of m. creep   275:8
deep sea ... m. in its roar   69:9
fled is that m.   150:6
have m. wherever she goes   193:1
how sour sweet m. is!   284:7
if m. be the food of love   290:10
like m. on my heart   87:1
linnet, how sweet his m.!   335:5
man that hath no m.   275:10
m. and women I ... give way to   199:11
m. has charms to soothe   89:5
m. that gentlier on the spirit lies   314:2

Nation (*continued*)
n. of shopkeepers   185:12, 303:4
n. ... perpetually to be conquered   64:5
n. shall not lift up sword agst. n.   40:18
no n. was ever ruined by trade   112:14
noble and puissant n. rousing herself   182:8
once to every man and n.   162:14
one third of a n. ill-housed   235:2
righteousness exalteth a n.   38:15
that this n. ... shall have a new birth   159:13
we are a musical n.   316:5
Nations: day of small n. ... passed away   78:8
eclipsed the gaiety of n.   145:1
equal rights ... of n., large and small   319:5
happiest n. have no history   105:15
in thy seed shall all the n. ... blessed   31:5
languages are the pedigree of n.   144:23
lasting peace ... with all n.   159:15
lightning of the n.   299:2
many n. and three continents   102:2
n. are as a drop of a bucket   41:1
n. which have put mankind ... in their debt   138:8
Privileged ... People ... Two N.   100:12
Native: content to breathe his n. air   203:20
fast by their n. shore   93:1
my n. Land—Good Night   69:2
n. hue of resolution   250–1:20
though I am n. here   249:2
Natives: the bulk of your n. ... vermin   308:16
Nativity: in n., chance, or death   276:8
Natural: as n. to die as to be born   21:10
I do it more n.   291:3
in him alone, 'twas n. to please   102:15
n., simple, affecting   123:5
Natural Philosophy [makes men] deep   23:9
Natural Selection: called this principle ... N.   95:11
Naturalists: so, n. observe, a flea   309:4
Naturally: if Poetry come not as n. as the Leaves   151:15
not n. honest   293:6
Nature: a friend ... masterpiece of N.   108:4
accuse not N.!   179:4
all n. is but art   203:4
allow not n. more than n. needs   266:2
are God and N. then at strife?   312:16
as old and new ... as N.'s self   60:13
broken N.'s social union   66:11
creatures that by a rule in n. teach   258:8
cunning'st pattern of excelling n.   280:11
disguise fair n. with ... rage   259:3
first follow N.   202:3
Force of N. cd. no farther go   104:11
fortress built by N. for herself   282:5
great n.'s second course   270:11
his n. is too noble   246:10
human n. is so well disposed   20:9
I have learned to look on n.   335:14
I love not Man the less, but N. more   69:9
in human n. ... more of the fool   22:3
in thy green lap was N.'s darling   127:1
let N. be your teacher   335:6
little we see in N.   333:3
loathed ... life that age ... can lay on n.   273:11
man is N.'s sole mistake   120:10
mute N. mourns her worshipper   239:14
N. always does contrive   117:8

Nature (*continued*)
N. and N.'s Laws lay hid   201:21
N. I loved   156:11
n. in you stands on the very verge   265:22
n. is but a name for an effect   93:11
n. is often hidden, sometimes overcome   22:26
n. is the art of God   59:13
n. lends such evil dreams   312:16
N. might stand up and say   264:7
n. ... must be obeyed   23:17
n. never did betray the heart   336:1
n. of a tragic volume   256:6
n., red in tooth and claw   312:17
n.'s law ... man was made to mourn   66:7
n.'s soft nurse   257:2
N. that framed us   166:10
o'erstep not the modesty of n.   251:9
on N., and on human life, musing   331:3
one touch of n. ... whole world kin   290:7
passing through n. to eternity   247:20
scenery is fine ... human n. is finer   151:16
spectacles of books to read n.   104:4
that N. yet remembers ... fugitive   332:4
the more man's n. runs to   21:12
the n. of an insurrection   262:13
the purpose and n. of miracles   297:3
the rest [hours] on N. fix   85:9
then Nature said, 'A lovelier flower'   335:9
to write and read comes by n.   278:4
true wit is n. to advantage dress'd   202:8
unerring N., still divinely bright   202:3
where man is not, n. is barren   57:6
whose body N. is, and God the soul   203:3
woman ... one of N.'s agreeable blunders   91:14
words, like N., half reveal   312:12
yet do I fear thy n.   270:1
youth ... still is N.'s priest   332:2
Natures: men's n. are alike   89:2
Naught: it is n., it is n., saith the buyer   38:24
Naughty: a n. night to swim in   266:15
good deed in a n. world   275:11
n. girl to disobey   191:9
Navy: Ruler of the Queen's N.   119:15,16
Nazareth: can ... any good thing come out of N.?   46:18
Neaera: tangles of N.'s hair   174:16
Near: call ... while he is n.   41:8
he seems so n. and yet so far   313:2
Nearer, my God, to thee   9:3
Neat: still to be n. ... be drest   145:9
Necessary: is yr. journey really n.?   11:5
Necessities: give us the luxuries ... will dispense with ... n.   184:11
Necessity: by n. ... we all quote   108:15
make a virtue of n.   229:20
n. hath no law   221:23
n. ... is the argument of tyrants   200:8
n. is the mother of invention   221:24
no virtue like n.   281:14
sworn brother ... to grim N.   284:4
teach thy n. to reason thus   281:14
thy n. is greater than mine   302:7
Neck: a n. God made for other use   136:4
England will have her n. wrung   83:4
my n. is very short   184:5
n. or nothing   221:25
some chicken! Some n.!   83:4
Need: all we n. of hell   99:15

Need (*continued*)
friend in n. is a friend indeed   214:18
in thy most n. ... by thy side   13:5
n. to pray for fair weather   22:8
O, reason not the n.   266:2
Needle: man for the sword and for the n. she   314:18
plying her n. and thread   135:3
through the eye of a n.   44:23
Needlessly sets foot upon a worm   93:12
Needs: all this sad world n.   326:11
more than nature n.   266:2
to each according to his n.   168:7
Negative Capability   151:11
Negatives: two n. make an affirmative   229:3
Neglect: n. the creeping hours   244:10
such sweet n. more taketh me   145:10
Negligent: celerity ... admir'd than by the n.   242:19
Neiges: où sont les n. d'antan?   320:15
Neighbour: false witness against thy n.   32:8
lov'd his wicked n. as himself   103:7
love thy n. as thyself   32:16
policy of a good n.   235:1
thy n.'s wife ... manservant ... ox ... ass   32:9
worketh no ill to his n.   47:29
Neighbours: good fences make good n.   113:13
in peace ... as good n.   319:5
live without friends ... not without ... n.   219:21
Nelly: let not poor N. starve   78:16
Neptune: do choose the ebbing N.   289:4
envious siege of wat'ry N.   282:6
he wd. not flatter N.   246:10
will all great N.'s ocean wash this blood?   270:12
Nerissa, my little body is aweary   274:5
Nerves: when ... the n. prick   312:14
Nervous: Bradshaw—n. and terse but limited   102:6
Nest: to find a mare's n.   220:24
Nests: birds in their little n. agree   323:3
birds in their ... n. agree with Chinamen   27:11
built their n. in my beard   158:13
Nettle: out of this n., danger   254:10
Never: and ... n. called me mother   330:7
better late than n.   207:30
books n. die   235:5
dead men rise up n.   310:1
don't mourn for me n.   12:1
I n. shall love the snow again   58:5
limericks n. wd. scan   13:1
love that n. told can be   55:10
me and my true love will n. meet   16:10
my apple trees will n.   113:13
n. a spray of yew   18:16
n. begin than n. make an end   207:32
n. broke the Sabbath, but for gain   103:6
n. glad confident morning again   61:9
n., I ween, was a prouder   24:5
n. lov'd ... met ... parted   65:10
n., n., n., n., n.   268:4
n., n. thinks of me   17:3
n. seek to tell thy love   55:10
n. send to know for whom the bell   101:8
n. the time and the place   61:11
n. the twain shall meet   154:8

Never (*continued*)
n. to have lost at all   68:12
n. to have loved at all   312:13
n. turned his back ... n. doubted   60:12
seldom or n. the two hit it off   330:10
This England n. did nor n. shall   265:4
what, n.? No, n.!   119:11
who n. made a foe   312:5
Nevermore: quoth the Raven, N.   200:19
New: a n. broom sweeps clean   221:37
a n. commandment I give   46:29
a n. heaven and a n. earth   51:1
a n. master—get a n. man   288:10
among n. men, strange faces   312:7
as old and n. ... as Nature's self   60:13
before you are on with the n.   16:1
called the N. World into existence   72:15
[compassions] are n. every morning   41:19
conservatism? ... is ... against the n.   159:11
how strange it seems, and n.!   61:10
n. king ... knew not Joseph   31:15
n. man ... raised up in him   53:10
n. nobility ... act of power   22:7
n. philosophy calls all in doubt   100:16
n. wine into old bottles   45:25
no n. thing under the sun   39:12
old lamps for n.   18:1
old order ... yielding place to n.   312:8
piping songs for ever n.   149:9
ring in the n.   313:4
sing unto him a n. song   36:5
will not apply n. remedies   22:18
New Way to Pay Old Debts   169:3
Newcastle: coals to N.   209:8
Newcomer: O, blithe N.!   336:2
New-fangled: May's n. shows   268:9
their garments, though n. ill   294:2
News: all the n. that's fit to print   196:9
first bringer of unwelcome n.   256:7
for there is good n. yet to hear   81:8
good n. from a far country   38:29
he that tells his wife n.   227:21
ill n. comes too soon   217:18
man bites a dog, that is n.   95:5
master-passion ... love of n.   93:18
nature of bad n. infects   242:11
never good to bring bad n.   242:16
no n. is good n.   222:4
nowadays truth ... greatest n.   222:20
talk of court n.   267:13
Newspapers: n. always excite curiosity   156:8
successful n. are ceaselessly querulous   169:12
Newton: another N., a new Donne   137:14
God said, Let N. be!   201:21
Nice: a n. man ... of nasty ideas   309:10
n. to get up in the mornin'   157:6
sugar and spice and all that's n.   195:6
too n. for a statesman   123:2
Nicely: n.-calculated less or more   330:11
sick men play so n. with their names   282:7
Nickname: a n. is the heaviest stone   129:14
Nigh: the Lord is n.   36:7
Night: a braw, bricht, moonlicht n.   157:4
a casement ope at n.   150:7
a naughty n. to swim in   266:15
afraid for the terror by n.   36:26
all n. long ... on sentry-go   117:6
and darkness N. he named   178:21

Noise (*continued*)
dreadful n. of waters 285:1
Fifth Symphony ... most sublime n. 112:1
never valued till they make a n. 94:1
Noises: like n. in a swound 86:2
this isle is full of n. 288:13
Noll: for shortness called N. 115:2
No-More, Too-Late, Farewell 236:8
Nonconformist: whoso wd. be a man must be
a n. 108:11
None: n. of us liveth to himself 47:30
n. that ... trust in him shall be overcome
52:9
so the poor dog had n. 192:2
some believe they've n. at all 68:2
then n. was for a party 163:12
this little pig had n. 194:7
Nonsense: sounds like n., my dear 240:11
through ... realms of N. absolute 104:13
Noon: dark, amid the blaze of n. 180:10
far from the fiery n. 148:4
from morn to n. he fell 176:14
sun has not attained his n. 132:1
Noon-day, upon the market-place 262:12
Noose: in a N. of Light 109:13
naked to the hangman's n. 136:4
Normal: yes, thank God, we're n. 197:9
Norman: simple faith than N. blood 313:10
North-north-west: am but mad n. 250:8
Nor(o)way: to N., N. ... o'er the faem 11:14
Norwich: asked his way to N. 191:6
Nose: custom ... hateful to the n. 138:14
cut off one's n. to spite one's face 210:29
Dong with a luminous N. 158:3
ever and anon he gave his n. 254:1
had Cleopatra's n. been shorter 198:7
led by the n. with gold 293:8
Marian's n. looks red and raw 269:1
n. was as sharp as a pen 259:2
one's n. to the grindstone 222:10
pay through the n. 28:9, 222:38
ring at the end of his n. 158:8
snapped off her n. 193:5
to turn up one's n. 228:33
wipe a bloody n. 115:11
Noses: athwart men's n. as they lie asleep
286:1
n., ... but they smell not 37:9
nothing pay for wearing our own n.
247:1
Note: as the gen'l'm'n said to the fi' pun' n.
99:2
his merry n. unto ... bird's throat 244:4
not a funeral n. 330:3
when found, make a n. 98:3
Notes: I heard a thousand blended n. 332:7
the sound is forced, the n. are few 56:14
Nothing: book although there's n. in't 70:12
certain of n. but ... holiness 151:9
civility costs n. 209:29
days ... when ... n. goes wrong 120:13
devil, having n. else to do 27:8
did n. in particular 117:11
do n. for ever and ever 12:1
doing n. for a bribe 247:3
doings without charity are n. worth 53:3
easy to take *more* than n. 74:10
everything by starts and n. long 103:4
gives to airy n. ... habitation 277:6
he n. common did or mean 168:4

Nothing (*continued*)
he that knows n., doubts n. 218:15
I am n. if not critical 279:7
I do n. upon myself 101:6
is it n. to ... ye that pass by ? 41:17
know this only, that he n. knew 180:4
learnt n., and forgotten n. 310:12
let n. you dismay 15:3
looked at for n. Nohow! 75:13
mind's cluttered up with n. 324:17
neck or n. 221:25
n. a year, paid quarterly 308:9
n—absolutely n.—half so much worth
doing 124:12
n. begins and n. ends 316:8
n. beside remains. Round the decay 299:8
n. can bring you peace 108:13
n. destroyeth authority so much 22:15
n. except a battle lost 324:6
n. for n. 222:12
n. for n. 'ere 231:24
n. great ... without enthusiasm 108:3
n. happens, nobody comes 25:11
n. in excess 17:10
n. in his life became him 269:11
n. is certain but death and taxes 113:3
n. is certain but uncertainty 222:13
n. is had for n. 84:12
n. is ours but time 222:14
n. of him that doth fade 288:1
n. of itself will come 331:5
n. pay for wearing our own noses 247:1
n. seek, n. find 222:16
n. so absurd but some philosopher has said
it 84:1
n. so sharply reminds 96:5
n.'s truer than them [taxes] 97:19
n. succeeds like excess 328:14
n. succeeds like success 222:17
n. to declare except my genius 328:16
n. to do but work 153:10
n. to eat but food 153:10
n. to look backward [forward] to 113:10
n. to say—say n. 88:18
n. to wear but clothes 153:10
n. venture, n. win 222:19
n. ... violent is permanent 222:18
n. went unrewarded but Desert 103:5
n. whatever to grumble at 120:13
n. will come of n. 265:6
questioneth n., learneth 222:15
sea ... n. but to make him sick 101:2
smattering of everything ... knowledge of n.
99:11
sound and fury signifying n. 272:10
speak ... as I am; n. extenuate 280:14
think n. done while aught remains 234:14
'tis something, n. 279:15
we brought n. into this world 49:13
yeomanry ... with whom ... n. to do 20:6
Nothingness: love and fame to n. 151:8
will never pass into n. 147:8
Notice ... you have been pleased to take 142:1
Notorious: open and n. evil liver 53:9
Nought: knows n. that knows not this 289:15
Noun: talk of a n. and a verb 260:11
Nourished: how begot, how n. 274:18
Novel: I've read in many a n. 72:2
only obligation to which ... we may hold a n.
139:3

Novel (*continued*)
    when I want to read a n. 100:15
Novels: catalogue ... more entertaining than
    ... n. 169:6
    how much wd. n. gain 70:10
November's sky ... November's leaf 240:3
Novice: young, a N. in the Trade 104:15
Now: in England—n.! 61:1
Nowhere: and n. did abide 86:12
    one really lives n. 65:5
Nude: keep one from going n. 153:10
Nuisances who write for autographs 118:4
Number: count the n. of the beast 50:26
    greatest happiness of the greatest n. 29:1
    so teach us to n. our days 36:24
Numbers: achiever brings home full n. 277:9
    divinity in odd n. 276:8
    I lisp'd in n., for the n. came 201:13
    perhaps the plaintive n. flow 334:17
    tell me not, in mournful n. 160:14
Numbness: drowsy n. pains my sense 149:13
Nun: holy time is quiet as a n. 333:2
Nuncheon: crunch on, take your n. 62:4
Nunnery: get thee to a n. 251:2
    n. of thy chaste breast 162:6
Nuns fret not at ... narrow cell 332:13
Nuptials: prone to any iteration of n. 90:1
Nurse: baby ... that sucks the n. asleep 243:11
    nature's soft n. 257:2
    this n., this teeming womb of ... kings
    282:5
Nurseries: in the n. of Heaven 316:11
    n. of all vice and immorality 109:10
Nurses: wives are ... old men's n. 21:20
Nursing the unconquerable hope 19:1
Nursling: I am ... the n. of the Sky 298:6
Nurslings of immortality 299:11
Nut: hard n. to crack 216:14
    I had a little n. tree 190:1
Nutmeg: silver n. and a golden pear 190:1
Nuts: Brazil, where the n. come from 315:1
    gathering n. in May 15:7
    may be n. for Mary Ann 12:6
Nymph: haste thee, N. 173:16
    mountain-n., sweet Liberty 173:18

O: cram within this wooden O 258:6
Oak: bend a knotted o. 89:5
    grave where English o. and holly 129:2
    hearts of o. are our ships 115:1
Oaks: tall o., branch-charmed 148:6
Oars: the o. were silver 242:14
    with falling o. ... kept the time 167:10
Oath: a good mouth-filling o. 255:9
Oaths: full of strange o. 244:11
    o. are but words 67:16
Oats: o. ... in England ... given to horses
    140:9
    sow one's wild o. 230:16
Obedience: as honour, love, o. 272:5
    o. is ... seen in little things 222:21
    resistance to tyrants is o. to God 139:11
Obey: safer to o. than to rule 152:16
    to love, cherish, and to o. 53:23
    woman to o. 314:18
Object: my o. all sublime 118:10
    only legitimate o. of government 139:10
    'tis for o. strange and high 167:16
Obligation: only o. to which ... we may hold a
    novel 139:3

Obligations: nobility imposes its own o. 159:4
    respect for the o. arising from treaties
    319:5
Oblivion: put alms for o. 290:6
    second childishness and mere o. 244–5:11
    the rest ... commend to cold o. 298:8
Oblivious: some sweet o. antidote 272:6
Obsequies: Nature ... celebrates his o. 239:14
Observance: more honour'd in the breach than
    the o. 249:2
    with this special o. 251:9
Observation: let o. with extensive view 141:9
Observations which ourselves we make
    203:13
Observed: the o. of all observers 251:5
Obstruction: to lie in cold o. and to rot 273:10
Occasion: courage mounteth with o. 264:10
Occasions: all o. do inform against me 252:17
    there is o. and causes 260:3
Occupation: absence of o. is not rest 93:4
    line of o. in the central sector 83:10
Occupations: worse o. in the world 306:14
Occupied: how my parents were o. and all
    237:13
Ocean: a life on the o. wave 238:8
    dark unfathom'd caves of o. 126:10
    great Neptune's o. wash this blood 270:12
    in the o.'s bosom unespied 167:8
    make the mighty o. 73:13
    on the o. of life we pass 161:7
    painted ship upon a painted o. 86:5
    pores of the o. and shores 298:6
    we sail the o. blue 119:8
Odd: creators of o. volumes 156:3
    divinity in o. numbers 276:8
    o. because ... middle of the night 75–6:16
    scarcely o. because they'd eaten every one
    76:6
    think it exceedingly o. 155:14
Odds: die better than facing fearful o. 163:10
    the o. is gone 243:6
Odi et amo. Quare ... nescio 77:16
Odium: the o. of having discovered sodium
    29:5
Odorous: comparisons are o. 278:8
Odour: in the o. of sanctity died 24:6
    stealing and giving o. 290:10
Odours, when sweet violets sicken 300:6
O'erpeer: for truth to o. 246:8
Off: o. with his head! 74:11
    o. with the old love 16:1
    only that when ... o. [stage] he was acting
    123:5
Offence: beauty ... after o. returning 181:5
    dire o. from am'rous causes springs 204:5
    my o. is rank 252:10
Offend: if thine eye o. thee 44:21
    o. one of these little ones 44:20
Offended: for him have I o. 263:10
Offender: Clinker ... a most notorious o.
    303:19
Offenders: little list of Society o. 118:4
    the more laws, the more o. 218:25
Offer: never refuse a good o. 221:32
    nothing to o. but blood, toil, tears 82:11
Office: hath but a losing o. 256:7
    heresy ... that ... o. sanctifies 9:1
    o. and affairs of love 277:15
    o. and custom, in all line 290:1
    the insolence of o. 250–1:20

Office boy: as o. to an Attorney's firm 119:15
Officers: a King, and o. of sorts 258:8
Official: what is o. is incontestable 114:3
Officious, innocent, sincere 140:14
Officiously to keep alive 84:16
Offspring: o. of Heaven first-born! 177:9
  true source of human o. 178:8
Oft: many a time and o. 274:9
  o., when on my couch I lie 331:11
Oil: lingering, with boiling o. 118:14
  o'er books consumed the midnight o. 115:9
  pour o. upon the waters 222:22
Ointment: good name ... better than precious
  o. 39:18
Old: a liking o. for thee 72:4
  adherence to the o. and tried 159:11
  all things worn out and o. 337:7
  an o. abusing of ... patience 276:3
  an o. man in a dry month 106:5
  an o. man in a hurry 82:5
  an o. maxim in the schools 308:12
  as o. and new ... as Nature's self 60:13
  call for his o. shoes 241:1
  grow o. along with me 62:9
  grow o. with a good grace 306:7
  half as o. as time 64:3
  I grow o. ... I grow o. 106:15
  I love everything that's o. 123:6
  if I ever grow to be o. 28:3
  man ... as o. as he's feeling 88:7
  never too o. to learn 221:35
  new book is published, read an o. one
    234:13
  o. age shd. burn 315:15
  o. and godly and grave 337:6
  o. as he feels ... o. as she looks 220:17
  o. as the hills 222:23
  o. books, o. wine 123:6
  o. friends and o. wine are best 222:24
  o. friends are best 241:1
  o. friends, o. times, o. manners 123:6
  o. head on young shoulders 222:25
  o. lamps for new 18:1
  o. men forget 260:1
  o. poacher ... good game-keeper 222:26
  o. soldiers ... only fade away 16:7
  o. soldiers, sweethearts ... lovers 324:1
  o., unhappy, far-off things 334:17
  o. wine ... o. pippins ... o. wood 324:1
  one of them is fat and grows o. 254:14
  ring out the o. 313:4
  so o., and so profane 258:3
  summits o. in story 314:14
  tell me the o., o. story 128:4
  the grand o. name of gentleman 313:8
  the mighty minds of o. 304:10
  the o. gang 82:4
  the o. order changeth 312:8
  the thousand wars of o. 313:6
  they shall grow not o. 54:5
  they think he is growing o. 138:10
  when thou art o. ... grief enough 127:5
  when you are o. and grey 337:10
  woman as o. as she looks 88:7
  young in years ... o. in hours 23:1
Old Bailey: say the bells of O. 192:4
Old Kent Road: knock'd 'em in the O. 81:13
Old Testament: prosperity is the blessing of
  the O. 21:13
Olive-leaf: an o. he brings, pacific sign 179:16

Olive-leaf (*continued*)
  in her mouth was an o. 30:22
Oliver Twist has asked for more 98:12
Olivia: air cry out 'O.!' 290:15
Olympiades: l'important dans ces o. 91:2
Olympic Games: important thing in the O. is
  91:2
Omnia vincit amor ... cedamus 321:5
On: before you are o. with the new 16:1
  o., o., you noblest English 259:4
  o., Stanley, o.! 240:10
Once: children ... call yet o. 18:12
One: all for o., and o. for all 105:3
  animals went in o. by o. 14:9
  but the O. was Me 137:14
  clock struck o., the mouse ran down 189:6
  dead men ... shall be o. 315:14
  he replied, O.'s absurd 183:1
  how to be o. up 204:16
  Liberty and Union ... o. and inseparable
    323:10
  o. for the master ... o. for the dame 188:4
  o. God, o. law, o. element 313:9
  o. ... is rather coarse 13:11
  o. more river to cross 14:9
  o. thing ... worse than being talked about
    328:6
  O., two, buckle my shoe 192:3
  o. to watch and o. to pray 9:13
  the O. remains, the many change 298:2
  to lose o. parent 327:12
  true it is she had o. failing 66:6
  two hearts that beat as o. 162:8
One-and-twenty: long expected, o. ... is flown
  140:18
  when I was o. 136:5
Oneself: to love o. ... lifelong romance 327:5
Only: not by eastern windows o. 85:3
  o. thing that I ever did wrong 16:3
Onward: a little o. lend thy ... hand 180:8
  O. Christian soldiers 24:9
  O., the sailors cry 57:12
Open: o. and notorious evil liver 53:9
  o. not thine heart 51:18
  o. Sesame! 18:2
Ophir: quinquireme ... from distant O.
  168:13
Opinion: error of o. may be tolerated 139:8
  never in touch with public o. 328:11
  no o. of God at all 22:12
  of his own o. still 68:1
  think the last o. right 202:12
Opinions: halt ye between two o. 34:19
  proper o. for the time of year 20:4
  so many men, so many o. 315:4
  stiff in o., ... in the wrong 103:4
Opium: religion ... is the o. of the people
  168:8
Opportunity makes the thief 222:29
Opposed: bear't that th' o. may beware
  248:16
Opposing: sea of troubles and by o., end them
  250–1:20
Opposition: conjunction of the mind, and o. of
  the stars 167:17
Oppression: lack gall to make o. bitter 250:17
Oppressor: who wd. bear ... th' o.'s wrong?
  250–1:20
Oracle: I am Sir O. 274:3
Orange: ruled by an O. 241:12

Oranges and lemons 192:4

Orator: beauty ... doth ... persuade ... without an o. 295:5

Orb: monthly changes in her circled o. 286:10

   smallest o. which thou behold'st 275:8

Orchard: chaffinch sings on the o. bough 61:1

Order: good o. is the foundation 64:14

   in all line of o. 290:1

   o. ... this matter better in France 306:11

   stand not upon the o. of your going 271:9

   the old o. changeth 312:8

   to o. myself ... reverently 53:13

   words in the (their) best 88:3

Ordered: God ... o. their estate 10:5

Ore: load ... yr. subject with o. 152:12

Organ: O. Morgan ... o. o. all the time 316:6

   playing of the merry o. 15:8

Organism to live beyond its income 68:7

Organized: no mind is thoroughly well o. 88:4

Organs: hath not a Jew hands, o.? 274:17

Orgies are vile 186:3

Origin: dancing? Oh, dreadful! ... of savage o. 65:4

   indelible stamp of his lowly o. 95:10

Original: a thought is often o. 134:4

   their great O. proclaim 9:9

Originality: all good things ... are the fruits of o. 170:10

Originator: next to the o. of a good sentence 108:14

Orlando: run, run O. 245:2

Ormus: wealth of O. and of Ind 176:15

Ornament: rhyme being no ... true o. 175:14

Ornavit: nullum quod tetigit non o. 144:22

Orpheus with his lute 261:6

Oscar: you will, O., you will 325:7

Ostrich: America cannot be an o. 329:8

Other: after the first death ... no o. 316:1

   bunch of o. men's flowers 183:6

   or any o. reason why 10:3

   o. times, o. manners 206:29

   since then I have used no o. 232:2

Others: a corner ... for o.' uses 279:17

   be not false to o. 22:17

   best and distinguished above o. 134:9

   England ... wont to conquer o. 282:6

   fly to o. that we know not of 250–1:20

   misfortunes and pains of o. 65:1

   o. abide our question 19:2

   pleased ourselves, we ... please o. 223:11

   some ... are more equal than o. 197:1

   to encourage the o. 321:10

Otherwise: some ... wise, and some ... o. 225:38, 303:20

Ounce: an o. of discretion 222:30

Ours: little we see in nature that is o. 333:3

Ourselves: fault ... not in our stars, but in o. 262:8

   praise o. in other men 202:13

Out: include me o. 124:5

   mordre wol o. 80:2

   murder will o. 221:21

   O., damned spot! o., I say! 272:2

   o. of sight, o. of mind 222:31

   o., o., brief candle! 272:10

   o., o., hyaena! 180:16

   who's in, who's o. 267:13

Outgrabe: mome raths o. 75:9

Outlive: desire shd. so ... o. performance? 256:19

Outrun: we may o. by violent swiftness 261:3

Outside: I am just going o. 196:7

Outsoared: he has o. the shadow of our night 297:16

Outward: hope from o. forms to win 87:9

   o. and visible sign 53:16

Oven: in the o. for baby and me 192:5

Over: now the day is o. 24:8

   'O. the hills and far away' 195:3

   until it doth run o. 14:14

Over much: be not righteous o. 39:21

Over-canopied with luscious woodbine 276:20

Overcast: since first our sky was o. 93:13

Overcoat: only argument ... put on yr. o. 163:1

Overcome: nature ... sometimes o. 22:26

   o. evil with good 47:27

   to o. pleasure ... greatest pleasure 223:13

   what is else not to be o.? 175:18

Overcomes: who o. by force 176:13

O(v)erjoyed was he to find 92:8

Overpaid: high official ... grossly o. 131:6

Overset the brain, or break the heart 332:12

Overthrow: those ... thou thinkest thou dost o. 101:4

Overwhelm myself in poesy 150:10

Overwhelmed all her litter but one 256:8

Owed: so much o. by so many to so few 82:15

Owes: he o. not any man 161:10

   o. its pleasure to another's pain 93:9

Owl: moping o. does to the moon complain 126:5

   nightly sings the staring o. 269:1

   old o. lived in an oak 231:26

   o., for all his feathers, was a-cold 147:12

   the O. and the Pussy-Cat 158:7

Owls: I couch when o. do fly 289:6

   two O. and a Hen 158:13

Own: came unto his o. and his o. received him not 46:16

   every country but his o. 118:5

   our watches ... each believes his o. 202:2

   room of one's o. 330:9

   we mean to hold our o. 83:6

Owner: the o. whereof was Giant Despair 63:11

   the ox knoweth his o. 40:16

Ox: a stalled o. and hatred 38:18

   nor his o., nor his ass 32:9

   o. knoweth his owner 40:16

   thou shalt not muzzle the o. 33:4

Oxenford: a Clerk ther was of O. 79:7

Oxford: ahead ... either O. or Cambridge 304:4

   the clever men at O. 124:13

   the king to O. sent a troop 60:4

   to ... O. I acknowledge no obligation 116:1

   to O. sent a troop of horse 318:1

Oxlips and the nodding violet 276:20

Oyster: an o. may be crossed in love 301:3

   the world's mine o. 276:4

Oysters: 'O, O.,' said the Carpenter 76:6

   poverty and o. 99:1

Ozymandias, king of kings 299:8

P's and Q's: to mind one's P. 222:32

Pace: creeps in this petty p. 272:10

Paced: bride hath p. into the hall 86:1
Pacem: qui desiderat p. 320:8
Paces about her room ... alone 107:5
Pacific: he stared at the P. 150–1:15
Pack: can p. the cards 22:16
Paddington: as London is to P. 72:17
Paddle: every man p. his own canoe 167:7
Padlock: clap yr. p. on her mind 205:5
  wedlock is a p. 230:3
Pagan suckled in a creed outworn 333:4
Pagans: to chase these p. in those holy fields
  253:14
Page: on a beautiful quarto p. 301:13
Pageant: this insubstantial p. faded 288:16
Paid: at cards for kisses—Cupid p. 163:3
  p. at the Greek Kalends 71:10
  two I am sure I have p. 254:15
  well p. that is well satisfied 275:7
Pail: to fetch a p. of water 190:6
Pain: a stranger yet to p. 125:13
  although p. isn't real 12:9
  cease upon the midnight with no p. 150:3
  hour of p. ... long as a day 217:7
  I feel no p., dear mother 15:9
  I love to give p. 89:12
  laughter with some p. is fraught 300:2
  long grief and p. 314:5
  neither shall there be any more p. 51:3
  not because it gave p. to the bear 164:7
  not in pleasure, but in rest from p. 104:9
  one who never inflicts p. 187:13
  owes its pleasure to another's p. 93:9
  p. clings cruelly to us 147:9
  sweet is pleasure after p. 103:14
  we are born in others' p. 316:8
  what p. it was to drown! 285:1
  when p. and anguish wring the brow 240:9
  who wd. lose, though full of p., this ... being
  176:19
  with p. purchas'd, doth inherit p. 268:7
Painful: no p. inch to gain 85:2
  one ... as p. as the other 21:10
Pains: for my p. a world of sighs 279:2
Paint: cheeks are covered with p. 186:1
  good face needs no p. 215:17
  looking as fresh as p. 303:2
  p. my picture truly like me 94:10
  p. the meadows with delight 268:17
  to p. the lily 264:19
Painted: face with nature's own hand p.
  293:16
  idle as a p. ship upon a p. ocean 86:5
  not so young as ... p. 26:7
Painters and poets ... lie 222:33
Painting a face ... not washing 114:7
Paintings: I have heard of your p. 251:4
Palace: a p. and a prison on each hand 69:6
  love in a p. 149:1
  my gorgeous p. for a hermitage 283:7
Palaces: cottages, princes' p. 274:6
Pale: p. cold cowardice 281:10
  p. grew thy cheek and cold 71:5
Palestine: to haven in sunny P. 168:13
Pall Mall Gazette is written by gentlemen
  315:8
Palladium of all the ... rights 146:5
Palm: an itching p. 263:22
  bear the p. alone 262:7
Palms: before my feet 81:3
Palpable: a very p. hit 253:7

Pan: what ... doing, the great god P. ? 60:9
Pancake: as flat as a p. 213:37
Pangs: more p. ... than wars or women have
  261:10
  p. of despis'd love 250–1:20
Panic: what a p.'s in thy breastie 66:10
Pansies, that's for thoughts 252:23
Pantaloon: lean and slipper'd p. 244:11
Paper: both sides of the p. at once 241:14
  he hath not eat p. 268:11
  if all the world were p. 14:1
  make dust our p. 283:5
Paper-mill: thou hast built a p. 260:11
Paradise: a p. to what we fear of death 273:11
  called the P. of Fools 177:11
  drunk the milk of P. 87:16
  England ... p. of women, the hell of horses
  67:10, 212:24
  P. of exiles, Italy 298:12
  such are the gates of P. 55:3
  this other Eden, demi-p. 282:5
  to P. by way of Kensal Green 81:8
  weave a p. for a sect 148:1
  Wilderness is P. enow 109:15
Paragon: the p. of animals! 250:6
Parchment: inky blots and rotten p. bonds
  282:6
Pard: bearded like the p. 244:11
Pardon: bret-ful of p. ... from Rome 79:19
  never ask p. before ... accused 221:30
Parent: to lose one p., Mr. Worthing 327:12
Parents: joys of p. are secret 21:17
  of p. good, of fist most valiant 259:9
  p. we can have but once 142:17
  what p. were created for 186:6
Paris: good Americans ... go to P. 328:8
  P. is well worth a mass 130:12
  P. vaut bien une messe 130:12
  the last time I saw P. 128:1
Parish: all the world as my p. 325:4
  born ... hanged ... in the same p. 12:5
Parliament: in the P. of man 313:17
Parliaments: England ... mother of p. 58:9
Parlour: 'tis the prettiest little p. 136:10
  will you walk into my p. ? 136:10
Parmaceti for an inward bruise 254:2
Parochial: worse than provincial—he was p.
  139:5
Parody: the devil's walking p. 81:2
Parole ... donnée à l'homme pour déguiser 311:1
Paroles ... pour déguiser leurs pensées 321:12
Parson: a p. much bemused in beer 201:11
  coughing drowns the p.'s saw 269:1
Part: every man must play a p. 274:1
  I have forgot my p. 246:11
  if ought but death p. thee and me 33:26
  kiss and p. 102:12
  p. of education ... p. of experience 22:13
  till death us do p. 53:22
Parted: when we two p. 71:5
Partial: more p. for the observer's sake 203:13
Particle: very fiery p. ... snuff'd out 70:6
Particular: a London p.—a fog, miss 97:9
  called away by p. business 301:16
Particulars: [do good] in Minute P. 55:6
Parties: both p. nobly are subdu'd 257:12
  hear all p. 216:23
Parting: do not let this p. grieve thee 17:4
  p. is all we know of heaven 99:15
  p. is such sweet sorrow 286:14

Parting (*continued*)
  stood at the p. of the way 41:22
  this p. was well made 264:4
Partitions: thin p. do their bounds divide
  102–3:17
Partridge in a pear tree 194:2
Parts: one man ... plays many p. 244:11
Party: ancient forms of p. strife 313:5
  neither p. ioser 257:12
  then none was for a p. 163:12
  there was an old p. of Lyme 183:1
  to p. gave up what was ... for mankind
  123:1
  true patriotism is of no p. 304:2
Pass: his ghost. O, let him p. 268:5
  I p. through the pores of the ocean 298:6
  she may ... p. for forty-three 120:15
  they shall not p. 199:16
Passed: he p. by on the other side 45:29
  so he p. over 63:16
  [time] wd. have p. in any case 26:1
Passeront: ils ne p. pas 199:16
Passes: everything p. ... perishes ... palls
  228:16
  p. at girls who wear glasses 198:2
Passing: did but see her p. by 17:2
  P. of the Third Floor Back 139:16
  p. the love of women 34:12
Passion: a master-p. is the love of news 93:18
  calm of mind, all p. spent 181:8
  in her first p. woman 69:17
  man that is not p.'s slave 252:1
  master mistress of my p. 293:16
  Queen was in a furious p. 74:11
  ruling p. conquers reason still 203:19
  strange fits of p. 335:2
  the p. and the life 87:9
Passion-flower: the p. at the gate 314:4
Passionless: hopeless grief is p. 60:8
Passions: all thy p., match'd with mine
  313:19
  hath not a Jew ... p.? 274:17
  in truth but two p., vanity and love 80:16
Past: a mischief that is p. and gone 279:3
  leave thy low-vaulted p. 134:5
  p. and to come seems best 256:13
  p. cure, p. care 222:34
  p. help ... p. grief 292:14
  p. my help ... p. my care 25:9
  remembrance of things p. 293:18
  study the p. ... divine the future 89:3
'Pastern' as the 'knee of a horse' 142:4
Pastoral-comical, historical-p. 250:9
Pastors: as some ungracious p. do 248:14
Pasture: sell the p. now to buy the horse
  258:9
Pastures: fresh woods, and p. new 175:6
  lie down in green p. 35:28
  on England's pleasant p. seen 55:8
Pat-a-cake, baker's man 192:5
Path: a beaten p. to his door 108:23
  p. of duty ... way to glory 314:11
Pathetic: That's what it is, P. 172:5
Pathless: pleasure in the p. woods 69:9
Paths: so many p. that wind 326:11
Patience: abusing of God's p. 276:3
  how poor ... that have not p.! 279:12
  in mean men we entitle p. 281:10
  p. is a flower 222:35
  p., money ... bring all ... to pass 222:36

Patience (*continued*)
  p. under ... sufferings 52:30
  sat like P. on a monument 291:7
  though p. be a tired mare 258:11
  though with p. He stands waiting 161:3
  ye have heard of the p. of Job 50:3
Patient: a p. etherised upon a table 106:11
  fury of a p. man 103:9
Patines: inlaid with p. of bright gold 275:8
Patria: dulce et decorum est pro p. mori 136:1
  pro p. ... liberis ... aris 238:1
Patrie: allons, enfants de la p. 236:11
Patriot: for a p., too cool 123:2
  such is the p.'s boast 123:14
Patriotic: if p. sentiment is wanted 118:1
Patriotism: I realize ... p. is not enough 78:1
  p. ... last refuge of a scoundrel 143:17
  true p. is of no party 304:2
Patriots: true p. we 25:2
Patron: a P., ... looks with unconcern 142:1
  p. ... a wretch ... with insolence 140:10
Pattern: thou cunning'st p. of ... nature
  280:11
Paul: one named Peter, the other named P.
  195:5
  rob Peter to pay P. 224:24
Pause: what dreams ... must give us p.
  250–1:20
Pawn: p. the Bechstein Grand 91:6
  you p. your intelligence 94:14
Pay: God make me able to p. 199:9
  p. ... in his own coin 222:37
  p. through the nose 222:38
  what one can p. others to do 169:7
  when will you p. me? 192:4
  you ought to p., you know 75:13
Pays: he who p. the piper 222:39
  p. yr. money ... takes yr. choice 231:18
Peace: a hard and bitter p. 153:1
  a p. above all earthly dignities 261:11
  a p. I hope with honour 100:7
  all her paths are p. 38:3
  better a lean p. 207:17
  blood of Jesus whispers p. 54:4
  calm world and a long p. 255:16
  cherish a just and lasting p. 159:15
  create desolation, call it p. 310:8
  for ever hold his p. 53:20
  for p. comes dropping slow 337:5
  give p. in our time, O Lord 52:16
  I am for p. ... they ... for war 37:14
  I shall have some p. there 337:5
  if p. cannot be ... with honour 237:7
  in P., Goodwill 83:13
  in what p. a Christian can die 9:12
  inglorious arts of p. 168:3
  live together in p. ... as good neighbours
  319:5
  never was ... a bad p. 113:2
  no p. ... unto the wicked 41:3
  nothing can bring you p. but yourself
  108:13
  on earth p., good will 45:22
  our p., our fearful innocence 333:11
  p., commerce, and honest friendship 139:9
  p. for our time ... p. with honour 78:10
  p. hath her victories 181:13
  p. is indivisible 160:3
  p. is of the nature of a conquest 257:12
  p. is poor reading 128:7

Peace (*continued*)
p. makes plenty 222:40
p. of God ... passeth all understanding 48:31
p. on earth and mercy mild 325:2
p., p., when there is no p. 41:12
p., perfect p. 54:4
p. shall go sleep with Turks 283:8
the Lord ... give thee p. 32:18
the Prince of P. 40:23
the soft phrase of p. 278:21
the thousand years of p. 313:6
their bodies are buried in p. 52:8
weak piping time of p. 284:11
when ... p. he was for p. 20:4
who desires p., prepare for war 320:8
Peaceably: living p. in their habitations 52:6
Peaceful: p. hours I once enjoyed 92:14
welcome p. evening in 93:10
Peace-maker: yr. If is the only p. 246:3
Peach: do I dare to eat a p.? 106:16
p. was once a bitter almond 318:16
Peacock: as proud as a p. 223:33
Peacocks and lilies for instance 237:3
Pear: and a golden p. 190:1
Pearl: barbaric p. and gold 176:15
heaps of p., inestimable stones 285:1
hillside's dew-p.'d 62:7
like the base Indian, threw a p. away 280–1:14
one p. of great price 44:13
sowed the earth with orient p. 178:12
Pearls: he who wd. search for p. must dive 103:16
neither cast ... p. before swine 44:6
p. that were his eyes 288:1
teeth like p. 62:6
Peas: I always eat p. with honey 13:10
Peccavi [I have Sind] 185:9
Pécher en silence 182:16
Pedigree: languages ... p. of nations 144:23
Peep about to find ... graves 262:8
Peeping: came p. in at morn 134:14
Peepshow: a ticket for the p. 164:14
Peer: a rhyming p. 201:11
when daffodils begin to p. 292:17
Peg: take one down a p. 227:2
Pelican: wonderful bird is the p. 170:6
Pelting: bide the p. of this pitiless storm 266:13
Pen: before my p. has glean'd 151:7
biting my truant p. 302:3
more cruel ... p. is than ... sword 67:9
p. is mightier than the sword 63:3
poet's p. turns them to shapes 277:6
Penance: hath p. done and p. more will do 86:15
Pence: take care of the p. 227:1
Penny: back again, like a bad p. 206:32
I spent a p. ... I lent a p. 190:2
in for a p., in for a pound 217:21
not given a p. for a song 337:3
p. and p. laid up 223:1
p. for yr. thoughts 223:2
p. wise, pound foolish 223:3
shall have but a p. a day 193:3
show me first yr. p. 193:4
turn an honest p. 228:29
two a p., hot cross buns 189:7
Pens: let other p. dwell on guilt 20:13

Pensée: se servent de la p. ... pour autoriser ... injustices 321:12
Pensées: paroles ... pour déguiser ... p. 321:12
Pension: p. never enriched a young man 223:4
p. ... pay given to a state hireling 140:11
Pensive: in vacant or in p. mood 331:11
Pent: long in city p. 151:6
long in populous city p. 179:9
Penury: age, ache, p., and imprisonment 273:11
People: a glorious p. vibrated again 299:2
all p. that on earth do dwell 153:4
among a p. generally corrupt 64:19
Continental p. have sex life 170:8
decent godless p. 107:1
for God's sake look after our p. 239:2
good of the p. ... chief law 84:2
good p. all, of every sort 122:18
government of the p., by the p. 159:13
if the good p. in their wisdom 159:6
indictment against an whole p. 64:6
it is what the p. think so 64:17
let my p. go 31:21
no p. do so much harm as 94:4
no vision, the p. perish 39:5
nor is the p.'s judgment ... true 103:8
observe the condition of the p. 146:6
p. agree with me ... I must be wrong 327:3
p. are ... charming or tedious 328:1
p. have good food ... table manners 170:7
p. who like this sort of thing 160:2
p.'s mothers ... bore me 328:13
raising up a p. of customers 303:4
such trivial p. shd. muse 157:11
the Irish are a fair p. 143:11
the p. all exulting 325:12
the p. are the masters 64:8
the p. that walked in darkness 40:22
thou art a stiffnecked p. 32:12
thy p. shall be my p. 33:25
Top P. 11:9
voice of the p. 10:2
what kind of a p. do they think 83:3
wholesome ... nice English p. 295:17
win friends and influence p. 73:12
wd. all have some p. under them 142:12
you can fool some of the p. 160:1
you live with rich p. 303:7
Peopled: the world must be p. 278:1
Pepper: enjoy the p. when he pleases 74:7
peck of pickled p. 192:6
Peppered: I have p. two of them 254:15
Perceives: the Man p. it die away 332:2
Perceiving *how not to do it* 98:4
Perception: if the doors of p. were cleansed 57:7
p. that something ought to be done 324:15
Percy: I am not yet of P.'s mind 254:12
old song of P. and Douglas 302:6
Perdition catch my soul 279:14
Perfect: he was a p. cavaliero 68:16
I had else been p. 271:6
p. little body 58:6
practice makes p. 223:22
Perfection: the pursuit of p. ... is 19:5
Performance: provokes desire ... takes away ... p. 270:14
Perfume: throw a p. on the violet 264:19
Perfumed: he was p. like a milliner 254:1

Perfumes: all the p. of Arabia will not sweeten
272:3

Perhaps: in search of a great p.   232:9

Perilous: bright stars, through the p. fight
153:6

cleanse ... bosom of that p. stuff   272:6

thought without learning is p.   89:4

Perils and dangers of this night   52:21

Perish: name ... will not p. in the dust   304:11

no vision, the people p.   39:5

shall not p. from the earth   159:13

thy money p. with thee   47:2

to p. ... swallowed up and lost   176–7:19

when your time has come to p.   118:9

whosoever believeth ... shd. not p.   46:21

Periwig: new p., make a great show   199:12

Perjured, murd'rous, bloody   294:11

Perk'd up in a glist'ring grief   261:4

Perplexed: being wrought, p. in the extreme
280–1:14

p. in a world of doubts   151:12

Persecuted: I am p. with letters   89:11

Persepolis: in triumph through P. ?   166:9

Persians and the Medes: among the laws of the
P.   34:26

Persons: comprehended two aspicious p.
278:10

God is no respecter of p.   47:5

no respect of place, p., nor time   291:4

should certain p. die before they sing   87:10

you tossed and gored several p.   143:3

Perspiration: genius ... ninety-nine per cent p.
105:8

Persuade: beauty ... doth of itself p.   295:5

Persuadest: almost thou p. me   47:14

Persuading others we convince ourselves
146:7

Persuasive: case [against wealth] never proved
widely p.   114:13

Pert as a school-girl   118:6

Perturbation: O polish'd p.! golden care!
257:16

Peru: mankind from China to P.   141:9

Pestilence: he ... breeds p.   57:2

p. that walketh in darkness   36:27

Petard: hoist with his own p.   216:35

Peter: dicky birds ... one named P.   195:5

rob P. to pay Paul   224:24

Shock-headed P.   133:11

thou art P., and upon this rock   44:16

Peter Piper picked a peck   192:6

Petty: a p. sneaking knave   56:1

Peut-être: chercher un grand p.   232:9

Phagocytes: stimulate the p.   295:16

Phantasma: like a p. or a hideous dream
262:13

Phantom: she was a P. of delight   334:12

Pharaoh: the Lord hardened P.'s heart   31:24

Philistian: resist P. gold   181:1

Philistines: Barbarians, P., Populace   19:6

Philosopher: all be that he was a p.   79:9

guide, p. and friend   203:11

nothing so absurd but some p. has said   84:1

there was never yet ...   278:17

tried ... in my time to be a p.   105:11

Philosophers: English are ... the least ... pure
p.   23:20

Philosophic: gild the p. pill!   121:3

Philosophy: a little p. inclineth ... to atheism
22:11

Philosophy (*continued*)

are dreamt of in your p.   249:12

history is p. teaching by examples   100:1

how charming is divine P.!   172:18

mere touch of cold p.   149:2

new p. calls all in doubt   100:16

p. is nothing but discretion   241:3

p. will clip an angel's wings   149:3

Phoebus: and P. 'gins arise   246:13

Delos rose, and P. sprung   69–70:21

Phrase: proverb'd with a grandsire p.   285:20

the soft p. of peace   278:21

Physic: for p. and farces   114:17

take p., pomp   266:14

Physician: honour a p.   52:3

is there no p. there ?   41:13

p., heal thyself   45:24

they that are whole ... no need of the p.
45:5

Physicians: few p. live well   213:22

p. of the utmost fame   27:3

Pianist: do not shoot the p.   327:19

Piccadilly: good-bye, P.   329:1

Picked a peck of pickled pepper   192:6

Picket: the p.'s off duty forever   26:10

Picking and stealing   53:14

Pickwick: Mr. P.   98:20, 22; 99:7

P., ... Owl ... Waverley pen   11:8

Pictures: book without p. and conversation
73:14

cutting all the p. out   26:14

Pie: blackbirds baked in a p.   193:5

eating a Christmas p.   191:2

finger in the p.   213:27

some of a pudding ... none of a p.   207:33

Pieces: broke into a thousand p.   24:11

Pie-crust: promises and p. ... to be broken
309:5

Pieman: Simple Simon met a p.   193:4

Pierian spring: taste not the P.   202:5

Pies: eat one of Bellamy's veal p.   200:11

Piety: nor all thy p. nor wit   110:12

renowned for larnin' and p.   125:4

Pig: a p. in a poke   209:1

stole a p. and away he run   195:4

the p. was eat   195:4

this little p. went to market   194:7

Pigeon: crooning like a bilious p.   296:18

Pigeon-livered: am p., and lack gall   250:17

Piggy-wig: a P. stood   158:8

Pigmy: darling of a p. size   332:3

fretted the p. body   102:17

Pigs: and whether p. have wings   76:4

p. might fly   223:5

Pike-staff: as plain as a p.   223:7

Pilate: P. saith ... What is truth ?   46:33

what is truth ? said jesting P.   21:8

Pilgrim: Honour comes, a p. grey   88:11

p. through this barren land   329:2

the P. of Eternity   297:13

to be a p.   63:13,14

Pilgrim's Progress ... interesting but tough
318:7

Pilgrimage: thus I'll take my p.   232:12

Pilgrims: we ben p.   79:21

Pill: gild the philosophic p.   121:3

Pillage ... with merry march bring home
258:8

Pillar: from p. to post   223:6

in his rising seemed a p. of state   177:3

Pillar (*continued*)
    she became a p. of salt 31:4
    triple p. of the world transform'd 242:9
Pillars: the four p. of government 22:8
    wisdom ... hewn out her seven p. 38:6
Pillows his chin upon ... wave 175:10
Pilot: a daring p. in extremity 102–3:17
Pimples: remark these roughnesses, p. 94:10
Pin: if I sit on a p. 12:9
    might have heard a p. drop 216:25
    my life at a p.'s fee 249:4
    serve to p. up one's hair 89:11
    with a little p. bores ... castle wall 283:6
    you might have heard a p. drop 234:15
Pinafore: Captain of the *P.* 119:10, 119:13
Pinch: one P., a ... lean-fac'd villain 246:5
Pine: p. for what is not 300:2
    this spray of Western p. 129:2
Pined: she p. in thought 291:7
Pines: eat the cones under his p. 113:13
Pink: the very p. of courtesy 286:17
Pint: drinka p.'a milka day 11:2
Pipe: a three-p. problem 101:13
    blow your p. ... till you burst 62:5
    he called for his p. 192:1
    in yr. p. and smoke it 223:37
    p. a song about a lamb 56:8
    p. to the spirit ditties 149:7
Piped: so I p. with merry cheer 56:8
Piper: Tom, he was a p.'s son 195:3
    Tom, Tom, the p.'s son 195:4
    who pays the p. may call the tune 222:39
Pipers: ten p. piping 194:2
Pipes: p. and whistles in his sound 244–5:11
    scrannel p. of wretched straw 175:4
    ye soft p., play on 149:7
Piping: helpless, naked, p. loud 56:3
    p. down the valleys wild 56:7
    p. songs of pleasant glee 56:7
    weak p. time of peace 284:11
Pippin: right as a Ribstone p. 27:9
Pippins: old p. toothsomest 324:1
Pistol: if his p. misses fire 124:2
Pistols: young ... carry p. ... old ones grub 295:7
Pit: black as the p. from pole to pole 130:8
    the bottomless p. 50:24
    what is in the p. 55:2
    whoso diggeth a p. 39:1
Pitch: bumping p. and a blinding light 187:11
    he that toucheth p. ... defiled 51:22
Pith: arms ... had seven years' p. 278:21
    enterprises of ... p. and moment 250–1:20
    my rhyme ... hath in it some p. 302:11
Pitied: better be envied than p. 207:22
Pitieth: the Lord p. them that fear 36:28
Pitiful: 'twas p., 'twas wondrous p. 279:2
Pitt is to Addington 72:17
Pity: a p. beyond all telling 337:9
    and never a saint took p. 86:10
    and p. 'tis 'tis true 249:17
    I p. the man who can travel 306:13
    loved her that she did p. them 279:2
    p. my simplicity 325:1
    the p. of it, Iago! ... the p.! 280:4
Place: a p. called ... Armageddon 50:27
    earth's the right p. for love 113:8
    give me a firm p. 18:3
    grave's a fine and private p. 167:14
    Great God! this is an awful p.! 239:1

Place (*continued*)
    love a p. the less for having suffered 20:16
    never the time and the p. 61:11
    p. of justice ... hallowed p. 23:11
    reign in this horrible p. 93:15
    savage p., as holy and enchanted 87:12
    the mind is its own p. 176:5
    vicious p. where thee he got 267:14
Places: all p. thou 179:17
    men in great p. 22:2
    praising ... exactly in the right p. 68:10
    proper words in proper p. 309:2
Placid: animals ... so p. and self-contained 326:2
Plague: a p. o' both your houses! 286:19
    a p. of all cowards! 254:13
    a p. of sighing and grief! 254:17
    make instruments to p. us 267:14
    p. o' these pickle-herring! 290:14
    the red p. rid you 287:19
Plagues: of all p. ... thy wrath can send 72:16.
    of all the p. ... woman ... worst 125:3
    p. that are written 51:4
    p. with which mankind are curst 96:10
Plain: all doctrines p. and clear 67:17
    did you ... see Shelley p. ? 61:10
    in meadow or p. 309:14
    p. as a pike-staff 223:7
    p. living and high thinking 333:11
    pricking on the plain 305:10
    virtue is ... best p. set 23:2
Plainly: honest tale ... p. told 285:9
Plaintive: the p. numbers flow 334:17
Plan: mighty maze! but not without a p. 202:17
Planet: measure every wandering p.'s course 166:10
    when a new p. swims into his ken 150:15
    while Jove's p. rises 61:5
Planets: the p., and this centre, observe degree 290:1
Planned: Who saith 'A whole I p.' 62:9
Plant: a Sensitive P. in a garden grew 299:14
Planted: feet firmly p. in the air 235:3
    I have p., Apollos watered 47:32
Platitude: a longitude with no p. 114:4
Plato: attachment *à la* P. 119:5
    P. is dear to me 18:7
Platter: they licked the p. clean 190:7
Play: all work and no p. 230:40
    an hour to p. ... last man in 187:11
    at Christmas p. and make good cheer 318:5
    better than a p. 78:17
    boys and girls come out to p. 188:6
    can pack ... cards ... cannot p. well 22:16
    good p. needs no epilogue 246:4
    I doubt some foul p. 248:12
    learnt to p. when he was young 195:3
    never ... go to a p. together 89:17
    p. first (second) fiddle 223:8
    p. up! and p. the game 187:12
    p. with the gypsies in the wood 191:9
    the p. ... pleas'd not the million 250:10
    the p.'s the thing wherein 250:19
    they p. from ten till four 231:12
    two can p. at that game 228:38
    where every man must p. a part 274:1
    Zephyrus did softly p. 305:15

Played: marks ... how you p. the game 233:12
Player: a walking shadow, a poor p. 272:10
Players: men and women merely p. 244:11
  mouth it, as ... p. do 251:7
Playing of the merry organ 15:8
Playmates: I have had p. ... old familiar faces 156:9
Plays: he p. best (well) that wins 223:9
  old p. begin to disgust 109:2
Plea: general good ... p. of the scoundrel 55:6
Pleasance: youth is full of p. 295:1
Pleasant: a few think him p. enough 158:6
  a p. fire our souls to regale 56:4
  abridgement of all ... p. in man 123:3
  green and p. land 55:8
  how p. to know Mr. Lear! 158:6
  on England's p. pastures seen ? 55:8
  p. in their lives 34:11
  p. thoughts bring sad 332:7
  p. ... to see ... name in print 70:12
  some day be p. to remember 321:1
  songs of p. glee 56:7
  standing on this p. lea 333:4
Pleasantest: one of the p. things ... a journey 129:11
Pleasantness: her ways are ways of p. 38:3
  the p. of an employment 21:3
Please: books cannot always p. 93:17
  in him alone 'twas natural to p. 102:15
  live to p., must p. to live 141:1
  say what they p. ... do what I p. 113:6
  seeketh not itself to p. 56:2
Pleased: as p. as Punch 223:10
  p. with what he gets 244:6
  when ... p. ourselves, we ... please 223:11
Pleases: every prospect p. 130:2
  one makes lovers ... as one p. 89:13
Pleasing: art of p. ... being pleased 129:13
Pleasure: a p. in the pathless woods 69:9
  business before p. 208:39
  but the privilege and p. 116:13
  dissipation without p. 116:2
  drinking is the soldier's p. 103:14
  every p. is of itself a good 144:13
  friend of P., Wisdom's aid 88:14
  gave p. to the spectators 164:7
  good, p., ease, content! 203:7
  great source of p. is variety 144:26
  happiness ... not in p. but in rest from pain 104:9
  hatred ... the longest p. 70:7
  love ceases to be a p. 26:11
  money gives me p. 27:10
  more p. in loving than ... loved 223:12
  no p. without pain 222:5
  no profit ... where is no p. 287:6
  owes its p. to another's pain 93:9
  p. ... is lost by coveting more 223:14
  p. is oft a visitant 147:9
  p. never is at home 148:3
  p. of the fleeting year 294:4
  p.'s a sin ... sin's a p. 69:13
  public stock of harmless p. 145:1
  refrain from the unholy p. 26:14
  short p., long lament 225:20
  some to business, some to p. take 203:15
  sweet is p. after pain 103:14
  though on p. she was bent 92:8
  to overcome p. is the greatest p. 223:13
  'twas for your p. you came 92:12

Pleasure (*continued*)
  variety ... soul of p. 26:12
  when Youth and P. meet 69:4
  written without effort ... read without p. 144:25
Pleasure-dome: a stately p. 87:11
  sunny p. with caves of ice 87:15
Pleasures: all the p. prove 167:1
  cannot understand the p. 20:7
  can sympathise ... not with their p. 137:11
  in unreproved p. free 174:1
  'mid p. and palaces 199:2
  no man is a hypocrite in his p. 144:20
  p. are like poppies spread 67:4
  the purest of human p. 23:4
  these p., Melancholy, give 173:13
  these pretty p. might me move 232:14
  we will some new p. prove 100:17
Pledge: I will p. with mine 145:7
  p. to each other our lives, our fortunes 139:7
Plenty: however p. silver dollars may become 84:10
  in delay there lies no p. 291:2
  p. makes me 197:15
  wasna fou, but just had p. 65:16
Pleure: il p. dans mon cœur 320:10
Plodders: small have continual p. ... won 268:8
Plot: the sonnet's scanty p. of ground 332:14
  this blessed p., this earth 282:5
Plough: having put his hand to the p. 45:26
Ploughman: heavy steps of the p. 337:7
  the p., near at hand 174:3
Plowman homeward plods 126:3
Pluck: p. from the memory a rooted sorrow 272:6
  sin will p. on sin 285:6
  we p. this flower, safety 254:10
Plucked: when I have p. thy rose 280:11
Plum: and pulled out a p. 191:2
  supping cold p. porridge 191:6
Poacher: a p. is a keeper 154:6
  old p. makes a good game-keeper 222:26
Pocket: a p. full of posies 193:2
  a p. full of rye 193:5
Pocket borough: by a p. into Parliament 119:16
Pocket-handkerchief: holding his p. 76:5
Pockets: p. in none of his clothes 28:9
  to line one's p. 219:14
Poem: I would rather have written that p. 330:5
  ought himself to be a true p. 182:1
  p. lovely as a tree 153:8
  p. must ride on ... melting 113:16
  p. ... worked ... not worried 113:16
Poems: dictionaries, and temporary p. 140:6
  Gert's p. are bunk 13:4
  p. are made by fools like me 153:9
Poesy: drainless shower of light is p. 150:12
  great end of p. ... shd. be a friend 150:13
  on the viewless wings of P. 149:16
  overwhelm myself in p. 150:10
Poet: a p. cd. not but be gay 331:10
  business of a p., said Imlac 141:5
  consecration, and the p.'s dream 331:1
  lunatic, the lover, and the p. 277:5
  p. and the dreamer are distinct 148:2
  p.'s eye, in a fine frenzy rolling 277:6

Poet (continued)
  p.'s pen turns ... to shapes   277:6
  say that when the P. dies   239:14
  Swift, you will never be a p.   104:12
  the p. sing it with such airs   337:3
  the p.'s inward pride   96:6
Poetess: a maudlin p., a rhyming peer   201:11
Poetic: which constitutes p. faith   87:19
Poetical: gods had made thee p.   245:9
Poetry: Fleshly School of P.   62:12
  homely definitions of prose and p.   88:3
  if P. comes not as naturally   151:15
  in p. ... in life ... ineffectual angel   19:9
  mincing p.   255:7
  not P., but prose run mad   201:15
  p. is the record of the best   300:10
  p. is the spontaneous overflow   336:7
  p. lifts the veil   300:9
  p. of earth is never dead   151:1
  p. shd. be great and unobtrusive   151:13
  p. shd. surprise by ... excess   151:14
  p.'s unnat'ral; no man ever talked p.   99:5
  truest p. is the most feigning   245:10
Poets: I shall be among the English P.   152:5
  our clever young p.   88:3
  painters and p. ... lie   222:33
  p. are the unacknowledged legislators   300:11
  p. [make men] witty   23:9
  p. that lasting marble seek   322:2
  souls of p. dead and gone   149:4
  such sights as youthful p. dream   174:7
  three p. in three distant Ages   104:11
  translunary things ... first p. had   102:11
Point: missed the p. completely, Julia   107:7
  p. his slow unmoving finger   280:5
  thus I bore my p.   254:15
  touch'd the highest p. of all my greatness   261:8
Poison: if you p. us, do we not die?   274:17
Poissons: nous attendons ... les p. aussi   83:1
Poke: buy a pig in a p.   209:1
  p. poor Billy   124:10
Poker: stiff as a p.   226:19
Pole: beloved from p. to p.   86:13
  soldier's p. is fall'n!   243:6
Police: friendship recognised by the p.   307:7
Policeman: a p.'s lot is not a happy one   120:6
  want to know the time, ask a P.   234:12
Policemen: sadists ... p. or butchers   90:4
Policy: honesty is the best p.   216:5
  p. of a good neighbour   235:1
  turn him to any cause of p.   258:7
Polished up the silver plate   184:8
Politely: hang you ... most p.   120:9
Political: man is ... a p. animal   18:5
  retired into ... p. Cave of Adullam   58:10
Politician: coffee, which makes the p. wise   204:10
  like a scurvy p. seem   267:7
  p. is an arse   94:12
Politicians: for P. neither love nor hate   103:2
  whole race of p. put together   309:1
Politics: confound their p.   73:2
  holy, mistaken zeal in p.   146:7
  my p., like my religion ... accommodatin'   322:10
  p. we bar ... not our bent   120:8
Poll: but talked like poor P.   115:2

Polly-wolly-doodle all the day   16:5
Poltagrue: My Lady P.   27:8
Polygamy: before p. was made a sin   102:14
Pomp: grinning at his p.   283:6
  p., and circumstance, of ... war   280:2
  take physic, p.   266:14
  the p. of power   126:8
  vain p. and glory of this world   261:10
Pompous: man is ... p. in the grave   60:3
Pomps and vanity of ... world   53:12
Poniards: she speaks p.   277:16
Pony: to town riding on a p.   196:4
Pooh: three cheers for P.!   172:11
Pooh-Bah (Lord High Everything Else)   117:14
Poor: a certain p. widow   45:15
  as p. as Job   223:15
  decent means p.   199:3
  leave [grapes] for the p. and stranger   32:15
  grind the faces of the p.   40:19
  he that considereth the P.   36:12
  how apt the p. are to be proud   291:11
  how p. ... that have not patience!   279:12
  Im one of the undeserving p.   296:21
  inconvenient to be p.   92:3
  it's the p. wot gets   16:13
  laws grind the p.   123:16
  makes me p. indeed   279:15
  my friends were p. but honest   242:3
  none so p. to do him reverence   263:14
  plenty makes me p.   197:15
  p. ... maimed ... halt ... blind   46:1
  p. old Joe   112:11
  poverty consists in feeling p.   108:19
  simple annals of the p.   126:7
  the p. man at his gate   10:5
  the p. shall never cease   33:3
  the riches of the p.!   145:18
  to be p. and independent   85:4
  too p. for a bribe   127:3
  ye have the p. always   45:1
Poor relations: even great men have their p.   97:11
Pop goes the weasel   165:5
Pope: better to err with P.   70:15
Poppies: in Flanders fields the p. blow   164:8
  pleasures are like p. spread   67:4
Populace: Barbarians, Philistines, P.   19:6
Population: only talked of p.   123:19
Porpentine: quills upon the fretful p.   249:7
Porpoise: there's a p. close behind us   75:2
Porridge: comfort like cold p.   288:3
  supping cold plum p.   191:6
Port: any p. in a storm   206:17
  p. after stormy seas   305:11
  p. for men   144:15
  the p. is near, the bells I hear   325:12
Porte: il faut qu'une p. soit ouverte ou fermée   185:5
Portend: late eclipses ... p. no good   265:9
Porter: Oh, mister P.   160:7
Porters: mechanic p. crowding in   258:8
Portion: any p. of the foreign world   322:16
  best p. of a good man's life   335:10
  he is a p. of the loveliness   298:1
Portrait of the Artist as a Young Man   146:4
Ports: all places ... are ... p. and happy havens   281:14
  p. of slumber open wide   257:16
Possessed: liberty ... limited ... to be p.   64:18

Prepare to meet Thy God 42:16

Preposterous? A thorough-paced absurdity 119:3

Presbyter: new P. is but old Priest 181:12

Presence: from whose unseen p. the leaves dead 299:3
lord of thy p. and no land 264:9
p. strengthens [love] 205:8
scanter of yr. maiden p. 249:1

Present: a very p. help in trouble 36:13
both perhaps p. in time future 106:3
no time like the p. 228:4
p. mirth hath p. laughter 291:2
p. only toucheth thee 66:13
things p., worst 256:13
un-birthday p. 76:9

Presents ... endear Absents 156:5

Preservation: creation, p., and all the blessings 53:1

President: rather be right than be P. 84:9

Press: god of our idolatry, the p. 93:3
misused the King's p. damnably 255:15
written of the power of the p. 319:6

Pressed: if it were p., would run 27:14
power p. too far and relaxed too much 22:15

Pretender: who P. is, or who is King 68:15

Pretty: where the girls are so p. 15:10

Prevail: gates of hell shall not p. 44:16
passion for making them p. 19:10

Prevention is better than cure 199:5, 223:26

Prey: have they not divided the p.? 33:16
smaller fleas that on him p. 309:4
to hastening ills a p. 122:5

Price: all those men have their p. 322:4
p. of everything ... value of nothing 328:4
p. of wisdom is above rubies 35:9
virtuous woman ... p. ... above rubies 39:8

Prick: how if honour p. me off? 255:21
if you p. us, do we not bleed? 274:17
no spur to p. the sides of my intent 270:6
pat it and p. it 192:5
when ... the nerves p. 312:14

Pricking: a gentle knight was p. on the plain 305:10

Pricks: kick against the p. 47:4

Pride: he that is low, no p. 63:15
look backward to with p. 113:10
perished in his p. 334:8
p. goeth before destruction 38:19
p. of kingly sway from out my heart 284:2
p., pomp, and circumstance, of ... war 280:2
p. that licks the dust 201:19
p., the ... vice of fools 202:4
p. will have a fall 223:27
the poet's inward p. 96:6
the p. of that country side 24:6

Priest: am I both p. and clerk? 284:1
free me of this turbulent p. 130:14
I tell thee, churlish p. 253:3
p. all shaven and shorn 194:8
p. is at the bottom of it [mischief] 222:1
youth ... still is Nature's p. 332:2

Priest-craft: ere p. did begin 102:14

Priests: of p. ... a charmin' variety 125:4

Prime: having lost but once yr. p. 132:8

Primrose: p. path of dalliance treads 248:14
p. way to th' everlasting bonfire 270:13
rathe p. that forsaken dies 175:5

Prince: the P. of Peace 40:23

Princes: hangs on p.' favours 261:10
put not yr. trust in p. 37:31
that sweet aspect of p. 261:10

Principalities: against p., against powers ... rulers 48:27

Principle: a p. in life with me, sir 297:7
don't believe in p. ... *do* in interest 162:11
fundamental p. of ... constitution 54:10
what is p. against ... flattery? 301:18

Principles: first, religious and moral p. 19:12
these two p.—right and wrong 159:10
they speak of p.—look out 20:1

Print: some said, John, p. it 63:5
to see one's name in p. 70:12

Printer: almost hear the p. saying damn 319:9

Printers: books by which the p. have lost 114:10

Printing: barbarous where there is no p. 143:8
cogent reasons for not p. ... subscribers 144:17
thou hast caused p. to be used 260:11

Priority: observe degree, p., and place 290:1

Prison: come, let's away to p. 267:13
dock in a pestilential p. 118:7
Lime-tree Bower my p. 87:17
palace ... p. on each hand 69:6
stone walls do not a p. make 162:5
this p. where I live 284:6

Prisoner: the jury, passing on the p.'s life 273:1

Prison-house: secrets of my p. 249:7
shades of the p. begin to close 332:1

Prithee, pretty maiden 119:6

Private: to the public good p. respects ... yield 181:2

Privilege: accursed power which stands on p. 27:7
but the p. and pleasure ... little errands 116:13

Privileged: the p. and the people ... two nations 100:12

Prize: men p. the thing ungain'd 289:15
not all that tempts ... is lawful p. 125:12
rain influence, and judge the p. 174:6
the p. we sought is won 325:12
too light winning make the p. light 288:2
what we have we p. not 278:12

Problem: quite a three-pipe p. 101:13

Problems: the p. of victory are more agreeable 83:8

Proceedings: subsequent p. interested him no more 129:3

Process: one long p. of getting tired 68:5

Procrastination is the thief of time 337:14

Procreate: we might p. like trees 60:1

Proctors: with prudes for p. 314:12

Prodigal: chariest maid is p. enough 248:13
Shimei, though not p. of pelf 103:7

Profane: O p. one! 58:2
so old, and so p. 258:3

Profaned: province ... desolated and p. 121:8

Profess: all who p. ... themselves Christians 52:28

Professions: let in some of all p. 270:13

Profit: my p. on't is, I know how to curse 287:19
no p. ... where ... no pleasure 287:6
the winds will blow the p. 164:15

Profit (*continued*)
 what p. hath a man of ... labour   39:10
 what shall it p. a man ?   45:10
Profits: small p. and quick returns   225:32
Progeny: a p. of learning   301:8
Prognostics do not ... prove prophecies   322:8
Progress: all p. ... desire ... to live beyond ...
 income   68:7
 history of England ... history of p.   164:5
 to promote social p.   319:5
Promethean: I know not where is that P. heat
 280:11
Promise of strength and manhood   58:6
Promises: he p. himself too much   142:17
 p. and pie-crust ... to be broken   309:5
 p. too much ... means nothing   223:28
Promising: pretty Thomasina ... once ... so p.
 113:17
Promontory: I sat upon a p.   276:18
Promotion: none will sweat but for p.   243:19
Prone to any iteration of nuptials   90:1
Pronounce: spell better than they p.   318:13
Proof of the pudding   223:29
Prop: you take my house ... take the p.   275:6
Propagate: endeavour to ... p. the best   19:8
Proper words in p. places   309:2
Properties: general p. and large appearances
 141:5
Property has its duties ... rights   102:13
Prophecies: prognostics do not always prove p.
 322:8
Prophecy: the trumpet of a p.   299:6
Prophesy: if you crown him, let me p.   283:8
Prophesying: ancestral voices p. war   87:14
Prophet: a p. is not without honour   44:14
 methinks I am a p. new inspir'd   282:4
 sons of the p. were brave   16:15
Prophetess: more than a p. ... uncommon
 pretty   105:13
Prophetic: O my p. soul!   249:10
 to something like p. strain   173:12
Prophets: beware of false p.   44:9
 is Saul ... among the p.   34:2
 wisest p. ... sure of the event first   322:8
Proportion: time is broke and no p. kept!
 284:7
Propose: whoever loves ... do not p.   101:2
Propriety: pleasantness ... does not ... evince ...
 p.   21:3
Proprium humani ingenii ... odisse   310:9
Prose: homely definitions of p. and poetry
 88:3
 in p. and verse was own'd ... absolute
 104:13
 je dis de la p.   182:13
 p. run mad   201:15
 talking p. for over forty years   182:13
 unattempted yet in p. or rhyme   175:16
Prospect: noblest p. ... Scotchman ever sees
 142:8
 p. is ... better than possession   223:30
 though every p. pleases   130:2
Prospects: died when his p. ... brightening
 11:18
 on p. drear   66:13
Prosper: treason doth never p.   128:13
Prosperity: a jest's p. lies in the ear   268:16
 a man to have been in p.   80:5
 him that stood in greet p.   80:1
 p. doth best discover vice   21:15

Prosperity (*continued*)
 p. has damned more ... than ... devils
 223:31
 p. is the blessing of the Old Testament
 21:13
 p.'s the very bond of love   293:5
 you will see a state of p.   164:12
Prospers: Hope ... turns Ashes—or it p.
 110:1
Protest: the lady doth p. too much   252:4
Proteus rising from the sea   333:4
Protracted: life p. is p. woe   141:12
Proud: Americans ... p. of ... ancient heritage
 153:1
 as p. as Lucifer   223:32
 as p. as a peacock   223:33
 being too p. to fight   329:7
 death, be not p.   101:4
 how apt the poor are to be p.   291:11
 I might grow p. the while   132:2
 p. me no prouds   287:1
 too p. for a wit   123:2
 too p. to importune   127:3
Prouder: never, I ween, was a p. seen   24:5
Prove: might p. anything by figures   73:4
 prov'd true before, p. false again   67:17
Proved: likely ... to have p. most royal
 253:12
 p. true before, prove false again   67:17
 which was to be p.   108:26
Proverb: a p. is much matter   114:8
 the p. is something musty   252:6
Providence: assert Eternal P.   175:17
 P. their guide   179:18
 reasoned high of P., Foreknowledge   177:6
Province: all knowledge to be my p.   23:14
 p. they [Turks] have desolated   121:8
Provincial: worse than p.—he was parochial
 139:5
Prudes: with p. for proctors   314:12
Pruning-hooks: swords into plowshares, ...
 spears into p.   40:18
Prussia: war ... national industry of P.   182:12
Prussian: French, or Turk, or P.   120:3
Psalmist: the sweet p. of Israel   34:15
Psaltery: sing unto him with the p.   36:4
Public: British p. in one of its ... fits   164:6
 deliberation sat, and p. care   177:3
 dislike the favour of the p.   152:9
 how p., like a frog   99:14
 mean, stupid, dastardly, ... p.   129:12
 never in touch with p. opinion   328:11
 reasons for ... not speaking in p.   143:15
 the sound of p. scorn   179:12
 wash clean linen in p.   229:29
 washing ... dirty linen in p.   327:9
Public house: vidders ... if they've kept a p.
 98:24
Public meeting: speaks ... as if I was a p.
 320:12
Public opinion: researchers into p.   20:4
Public schools are the nurseries of vice
 109:10
Publican: how like a fawning p.   274:7
Publish: I'll p., right or wrong   70:11
 p. and be damned   324:11
 p. it not in the streets   34:10
Publisher: now Barabbas was a p.   72:11
Publishers: with irrational fear of life become
 p.   90:4

Pudding: a p. hath two [ends] 212:37
  better some of a p. 207:33
  proof of the p. is in the eating 223:29
Puff direct ... preliminary ... collateral 301:1
Puffing is of various sorts 301:1
Puissant et solitaire 320:13
Puking: infant, mewling and p. 244:11
Pullet-sperm: no p. in my brewage 276:7
Pulse: feeling a woman's p. 306:14
  two people with one p. 165:2
  when the p. begins to throb 58:15
Pumpkins: where the early p. blow 158:2
Punch: as pleased as P. 223:10
Punctuality is the politeness of kings 162:4
Punctures: pin ... p. my skin 12:9
Punishment: as I deserve, pay on my p.
  180:14
  the p. fit the crime 118:10
Puppets: God, whose p. ... are we 62:8
Purchased: thought ... gift of God may be p.
  47:2
Pure: as p. as snow 251:3
  because my heart is p. 314:19
  blessed are the p. in heart 43:16
  more p. than his Maker 35:2
  p. as an angel 310:11
  p. as the naked heavens 333:13
  p. unbounded love thou art 325:3
  things are p. ... lovely ... of good report
    49:1
  unto the p. all things are p. 49:18
Purest: garden ... p. of human pleasures 23:4
Purgatory: England ... p. of men 111:4
  no other p. but a woman 25:10
Purge: I'll p., and leave sack 256:5
  p. me with hyssop 36:14
Puritan: saw a P.-one hanging of his cat 58:2
  the P. hated bear-baiting 164:7
Purlieus: dusty p. of the law 312:18
Purple: I never saw a P. Cow 64:1
  I wrote the 'P. Cow' 64:2
  p. the sails, and so perfumed 242:14
Purpose: cite Scripture for his p. 274:8
Purse; ask thy p. what thou shdst. buy 206:25
  heavy p. ... light heart 216:27
  light p. ... heavy heart 219:9
  little and often fills the p. 219:17
  p. ... full of other men's money 212:21
  put money in thy p. 279:6
  remedy against ... consumption of the p.
    256:12
  silk p. out of a sow's ear 225:24
  who steals my p. steals trash 279:15
Purses: our p. shall be proud 287:11
  wine and wenches empty ... p. 230:19
Purse-strings are ... common ties 223:36
Pursuing: faint, yet p. 33:17
Pursuit of perfection ... is the p. of sweetness
  19:5
Pussy: Owl and the P.-cat 158:7
  P. cat, where have you been? 192:7
  P.'s in the well 188:9
Put: p. off holiness and p. on intellect 55:7
  up with which I will not p. 83:12
Putting milk into babies 83:9
Pye: than shine with P. 70:15
Pyramides: du haut de ces p. 185:10
Pyramids: from the summit of these p.
  185:10
Pyramus: Death of P. and Thisby 276:13

Pyrénées: il n'y a plus de P. 162:3
Pyrenees no longer exist 162:3

Quad: no one about in the Q. 155:14
Quadruplets, not twins 13:2
Qualified: few are q. to shine in company
  309:9
Qualities: man, with all his noble q. 95:10
  such q. as wd. wear well 123:20
Quality: men of good q. 322:17
  q. of mercy is not strain'd 275:1
  royal banner and all q. 280:2
Quantities: wept ... to see such q. of sand 76:2
Quarrel: beware of entrance to a q. 248:16
  find q. in a straw 252:19
  sudden and quick in q. 244:11
  takes two to make a q. 229:6
Quarrelling: satisfaction in q. with her 301:14
Quarrels: bad workman q. with his tools
  206:34
  lovers' q. ... renewal of love 315:2
  those who in q. interpose 115:11
Quarter: any mistake ... in any q. 83:6
Quarterly: 'I', says the Q. 70:17
  nothing a year, paid q. 308:9
Quarto: on a beautiful q. page 301:13
Quean: the flaunting, extravagant q. 301:17
Quebec: rather have written ... poem ... than
  take Q. 330:5
Queen: another Sheba Q. 329:10
  cruel q. died ... post-mortem ... revealed
    241:11
  goddess and maiden and q. 310:3
  I'm to be Q. of the May 314:7
  I wd. not be a q. 261:5
  in good Q. Bess's glorious days 117:10
  'leg of mutton,' said the Red Q. 77:10
  'no!' said the Q. 'Sentence first' 75:8
  q. and huntress, chaste and fair 145:8
  Q. Anne is dead 223:39
  Q. asked the Dairymaid 171:11
  Q. of Hearts, she made some tarts 75:6,
    192:8
  q. was in a furious passion 74:11
  q. was in the parlour 193:5
  Red Q. sharply interrupted 77:8
  Ruler of the Q.'s Navee 119:15,16
  the mobled q. 250:11
  to London to look at the q. 192:7
Queens have died young and fair 186:12
Queer: all ... q. save thee and me 197:17
  drink to the q. old Dean 305:20
  ill-tempered and q. 158:6
Quench: foul water will q. fire 214:14
  if I q. thee, thou flaming minister 280:11
  many waters cannot q. love 40:15
  smoking flax ... not q. 41:2
  wine in the bottle does not q. 230:20
Question: others abide our q. Thou art free
  19:2
  sees both sides of q. ... sees ... nothing 327:1
  the q. ... wd. it bring a blush 98:16
  two sides to every q. 229:4
Questions: animals ... ask no q. 105:16
  answered three q. and that is enough 74:4
  ask me no q. 123:10
  ask no q. ... be told no lies 206:24
  education ... asking q. all the time 324:18
  not one of us is asking q. 324:18
Queue: an orderly q. of one 170:9

Quickly: gives twice who gives q. 214:35
  good and q. seldom meet 215:14
Quiet: all q. along the Potomac 26:10
  All Q. on the Western Front 233:7
  anything for a q. life 206:18
  holy time is q. as a nun 333:2
  in q. she reposes 18:16
  made q. by the power of harmony 335:12
  my scallop-shell of q. 232:12
  Saturn, q. as a stone 148:4
Quietness: bride of q. 149:6
  king ... men ... made ... for q.' sake 241:5
Quietus: he himself might his q. make
  250–1:20
Quills upon the fretful porpentine 249:7
Quince: mince and slices of q. 158:9
Quinquireme of Nineveh 168:13
Quintessence: what is this q. of dust? 250:6
Quintili Vare, legiones redde 71:9
Quintilius Varus, give me ... my legions 71:9
Quip: second, the Q. Modest 246:2
Quips and Cranks and wanton Wiles 173:16
Quires and places where they sing 52:18
Quiring to the young-ey'd cherubins 275:8
Quit: like doth q. like 273:14
  q. yourselves like men 34:1
Quiver: willows whiten, aspens q. 313:12
Quod erat demonstrandum 108:26
Quotation: every q. contributes something
  140:3
Quotations: a book that furnishes no q. 199:4
Quote: by necessity ... delight, we all q.
  108:15
  grow immortal as they q. 337:11
  I'll kill you if you q. it 64:2
  I q. the fights historical 120:4
Quoter: next to originator ... is the first q.
  108:14

Rabbit: the r. has a charming face 14:6
Race: earth ... will no longer tolerate the r.
  23:23
  he rides a r. 92:9
  pernicious r. ... of odious vermin 308:16
  slow and steady wins the r. 160:8
  some new r., called Man 177:4
  the human r., to which so many ... belong
  81:12
  the r. dwelling all round the globe 83:14
  the r. is not to the swift 39:23
  whole r. of politicians 309:1
Races: human species ... two distinct r. 156:2
Rachel weeping for her children 43:9
Rack: leave not a r. behind 288:16
  ship has weather'd every r. 325:12
  the r. of this tough world 268:5
  then we r. the value 278:12
Radical ... with both feet ... in the air 235:3
Rage: disguise ... nature with hard-favour'd r.
  259:3
  puts all Heaven in a r. 54:13
  r., r., against the dying 315:15
Ragged: though my ryme be r., tattered
  302:11
Raggedness: loop'd and window'd r. 266:13
Rags: heaven in r. than to hell in embroidery
  207:29
  no scandal like r. 109:3
  sat in unwomanly r. 135:3
Rail: I'll r. against ... first-born 244:7

Rail (*continued*)
  whiles I am a beggar, I will r. 264:14
Rain: being read to ... waiting for r. 106:5
  droppeth as the gentle r. from heaven
  275:1
  hath the r. a father? 35:13
  I dissolve it in r. 298:5
  in thunder, lightning, or in r. 269:3
  nor r., wind, thunder ... my daughters
  266:7
  r. before seven; fine before eleven 224:1
  r., r., go to Spain 224:2
  right as r. 224:21
  ripple of r. 309:16
  rudely r. beaten ... moth-eaten 302:11
  sendeth r. on ... just ... unjust 43:21
  still falls the r. 302:9
  stirring ... roots with spring r. 107:3
  the r. came heavily ... in floods 334:7
  the r. is full of ghosts 170:14
  the r. is over and gone 40:8
  the r. it raineth every day 292:3
  the r. it raineth on the just 57:14
  the wind and the r. 292:3
Rainbow: a r. in the sky 333:8
  add another hue unto the r. 264:19
  the r. comes and goes 331:13
Rains: it never r. but it pours 224:3
Rainy: lay it up for a r. day 224:4
  the weather when it is not r. 68:17
Raisons que la raison ne connaît point 198:8
Rake: every woman is at heart a r. 203:15
  excuse for thus playing the r. 184:3
  lean as a r. 218:29
  lene was his hors as is a r. 79:8
  man's a ribald ... a r. 120:10
Rampallion: you r.! 256:14
Rampart: his corse to the r. we hurried
  330:3
Ramparts: o'er the r. we watched 153:6
Ran: Georgie Porgie r. away 189:3
  grief with a glass that r. 309:15
  the sacred river r. 87:11, 87:13
Range with humble livers in content 261:4
Rank is good, and gold is fair 326:6
Rankers: gentlemen r. 154:15
Ranks: all service r. the same with God
  62:8
  even the r. of Tuscany 164:1
Rap and knock and enter in our soul 60:13
Rapidity: travelling ... dull in ... proportion to
  its r. 237:1
Rapidly: yes, but not so r. 26:1
Rapscallions: all kings is mostly r. 318:9
Rapture: a r. on the lonely shore 69:9
  first fine careless r. 61:3
Raptures: the r. and roses of vice 309:17
Rare: I think my love as r. 294:14
  she was indeed a r. one 329:10
Rarely, rarely, comest thou 300:4
Rascal: a dull and muddy-mettl'd r. 250:16
  get down you dirty r. 190:3
Rashes: green grow the r. 66:1
Rasselas, prince of Abyssinia 141:3
Rat: a dog, a horse, a r. have life 268:4
  a r.? Dead, for a ducat 252:12
  cat that killed the r. 194–5:8
  Mr. Speaker, I smell a r. 234:3
  to smell a r. 225:33
Rate: brings down the r. of usance 274:7

Rated: in the Rialto you have r. me 274:9
Rather: he had r. have a turnip 140:17
  I live ... r. as a Spectator 9:6
Rationed: liberty ... so precious ... it must be r. 159:3
Rats: out ... the r. came tumbling 62:3
  r. desert a sinking ship 224:5
  r.! they fought the dogs 61:17
  rid your town of r. 62:2
Rattle: spoiled his nice new r. 75:14
Rave: old age shd. burn and r. 315:15
Raven: quoth the R., Nevermore 200:19
  yr. locks were like the r. 66:5
Ravens: there were three r. 11:15
Ray: gem of purest r. serene 126:10
Raze out the ... troubles of the brain 272:6
Reach: man's r. shd. exceed his grasp 60:11
Read: classic ... everybody wants to have r. 319:2
  classic ... nobody wants to r. 319:2
  I r. much of the night 107:4
  I've r. in many a novel 72:2
  r. ... as inclination leads him 142:9
  r., mark, learn 53:2
  sins were scarlet ... books were r. 27:5
  sooner r. a time-table ... than nothing 169:6
  what do you r., my lord? 250:2
  without an intention to r. it 143:10
Reader: last r. reads no more 13:12
Readers: the human race, to which ... r. belong 81:12
Reading: I prefer r. 303:8
  peace is poor r. 128:7
  r. is to the mind 306:8
  r. maketh a full man 23:8
  when ... not walking, I am r. 156:6
  writer's time is spent in r. 143:16
Ready: conference [maketh] a r. man 23:8
  we always are r. 115:1
Real: although pain isn't r. 12:9
Realistic: when statesmen ... say ... r. 20:1
Reality: between the idea and the r. 106:8
  cannot bear very much r. 106:4
Realm: this earth, this r., this England 282:5
Realms: constancy lives in r. above 87:7
  who dwell in r. of day 55:1
Reap: men that sow to r. 309:18
  shall r. the whirlwind 42:9
Reaped: wheat which never shd. be r. 317:17
Reason: all r. is against it 68:8
  Cornish men will know the r. why 129:4
  divorced old barren R. 110:9
  do ... r. themselves out again 260:4
  have I not r. to lament 332:8
  in erring r.'s spite 203:4
  no other but a woman's r. 292:5
  O, r. not the need 266:2
  or any other r. why 10:2
  r. and energy, love and hate 56:15
  r. is left free to combat it 139:8
  r. is our soul's left hand 100:18
  r. why I cannot tell 59:9
  reasons which r. does not know 198:8
  right deed for the wrong r. 107:10
  ruling passion conquers r. still 203:19
  teach my necessity to r. thus 281:14
  theirs not to r. why 311:11
  worse appear the better r. 176:18
Reasonable: a r. good ear in music 277:4

Reasoned high of Providence 177:6
Reasons: the heart has its r. 198:8
Rebel: thinking man is bound to r. 138:3
Rebellion lay in his way 255:19
Rebels: dear earth ... though r. wound thee 283:1
Rebuke: boldly r. vice 53:8
  open r. is better than secret love 39:2
Recapture: think he never could r. 61:3
Reckless what I do to spite the world 271:2
Recommendation: self-praise is no r. 225:12
Recompense: heaven did a r. ... send 126:14
Record: puts a r. on the gramophone 107:5
Recover: die of it do seldom ... r. 243:8
Recte: si possis r., si non, quocumque modo rem 135:11
Reculer: il faut r. pour mieux sauter 217:15
Red: coral is far more r. than her lips' r. 294:13
  grace to get ... r. in the face 29:7
  her lips were r., her looks were free 86:8
  keep the R. Flag flying 90:3
  like a r. r. rose 66:15
  making the green one r. 270:12
  nature, r. in tooth and claw 312:17
  r. as a rose 224:6
  r. as a rose is she 86:1
  r. rag to a bull 224:7
  sun ... curtained with cloudy r. 175:10
  sunset ... one glorious blood-r. 61:4
  the one in r. cravat 99:18
  the r. plague rid you 287:19
  the R. Queen 77:8,10
Red brick: not even r., but white tile 197:12
Red-breast: the r. whistles 147:5
Rede: recks not his own r. 248:14
Redeemer: I know that my r. liveth 35:8
Redemption: condemn'd into everlasting r. 278:15
  no r. from hell 224:8
Redress: things past r. ... past care 282:11
Reed: a bruised r. shall he not break 41:2
  r. shaken with the wind 44:11
Reeds: down in the r. by the river 60:9
Reeking into Cadiz Bay 61:4
Reeling and Writhing 74:15
References: always verify yr. r. 236:13
Reflect: when I r. that God is just 139:13
Reformation: reforming of R. itself 182:7
Reforming: nothing so needs r. as ... habits 319:1
Refrain: did ... from expensive sins r. 103:6
Refreshment: the most perfect r. 20:12
Refuge: eternal God is thy r. 33:9
  God is our r. and strength 36:13
  idleness ... r. of weak minds 80:15
Refugees: the guttural sorrow of the r. 165:1
Regard: where ... least r. for human freedom 305:6
Regiment: four elements warring ... for r. 166:10
  led his r. from behind 116:6
  Monstrous R. of Women 155:13
Region: in thrilling r. of thick-ribbed ice 273:10
Regions: double lived in r. new 147:6
  r. Caesar never knew 92:2
Regret: youth is a blunder ... old age a r. 100:9
Regrets: past R. and future Fears 110:2

Requests: thou wilt grant their r.   52:19
Require: what doth the Lord r.?   42:24
Requires: all the human frame r.   27:4
Researchers: our r. into public opinion   20:4
Resemble: when I r. her to thee   322:1
Resent: no individual cd. r. ... thousands ... meant   308:13
Resist: can r. everything except temptation   328:2
  r. the devil and he will flee   50:2
Resisting: not over-fond of r. temptation   26:3
Resolute: be bloody, bold and r.   271:15
Resolution: in War: R.   83:13
  native hue of r.   250-1:20
  what r. from despair   176:3
Resolved to live a fool   25:7
Resolves; and re-resolves; then dies the same   338:1
Resort: far from all r. of mirth   173:9
Resource: infinite—r.—and—sagacity   155:10
Respect: is there no r. of place ... time?   291:4
  the r. that makes calamity   250-1:20
Respectable: r. means rich   199:3
  when was genius found r.?   60:6
Respecter of persons   47:5
Respects: he that r. not is not respected   224:14
Responsibility: liberty means r. ... men dread it   296:12
  no sense of r. [baby]   155:15
Rest: absence of occupation is not r.   93:4
  angels sing thee to thy r.   253:11
  far better r. that I go to   99:12
  God ... ordain'd no r.   320:6
  run far faster than the r.   27:14
  set up my everlasting r.   287:4
  she's at r., and so am I   104:5
  so may he r.   261:14
  some ill a-brewing towards my r.   274:13
  the r. is silence   253:16
  the r. of his dull life   25:7
  wear ourselves, and never r.   166:10
Restoration: the Church's R. in 1883   29:11
Restraint: firm r. with which they write   72:6
Resumed: democracy r. her reign   27:7
Reticulated or decussated   140:8
Retire me to my Milan   289:8
Retired into ... political Cave of Adullam   58:10
Retirement: short r. urges sweet return   179:8
Retort: first the R. Courteous   246:2
Retreat: let us make an honourable r.   245:4
Return: art gone, and never must r.   174:14
  departed never to r.   67:6
  short retirement urges sweet r.   179:8
  unto dust shalt thou r.   30:14
Returns: and the day r. too soon   71:4
  small profits and quick r.   225:32
Reveal: words ... half r. ... half conceal   312:12
Reveals: soberness conceals what drunkenness r.   225:37
Revelry: sound of r. by night   69:3
Revels: our r. now are ended   288:16
Revenge: prompted to my r. by heaven   250:18
  r., at first though sweet   179:7
  r. his foul ... unnatural murder   249:8
  r. is a kind of wild justice   21:12
  r. is sweet   224:15
  r. never repairs   224:16

Revenge (*continued*)
  shall we not r.?   274:17
  spur my dull r.   252:17
  study of r., immortal hate   175:18
  sweet is r.—especially to women   69:12
  sweet r. grows harsh   280:12
Revenges: time brings in his r.   292:2
Reverence: none so poor to do him r.   263:14
  yet r. ... doth make distinction   247:7
Reviewing: read a book before r. it   303:16
Revolt: a r.? No, Sire, ... a revolution   234:10
  inferiors r. in order that   18:6
Révolte: c'est une r.? non ... une révolution   234:10
Revolution: a revolt? No, sire, ... a r.   234:10
Révolution: une révolte? Non ... une r.   234:10
Revolutionist: not a r., is an inferior   296:9
Revolutions: state of mind which creates r.   18:6
Reward: only r. of virtue is virtue   108:5
  r. of a thing well done   108:8
  the Lord shall r. thee   38:28
  virtue is its own r.   229:18
Rheims: Cardinal Lord Archbishop of R.   24:5
Rhetorician: a sophistical r. inebriated [Gladstone]   100:8
Rheumatic of shoulder   57:15
Rhodope: brighter than is ... R.   166:7
Rhyme: build the lofty r.   174:13
  r. being no necessary adjunct   175:14
  r. themselves into ladies' favours   260:4
  soft names in many a mused r.   150:3
  still more tired of r.   27:10
  though my r. be ragged   302:11
Rialto: in the R. you have rated me   274:9
Rib: r. ... made he a woman   30:8
  smote him under the fifth r.   34:13
Riband: just for a r. ... in his coat   61:8
  r. in the cap of youth   252:24
Ribstone pippin: right as a R.   27:9
Rich: adversity makes ... not r.   206:5
  being r., my virtue ... shall be   264:14
  better to live r. than to die r.   144:11
  born lucky than r.   207:21
  good workmen are seldom r.   215:25
  God help the r.   215:6
  grew so r. that I was sent   119:16
  he is r. that is satisfied   224:18
  health! the blessing of the r.!   145:18
  if I ever become a r. man   28:3
  maketh haste to be r.   39:4
  never be handsome, strong, r.   216:3
  no sin but to be r.   264:14
  one law for the r.   218:23
  over the r. Dead   59:1
  passing r. with forty pounds a year   122:9
  Poor Little R. Girl   91:11
  poverty is an anomaly to r. people   23:21
  respectable means r.   199:3
  r. can help themselves   215:5
  r. man to enter ... kingdom of God   44:23
  r. men have no faults   224:17
  r. men rule the law   123:16
  r. not gaudy   248:16
  r. what gets the gravy   16:13
  seems it r. to die   150:3
  the r. man in his castle   10:5
  victim of a r. man's game   16:11
  when I grow r., say the bells   192:4

Rich (*continued*)
  widows are always r. 230:14
  wretchedness of being r. 303:7
Richard: body of R. Hind 12:3
  we came in with R. Conqueror 287:5
Richer: for r. for poorer 53:22
  r. than doing nothing for a bribe 247:3
Riches: infinite r. in a little room 166:4
  of great r. ... no real use 22:25
  r. are for spending 22:22
  r. I hold in light esteem 58:14
  r. of the mind ... make ... rich 224:19
  to r., dignity and power 28:1
Richly: a lady r. left 274:4
Rickshaw: it's no go the r. 164:14
Rid: idea of getting r. of it [work] 139:15
  if I can r. your town 62:2
Riddle: r. wrapped in a mystery 82:10
Ride: a poem must r. 113:16
  Haggards r. no more 306:10
  r. a cock-horse 193:1
  r. in triumph through Persepolis 166:9
  went for a r. on a tiger 12:10
  when he next doth r. abroad 92:13
Rideau: tirez le r., la farce est jouée 232:8
Rider: secret ... between a r. and his horse 308:10
Rides: and r. upon the storm 92:15
Ridicule: easier to r. than commend 224:20
Ridiculous: is not this r. ? 119:3
  one step above the r. 197:18
  sublime to the r. 185:11
  the sublime and the r. ... nearly related 197:18
Riding: r. to and from his wife 325:8
  Yankee Doodle ... r. on a pony 196:4
Ridley: be of good comfort, Master R. 157:2
Rien appris ... oublié 310:12
Rifle all the breathing spring 88:8
Rift: load every r. of yr. subject 152:12
Riga: young lady of R. 12:10
Right: a r. judgement in all things 53:5
  all goes r. and nothing ... wrong 120:13
  all's r. with the world 62:7
  an earl by r., by courtesy a man 21:5
  defend to the death your r. 321:18
  do the r. deed for the wrong reason 107:10
  earth's the r. place for love 113:8
  great r. ... a little wrong 275:2
  I'll publish, r. or wrong 70:11
  it must be r. I've done it from my youth 93:16
  know not whether laws be r. 326:15
  majority never has r. on its side 138:3
  my r. there is none to dispute 93:14
  never dreamed, though r. were worsted 60:12
  no r. to strike against the public safety 90:10
  our country, r. or wrong 96:7
  rather be r. than be President 84:9
  r. as a Ribstone Pippin 27:9
  r. as rain 224:21
  r. divine of kings to govern wrong 201:3
  r. in his own eyes 33:24
  shall not the Judge ... do r. ? 31:2
  think at yr. age, it is r. ? 74:3
  think the last opinion r. 202:12
  too fond of the r. 123:2
  two wrongs don't make a r. 229:7
  with firmness in the r. 159:15

Righteous: be not r. over much 39:21
  die the death of the r. 32:20
  if I find ... fifty r. 31:3
  judge r. judgment 46:23
  souls of the r. are in the hand of God 51:12
Righteousness: r. exalteth a nation 38:15
  the Sun of r. arise 43:7
Rights: endowed ... with certain unalienable r. 139:6
  property has its duties ... its r. 102:13
  reaffirm faith in fundamental ... r. 319:5
Rigol: from this golden r. hath divorc'd 257:17
Rigour of the game 156:4
Ring: r. at the end of his nose 158:8
  spring ... the only pretty r. time 245:16
  with this r. I thee wed 53:24
Ring-a-ring o' roses 193:2
Rings: my true love sent ... five gold r. 194:2
  r. on her fingers 193:1
Riot: rash fierce blaze of r. cannot last 282:4
  r. and dishonour stain the brow 253:15
Ripe: from hour to hour, we r. and r. 244:9
  scholar ... r. and good one 262:2
Ripeness is all 267:12
Rise: r. up before the hoary head 32:17
  r. up, my love, my fair one 40:7
  some r. by sin ... by virtue fall 273:2
Rises: hoo-ray and up she r. 17:7
  while Jove's planet r. yonder 61:5
Rising: in his r. seemed a pillar 177:3
River: Alph, the sacred r., ran 87:11
  away, you rolling r. 16:9
  dat ol' man r. 128:2
  even the weariest r. 310:1
  fame is like a r. 23:10
  follow the r. ... to the sea 214:1
  in the reeds by the r. 60:9
  lived on the r. Dee 54:1
  on either side the r. lie 313:11
  one more r. to cross 14:9
  r. Weser, deep and wide 61:16
  snow falls in the r. 67:4
  the rush of the r. 26:10
  through wood and dale the sacred r. 87:13
Rivers: washed by the r., blest by suns 59:6
Rivulet: a neat r. of text shall meander 301:13
Road: does the r. wind up-hill ? 236:3
  good to be out on the r. 169:1
  however long and hard the r. 82:12
  O ye'll tak' the high r. 16:10
  on a lonesome r. 86:16
  on to the end of the r. 157:5
  their ... monument the asphalt r. 107:1
  watched the ads and not the r. 186:4
Roads: all r. lead to Rome 224:22
Roam: a dunce that has been sent to r. 93:2
  ever let the fancy r. 148:3
  gave, once, her ... ways to r. 59:6
Roamin' in the gloamin' 157:7
Roaming: mistress mine, where are you r. ? 291:1
Roar: called upon to give the r. 83:14
  r. like a bull 224:23
Roared: cracked and growled and r. and howled 86:2
Roaring: a r. in the wind all night 334:7
Rob Peter to pay Paul 224:24
Robbed: he that is r. ... not r. at all 280:1
  r. that smiles steals something 279:4

Robbery: fair exchange is no r.   213:11
Robbing: forbids the r. of a foe   82:3
Robe: the marshal's truncheon nor the judge's
r.   273:4
Robes: lever ... bokes ... than r. riche   79:9
r. and furr'd gowns hide all   267:6
Robin: a r. redbreast in a cage   54:13
call for the r. redbreast   324:3
Robins: alive when the r. come   99:18
Rock: R. of Ages, cleft for me   317:15
upon this r. ... my church   44:16
whole as the marble, founded as the r.
271:6
Rocks: soften r., or bend a knotted oak   89:5
with r., and stones, and trees   334:15
Rod: a r. for his own back   224:25
a r. to check the erring   334:3
can wisdom be put in a silver r. ?   55:2
spareth his r. hateth his son   38:14
thy r. and thy staff they comfort me   35:29
Rode: r. madly off in all directions   157:13
r. the six hundred   311:9
she r. forth, clothed on with chastity   312:3
Roe: chasing ... deer and following the r.
66:14
Rogue: bewitch'd with the r.'s company
254:6
r. and peasant slave am I!   250:14
Rogues in buckram   254:15
Roll: not in the r. of common men   255:4
r. up that map   200:10
Rolling: just keeps r., he keeps on r.   128:2
r. English drunkard ... r. English road   81:6
Romae: si fueris R.   10:10
Romam: O fortunatam ... me consule R.!   84:8
Roman: a R.'s life, a R.'s arms   163:14
before the R. came to Rye   81:6
I am a R. citizen   84:7
neither holy, nor R.   321:16
rather be a dog ... than such a R.   263:23
Roman Conquest ... a *Good Thing*   241:8
Romance: to love oneself ... lifelong r.   327:5
Romano: si fueris Romae, R. vivito more   10:10
Romans: Friends, R., countrymen   263:11
live as the R. do   10:10
the R. counted *backwards*   241:9
Tiber, to whom the R. pray   163:14
which came first, the Greeks or ... R.
100:14
Rome: all roads lead to R.   224:22
fiddle while R. is burning   213:25
happy R., born when I was consul   84:8
I lov'd R. more   263:9
pardoun come from R.   79:19
R. shall fall; and when R. falls   69:8
R. was not built in a day   224:27
the grandeur that was R.   200:18
the hook-nos'd fellow of R.   257:13
when in R., live as the Romans do   10:10
Romeo: wherefore art thou R. ?   286:8
Ronald: Lord R. said nothing ... rode ... off
157:13
Rood: when every r. ... maintained its man
122:6
Roofs: masons building r. of gold   258:8
Room: all before my little r.   59:2
although the r. grows chilly   124:10
always r. at the top   323:12
convent's narrow r.   332:13
infinite riches in a little r.   166:4

Room (*continued*)
no r. ... for hyphenated Americanism
235:10
no r. for them in the inn   45:19
not r. to swing a cat   224:28
r. of one's own   330:9
r. with a view—and you   91:7
Roosevelt: here is the answer ... to President
R.   83:2
Roost (Roast): to rule the r.   224:31
Root of all evil. The want of money   68:3
Rooted: pluck from the memory a r. sorrow
272:6
Roots: stirring dull r. with spring rain   107:3
straight trees have crooked r.   226:28
Rope: a r. to hang himself   15:6
give a thief r. enough   224:29
Ropes: know the r.   218:9
Rose: a sadder ... man he r.   87:5
and lovely is the r.   331:13
as red as a r.   224:6
At Christmas I no more desire a r.   268:9
beauty's r. might never die   293:10
go, lovely r.   322:1
he's mighty lak' a r.   306:5
I am the r. of Sharon   40:4
in a twilight dim with r.   97:1
my fause lover stole my r.   67:7
my love ... like a red red r.   66:15
no r. without a thorn   222:6
not to me returns ... summer's r.   177:10
red as a r. is she   86:1
r. by any other name   286:9
r. leaves, when the r. is dead   300:6
r. of the fair state   251:5
r. or rue or laurel   309:16
the last r. of summer   184:1
the r. of youth upon him   242:20
when I have pluck'd thy r.   280:11
your image that blossoms a r.   337:7
Rosebuds: gather ye r. while ye may   132:7
r., before they be withered   51:10
Rosemary: for you there's r. and rue   293:1
r., that's for remembrance   252:23
Rose-moles all in stipple upon trout   135:7
Rose-red city half as old as time   64:3
Roses: as soon seek r. in December   70:14
ash the burnt r. leave   106:10
it was r., r., all the way   61:15
raptures and r. of vice   309:17
strew on her r., r.   18:16
their lips were four red r.   285:8
twin r. by the zephyr blown apart   148:10
where r. and white lilies grow   72:13
Rosy cheeks and flaxen curls   62:6
Rot: from hour to hour, we r. and r.   244:9
lie in cold obstruction and to r.   273:10
r. inwardly, and foul contagion spread
175:4
Rotted: do you think my mind ... r. early ?
186:5
Rotten: something is r. in the state of
Denmark   249:5
soon ripe, soon r.   226:1
Rotting: mean and mighty r. together   247:7
Rough: take the r. with the smooth   224:30
Rough-hew them how we will   253:6
Round: in a light fantastic r.   172:16
Rounded: our little life is r. with a sleep
288:16

Sceptre (*continued*)
  this unwieldy s. from my hand 284:2
Sceptred: what avails the s. race? 156:13
Schemes: best laid s. o' mice and men 66:12
Scholar: he was a s. and a ripe 262:2
  what ills the s.'s life assail 141:10
Scholars: great men ... not commonly ... great
    s. 134:6
  s. dispute ... case is still before the courts
    135:9
School: every day in the life of a s. 157:12
  example ... the s. of mankind 64:15
  extreme busyness ... at s. or college 307:8
  like snail unwillingly to s. 244:11
  s. of Stratford atte Bowe 79:4
  tell tales out of s. 227:8
  toward s. with heavy looks 286:12
  village master taught his little s. 122:11
Schoolboy: every s. knows who imprisoned
    Montezuma 164:2
  whining s., with his satchel 244:11
Schoolboys: as s. from their books 286:12
Schooldays: in my joyful s. 156:9
Schoolgirl: pert as a s. 118:6
  that s. complexion 11:6
Schoolman's subtle art 201:20
Schoolmaster: average s. ... essentially an ass
    169:13
Schools: 'tis an old maxim in the s. 308:12
Schooner: the s. Hesperus 161:12
Science: fair S. frowned not on his ... birth
    126:13
  S. is organised knowledge 305:1
Scoff: fools, who came to s. 122:10
Scoffing: antic sits s. his state 283:6
Scorer: when the one Great S. comes 233:12
Scorn: fixed figure for the time of s. 280:5
  I can s. and let her go 330:1
  I s. to change my state 293:17
  in s. of eyes, reflecting gems 285:1
  love he laugh'd to s. 295:4
  love I laugh to s. 58:14
  s. not the sonnet 333:5
  the sound of public s. 179:12
Scorned: nor hell a fury like a woman s. 89:6
Scorns: how Stanley s., the glance 63:2
Scorpions: they had tails like unto s. 50:25
Scotchman: a S., if he be caught young 143:9
Scot-free: to go s. 225:2
Scotland: I do indeed come from S. 142:6
  I'll be in S. afore ye 16:10
  oats ... in S., supports the people 140:9
  stands S. where it did? 271:19
Scots: Kills me ... S. at a breakfast 254:12
  S. wha hae wi' Wallace bled 67:1
  S. whom Bruce has ... led 67:1
Scotsman: grandest moral attribute of a S.
    25:1
Scott: not even Sir Walter S. 297:8
Scotus or Aquinas 182:5
Scoundrel: every man over forty is a s. 296:16
  general good ... plea of the s. 55:6
  patriotism ... last refuge of a s. 143:17
Scourge: daughter of Jove ... whose iron s.
    126:16
Scratch: come up to the s. 225:3
  s. my back and I'll s. yours 225:4
Scratching: cure ... but the s. of a pen 162:9
  wd. ... I had the s. of thee 290:4
Scream: a s., a splash 16:12

Screw: a s. loose somewhere 225:5
  s. may twist ... rack may turn 120:16
  s. yr. courage to the sticking place 270:7
Scribble: always s., s., s.! ... Mr. Gibbon
    121:13
Scrip and scrippage 245:4
Scripture: all s. is ... by inspiration of God
    49:16
  devil can cite S. for his purpose 274:8
Scriptures: life like the s.—figurative 152:7
Scruple: some craven s. 252:18
  wd. not s. to pick a pocket 97:5
Scullion: away, you s.! 256:14
Sculpture: beauty cold ... like that of s. 237:9
Scum: [our army] ... s. of the earth 324:8
Scutcheon: honour is a mere s. 255:21
Scylla: between S. and Charybdis 207:38
Scythe: mower whets his s. 174:3
Scythian: snow on S. hills 166:7
Sea: all the s. were ink 14:1
  alone on a wide, wide s. 86:10, 87:2
  and there was no more s. 51:1
  between France and England ... the s.
    139:18
  devil and the deep s. 211:17
  down to a sunless s. 87:11
  down to the s. in ships 37:4
  England ... with the triumphant s. 282:6
  first ... into that silent s. 86:4
  from s. to shining s. 25:4
  into the midst of the s. 31:26
  learn the secret of the s.? 161:4
  mother and lover ... the s. 310:6
  my Bonnie is over the s. 16:2
  never, never sick at s.! 119:11
  not all the water in the rough, rude s. 283:2
  on such a full s. are we now afloat 264:3
  one foot in s. 277:21
  one that goes to s. for nothing 101:2
  out of the s. came he 85:13
  over the s. to Skye 57:12, 307:3
  plants His footsteps in the s. 92:15
  precious stone set in the silver s. 282:5
  sailed the wintry s. 161:12
  scatter'd in the bottom of the s. 285:1
  the kings of the s. 18:13
  the rude s. grew civil 276:18
  the s. is calm to-night 18:9
  the s. never changes 90:8
  the s.! the s.! 337:2
  the wrinkled s. beneath him crawls 312:1
  there is Society ... by the deep s. 69:9
  till the s. ... floweth in yr. veins 317:16
  to s. for nothing but to make him sick
    101:2
  to s. in a ... pea-green boat 158:7
  two Voices ... one is of the s. 333:10
  went down into the s. 85:13
  went to s. in a sieve 158:4
  when I put out to s. 311:13
  where no s. runs 315:18
  whose sound was like the s. 333:13
  why the s. is boiling hot 76:4
  wind of the Western S. 314:13
  winds somewhere safe to s. 310:1
  within a walk of the s. 28:4
  worse things happen at s. 231:2
Sea-boy: wet s. in an hour so rude 257:3
Seagreen Incorruptible 73:7
Seal: all right ... you heard a s. bark 317:7

Seal (*continued*)
  opened the seventh s. 50:23
Sealing-wax: ships and s. 76:4
Seals of love, but seal'd in vain 273:12
Sea-maid: to hear the s.'s music 276:18
Sea-mark: very s. of my utmost sail 280:13
Sea-monster: ingratitude ... more hideous ... than the s. 265:14
Search will find it out 132:5
Seas: foam of perilous s. 150:4
  guard our native s. 72:10
  I must down to the s. again 168:15–17
  port after stormy s. 305:11
  the multitudinous s. incarnadine 270:12
  we shall fight on the s. and oceans 82:13
Seaside: I do like to be beside the s. 121:14
Season: a dry brain in a dry s. 106:6
  givest ... meat in due s. 37:30
  in the s. of the year 16:6
  to every thing ... a s. 39:14
Seasons: as the swift s. roll 134:5
  defend you from s. such as these 266:13
  four s. fill the measure 151:4
  four s. in the mind of man 151:4
  thus with the year s. return 177:10
  when mercy s. justice 275:1
Seat: regain the blissful s. 175:15
  this is the seat of Mars 282:5
Seats: you want the best s.; we have them 11:11
Seconds: sixty s.' worth of distance run 154:20
Secrecy: for s., no lady closer 254:11
Secret: bread eaten in s. is pleasant 38:7
  digestion ... great s. of life 303:17
  it [love] ceases to be a s. 26:11
  joys of parents are s. 21:17
  learn the s. of the sea? 161:4
  s., black, and midnight hags! 271:13
  there is no s. so close 308:10
Secrets: s. with girls ... never valued 94:1
  tell the s. of my prison-house 249:7
Sect: attached to that great s. 298:8
  paradise for a s. 148:1
Sects: two-and-seventy jarring s. confute 110:10
Secure: safe ... never to be s. 229:37
  s., and never now can mourn 297:16
Sedge is wither'd from the lake 148:14
See: and no man s. me more 261:8
  blind as those who won't s. 208:9
  come up and s. me sometime 325:5
  content to s. no other verdure 151:2
  did you once s. Shelley plain? 61:10
  ever s. such a thing in yr. life? 195:1
  forward tho' I canna s. 66:13
  I did but s. her passing by 17:2
  I s. the moon ... moon sees me 190:5
  if thou hast eyes to s. 279:5
  may I be there to s. 92:13
  O! say can you s. 153:6
  rather s. than be one 64:1
  s. all, nor be afraid 62:9
  s. her on the bridge at midnight 16:12
  s., not feel, how beautiful 87:8
  s. what we shall s. 225:9
  shall never s. a billboard 186:10
  the eye begins to s. 58:15
  to s. beyond our bourn 147:11
  to s. her was to love her 65:9

See (*continued*)
  wait and s. 19:15, 229:22
  we s. through a glass darkly 48:7
Seed: groweth s. and bloweth med 14:7
  in thy s. ... all nations ... blessed 31:5
  robs not one light s. 148:5
  s. begging their bread 36:9
Seeds: if you can look into the s. of time 269:8
Seeing: s. is believing 225:10
  worth s. ? Yes; but not ... going 144:16
Seek: nothing s., nothing find 222:16
  s. ye the Lord 41:8
Seeking: s. the food he eats 244:6
  s. whom he may devour 50:8
  we must still be s. 331:5
Seeks: he that s. trouble 225:11
  whoever s. abroad may find 147:3
Seem: free we s. ... fettered ... are 60:10
  s. here no painful inch to gain 85:2
  s. wiser than they are 22:20
  things are not what they s. 160:14
Seeming: keep s. ... all the winter 293:1
Seems: he s. so near and yet so far 313:2
  how sweet and fair she s. to be 322:1
  so careful of the type she s. 312:16
Seen: because thou art not s. 245:1
  s. and not heard 209:21
  to be hated needs but to be s. 203:6
  who hath not s. thee ? 147:3
See-saw, Margery Daw 193:3
Seidlitz powder: burst while drinking a s. 12:4
Seize the flow'r, its bloom is shed 67:4
Self: from thee to my sole s. 150:5
  nothing ... greater to one than ... s. 326:4
  to thine own s. be true 248–9:17
  wretch, concentred all in s. 240:1
Self-evident: we hold these truths to be s. 139:6
Self-praise is no recommendation 225:12
Self-preservation ... first law of nature 225:13
Self-sacrifice: the spirit of s. 334:4
Self-sufficient: know how to be s. 183:3
Seldom: a woman s. asks advice 9:10
  s. or never the two hit it off· 330:10
Sempronius: we'll do more, S. 9:4
Senators: green-rob'd s. of mighty woods 148:6
Sensation of a short sharp shock 118:7
Sensations: Life of S. rather than of Thoughts 151:10
Sense: devoid of s. and motion 176–7:19
  fools admire, but men of s. approve 202:11
  live within the s. they question 300:6
  man of s. ... trifles with [women] 80:14
  Shadwell never deviates into s. 104:14
  so sweet that the s. aches 280:6
  sound ... an echo to the s. 202:10
  take care of the s. 74:13
Sense of humour: mind ... deficient in a s. 88:4
Senseless: the most s. and fit man 278:5
Senses: steep my s. in forgetfulness 257:2
Sensibility: fine sense, yet wanting s. 93:12
Sensible: moral, s., and well-bred 92:4
Sentence: my s. is for open war 176:16
  originator of a good s. 108:14
  s. first—verdict afterwards 75:8
Sentimental: carry ... body around because of its s. value 114:1

She (*continued*)
  that not impossible s. 94:3
  the fair ... and unexpressive s. 245:2
Sheba: another S. Queen 329:10
Shed: a lowly cattle s. 10:6
  by man shall his blood be s. 30:24
  tears, prepare to s. them now 263:16
  with ... [Edmund Burke] beneath a s. 145:4
Sheep: an old half-witted s. 306:9
  baa, baa, black s. 188:4
  black s. in every flock 208:6
  divideth ... s. from ... goats 44:29
  hanged for a s. as a lamb 216:5
  hungry s. look up, and are not fed 175:4
  Little Bo-peep has lost her s. 190:10
  looking on their silly s. 260:14
  mountain s. are sweeter 199:6
  noble ensample to his s. he yaf 79:16
  return to our s. 17:9
  strayed from thy ways like lost s. 52:12
  the s.'s in the meadow 191:1
Sheep-hook: know how to hold a s. 175:3
Sheet: a wet s. and a flowing sea 95:1
Sheets: better wear out shoes than s. 207:37
Shelley: did you once see S. plain? 61:10
Shelter: I will build a house ... to s. me 28:3
  our s. from the stormy blast 323:4
Shenandoah: O, S. I long to hear you 16:9
Shepherd: as a s. divideth his sheep 44:29
  Dick the s. blows his nail 269:1
  every s. tells his tale 174:3
  go, for they call you, S. 18:18
  good s. giveth his life 46:27
  homely, slighted, s.'s trade 174:15
  Old Nod the s. goes 97:1
  truth in every s.'s tongue 232:14
Shepherds: a sweeter shade to s. 260:14
  s. abiding in the field 45:20
  while s. watched their flocks 311:4
Sheridan was listened to 234:15
Shibboleth: say now S. 33:18
Shift: let me s. for myself 184:4
Shilling: better give a s. 207:28
  cut off with a s. 210:30
Shillings: rather than forty s. ... Book of Songs 276:2
Shimei, though not prodigal of pelf 103:7
Shine: err with Pope ... s. with Pye 70:15
  few are qualified to s. 309:9
  I see Heaven's glories s. 58:12
  moon doth s. as bright as day 188:6
  s. so brisk, and smell so sweet 254:2
  sun that warms you ... s. on me 281:11
Shines: light ... where no sun s. 315:18
Shining: from sea to s. sea 25:4
  s. with all his might 75:16
Ship: a s. in a black storm 324:4
  a s. is worse than a gaol 143:21
  a stately s. of Tarsus 180:15
  all I ask is a tall s. 168:15
  as idle as a painted s. 86:5
  our saucy s.'s a beauty 119:8
  rats desert a sinking s. 224:5
  sail on, O S. of State 160:11
  the s. has weathered every rack 325:12
Ships: face that launch'd a thousand s. 165:8
  I saw three s. come sailing by 190:4
  our bloody s. today 25:6
  seen old s. sail like swans 111:3

Ships (*continued*)
  s. that pass in the night 161:7
  s., towers, domes, theatres 333:6
  spied three s. come sailing by 14:10
  we've got the s., we've got the men 137:4
Shires and towns from Airly Beacon 154:1
Shirt: no s. or collar ... comes back twice 157:15
Shive: cut loaf to steal a s. 289:13
Shiver: little breezes dusk and s. 313:12
Shivering: grass ... s.-sweet to the touch 90–1:16
Shoal: a s. of fools for tenders 89:10
  bank and s. of time 270:5
Shock: short sharp s. 118:7
Shock-headed Peter 133:11
Shocks: natural s. that flesh is heir to 250–1:20
Shoe: I kiss his dirty s. 259:9
  know where the s. pinches 225:16
  my dame has lost her s. 188:7
  old woman ... lived in a s. 194:5
  one, two, buckle my s. 192:3
Shoemakers: brave s. ... of the gentle craft 96:12
Shoe-string: a careless s. in whose tie 131:15
Shoes: better wear out s. than sheets 207:37
  her s. were number nine 183:9
  old s. ... easiest for his feet 241:1
  s.—and ships—and sealing-wax 76:4
Shone like a meteor streaming 176:9
Shoot: do not s. the pianist 327:19
  s., if you must, this old gray head 326:7
Shopkeepers: England is a nation of s. 185:12
  fit only for a nation of s. 303:4
  nation that is governed by s. 303:4
Shops: that men might shun the awful s. 81:10
Shore: adieu, my native s. 69:1
  fast by their native s. 93:1
  now upon the farther s. 107:16
  rapture on the lonely s. 69:9
  rocky s. beats back the envious siege 282:6
  s. of the wide world 151:8
  the lights around the s. 236:10
  waves make towards the pebbled s. 294:1
Shoreditch: say the bells of S. 192:4
Short: if you find it wond'rous s. 122:18
  s. and sweet 225:17
  sweet discourse makes s. days 226:34
  take a long while to make it s. 317:4
Shorter: had Cleopatra's nose been s. 198:7
  make you s. by a head 107:12
Shortly: I expect a judgment. S. 97:10
Shortness: to spend that s. basely 255:22
Shot: I s. the albatross 86:3
  not a soldier discharged his farewell s. 330:3
Shoulder: give the cold s. 210:3
  put yr. s. to the wheel 223:38
Shoulder-blade: I have a left s. ... a miracle 118:13
Shoulders: old head on young s. 222:25
Shout: s. that tore Hell's concave 176:10
  's. with the largest' [mob] 98:20
  there was a s. about my ears 81:3
Shouting: after the ... music with s. and laughter 62:6
  all is over bar the s. 206:13

Shovel them [bodies] under and let me work 238:5

Show: s. and gaze o' th' time 272:13
that within which passes s. 248:1
to offer it the s. of violence 247:15

Shower: drainless s. of light is poesy 150:12
this was our finest s.! 197:9

Showers: Aprille with his s. sote 79:1
fresh s. for thirsting flowers 298:4
small s. last long 282:4

Shows: May's new-fangled s. 268:9

Shreds: king of s. and patches 252:13
thing of s. and patches 117:16

Shrieking: with s. and squeaking 62:1

Shrink: all the boards did s. 86:6

Shroud: my s. ... stuck all with yew 291:6

Shrug: borne it with a patient s. 274:10

Shuffled off this mortal coil 250–1:20

Shun: s. the heaven that leads ... to ... hell 294:12
that men might s. the awful shops 81:10

Shut, shut the door, good John 201:10

Shutters: now ... close the s. fast 93:10

Shy: once bitten, twice s. 222:27
you look a little s. 77:10

Sick: can s. men play so nicely? 282:7
for I am s. of love 40:6
hope deferred maketh the heart s. 38:13
I am s. at heart 247:13
never, never s. at sea! 119:11
s. hurry ... divided aims 18:21
the devil was s. 185:1
the enterprise is s.! 290:2
tie up the knocker, say I'm s. 201:10
to sea for nothing but to make him s. 101:2
when ... the heart is s. 312:14
when we are s. in fortune 265:10

Sicklied o'er with the pale cast 250–1:20

Sickness: he hath the falling s. 262:10
in s. and in health 53:22
s. is better than sadness 225:21

Side: courtesy on one s. only 210:15
hear the other s. 206:27
look on the bright s. 219:28
nobody is on my s. 21:2
trumpets sounded ... on the other s. 63:16
which s. one's bread is buttered 218:8

Sides: buttered on both s. 208:29
laughter holding both his s. 173:17
your ... unfed s. 266:13

Siècles: quarante s. vous contemplent 185:10

Siege: rocky shore beats back the envious s. 282:6

Sieve: carry water in a s. 229:33
in a s. they went to sea 158:4

Sigh: a s. is the sword 55:5
a s. like Tom o' Bedlam 265:11
s. no more, ladies, s. no more 277:21
s. the lack of many a thing 293:18
something ... prompts th' eternal s. 203:7

Sighed: no sooner s. but they ask'd 245:14
she s., she cried 16:4
s. for ... love of a ladye 121:2

Sighing: a plague of s. and grief! 254:17
fell a-s. and a-sobbing 196:3

Sighs: for my pains a world of s. 279:2
s. are the natural language 241:18

Sight: a s. to dream of 87:6
and 'tis a shameful s. 323:3
every common s. to me did seem 331:12

Sight (*continued*)
Oh the pleasant s. to see 154:1
she gleamed upon my s. 334:12
s. for sore eyes 225:22
s. ... good for sore eyes 309:6
s. of means to do ill deeds 265:2
s. of vernal bloom 177:10
s. so touching in its majesty 333:6
to s. or thought be formed 179:10
who ever lov'd that lov'd not at first s.? 166:15

Sights: such s. as youthful poets dream 174:7
what s. of ugly death! 285:1

Sign: an olive-leaf ... pacific s. 179:16
an outward and visible s. 53:16
God made the wicked Grocer for a ... s. 81:10

Signal: only a s. shown 161:7

Silence: but oh! the s. sank 87:1
darkness again and a s. 161:7
dusky hour friendliest to ... s. 178:17
foster-child of s. 149:6
greet thee? With s. and tears 71:6
let yr. women keep s. in ... churches 48:9
mourn'd in s. and was Di-do-Dum 204:12
my gracious s., hail! 246:6
no wisdom like s. 230:22
seul le s. est grand 320:14
s. gives consent 225:23
s. is golden 226:9
s., like a poultice, comes 133:13
s. ... perfectest herald of joy 277:17
the rest is s. 253:10
there was s. in heaven 50:23
to sit in solemn s. in ... dock 118:7

Silent: burst into that s. sea 86:4
s. as the moon, when she deserts 180:11
s., flooding in, the main 85:2
s. over Africa 61:5
s. stars go by 59:8
s., upon a peak in Darien 150–1:15
s. was the flock 147:12

Silently: s., and with how wan a face! 302:4
s., invisibly he took her 55:11
wind does move s., invisibly 55:10

Silk: rustling in unpaid-for s. 247:3

Silken: s. dalliance in the wardrobe lies 258:9
s. lines and silver hooks 100:17

Silks: whenas in s. my Julia goes 132:6

Silver: can wisdom be put in a s. rod? 55:2
every cloud has a s. lining 209:34
how s.-sweet sound lovers' tongues 286:13
just for a handful of s. 61:8
polished up the s. plate 184:8
precious stone set in the s. sea 282:5
seated in thy s. chair 145:8
s. and gold have I none 47:1
s. bells and cockle shells 191:7
s. buckles at his knee 188:5
s. nutmeg and a golden pear 190:1
the oars were s. 242:14
the s. Rhodope 166:7
when gold and s. becks me 264:16

Silvia: who is S.? What is she? 292:8

Simon: Simple S. met a pieman 193:4

Simplicity: in low s. he lends out ... gratis 274:7
in ... s. a child 201:22
pity my s. 325:1

Simplify, simplify 317:1

Sin: a private s. is not so prejudicial 78:5
  a s. to covet honour 259:14
  as ugly as s. 229:8
  before polygamy was made a s. 102:14
  he that is without s. among you 46:24
  hold there is no s. but ignorance 166:3
  no s. but to be rich 264:14
  no s. except stupidity 327:4
  no s. to s. in secret 182:16
  pleasure's a s. ... s.'s a pleasure 69:13
  some rise by s. 273:2
  some will pluck on s. 285:6
  this dark world of s. 54:4
  wages of s. is death 47:18
  whose s. ... dipt me in ink? 201:13
Sincere: a wit shd. be no more s. 89:9
Sincerely: comes as s. from the author's soul
  137:13
Sincerity: a little s. is a dangerous thing 327:2
Sind: *Peccavi* (I have S.) 185:9
Sinews: stiffen the s., summon up the blood
  259:3
Sing: and I will s. of the sun 205:3
  arms and the man I s. 105:1
  himself to s., and build the lofty rhyme
  174:13
  I celebrate ... and s. myself 325:13
  I do not think that they will s. to me 106:17
  I'll s. ... in thy praise 65:11
  I s. the sofa 93:5
  lhude s. Goddamm 205:2
  love, and pray, and s. 267:13
  more safe I s. 178:20
  now let us s., Long live the King 92:13
  ord'ring yr. affairs, to s. them too 293:2
  Quires and Places where they s. 52:18
  s. both high and low 291:1
  s., choirs of Angels, s. in exultation 196:5
  s., Heavenly Muse 175:15
  s. me a song ... lad that is gone 307:3
  s. me a song, O! 121:1
  s. no sad songs for me 236:4
  s. 'polly-wolly-doodle' 16:5
  s. them loud ... dead of night 290:15
  s. to the Lord with cheerful voice 153:4
  swans s. before they die 87:10
  used to s. it—fifty thousand strong 336:9
  we'd s. and pray ... livelong day 56:4
  we'll s. another song 336:9
  when you s., I'd have you buy 293:2
Singe: so hot ... it doth s. yourself 261:3
Singed: I have s. ... king's beard 102:7
Singing: everyone suddenly burst out s.
  238:10
  I'll be quit of the s. 12:1
  maid s. in the valley below 15:1
  s. in the Wilderness 109:15
  sweet s. in the choir 15:8
Single: continued s. ... only talked of population 123:19
Sings: chaffinch s. on the orchard bough 61:1
  in his motion like an angel s. 275:8
  in me [summer] s. no more 170:15
  lark at heaven's gate s. 246:13
  s. for his supper 191:4
  tell me what she s. 334:17
  thrush, he s. each song twice over 61:3
Singularity: surprise by ... excess ... not by S.
  151:14
Sinks: it s., and I am ready 156:11

Sinner: joy ... over one s. that repenteth 46:2
Sinners: God and s. reconciled 325:2
  mercy upon us miserable s. 52:22
Sinning: more sinn'd against than s. 266:11
Sins: did ... from expensive s. refrain 103:6
  few love to hear the s. they love to act 281:3
  his s. were scarlet, but his books 27:5
  oldest s. the newest kind of ways 257:19
  other s. only speak; murder shrieks out
  323:15
  result of her s. was quadruplets 13:2
  the multitude of s. 50:7
  though yr. s. be as scarlet 40:17
Sirens: blest pair of S. 172:12
Sisera: stars ... fought against S. 33:14
Sister: a barren s. all your life 276:9
  but I kissed her little s. 183:10
Sisters: his s., and his cousins, and his aunts
  119:14
  sphere-born harmonious s. 172:12
  two s. embrace like one brother 234:1
Sit: can s. and look at it [work] for hours
  139:15
  here I and sorrows s. 264:15
  I will s. down now, but 100:2
  if I s. on a pin 12:9
  not fit that you shd. s. here 94:9
  shall s. and drink with me 28:4
  s. every man under his vine 42:22
  s. on a cushion and sew 188:8
  s. upon the murdered reputations 89:7
  so I did s. and eat 131:11
  test my bath before I s. 186:9
  there we s. in peaceful calm 137:15
  to s. in ... shade ... look upon verdure 20:12
  to s. upon a hill, as I do now 260:13
Sitivation at the lighthouse 99:10
Sitting: thee s. careless on ... granary floor
  147:3
Situation excellent. I shall attack 111:5
Six: it's just s. of one 167:6
  s. days shalt thou labour 32:3
  s. hours in sleep, in ... study s. 85:9
  s. of one and half a dozen ... other 225:26
Sixes and sevens: to be at s. 225:27
Sixpence: bang—went s.!!! 231:23
  buy a thing that costs even s. 143:10
  he found a crooked s. 194:3
  I love s., jolly little s. 190:2
  nothink for nothink ... little for s. 231:24
  sing a song of s. 193:5
Skating over thin ice 108:10
Skies: cloudless climes and starry s. 71:2
  for s. of couple-colour 135:7
  his watch-tower in the s. 174:2
  in summer s. to mourn 147:11
  some watcher of the s. 150:15
Skill: simple truth his utmost s. 336:13
Skills: create by means of new s. 237:8
Skin: and it punctures my s. 12:9
  by the s. of one's teeth 225:28
  can the Ethiopian change his s.? 41:14
  her s. was white as leprosy 86:8
  I stuff my s. so full within 307:12
  saw the skull beneath the s. 107:6
  why, my s. hangs about me 255:11
Skins: all ... fancy dress ... except our ... s. 297:6
Skipped: the mountains s. like rams 37:7
Skipper: the s. had taken his little daughter
  161:12

Solitude (*continued*)
  in s. what happiness ? 179:3
  O S.! where are the charms ? 93:15
  race ... has ... disturbed its s. 23–4:23
  s. sometimes is best society 179:8
  which is the bliss of s. 331:11
  whosoever is delighted in s. 22:21
Solitudinem faciunt, pacem appellant 310:8
Solomon: S. Grundy, born on a Monday
    193:6
  the wisdom of S. 34:17
Some: S. chicken! S. neck! 83:4
  s. ... fou o' love ... s. ... o' brandy 66:4
  s. glory in their birth 294:2
  s. hae meat ... s. wad eat 67:3
  s. talk of Alexander 16:14
Somebody: how dreary to be s. 99:14
  s. bet on de bay 112:4
  when every one is s. 116:15
Somer: in a s. season 157:1
Something: a man's worth s. 60:14
  add s. more to this wonderful year 115:1
  always doing s. for posterity 9:11
  in our embers is s. that doth live 332:4
  s. left to treat my friends 165:4
  s. rich and strange 288:1
  s. sensational to read in the train 327:16
  s. ... that doesn't love a wall 113:14
  s. was dead in each of us 326:13
  that s. ... which prompts th' eternal sigh
    203:7
  time for a little s. 172:7
  'tis s., nothing 279:15
  what's s. rarish 12:5
Sometime: come up and see me s. 325:5
Somewhat: more than s. 236:15
Somewhere: time was away and s. else 165:2
Son: a foolish s. ... heaviness 38:8
  a virgin shall ... bear a s. 40:21
  a wise s. ... a glad father 38:8
  as a man chasteneth his s. 32:24
  he gave his only begotten S. 46:21
  Jehu ... s. of Nimshi ... driveth 34:25
  marry yr. s. when you will 220:34
  my s., if thou come to serve 51:15
  O Absalom, my s., my s.! 34:14
  O Lucifer, s. of the morning 40:25
  she will ... renounce me for a s. 116:1
  spareth his rod hateth his s. 38:14
  unto us a s. is given 40:23
Song: a s. to sing, O! 121:1
  burst into a quavering s. 324:12
  fierce wars ... shall moralize my s. 305:9
  give ear unto my s. 122:18
  glorious the s. when God's the theme
    302:13
  he sings each s. twice over 61:3
  let satire be my s. 70:11
  not given a penny for a s. 337:3
  old s. of Percy and Douglas 302:6
  one grand, sweet s. 154:2
  pipe a s. about a lamb 56:8
  run softly till I end my S. 305:16
  sang a most topical s. 12:11
  sea grew civil at her s. 276:18
  self-same s. that found a path 150:4
  sold my Reputation for a S. 110:15
  s. for yr. delight 76:11
  suck melancholy out of a s. 244:5
  that glorious s. of old 240:14

Song (*continued*)
  the Lord's s. in a strange land 37:25
  this subject for heroic s. 179:6
  unlike my subject ... frame my s. 80:18
  we'll sing another s. 336:9
Songs: Book of S. and Sonnets here 276:2
  for ever piping s. for ever new 149:9
  our sweetest s. ... saddest thought 300:2
  piping s. of pleasant glee 56:7
  sing no sad s. for me 236:4
  the s. of Apollo 269:2
  their lean and flashy s. 175:4
  there shall the Sussex s. be sung 28:3
  where are the s. of Spring ? 147:4
Sonne: when soft was the s. 157:1
Sonnet: a s. is a moment's monument 236:6
  scorn not the s. 333:5
  s.'s scanty plot of ground 332:14
Sonnets: onlie begetter of ... insuing s. 293:9
Sons: bears all its s. away 323:6
  free as the s. of the waves 115:1
  s. of Belial, flown with insolence 176:8
  s. of Belial had a Glorious Time 103:7
  the s. of the prophet were brave 16:15
  things are the s. of heaven 140:2
Soon: belovèd Night ... come s., s. 299:1
  day returns too s. 71:4
  it [the future] comes s. enough 105:12
  s. as she was gone ... a traveller came 55:11
  s. got, s. spent 225:40
  s. hot, s. cold 225:41
  s. ripe, s. rotten 226:1
  you have waked me too s. 323:7
Sooner it's over, the s. to sleep 154:3
Soot: black as s. 208:4
Sooth: poesy ... friend to s. the cares 150:13
Sophisters: age ... of s., economists, calculators
    64:11
Sore: sight ... good for s. eyes 309:6
  sleep ... s. labour's bath 270:11
  trust in critics who themselves are s. 70:14
Sorrow: and not be in s. too 56:12
  and wear a golden s. 261:4
  any s. like unto my s. 41:17
  brief s., short-lived care 186:13
  down, thou climbing s. 265:21
  ere the s. comes with years 60:7
  from the sphere of our s. 300:8
  has brought [war] untold s. to mankind
    319:5
  I feel it when I s. most 312:13
  increaseth knowledge increaseth s. 39:13
  more in s. than in anger 248:10
  no more death, neither s. 51:3
  O S., why dost borrow ? 147:10
  parting is such sweet s. 286:14
  pluck from the memory a rooted s. 272:6
  pure and complete s. 317:14
  s. comes unsent for 226:2
  s. goes, and pleasure tarries 116:11
  s. will come fast enough 215:9
  the guttural s. of the refugees 165:1
  then to come, in spite of s. 174:2
  there is no greater s. 95:7
  to think is to be full of s. 149:15
  truly that hour foretold s. 71:5
  write s. on the bosom of the earth 283:5
Sorrows: a man of s. ... acquainted with grief
    41:5
  here I and s. sit 264:15

Sorrows (*continued*)

losses are restor'd and s. end 293:19

s. come ... not single spies 252:21

there are few s. ... in which 303:6

when age, disease, or s. strike him 84:14

Sorry: better ... safe than s. 207:24

dreadful s., Clementine 183:8

truly s. man's dominion 66:11

Sort: a s. of men whose visages 274:2

travel, in the younger s. 22:13

Sorts: all s. and conditions of men 52:27

Sought: that I s. to destroy institutions 325:10

the prize we s. is won 325:12

those men that s. him 262:2

Soul: a day for a man to afflict his s. 41:10

a thing which enters ... s. 151:13

all thy heart ... all thy s. 33:1

and his s. sincere 126:14

as if that s. were fled 183:11

asleep in body ... become a living s. 335:12

body Nature is, and God the s. 203:3

body presseth down the s. 51:13

breathes there the man, with s. so dead 239:16

build ... stately mansions, O my s. 134:5

call upon my s. within the house 290:15

cold waters to a thirsty s. 38:29

confession is good for the s. 210:6

distress hath humanised my s. 321:2

dull wd. he be of s. 333:6

for my s., what can it do to that? 249:4

for my unconquerable s. 130:8

foredoom'd his father's s. to cross 201:11

gain the ... world, and lose his own s. 45:10

give not thy s. unto a woman 51:19

hae mercy o' my s., Lord God 164:10

half conceal the S. within 312:12

harrow up thy s., freeze thy young blood 249:7

Helen, ... give me my s. again 165:8

her lips suck forth my s. 165:8

hidden s. of harmony 174:9

his s. is marching on! 127:13

I am black ... my s. is white 56:10

I am the captain of my s. 130:10

I ... invite my s. 326:1

iron entered [into] his s. 37:3, 217:23

it is the cause, my s. 280:10

joy's s. lies in the doing 289:15

King Cole was a merry old s. 192:1

largest and most comprehensive s. 104:3

lose his own s. 45:10

memorial from the S.'s eternity 236:6

merit wins the s. 204:11

most offending s. alive 259:14

my prophetic s.! My uncle! 249:10

my s. in agony 86:10

my s. into the boughs does glide 168:2

my s., like to a ship 324:4

my s., there is a country 320:7

no coward s. is mine 58:12

our s.'s left hand 100:18

perdition catch my s. 279:14

pouring forth thy s. abroad 150:3

praise my s., the King of Heaven 163:8

pray for my s. 312:9

prepare thy s. for temptation 51:15

rap and knock and enter in our s. 60:13

sleepless S. that perished 334:8

Soul (*continued*)

s. and ... gift of articulate speech 296:18

s. hath been alone 87:2

s. is dead that slumbers 160:14

s. is in a ferment 147:7

s. is not more than the body 326:4

s. of the Age! 145:11

s. rememb'ring my good friends 282:8

s. was sad ... glance was glum 121:2

the s. of Adonais, like a star 298:3

the s. that rises with us 332:1

the s. to feel the flesh 58:15

thou art a s. in bliss 267:10

thy rapt s. sitting in thine eyes 173:7

thy s. was like a Star 333:13

to bear my s. away 9:13

was not spoken of the s. 160:14

what a dusty answer gets the s. 170:2

what of s. was left 62:11

with all thy s. ... all thy might 32:22

yet my s. drew back 131:10

Souls: fire our s. to regale 56:4

have ye s. in heaven too? 147:6

immediate jewel of their s. 279:15

Lord, thou lover of s. 51:14

our s., whose faculties can comprehend 166:10

poor s. who dwell in Night 55:1

prosperity has damned more s. 223:31

s. of Poets dead and gone 149:4

s. of the righteous ... in the hand of God 51:12

s. of women are so small 68:2

such harmony is in immortal s. 275:8

two s. with but a single thought 162:8

unless they've s. that grovel 72:2

we that have free s. 252:5

ye have left yr. s. on earth 147:6

Sound: full of s. and fury 272:10

hear dat mournful s. 112:6

no s. save the rush of the river 26:10

sighing s., the lights around the shore 236:10

s. must seem an echo to the sense 202:10

s. of a voice that is still 311:6

s. of public scorn 179:12

s. of revelry by night 69:3

s. upon the bugle-horn 313:14

the s. is forc'd, the notes are few 56:14

the s. of his horn 125:6

to heal the blows of s. 133:13

Sounds: s. will take care of themselves 74:13

with s. that echo still 311:14

Soup: he screamed out, 'Take the s. away!' 133:8

of s. and love, the first 226:3

s. of the evening, beautiful s. 75:5

Sour: how s. sweet music is 284:7

lost his taste, sweet is s. 219:32

love is ... s. in the ending 219:39

things sweet ... prove in digestion s. 281:13

will not taste the s. 211:14

Source: true s. of human offspring 178:8

South: beaker full of the warm S. 149:14

he went by the s. 191:6

I ... go s. in the winter 107:4

Oh, I went down S. 16:5

yes, but not in the S. 205:1

South country: great hills of the S. 28:2

Southern: bore me in the s. wild 56:10
  walls on the s. side 61:16
Sovereign: servants of the s. or state 22:2
Sovereignest thing on earth 254:2
Soviet power into the heart of W. Europe
  83:10
Sow (noun): I do ... walk before thee like a s.
  256:8
  s. that was washed ... wallowing 50:9
Sow (verb): men that s. to reap 309:18
  s. one's wild oats 230:16
  they that s. in tears 37:18
Soweth: whatsoever ... s. ... shall he also reap
  48:23
Sown the wind ... reap the whirlwind 42:9
Spade: call a s. a s. 209:5
Spain: build castles in S. 209:11
  King of S.'s daughter came to visit 190:1
  rain, rain, go to S. 224:2
Span: when Adam delved and Eve s. 24:2
Spaniards: S. seem wiser than they are 22:20
  win this game ... thrash the S. 102:8
Spanish: I speak S. to God 78:18
Spare: I will s. all the place 31:3
  s. all I have ... take my life 109:5
  woodman, s. the beechen tree 72:7
Sparkling: pair of s. eyes 116:14
Sparks: born unto trouble as the s. fly 35:3
Sparrow: I, said the S. 196:2
Speak: did he stop and s. to you? 61:10
  I only s. right on 263:20
  I s. severely to my boy 74:7
  I s. Spanish to God 78:18
  never s. well of one another 143:11
  now s., or ... hold his peace 53:20
  one to s., ... another to hear 317:3
  other sins only s.; murder shrieks 323:15
  s. each other in passing 161:7
  s., Lord; for thy servant heareth 33:28
  s. not of my debts unless 226:5
  s. of me as I am 280:14
  s. roughly to your little boy 74:6
  s. the speech ... as I pronounc'd 251:7
  s. well of yr. friend 226:6
  s. when you are spoken to 77:8, 226:7
  think to-day and s. tomorrow 227:30
  when I think, I must s. 245:6
  when you s., ... I'd have you do it ever 293:2
Speaking: he ... [Adam] thought him still s.
  179:1
Speaks: s. ill of his wife 226:8
  when he s., the air ... is still 258:7
Spear: bring me my s. 55:8
Spears: stars threw down their s. 56:6
Species: especially the male of the s. 157:8
  female of the s. is more deadly 154:14
  not the individual, but the s. 141:5
  our self-tormented s. 237:8
Spectacles: her s. ... on her aproned knees
  71:16
  needed not the s. of books 104:4
  s. on nose and pouch on side 244–5:11
Spectator: I live ... as a S. 9:6
Spectre: grows pale and s.-thin 149:15
Speculator: I was raised by a s. 307:14
Speech: be ... never tax'd for s. 242:1
  found our s. copious without order 140:1
  freedom of s. and expression 235:4
  let thy s. be short 52:2
  rude am I in my s. 278:21

Speech (continued)
  soul and ... gift of articulate s. 296:18
  souninge in moral vertu was his s. 79:10
  s. ... given to ... disguise thoughts 311:1
  s. is silver 226:9
Speed: s., bonny boat, like a bird 57:12
  our safety is in our s. 108:10
  whose s. ... faster than light 63:1
Spell: foreigners always s. better 318:13
Spend: to s. too much time in studies 23:6
  what we yet may s. 110:3
Spending: getting and s., we lay waste our
  powers 333:3
  riches are for s. 22:22
Spends: commuter—one who s. his life 325:8
Spenser: sage and serious poet S. 182:5
Spent: all passion s. 181:8
  how my light is s. 181:10
  soon got, soon s. 225:40
Speranza: lasciate ogni s. 95:6
Spermatozoa: a million million s., all ... alive
  137:14
Sphere: from the s. of our sorrow 300:8
  their motion in one s. 255:23
  world's storm-troubled s. 58:12
Spheres: as the restless s. 166:10
  stand still, you ever-moving s. 165:10
  stars shot madly from their s. 276:18
Spice: variety's the very s. of life 93:8
Spick and span 226:10
Spider: said a s. to a fly 136:10
  there came a big s. 191:3
Spies: as if we were God's s. 267:13
  sorrows ... come not single s. 252:21
Spires: City with her dreaming s. 19:4
  dim-discover'd s. 88:9
Spirit: a bold s. in a loyal breast 281:8
  a pardlike S. beautiful and swift 297:14
  a S. still, and bright 334:14
  a S., yet a Woman too 334:13
  expense of s. in a waste 294:11
  follow your s., and upon this charge 259:5
  give me the s. 257:9
  hail to thee, blithe s. 300:1
  have not that alacrity of s. 285:14
  history of the human s. 19:11
  how oft, in s. ... sylvan Wye 335:13
  I am thy father's s. 249:6
  life-blood of a master s. 182:3
  music ... gentlier on the s. lies 314:2
  my s. is too deeply laden 300:7
  pipe to the s. ditties of no tone 149:7
  present in s. 47:33
  rarely comest thou, S. of Delight 300:4
  same s. that its author writ 202:6
  s. ... is willing ... flesh is weak 45:2
  s. of health or goblin damn'd 249:3
  s. that will start the world along 336:9
  s. to bathe in fiery floods 273:10
  spur that the clear s. doth raise 175:1
  the worser s. ... a woman 294:16
  Wild S. ... moving everywhere 299:4
Spirits: actors ... were all s. 288:16
  choice and master s. of this age 263:6
  comfort and despair, which like two s.
  294:16
  her wanton s. look out 290:8
  I can call s. from the ... deep 255:5
  pluck up thy s., man 184:5
Spit: 'Please don't s. on the floor 13:3

Spit (*continued*)
  s. fire; spout rain 266:7
  s. in my face, call me horse 254:15
  s. upon my Jewish gaberdine 274:10
Spite: cursed s., that ... I was born 249:14
  cut off ... nose to s. ... face 210:29
  reckless what I do to s. the world 271:2
  S. of cormorant devouring Time 268:6
  s. of pride, in erring reason's s. 203:4
  victory in s. of all terror 82:12
Splash: a scream, a s. 16:12
Spleen or Vapors 104:2
Splendid: and by the vision s. 332:2
  in ... our s. isolation 124:7
  man is ... s. in ashes 60:3
  s. tear from the passion-flower 314:4
Splendour: the s. falls on castle walls 314:14
Split: part ... to make all s. 276:14
Spoil: come and s. the fun 76:1
  company ... hath been the s. of me 255:12
Spoiled: had s. his nice new rattle 75:14
Spoilers of ... symmetry of shelves 156:3
Spoils: it s. the singing of the nightingale 147:11
Spoke: English as she is s. 318:14
  less he s., the more he heard 231:26
  put a s. in one's wheel 226:12
Spoken: sure of being kindly s. of 20:9
Spoon: dish ran away with the s. 189:5
  have a long s. that sups with the devil 219:25
  silver s. in his mouth 208:22
Spoons: measured out my life with coffee s. 106:14
  the faster we counted our s. 108:2
Sport: detested s., that owes its pleasure 93:9
  dog laughed to see such s. 189:5
  S. that wrinkled Care derides 173:17
  s. with Amaryllis in the shade 174:16
  the chase, the s. of kings 304:8
  they kill us for their s. 266:20
  to s. wd. be as tedious as to work 253:21
Sported: and by him s. on the green 304:13
Sports: let us prove ... the s. of love 146:1
Spot: Out, damned s.! out, I say! 272:2
Spout: cataracts and hurricanoes s. 266:6
  spit fire; s. rain 266:7
Sprang: I s. to the stirrup 61:6
Sprat: a s. to catch a mackerel (whale) 226:13
Spray: never a s. of yew 18:16
Spread: money ... like muck ... be s. 22:9
Sprightly: tossing their heads in s. dance 331:9
Spring: a linnet courting ... in the s. 58:4
  absent in the s. 294:5
  all the breathing s. 88:8
  apparell'd like the s. 281:2
  can S. be far behind? 299:6
  how this s. of love resembleth 292:6
  in s., when woods are getting green 76:12
  in the Fire of S. 109:14
  in the s. a young man's fancy 313:15
  it is s., moonless night 316:2
  lived light in the s. 18:10
  no s. ... beauty hath such grace 101:1
  sweet lovers love the s. 245–6:16
  the year's at the s. 62:7
  when the hounds of s. 309:14
  where are the songs of S.? 147:4

Springs: four wanton s. end in a word 281:12
  steeds to water at those s. 246:13
Sprites: [tale] ... of s. and goblins 292:13
Spur: do not s. a free horse 226:14
  fame is the s. 175:1
  no s. to prick the sides of my intent 270:6
  on the s. of the moment 226:15
Spurns that patient merit ... takes 250–1:20
Spurs: let the boy win his s. 105:9
Squandering wealth was his peculiar art 103:5
Squeaking: with shrieking and s. 62:1
Squeals: if he s., let him go 189:1
Squeers, Mr. Wackford 98:9
Stable: nothing s. in the world 151:12
Stables: the s. are ... centre of the household 295:17
Stabs: with bemock'd-at s. kill ... waters 288:15
Staff: I'll break my s. 289:5
  my s. of faith to walk upon 232:12
Stag at eve had drunk his fill 239:6
Stage: after a well-grac'd actor leaves the s. 284:5
  all the world's a s. 244:11
  frets his hour upon the s. 272:10
  if ... played upon a s. now 291:14
  mellow glory of the Attic s. 18:14
  on the s. he was natural 123:5
  s. where every man must play a part 274:1
  the wonder of our S. 145:11
  to this great s. of fools 267:8
  two hours' traffic of our s. 285:18
  your daughter on the s. 91:10
Stages: where'er his s. may have been 300:12
Stagger: they reel ... s. like a drunken man 37:5
Stain: true blue will never s. 228:21
  without fault or s. on thee 58:6
Stairs: somebody stopped the moving s. 165:2
Stake: when honour's at the s. 252:19
Stamford: bullocks at S. fair? 257:6
Stamp: s. of his lowly origin 95:10
  too late to save the s. 124:9
Stand: s. still, you ever-moving spheres 165:10
  s. up for Jesus! 105:2
  Sun, s. thou still 33:12
  who will s. on either hand? 163:11
Standard: raise the scarlet s. high 90:3
Standing: Jackson s. like a stone wall 26:5
Stanley: here S. meets,—how S. scorns 63:2
  on, S., on! 240:10
Stanza: pens s. when he shd. engross 201:11
Star: and a s. or two beside 86:12
  desire of the moth for the s. 300:8
  dropped from the zenith, like a falling s. 176:14
  eve's one s. 148:4
  go and catch a falling s. 101:5
  hitch yr. wagon to a s. 108:18
  Soul ... rises with us, our life's S. 332:1
  s. to steer her by 168:15
  there was a s. danc'd 277:20
  thy soul was like a S. 333:13
  twinkle, twinkle, little s. 311:5
  we have seen his s. 43:8
Star Chamber matter of it 276:1
Star-crossed: a pair of s. lovers 285:17

Stomach (continued)
    have the ... s. ... of a King of England
      107:13
    my s. is not good 307:11
Stone: heaviest s. ... the devil can throw
    129:14
    kill two birds with one s. 217:38
    leave no s. unturned 218:34
    let him first cast a s. at her 46:24
    not a s. tell where I lie 204:1
    precious s. set in the silver sea 282:5
    rolling s. gathers no moss 224:26
    s. that lieth not in yr. way 226:26
    s. which the builders refused 37:13
    virtue is like a rich s. 23:2
    water like a s. 235:15
    we raised not a s. 330:4
Stones: in glass houses ... never throw s.
    214:37
    inestimable s., unvalued jewels 285:1
    labour of an age in piled s. 175:11
    o, ye are men of s. 268:2
    sermons in s. 243:15
    you blocks, you s.! 262:4
Stools: between two s. one falls 207:39
Stop: Shelley ... did he s. and speak? 61:10
    s.; look; listen 319:7
    s. me and buy one 11:7
    time ... must have a s. 256:1
    when the kissing had to s. 62:11
Stopped: he [Death] kindly s. for me 99:17
    it s. short—never to go again 336:8
Stoppeth: he s. one of three 85:11
Store: oft amid thy s. 147:3
    s. of ladies, whose bright eyes 174:6
Storied windows richly dight 173:11
Stories: s. ... not to thy credit 72:4
    tell sad s. of the death of kings 283:6
Storm: after a s. ... a calm 206:8
    and rides upon the s. 92:15
    any port in a s. 206:17
    S. and Stress 155:12
    S. in a Teacup 29:10, 226:27
    lovers fled ... into the s. 147:14
    the pelting of this pitiless s. 266:13
Storms: he sought the s. 102–3:17
    sudden s. are short 282:4
    vows made in s. are forgotten 229:21
Story: honour is the subject of my s. 262:6
    in pain, to tell my s. 253:9
    not that the s. need be long 317:4
    our rough island-s. 314:11
    place where a s. ended 106:10
    shuts up the s. of our days 232:11
    summits old in s. 314:14
    teach him how to tell my s. 279:2
    tell me the old, old s. 128:4
    the s. of Sussex told 28:3
Stove: like ... ice on a hot s. 113:16
Straight trees ... crooked roots 226:28
Strain: attain to something like prophetic s.
    173:12
    that s. again 290:10
Strained: quality of mercy is not s. 275:1
Straining upon the start 259:5
Strains: such s. as wd. have won the ear
    174:10
Straits: moon lies fair upon the S. 18:9
Strand: India's coral s. 130:1
    let's all go down the S. 77:12

Strange: how s. it seems, and new! 61:10
    how s. now, looks the life 60:10
    misery acquaints ... with s. bedfellows
      288:7
    something rich and s. 288:1
    s. as if ... married a great while 89:17
    'tis s. but true 70:10
    truth is always s. 70:10
    'twas s., 'twas passing s. 279:2
    very s. and wellbred 89:17
Stranger: a s. in a strange land 31:16
    a s. yet to pain 125:13
    love ye ... the s. 33:2
    s. than fiction 70:10
    the wiles of the s. 186:2
Strangers: gracious and courteous to s. 22:6
    s. in the land of Egypt 33:2
    we may be better s. 245:7
Strangling: other use than s. in a string 136:4
Stratford: the scole of S. atte Bowe 79:4
Straw: drowning man ... catch at a s. 211:35
    find quarrel in a s. 252:19
    headpiece filled with s. 106:7
    last s. breaks the camel's back 218:20
    scrannel pipes of wretched s. 175:4
Strawberries: feed upon s., sugar and cream
    188:8
    in Holborn I saw good s. 285:3
Straws: errors, like s. 103:16
Stray: if with me you'd fondly s. 115:6
    nor ever ... from the Church to s. 56:4
Streaks: number the s. of the tulip 141:5
Stream: hoar leaves in the glassy s. 253:1
    still glides the S. 334:9
    time, like an ever-rolling s. 323:6
Streamers: sails filled and s. waving 180:15
Streams: fresh showers ... from ... the s. 298:4
    thy banner ... s. ... against the wind 69:7
Street: have yer bought the s.? 81:13
    man in the s. 220:15
Streets: through s. broad and narrow 15:10
    we shall fight ... in the s. 82:13
Strength: as thy days, so shall thy s. be 33:8
    better than the s. of Samson 221:1
    Christ is thy s. 183:2
    comfort in the s. of love 332:12
    fall'n ... that tower of s. 314:10
    glory of young men is their s. 38:25
    if I be shaven ... s. will go 33:21
    Ignorance is S. 197:4
    king's name is a tower of s. 285:13
    my s. is as the s. of ten 314:19
    my s. is made perfect in weakness 48:19
    promise of s. and manhood 58:6
    s. to bear the misfortunes of others 234:4
    their s. labour and sorrow 36:23
    they go from s. to s. 36:20
    to have a giant's s. 273:6
    unity is s. 229:12
    we shall fight with growing ... s. 82:13
Stretch: upon the rack ... s. him out longer
    268:5
Stretched: there was things ... he s. 318:6
    when I s. out my hand 306:16
Strew: shall I s. ... rose or rue or laurel?
    309:16
    s. on her roses, roses 18:16
Strife: agonies, the s. of human hearts 150:11
    ancient forms of party s. 313:5
    are God and Nature ... at s. 312:16

Strife (*continued*)
  books ... dull and endless s. 335:5
  ignoble s. 126:12
  in the s. of Truth with Falsehood 162:14
  poverty breeds s. 223:19
Strike: no right to s. against the public safety
  90:10
  s. while the iron is hot 226:29
  take heed ... thou s. not awry 184:5
String: chewing little bits of s. 27:2
  harp not on that s. 285:10
  provided ... s. to tie them together 183:6
  strangling in a s. 136:4
  untune that s. 290:3
Strings: the languid s. do scarcely move 56:14
  there are s. in the human heart 97:8
Stripes: whose broad s. and bright stars 153:6
Strive: four champions fierce, s. here 177:8
  s. to set the crooked straight ? 184:9
Striving to better, mar what's well 265:16
Strode: out to Severn s. 81:6
Stroke: tune of flutes kept s. 242:14
Strong: be s. and of a good courage 33:10
  but wants that little s. 134:2
  out of the s. ... sweetness 33:19
  s.-backed and neat-bound 156:7
  we know ... that the wall is s. 326–7:15
  we then that are s. 47:31
  what will it help ... once you were s. ? 57:15
Strove: a little still she s. 69:11
  I s. with none 156:11
Struggle: manhood a s. 100:9
  say not the s. naught availeth 85:1
Struggling for life in the water 142:1
Strumpet: transform'd into a s.'s fool 242:9
Struts: that s. and frets his hour 272:10
Stubble: chin ... show'd like a s. land 254:1
  he lies in the s. 11:18
Studies: s. serve for delight, for ornament 23:5
  too much time in s. 23:6
Study: every Jack ... must s. the knack 121:6
  his s. was but litel on the bible 79:13
  I am slow of s. 276:15
  much s. ... weariness of the flesh 39:28
  proper s. of Mankind is Man 203:5
  s. what you most affect 287:6
Stuff: ambition ... made of sterner s. 263:13
  listen all day to such s. 74:4
  'S. and nonsense!' said Alice 75:8
  s. of life to knit me 136:7
  such s. as dreams are made on 288–9:16
  written such volumes of s.! 158:6
Stumble: they s. that run fast 286:15
Stupidity: confirm'd in full s. 104:14
  no sin except s. 327:4
Sturm und Drang 155:12
Stygian: in S. cave forlorn 173:14
  s. smoke of the pit 138:14
Style: le s. est l'homme 62:14
Style: s. is the man himself 62:14
  true definition of a s. 309:2
Subdue: it [force] may s. for a moment 64:5
Subject: every s.'s duty ... soul 259:11
  load every rift of yr. s. 152:12
  poetry ... startle ... with its s. 151:13
  s. to the same diseases 274:17
  s. we old men are to ... lying 257:10
  this s. for heroic song 179:6
Subjects: my s. for a pair of carved saints
  283:7

Subjects (*continued*)
  poorest s. are at this hour asleep! 257:2
Sublime: du s. au ridicule ... un pas 185:11
Sublime: from the s. to the ridiculous 185:11
  my object all s. 118:10
  one step above the s. 197:18
  s. and the ridiculous are ... related 197:18
  we can make our lives s. 161:1
Sublimity: a S. to welcome me home 152:6
Submit: King do now ? Must he s. ? 283:7
Subscribers: he for s. baits his hook 82:3
  not printing any list of s. 144:17
Substance of things hoped for 49:21
Subtlety is better than force 226:30
Succeed: if at first you don't s. 132:11
  those who ne'er s. 99:13
Succeeds: nothing s. like excess 328:14
  nothing s. like success 222:17
Success: s. and miscarriage are empty sounds
  140:4
  s. is counted sweetest 99:13
  this ecstasy, is s. in life 198:9
  to command s. 9:4
  to make a marriage a s. 238:2
  true s. is to labour 307:10
  yours [religion] is S. 24:15
Sucked: I s. the blood 86:7
Sucker: a s. born every minute 24:10
Sucks: my baby ... s. the nurse asleep 243:11
  where the bee s., there suck I 289:6
Sudden storms are short 282:4
Suddenly: shall s. come to his temple 43:6
Sudetenland is the last ... claim 132:14
Sue: less used to s. than to command 239:8
  we were not born to s. 281:9
Suez: somewhere East of Suez 155:2
Suffer: but doth s. a sea-change 288:1
  not s. a witch to live 32:11
  s. for the truth's sake 53:8
  s. me to come to thee 325:1
  s. the little children to come 45:13
  than one innocent s. 54:11
  ye s. fools gladly ... yourselves are wise 48:17
Sufferance is the badge of all our tribe 274:10
Suffered: Lord Hippo s. fearful loss 27:14
  love a place the less for having s. 20:16
Suffering: been s., nothing but s. 20:16
Sufficiency: an elegant s., content 316:13
Sufficient: s. conclusions from insufficient
  premises 68:6
  s. unto the day is the evil 44:6
Sugar: I must s. my hair 75:4
  s. and spice and all that's nice 195:6
Suggests: the word Intellectual s. 20:3
Suit: silk s. ... cost me much money 199:9
Sultry: more common where the climate's s.
  69:10
Summer: a wind in s. 150:8
  after s., merrily, merrily 289:6
  all on a s.'s day 192–3:8
  bud of love by s.'s ripening breath 286:11
  compare thee to a s.'s day 293:13
  dry as s. dust 331:4
  eternal s. gilds them 69–70:21
  haunt of flies on s. eves 150:2
  I only know that s. sang in me 170:15
  in their s. beauty kiss'd 285:8
  last rose of s. 184:1
  live murmur of a s.'s day 18:19
  on s. eves by haunted stream 174:7

Summer (*continued*)
one swallow does not make a s.   226:33
s. and winter ... shall not cease   30:23
s. by this sun of York   284:8
s. has o'er-brimm'd ... clammy cells   147:2
s. has set in with ... severity   88:2
s. is icumen in   14:7
s.'s lease ... too short a date   293:13
s.'s velvet buds   258:8
thinking on fantastic s.'s heat   282:1
thy eternal s. shall not fade   293:14
to ... men that sought him sweet as s.   262:2
warmed ... by the same ... s.   274:17
with love in s.'s wonderland   188:1
Summits: snowy s. old in story   314:14
Sun (*see also* Sonne): all, except their s., is set   69–70:21
and I will sing of the s.   205:3
at the going down of the s.   54:5
before the rising s.   323:5
between me and the s.   99:19
birds are faint with the hot s.   151:1
cannot make our s. stand still   167:15
close to the s. in lonely lands   312:1
dominions, on which the s. never sets   187:16
early-rising s. has not attained   132:1
eyes are nothing like the s.   294:13
far from the s. and summer-gale   127:1
follow thy fair s.   72:12
furnish'd ... by Aldershot S.   29:12
glory of the s. will be dimmed   23:23
go out in the midday s.   91:8
hath Britain all the s.?   247:5
I am too much in the s.   247:19
I gin to be aweary of the s.   272:11
just as the s. was rising   15:1
late eclipses in the s. and moon   265:9
light ... dies with the dying s.   57:13
light ... where no s. shines   315:18
love that moves the s.   95:8
loves to live i' th' s.   244:6
make guilty ... the s.   265:10
make hay while the s. shines   220:12
Mother, give me the s.   138:5
never shall s. that morrow see   270:3
no new thing under the s.   39:12
now the s. is laid to sleep   145:8
self-same s. that shines   293:4
she grew in s. and shower   335:9
so when the s. in bed   175:10
s. breaks through the darkest clouds   287:11
s. came up upon the left   85:13
s. climbs slow, how slowly   85:3
s. go down upon your wrath   48:24
s. shines upon all alike   226:31
S., stand thou still   33:12
s. that warms you ... shine on me   281:11
s. was shining on the sea   75:16
thank heavens, the s. has gone in   303:9
the chambers of the s.   56:13
the maturing s.   147:1
the rising of the s.   15:8
the s. is lost, and th' earth   100:16
the s. of righteousness arise   43:7
the s. shall not smite thee   37:16
this s. of York   284:8
to have enjoy'd the s.   18:10
white founts ... in the Courts of the s.   81:4
with the setting s. dropped from the zenith   176:14

Sunday: golf may be played on S.   157:14
here of a S. morning   136:6
killing ... mouse on S.   58:2
shot through his heart on S.   307:1
S. clears away the rust   9:7
Sunk: all s. beneath the wave   93:1
Sunless: down to a s. sea   87:11
Sunny Jim: they called him S.   128:3
Sunny pleasure-dome   87:15
Sunrise: in eternity's s.   55:4
Suns: blest by s. of home   59:6
Sunset: s. and evening star   311:13
s. ran, one glorious blood-red   61:4
Sunshine: no s. but has some shadow   222:8
the s. is a glorious birth   331:14
Sup: who sipped no s.   121:2
Supercilious: a s. knowledge in accounts   301:9
Superfluity of good things   10:8
Superfluous: in the poorest thing s.   266:2
Superior: revolt ... that they may be s.   18:6
Superiority: one shall acquire an evident s.   143:2
Superstition is the religion of feeble minds   64:13
Superstitions: new truths ... end as s.   138:1
Supper: hope is ... a bad s.   23:13
sings for his s.   191:4
to s. with a flood of tears   97:15
Support: help the feeble ... s. him after   289:9
Sure: his mercy is for ever s.   153:5
s. way to see it lost ... last ditch   65:3
Surfeit: feast ... where no crude s. reigns   172:18
Surfeit-swelled: so s., so old   258:3
Surfeiting: give me excess ... that s.   290:10
Surfeits: the s. of our own behaviour   265:10
Surgery: honour hath no skill in s.   255:21
Surmise: with a wild s.   150–1:15
Surprise: poetry shd. s. by a fine excess   151:14
Surprised by joy ... I turned   333:1
Surrender: unconditional and immediate s.   125:1
we shall never s.   82:13
Survey: monarch of all I s.   93:14
time that takes s.   256:1
Survival: s. of the fittest   95:12, 305:3
without victory there is no s.   82:12
Survive: but one ... Noah dare hope to s.   137:14
Suspects: man s. himself a fool   338:1
Suspension: willing s. of disbelief   87:19
Suspicion: Caesar's wife ... above s.   71:15
s. ... haunts the guilty mind   261:1
Suspicions amongst thoughts ... bats amongst birds   22:24
Sussex: and the story of S. told   28:3
there shall the S. songs be sung   28:3
Swagman: jolly s. camped by a billabong   198:10
Swain: no better than a homely s.   260:13
Swains: all our s. commend her   292:8
Swallow: hope ... flies with s.'s wings   285:12
one s. does not make a summer   226:33
Swallows: gathering s. twitter   147:5
whitethroat builds and all the s.   61:2
Swan: Sweet S. of Avon   145:16
Swanee Ribber: 'way down upon de S.   112:8
Swans: all his geese are s.   214:29

Swans (continued)
  seven s. a-swimming   194:2
  s. sing before they die   87:10
Swap horses in mid-stream   159:14
Swat: Akond of S.   158:1
Sway: mercy is above this sceptred s.   275:1
  regions ... thy posterity shall s.   92:2
  truth ... prevailed with double s.   122:10
Swear: s. me, Kate, like a lady   255:9
  when very angry, s.   318:18
Sweat: blood, toil, tears and s.   82:11
  in the s. of thy face   30:13
  none will s. but for promotion   243:19
  s. for duty not for meed   243:19
Sweating: quietly s. palm to palm   137:15
Sweats: Falstaff s. to death   254:9
Sweep on, you fat and greasy citizens   243:16
Sweet: a lady s. and kind   17:2
  and s. girl-graduates   314:12
  back to the great s. mother   310:6
  both s. things ... all s. things   57:8
  but then, how it was s.!   60:16
  by any other name wd. smell as s.   286:9
  deserves not the s.   211:14
  each op'ning s. of earliest bloom   88:8
  how sour s. music is!   284:7
  how s. and fair she seems to be   322:1
  how s. the moonlight sleeps   275:8
  how s. their memory still   92:14
  law beyond its own s. will   326:6
  little s. ... kill much bitterness   148:11
  love is s. for a day   310:4
  love is s., given or returned   299:12
  naught so s. as Melancholy   67:8
  revenge is s.   224:15
  sessions of s. silent thought   293:18
  sleep of labouring man is s.   39:17
  stolen waters are s.   38:7
  s. as love   310:11
  s. breathing Zephyrus did ... play   305:15
  s. is pleasure after pain   103:14
  s. is revenge—especially to women   69:12
  s. Little Buttercup I   119:9
  s. singing in the choir   15:8
  s. Stay-at-Home, s. Well-content   96:3
  s. Thames! run softly   305:16
  s. to look into ... face of heaven   151:6
  s. to taste ... indigestion sour   281:13
  swing low, s. chariot   17:1
  the s. o' the year   292:17
  to have a s. tooth   226:35
  when you speak, s.   293:2
  you'll look s. upon the seat   95:4
Sweet and twenty: kiss me, s.   291:2
Sweet-briar: through the s. or the vine   174:2
Sweeten: children s. labours   21:18
  civet ... to s. my imagination   267:5
  perfumes of Arabia will not s.   272:3
Sweeter: anything to me is s.   133:11
  s. manners, purer laws   313:5
  s. than the berry   115:4
Sweetest: last taste of sweets is s. last   282:3
  s. li'l feller   306:5
  s. thing that ever grew   332:10
Sweethearts: old soldiers, s., are surest   324:1
Sweeting: trip no further, pretty s.   291:1
Sweetly flows that liquefaction   132:6
Sweetness: out of the strong came forth s.   33:19
  passion for s. and light   19:10

Sweetness (continued)
  pursuit of s. and light   19:5
  two noblest things ... s. and light   308:11
  waste its s. on the desert air   126:10
Sweets: as the last taste of s., is sweetest last   282:3
  perpetual feast of nectared s.   172:18
  stolen s. are best   83:16
  s. and a ride in the train   171:10
  s. to the sweet; farewell!   253:4
Swept: if seven maids ... s. it   76:3
Swift: Cousin S., you will never be a poet   104:12
  too s. ... as tardy as too slow   286:18
Swifter than eagles, ... stronger than lions   34:11
Swim: a naughty night to s. in   266:15
  but said I cd. not s.   75:7
Swine: nor yet feed the s.   188:8
  pearls before s.   44:6
  s., women and bees cannot be turned   226:36
Swing low, sweet chariot   17:1
Swoon: at twelve noon the natives s.   91:8
Swoons: wearied band s. to a waltz   137:15
Swop for my dear old Dutch   81:14
Sword: a Sigh is the s. of an angel king   55:5
  believed he had a s. upstairs   337:3
  his father's s. ... girded on   184:2
  I with s. will open   276:4
  is the s. unsway'd?   285:11
  man for the s.   314:18
  more cruel the pen ... than ... s.   67:9
  nor shall my s. sleep   55:8
  nor the deputed s.   273:4
  pen is mightier than the s.   63:3
Swords: beat ... s. into plowshares   40:18
  with paper hats and wooden s.   320:1
Swore: Frankie and Johnny ... s. to be true   15:2
Swound: like noises in a s.   86:2
Syllable: last s. of recorded time   272:10
Symmetry: frame thy fearful s.   56:5
  spoilers of the s. of shelves   156:3
Sympathise: the Walrus said: 'I deeply s.'   76:5
  s. with ... pains ... not ... pleasures   137:11
Sympathy: without feeling or exciting s.   141:8
System: energies of our s. will decay   23:23
Systems: our little s. have their day   312:10

Ta-ra-ra-boom-de-ay   238:11
Table: crumbs ... from the rich man's t.   46:8
Tables: to turn the t.   228:32
Tabor: as to the t.'s sound   331:15
Tail: better ... than the t. of a lion   207:25
  he's treading on my t.   75:2
  improve his shining t.   73:17
  sting is in the t.   226:22
  such a little t. behind   27:1
  thereby hangs a t.   279:13
Tails: and bring their t. behind them   190:10
  cut off their t. with a carving knife   195:1
  frogs and snails and puppy-dogs' t.   195:6
  stings in their t.   50:25
  t. like unto scorpions   50:25
Take: t. a farthing away   226:37
  t. any man's horses   258:2
  t. away my good name   226:39
Taken: when t. to be well shaken   88:16

Teases: he knows it t. 74:6
Tedious: people are ... charming or t. 328:1
  returning were as t. as go o'er 271:10
  scandal is gossip made t. 328:3
  t. as a twice-told tale 264:17
  thinking his prattle to be t. 284:5
Teeth: bid them ... keep their t. clean 246:7
  by the skin of one's t. 225:28
  children's t. are set on edge 41:16
  escaped with the skin of my t. 35:7
  sparkling eyes, and t. like pearls 62:6
Teetotaller: I'm only a beer t. 295:13
Tell: I can t. you anyhow 64:2
  I cannot t. what you ... think 262:6
  never seek to t. thy love 55:10
  our dead bodies must t. the tale 239:3
  t. it not in Gath 34:10
  t. me not, in mournful numbers 160:14
  t. me not, sweet, I am unkind 162:6
  t. me what she sings ? 334:17
  t. thee what thou art 78:6
  to dream of, not to t. 87:6
  when or how I cannot t. 236:10
Telling: not arguing ... I am t. you 325:6
Temper: I shall t. ... justice with mercy
    179:11
  keep me in t.; I wd. not be mad! 265:17
  man of such a feeble t. 262:7
Temperance hotels: I prefer t. 322:12
Temperate: more lovely and more t. 293:13
Tempered by war, disciplined by ... peace
    153:1
Tempers: God t. the wind 306:15
Tempests: looks on t. and is never shaken
    294:8
Temple: shall suddenly come to his t. 43:6
Temples: for ... the t. of his gods 163:10
  mortal t. of a king 283:6
  solemn t., the great globe itself 288:16
Tempora: O t.! O mores! 84:6
  t. mutantur et nos mutamur 17:14
Temporary: use of force alone is but *t.* 64:5
Tempt: t. me no more 96:6
  to t. my Lady Poltagrue 27:8
Temptation: can resist everything except t.
    328:2
  lead us not into t. 43:24
  maximum of t. ... of opportunity 296:14
  not over-fond of resisting t. 26:3
  prepare thy soul for t. 51:15
  the last t. is the greatest treason 107:10
  watch ... that ye enter not into t. 45:2
  way to get rid of a t. 328:7
Tempted: My Lady, t. by a ... whim 27:8
  one thing to be t., Escalus 273:1
  to his ... annoyance t. him 27:8
Tempts: all that t. yr. wand'ring eyes 125:12
Tempus: fugit ... inreparabile t. 321:8
  t. edax rerum 197:16
  t. fugit 227:22
Ten: as the strength of t. 314:19
  better that t. guilty ... escape 54:11
  t. to make ... match to win 187:11
Tender is the night 149:16
Tenderly: take her up t. 134:10
Tenders: a shoal of fools for t. 89:10
Tenement: o'r informed the T. of clay
    102–3:17
Tennis: we are ... the star's t. balls 323:17
Ten-sixty-six and All That 241:7

Tenterhooks: to be on t. 227:23
Tent-royal of their emperor 258:8
Terminological: some risk of t. inexactitude
    82:7
Terms: fair t. and a villain's mind 274:11
Terrible as an army with banners 40:13
Territorial: last t. claim ... in Europe 132:14
Terror: so full of dismal t. was the time
    284:15
  victory in spite of all t. 82:12
Test: source, and end, and t. of Art 202:3
Text: of that t. a pulled hen 79:5
Thais: lovely T. by his side 103:11
Thames: every drop of the T. is liquid history
    65:7
  set the T. on fire 225:14
  sweet T.! run softly 305:16
Thank: I t. whatever gods may be 130:8
  t. me no thankings 287:1
  we t. with brief thanksgiving 310:1
Thankless: to have a t. child 265:15
Thatch: build a house with a deep t. 28:3
Thaw and resolve itself into a dew 248:2
The Times: T. has made many ministries
    23:18
  Top People take T. 11:9
Theatre: as in a t. the eyes of man 284:5
  Idols of the T. 23:16
Theatres: domes, t. and temples 333:6
  in t. of crowded men 148:7
Their's not to reason why 311:11
Theme: fools are my t. 70:11
Themselves: are a law unto t. 47:16
Them's my sentiments 315:11
There: haven't been t. to attend to the case
    117:5
  is t. anybody t. ? 96:14
  met a man who wasn't t. 169:8
Thereby hangs a tail 279:13
Thersites' body is as good as Ajax' 247:8
Thespian: bathed in the T. springs 102:11
Thick: as t. as thieves 227:25
  one can lay it on so t. 68:10
Thief: Aram ... t. ... liar ... murderer 72:3
  give a t. rope enough 224:29
  jury ... may ... have a t. or two 273:1
  opportunity makes the t. 222:29
  poor man, beggarman, t. 195:2
  set a t. to catch a t. 227:26
  steals something from the t. 279:4
  the t. doth fear each bush 261:1
Thieves: as thick as t. 227:25
  beauty provoketh t. 243:14
  fell among t. 45:28
  made it a den of t. 45:14
  there is honour among t. 217:1
Thin end of the wedge 227:27
Thing: a lovely and a fearful t. 69:16
  a most unattractive old t. 118–9:15
  a tear is an intellectual t. 55:5
  a terrible t., thank God 316:4
  a t. of shreds and patches 117:16
  a t. she had frequently done 71:16
  an excellent t. in woman 268:3
  any good t. come out of Nazareth ? 46:18
  any t. that is thy neighbour's 32:9
  excuse my having such a t. 297:7
  far, far better t. ... I do 99:12
  first t. you'll ... want to know 237:13
  foolish t. was but a toy 292:3

Thing (*continued*)

has this t. appear'd again ? 247:14
if you want a t. well done 229:24
ill-favour'd t., ... but mine own 246:1
in the poorest t. superfluous 266:2
lack of many a t. I sought 293:18
laugh at any mortal t. 70:2
like this sort of t. 160:2
moderation ... a fatal t. 328:14
one damned t. after another 136:12
one t. is certain ... Life flies 110:4
only t. ... to fear is fear itself 234:18
see such a t. in yr. life ? 195:1
sincerity is a dangerous t. 327:2
sleep! it is a gentle t. 86:13
spirit of youth in every t. 294:5
such a t. as I myself 262:6
swans sing ... 'twere no bad t. 87:10
sweetest t. that ever grew 332:10
the acting of a dreadful t. 262:13
the play's the t. wherein 250:19
t. immortal as itself 249:4
throw away the dearest t. 269:11
to one t. constant never 277:21
what t. of sea or land ? 180:15
who Pretender ... quite another t. 68:15

Things: a thousand thousand slimy t. 86:11
a time for all t. 228:3
all good t. ... fruits of originality 170:10
all t. are artificial 59:13
all t. are lawful ... all t. not expedient 48:2
all t. both great and small 87:4
all t. bright and beautiful 10:4
all t. to all men 48:4
all t. uncomely ... broken ... worn out 337:7
all t. wise and wonderful 10:4
as t. have been, t. remain 85:1
few t. to desire ... many t. to fear 22:14
former t. are passed away 51:3
forms of t. unknown 277:6
foundation of all good t. 64:14
four t. greater than all t. 154:9
giver of all good t. 53:6
I put away childish t. 48:6
like and dislike the same t. 237:15
little t. please little minds 219:18
little t. ... the most important 101:12
look thy last on all t. lovely 96:13
Man is the master of all t. 310:2
men may rise ... to higher t. 312:11
mighty sum of t. forever speaking 331:5
more t. are wrought by prayer 312:9
more t. in heaven and earth 249:12
night and day ... both sweet t. 57:8
old, unhappy, far-off t. 334:17
remembrance of t. past 293:18
right judgement in all t. 53:5
river ... drowns t. weighty 23:10
see the t. thou dost not 267:7
set yr. affection on t. above 49:4
Shape of T. to Come 324:16
sweetest t. turn sourest 294:3
sympathiseth with all t. 59:14
take upon's the mystery of t. 267:13
the day of small t. 43:3
the more t. change 146:12
the two noblest of t. 308:11
there was t. ... he stretched 318:6
t. are not what they seem 160:14
t. are the sons of heaven 140:2

Things (*continued*)

t. hoped for ... t. not seen 49:21
t. past redress ... past care 282:11
t. sweet to taste prove ... sour 281:13
t. that go bump in the night 13:7
t. that wd. astonish you 117:7
t. ... true, t. ... honest ... just ... think on these t. 49:1
t. ... we ought not to have done 52:13
t. won are done 289:15
those brave translunary t. 102:11
thou ... art all t. under Heaven 179:17
to talk of many t. 76:4
two t. about the horse 13:11
two t. stand like stone 124:6
unseen t. above 128:4
unto the pure all t. are pure 49:18
what t. ... done at the Mermaid 25:7
you worse than senseless t.! 262:4
you'll understand a good many t. 99:3

Think: books t. for me 156:6
first t., and then speak 213:33
I cannot sit and t. 156:6
I stand alone, and t. 151:8
I t. him so, because I t. him so 292:5
I t., therefore I am 97:7
if ... I t. on thee, dear friend 293:19
not so t. as you drunk 306:3
t. of yr. forefathers ... posterity! 9:2
t. to-day and speak tomorrow 227:30
t. too little ... talk too much 103:3
t. well of all men 227:31
t. with the wise 227:32
to t. is to be full of sorrow 149:15
we cannot t. alike 104:7
when I t., I must speak 245:6
world is a comedy to those who t. 322:7

Thinking: dogged as does it. It ain't t. 318:2
good or bad, ... t. makes it so 250:5
never thought of t. for myself 119:10
plain living and high t. 333:11
put on one's t. cap 223:34
talk without t. ... shoot without aiming 227:11
t. is very far from knowing 227:33
t. jest what a Rum Go 324:14
t. on fantastic summer's heat 282:1
t. on the frosty Caucasus 282:1
t. too precisely on th' event 252:18

Thinks: he t. too much. Such men are dangerous 262:9
t. what ne'er was, nor is 202:7
you do anything, he t. no ill 293:20

Third: to make a t. she joined the former two 104:11
unto the t. and fourth generation 32:1

Thirst: a man can raise a t. 155:2

Thirsty: if he be t., give him water 38:28
when you are t., to cure it 199:5

Thirteen: the clocks were striking t. 197:2

Thirty: at t. man suspects 338:1
person under ... t. ... not a revolutionist 296:9
t. days hath September 194:6

Thomasin once ... so promising 113:17

Thorn: a t. in the flesh 48:18
day as sharp to them as t. 284:3
figs grew upon t. 81:1
he left the t. wi' me 67:7
no rose without a t. 222:6

Thorn (*continued*)
  snail's on the t.   62:7
Thorns: I fall upon the t. of life!   299:5
Thorny: life is t.; and youth is vain   87:7
Thou: and T. beside me singing   109:15
Thought: an holy and a good t.   52:11
  best that is known and t.   19:8
  every third t. ... my grave   289:8
  evil is wrought by want of T.   135:1
  green t. in a green shade   168:1
  he t. I t. he t. I slept   198:11
  I t. so little   119:16
  learning without t. ... t. without learning
    89:4
  never t. of thinking for myself   119:16
  oft was t., but ne'er so well express'd   202:8
  pale cast of t.   250–1:20
  sessions of sweet silent t.   293:18
  sweetest songs ... tell of saddest t.   300:2
  t. does not become a young woman   301:4
  t. is free   227:35
  to have loved ... t. ... done   18:10
  two lads that t. ... no more behind   292:12
  two souls with but a single t.   162:8
  use t. ... to justify ... wrong-doing   321:12
  use ... words ... to conceal ... t.   321:12
  whose armour ... honest t.   336:13
  wish was father ... to that t.   257:18
Thoughtless: the hour of t. youth   335:14
Thoughts: give thy t. no tongue   248:15
  in t. more elevate   177:6
  lift the t. of man   150:13
  my t. are not yr.   41:9
  my t. remain below   252:11
  pansies, that's for t.   252:23
  penny for yr. t.   223:2
  second t. are best   225:6
  Sensations rather than of T.!   151:10
  speech was given ... to disguise his t.   311:1
  suspicions among t. are like bats   22:24
  t. of a dry brain   106:6
  t. that wander through eternity   176:19
  t. ... too deep for tears   332:6
  thy t., when thou art gone   300:6
  turns to t. of love   313:15
  what fond and wayward t.   335:3
  when pleasant t. bring sad t.   332:7
  wording of his own highest t.   151:14
  words without t. never to heaven go   252:11
Thousand: a race, 'tis for a t. pound   92:9
  a t. ages in thy sight   323:5
  a t. lost golf balls   107:2
  a t. t. slimy things   86:11
  a t. years as one day   50:10
  a t. years in thy sight   36:22
  after t. aves told   147:15
  difference of forty t. men   324:7
  face that launch'd a t. ships?   165:8
  give me a t. kisses   77:15
  heart-ache ... t. natural shocks   250–1:20
  here's twenty t. Cornish men   129:4
  I heard a t. blended notes   332:7
  I, in twelve t., none   284:1
  if I had five t. a year   315:12
  laugh broke into a t. pieces   24:11
  more than sixscore t.   42:21
  my conscience hath a t. ... tongues   285:15
  night has a t. eyes   57:13
  O that we now had ... ten t. of those men
    259:12

Thousand (*continued*)
  of many t. kisses the poor last   243:5
  one day ... as a t. years   50:10
  one man ... out of ten t.   250:1
  Shallow, I owe you a t. pound   258:4
  take a farthing ... from a t. pounds   226:37
  ten t. saw I at a glance   331:9
  the t. creeds   58:13
  the t. years of peace   313:6
  t. fearful wrecks, a t. men   285:1
  used to sing it—fifty t. strong   336:9
  what a t. pities ... that Adam   135:2
  will you give ... t. guilders?   62:2
  Yesterday's Sev'n T. Years   110:2
Thousands: has been slave to t.   279:15
  Jesu ... the t. He hath freed   78:12
  makes countless t. mourn   66:8
  slain his t. ... his ten t.   34:7
  t. at his bidding speed   181:11
  where t. equally were meant   308:13
Threadneedle Street: the old lady of T.
    227:37
Threaten: you t. us, fellow?   62:5
Threatened men live long   227:38
Three: a t.-pipe problem   101:13
  actors are ... the usual t.   169:16
  all Gaul ... in t. parts   71:11
  Church clock at ten to t.   59:4
  going on ... for t. hundred years   328:9
  handsome in t. hundred pounds a year
    276:6
  he stoppeth one of t.   85:11
  I have answered t. questions   74:4
  I spied t. ships   14:10
  in married life t. is company   327:10
  indicates that two and one are t.   306:9
  is without t. good friends   245:3
  lives not t. good men unhanged   254:14
  loved t. whole days together   308:2
  there are t. sexes   303:14
  though he was only t.   171:8
  t. acres and a cow   88:6
  t. cheers and one cheer more   119:13
  t. distinct terms, Barbarians   19:6
  t., four, knock at the door   192:3
  t. hours a day will produce   318:3
  t. is company and two is none   327:10
  t. jolly farmers   97:2
  t. little maids from school   118:6
  t. may keep counsel if two be away   227:39
  t. poets in t. distant Ages   104:11
  t. ravens sat on a tree   11:15
  t. ships come sailing by   190:4
  t. things I never lends   308:7
  t. things ... too wonderful for me   39:7
  t. years she grew in sun   335:9
  we galloped all t.   61:6
  when shall we t. meet again?   269:3
Threefold: a t. cord is not ... broken   39:15
Threescore: the days of our years are t. years
    and ten   36:23
Threshold: starry t. of Jove's court   172:13
Thrice: men in great places are t. servants
    22:2
  t. welcome darling of the Spring   336:3
  weave a circle round him t.   87:16
Thrift, thrift, Horatio!   248:8
Thrifty: the housewife that's t.   301:17
Thrilling: in t. region of thick-ribbed ice
    273:10

Thrive: only the strong shall t. 241:15

Throat: took by the t. the circumcised dog 280–1:14

   unto the sweet bird's t. 244:4

Throne: here is my t., bid kings come 264:15

   high on a t. of royal state 176:15

   Queen-Moon is on her t. 149:16

Throw good money after bad 227:41

Thrush: that's the wise t. 61:3

Thumb: he put in his t. 191:2

   'twixt his finger and his t. 254:1

Thunder: glorious the t.'s roar 302:13

   laugh as I pass in t. 298:5

   t. in such lovely language 157:11

   t., lightning, or in rain? 269:3

Thunderbolt: like a t. he falls 312:1

Thunderstorm: dying duck in a t. 212:6

   streams like the t. 69:7

Thursday: T.'s child has far to go 191:8

   took ill on T. 193:6

Thus: why ... t? ... reason of this thusness? 322:13

Thwackum was for doing justice 109:11

Thyme: the wild t. blows 276:20

Thyself: love thy neighbour as t. 32:16

   when T. with shining Foot 111:1

Tiber: Oh, T., father T. 163:14

Tickle: if you t. us, do we not laugh? 274:17

   I'll t. your catastrophe 256:14

Tickling commodity 264:13

Tide: a t. in the affairs of men 264:3

   a t. in the affairs of women 70:3

   call of the running t. 168:16

   ev'n at the turning o' th' t. 259:1

   lived in the t. of times 263:7

   the t. is full, the moon lies fair 18:9

Tidings: glad t. of great joy 311:4

Tie: educational relations ... strongest t. 233:11

Ties: purse-strings ... common t. of friendship 223:36

Tiger: imitate the action of the t. 259:3

   smile on the face of the t. 12:10

   t., t., burning bright 56:5

   t.'s heart ... in a player's hide 127:6

   went for a ride on a t. 12:10

Tigers: there were no t. That was the point 107:7

Tiggers don't like honey 171:2

Time: a man must serve his t. 70:13

   a t. for all things 228:3

   a t. for such a word 272:10

   a t. to every purpose 39:14

   a t. when meadow, grove, and stream 331:12

   almost fairy t. 277:8

   ancient nobility ... act of t. 22:7

   and in good t. you gave it 266:1

   Art is long, and T. is fleeting 160:15

   bank and shoal of t. 270:5

   be not coy, but use yr. t. 132:8

   bid t. return 283:3

   busiest man who has t. to spare 198:5

   but a short t. to live 53:28

   conspiracy his t. doth take 288:5

   cormorant devouring T. 268:6

   creeping hours of t. 244:10

   dark backward and abysm of t. 287:15

   dust on antique t. 246:8

Time (*continued*)

   fixed figure for the t. of scorn 280:5

   fleet the t. carelessly 243:12

   fly envious T. 181:15

   fool all the people all the t. 160:1

   footprints in the sands of t. 161:1

   friends are thieves of t. 214:21

   full of dismal terror was the t. 284:15

   greatest part of a writer's t. 143:16

   half as old as t. 64:3

   happiness takes no account of t. 216:7

   he hath shook hands with t. 111:10

   how long a t. lies in one ... word 281:12

   I had liv'd a blessed t. 270:15

   in t. all haggard hawks 155:16

   in t. small wedges cleave 155:16

   in t. the flint is pierced 155:16

   in t. the savage bull 155:16

   inaudible and noiseless foot of T. 242:8

   just going outside ... may be some t. 196:7

   life, t.'s fool 256:1

   look into the seeds of t. 269:8

   many a t. and oft 274:9

   never the t. and the place 61:11

   new wail my dear t.'s waste 293:18

   no t. like the present 228:4

   no t. to stand and stare 96:2

   not of an age but for all t.! 145:15

   nothing is ours but t. 222:14

   old in hours if he have lost no t. 23:1

   old t. is still a-flying 132:7

   panting t. toiled after him 140:19

   patience, money and t. 222:36

   remember that t. is money 112:13

   repeat how T. is slipping 110:7

   seen better faces in my t. 265:19

   sent before my t. into this ... world 284:10

   such is T. that takes in trust 232:11

   that passed the t. It wd. have passed 26:1

   that t. may cease, and midnight 165:10

   the Bird of T. has but a little way 109:14

   the holy t. is quiet as a nun 333:2

   the last syllable of recorded t. 272:10

   the show and gaze o' th' t. 272:13

   'the t. has come,' the Walrus said 76:4

   the t. is out of joint 249:14

   the t. of our Ford 137:8

   the t. will come ... you will hear me 100:2

   thief of t. 337:14

   this bloody tyrant T. 293:12

   T. ambles ... trots ... gallops 245:8

   t. and chance happeneth to ... all 39:23

   t. and the hour 269:10

   t. and thinking tame ... grief 228:1

   t. and tide wait for no man 228:2

   t. enough to think of the future 296:20

   t. flies 227:22

   t. future contained in t. past 106:3

   t. hath ... a wallet 290:6

   t. is broke and no proportion kept 284:7

   t. is flying 321:8

   t. is on our side 121:7

   t. is the greatest innovator 22:18

   t., like an ever-rolling stream 323:6

   t. ... man is always trying to kill 304:16

   t. ... must have a stop 256:1

   t. of life is short 255:22

   t. of the singing of birds 40:9

   t. present and t. past are both 106:3

   t. spent on any item of the agenda 198:6

Tongue (*continued*)
  fellows of infinite t.   260:4
  give thy thoughts no t.   248:15
  iron t. of midnight   277:8
  keep one's t. between one's teeth   217:33
  keep wel thy t. ... keep thy freend   80:3
  no venom to that of the t.   229:15
  one t. is enough for a woman   228:8
  our English t. a gallimaufry   305:17
  sad words of t. or pen   326:8
  sharp t. ... edged tool ... grows keener   138:12
  though his t. dropped manna   176:18
  t. can no man tame   50:1
  t. cleave to ... roof of my mouth   37:27
  t. is not steel ... it cuts   228:9
  t. of idle people   228:10
  t. sounds ... as a sullen bell   256:7
  t. that Shakespeare spake   334:1
  use of my oracular t.   301:10
  virtue dwells not in the t.   229:17
Tongues: conscience ... thousand several t.   285:15
  done to death by slanderous t.   278:19
  finds t. in trees   243:15
  lack t. to praise   294:7
  silver-sweet ... lovers' t. by night   286:13
  these poor t. ... shall be silent   159:10
Tonight: along the Potomac t.   26:10
  t. we'll merry be   14:14
Too: this t., t. solid flesh   248:2
  t. nice ... t. proud ... cool ... fond   123:2
Tool: man is a t.-making animal   113:4
  sharp tongue ... edged t. ... grows keener   138:12
Tools: bad workman quarrels with his t.   206:34
  give us the t. ... finish the job   83:2
  t. to work ... for those who will   162:12
Tooth: a t. for a t.   43:18
  Nature, red in t. and claw   312:17
  sharper than a serpent's t.   265:15
  t. for t., hand for hand   32:10
  to have a sweet t.   226:35
  thy t. is not so keen   245:1
Toothache: endure the t. patiently   278:17
Top: always room at the t.   323:12
  I shall die at the t.   309:12
  sleep like a t.   95:13
  t. of it reached to heaven   31:9
  T. People take *The Times*   11:9
Topical: sang a most t. song   12:11
Topics: high life ... other fashionable t.   123:23
Tops: mountain t. that freeze   261:5
  t. were close against the sky   134–5:15
Topses: herring boxes without t.   183:9
Topsy: persisted T., 'never had no father'   307:14
Torch: a bright t. and a casement   150:7
  t. ... passed to a new generation   153:1
Torches: doth teach the t. to burn bright   286:3
Tories own no argument but force   60:4
Torment: love in a palace ... grievous t.   149:1
  there shall no t. touch them   51:12
Torments: our t. ... may ... become our elements   177:2
Torn: man all tattered and t.   194:8
Tortoise: why did you call him T.?   74:14

Torture: touch him not and t. not again   297:16
Tory ... with more propriety ... the Conservative   94:6
Tossed: you t. and gored several persons   143:3
Tossing their heads in sprightly dance   331:9
Totter: charming to t. into vogue   322:6
Totters: the state t.   288:11
Touch: men t. them and change   309:17
  O for the t. of a vanish'd hand   311:6
  one t. of nature   290:7
  that I might t. that cheek   286:7
  t. him with a pair of tongs   228:14
  t. not, taste not, handle not   49:3
  t. wood   228:15
  unkind as the t. of sweating metal   96:5
Touching: a sight so t. in its majesty   333:6
Toujours gai archy   167:3
Tous pour un, un pour tous   105:3
Tout passe, t. casse, t. lasse   228:16
Toves: the slithy t.   75:9
Tower: fall'n ... that t. of strength   314:10
  King's name is a t. of strength   285:13
  to the dark t. came   266:17
  yonder ivy-mantled t.   126:5
Towers: burnt the topless t. of Ilium?   165:8
  cloud-capp'd t., ... gorgeous palaces   288:8
Town: a tavern in the t.   17:3
  in Scarlet t., where I was born   11:12
  King sits in Dunfermline t.   11:13
  lived in a pretty how t.   94:13
  O little t. of Bethlehem   59:8
  spring, moonless night ... small t.   316:2
  t. ... is lighter than vanity   63:9
Town-crier: as lief the t. spoke   251:7
Toy: foolish thing was but a t.   292:3
  I count religion ... childish t.   166:3
Toys: all is but t.   270:15
Trace: learned to t. the day's disasters   122:11
Traces: hounds of spring are on winter's t.   309:14
Trade: and now there isn't any t.   131:6
  every t. save censure   70:13
  half a t. and half an art   138:7
  homely, slighted, shepherd's t.   174:15
  no nation was ever ruined by t.   112:14
  others ... venture t. abroad   258:8
  where the old t.'s plying   187:10
Tradesmen: bow, ye t., bow, ye masses   117:1
  lying ... becomes none but t.   293:7
Tradition: t. approves all forms of competition   84:17
  youth of America ... oldest t.   328:9
Traduced: beat a Venetian and t. the state   280–1:14
Trafalgar Square fountains like Government Clerks   231:22
Traffic: the two hours' t. of our stage   285:18
Tragedies: all t. are finished by a death   69:19
  there are two t. in life   296:8
Tragedy: go litel myn t.   80:6
  t. is ... a certeyn storie   80:1
  world ... a t. to those who feel   322:7
Tragical - historical,   t. - comical - historical -   250:9
Trail: long, long t. a-winding   153:11
Train: a man who shaves and takes a t.   325:8
  something ... to read in the t.   327:16
Train-band: a t. captain eke was he   92:6

16*

Trouble (*continued*)

has t. enough of its own   326:9
he that seeks t.   225:11
kindness in another's t.   124:6
man is born unto t.   35:3
man ... of few days ... full of t.   35:5
never t. t. until t. troubles   221:36
where there's a will, there's t.   230:18

Troubles: arms against a sea of t.   250–1:20
don't meet t. half-way   220:38
pack up yr. t.   19:14
the written t. of the brain   272:6

Trousers: bottoms of my t. rolled   106:15
I shall wear white flannel t.   106:16
shd. never put on his best t.   138:4

Trout: rose-moles ... upon t.   135:7

Trowel: lay it on with a t.   218:27
that was laid on with a t.   243:13

Truant: a t. disposition   248:7
and every t. knew   122:11

True: a truism ... none the less t.   238:3
as t. ... as taxes is   97:19
be so t. to thyself   22:17
dare to be t.   131:9
faith unfaithful ... falsely t.   312:4
good to be honest and t.   16:1
he's mad, 'tis t.: 'tis t. 'tis pity   249:17
if all be t. that I do think   10:3
me and my t. love   16:10
nor ... people's judgment always t.   103:8
one religion is as t. as another   67:11
ring in the t.   313:4
sad reflection but a t. one   142:11
so young, my lord, and t.   265:7
to thine own self be t.   248–9:17
t. as the stars above   15:2
which was prov'd t. ... prove false   67:17

Truism: a t. is ... none the less true   238:3

Truly: whom t. to know is everlasting life   53:7

Trumpet: moved more than with a t.   302:6
the t. of a prophecy! O, Wind   299:6
to blow one's own t.   208:12

Trumpets: all the t. sounded for him   63:16
sound the t., beat the drums   103:13, 184:6

Trumps: to turn up t.   228:34

Truncheon: marshal's t. ... judge's robe   273:4

Trunk: so large a t. before   27:1

Trust: better to t. in the Lord   37:12
extreme, rude, cruel, not to t.   294:11
failing to t. everybody ... t. nobody   213:8
men dare t. themselves with men   289:10
never t. a woman who tells one her real age   328:12
none that put ... t. in him   52:9
put not your t. in princes   37:31
some t. in chariots   35:26
though he slay me yet will I t.   35:4
t. God: see all   62:9
t. not a new friend ... old enemy   228:23
under his wings shalt thou t.   36:25

Truth: a melancholy t. ... poor relations   97:11
beauty is t., beauty   149:10
constantly speak the t.   53:8
error ... highly heap'd for t. to o'erpeer   246:8
found t. in all but one   284:1
great is T., and mighty   51:6
greater the t., the greater the libel   215:31
habit ... all the test of t.   93:16

Truth (*continued*)

he is less remote from the t.   139:12
his t. at all times firmly stood   153:5
however improbable ... the t.   102:3
it is a t. universally acknowledged   20:17
love swears that she is made of t.   294:15
mainly he told the t.   318:6
mathematics possesses not only t.   237:9
my way of joking ... tell the t.   295:20
nowadays t. ... greatest news   222:20
one t. is clear   203:4
patiently suffer for the t.'s sake   53:8
Pilate saith ... What is t.?   46:33
Plato is dear ... dearer still is t.   18:7
simple t. his utmost skill   336:13
single hast maintained ... the cause of t.   178:19
so few enthusiasts ... speak the t.   24:1
speaking nothing but the t.   327:18
strife of T. with Falsehood   162:14
takes two to speak the t.   317:3
tell the t. and shame the devil   227:20
the t. is rarely pure   327:7
the unclouded face of t.   238:15
T. beareth away the victory   51:5
t. comes out in wine   200:17
t. fears no colours   228:24
t. from his lips prevailed   122:10
t. has such a face   104:6
t. in every shepherd's tongue   232:14
t. in masquerade   70:5
t. is always strange   70:10
t. is stranger than fiction   228:25
t. is the daughter of God   228:26
t. never grows old   228:27
t. of Imagination   151:9
t. sits upon the lips of dying men   19:3
t. ... told with bad intent   54:14
what is t.? said jesting Pilate   21:8
who ever knew T. put to the worse   182:10
whole t. and nothing but the t.   228:28
wine in, t. out   230:21

Tulip: not number the streaks of the t.   141:5

Tune: all the t. that he cd. play   195:3
Cassio kill'd! ... murder's out of t.   280:12
Heaven tries earth if it be in t.   162:15
pays the piper ... call the t.   222:39
sweetly played in t.   66:15
to the t. of flutes kept stroke   242:14

Tunes: devil shd. have all the good t.   132:12
weight of Cathedral t.   99:16

Tupman: Mr. T.   98:22

Turbulent: free me of this t. priest?   130:14
Sagacious, Bold, and T. of wit   102:16

Turk: a malignant and a turban'd T.   280–1:14
French, or T., or Proosian   120:3

Turks: peace shall go sleep with T.   283:8

Turn: fortune ... t. thy wheel   265:20
let not each gay t. ... move   202:11
one good t. deserves another   215:21
person t. in his grave   228:30
tread on a worm ... will t.   228:19
t. an honest penny   228:29
t. over a new leaf   228:31
t. the tables   228:32
t. to God to praise and pray   61:5
t. up one's nose   228:33
t. up trumps   228:34

Turned: having once t. round walks on   86:16
'in case anything t. up'   97:15

Turnips: if the man who t. cries 140:17
Turns: t. no more his head 86:16
    whoso t. as I, this evening 61:5
Turpissimus: nemo repente fuit t. 146:8
Turret: Sultan's T. in a Noose of Light 109:13
Turtle: the t. lives 'twixt plated decks 186:11
    voice of the t. is heard 40:9
Turtle-doves: two t. and a partridge 194:2
Tuscany: even the ranks of T. 164:1
Tutor: irreverent to my t. 141:14
Tweedledee: 'Contrariwise,' continued T. 75:15
    Tweedledum and T. 75:14
Twelve: 'a parted ... between t. and one 259:1
    at t. noon the natives swoon 91:8
    he in t. found truth in all but one 284:1
    I in t. thousand, none 284:1
    in the sworn t. have a thief or two 273:1
Twenty: expenditure t. pounds ought and six 97:16
Twice: a victory is t. itself 277:9
    he sings each song t. over 61:3
    hear t. before you speak once 216:24
    it is t. blest 275:1
Twig: as the t. is bent, the tree's inclined 203:14
Twilight: a t. dim with rose 97:1
    bats ... they ever fly by t. 22:24
    by the t.'s last gleaming 153:6
    t. grey ... in her sober livery 178:6
Twin roses by the zephyr blown apart 148:10
Twinkle: t. on the milky way 331:8
    t., t., little bat 74:8
    t., t., little star 311:5
Twinkling: in the t. of a bed-staff 241:20
Twins: quadruplets, not t. 13:2
Twist: neither t. wolf's-bane 149:11
Twitched: rose, and t. his mantle blue 175:6
Two: a trick worth t. of that 254:5
    bicycle made for t. 95:4
    human species ... t. distinct races 156:2
    I like t. months of every year 68:17
    if t. are in the churchyard laid 336:6
    in t. words: im-possible 124:4
    only t. families in the world 78:4
    only t. sorts of boys 98:14
    takes t. to speak the truth 317:3
    the t. noblest of things 308:11
    there went in t. and t. unto Noah 30:20
    t. can play at that game 228:38
    t. cheers for Democracy 112:2
    t. glasses ... t. chairs ... t. people 165:2
    t. luxuries to brood over 152:8
    t. men look out 156:15
    t. mites, which make a farthing 45:15
    t. things stand like stone 124:6
    t. to bear my soul away 9:13
    t. to make a marriage a success 238:2
    when t. or three are gathered together 52:19
Type: so careful of the t. she seems 312:16
Tyrannies: of all the T. on humane kind 104:7
Tyrannous to use it like a giant 273:6
Tyranny: ecclesiastic t.'s the worst 96:10
    taxation without representation is t. 197:13
Tyrant: little t. of his fields withstood 126:11
    professed t. to their sex 277:12
    this bloody t., Time 293:12

Tyrants: necessity ... argument of t. 200:8
    resistance to t. is obedience 139:11
Tyre: village which men still call T. 111:3

U and Non-U ... Sociological Linguistics 235:14
Uglier yet is the hump 155:9
Uglification and Derision 74:15
Ugly: beauty ... that makes me u. 280:8
    The U. Duckling 10:11
Umbrella: unjust steals the just's u. 57:14
Unadorned: beauty u. 26:13
Unarm, Eros ... day's task is done 243:4
Unattempted yet in prose or rhyme 175:16
Unbaptized: any that die u. 53:27
Unbelief: help thou mine u. 45:11
Unbidden guests ... welcomest when ... gone 260:6
Un-birthday: an u. present 76:9
Unborn: the children yet u. shall feel 284:3
Unburied: bodies of u. men 324:3
Uncertain: u., coy, and hard to please 240:9
    u. glory of an April day 292:6
Uncharitableness: envy, hatred, ... and all u. 52:23
Uncle: my prophetic soul! My u.! 249:10
    u. me no u. 282:9
Uncle Toby: our armies swore ... cried my U. 306:17
Uncle Tom Cobbleigh and all 17:5
Unclubbable: a very u. man 142:16
Uncomely: all things u. and broken 337:6
Uncomfortable: thinks he is moral ... is only u. 296:7
    we u. feel 120:5
Uncommon: the thing that's most u. 204:3
Unconfined: let joy be u. 69:4
Unconscionable time dying 78:14
Uncover, dogs, and lap 289:11
Under-belly: the soft u. of the Axis 83:7
Underlings: fault ... in ourselves that we are u. 262:8
Underneath are the everlasting arms 33:9
Underpaying: better than the u. instinct 295:12
Underrate ... the duty of being happy 307:9
Understand: a man will ne'er quite u. 198:12
    I u. thy kisses, and thou mine 255:8
    no one can u. Ein 13:4
    one half ... world cannot u. 20:7
Understanding: brute beasts that have no u. 53:19
    Donne's verses ... pass all u. 138:15
    give it an u., but no tongue 248:11
    light a candle of u. 51:7
    peace of God, which passeth all u. 48:31
Undeserver may sleep 257:1
Undeserving: Im one of the u. poor 296:21
Undo: pray you u. this button 268:4
Undone: u. those things we ought to have done 52:13
    what's done cannot be u. 272:4
    wish th' estate of th' world were now u. 272:11
Uneasy: this swift business I must u. make 288:2
    u. lies the head that wears a crown 257:3
Uneatable: in full pursuit of the u. 328:10
Unexpected: moment foreseen may be u. 107:11

Unexpected (*continued*)
the u. ... always happens   229:11
Unfaithful: faith u. ... falsely true   312:4
Unfit: worse man ... u. for the married state
   144:2
Unfold: O clouds, u.!   55:8
Unfortunate: one more U., weary of breath
   134:10
Unfriendly to society's chief joys   92:5
Unhanged: not three good men u.   254:14
Unhappy: had been very u. in marriage   143:6
   instinct for being u. highly developed
   237:11
   no one till his death ... called u.   60:5
   u. family is u. in its own way   317:13
Unheard: heard melodies are sweet, but those
   u.   149:7
Unholy: refrain from the u. pleasure   26:14
   shrieks, and sights u.!   173:14
Unicorn: lion and the u. were fighting   190:9
Unintelligible: weary weight of ... this u.
   world   335:11
Union: broken Nature's social u.   66:11
   Liberty and U., now ... for ever ... in-
   separable   323:10
   O U., strong and great!   160:11
Unite: workers of the world, u.   168:10
United Nations: we the peoples of the U.
   319:5
Unity: brethren ... dwell together in u.   37:21
   u. is strength   229:12
Universally acknowledged ... a single man
   20:17
Universe: born for the U. [Burke]   123:1
   wide vessel of the u.   259:8
Universities: state of both his u.   318:1
University: don't think one 'comes down' from
   Jimmy's u.   197:12
   true U. ... is a collection of books   73:9
   we are the U.   306:1
Unjust steals the just's umbrella   57:14
Unkind: Midlands ... sodden and u.   28:2
   not so u. as man's ingratitude   245:1
   tell me not, sweet, I am u.   162:6
   when givers prove u.   251:1
Unkindest: the most u. cut of all   263:18
Unkindness: I tax not ... elements with u.
   266:7
Unknown: forms of things u.   277:6
   I travelled among u. men   331:6
   not to know me argues yourselves u.   178:9
   Paradise of Fools; to few u.   177:11
Unlamented let me die   204:1
Unlearned, he knew no schoolman's ... art
   201:20
Unlucky: so u. that he runs into accidents
   167:4
   when you shall these u. deeds relate   280:14
Unnatural: foul, strange, and u.   249:9
   let me be cruel, not u.   252:9
   poetry's u.   99:5
Unobserved, home to his mother's house
   180:6
Unperfect, unfinished, inartistic [of Thoreau]
   139:5
Unpremeditated: my u. verse   179:5
Unprofitable: months ... most idle and u.
   116:1
   stale, flat, and u.   248:2
Unrespited, unpitied, unreprieved   177:1

Unrewarded: nothing went u. but desert
   103:5
   wit shall not go u.   289:1
Unseen: born to blush u.   126:10
   leave the world u.   149:14
Unsought: Beadsman ... u. for slept   147:15
   [love] given u.   291:12
Unspeakable: the u. in ... pursuit of ... un-
   eatable   328:10
Unstable as water   31:14
Unsubstantial: an u. faery place   336:4
Untaught: better u. than ill-taught   207:36
Untimely: was from his mother's womb u.
   ripp'd   272:12
Untrue to his wife   20:3
Untruths: they have spoken u. ... are slanders
   278:18
Untune that string   290:3
Unturned: leave no stone u.   218:34
Unvarnished: a round u. tale deliver   279:1
Unwept, unhonour'd, and unsung   240:1
Unworthy: an opinion ... u. of him   22:12
   spurns that ... merit of th' u. takes
   250—1:20
Up: they cannot bear levelling u.   142:12
   U., Guards, and at 'em   324:9
   u. so floating many bells down   94:13
   U., u.! my friend ... quit your books   335:4
   u. with which I will not put   83:12
Up-hill: road wind u. all the way?   236:3
Uphold: will u. the unyok'd humour   253:20
Upper classes have ... u. hand   91:5
Uproar's your only music   151:12
Upstairs and downstairs   189:4
Urn: bubbling and loud-hissing u.   93:10
Us: how different from u.   14:4
Usance: rate of u. here ... in Venice   274:7
Use: beauty too rich for u.   286:3
   great riches ... no real u.   22:25
   how u. doth breed a habit!   292:10
   soil'd with all ignoble u.   313:8
   u. a poor maiden so   15:1
   u. every man after his desert   250:13
   what's the u. of worrying?   19:14
Used: not what there u. to be   29:11
Useless: all art is quite u.   328:5
   most beautiful things ... most u.   237:3
   talent ... lodged with me u.   181:10
   u. each without the other   161:6
Uses: all the u. of this world!   248:2
   keep a corner ... for others' u.   279:17
   sweet are the u. of adversity   243:15
Usurpation: I dare, without u.   59:12
Utter: not u. what thou dost not know   254:11

Vacant: in v. or in pensive mood   331:11
   loud laugh ... spoke the v. mind   122:8
Vacations: Dotheboys Hall ... no extras, no v.
   98:9
Vae victis   160:4
Vaguery: medal 'For V. in the Field'   197:11
Vain: hour when you too learn that all is v.
   236:7
   labour and the wounds are v.   85:1
   mock on, 'tis all in v.   55:9
   name of the Lord thy God in v.   32:2
   no great man lives in v.   73:8
   they labour in v. that build   37:19
   use not v. repetitions   43:23
   v. are the thousand creeds   58:13

Vain (*continued*)
  v. for you to rise up early 37:20
  Why, all delights are v. 268:7
  youth is v. 87:7
Vaincre sans péril ... triomphe sans gloire 90:14
Vainly: tired waves, v. breaking 85:2
Valet: no man is a hero to his v. 91:1
  to his very v. ... a hero 68:16
Valiant: as he was v., I honour him 263:10
  he who would v. be 63:13
  the v. man and free 313:7
  v. ... taste of death but once 262:15
Valley: all in the v. of Death 311:9
  in the v. of decision 42:14
  maid singing in the v. 15:1
  v. of the shadow of death 35:29
Valleys: piping down the v. wild 56:7
Valour: better part of v. is discretion 256:3
  discretion ... better part of v. 211:21
  for contemplation he and v. 178:3
Value: price of everything ... v. of nothing 328:4
  then we rack the v. 278:12
Valued: never v. till they make a noise 94:1
Van Dycks have to go 91:6
Vanish: ah, wd. the scandal v. 282:6
Vanished: dream that v. with the morn 58:14
  the touch of a v. hand 311:6
Vanity: it beareth the name of V. Fair 63:9
  that v. in years 255:1
  two passions, v. and love 80:16
  v. of vanities, saith the Preacher 39:9
Vanquished: woe to the v. 160:4
Variable: Woman ... v. as the shade 240:9
Variation: each slight v., if useful 95:11
Variety: great source of pleasure is v. 144:26
  nor custom stale her infinite v. 242:15
  v. is pleasing 229:13
  v. is the mother of enjoyment 100:13
  v. is the soul of pleasure 26:12
  v.'s the very spice of life 93:8
Various: as you are woman ... so be v. 125:8
  so v., that he seem'd ... Epitome 103:4
Varium et mutabile ... femina 321:3
Vase: 'twas on a lofty v.'s side 125:9
Vassals and serfs at my side 63:4
Vasty fields of France 258:6
Vault: that heaven's v. should crack 268:2
Vaults: been in these here v. 11:17
Vegetable: my v. love shd. grow 167:12
  v., animal, and mineral 120:4
Vegetate: one does but v. 65:5
Veil: this that was the v. of thee 309:16
  V. past which I cd. not see 110:6
Veils: peace ... dropping from the v. of the morning 337:5
Vein: not in the giving v. today 285:7
Veins: jigging v. of rhyming mother-wits 166:6
Venetian: Turk beat a V. 280–1:14
Vengeance: noblest v. is to forgive 229:14
  rarer action ... virtue than in v. 289:3
  v. is mine ... saith the Lord 47:26
Veni, vidi, vici 71:13
Venice: here with us in V. 274:7
  in V., on the Bridge of Sighs 69:6
Venom: no v. to that of the tongue 229:15
Vent: ce qu'est au feu le v. 67:13
Vent: what his breast forges, that his tongue must v. 246:10

Venture: nothing v., nothing win 222:19
Ventures: take the current ... or lose our v. 264:3
'Verboojuice': 'Sesquippledan v.' 324:13
Verbum sapienti sat est 229:16
Verdict: Sentence first—v. afterwards 75:8
Verdure: content to see no other v. 151:2
  different shades in the v. 141:5
Verge: on the very v. of her confine 265:22
Verified: they have v. unjust things 278:18
Verify: always v. yr. references 236:13
Veritas: in vino v. 200:17
Vermin: yr. natives ... race of little odious v. 308:16
Verse: bumbast out a blank v. 127:6
  curst be the v. 201:18
  Flask of Wine, a Book of V. 109:15
  my unpremeditated v. 179:5
  ornament of poem or good v. 175:14
  the v. you grave for me 307:6
Verses: Donne's v. ... pass all understanding 138:15
  tear him for his bad v.! 263:21
Vessel: wide v. of the universe 259:8
Vessels: empty v. make the most noise 212:22
Vest: casting the body's v. aside 168:2
Vestal: happy is the blameless v.'s lot 201:9
Vestry: see you in the v. after the service 303:13
Vesture: this muddy v. of decay 275:8
Veterans: how the world its v. rewards 203:16
Vex not his ghost. O, let him pass! 268:5
Vexes: the other v. it 148:2
Vexing the dull ear of a drowsy man 264:17
Vibrated: strings ... better not ... v. 97:8
Vibrates: music ... v. in the memory 300:6
Vicar: I'll be the V. of Bray, Sir 15:13
Vice: any taint of v., whose ... corruption 292:1
  boldly rebuke v. 53:8
  homage paid by v. to virtue 234:7
  hypocrisy ... homage that v. pays 217:12
  in v. their [king's] law's their will 281:4
  lash'd the v., but spared the name 308:13
  mutual forgiveness of each v. 55:3
  no v. but beggary 264:14
  prosperity doth best discover v. 21:15
  public schools ... nurseries of all v. 109:10
  subject ... to this v. of lying! 257:12
  that reverend v., that grey iniquity 255:1
  the raptures and roses of v. 309:17
  v. is a master of so frightful mien 203:6
Vice versa: good for General Motors and v. 329:4
Vices: of our pleasant v. make instruments 267:14
  through tatter'd clothes small v. 267:6
Vicious: restraint of ten v. 182:6
Victim: some day ... a v. must be found 118:4
  v. of a rich man's game 16:11
Victoria Station: the cloak-room at V.? 327:14
Victorious, happy and glorious 73:1
Victory: a v. is twice itself 277:9
  and shouted V.! 240:10
  better a lean peace than a fat v. 207:17
  but 'twas a famous v. 304:15
  grave, where is thy v.? 48:13
  however long ... for without v. ... no survival 82:12

Victory (*continued*)
in V., Magnanimity 83:13
O Grave! where is thy V.? 201:4
peace hath her v. 181:13
problems of v. are more agreeable 83:8
v. in spite of all terror 82:12
welcome to yr. gory bed, or to v. 67:1
Westminster Abbey or v. 187:4
where, grave, thy v.? 163:7
Victuals: picks it up and buys v. 142:7
the German dictator, instead of snatching
the v. 82:9
Vieillesse: si v. pouvait 108:25
View: observation with extensive v. 141:9
View halloo: Peel's v. wd. a-waken the dead
125:6
Vigilance: condition ... liberty ... eternal v.
95:3
Vigorous: shd. feel fresh and v. enough
322:14
Vile: better to be v. than v. esteemed 294:10
cd. make so v. a pun 97:5
from living in a v. hotel 28:1
out, v. jelly! 266:18
v., but viler George the Second 156:10
wisdom and goodness to the v. seem v.
266:21
Viilage: loveliest v. of the plain 122:4
through an Alpine v. passed 160:12
v. ... men still call Tyre 111:13
Villages: dollar ... no ... devotees in these ... v.
138:13
Villain: condemns me for a v. 285:15
determined to prove a v. 284:12
fair terms and a v.'s mind 274:11
hungry, lean-fac'd v. 246:5
O v. ... condemned into ... redemption
278:15
Villainous: foreheads v. low 289:2
Villains: God shd. go before such v. 278:14
Villainy: thus I clothe my naked v. 284:14
Vinci: they spell it V. 318:12
Vindicate the ways of God to Man 202:18
Vine: Daughter of the V. 110:9
every man under his v. 42:22
Vines: bless with fruit the v. 147:1
our v. have tender grapes 40:10
Vineyard: thou shalt not glean thy v. 32:15
Violence: to offer it the show of v. 247:15
Violent: laid v. hands upon themselves 53:27
nothing ... v. is permanent 222:18
so over v. or over civil 103:5
Violet: the nodding v. grows 276:20
the v. smells to him as ... to me 259:10
throw a perfume on the v. 264:19
Violets: breathes upon a bank of v. 290:10
daisies pied and v. blue 268:17
from her ... flesh may v. spring 253:3
odours, when sweet v. sicken 300:6
Vipers: generation of v. 43:12
Virgin: a v. shall conceive, and bear 40:21
Virtue: a fugitive and cloistered v. 182:4
admire v. ... follow not her lore 180:1
assume a v. if you have it not 252:14
enterprises ... of v. or mischief 21:19
every v. ... founded on compromise 64:7
forbearance ceases to be a v. 64:10
if V. feeble were 173:4
lilies and languours of v. 309:17
love V., she alone is free 173:4

Virtue (*continued*)
much v. in If 246:3
O infinite v., com'st thou smiling? 243:3
only reward of v. is v. 108:4
power ... extirpates ... gentle v. 65:2
rarer ... in v. than in vengeance 289:3
saw v. in her shape how lovely 178:10
some rise by sin, and some by v. fall 273:2
there is no v. like necessity 281:14
useful life, progressive v. 316:13
v. dwells not in the tongue 229:17
v. is ... best plain set 23:2
v. is its own reward 229:18
v. never grows old 229:19
v. of necessity 229:20
v. only makes our bliss below 203:12
v. that possession wd. not show 278:12
wars that makes ambition v. 280:2
Virtues: be to her v. very kind 205:5
lady ... of wondrous v. 274:4
their v. we write in water 262:1
world to hide v. in? 290:12
Virtuous: be in general v., and ... happy
112:15
think, because thou art v. 291:5
Visages: whose v. do cream and mantle 274:2
Vision: a v. or a waking dream? 150:6
baseless fabric of this v. 288:16
by the v. splendid ... attended 332:2
not disobedient unto ... heavenly v. 47:13
saw the V. of the world 313:16
where ... no v., the people perish 39:5
write the v., ... make it plain 42:26
Visionary: whither is fled the v. gleam?
331:16
Visions: young men shall see v. 42:13
Visit: let us never v. together 89:17
v. us with thy salvation 325:3
Visiting the iniquity of the fathers 32:1
Vital: I cannot give it v. growth again 280:11
Vitality: extreme busyness ... deficient v.
307:8
Vive: Napoleon's armies ... shouting 'V.
l'intérieur' 241:13
Vocabulary: the v. of Bradshaw is nervous
102:6
Vocation: no sin ... to labour in his v. 253:18
'tis my v., Hal 253:18
Vogue: charming to totter into v. 322:6
Voice: a certain what-is-it in his v. 330:2
a distant v. in the darkness 161:7
a still small v. 34:21
a v. cry, Sleep no more 270:11
bird, or but a wandering v.? 336:2
every man thy ear, but few thy v. 248:16
harmonious sisters, V. and Verse 172:12
hear a v. in every wind 126:1
heart and soul and v. 186:14
her v., and her hair, and eyes 168:12
her v. was ever soft 168:12
his big manly v. 244–5:11
I sing with mortal v. 178:20
its familiar v. wearies not ever 299:12
lost my v. most irrecoverably 324:5
my v. ... lost it with hallooing 256:9
no v.; but oh! the silence sank 87:1
no v. but the v. of complaining 184:10
no v. I'll be quit of the singing 12:1
sing to the Lord with cheerful v. 153:4
so charming left his v. 179:1

Voice (*continued*)
  sound of a v. that is still   311:6
  still raise ... the supplicating v.   141:13
  the v. is Jacob's v.   31:8
  the v. of all the gods   268:13
  the watchdog's v. that bayed   122:8
  'tis the v. of the Lobster   75:4
  'tis the v. of the sluggard   323:7
  v. ... crying in the wilderness   43:11
  v. I hear this passing night   150:4
  v. of the people ... of God   10:2
  v. of the turtle is heard   40:9
  v. ... run from hedge to hedge   151:1
  v. whose sound was like the sea   333:13
  warm, thrilling v. cry out   197:10
Voices: ancestral v. prophesying war   87:14
  I hear the gentle v. calling   112:11
  music, when soft v. die   300:6
  two v. are there   333:10
  two v. are there ... of ... deep ... of sheep   306:9
  v. of children ... on the green   56:11
  v. telling me what to do   297:2
Void: have left an aching v.   92:14
  without form, and v.   30:1
Volscians: flutter'd yr. V. in Corioli   246:12
Voltaire: mock on, V., Rousseau   55:9
Volume: desideratum of a v.   156:7
  foretells ... a tragic v.   256:6
Volumes: borrowers ... creators of odd v.   156:3
  written such v. of stuff!   158:6
Vomit: dog is turned to his ... v.   50:9
  dog returneth to ... v., ... fool ... to ... folly   38:31
Vorpal blade went snicker-snack   75:10
Vote: v. ... as ... leaders tell 'em to   117:9
Voted at my party's call   119:16
Votes: anyone who v. Labour   183:7
Vow: I v. to thee, my country   305:22
Vows made in storms are forgotten   229:21
Vox populi, vox dei   10:2
Voyage: about to take my last v.   133:4
Voyager: lands the v. at last   107:16
Vulgar: familiar, but by no means v.   248:15
  think with the wise, but talk with the v.   227:32

Wabe: gimble in the w.   75:9
Wacht am Rhein   238:14
Wade: shd. I w. no more   271:10
Wages: be content with your w.   45:23
  home art gone, and ta'en thy w.   247:9
  w. of sin is death   47:18
Wagon: hitch yr. w. to a star   108:18
Wail: with old woes new w. ... time's waste   293:18
Wailing for her demon lover   87:12
Wait: learn to labour and to w.   161:2
  make 'em laugh ... cry ... w.   233:5
  time and tide w. for no man   228:2
  w. and see   19:15, 229:22
  who only stand and w.   181:11
Waiter roars it through the hall   156:14
Waiting for the long-promised invasion   83:1
Waiting-gentlewoman: talk so like a w.   254:2
Waits: everything comes to him who w.   212:36
  the dinner w., and we are tired   92:10
Wake: do I w. or sleep ?   150:6

Wake (*continued*)
  held we ... sleep to w.   60:12
  w. up, America   114:16
  w. up, England   115:15
  you must w. and call me early   314:6
Waked: you have w. me too soon   323:7
Wakes: and whoever w. in England   61:1
Walcum: a little talcum is always w.   186:7
Walk: can two w. together ?   42:15
  doth w. in fear and dread   86:16
  w. humbly with thy God   42:24
  w. upon England's mountains green   55:8
  we w. by faith, not by sight   48:15
  where'er you w., cool gales   204:4
  will you w. a little faster ?   75:2
  will you w. into my parlour ?   136:10
  within a w. of the sea   28:4
Walked: as I w. through the wilderness   63:6
  when she has w. before   122:16
Walking: I nauseate w.   89:16
  life's but a w. shadow   272:10
Walks: having once turned round w. on   86:16
  I wish I liked the way it w.   233:1
  she w. in beauty, like the night   71:2
  w. the night in her silver shoon   97:3
Wall: green hill ... without a city w.   10:7
  Jackson standing like a stone w.   26:5
  know ... the w. is strong   326–7:15
  little pin bores through his castle w.   283:6
  serves it in the office of a w.   282:5
  something ... that doesn't love a w.   113:14
  washes its w. on the southern side   61:16
  weakest goes to the w.   229:38
Wallet: his w. lay ... in his lappe   79:19
  time hath ... a w. at his back   290:6
Wallow naked in December snow   282:1
Wallowing: sow ... to her w. in the mire   50:9
Walls: banners on the outward w.   272:8
  stone w. do not a prison make   162:5
  w. have ears   229:23
  watches from his mountain w.   312:1
Walrus and the Carpenter   76:2–6
Waltzing: you'll come a-w., Matilda   198:10
Wander: whither shall I w. ?   189:4
  you shall w. hand in hand   188:1
Wandered: I w. lonely as a cloud   331:7
  when we have w. all our ways   232:11
Wandering: a w. minstrel I   117:16
  w. between two worlds   18:15
  w. Dong through the forest goes!   158:3
Want: Adam ... did not w. the apple   318:15
  all we w. is a limousine   164:14
  freedom from w. ... everywhere   235:4
  I shall not w.   35:27
  if you w. to get somewhere else   75:12
  not good to w. and to have   215:20
  the w. of money is so [the root of all evil]   68:3
  w. it [advice] most ... like it least   80:12
  w. of a thing is perplexing   320:3
  w. of Thought ... w. of Heart   135:1
  waste not, w. not   229:31
  worth ... best known by w.   231:4
  you w. the best seats   11:11
Wanted: every man is w., ... no man is w. much   108:9
  map ... not be w. these ten years   200:10
Wanting: robb'd, not w. what is stol'n   280:1
  weighed ... and art found w.   42:2
Wanton: w. love corrupteth   22:1

Wanton (*continued*)
  weep not, my w.   127:5
Wantonness: kindles in clothes a w.   131:14
Wants: but w. that little strong   134:2
  man w. but little here below   122:15
  w. money, means, and content   245:3
War: advise none to ... go to w.   206:7
  all is fair in love and w.   206:11
  Americans ... tempered by w.   153:1
  ancestral voices prophesying w.   87:14
  desires peace, prepare for w.   320:8
  Don John of Austria is going to the w.   81:5
  ease after w., death after life   305:11
  he that first invented w.   166:8
  I know the disciplines of w.   259:7
  image of w. without its guilt   304:8
  in w. ... no winners, ... all are losers   78:9
  in W.: Resolution. In Defeat: Defiance   83:13
  infection and the hand of w.   282:5
  let slip the dogs of w.   263:8
  looks on w. as all glory   301:20
  love ... is exactly like w.   307:1
  magnificent, but ... not w.   57:9
  marching as to w.   24:9
  my sentence is for open w.   176:16
  neither shall they learn w.   40:18
  never was a good w.   113:2
  pride, pomp, and circumstance of ... w.   280:2
  so dauntless in w.   240:6
  some ... depos'd, some slain in w.   283:6
  stupid crime ... devil's madness—W.   241:16
  succeeding generations from ... scourge of w.   319:5
  the arts of w. and peace   69–70:21
  The W. between Men and Women   317:9
  to w. and arms I fly   162:6
  w. ... endless w. still breed?   181:14
  w. is done and youth stone dead   238:9
  w. is ... national industry of Prussia   182:12
  W. is Peace, Freedom is Slavery   197:4
  w. makes rattling good history   128:7
  w. ... too serious ... to be left to military   311:3
  w. upon this bloody tyrant, Time   293:12
  when I speak, they are for w.   37:14
  when the blast of w. blows   259:3
  when there was w., he went   20:4
  when w. begins, hell opens   229:26
  wither'd is the garland of the w.   243:6
  Women ... and Power and W.   154:9
Warble his native wood-notes wild   174:8
Ward: thou knowest my old w.   254:15
Ware: I shd. dine at W.   92:11
Warm: let the w. Love in   150:7
  this sensible w. motion to become   273:10
Warmed: w. and cooled ... winter and summer   274:17
  w. both hands ... fire of life   156:11
Warn: to w., to comfort, and command   334:14
Warned: be w. by me that breakfast   27:4
Warring within our breasts   166:10
Wars: end to the beginnings of all w.   235:6
  fierce w. and faithful loves   305:9
  let w. give way to peace   84:4
  more ... fears than w. or women   261:10
  still w. and lechery!   290:9

Wars (*continued*)
  the thousand w. of old   313:6
  w. and rumours of w.   44:27
  w. bring scars   229:27
  w. that makes ambition virtue   280:2
Wars of the Roses: leave Moses out of the W.   29:8
Warts: roughnesses, pimples, and w.   94:10
Wash: bid them w. their faces   246:7
  I w. away my balm   284:2
  tears ... w. out a word of it   110:12
  w. dirty linen in public   229:29
  w. me ... whiter than snow   36:14
  w. the balm ... from ... anointed king   283:2
  w. ... yr. feet seldom ... head never   229:30
  will all great Neptune's ocean w. this blood   270:12
Washed the dishes with his wife   184:8
Washes: river Weser ... w. its wall   61:16
Washing: no cooking, or w., or sewing   12:1
  painting a face ... not w. it   114:7
  w. ... clean linen in public   327:9
Waste: barrel of meal shall not w.   34:18
  in a w. of shame   294:11
  wail my dear time's w.   293:18
  w. not, want not   229:31
Wasted: some nine moons w.   278:21
Wasteful and ridiculous excess   264:19
Wastes: tell her that w. her time and me   322:1
Watch: has a w. and chain, of course   234:12
  keeping w. over ... flock by night   45:20
  one to w., and one to pray   9:13
  our w. ... have indeed comprehended   278:10
  secret whispers of each other's w.   259:8
  take ye heed, w. and pray   45:16
  w. and pray, that ye enter not   45:2
  W. on the Rhine   238:14
  w. that ends the night   323:5
  w. to babble and to talk   278:6
Watchdog: the w.'s voice that bayed   122:8
Watched: he w. the ads and not the road   186:4
  o'er the ramparts we w.   153:6
  w. pot never boils   229:32
Watcher of the skies   150:15
Watches: a heart that w. and receives   335:8
  he w. from his mountain walls   312:1
  with our judgments as our w.   202:2
Watching: Big Brother is w. you   197:3
Watchman, what of the night?   40:26
Watch-tower: from his w. in the skies   174:2
Water: as w. unto wine   313:19
  blood is thicker than w.   208:13
  by w. and the Word   307:13
  carry w. in a sieve   229:33
  deepest w. ... best fishing   211:12
  Eeyore ... looked at himself in the w.   172:5
  give him w. to drink   38:28
  I came like W.   110:5
  I don't care where the w. goes   81:11
  like w. off a duck's back   229:34
  may lead a horse to the w.   218:28
  more w. glideth by the mill   289:13
  name was writ in w.   152:13
  never know the worth of w.   218:10
  not all the w. in the rough rude sea   283:2
  smooth ... w. where the brook is deep   260:8
  unstable as w. ... shalt not excel   31:14

Water (*continued*)
  virtues we write in w.   262:1
  w. is best   200:5
  w. out of a stone   229:35
  w., w. every where   86:6
Watered heaven with ... tears   56:6
Waterfall: from the w. he named her   161:5
(A)-Watering the last year's crop   105:14
Waterloo: battle of W. was won ... Eton
    324:10
  bodies high at Austerlitz and W.   238:5
  every man meets his W. at last   200:4
  Marathon to W.   120:4
Water-mill: noise like that of a w.   308:14
Water-rugs: shoughs, w., and demi-wolves
    271:1
Waters: a fen of stagnant w.   333:12
  beside the still w.   35:28
  cast thy bread upon the w.   39:24
  cold w. to a thirsty soul   38:29
  dreadful noise of w. in my ears   285:1
  fades o'er the w. blue   69:1
  kill the still-closing w.   288:15
  many w. cannot quench love   40:15
  still w. run deep   226:21
  stolen w. are sweet   38:7
  w. of the heart push in their tides   315:18
Watson: you know my methods, W.   101:14
Wave: all sunk beneath the w.   93:1
  chin upon an orient w.   175:10
  glassy, cool, translucent   173:3
  lift me as a w., a leaf   299:5
  walk o'er the western w.   298:15
Waved: long has it w. on high   134:1
Waves: sons of the w.   115:1
  the tired w., vainly breaking   85:2
  w. make towards the pebbled shore   294:1
  when ... w. went high ... sought ... storms
    102–3:17
Wax-works: if you think we're w.   75:13
Way: a damned long, dark ... w.   123:7
  all taking the easiest w. out   324:18
  catch the nearest w.   270:1
  every day, in every w. ... better   91:3
  go by the king's high w.   32:19
  gull's w. and the whale's w.   168:17
  keep his distant w. [Milton]   127:2
  long is the w. and hard   177:5
  love will find a w.   220:7
  perilous w. from a tree's summit   150:9
  plods his weary w.   126:3
  primrose w. to the ... bonfire   270:13
  roses, roses all the w.   61:15
  set out ... in a relative w.   63:1
  steep and thorny w. to heaven   248:14
  the w. of all flesh   324:2
  the w. to dusty death   272:10
  travel on life's common w.   333:13
  w. of an eagle ... serpent   39:7
  w. was long, the wind was cold   239:11
  where there's a will ... a w.   230:17
  which w. shall I fly?   177:13
Ways: among the untrodden w.   334:11
  gave once ... her w. to roam   59:6
  he had his little w.   171:4
  her w. are w. of pleasantness   38:3
  let all her w. be unconfined   205:5
  Mr. Facing-both-w.   63:10
  neither are yr. w. my w.   41:9
  oldest sins the newest ... w.   257:19

Ways (*continued*)
  when ... w. be foul   269:1
We: put it down a w., my lord   99:8
Weak: bear the infirmities of the w.   47:31
  concessions of the w.   64:4
  idleness ... refuge of w. minds   80:15
  surely the w. shall perish   241:15
  to be w. is miserable   176:1
  w. and therefore pacifistic   20:1
Weakest goes to the wall   229:38
Weakness: show no more w. than is natura
    317:5
  silence ... all else is w.   320:14
  w. is thy excuse   181:1
Wealth: as their w. increaseth, so inclose
    166:4
  bear w.   207:4
  consume w. without producing it   295:11
  he that marries for w.   220:27
  health is better than w.   216:21
  let w. and commerce ... die   237:10
  love rememb'red such w. brings   293:17
  neither wit nor w.   15:6
  squandering w. ... his ... art   103:5
  there is no w. but life   237:6
  w. accumulates and men decay   122:5
  w. is contentment with a little   229:39
  w. is not without its advantages   114:13
  w. maketh many friends   38:21
  where w. and freedom reign   123:15
Weapons: hurt with the same w.   274:17
  in this war ... books are w.   235:5
  women's w., water-drops   266:3
Wear: better to w. out than ... rust out   94:11
  better w. out shoes than sheets   207:37
  if the cap fits, w. it   209:6
  our souls ... will us to w. ourselves   166:10
  to w. the breeches   230:2
  w. him in my heart's core   252:1
Wearied: wherein have I w. thee?   42:23
Weariest: even the w. river ... safe to sea
    310:1
Weariness: much study ... a w. of the flesh
    39:28
Wearing: everything is the worse for w.
    212:38
Weary: age shall not w. them   54:5
  how my heart grows   112:9
  how w., stale ... uses of this world   248:2
  long w. day have end   305:8
  sae w., fu' o' care   67:5
  Unfortunate, w. of breath   134:10
Weasel: as a w. sucks eggs   244:5
  pop goes the w.!   165:5
Weather: I like the w.   68:17
  if it prove fair w.   308:2
  need to pray for fair w.   22:8
  no enemy but winter and rough w.   244:4
  the w. the cuckoo likes   128:10
  two Englishmen ... talk is of the w.   140:12
  what dreadful hot w.!   21:4
  who's there, besides foul w.?   266:5
  you won't hold up the w.   164:15
Weave: tangled web we w.   240:8
  w. a circle round him thrice   87:16
Weaving: I work at the w. trade   16:3
Web: w. of our life ... mingled yarn   242:6
  what a tangled w. we weave   240:8
Webster was ... possessed by death   107:6
Wed: with this ring I thee w.   53:24

Whig: first W. was the Devil   144:12
Whigs: caught the W. bathing   100:3
W. ... no force but argument   60:4
Whim: tempted by a private w.   27:8
the strangest w. has seized me   80:20
Whimper: not with a bang but a w.   106:9
'twixt a smile and a w.   299:10
Whipped: she w. them all soundly   194:5
Whipping: who shall 'scape w. ?   250:13
Whips and scorns of time   250–1:20
Whirligig of time brings ... revenges   292:2
Whiskers: runcible cat with crimson w.   158:10
Whisky: freedom and W. ... thegither   65:14
Whisper: hush! hush! w. who dares!   172:2
Whispering: where there is w. ... lying   230:13
Whispers: blood of Jesus w. peace   54:4
secret w. of each other's watch   259:8
Whist: loved a good game of w.   156:4
Whistle: as clean as a w.   209:30
hir joly w. wel y-wet   79:22
to wet one's w.   230:6
Whistles o'er the furrowed land   174:3
White: a moment w., then melts   67:4
as w. as leprosy   86:8
fleece was w. as snow   127:11
I shall wear w. flannel trousers   106:16
in winter, when the fields are w.   76:11
my soul is w.   56:10
one w., and two khaki   13:2
[sins] shall be ... w. as snow   40:17
some gave them w. bread   190:9
the w. foam flew   86:4
the W. Man's Burden   155:6
two blacks do not make a w.   228:37
w. radiance of Eternity   298:2
yr. hair has become very w.   74:3
Whiten: w. the green plains under   298:5
willows w., aspens quiver   313:12
Whiter: I shall be w. than snow   36:14
Whites: don't fire ... see the w. of their eyes   205:4
Whitethroat builds, and all the swallows   61:2
Whither: one knows not w. nor why   169:1
soul ... driven ... I know not w.   324:4
w. goest thou ?   46:32
w. is fled the visionary gleam ?   331:16
Whiting: said a w. to a snail   75:2
Who: w. killed Cock Robin ?   196:2
w. kill'd John Keats ?   70:17
w., or why, or which   151:1
w. was then the gentleman ?   24:2
Whole: all ... parts of one stupendous w.   203:3
saw life steadily, and saw it w.   18:14
they that are w.   45:5
Who saith 'A w. I planned'   62:9
Whooping: wonderful ... out of all w.   245:5
Whore: like a w., unpack my heart   250:18
'Tis Pity She's a W.   111:11
Wicked: God made the w. Grocer   81:10
lov'd his w. neighbour as himself   103:7
no peace ... unto the w.   41:3
pomps ... of this w. world   53:12
Wickedness: men alone ... capable of every w.   90:9
spiritual w. in high places   48:27
w. of a woman   52:1
Wicklow: chink in the floor of the old W. house   310:7

Widdicombe Fair: for to go to W.   17:5
Wide: alone on a w. w. sea   86:10, 87:2
Wider still and wider shall thy bounds be set   28:10
Widow: a certain poor w. ... threw in two mites   45:15
care for ... his w. and his orphan   159:15
here's to the w. of fifty   301:17
Widows: be very careful o' w. (vidders)   98:24
when w. exclaim ... against second marriage   109:7
w. are always rich   230:14
Wife: a light w., a heavy husband   275:12
all the world and his w.   231:1
and Noah he often said to his w.   81:11
by degrees dwindle into a w.   89:18
Caesar's w. ... above suspicion   71:15
choose a w. ... by yr. ear   209:24
chose my w. ... not for ... glossy surface   123:20
good w. and health ... best wealth   215:22
good w. makes a good husband   215:23
has a w., has a master   230:15
he that hath w. and children   21:19
he that speaks ill of his w.   226:8
he that tells his w. news   227:21
here lies my w.—hallelujah!   12:2
his w. cd. eat no lean   190:7
his w. looked back   31:4
honour unto ... w. as ... weaker vessel   50:6
horse made ... w. to make   209:23
how ... be married without a w. ?   191:4
if w. shd. dine at Edmonton   92:11
Intellectual suggests ... untrue to his w.   20:3
kill a w. with kindness   287:10
married, but I'd have no w.   94:2
must be in want of a w.   20:17
naked, the man and his w.   30:10
need makes the old w. trot   221:26
never lend—'oss, ... w., ... name   308:7
not covet thy neighbour's w.   32:9
remember Lot's w.   46:10
riding to and from his w.   325:8
roaring of the wind is my w.   152:6
tell his w. all he knows   114:9
this is my w.—look well at her   306:1
took fourpence home to my w.   190:2
when his w. talks Greek   145:3
whose w. shall I take ?   184:3
Wights: descriptions of the fairest w.   294:6
Wild: and her eyes were w.   148:15
bore me in the southern w.   56:10
kind of w. justice   21:12
piping down the valleys w.   56:7
Wilderness: one crying in the w.   43:11
scapegoat into the w.   32:13
the w. of this world   63:6
W. is Paradise enow   109:15
Wiles: of w., more unexpert, I boast not   176:16
Quips and Cranks and wanton W.   173:16
Will: a man's ... w. ... invalidated by marriage   68:11
complies against his w.   68:1
law beyond its own sweet w.   326:6
man has his w. ... woman has her way   134:3
puzzles the w.   250–1:20
serveth not another's w.   336:13
the w.! the w.! ... Caesar's w.!   263:15

Will (*continued*)
the w. to do, the soul to dare   239:7
their law's their w.   281:4
thy w. be done   43:24
unconquerable w., and study of revenge   175:18
where there's a w. there's a way   230:17
where there's a w., there's trouble   230:18
w. in us is over-rul'd by fate   166:14
William: you are old, Father W.   74:3
Williamanmary ... ruled by an Orange   241:12
Willow: a w. cabin at yr. gate   290:12
a w. grows aslant the brook   253:1
w., titwillow   119:1
w. w. waly   119:6
Willows: our harps upon the w.   37:23
w. whiten, aspens quiver   313:12
Wills: choose executors and talk of w.   283:5
the w. above be done   287:14
women must have their w.   230:36
Win: heads I w., tails you lose   94:5, 216:20
hope from outward forms to w.   87:9
nothing ... foul to those that w.   255:18
Wind: a roaring in the w. all night   334:7
absence is to love what w. is to fire   67:13
all aloud the w. doth blow   269:1
and the w. shall say   107:1
bayed the whispering w.   122:8
blow, blow, thou winter w.   245:1
blow w., come wrack   272:11
fair stood the w. for France   102:9
frosty w. made moan   235:15
gentle w. doth move   55:10
God tempers the w. ... shorn lamb   215:11
hey, ho, the w. and the rain   292:3
hope constancy in w.   70:14
how the w. doth ramm!   205:2
ill w. that blows nobody good   217:19
impatient as the W.   333:1
know which way the w. blows   218:11
like W. I go   110:5
likewise a w. on the heath   57:8
man in the w.   315:14
more gentle than a w. in summer   150:8
O Wild West W.   299:3
only argument ... with an east w.   163:1
readers ... sway in the w.   106:2
reed shaken with the w.   44:11
roaring of the w. is my wife   152:6
sail near the w.   224:35
shorter in w., as in memory long   57:15
streams ... *against* the w.   69:7
swoln with w. and the rank mist   175:4
tempers the w. ... to the shorn lamb   306:15
the w. of. change is blowing   164:13
they have sown the w.   42:9
when the w. is southerly   250:8
where the w. comes from ... goes   171:5
w. bloweth where it listeth   46:20
w. blows it back again   55:9
w. blows, the cradle will rock   189:10
w. of the Western Sea   314:13
w. out of one's sails   227:6
w. that follows fast   95:1
w.'s like a whetted knife   168:17
words but w.   67:16
Window: at my w. bid good morrow   174:2
love comes in at the w.   219:37
the little w. where the sun   134:14
what light through yonder w. ?   286:6

Windowed: loop'd and w. raggedness   266:13
Window-panes: fog ... rubs its back upon the w.   106:13
Windows: cleaned the w., ... swept the floor   119:15
not by eastern w. only   85:3
storied w. richly dight   173:11
Winds: blow, w., and crack yr. cheeks   266:6
courted by all the w.   180:15
four-square to all the w.   314:10
rough w. do shake the darling buds   293:13
so perfumed that the w. were love-sick   242:14
the w. will blow the profit   164:15
w. somewhere safe to sea   310:1
wound the loud w.   288:15
young w. fed it with ... dew   299:14
Windy: keep o' th' w. side of the law   291:16
Wine: a little w. for thy stomach's sake   49:12
as water unto w.   313:19
bring me flesh ... wine   187:2
cedarwood, and sweet white w.   168:13
conversations over the w.   317:2
good w.—a friend—or being dry   10:3
good w. needs no bush   215:24
happiness ... w. of the rarest vintage   303:5
I love ... old books, old w.   123:6
I'll not look for w.   145:7
if it doesn't get into the w.   81:11
mine host's Canary w.   149:4
new w. into old bottles   45:25
old friends and old w. are best   222:24
old w. wholesomest   324:1
Sans W., sans Song   110:3
sour grapes can ne'er make sweet w.   226:4
the blude-red w.   11:13
thy love is better than w.   40:2
truth comes out in w.   200:17
w. and wenches empty men's purses   230:19
w. gives great pleasure   144:13
w. in the bottle does not quench   230:20
w. in, truth out   230:21
w. is a good familiar creature   279:11
w. is a mocker   38:22
w. is in ... wit is out   26:4
w. is the strongest   51:5
w. that maketh glad the heart   37:2
w. ... the gout; ... no w. ... the gout   211:34
wolf's-bane, ... for its poisonous w.   149:11
Wine, woman and song: who loves not w.   163:2
Wing: got to take under my w., tra la   118:15
Lo! the Bird is on the W.   109:14
the lark's on the w.   62:7
Winged Cupid painted blind   276:12
Wings: and whether pigs have w.   76:4
beating ... his luminous w. in vain   19:9
beating of his [Death's] w.   58:8
cloying treacle to the w.   152:9
golden hours on angel w.   66:3
ill news hath w.   102:10
in the shade of your soft w.   238:12
love ... spreads his light w.   201:8
O for a horse with w.!   247:2
Oh that I had w.   36:16
under his w. shalt thou trust   36:25
under the shadow of thy w.   35:21
viewless w. of Poesy   149:16
with healing in his w.   43:7
Wink: I have not slept one w.   247:4

Wink (*continued*)
w. and hold out mine iron 258:10
Winners: in war ... no w., ... all are losers 78:9
Winning: not w., but taking part 91:2
  too light w. make the prize light 288:2
Wins: and Mammon w. his way 68:18
  plays best (well) that w. 223:9
  who loses and who w. 267:13
Winter: a sad tale's best for w. 292:13
  cold ... heat ... summer ... w. 30:23
  cooled by the same w. 274:17
  English w.—ending in July 70:8
  for, lo, the w. is past 40:8
  her w. weeds outworn 298:11
  hounds of spring are on w.'s traces 309:14
  I ... go south in the w. 107:4
  if W. comes, can Spring be far behind?
    299:6
  in w., when the fields are white 76:11
  it was the w. wild 175:8
  like a w. hath my absence been 294:4
  my age is as a lusty w. 243:18
  nor the furious w.'s rages 247:9
  red blood ... in the w.'s pale 292:17
  savour all the w. long 293:1
  the w. evening settles down 106:19
  w. and rough weather 244:4
  w. is come and gone 297:10
  w. is icummen in 205:2
  w. of our discontent 284:8
Winters: four lagging w. ... wanton springs
  281:12
Wisdom: apply our hearts unto w. 36:24
  can w. be put in a silver rod? 55:2
  excess leads to ... palace of w. 57:1
  fear of the Lord ... beginning of w. 37:6
  for w. is better than rubies 38:5
  friend of Pleasure, W.'s aid 88:14
  how can he get w.? 52:4
  in much w. is much grief 39:13
  knowledge comes ... w. lingers 313:18
  more of w. in it 335:5
  no w. like silence 230:22
  the price of w. ... above rubies 35:9
  to hear the w. of Solomon 34:17
  unsearchable dispose of Highest W. 181:7
  w. and goodness to the vile 266:21
  w. hath builded her house 38:6
Wise: a word is enough to the w. 229:16
  all things w. and wonderful 10:4
  be not w. in yr. own conceits 47:25
  be w. today ... madness to defer 337:13
  be w. with speed 337:12
  better ... happy than w. 207:23
  exceeding w., fair-spoken 262:2
  fool ... holdeth his peace is counted w.
    38:20
  give unto me made lowly w. 334:4
  good to be merry and w. 16:1
  great men are not always w. 35:11
  he that is not ... w. at fifty 216:3
  histories make men w. 23:9
  holy, fair and w. is she 292:8
  I care whether ... w. man or a fool 55:7
  I heard a w. man say 136:5
  more of the fool than of the w. 22:3
  nor ever did a w. one 234:11
  reputed one of the w. men 21:21
  same tree ... a w. man sees 57:3
  so w., so young ... never live long 285:2

Wise (*continued*)
  some are w., ... some are otherwise 225:38
  some folk are w. ... some are otherwise
    303:20
  that's the w. thrush 61:3
  the least foolish is w. 218:31
  the only wretched are the w. 205:7
  'tis folly to be w. 126:2
  to a w. man ports ... havens 281:14
  to be w. and love 290:5
  w. after the event 212:13
  w. father ... knows his own child 274:12
  w. man that marries a harlot 241:19
  w. ones [marry] not at all 216:38
Wisely: one that lov'd not w., but too well
  280:14
  thou dost not inquire w. 39:20
Wiser: be w. ... but do not tell 80:8
  French are w. than they seem 22:20
  sadder and a w. man 87:5
  Spaniards seem w. than they are 22:20
  world would be w. than ever 330:10
Wisest: fool ... ask more than ... w. ... can
  answer 88:20
  in the mouths of w. men 181:2
Wish: I w. I had said that. You will 325:7
  I w. our clever young poets 88:3
  my oft-expressed personal w. 159:12
  who wd. w. to die? 57:8
  w. is father to the thought 230:26
  w. was father ... to that thought 257:18
Wished she had not heard it, yet she wished
  279:2
Wishes: everything ... exact to my w. 12:1
Wit: a w. shd. be no more sincere 89:9
  age is in, the w. is out 278:9
  bold and turbulent of w. 102:16
  brevity is the soul of w. 249:15
  he is only a w. among Lords 141:18
  his whole w. in a jest 25:7
  I wish him neither w. nor wealth 15:6
  impropriety ... soul of w. 169:5
  in w. a man: simplicity a child 201:22
  neither w., nor words, nor worth 263:20
  no man's w. can well direct 100:16
  nor all thy piety nor w. 110:12
  prize of w. or arms 174:6
  too proud for a w. 123:2
  true w. is nature to advantage 202:8
  want of w. is worse 229:25
  wine is in ... w. is out 26:4
  w., if not first, in ... first line 123:4
  w. shall not go unrewarded 289:1
  w. that can creep 201:19
  w. with dunces ... dunce with wits 201:2
  your men of w. will condescend 308:12
Witch: not suffer a w. to live 32:11
Witchcraft: only ... w. I have used 279:2
Witching: very w. time of night 252:8
With: not w. me is against me 44:12
Withal: Time ambles w., ... trots w. 245:8
Withered: rosebuds, before they be w. 51:10
  so w., ... wild in their attire 269:7
Withers: our w. are unwrung 252:5
Within: life whose fountains are w. 87:9
Witness: shalt not bear false w. 32:8
  such weak w. of thy name 175:12
Wits: great w. .... to madness near allied 102–3:17
  home-keeping youth ... homely w. 292:4
Witty: a w. statesman ... prove anything 73:4

Witty (*continued*)

  it shall be w. and it shan't be long   80:18

  not only w. in myself   256:8

Wive: hard to w. and thrive ... in a year   230:27

Wives: a man with seven w.   188:3

  married three w. at one time   183:1

  profane and old w.' fables   49:10

  sky changes when they are w.   245:13

  some poison'd by their w.   283:6

  w. are young men's mistresses   21:20

  w. must be had ... good or bad   230:28

Wiving: hanging and w. goes by destiny   274:15

Wobbly: my spelling is w.   172:8

Woe: a thurghfare ful of w.   79:21

  all our w., with loss of Eden   175:15

  bitter groan of a martyr's w.   55:5

  can I see another's w.?   56:12

  cry w., destruction, ruin   283:4

  life protracted is protracted   141:12

  man was made for joy and w.   54:15

  the w.'s to come   284:3

  trappings and the suits of w.   248:1

  Wednesday's child is full of w.   191:8

  w. to the vanquished   160:4

  w. to them ... at ease in Zion   42:17

  w. unto them that call ... good evil   40:20

Woes: with all w. new wail   293:18

Wold: fields ... that clothe the w.   313:11

Wolf: keep the w. from the door   230:29

  to cry 'W.'   210:23

  w. ... shall dwell with the lamb   40:24

Wolf's-bane, tight-rooted   149:11

Wolves: inwardly ... ravening w.   44:9

Woman: a fair w. ... without discretion   38:11

  a perfect W., nobly planned   334:14

  a Spirit, yet a W. too   334:13

  a virtuous w. is a crown   38:12

  a w. is a foreign land   198:12

  a w. is only a w.   154:10

  A W. Killed with Kindness   132:10

  a w. mov'd ... a fountain troubled   287:12

  a w. sat, in unwomanly rags   135:3

  a w. seldom asks advice   9:10

  a w.'s face ... hast thou   293:16

  a w.'s preaching is like   142:13

  a w.'s whole history   138:11

  a w., therefore to be won   260:7

  a w. who tells her ... age   328:12

  a w. with fair opportunities   315:9

  a w. yet think him an angel   315:7

  a worthy w. al hir lyve   79:15

  a young w. called Starkie   13:2

  an uncommon pretty young w.   105:13

  as you are w., so be lovely   125:8

  believe a w. or an epitaph   70:14

  but what is w.?   91:14

  but w. has her way   134:3

  constant ... but yet a w.   254:11

  die because a w.'s fair   329:11

  do you not know I am a w.?   245:6

  dumb jewels ... move a w.'s mind   292:7

  every w. false like thee   180:16

  every w. is at heart a rake   203:15

  every w. is ... to be gained by ... flattery   80:17

  every w. shd. marry—and no man   100:10

  fat white w. whom nobody loves   90–1:16

  frailty, thy name is w.   248:5

Woman (*continued*)

  give not thy soul unto a w.   51:19

  God made the w. for the man   312:2

  great glory in a w.   317:5

  had a w. ever less?   66:6

  her voice ... soft—an excellent thing in w.   268:3

  I could be a good w. if   315:12

  I know a reasonable w.   204:3

  if a w. have long hair   48:5

  in a post-chaise with a pretty w.   144:7

  in argument with men a w.   181:3

  in her first passion w.   69:17

  lays his hand upon a w.   317:12

  love and good company improves a w.   109:4

  man that is born of a w.   35:5, 53:28

  never yet fair w. but   266:9

  no other but a w.'s reason   292:5

  no other purgatory but a w.   25:10

  no w. shd. ... be quite accurate   327:17

  no w. shd. have a memory   328:15

  none of w. born shall harm Macbeth   271:15

  nor hell a fury like a w. scorned   89:6

  O W.! in our hours of ease   240:9

  of every ill, a w. is the worst   125:3

  old w. lived under a hill   194:4

  old w. who lived in a shoe   194:5

  one tongue is enough for a w.   228:8

  poor w. who was always tired   12:1

  seven [hours' sleep] for a w.   225:25

  she is a w., ... may be woo'd ... won   289:13

  teaches such beauty as a w.'s eye   268:12

  the rib ... made he a w.   30:8

  the worser spirit a w. colour'd ill   294:16

  there's a broken-hearted w.   129:6

  this w. to thy wedded wife   53:21

  thought does not become a young w.   301:4

  'tis w.'s whole existence   69:14

  to show a w. when he loves   61:14

  wavers ... in a word, she is a w.   232:10

  when lovely w. stoops to folly   107:5, 124:1

  who can find a virtuous w.?   39:8

  wickedness of a w.   52:1

  wit no more ... sincere than a w. constant   89:9

  without the ... w. I love   105:10

  w. as old as she looks   88:7

  w. ... at the bottom of [mischief]   222:1

  w. conceals what she knows not   230:30

  w. ... fickle and changing   321:3

  w. for the hearth   314:18

  w. ... if she have the misfortune   20:15

  w. in this humour woo'd ... won?   284:13

  w. is his game   314:17

  w. is the lesser man   313:19

  w.'s at best a contradiction   203:18

  w.'s happiest knowledge   178:7

  w. that deliberates is lost   9:5

  w. to obey   314:18

  w. wailing for her demon-lover   87:12

  w. will be the last thing civilized   170:3

  w. with the heart   314:18

  worse occupations ... than feeling a w.'s pulse   306:14

  yield to one of w. born   272:12

Womb: from his mother's w. untimely ripp'd   272:12

  this teeming w. of royal kings   282:5

Womb (*continued*)
  through the foul w. of night   259:8
Women: a bevy of fair w.   179:15
  alas! the love of w.   69:16
  an experience of w. which extends   102:2
  Bah! I have sung w.   205:3
  by bad w. been deceived   180:12
  dally not with money or w.   210:33
  discreet w. ... neither eyes nor ears   211:20
  England ... a paradise for w.   67:10
  England is the paradise of w.   111:4, 212:24
  fair w. and brave men   69:3
  for w. to keep counsel   263:1
  from w.'s eyes this doctrine I derive   268:14
  goes with w., and champagne   27:7
  happiest w. ... have no history   105:15
  how w. pass the time when ... alone   131:2
  I speak ... Italian to w.   78:18
  Italy ... hell for w.   67:10
  let your w. keep silence in ... churches   48:9
  loved Esther above all the w.   34:27
  Monstrous Regiment of W.   155:13
  most w. are not so young as ... painted   26:7
  music and w. I ... give way to   199:11
  other w. cloy the appetites   242:15
  passing the love of w.   34:12
  souls of w. are so small   68:2
  sweet is revenge—especially to w.   69:12
  the more w. look in ... glass   230:35
  the third wrote, W. are strongest   51:5
  three w. ... goose make a market   227:40
  tide in the affairs of w.   70:3
  where there are w. and geese   230:32
  W. and Horses and Power   154:9
  w. and music shd. never be dated   123:11
  w. are always in extremes   230:33
  w. are angels, wooing   289:15
  w. are glad to have been asked   197:14
  w. are necessary evils   230:34
  w. become like their mothers   328:13
  w. ... care ... more for a marriage   23:19
  w. in London who flirt   327:9
  w. ... more like each other than men   80:16
  w. must have the last word   230:37
  w. must have their wills   230:36
  w. must weep   154:3
  w. never look so well as when   308:8
  w. require both   68:13
  w. sit or move to and fro   325:9
  w.'s letters ... pith is in the postscript   129:7
  w.'s weapons, water-drops   266:3
  w. ... talking of Michelangelo   106:12
  w., worst and best   312:6
Won: a woman, therefore to be w.   260:7
  marks—not that you w. or lost   233:12
  melancholy as a battle w.   324:6
  prize we sought is w.   325:12
  things w. are done   289:15
  woman, therefore may be w.   289:13
  w. on the playing fields of Eton   324:10
Wonder: all the w. that wd. be   313:16
  and still the w. grew   122:12
  how I w. what you are!   311:5
  how I w. what you're at   74:8
  the common w. of all men   59:15
  we ... have eyes to w.   294:7
Wonderful: all things wise and w.   10:4
  how w. is Death!   298:7
  O w., w. ... out of all whooping   245:5

Wonderful (*continued*)
  W., Counsellor, The Mighty God   40:23
Wonderment: I'm always moved to w.   186:9
Wonders: His w. to perform   92:15
  w. will never cease   230:38
Won't: will you, w. you, will you, w. you?   75:3
Woo: was to w. a fair young maid   16:3
Wood: my house in the high w.   28:4
  old w. burn brightest   324:1
  one impulse from a vernal w.   335:7
  see the w. for the trees   225:8
  springeth the w. new   14:7
  through w. and dale the sacred river   87:13
Woodbine: over-canopied with luscious w.   276:20
Woodman, spare the beechen tree   72:7
Wood-notes: his native w. wild   174:8
Woods: a pleasure in the pathless w.   69:9
  and the w. have no voice   184:10
  in spring, when w. are getting green   76:12
  senators of mighty w.   148:6
  the w. shall to me answer   305:7
  though he build his house in the w.   108:23
  tomorrow to fresh w.   175:6
  we'll to the w. no more   136:3
  w. or steepy mountain yields   167:1
Woodshed: something nasty in the w.   116:5
Wooed: beautiful, and therefore to be w.   260:7
  woman in this humour w.   284:13
  woman, therefore may be w.   289:13
Wooing: a frog he wd. a-w. go   189:2
  women are angels, w.   289:15
Wool: have you any w. ?   188:4
  pull the w. over a person's eyes   230:39
Word: a character dead at every w.   301:15
  a tale unfold whose lightest w.   249:7
  at every w. a reputation dies   204:8
  by water and the W.   307:13
  every w. stabs   277:16
  every w. that proceedeth   32:23
  fairer than that w.   274:4
  four ... winters ... springs end in a w   281:12
  Greeks had a w. for it   10:1
  his w. was still 'Fie, foh, and fum'   266:17
  in the captain's but a choleric w.   273:8
  in w. mightier   178:19
  Latin w. for three farthings   268:10
  let the w. go forth   153:1
  many a true w. ... in jest   228:22
  Mum's the w.   88:15
  nor all thy tears wash out a w. of it   110:12
  some with a flattering w.   326:12
  suit ... the w. to the action   251:9
  that I kept my w., he said   96:15
  the W., and the W. was with God   46:14
  the W. was made flesh   46:17
  there wd. have been a time for such a w.   272:10
  what is honour ? A w.   255:21
  'when I use a w.,' Humpty Dumpty said   76:10
  whose w. no man relies on   234:11
  women must have the last w.   230:37
  w. for w. without book   290:11
  w. is as good as his bond   216:37
  w. ... teems with hidden meaning   120:14
  yawning at every other w.   77:6

Word (continued)
  yesterday the w. of Caesar 263:14
Words: actions speak louder than w. 206:4
  all sad w. of tongue or pen 326:8
  as many w. into the last line 13:1
  best w. in the best order 88:3
  comprehending much in few w. 52:2
  dumb jewels ... more than quick w. do move 292:7
  eat one's w. 212:15
  few w. are best 213:23
  her last w. on earth 12:1
  in two w.: im-possible 124:4
  let the w. of my mouth ... be acceptable 35:25
  let thy w. be few 39:16
  like a whore, unpack my heart with w. 250:18
  long w. Bother me 172:4
  men of few w. ... best men 259:6
  much matter decorated into few w. 114:8
  my w. fly up, my thoughts remain 252:11
  neither wit, nor w., nor worth 263:20
  noun ... verb ... abominable w. 260:11
  oaths are but w. ..., w. but wind 67:16
  on the pedestal these w. appear 299:8
  proper w. in proper places 309:2
  report thy w. by adding fuel 181:6
  scatter ... my w. among mankind 299:6
  the w. of Mercury are harsh 269:2
  use ... w. only to conceal ... thoughts 321:12
  what do you read ... ? W., w., w. 250:2
  when you let proud w. go 238:6
  w. are the daughters of earth 140:2
  w., like Nature, half reveal 312:12
  w. may be false 241:18
  w. ... so nimble ... full of ... flame 25:7
  w. that frightened the birds 12:11
  w. will never hurt me 226:18
  w. without thoughts never to heaven go 252:11
Wore enough for modesty 62:13
Work: a w. that aspires to ... art 90:7
  all in the day's w. 206:10
  all things w. together for good 47:20
  all w. and no play 230:40
  because he can't w. any faster 193:3
  day is short ... w. is long 210:35
  doing more w. than I shd. do 139:15
  I have left no immortal w. 152:11
  I have protracted my w. 140:4
  I like w.; it fascinates me 139:15
  I w. at the weaving trade 16:3
  if any wd. not w., neither shd. he eat 49:8
  men must w. and women must weep 154:3
  my w. is left behind 28:2
  night ... when no man can w. 46:26
  no more hard w. for poor old Ned 112:12
  nothing to do but w. 153:10
  old Kaspar's w. was done 304:12
  smile his w. to see 56:6
  so w. the honey bees 258:8
  sport wd. be as tedious as to w. 253:21
  strive on to finish the w. 159:15
  the way to spread a w. 143:10
  there is always w. and tools to w. 162:12
  to w. is to pray 218:16
  whose w. is not born with him 162:12
  woman's w. is never done 230:31
  w. ... curse of the drinking classes 328:18

Work (continued)
  w. expands so as to fill the time 198:5
  w. like madness in the brain 87:7
  w. yr. hands from day to day 164:15
Workers of the world, unite 168:10
Workhouse: Christmas Day in the W. 302:8
Working: another for w.-days 277:18
  fiery Soul, which w. out its way 102:17
Workman: a bad w. quarrels ... tools 206:34
Workmen: good w. are seldom rich 215:25
Works: devil and all his w. 53:11
  faith without w. is dead 49:25
  its [sea's] w. ... are wrapped in mystery 90:8
  Saturday's child w. hard for his living 191:8
World: a balm upon the w. 148:2
  a citizen ... of the w. 304:5
  a man if he shall gain the whole w. 45:10
  a w. in a grain of sand 54:12
  a w. of happy days 284:15
  a w. too wide for his shrunk shank 244–5:11
  a w. where nothing is had for nothing 84:12
  aching void the w. can never fill 92:14
  all de w. am sad 112:9
  all sorts to make a w. 206:16
  all's right with the w. 62:7
  all the uses of this w.! 248:2
  all the w. and his wife 231:1
  all the w. as my parish 325:4
  all the w. is queer 197:17
  all the w.'s a stage 244:11
  all this sad w. needs 326:11
  all this the w. well knows 294:12
  an excellent foppery of the w. 265:10
  and all the w. would stare 92:11
  another W., the happy seat 177:4
  any author in the w. 268:12
  any portion of the foreign w. 322:16
  any way to perpetuate the w. 60:1
  as good be out of the w. 83:15
  as they did in the golden w. 243:12
  banish ... Jack and banish all the w. 255:2
  before my time into this breathing w. 284:10
  body is aweary of this great w. 274:5
  brave new w. ... such people in't 289:7
  Britain is a w. by itself 247:1
  called from the w. 12:4
  cankers of a calm w. 255:16
  Clearing-house of the w. 78:7
  commodity, the bias of the w. 264:13
  compare this prison ... unto the w. 284:6
  consider the w. as made for me 304:1
  constant service of the antique w. 243:19
  contain and nourish all the w. 268:14
  deceits of the w., the flesh, and the devil 52:24
  enthusiasm moves the w. 24:1
  ever shall be: w. without end 52:14
  fast, and the w. goes by 326:10
  flash in this w. of trouble 11:18
  funniest joke in the w. 295:20
  gave me ... a w. of sighs 279:2
  get the start of the majestic w. 262:7
  gone into the w. of light 320:5
  greatest thing in the w. 183:3
  had we but w. enough, and time 167:11
  he doth bestride the narrow w. 262:8

World (*continued*)

he is a citizen of the w. 22:6
hold the w. but as the w. 274:1
hope before you blacken their w. 319:8
how the w. its veterans rewards 203:16
how this w. is given to lying! 256:4
I called the New W. into existence 72:14
if all the w. were paper 14:1
in this harsh w. draw thy breath in pain 253:9
into the dangerous w. I leapt 56:3
justice ... though the w. perish 109:6
knaves and fools divide the w. 218:6
laugh, and the w. laughs with you 326:9
leaves the w. to darkness and to me 126:3
light of the bright w. dies 57:13
love is enough though the w. 184:10
love makes the w. go round 220:2
mad w.! mad kings! 264:12
more ... wrought by prayer than this w. dreams 312:9
nature is too noble for the w. 246:10
never enjoy the w. aright 317:16
no enjoying the w. without [health] 145:18
not loved the w., nor the w. me 69:5
nothing stable in the w. 151:12
official ... undercuts the problematical w. 114:3
on ... shore of the wide w. 151:8
one half ... w. cannot understand 20:7
reckless what I do to spite the w. 271:2
ring'd with the azure w. he stands 312:1
same the whole w. over 16:13
Saviour of the w. 68:14
saw the Vision of the w. 313:16
so shines a good deed in a naughty w. 275:11
some say the w. will end in fire 113:12
the correction of the w. 182:14
the Federation of the W. 313:17
the ... increase of the w. 312:2
the light of the w. 46:25
the rack of this tough w. 268:5
the workers ... have a w. to gain 168:10
the wilderness of this w. 63:6
the w. forgetting, by the w. forgot 201:9
the w. is too much with us 333:3
the w. must be peopled 278:1
the w. shd. listen then 300:3
the w.'s great age begins anew 298:11
the w.'s grown honest 250:4
the w.'s mine oyster 276:4
the w. was all before them 179:18
this dark w. and wide 181:10
this dark w. of sin 54:4
this happy breed ... this little w. 282:5
this is the way the w. ends 106:9
this w. ... a thurghfare ful of wo 79:21
thro' the w. we safely go 54:15
to save your w. you asked 19:16
two soul-sides, one to face the w. 61:14
up above the w. so high 311:5
vanity of this wicked w. 53:12
vile blows and buffets of the w. 271:2
weight of ... unintelligible w. 335:11
when all the w. is young 154:4
when Rome falls—the W. 69:8
where in all this small-talking w. 114:4
whole w.'s in a state o' chassis 196:8
wondrous architecture of the w. 166:10

World (*continued*)

word of Caesar ... against the w. 263:14
w. grew pale 141:11
w. history is the w.'s judgment 238:13
w. is a comedy ... a tragedy 322:7
w. is charged with the grandeur 135:6
w. must be made safe for democracy 329:9
w. of doubts and fancies 151:12
w. of vile, ill-favour'd thoughts 276:6
w.'s great snare uncaught 243:3
w.'s storm-troubled sphere 58:12
w. to hide virtues in 290:12
w. wd. be wiser than ever 330:10
w. wd. go round ... faster 74:5
you shut out the w. 324:17
Worldly: name ... was Mr. W. Wiseman 63:8
with all my w. goods 53:24
Worlds: best of possible w. 321:9
exhausted w., and then imagin'd new 140:19
the little less, ... what w. away 60:15
wandering between two w. 18:15
Worm: concealment, like a w. i' th' bud 291:7
early bird catches the w. 212:8
tread on a w. and it will turn 228:19
who ... sets foot upon a w. 93:12
wish you joy o' th' w. 243:9
Worms: have made w.' meat of me 286:19
I was one of the w. 90:5
talk of graves, of w. and epitaphs 283:5
w. have eaten them 245:12
you have tasted two whole w. 305:19
Wormwood and the gall 41:18
Worried: poem ... not ... w. into being 113:16
w. the cat that killed the rat 194–5:8
Worry: no one to w. ... to hurry us 91:7
Worse: as Heaven made him, and ... w. 78:3
goes by the w., whatever be her cause 181:3
make the w. appear the better 176:18
really w. than interrupting 107:8
remedy is w. than the disease 22:10
sell w. kinds of liquor 322:12
there is no w. heresy 9:1
w. than being talked about 328:6
Worship: are come to w. him 43:8
with my body I thee w. 53:24
Worshipper: Nature mourns her w. 239:14
Worst: do your w., blow your pipe 62:5
hope ... best and prepare for the w. 217:3
so long as we can say 'This is the w.' 266:19
so much good in the w. of us 133:5
things at the w. will mend 227:29
things present, w. 256:13
whose puppets, best and w. 62:8
women, w. and best 312:6
Worth: doings without charity are nothing w. 53:3
none was w. my strife 156:11
slow rises w., by poverty depressed 140:16
w. a guinea a box 11:10
w. ... best known by the want 231:4
w. doing ... w. doing well 80:9, 230:8
w. of a State ... w. of ... individuals 170:11
w. reading ... w. buying 237:2
w. seeing ... not w. going to see 144:16
Worthington: daughter on the stage, Mrs. W. 91:10
Worthless as wither'd weeds 58:13

Worthy: labourer is w. of his hire 45:27
Worts: went to W. 204:13
Wound: did help to w. itself 265:4
  jests at scars that never felt a w. 286:6
  take away the grief of a w. 255:21
  what w. did ever heal? 279:12
  w. the loud winds 288:15
Wounds: bind up the nation's w. 159:15
  faithful ... the w. of a friend 39:3
  gash is added to her w. 271:18
  labour and the w. are vain 85:1
  talk ... of guns ... and w. 254:2
  these w. in thine hands 43:4
Wrangle: men will w. for religion 88:17
Wrapped up in a five-pound note 158:7
Wrath: day of w., that dreadful day 240:2
  infinite w. and infinite despair 177:13
  sun go down upon your w. 48:24
  the w. to come 43:12
Wreck: decay of that colossal w. 299:8
Wrecks: like w. of a dissolving dream 298:11
Wren: four Larks and a W. 158:13
  robin redbreast and the w. 324:3
  Sir Christopher W. said 29:3
  the w. goes to't 267:4
Wrestle: we w. not against flesh 48:27
Wretch: excellent w.! 279:14
  needy, hollow-ey'd ... w. 246:5
  patron.—commonly a w. 140:10
  w., concentred all in self 240:1
Wretched: scrannel pipes of w. straw 175:4
  the only w. are the wise 205:7
  the w. child expires 27:4
  w. matter and lame metre 175:14
Wretchedness: the w. of being rich 303:7
Wretches: poor naked w., wheresoe'er you are 266:13
  to feel what w. feel 266:14
Wrinkled: the w. sea beneath him 312:1
  w. with age ... Old Nod 97:1
Writ: if this be error ... I never w. 294:9
  over that same door was ... w. 305:12
Write: as much as a man ought to w. 318:3
  contrive to w. so even 20:19
  firm restraint with which they w. 72:6
  hope to w. well hereafter 182:1
  I never read books—I *w.* them 232:1
  look in thy heart and w. 302:3
  to w. and read comes by nature 278:4
  when I want ... novel I w. one 100:15
  why did I w.? 201:13
  w. God first 278:13
  w. me down an ass 278:16
Writers of small histories, dictionaries 140:6
Writes: the moving finger w. 110:12
Writing: in w. or in judging ill 202:1
  true ease in w. comes from art 202:10
  w. [maketh] an exact man 23:8
Written: what I have w. I have w. 46:34
  w. such volumes of stuff 158:6
Wrong: and if you w. us, shall we not revenge? 274:17
  but he done her w. 15:2
  fifty million Frenchmen can't be w. 127:10
  for telling a man he was w. 85:6
  house of Tarquin ... suffer w. no more 163:9
  I always feel I must be w. 327:3
  King can do no w. 54:10, 218:1
  losers are always in the w. 219:30

Wrong (*continued*)
  never dreamed ... w. wd. triumph 60:2
  only thing that I ever did w. 16:3
  or whether laws be w. 326:15
  our country, right or w. 96:7
  physical effect is good ... action ... w. 142:7
  right divine of kings to govern w. 201:3
  something ... w., however slightly 204:16
  something w. with ... ships 25:6
  stiff in opinions, always in the w. 103:4
  to do a great right do a little w. 275:2
  we do it w., being so majestical 247:15
  w. never comes right 231:5
Wrong number: if I called the w., why ... answer? 317:8
Wrote: no man ... ever w. except for money 144:5
  who w. like an angel 115:2
Wroth: to be w. with one we love 87:7
Wrought: being w., perplexed in the extreme 280–1:14
  first he w., ... afterwards he taughte 79:16
  more things are w. by prayer 312:9
Wye: turned to thee, O sylvan W. 335:13

Xanadu: in X. did Kubla Khan 87:11

Yankee Doodle came to town 196:4
Yarn: all I ask is a merry y. 168:17
  web of our life ... a mingled y. 242:6
Year: about two hundred pounds a y. 67:17
  add ... to this wonderful y. 115:1
  any book ... not a y. old 108:17
  before the mellowing y. 174:12
  each day is like a y. 326–7:15
  grief returns with the revolving y. 297:10
  how many days will finish ... y. 260:13
  I like two months of ... y. 68:17
  if ... y. were playing holidays 253:21
  in the season of the y. 16:6
  measure of the y. 151:4
  pleasure of the fleeting y. 294:4
  proper opinions for ... time of y. 20:4
  say no ill of the y. 224:40
  stolen ... my three-and-twentieth y. 181:9
  sweet o' the y. 292:17
  the y. is going, let him go 313:4
  the y.'s at the spring 62:7
  twentieth y. is well-nigh past 93:13
  wive and thrive both in a y. 230:27
Yearning: man of y. ... aspiration 236:9
Yearnings for equal division 107:18
Years: a thousand y. as one day 50:10
  age ... not weary ... nor the y. condemn 54:5
  alas, Postumus, the fleeting y. 135:15
  all the hopes of future y. 160:11
  before the beginning of y. 309:15
  come to the dignity of discretion 53:17
  cuts off twenty y. of life 263:3
  eight y. with a strange man 138:2
  evil days come not ... y. draw nigh 39:26
  forty y. on 57:15
  fourteen hundred y. ago were nail'd 253:14
  hasn't been kissed for forty y. 236:14
  if the British Empire ... last for a thousand y. 82:14
  Myself with Yesterday's Sev'n Thousand Y. 110:2
  O for ten y. 150:10